CHALLENGING THE CHRISTIAN LIFE

Volume Five

By

Rayola Kelley

Hidden Manna Publications

Challenging the Christian Life
Volume Five
Copyright © 2014 and 2023 by Rayola Kelley

ISBN: 978-0-9891683-5-9

All rights reserved. No part of this publication may be reproduced or transmitted in any form or by any means without written permission of Gentle Shepherd Ministries.

Except where otherwise indicated, all Scripture quotations in this book have been taken from the King James Version of the Bible.

Featuring the Following Books:

The Issues of Life
Presentation of the Gospel
For the Purpose of Edification
Whatever Happened to the Church?
Women's Place in the Kingdom of God

You can obtain a study reference book to complement your studies of the books in this volume at Gentle Shepherd Ministries' website at www.gentleshepherd.com

Hidden Manna Publications
P.O. Box 3572
Oldtown, ID. 83822
www.gentleshepherd.com

Facebook:
https://www.facebook.com/HiddenMannaPublications/

Dedication:

I want to dedicate this book to the
true Church of Jesus Christ
that will never be silenced because
it is living, universal, and eternal, for
it possesses the eternal life of
Jesus. It is also marked by the power
of the Holy Spirit, singular in devotion,
clear about its commission, and
serving as a living testimony of
the faithfulness and glory of
the true and only God.

Acknowledgment:

I want to acknowledge the
editing work of Jo Reaves and
Sarah Rick. Thank you, Jo
and Sarah for seeing such
a large commitment through to the end.
I also want to thank my
co-laborer, Jeannette Haley,
for all of her
hard work on these different
book projects.

Contents

Volume Five Introduction
Volume Introduction 9

Book One: THE ISSUES OF LIFE 13

	Introduction	15
1	The Essence of Christianity	16
2	Becoming a Philosopher	20
3	Looking For Life	24
4	Lessons of Life	29
5	The Reality of It All	37
6	The Tragedy of It All	43
7	Making the Connection	49
8	Order in the Environment	54
9	Point of Reliance	59
10	Gaining Life	66
11	Reaching Our Potential	71
12	Transforming the Mind	75
13	Reckoning a Matter As So	79
14	A Living Memorial for God	84

Book Two: PRESENTATION OF THE GOSPEL 89

	Introduction	91
1.	What is the Gospel?	92
2.	The Preparation of the Gospel	101
3.	The Gospel in Action	110
4.	The Power of the Gospel	119
5.	The Gospel and Carnality	130
6.	The Perverted Gospel	142
7.	The Inheritance of the Gospel	154
8.	The Fellowship of the Gospel	162
9.	The Hope of the Gospel	172
10.	The Assurance of the Gospel	183
11.	The Glorious Gospel	195
12.	The Disciplines of the Gospel	203
13.	The Product of the Gospel	212
14.	The Purpose of the Gospel	223
15.	The Revelation of the Gospel	230

Challenging the Christian Life

Book Three: FOR THE PURPOSE OF EDIFICATION.........239

	Introduction	241
1.	Edification	242
2.	The Giver	247
3.	The Design	253
4.	The Positions	258
5.	A Servant of All	265
6.	The Gifts of Grace	272
7.	Gifts of Benevolence	277
8.	Supernatural Gifts	284
9.	Diversity of Gifts	288
10.	Word of Wisdom	291
11.	Word of Knowledge	295
12.	Discerning of Spirits	298
13.	Gift of Faith	302
14.	Healing and Miracles	307
15.	Gift of Prophecy	316
16.	Tongues and Interpretation	323
17.	The Challenge	332

Book Four: WHATEVER HAPPENED TO THE CHURCH?..........................337

	Introduction	339
	Part I: Laying A Foundation	341
1.	What is the Church?	341
2.	A Bit of History	348
3.	What is Missing?	352
4.	The Replacement	358
	Part II: The Shift From Center	365
5.	The Open Door	365
6.	The Shift in Leadership	372
7.	Foundation Redefined	382
8.	Cornerstone Readjusted	393
9.	Perverting the Gospel	400
10.	Reprobate Faith	407
	Part III: The Powerless Pulpit	416
11.	The Purpose	416
12.	The Place of Witness	420
13.	The Sword	425
14.	Place of Authority	431
15.	Vision	436

	Part IV: Coming Back To Center	443
16.	Arise Sleeping Church	443
17.	Unveiling the Mystery	449
18.	Divide and Conquer	455
19.	The Gates of Hell Will Not Prevail	466

Book Five: WOMEN'S PLACE IN THE KINGDOM OF GOD.................473

	Introduction	475
1	Inspiration or Tradition?	477
2	A Woman Called "Adam"	481
3	Cursed or Blessed?	486
4	The Struggle Intensifies	492
5	The Truth about Marriage	496
6	Unveiling the Truth	502
7	Restraint or Persecution?	508
8	Between a Rock and a Hard Place	513
9	The Last Shall Be First	517
10	Can Women Be Entrusted?	523
11	Let My Handmaidens Go!	528

Bibliography **533**

About the Author **535**

INTRODUCTION

Challenging the Christian Life is the fifth volume in the Gentle Shepherd Ministries' advanced Discipleship Course. Volume five is meant to deal with subjects that are capable of challenging our religious comfort zones. These comfort zones can include theology, doctrine, or religious affiliations. Since the different subjects in this volume can sometimes be found at the core of discussion, disagreement, and division among the Christian denominations, they clearly have the capacity to challenge and shake our spiritual foundations, as well as expose our prejudices, character, and quality of Christianity.

Although the subjects of this volume have become controversial in the Church, the Bible does present a clear picture as to how we, as believers, should regard these different matters. It is man, with his theological opinions, worldly influences, and intellectual arrogance that often causes extreme approaches towards spiritual issues. By maintaining the intent of the Bible, controversial matters can be brought into a proper perspective.

The Issues of Life is the first book in this volume. Life clearly challenges each of us with situations that prove to be notorious and overwhelming. It is a tough teacher that teaches hard lessons as it reveals people's attitudes and character. It represents the essence of reality that is often ignored and dreaded. Since life comes from outside of man, he must choose the type of life he will pursue and embrace. However, people's attitudes towards life often cause conflict in regard to the responsibilities that surround this subject. Due to personal preferences, they often refuse to become responsible for the life which they end up preferring and pursing.

This brings us to a very important aspect of Christianity. Christianity is not a religion, but it is a life that must be lived out in practical ways. Such a life points to a lifestyle that is clearly expressed in disposition and attitude, and must be walked out in sincere faith and conduct. In this book, the author candidly addresses the different aspects of life that believers must confront in order to come to terms with their personal life in Christ and to avoid making Christianity "religious", while pursuing the vanity of this present world.

Another area that is controversial is the Gospel message. Although there seems to be a general consensus among Christian denominations about the essence of this message, there are still various presentations of the Gospel inundating the Church world, causing confusion. Obviously, the real Church of Jesus Christ must come to terms with the reality that there is only one true Gospel of Jesus Christ, and the presentation of it will determine whether the integrity and power behind it is maintained. According to the Apostle Paul, the true Gospel is the power of God unto salvation.

The Presentation of the Gospel presents the true Gospel in light of the many false messages that have found inroads into the Church. These false gospels are undermining the authority of the real Gospel, rendering it powerless and ineffective to save.

These pseudo-gospels may even contain some of the message of the true Gospel, but they downplay, take away from, or have been adjusted to become attractive and palatable to those of the world. Such attempts have redefined the true message that has been secured by Jesus' redemption, thereby causing confusion and controversy in the Church.

The Presentation of the Gospel will challenge any weak or wrong presentation of this incredible message. In some cases, the challenges in this book may insult those who have been promoting a gospel that is so weak that it is incapable of saving a person, or it might infuriate those who are promoting a wrong gospel that is leading individuals down the path of destruction. Clearly, this book will challenge the reader to consider how far the different gospel messages have strayed from the true message that is marked by the very power of God.

One of the most controversial issues in the Church is the manifestation of the Holy Spirit. God has provided the necessary means for the Church to spiritually grow and develop as a powerful Body and living representative of Jesus Christ. These avenues, or tools of edification, include the sovereign work of the Spirit, which includes the placing or distributing of spiritual positions and gifts in the Church. These positions and gifts clearly show God's order and His heart towards the redeemed Church.

Sadly, these avenues or tools have become controversial; therefore, they have become neglected, mishandled, and improperly presented. *For the Purpose of Edification* deals with each area that has been abused or misrepresented by man's personal conclusions, theology, or traditions. It is a book that is capable of bringing balance to this subject, as well as edifying the reader as he or she considers the orderly and incredible ways in which God ministers to the Body through the work and manifestation of His Spirit.

Since there is confusion about the Christian life, the true Gospel is being rendered powerless by counterfeit messages, and the tools used for edification have been considered as being obsolete and are often treated in an abusive manner. This has created an environment where the teaching and representation of the true Church has become the real casualty. The Body of Jesus has found itself in an identity crisis. The fourth book in this volume, *Whatever Happened to the Church?* candidly reveals how far away from the center the concepts, workings, and functions of the visible Church have fallen from their original introduction.

The Church, which has been empowered to express the life of Jesus, commissioned to preach the Gospel, and entrusted with the tools to ensure spiritual growth and a living, powerful testimony in this world, now appears to have a different foundation. As a result, it is no longer aligned to the cornerstone, as it walks according to a pseudo-faith. This visible Church clearly expresses the ways of the world more than the ways of its Lord and Redeemer.

The influence of the world upon the Church not only reveals that an unholy agreement has and is now taking place in the religious realm; but it also explains why so many of the pulpits remain powerless to make an eternal impact on people's lives. Although not part of the original book, a section entitled "powerless pulpit", along with two other chapters that challenge the Church to arise from its present condition and allow the incredible mystery of heaven to be unveiled in it, has also been added to this book. These additions bring a clearer picture of how much of what is now considered the Church in America fails to stand distinct from the world and has been consecrated unto the Lord as His chaste Bride.

The book about the true Church of Jesus has the potential to challenge the religious perception of the reader, causing him or her to reconsider what the Word has established about the Body of Christ. However, the final book in this volume not only has the potential to challenge the reader, but to stretch and enlarge his or her understanding. *Women's Place in the Kingdom of God* deals with the controversial debate concerning women's position in God's kingdom and the Church. The Bible has clearly established the woman's place in the home, but there are examples and Scriptures in regard to women in the kingdom of God that collide with assumed attitudes and acceptable doctrine, causing confusion as to how women must be regarded in light of God's calling and work. Sadly, many of the Scriptural examples have been largely ignored, and the few Scriptures that make reference to this subject have been made into doctrines that have defined and limited women's place in God's kingdom, hindering His work in the great harvest field of humanity.

Women's Place in the Kingdom of God addresses the controversy concerning women in the kingdom of God from the perspective of Biblical examples and Scriptures in order to bring a balanced view. This exposition on this issue reveals how religious, political, and cultural practices influenced the few Scriptures that address this issue in the New Testament. Even though a person may approach this subject with his or her bias, limited view, opinion, or conclusion in place, this small book will challenge, shake, or, even in some cases, change a person's understanding about this subject.

Although many religious people have set ideas about the subjects that are covered in this book, the reader will find that these matters are not as black and white as he or she might have previously perceived. As believers in the Most High God, we must never resort to putting Him or His ways in religious boxes in order to fit into our bias or worldly views. It is important that we allow God to be big enough that personal prejudices can be rooted out and faulty foundations shaken to the ground to allow our minds to be truly cleansed by His Word and transformed by His Spirit

Challenging the Christian Life

as a means to ensure that we have the mind of Christ concerning each of these vital issues.

THE ISSUES OF LIFE

Book One

Copyright © 2006 by Rayola Kelley

INTRODUCTION

What is life? This is a subject we take for granted, but unless we consider this matter, we may never discover what this journey is all about.

As I have observed people, there are very few who seem to live life. Granted, people are living in some type of existence, but they are not living life. Such a situation will cause despair and hopelessness.

This book considers the issues of life. It is meant to cause people to look at, meditate upon, and regard this incredible odyssey that each of us are experiencing. What does the essence of our life say about our character, resolve, and worth? It is time people cease from simply going through the motions of life, and discover what it means to live the life they have been entrusted with.

It is my hope that people will seriously consider this matter. And, in doing so will come to terms with the source of genuine life—that of the Lord Jesus Christ.

1

THE ESSENCE OF CHRISTIANITY

Occasionally, there are Christians who stop and actually consider the essence of Christianity. Is it some religious exercise where you fine-tune beliefs and religious activities, line up to some moral code, or exhibit practices that speak of piousness? Is Christianity some vague concept?

It would serve believers well to consider their attitudes about what constitutes genuine Christianity. Clearly, a study of the Word of God would, first of all, identify Christ as being the source of Christianity. If Christ is missing from the equation, then there is no real practice or religious exercise called "Christianity." In fact, there is no substance or meaning behind the term. It will lack credibility and strength.

The harsh reality in many cases is that Christ has been replaced by religion, substituted with some false idea of who He is, and tacked on to different types of religious or charitable activities. However, if the Person of Christ is missing from the word "Christianity", there is no real Christianity to speak of.

Once you get past "Christ" in the word "Christianity," you have the letters "i-a-n." These three letters point to a person. Such a person must be identified or associated with Christ to be considered a Christian. When you study the word "Christian," it is first mentioned in Acts 11:26. As you consider the environment in Acts 11, you will see that believers were dispersed throughout the region due to persecution. The Gospel reached into the hearts of the Gentiles as the distinction of this new "Way" was being unveiled through the power of the Spirit. Identification with the "Way" distinguished such a person as being a follower of Jesus, the Christ.

Obviously, a Christian is totally identified to the Person of Jesus Christ and the way in which he or she is to walk. To be identified with Christ means there must be distinguishing characteristics that speak of His presence, influence, and attitude in a person's life.

The last part of the word "Christianity" is expressed in the three letters "i-t-y." These three letters imply action, activity, and application. Obviously, Christianity is where I apply the ways, teachings, and attitudes of Christ to my life. Such application means that it will be expressed in how I approach matters, and it will motivate or determine the type of activity with which I will be involved.

This brings us to the essence of Christianity. Obviously, it is not just a religion that I practice every Sunday. It is not just a matter of beliefs. After all, beliefs do not always produce outward action. It is not just a lot of pious activity. All such things can lack inward substance.

The Word of God shows that Christianity entails a walk. We are to walk out the reality of Christ in our lives. Yet, it is not just a matter of walking, rather it comes down to how one walks. Obviously, Christians must walk in the light of Jesus Christ. It is not a matter of just moving, but of going forward in character, approach, and practices. As believers we must be moving forward in establishing a relationship with God. Clearly, this walk is not just a matter of being busy doing good deeds, rather it is a matter of having a destination and purpose that will discipline the way one walks. Ultimately, such a walk will bring a person into communion and agreement with God and those who possess His Spirit.

Since walking is associated with Christianity, one must assume there is a spiritual journey involved with this Christian life. The Apostle Peter confirms that Christianity is a journey. He tells us we are sojourners or pilgrims in this world.[1] As a sojourner, we are strangers in our present status since we are simply passing through this present world. As pilgrims, we are searching for something in this world that will satisfy our seeking heart. Obviously, being sojourners and pilgrims will affect our attitudes towards the world and our approaches in regard to the matters of life.

The Apostle Peter explained why we are sojourners in his first epistle; we do not fit in this present world. We must, therefore, abstain from fleshly lusts that war against the Spirit. In other words, we should be uncomfortable in our present status in the midst of the unholy and corruptible practices of this world. Our conversations and lifestyles must prove contrary to the world. We must be honest in all that we do to ensure we bring glory to God. As Jesus said, the world will hate those who belong to Him. The reason is because the world is at enmity with God. There is no agreement in the realm of spirit or truth.[2]

Christianity is a journey, a walk, but what does this mean for you and me? It means Christianity is a way of life. In fact, it is distinguished by the activity of Jesus' life in us. Colossians 3:4 brings out the fact that life is associated with Jesus, "When Christ, who is our life, shall appear, then shall ye also appear with him in glory." (Emphasis added.)

Today, life is eluding many people. The reason for this is that they are simply surviving or getting by. They do not live out each moment, minute, or day; rather they live from one activity to another activity. For example, some people live for the weekend. Other people live for certain events. It is their way of existing until they can experience some type of sensationalism. Meanwhile, they simply exist until they can feel something called life or a bit of spark in the midst of what seems dead,

---

[1] 1 Peter 2:11
[2] John 15:18-25; James 4:4

useless drudgery. As a result, it's not uncommon for life to be too great of a burden for most people to bear.

Instead of experiencing life, people are despairing over their lives. They can never seem to get on top of life with all of its demands. Every aspect of this meaningless activity called "life" disillusions them. Such disillusionment often produces and surrounds unproductive or unfulfilling relationships. It seems that this experience called "life" deems such people failures because they cannot make anything work. These people end up walking under a cloud of depression. They see no hope, purpose, or reason for their present existence.

At times, they may question the purpose of their lives. They even try different things such as religion, New Age practices, and various activities to avoid facing the drudgery of what appears to be an existence of futility. At times the meaningless aspects of their lives result in the gut-wrenching reality that there is something missing. At the end of each attempt is the same old vacuum that seems to suck more of their will to live from every fiber of their being.

The struggle to live is a battle in which the mind becomes weary, the emotions become taxed with overwhelming stress and hopelessness, and the will loses its resolve to continue down the same dark corridor of hopelessness.

The question as to what constitutes life nags those who consider their despairing lot in life. What does it mean to live life? True living cannot mean merely existing, getting by in each struggle, or surviving the latest onset of hopelessness. Life must have greater meaning then simply wading through the maze of despair, disillusionment, and depression.

The reason people despair over life is that it is not just meant to be survived; rather, it is meant to be lived out. To live life, people must discover what life is all about. They must realize it is, in essence, a journey to discover the source or purpose of our existence.

The problem is people try to determine life on their terms, rather than discover what it really is. Since they are trying to determine their very existence, they become consumed by despair as they realize that they cannot influence or control life according to their plans. Rather than discovering it, life eludes them, leaving them in a state of confusion and uncertainty.

Once a person discovers the real essence of their journey through this world, then he or she embraces life. The harsh reality is that most people avoid the reality of life, rather than embracing it. Clearly, we must not despair over this odyssey; we must learn to cherish it. How do we learn to cherish life? We must learn to value that which truly brings substance to it. When life holds no value or purpose, it is because we value that which holds no real significance. Therefore, we end up holding an empty bag, rather than clinging to that which brings us purpose and meaning.

Once we begin to cherish our life, we will experience life. Needless to say, most people fail to experience it. As a result, they become skeptical towards it.

What does it mean to experience real life? It means facing this experience for what it is. Most people are running away from life. Facing it can prove to be frightening and disheartening. After all, life presents both sorrow and challenges to each of us. To experience this adventure, we must encounter the bad with the good. We must taste sorrow to experience the laughter of the soul. There is good and evil in every arena. Without the contrast, we would not be able to recognize the joy of goodness and the emptiness and condemnation of evil. Contrast often produces confusion and adversity to those who hold tightly to their Cinderella fantasy of life. However, as we experience life in its fullness, character can be forged, satisfaction can be discovered, and lasting hope can be realized.

Life is meant to be discovered, embraced, and experienced. Clearly, we must discover the source of it. We must embrace the reality of its origins and experience the essence of it.

What does it mean to discover life? In order to answer that question, we must consider the different aspects of life. In a way, it is like becoming a philosopher. A philosopher of life seeks to understand the purpose of it. If one can understand the purpose of life, the adventure through this world could actually make sense.

This brings us back to Christianity. I have embarked on many different approaches to life, only to find that life eluded me. However, the life established in Christianity not only established the purpose for my being, but it answered the many questions that haunt so many people. The essence of Christianity is life, and discovering this life leads us through the maze of the many different challenges that confront each of us on this incredible journey.

Granted, we may know the answers to this question, but we may not be living it. Some are attempting to make sense out of this adventure, but it is according to their personal perception. Instead of trying to make sense out of life according to a limited perception, each of us must stop and consider the reality of it. We must become a philosopher for a moment and face life head on. It is time we come back to the source of life to establish our very reason for existing.

2

BECOMING A PHILOSOPHER

There was a time when great minds were occupied with the consideration of life. These men's approach to life made them philosophers of life. They would consider every aspect of life and philosophize about the meaning and reason for it. They dissected, pursued, and made conclusions about it. We occasionally read or hear their conclusions.

These philosophers approached the concept of life from different angles. There was the popular approach of experience. For example, some of these individuals considered life solely from this perspective. What could their different experiences tell them about life?

These experiences would penetrate into the emotional arena, causing these individuals to feel something. What they felt was often associated with the idea of living and defining life. The conclusion to the matter was that these feelings were associated with the sensation of life, supposedly verifying that a person was indeed alive. Such conclusions were fleshly, sensual, and temporary.

Experience, no doubt, is important because it entails some reality. But one must consider if an individual is only pursuing a particular type of experience. In other words, did this person determine what he or she would experience to control his or her reality or conclusions about what would constitute life? Obviously, certain philosophers determined what they would experience, and called it life. Yet, their experience had nothing to do with coming to terms with the concept of living.

Life is an experience in and of itself, but we cannot determine what we will experience due to its unpredictable aspects. No one can control the experiences of life or how they might unexpectedly affect him or her. Life has its surprises, its points of joy and happiness, but at the core of it is a harsh reality that most people refuse to face. Most reality has to do with the workings, effects, and results of sin. The ultimate reality of sin is death to or the ruin of spiritual well-being, destruction of relationships, and separation from what is genuine life. Therefore, the normal outcome is that most people avoid experiencing the essence of this odyssey.

Life is also associated with understanding its value. What makes this experience valuable and worthwhile? Such an approach can pursue the ethical side of this subject. To consider life in light of social views brings us down to customs and cultural influences. This approach tries to identify the meaning and worth of life based upon how someone may live. But, does this type of identity enable us to understand this experience?

Life does not come from the outside sources of this present world; it must exist from within. In other words, culture, race, and customs have nothing to do with creating or providing life. Granted, such influences will encourage certain lifestyles, but they cannot give, ensure, or maintain life. These influences may attach certain requirements of how individuals should live, but they have no ability to bring real worth or meaning to life.

Another way people approach their present existence is from a religious perspective. Religion, in some arenas, causes us to consider life outside of our experiences, customs, and culture to explore the influence of the unseen and the unexplainable. Yet, man's religion can turn out to be practices and beliefs that can cause one to become superstitious, unrealistic, fanatical, and legalistic. The problem with most religion is that it stops with man defining life according to his religious attempts, self-righteous standards, and high opinions of personal "goodness".

Religion also serves as an attempt to make sense out of life according to some belief system or code. In fact, this is where most people develop a moral code that may keep them from doing bad, but it cannot change their disposition. Religion may make a person more spiritual in appearance while he or she remains ignorant about the unseen. It may make a person more rigid in lifestyle, but strict practices can make him or her legalistic and indifferent towards the plight of others.[1] It may also make a person more religious in activities, but religion that goes to the extreme can express itself in fanaticism that has no sanity or reality to it.

Another approach to life is that of wisdom.[2] Some perceive that if they could gain wisdom, they would understand the meaning of life. In this particular pursuit, people perceive that they can gain insight or enlightenment that will give them the upper hand in the meaning of their existence.

This type of person perceives that such enlightenment will give him or her the means to solve the problems of the world. A pursuit of this nature can prove to be dangerous because exploration beyond this physical world into an arena that has no basis in which to discern its validity will ensue.

Granted, the search for the meaning of life takes people beyond the fleshly realm, but there is no way to test whether conclusions are true. In such cases, people do not discover the meaning of this adventure, but they often encounter demonically inspired experiences that will seem more real than life itself.

However, the reality of life does not make sense in light of the happenings around us. There are no real formulas with which to

---

[1] Romans 7:6; 2 Corinthians 3:6; 2 Timothy 3:5
[2] Consider how God sees the wisdom of man in James 3:13-16

understand life. Granted, the real meaning of this existence is discovered beyond the physical arena, but life is experienced every day on the earthly, fleshly plain.

If the pursuit of life does not bring us back to the reality that surrounds us, we must deem such pursuits as lies or counterfeits. The problem is that a growing number of people are trying to live life in the supernatural arena. The results are frightening in that such people are unable to deal with or in reality.

The final way to pursue an understanding life is to analyze it from the basis of philosophies, concepts, or fundamental beliefs. Such perspectives will often determine how we interpret life, but will prove ineffective when it comes to living it. The reason these perspectives fail to result in living life is because they do not become truths. In essence, these ideas never penetrate the heart. If philosophies or beliefs lack heart, they will remain concepts. Concepts are indifferent to reality.

Beliefs that are not applied to life keep people from addressing reality. These beliefs become dogmatic, unrealistic, judgmental, and self-exalting. Since our different pursuits of life have proven to be all vain or empty, where does one look to experience life?

This is the question I finally came to in my search for life. When I considered this adventure in light of experience, all I discovered was that there was no real satisfaction in what proved to be vain experiences. I considered life in light of culture and found prejudices, injustice, and mocking. I tried man's various religious presentations, only to discover most were hypocritical and dead. I pursued worldly wisdom only to find it often led to foolishness. I even tried to define my existence according to my religious beliefs, but such a pursuit left me a bigger hypocrite than those I took liberty to judge in my arrogance.

As I struggled with my philosophy of life, I realized life did not make sense. It did not matter what angle I approached it from, it seemed as if it actually made a fool out of me. It exposed my weaknesses, unveiled my hypocrisy, and striped me of my personal strength. In the end, I discovered that all I possessed was the philosophy that was influenced by the world. It not only spoiled my ability to face reality, but it caused me to operate in deception. It may have been based on accepted traditions of customs and culture, but it was man-inspired. It was clearly influenced by the spirit of the world.[3]

The final result was that I ended up with a big question mark that translated into inward despair. Life as I understood it seemed so useless and a waste of time. It appeared to have no real purpose.

Where does one find life when all the doors to life appear to be closed? Sadly, people start from point "A" to see if they missed something in their pursuit. Perhaps, there was an experience they missed, a practice they overlooked, a religion that was genuine, or greater insight yet undiscovered.

---

[3] Ephesians 2:2; Colossians 2:8

As a philosopher, man may look for the meaning of life, but he may utterly fail to recognize it as it passes by. After all, he is too busy trying to create an existence that he can recognize, understand, or that will best serve his purpose. As a result, he not only fails to discover life, but he fails to understand and experience it by learning the lessons of life.

Where do people look to find life? Sadly, it is in the wrong places. Each time they look in such places, they are left more disillusioned about life, dissatisfied with their existence, and lost in uncertainty.

We all develop a philosophy about life that will affect our attitudes and approaches towards life and God. However, the purpose of life is not to philosophize about it, but to develop a philosophy that will allow each of us to experience, discover, and embrace it. Life will not be handed to us; rather, we must come to terms with what constitutes the real essence of life. Such a search produces the million-dollar question in regard to discovering the real purpose of life. And, finding the right answer guarantees that a person's attitude and direction will radically change.

How about you? Can you honestly answer this question? It could change the way you look at and walk out your life.

3

LOOKING FOR LIFE

The great challenge in life is to actually find the essence of it. People equate their existence to different elements. Most people think of life in terms of happiness. However, the idea of happiness varies according to the person. For one person the idea of happiness is to have a well-balanced family. For someone else, happiness is fishing or getting in touch with nature. Other people may equate happiness with wealth, pleasure, friendship, or a successful career.

The reality is that all such concepts of happiness prove to be illusive, empty, or disappointing. There was a man who perceived that if he could enjoy the great outdoors without any distractions, he would be happy. Needless to say, he lived for retirement. When retirement came, he pursued his idea of happiness. Later, he admitted that one could only do so much of the same activity before it became empty and boring.

It is the idea of how something will make one feel that becomes the proverbial carrot at the end of the stick. As long as the idea remains the carrot that is always out of reach, it can continue as the essence of hope. However, once it becomes a reality, it often proves to be as empty as the rest of all the selfish, worldly pursuits. At this time the individual realizes that he or she was caught up with an idea, rather than with reality.

Most pursuits for the majority of people are self-serving. These individuals calculate what will make them happy and pursue after it. They often conclude that, if they are happy and satisfied with their existence, they can begin to live a life that will have meaning and purpose. Such pursuits ultimately leave them disillusioned and confused when the idea or fantasy of happiness is stripped away by the daily challenges of life, responsibilities, and the intrusion of people.

As I have stood at different crossroads in my lifetime, I could not help but wonder what life was all about. My pursuits after the different ideas of happiness often left me disappointed by life. Happiness seemed fleeting and hope was dashed by the various challenges that would intrude into my existence. These experiences happened in the tender years of growing up, but in my immaturity, I remained an optimist. My logic was that since other people had control over my life, I would never reach the pinnacle of my life, and, once I was on my own, I could mold my life into what I desired it to be. However, this even proved to be an elusive carrot. At the end of each pursuit, I had to ask myself if all a person does is simply live an uneventful, hard life and then die, what was the significance or purpose behind this adventure called "life?"

Perhaps, I mused, the song that boasts, "I did it my way," had a grasp on life. Yet, I learned early in my experiences that doing it my way never guaranteed happiness, purpose, or meaning. In fact, when I did it my way, it ended in despair. The person that sang that song may have done it his or her way, but ultimately such a boast would fade into the background as it gave way to some other platitude or philosophy. It seemed that there were many catchy tunes and platitudes concerning life that would grab the attention of people according to the present wave of fads, times, and seasons. These songs and sayings always seemed to rush in like waves and then recede out in the midst of the ever-changing environment of fickle humanity. In examining this, I had to ask what kind of legacy did such boastings or attempts leave?

If you asked the question of where people find the real meaning of life, you would probably receive various answers. Some might advocate that life can be found in success. The idea of success varies with people, but success is often based on the culture we live in. For America, success means the power to influence. Some would declare that education is the means to ensure success. Having degrees supposedly help people climb the ladder to success. However, I have known of well-educated men who worked at sawmills and lived on the streets.

We could go on with one example after another of what would constitute success, as well as the disillusionment of each pursuit. Obviously, there is not one attempt on man's part that can guarantee what people would deem the pinnacle of all success. However, success is tied into the world's philosophies of what determines happiness in the present life. The world offers many avenues to so-called "happiness". If one pursuit fails to bring the desired experience, there are many other options available. Each option has its own form of glitter or hope behind it.

As you consider the pursuits of others, you will realize there are only four avenues that offer happiness: relationships, material wealth, religion, and God.

When we look to relationships for happiness, we are looking to others to make us happy. Whether it is a spouse, family, or friends, we perceive that others hold the key to our true happiness. However, others will always miserably fail to make us happy, let alone to maintain happiness.

Happiness is an attitude more than a state. People's attitudes will determine how they perceive happenings around them. When a person is miserable in attitude, he or she is incapable of being happy regardless of what is going on. When people look to others to make them happy, they expect these poor souls to placate their attitudes, appease their desires, and make them feel good about themselves.

The reality is that others cannot control our reality or change our attitude about an issue, no matter how much they may bow down to our expectations. In fact, the more others bow down to a person's way of thinking, the more tyrannical that individual becomes in his or her demands. Such demands become insatiable, arrogant, and indifferent.

This is why each of us must take responsibility for our personal well-being, as well as confront our wrong attitudes. By becoming responsible for wrong attitudes, we will be able to come to a place where we can know joy.

Joy is different than happiness. Joy serves as an anchor of the soul that allows a person to come to a place of well-being. Such joy does not depend on circumstances; rather, it depends on the type of state that is being maintained. Those who are joyful come from a state of contentment. Contentment knows how to be satisfied; therefore, it has the ability to delight in the small things, experience pleasure in the midst of challenges, and display happiness that is manifested in a right attitude.

The next place people look for life is in the things of the world. For example, the riches of the world will enable individuals to buy so-called "happiness" as they heap the things of the world upon themselves. The education of the world will help them succeed in reaching their goals in life. These goals will speak of success, meaning, and value. In the minds of these people, the things of the world will empower them to pursue and possess a life that will bring happiness and purpose.

The Bible tells us that the world is temporary.[1] Obviously, the world can only offer a temporary utopia before reality intrudes into its fragile fantasy. Jesus summarized the essence of the world's form of hope and purpose in this way, "...Take heed, and beware of covetousness; for a man's life consisteth not in the abundance of the things which he possesseth" (Luke 12:15). The world offers things such as wealth, power, prestige, importance, and influence. However, Jesus said not to covet such things for life does not consist of such matters.

The next place people look for the meaning of life is religion. It is within the makeup of man to be religious. He must worship something greater than himself. After all, to look to self makes a person prideful, indifferent, frustrated, or tyrannical. Ultimately, self leads people into a depressing reality that is not only isolated and lonely, but offers no hope. The main manifestation of the perspective of self is self-pity.

Self-pity is a morbid reality in which a person becomes impressed with his or her suffering. As the individual suffers through each crisis, he or she becomes a greater martyr in his or her mind. Self-pity often serves as a platform for such people to exalt their suffering as a means to show how noble they are in light of how unfairly life is treating them. In this sick reality, the person is always being exalted for the purpose of others bowing down to their pathetic reality. In fact, such people wear self-pity as a badge of courage when, in reality, it is a sick example of those who refuse to face life head on. After all, life is never going to adjust to our convenience. It is never going to bow down to our way of thinking or

---

[1] 1 John 2:17

doing. We can claim that we are unable to face the harshness of life, but what will we do? Sit down and die? Or, perhaps we can go insane and hide in some unrealistic world.

The reality is life will continue on whether we sit down to die or claim insanity. It will not bow down to what we are willing to accept. Granted, we can go the way of self-pity and make ourselves a depressing lump that many will barely tolerate, or we can turn around and face life.

As a Christian, the issue is not how unfair life is, but how faithful God is. The only sweetness that will come out of the problems of life for the Christian is the revelation of God's faithfulness. It is in the crisis of life that Christians' testimonies can grow as the sweetness of God's faithfulness is realized in the fiery ovens that test our faith.[2] A powerful testimony of God comes with a high price tag. However, that high price tag is discovering His faithfulness to deliver us from and through the matters of life that bring us to the abyss of destruction.

Consider for a moment the person who looks elsewhere for life. If he or she looks to the world to find life, he or she discovers emptiness. As people operate between different fantasies created by the images of the world, they become despairing, clueless, or unrealistic about their environment. Eventually, such an environment creates a tormenting vacuum in their soul.

Religion is supposed to answer the tough questions about life. However, man inspired or driven religion often proves to be hypocritical. It encourages outward conformity that is both legalistic and judgmental. It offers doctrines without Spirit, creeds without authority, and rules without power. Such religion becomes lifeless and has nothing to offer. Then people either become skeptical towards all manners of religion or, on the other hand, fanatical in a desperate attempt to find meaning, purpose, or sense in life.

Religion of this nature becomes idolatrous as man, doctrines, creeds, rules, and high opinions of personal self-righteousness are exalted. Obviously, man is being deified at some level, rather than God being honored. In such an environment, the religious pulpit becomes a platform for man to perform from, rather than an altar where the God of the universe is being considered, worshipped, and honored.

All these attempts ultimately prove to be dissatisfying. It is as though life mocks one's attempts to unlock its secrets. After all, is there a secret to living life? Is there some key to unlock some door to this experience? Where can one find life in the midst of that which is limited, temporary, and lifeless?

These questions mocked me in my attempts to discover life. I tried to find it within myself to change the world, only to find my reality creating hopelessness. I looked to the world for my existence, only to find it empty. I tried popular religion, only to discover it was a façade that had no real substance or life behind it.

---

[2] 1 Peter 1:6-8

My search for life seemed so hopeless to me, until one day a glimmer of hope reached into the recesses of my soul. To my surprise, I found that hope rested in a relationship, not with my family or friends, but with the living God of the universe. To my delight, I discovered I could possess treasures that would last forever. These treasures would bring meaning and purpose to my life. Also, and not least of all, I found a religion based not on man's doctrines or emphasis, but on a Person, the Lord Jesus Christ. This religion was living and pure. It was a walk that embraced a way of living. It was where my heart became an altar, and from that altar Jesus was lifted up in His redemption and glory.

What amazed me is that I did not find this life; rather it found me in the midst of my despairing plight.[3] I had been seeking something, but I did not realize what I was looking for. I was looking for the one true God of the universe. Eventually, I came up against the true God in an incredible way that testified of His love for and commitment to me, helping me to realize that He was the One I had been seeking all along. Clearly, I could not find Him in myself, nor could I understand Him in light of the world's philosophies or pursuits. He could not be found in dead, hypocritical, or heretical religion, for He lives in the midst of that which is alive with His Spirit, and in that which is holy, pure, righteous, and true.

Finding the essence of life marks the beginning of seeking this life out daily. People must seek God out in every situation and find Him in the midst of every tribulation. They must not look *for* God; rather, they must look *to* God. After all, once you are found by God, you now know what you are looking for. From this perspective, it is a matter of identifying Him in the midst of a situation, seeking out His will for a matter, and walking it out as you keep your eyes on Jesus.[4]

Are you looking for life? Are you looking in the wrong places? God has been looking for you, calling out your name, and longing for you to allow Him to find you in the midst of the devastating hopelessness that plagues those walking in darkness.

---

[3] Luke 15:3-7
[4] Jeremiah 29:13; Hebrews 12:2

4

LESSONS OF LIFE

In our attempt to establish life, we end up seeing life as a burden. We note that life robs us of the strength of our youth, enduring hope, and meaningful purpose. The real purpose of this experience seems to elude even the sincerest philosopher. Life is a struggle, and as one struggles with the issues of this adventure, he or she must conclude that life has a purpose. But what is that purpose? Clearly, if anyone is to live this life by discovering what it is, embracing what it must become, and experiencing what it must be, then he or she must come to terms with what life is truly offering to those who are bent on discovering its treasures. Granted, one must cease from defining or establishing his or her existence on his or her terms in an attempt to answer the questions of life.

The purpose of this experience has to do with the lessons of life. The world is one big classroom. The teacher in this great classroom is life itself. However, it is hard to decipher what this teacher is trying to reveal to us. Instead of learning the lessons of life, most people develop questions because of their existence. Life leaves in its wake unresolved issues. Such issues make life seem unfair. Therefore, it is hard to receive any real instruction from life since it seems to mock all attempts to make peace with the reality it brings with its changing tides. These unresolved issues also make one's existence seem senseless. In fact, nothing makes sense in the midst of sorrow, hurts, wounds, and despair.

This brings us to the lessons of life. What must we learn in order to resolve those nagging questions that leave us hopeless? There are three main lessons that life will teach the sober student, the serious philosopher, and the realistic seeker. These three lessons will constantly be reinforced as each of us struggles with the different challenges of life.

The first lesson we all must learn is that *we are not God*. Amazingly, we all start out with a great sense of self-sufficiency.[1] We feel strong and confident in such sufficiency. We think we have control over our worlds, and believe we can accomplish anything we put our minds to.

Consider such an attitude. It declares that the person is in control of his or her reality. The person is stating that he or she is God. However, life has a way of revealing that personal strength can be quickly ebbed away, and self-confidence can be turned into anxiety and despair.

---

[1] 2 Corinthians 3:5

Regardless of my attempts, life did not submit to my way of thinking. It did not bow down to my way of being, and it will never give way to my way of doing. Life not only opposed me, but it often continued on without me, leaving me in depression. Obviously, I discovered that I was at the mercy of something that proved to be indifferent to who I was and my personal plight.

Life is a current that will not be stopped, redirected, controlled, or conquered. This current is alive, and it carries the various aspects of life from the debris of sin, the destruction of the world, and the consequences of death. Rather than stopping the debris of sin, I often found myself giving in to it. Instead of redirecting the power of life, I found myself succumbing to it. Rather than controlling life, I found myself being subject to it. Instead of overruling and conquering death, I became a victim to its claims and entanglements as it slowly worked within every fiber of my being.

It was vital that I learn the first lesson of life. Although I had to avoid becoming skeptical or cynical towards life, I had to come to a point where I conceded that I was not God. I was not, nor would I ever be able to call the shots, nor did I have any power to do so. In fact, life does not consider me at all. It is not concerned that I am upset with its indifference, offended by its injustice, and shocked by its cruelty. It does not care that I am left with unresolved issues that appear to have no resolution.

However, these aspects of life teach each of us that we do not control our lives. All we can do is determine the attitude and philosophy we develop about life. This attitude will depend upon what attitude we develop towards God. Life is meant to teach us that there is a God, but that it is neither you nor I.

The reality that I am not God can be a harsh reality. After all, I perceived myself as always being on top of a matter when challenged, coming out on top of a situation when it seemed hopeless, or climbing to the top to claim actual victory when defeat seemed imminent. In each defeat and failure, I learned that I had to face the harsh fact that the world does not revolve around me, and that I am at the mercy of something that does not appear to have any boundaries.

It is in light of this first realization that I was able to learn the next lesson of life, which is that *I* need *God*. This brings me down to the lesson of reliance. If people could control their realities and worlds, they would have no need of God. Sadly, religion has developed so-called "methods" in its attempts to control God. This control is for the purpose of determining reality. For example, if I don't like my reality, I can just use one of the self-help methods to arm-wrestle God into my way of thinking. After all, if I cannot control my reality, then I must control the One who can change or adjust my reality. I will simply call such an attempt "faith" when, in reality, it is nothing more than unbelief towards the righteousness, faithfulness, and power of God.

Unbelief refuses to trust God in present reality. God never promised He would deliver us from the harsh realities of our existence. He only guaranteed that He would deliver us through the challenges of life. He proved this in the wilderness with the children of Israel. When the serpents were released among the people as a means of judgment, God did not deliver them from the bite of the deadly serpent; rather, He provided a point of deliverance. Ultimately, they were delivered through the judgment of the serpents by faith in what God actually provided.[2]

People want to be spared from the lessons of life. They do not want to put their reliance on God to deliver them through a situation; rather, they want God to change their reality so they do not have to trust Him with those things that they want to control. In this type of arena, God is viewed as a pawn to be used as a means of controlling the aspects of life that will not bow down to these individuals.

Hence, enter religious methods to control God. Whether people use His Word against Him to bend Him to their wills or make declarations that demand He comply, they must get God to see it their way. Such methods are not faith in the character of God; instead, they are faith in the ability to control His power.

Fear can enter the scene when such methods prove to have no power over God. Such fear dissipates the power of God, subdues all knowledge of His love, and causes confusion.[3] This fear comes from the reality that God may not do what is expected of Him. He just might let such misguided hope crash against the rocks of reality as the person experiences ruin and loss. Such ruin will expose the person's real character and level of faith.

We all can admire the words of Job, "Though he slay me, yet will I trust in him; but I will maintain mine own ways before him" (Job 13:15). But, how many of us would maintain our ways before God if we truly suffered the same loss as Job? We can always think highly of our faith as long as it is never tested.[4] But, allow life to test one's faith, and he or she will realize his or her true level of confidence in God.

Obviously, the first lesson reveals people's arrogant attitude. In our initial ill-tempered, unregenerate state, we all possess the same attitude Satan displayed in Isaiah 14:12-15. I *WILL* control my reality, my world, and my life. I *WILL* ascend in my arrogance in the matters concerning life. I *WILL* exalt my ways in regards to life. I *WILL* sit on the throne, ruling over the ways of life. I *WILL* ascend above the challenges of life, and in the end I *WILL* be like the Most High in the matters of life.

However, life proves otherwise. As each experience left me in the different wakes of challenges and destruction, my existence appeared to mock me. This is where my real source of confidence would be revealed.

---

[2] Numbers 21:5-9; John 3:14-15
[3] 2 Timothy 1:7; 1 John 4:18
[4] 1 Peter 1:6-9

Challenging the Christian Life

In the initial challenges of a person's newfound faith in Christ, he or she realizes that faith in Christ must be refined and matured if one is to grow in the knowledge of Christ. The natural tendency when faith is being tested, enlarged, and matured is to deem God unfair and become skeptical towards challenging experiences. However, it is in such testing that a person's character is revealed.

Attitude is the manifestation of character. When life's challenges put a person up against the wall, his or her attitude will reveal the depth of his or her character about the matters of life. If the attitude is wrong, people can get into destructive patterns that allow them to wallow in self-pity and despair. After all, life has succeeded in accomplishing its first objective; the person is no longer exalted in personal arrogance. He or she has been brought low by the action of life. Now the person must determine what attitude and philosophy he or she is going to adopt towards his or her experience. The person can rage against it, only to become bitter. The individual can become cynical, only to become hard and judgmental. The person can become a suffering martyr, only to become touchy, paranoid, and angry, or he or she can become depressed and eventually fall into hopelessness.

Needless to say, the initial attitude reveals our source of confidence. Such a revelation is to show each of us that our confidence is not yet founded on Jesus. Faith is a choice of the will. We must personally choose to trust Him in the midst of challenges. This means we do not expect Him to change our circumstances, rather we trust Him to be faithful to see us through the situation.

If I make the correct choice to trust Jesus in a matter, I will be able to discover the treasure of life. The treasure of life can only be found in the one source of life, Jesus Christ. Jesus stated that without Him we can do nothing.[5] He is the Vine and we are the branches. The only way we can possess life is by abiding in Him. Branches that are not connected to the Vine are dying, dead, and doomed. Regardless of how beautiful they may have been, how many leaves budded from them, or even the fruit that might have been evident, without the proper connection to the Vine, there is no current of life pulsating through them. Without life, all matters are considered dead and doomed. Eventually, the useless branches will be cut off, gathered, and burned.

The lessons of life clearly teach us that we need God. This means we must become connected to God. Our need for God brings us to salvation. We must be saved from our useless dead state. We must be saved from being cast into a fire of judgment because we have no purpose, no meaning, and no life outside of Jesus.

Our need for God will bring us to the foot of the cross, seeking Him as our source of life. It is here that we finally put all of our reliance on Him. When the great "I WILL" of arrogance has been brought down to the "I NEED" of humility, God is able to receive us. Reliance points to

---

[5] John 15:4-6

faith, and faith is what connects us to the great "I AM". The great "I AM' is the one who serves as the origin of all life.

It is important to point out that God is the giver of life. He actually gives us three types of life. First, *He has given us our physical life.* This life is a gift. It is hard for many to believe their burdensome life is a gift from God. However, it is a gift in which to experience all that God has intended for each of us. As a result, our present life serves as a test as to whether or not we are going to neglect, abuse, misuse, or use this gift properly. To use this gift properly means one day I will present it back to the Lord. The proper goal in regards to the gift of life is to bring glory to God in and with my physical life.

The second type of life *God desires to give us* is the life He has for each of us. In other words, God has designated our existence before the foundation of the world. This experience is meant to be holy, but it is marked by adoption into His heavenly family. In other words, it is marked by an eternal inheritance.[6] Such a life is a matter of choice. You must choose it in your heart to embrace this life.

God brought this choice out in the wilderness. In Deuteronomy 30:19 we read, "I call heaven and earth to record this day against you, that I have set before you life and death, blessing and cursing; therefore, choose life, that both thou and thy seed may live." The life God has prepared for each of us is a matter of choosing His way. Any way outside of this life puts one on the broad path of destruction. Such a path will prove to be cursed by darkness, hopelessness, destruction, and death.[7]

Needless to say, this second life is eternal life. To have this life, we must be born again from above. A new heart and a new spirit distinguish such a life. It is marked by resurrection power that one day will raise us up in the fullness of God to completely realize this incredible gift of God.[8]

The third life is the life God *wants to impart to us*. Such a life points to the abundant life. The eternal life that is in us will not be fully realized until we pass through the corruptible veil of this flesh to embark on the incorruptible reality of heaven. However, we are meant to experience the abundant or complete life of Christ here. Whether or not we experience the satisfaction of His abundance will depend on if we partake of Jesus' divine life.[9]

When it comes to eternal life, we must choose the way of heaven. However, when it comes to experiencing the abundant life, we must walk it out by faith.[10]

As you consider these three lives, you can begin to understand that the thief of our souls wants to rob us of our physical well-being, kill all that is marked for eternity in us, and destroy any aspect of the abundant

---

[6] Ephesians 1:4-14
[7] Matthew 7:13-14
[8] Ezekiel 36:25-27; John 3:3, 5; 5:21-29; 11:25-26
[9] John 10:10; 1 Corinthians 15:40-54; 2 Peter 1:3-4
[10] 2 Corinthians 5:7

life working in us. The great question is how do we maintain our physical well-being, preserve the mark of eternity in our present lives, and ensure the abundance of Christ's life in us? Jesus actually revealed what we must do with each aspect of the life He desires to give us, work within us, and bring forth through us. After all, the abundant life will be marked by its fruits. The first fruit being that of an attitude made evident by the fruit of the Spirit. The second type of fruit will be the life of Jesus being established and brought forth in others.[11]

Jesus gives us this instruction in regard to finding, receiving, and establishing His abundant life in us. You must deny yourself of any rights to a personal life. Denial in this text points to consecration of the life you are presently living in the flesh. Such an existence requires that you present your body as a living sacrifice to find and secure what is the acceptable, perfect will of God.[12]

After you deny yourself for the purpose of consecration, you must pick up your cross. Eternal life is marked by death that has given way to resurrection power. The cross points to the fact that we are becoming crucified to the world as we are mortifying the deeds of the flesh.[13]

It is only as the avenue of the flesh is closed down that we can be assured of the disciplined life. A disciplined life is what ensures us that we will follow Jesus into the abundant or complete life. It is in the environment of spiritual abundance that we can begin to truly experience and live out the life God has ordained for us. It is in the reality of the complete life that we will be able to discover the character and ways of God.

We must keep in mind that it is up to us to find this life, receive it, and walk it out. We can only find our real life when we come to terms with the fact that we are not God of our life. We cannot make our life, ensure it, or add to it. God is the author of it. He is the One who has our days numbered, as well as the One who knows what will add to and complete our journey.[14]

This brings us to the third lesson of life that *we need to let God be God*. People have a hard time of just letting God be God. They have this selfish tendency to want to control Him. Each lesson of life reveals that God's ways are ways that can be trusted. We may not want to be subject to His ways by faith, but such resistance has to do with unbelief and not the character of God. The only way we can learn this lesson is by following Jesus into an abundant life.

Once we learn these lessons, we can seek Him out in our need and prepare to receive from Him by faith. As we receive, we begin to learn of Him. As our confidence grows, we give way to Him being God in our lives. As we give way to Him, He is able to complete our life with the

---

[11] John 15:5-8; Galatians 5:22-23
[12] Romans 12:1-2
[13] Matthew 16:24; Romans 6:3-12; 8:13; Galatians 6:14
[14] Psalm 90:12

reality of His Son. It is in Jesus that we truly discover the abundance of heaven. In light of the abundance, all past issues of life become resolved as they dissipate. This dissipation is due to the satisfaction that is experienced from partaking of the Manna of heaven and freely drinking of the River of Living Waters.[15]

Let us consider the picture that has emerged from this chapter. Consider the following table.

UNRESOLVED ISSUES	LESSONS	LIVES	FORMS OF ATTACK	SOLUTION
Life is Unfair.	I am not God (Attitude)	Physical Life (Gift)	Robs you of the gift of life.	Deny Self
Life does not make sense.	I need God (Reliance)	The life He has for me. (Eternal)	Kills what is the eternal work of God in us.	Pick up the Cross.
Life mocks me.	Let God be God (Walk)	The life He wants to impart. (Abundant)	Destroy the abundance associated with the life of Christ in us.	Follow Jesus

As you consider the table, where do you fit in it? The solution to the unresolved issues is simple. It is Jesus Christ in His fullness. As our Creator, He gives us purpose in our present life. As our Savior, He gives us eternal life. As our Shepherd, He leads us to that which is abundant, and, as our Lord, He ensures that abundance.[16] Are you adhering to our Lord's call or are you allowing life to mark you as you walk according to your own ways of destruction? If you are walking in the ways of death, you need to know you are abusing your present life, missing the mark of

---

[15] John 6:32-35; 7:37-39
[16] John 1:1-3; 10:14-18; Colossians 1:13-19; 1 John 4:14

Challenging the Christian Life

that which is eternal, and failing to experience the abundance of the life that can only be found in Jesus Christ.

5

THE REALITY OF IT ALL

As you begin to consider the essence of life, you realize that most people look at life from the point of expectations. In other words, they must put their hope in some aspect of life. If they do not, they will see no purpose for going on. However, such expectations can fall short when hope is deferred. One of the greatest philosophers about life, Solomon, made this statement in Proverbs 13:12, "Hope deferred maketh the heart sick; but when the desire cometh, it is a tree of life."

Obviously, expectation must be established in something that is firm. However, what in this experience called life can be considered firm, immovable, or sure? In all honesty, there is nothing tangible in life that can be considered sure. Everything that can be seen proves to be in flux. What we may consider valuable or sure may change in seconds. If you don't believe me, watch the news. It seems that the world around us is shaking. No wonder people walk around in depression or hopelessness about the prospects of life.

This brings us to ask, what kind of changes in our lives can bring us to such a state? The answer is simple. It is reality. The reality of life is that it can catch one off guard. It can shake, shock, and bring a person to utter despair. It can appear as insignificant drudgery one moment, but in the next moment it can turn around and bring a person to a state of utter ecstasy or devastation.

The real struggle for most people in life is to control, change, or adjust reality. However, any real attempt to do so can end in defeat or delusion. The harsh reality is that life goes on without any regard to the devastation it may leave in its wake.

Some people realize that they cannot control, change, or adjust reality, but they live in denial about it. In other words, they ignore it. Eventually, life becomes a tidal wave of unresolved issues that dogs the heels of such people. They have a sense that if they stop long enough, they may be destroyed by the utter despair of it all. As a result, they continue to ignore those particular aspects of life until they feel themselves becoming insane. Such a state becomes tormenting and frightening.

Other people become martyrs in their reality. They walk around in a morbid state as they accept their terrible lot in life. Their attitude is, "This is what life has dished out to me. Therefore, like a good sport, I am accepting it in a state of martyrdom and self-pity." These people exist under a cloud of great suffering as they accept what they consider to be the unfair advancements of life.

Such people use their reality as a platform to somehow come out on top as far as their outward show of nobility goes. They see themselves as being quite noble in accepting their terrible lot in life. In fact, they are often exalted in such a way that can throw doubt on the very character of God. After all, how could God let such a poor person walk under a cloud of suffering? However, if you dare to explore beyond this nobility, you will not only find that it is fake, but it is morbid. Such a reality is morbid because this individual enjoys the attention it brings to him or her. This person likes how such a state makes him or her feel, as he or she glories in his or her so-called "suffering".

When you encounter such people, you initially think of them in a sympathetic way. You admire their nobility, incorrectly deeming it as courage. However, the more you are around the person, the more this person's suffering begins to suck your very will to live. After all, you feel responsible to somehow help him or her in his or her suffering.

Once you begin to try to alleviate these people's suffering, you find that they will always produce other aspects of life that bring more suffering to them. This causes you to realize that these people actually thrive in their morbid state. In fact, they have no other intention but to continue in their grand suffering. At this stage, you must conclude that if you do not flee, you will lose all sense of reality. Needless to say, if you do leave a person in such a state, you will also become another point of suffering for this most miserable individual.

There are other people who live in total delusion about reality. These people have the means to create their own temporary reality. However, if you enter into their world, you will discover that they are very fragile. In fact, these people's worlds are nothing more than images. If you peek behind the veil of their images, you will find a frightening reality. The reality is that these individuals live in a house of cards. It would not take much of a wind of adversity to knock their houses down, leaving them exposed and without any means to stand.

This brings us down to the avenues by which people handle reality. People either live in the past or the future, but few live in the present. Those who live in the past live according to select memories. These memories can bring great sentiment as they remember the "good, ole days", or bad experiences become excuses for failures in their present reality.

However, living in the past leaves the individual in a state of limbo. This state can torment the person because he or she cannot adjust to present reality. Also, a person might give way to anger because his or her past life was so unfair. After all, if it had been better, he or she would be a better person. Ultimately, either state will bring a person to complete despair, for he or she has no means to change the past or control the present by demanding that present life regard him or her in light of the past. In fact, life continues on without any regard to the person.

People who live in the future tend to live from one event to the next. They live for the future because the present does not bring any excitement or purpose to them. They appear to swing from one pinnacle to the next pinnacle of unrealistic expectation and wishful thinking. For example, some people live for weekends. Weekends represent partying, having fun, or enjoying the different fruits of their labors.

The problem with living in the future is those valleys of drudgery in-between. After the rush of the pinnacle comes the downward swing into the valley of despair. To live from event to event is like being on a roller coaster. For instance, you find yourself emotionally pushing yourself up to this pinnacle of expectation and excitement. At this time, your momentum is building along with your expectation in regard to the event and what it will do for you. Once you reach the pinnacle, you may or may not experience the expected rush as you immediately find yourself going down into the valley.

You sense there was some type of rush, but, after the event, many people end up saying to themselves, "Is this all there is?" Such a realization brings people to a state of disillusionment. To avoid utter depression, they begin to look for another event or project to stir them up to keep going. However, each episode of disillusionment ends in anger and despair. In their attempts to control reality, these people discover that nothing really changes and that all desired adjustments in their reality are temporary.

This brings us to the present. Why do people avoid reality? What are they running from, ignoring, or trying to control? The reality that people are trying to avoid is that at the core of life is the tragic reality of death. You cannot have life without death. In fact, death gives us a reality check as to whether or not we are alive, living, or experiencing life.

When people face the harsh reality of death, they must face loss, their own mortality, and the aspect of eternity. Let us face it. None of us wants to experience loss, yet death intrudes into our reality and declares there will be losses along the way. If we are honest, we will admit that it is the losses along the way that cause most of the unresolved issues in our lives.

On the other hand, how many of us want to face our own mortality? Such a prospect causes tremendous fear. We cannot accept the loss associated with mortality as being part of life. The writer of Hebrews made this statement in regard to such fear, "And deliver them who, through fear of death, were all their lifetime subject to bondage" (Hebrews 2:15).

Every funeral brings us face to face with the issue of mortality. Our natural attitude about death is that it always happens to the other guy, but never to me. After all, we are an exception to the rule. In our minds, we cannot imagine that death will ultimately win out in our lives.

Challenging the Christian Life

However, the writer of Hebrews declares that we have been appointed to die once and then experience judgment.[1]

Finally, we must face the fact that past this present life is eternity. Physical death simply serves as a door into this unknown realm. There are people who are banking on the idea that there is no eternity, that this present world represents the sum of all life. Granted, the present world represents life as we know it, but there is so much more to life. We only have this fleeting present time to discover the essence of true life.

People avoid the prospect of eternity because it implies that there is a reason for being here other than living for self. If there is a reason for being here, then there must be some form of accountability that will be required of them. Who or what will call each individual to personal accountability for the actions of his or her life?

This is a frightening prospect that some ignore, avoid, or deny. Certain people will try to control this prospect with religion, some will try to change it with personal goodness, and others will try to adjust to this possible reality by erecting their own god. However, the reality is that life or death cannot be controlled, changed, or adjusted, and that physical death is clearly in operation.

There are three types of death that people must face and almost all people will personally experience two of these deaths. The saint will experience the first two types of death while the unbeliever will surely experience the first and last deaths.

The first type of death that every human being will most likely experience is that of physical death. This is when the physical tabernacle (body) is put off. It is at this time that people will be ushered into eternity. Such a loss requires us to mourn the passing of this particular person.

The second death is the death to self. In other words, over the years, aspects of the self-life will die. These aspects can include dreams, plans, hopes, ideas, beliefs, etc. As you can see, that which is attached to my idea of personal worth and identity can die as the different storms of life rip at the very core of my character and resolve. This can cause great suffering and anger since it is hard to understand why I cannot live life on my terms.

The final death is spiritual death. If eternity exists and man is meant to live forever, then his soul will spend eternity somewhere. As believers, we know that there is heaven or hell. The way we are living or walking is actually preparing us to spend eternity within the blessings of God or the curses of damnation. The latter death ends in the type of loss that will bring utter despair to the individual in the form of total isolation, torment, and gnashing of teeth.[2]

Heaven represents the presence of God while damnation represents the reality of darkness. God is the essence of life and darkness is a mirror of that which is devoid of the life of God. Therefore, this eternal

---

[1] Hebrews 9:27
[2] Matthew 10:28; Luke 13:25-28; 16:23-25

darkness represents spiritual separation from God, which is defined as spiritual death.

As you consider death, you will realize that this is the aspect of life that no one can control, change, or adjust. Granted, people try to control their life to put off physical death. They strive hard to change the concept of life by avoiding death to the different aspects of the self-life. They try to adjust the idea of eternity by adjusting God to their ways of thinking. However, all of these attempts will prove to be futile. After all, it is God who has our days on earth numbered. Since God never changes, He cannot be adjusted to fit our reality. Therefore, life will continue to devastate the self-life along the way, always challenging our present reality.

People who live in the past or in the future often remain indifferent to the present. This indifference allows them to deceive themselves about their present lives. They perceive themselves as controlling life when, in reality, they are being controlled by influences around them. These people can try to change reality around them, but, until there is inward change on their part, everything will remain the same. Meanwhile, life challenges and affronts their self-life. They may try to adjust reality to serve personal agendas and ideas only to be faced with the aspects of that which is unseen and eternal.

As we consider the reality of life, we must come back to the lessons of life. We are not God, we indeed need God, and we must allow God to be God to resolve the matters of life. It is true that everything is in a state of flux in our present life except God. Hebrews 11:1 says, "Now faith is the substance of things hoped for, the evidence of things not seen."

Obviously, our expectations should and must be in God. He may be unseen, but He still can be known by putting our faith in His character. He is the one that provided the foundation upon which all can stand, the means by which the self-life can be properly addressed, and the right solution when facing eternity. He alone will resolve those unresolved issues that torment our lives. He is the great "I AM," the ever present reality that will enable us to learn the lessons of the past in order to stand firmly in the present as we prepare to meet the future.

If you relate to this chapter in any way, consider your present state. If you are failing to face your present reality, you need to know you are missing the opportunity to discover life. In fact, life is passing you by. You need to repent. Turn and face the hope of all life, Jesus Christ. You need to make peace with the present so that God can use your past sufferings to establish you in confidence, enabling you to confidently face the future with Him.

Types of Realities	Approaches To Reality	Attitude Towards Reality	Types of Deaths And Their Affects
Past (Sentimental or used as a platform for present excuses.)	Tries to control reality.	Lives in denial about reality.	Physical Life (Mourn loss of it.)
Present (Most avoid facing reality.)	Will try to adjust reality.	Becomes a martyr in reality.	Self-life (Experience suffering.)
Future (Lives according to future expectations.)	Will try to change reality.	Lives in delusion about reality.	Spiritual (Experience utter despair.)

6

THE TRAGEDY OF IT ALL

In my young years, I viewed much of life as a fantasy. In this fantasy, there were always the villains such as Cinderella's stepmother and stepsisters, but, ultimately, the Cinderella's of the world would always come out on top. After all, life had to be just and all injustices had to be exposed and rooted out by that which was good.

However, when you read the account of creation in the Bible, another story emerges. Instead of good triumphing over evil, evil took root to bring all mankind into spiritual darkness. Instead of man finding a perfect life, he actually fell from a state of innocence into imperfection and death. Instead of a happy ending, the harsh reality of man's life was actually pronounced. Consider what God told Adam after he rebelled and ate of the tree of knowledge of good and evil,

> ...cursed is the ground for thy sake; in sorrow shalt thou eat of it all the days of thy life; Thorns also and thistles shall it bring forth to thee; and thou shalt eat the herb of the field; In the sweat of thy face shalt thou eat bread, till thou return unto the ground; for out of it was thou taken: for dust thou art, and unto dust shalt thou return (Genesis 3:17c-19).

Death was passed down from Adam to each of us.[1] Instead of the promise of happiness, man became faced with the harshness of a condition that would bring mourning, sorrow, and despair as the various challenges of life affronted all attempts to discover its meaning. Thorns that wound and thistles that stung, as well as prove to be abrasive would mock man's attempts to secure paradise. Sweat would remind each of us that nothing would be accomplished without much labor. The bread would remind us that man's best could only produce that which was temporary. This struggle would remain until this corruptible body gave way to death and once again became dust in the earth.

Such struggles found in life and death point to pain and sorrow. Life is clearly dotted and plagued by suffering and pain. There are three types of pain: physical pain, emotional pain, and mental pain. Such pain brings mourning, suffering, and sorrow. Each aspect of pain tests a different area of character and resolve. Obviously, ongoing pain in any arena proves to be oppressive and depressing.

---

[1] Romans 5:12

Two men that give us insight into all three types of pain are Job and Jesus Christ. We can actually observe how all three types of pain affect a person. In the physical arena, physical suffering brought Job to a place of silent suffering. His wife told him to curse God so he would die, but, instead, he clung to his faith in God.[2] Clearly, God is the only place of rest when it comes to pain that attacks the body and a person's resolve to live in an unrelenting way. Resolve not only points to our will to live, but also to our sense of self-sufficiency that serves as our source of strength or as a point of reliance to see a matter through.

Physical pain not only robs the body of its strength, but it wears it down as it brings its captive victim to utter despair in the soul. Clearly, there is no way that the individual can maintain any self-sufficiency. People who experience the depth of this abyss can try to describe such pain, but no one can understand the havoc it is capable of wreaking on both the body and the soul.

For Jesus, physical pain brought Him to a place of physical thirst.[3] Pain robs the body of its ability to function, to stand, and withstand. He cried out in His thirst to endure the devastation plaguing His body. But one must note that He was not asking for deliverance, rather He was asking for the means to withstand such suffering. Jesus willingly faced the cross, so we could possess eternal life.

The second type of pain comes from emotional suffering, which proves to be an affront against the soul. There is only one source that can bring on this type of pain—others. The indifferent or cruel attitudes and actions of others will cause emotional pain. Job clearly experienced this with his friends. They supposedly came to comfort him. Instead, they accused him of sin and pressed him to agree with their evaluation of his suffering. Instead of being comforters, they came across as predators ready to attack and destroy Job in his week state. Job said of them, "I have heard many such things. Miserable comforters are ye all" (Job 16:2).

In Jesus' case, we see the same type of response from most of the people around Him. In His ordeal leading up to Calvary, many took the stance of predators. He was mocked in His state, accused in His silence, beaten in His submission, and crucified as He came into total subjection to the Father's will.[4]

Jesus' response was one of forgiveness. He made this statement, "...Father, forgive them; for they know not what they do" (Luke 23:34). The reality of such emotional chaos is that those who are the cause of it are often clueless. After all, they see it as a matter of what is right. When we think we are right in our own sight, we become indifferent to the plight of others. Subsequently, in our mind they deserve such suffering. Of

---

[2] Job 2:7-10
[3] John 19:28-30
[4] Philippians 2:8

course, such a perspective comes from the premise of pride. Pride is not only indifferent, but also cruel.

As you consider emotional pain, you begin to realize that it is associated with rejection, misunderstanding, and false accusation. It is not that people set out to do such acts, but they do them because they cannot properly discern what is really going on around them. For example, this is the type of thinking that operates within a crowd. Since the majority of the people in the crowd seem to be in agreement about a matter, then it must be right. Due to the fact that those in leadership positions are advocating it, it must not be wrong, for they would never lead one astray. Since it feels right, sounds correct, and justifies personal insecurities and doubts, a person cannot be wrong in deeming that such a reality is correct. Clearly, this is when people get into the flow of others' reality without discerning what is going on. In such cases, people prove that they are sheep often being led to the slaughter by those with their own wicked agendas.[5]

How does one contend with emotional pain? After all, it usually means there is a broken heart involved. A broken heart produces sadness and cannot operate in forgiveness. The sorrow of it weighs on a person who struggles with the lack of resolution. The key rests in the attitude we develop towards such pain. This type of pain is bound to come, especially if we decide to follow Jesus. The Apostle Paul summarized it in this way, "Yea, and all that will live godly in Christ Jesus shall suffer persecution" (2 Timothy 3:12).

The problem with emotional suffering is that it intrudes into our feelings about life. Feeling good about life becomes a source of personal hope. However, when the grief of emotional pain rocks our boats, we become hopeless. In such hopelessness we can put up walls of protection, make bad decisions in regard to trusting others, and become bitter about life.

To properly confront emotional pain, one must examine his or her attitude regarding such pain. For example, Job could have become hopeless and bitter because of his friends, but he decided to cling to the promises of God. At one point, he declared he would come forth as gold, and in another declaration, he stated this promise, "For I know that my redeemer liveth, and that he shall stand at the latter day upon the earth; And though after my skin worms destroy this body, yet in my flesh shall I see God" (Job 19:25-26).[6]

Job recognized that his ordeal was a test. He would come forth in a better state because he had confidence in the work of his Creator. He did not understand the reason for his ordeal, but he chose to put his faith in what he knew about the character of his God.

We see Jesus experiencing this sorrow on the cross. His heart was broken over it, signified by the blood and water coming forth from His

---

[5] Isaiah 53:6
[6] Job 23:10

side. The broken heart did not have to do with His actual suffering, but with man's reaction towards the work of God. Jesus could stand in confidence in what He was doing because it was according to the perfect will of the Father. He did not come to lose His life, but to willing give it.[7] He understood the hope that existed for mankind beyond His physical and emotional suffering.

The final type of pain is that of mental anguish. Others cause emotional suffering, but mental suffering proves to be an affront against our very spirits. Such suffering is caused by personal sins, limitations, struggles, and what is perceived to be personal failures. It is hard to face the limitations or deviations of our personal character and ways. We strive hard to do right, only to miserably fail. We try to show our affection by our concern, only to be hurt by those who are not open. We attempt to situate matters to ensure positive results, only to be met with devastation. We take two steps towards the resolution of a matter, only to be knocked backwards ten feet.

We attempt to understand the matters confronting our lives, only to end in confusion. Every personal failure and limitation bring us to a state of despair over life. It seems that, no matter how hard we try, we cannot get life to go our way or change a particular matter. It is hard to see that most attempts are quite selfish. They may appear to be right, but they lack the inspiration of the Spirit. They may look logical, but there is no room for reasoning as to whether it is truly beneficial for all parties involved. It may appear as if it is the best way to go, but it lacks regard for others who feel as if they are being imposed on to ensure someone else's selfish reality.

Job's mental anguish came because he could not understand the issues that surrounded his life. His creed about God had failed him. If he went with his unfeeling creed, he would have to agree with his friends that there was some type of sin in his life. However, he had examined every aspect of his life and found no conviction coming from above.

No doubt, Job had wrestled with every possible angle, only to encounter silence. His anguish had to be great because nothing made sense. It appeared as if life was mocking him. He stood alone in the midst of his struggle.

For Jesus, we cannot begin to imagine His personal anguish as He took the sins of the world upon Himself. We can only get a sense of such anguish when we consider the words He cried from the cross, "...My God, my God, why hast thou forsaken me?" (Matthew 27:46). Did Jesus feel forsaken? In His humanity, He felt every type of pain and anguish that could be experienced. He knew that the Father had not forsaken Him, but that did not stop Him from feeling the pain of the mental anguish that can be experienced in such times. This type of sorrow clearly isolates people and makes them feel alone and vulnerable. It can become unbearable in its silence and overwhelming in its utter despair.

---

[7] John 10:18; 19:32-37

The question is how did these two men handle such despair? Keep in mind, physical pain affronts the body, emotional pain tests the soul of man, and mental anguish exposes the spirit of man. Therefore, each type of pain tests the different aspects of man's resolve to live. For example, physical pain tests man's patience to continue on under such a burden, emotional pain reveals and tests the heart's attitude to maintain its purity and uprightness, and mental anguish tempts the will and character of man to take matters into his own hands to stop the despair.

As you consider Job's resolve in the midst of his mental anguish, he made this statement, "Though he slay me, yet will I trust in him; but I will maintain mine own ways before him" (Job 13:15). Job was resolved to accept his fate before God as he stood upon what he knew to be true about his own life in the eyes of God.

Jesus made this statement from the cross, "...Father, into thy hands I commend my spirit..." (Luke 23:46). Obviously, Jesus put the matters of His ordeal into the hands of His Father once He knew that redemption was paid in full.

Job clearly did not understand the reason for his suffering, but he chose to put his trust in the very character of God. Jesus knew the purpose and outcome of the cross, but He still committed all matters into the hands of the Father. There is only one way to resolve the matter of mental pain, and that is by giving way to that which is eternal. Matters that involve the issues of life cannot be understood from an earthly perspective. In fact, such understanding will elude people, causing anger and despair.

Mental anguish can only be resolved when our perspective is turned heavenward in faith. The deep matters of life belong to God. He chooses what we will understand, and where understanding eludes us, faith must be applied.[8] As Jesus told Thomas who wanted to see with his own eyes the truth about His resurrection, "...Thomas, because thou hast seen me, thou hast believed; blessed are they that have not seen, and yet have believed" (John 20:29).

Job never really understood the reason for his plight, but what he obtained was of greater value. He obtained a greater revelation of God, "I have heard of thee by the hearing of the ear, but now mine eye seeth thee" (Job 42:5).

At the end of all anguish is the beacon of hope, and that is our life in God. Healing and restoration belongs to God. Sometimes, physical healing ends in physical death, but, nevertheless, it ends in rejoicing in the patience and grace of our God. Jesus heals the broken hearted. Emotional healing causes us to become more effective in ministry as benevolence and compassion is established in us in greater measure.[9] At the end of mental anguish are the restoration of a wounded spirit and a greater revelation of Jesus. Such a blessing far exceeds the temporary

---

[8] 2 Corinthians 5:7
[9] Psalm 116:15; Luke 4:18; 2 Corinthians 1:3-7

Challenging the Christian Life

anguish that life brings us. The Apostle Paul understood this fact when he made this statement,

> For our light affliction, which is but for a moment, worketh for us a far more exceeding and eternal weight of glory, While we look not at the things which are seen, but at the things which are not seen; for the things which are seen are temporal, but the things which are not seen are eternal (2 Corinthians 4:17-18).

We all want to avoid the pain that life brings us. After all, we want to feel good about our life and about ourselves. However, Jesus never promised us an easy life. He guaranteed us tribulation, but also that, in it, we could be of good cheer for He has overcome the world. It is only through much tribulation that we will enter the kingdom of God.[10] Being established in the life of God requires us to travail before God when it comes to the matters of life. For life to be present, it requires the struggles that are associated with pain and death.

However, for the believer, such struggles imply a greater resurrection.[11] This promise is in light of the eternal. When we weigh the temporary with the eternal, we have no other choice but to cling to the eternal, knowing that the temporary will eventually give way to that which is unseen and everlasting.

---

[10] John 16:33; Acts 14:22
[11] Hebrews 11:35

7

MAKING THE CONNECTION

The harsh realities of life are death and pain. The Apostle Paul put it in this perspective, "It is a faithful saying, For if we be dead with him, we shall also live with him; If we suffer, we shall also reign with him; if we deny him, he also will deny us" (2 Timothy 2:11-12). There is no way to discover life unless we enter by way of death. This is a principle that is constantly upheld in Scripture. To avoid death to the self-life means an existence of rebellion and despair. To enter the door of physical death without Christ is to taste the death of eternal separation from God.

Suffering will always follow death in certain arenas of life. In other words, the dying-out process will cause pain and suffering. However, it is necessary for a person to become identified with Christ in the life He desires for each of us. As Paul declared in Romans 8:17, "And if children, then heirs—heirs of God, and joint heirs with Christ—if so be that we suffer with him, that we may be also glorified together." Obviously, we must face the issue of death and suffering throughout our journey through this present age.

These two issues bring us to how we respond to the challenges of life. There are two ways in which people handle life; they either *react to* their environment or they *interact with* it. As you consider these two different ways people respond to life, you will be able to see two types of motivation and results. It is vital that we understand these two ways.

Reaction comes from two different types of premises. One premise is that of uncertainty. For example, if something is out of control in your environment, your natural tendency is to be ready to react to whatever may confront you.

The second premise that produces reaction is that of selfishness. This self-serving disposition will oppose anything in its environment that will not bow down to its reality. As you can see, most people are reacting to or opposing challenging aspects of their environments. Needless to say, the world encourages such opposition with the teaching and philosophies of self-esteem, loving self, and finding self.

The Bible's philosophy is opposite. Jesus tells us to deny self and show the same regard for others that we would want shown to ourselves. This regard is nothing but preferring or honoring others over ourselves. He also stated we must be willing to lose this present life as we know it to find life that is real, has meaning, and is lasting.[1]

---

[1] Matthew 16:23-24; Mark 12:29-31

Since much of the visible Church has adopted the philosophies of the world, it is not unusual to see people who call themselves Christians constantly opposing their environment. No wonder the divorce rate of the Church is equal to that of the world. No wonder we are losing our children on the various altars of the world as they become more self-centered, rebellious, and lost in the ridiculousness of it all. After all, our environment must bow down to our personal reality, rather than the truth of Jesus Christ.[2]

To oppose the truth of Christ is to oppose any absolutes, as well as God's rule in our lives. It amazes me how many people call themselves Christians, but they oppose God's rule, the proper application of His Word, and the reality of the Son of God in their midst.[3]

As you watch them oppose the sure reality of God, you realize they are trying to adjust God and His Word to their ways of thinking. Yet, Scripture is clear and God is the same today as He was yesterday and will be tomorrow.[4] He never changes according to cultures, movements, or philosophies. He remains that immovable Rock of eternity that determines the validity of present reality, puts the past into proper perspective, and holds the future in His hands.

History clearly reveals that all cultures will eventually fall or give way to something else. Movements fade, while philosophies are forever changing as the terrain and landscapes of people's influence and beliefs are changed with the winds of time. However, there is one consistent truth that has remained unchanged and that is God and His Word.

God's Word has assured us that He will never change. It has promised us that it is eternal and will remain standing when all else falls into judgment and succumbs to destruction.[5] I, for one, rejoice in this reality, for the world is becoming more frightening and unrealistic as I write. It is no longer just in a state of flux; it is winding down to utter chaos and despair. The only means to stop its downward spiral is for Jesus to step on the scene as the ultimate Lord, King, and Judge.

Since most people are opposing their present environments, there is very little sanity to be found. People are angry because they cannot have life on their terms. The more they oppose their environment to get their own way, the more it spirals out of control. Since they cannot conquer their environment or reality, they find that any hope for change or deliverance from their present situation eludes them. Hence, depression enters.

How many people are fighting or running from depression? In fact, these people feel as if they are being consumed by their present reality, leaving them without any recourse, energy, or means to stop the tidal wave of despair.

---

[2] John 14:6
[3] 2 Corinthians 13:8
[4] Malachi 3:6; John 5:39; Hebrews 13:8; James 1:22-25
[5] Psalms 33:11; 119:89; Matthew 5:17-18; 1 Peter 1:23-25

The second way that people respond to life is to interact with their environment. In fact, the definition of life is the ability to interact with our surroundings. It is only through the ability of interacting within our atmosphere that we can be able to make a real connection with the reality around us.

Obviously, in order to interact with my environment, I must be connected to the real source of life. The real source of genuine life is God. Therefore, I must be born of Spirit and water to make such a connection.[6]

This connection is important to effectively interact with my surroundings. Clearly, the life of God must be in me before I can interact with life around me and with the life that is in others. As you can see, there must be three points of connection before I can address the real issues of life in me, before me, and around me.

Let us consider these points of connection. We already discussed the first one. The only way I can connect with God is by being born again. I must have a new disposition, that of a new heart and spirit to truly make a connection with the heart and mind of God. Keep in mind, this is a spiritual connection. To be able to interact with life, I must be able to discern the spirit in operation in my environment to properly interact with it.[7] However, most people judge their situation according to their own understanding, which ends in condemnation. Condemnation justifies opposing one's environment.

The next point of connection comes by way of truth. Once I make a connection with God, I must connect with the reality of my own inward state. It is at this point I must establish an environment of honesty where truth serves as the premise by which I discern my personal attitudes, approaches, and conduct. Without the truth, God cannot step onto the scene to change my present reality. It is important to point out that God does not necessarily change what is happening in my environment, rather He changes my perspective about it.

As God changes my perspective about my inward state, my attitude will align to His evaluation of a matter, my approach will have a different agenda, and my conduct will adjust to my changing attitude. It never ceases to amaze me that what needs to change in my present reality to bring about the necessary change to my environment is my own attitude and approach towards a matter.

Once truth connects me to the reality of my inward state, it then takes the love of God to connect me to the atmosphere around me. The love of God is a commitment to be right before God and do right by others. It is pure in its approach, wise in its attitude, and longsuffering in its ability to interact with others. It actually possesses compassion, or the ability to enter into the plight of others, as it becomes aware of people's environment.

---

[6] John 3:3, 5
[7] Ezekiel 36:26-27; 1 Corinthians 2:13-14; Hebrews 10:16-20

Once these three connections are made, one is able to actually discern his or her environment. When people are opposing their environments, all they can do is judge from the basis of how life or their circumstances are making them feel or personally affecting them. However, this is all fleshly, which means that it is self-serving and idolatrous.[8]

Sadly, the people who never connect to their environments come across as being rude, indifferent, and cruel. These people are rude because they are so into themselves that they have no concept of how ill-mannered they are towards others. I have seen Christians who are absolutely clueless in their environment. They may want to serve God, but they are rude to His people. They have no concept of how to interact with them. They are crude, obnoxious, or inconsiderate. Clearly, such people only operate from the small premise of their comfort zones and have shut down their senses so they do not have to come to terms with how they feel or think about matters that are left unresolved.

It is important to point out that discernment involves both the Spirit of God and the senses of a person. These senses must be under the control of the Spirit. Once they are under His control, the person will have the ability to hear what the Spirit is saying, see the path set before him or her, taste a bit of eternity, touch the unseen, and smell the fragrance of heaven.

Most people are closed to the spiritual connection of the Spirit because their senses are subject to fleshly appetites. Instead of being tempered, these undisciplined senses are subject to defining the environment around self according to feelings and personal conclusions. Jesus warned to take heed of how we hear a matter. He also instructed His followers to make sure that the light of their understanding was not darkness.[9]

People who do not ensure that the Holy Spirit tempers their senses find themselves losing credibility with those around them. They cannot connect to the real issues confronting life. Therefore, they cannot address them. Opportunity to become part of the solution passes them by. Since they lack the spiritual connection to what is going on around them, the Spirit of God has no platform in which to move in a situation to bring perspective and instruction.

There are people who insist on being indifferent to their environment. They want to judge from a fleshly perspective. The reason for this is because they want life on their terms, which means they must avoid all levels of accountability. After all, the truth would not only rip their realities to pieces, but it would call them to personal accountability for their lack of love. These people walk in unbelief towards the aspects of God that do not agree with their ideas about life.

---

[8] Matthew 7:1-4
[9] Matthew 6:22-23; Luke 8:18

I cannot begin to tell you of the Christians I have encountered that take pride in their form of unbelief, as well as their attempt to control their reality by being indifferent to it. Obviously, these people have no sensitivity to the Spirit; therefore, they remain clueless as to what is really going on around them. In many cases, they end up looking foolish or ridiculous because there is no real connection.

The next group of people is those who are cruel in their environments. These people strive to control their environments through tyrannical means. They intimidate, demean, mock, and cause chaos for others. They appear heartless as they use people's feelings, struggles, and weaknesses against them. They do not care that they leave devastation in their wake because they feel superior and justified.

The ones who are rude in their environments come across as inconsiderate. They are often anti-social or obnoxious because they can come out opposing anything in their environments that irritates or does not make sense according to their personal realities. These people's realities are very small and fragile.

The people who insist on being indifferent to reality come across as clueless and ridiculous. They do not want to be bothered with truth outside of their worlds. These people will become cynical, skeptical, and critical towards any truth that may challenge their controlled reality. Such people usually mock truth and twist it to suit their perverted perceptions.

Those who are cruel will look for any weakness to gain the upper hand over those in their environment. If these individuals fail to take control, they display great emotions in an attempt to get people to feel sorry for them. Once the guard is put down, these cruel individuals will quickly become offensive as they use any show of compassion and kindness from others to once again cause chaos. Clearly, these people's realities are treacherous and self-centered.

As you can gather, it takes integrity, honesty, and uprightness to face reality and gain the truth that enables each of us to interact with our environments. The question is, are you interacting with your environment or are you opposing it? The attitude that you have towards life will reveal how you are responding to it.

8

ORDER IN THE ENVIRONMENT

Whether we are interacting or reacting will determine the quality of our environments. The challenge that faces many people is that their environments are out of order due to the opposition that is present. If people's surroundings are out of order, they can be assured that there is fear, anxiety, and anger. People fear what they cannot control, become anxious over what will not submit to their particular reality, and are often plagued by anger that operates between depression and rage.

Such people are usually raging against life or are wallowing in self-pity. After all, their environment is out of control. There is no order to be found. Chaos threatens to not only expose their fragile reality, but to cause it to cave in around them.

As a result, people run from reality both physically and emotionally. This is where denial, deception, and drug and alcohol abuse can enter the scene. What you realize is that these people's realities are like a house of cards. They give the impression that they are too fragile to face reality. There are a couple of reasons why people are in this fragile state. The first reason is that those around them have pampered them, allowing them to refuse to face life for what it is. The second reason people appear fragile is because they have failed to face something in their personal world.

I knew of a person who refused to face the fact that her spouse was perverted and did not properly conduct himself around other women. He constantly touched them in inappropriate ways and made unbecoming statements to them. Meanwhile, he catered to his wife's fragile reality as she lived in denial about his problem. Needless to say, if a problem is left in the dark, it will eventually manifest itself. When the man's sin came to the light, the house of cards caved in around the woman. Regardless of her fragile state, she had to face the reality of her husband's problem.

Other people go into rebellion as they give way to every inhibition to drown out the conflict raging in their soul. They have tried to keep a lid on it as they consider different aspects of life, only to find it plaguing them. Eventually, they give up trying to keep a lid on their desires and wants. They open what we would consider Pandora's Box. After all, they feel miserable in their present reality. Therefore, they might just as well go all the way and have a real reason for feeling bad about life.

When an environment is out of order, there is no real peace to be found. People in this state can find themselves on the ocean of life being tossed by the different waves of life. They feel hopeless, for now they are at the mercy of whatever comes along. They cannot control the waves of life and they are weary of struggling to try and bring these different waves into submission to their reality. Since they are fair game for life to do with them as it will, they will give up and cave in to despair.

Granted, no one can control the waves of life, but they can be assured that there can be order in their environments. This order is vital if one is going to determine how the waves of life are going to affect them. This is the key to properly facing, embracing, and discovering life. It is necessary if one is going to learn the lessons of life. Obviously, there must be order.

For there to be order, we must come to terms with what is out of order. Can we declare life to be out of order? Life is life, with its various demands, circumstances, and challenges. It is neither out of order nor in order. We are the ones who determine how life affects our particular order.

We can say that the people in our environments are out of order. This could be true, but people do not determine whether we are opposing our environments or interacting with them. Obviously, if we are opposing our environments, there will be conflict at every turn. Conflict points to chaos.

What is out of order in our environments? The answer is obvious. We are out of order. Having order will be determined by how we respond to what is happening around us. Obviously, each of us must bring ourselves into order to ensure that there will be order in the environment.

"Order" in the environment means that we have submitted to that which is worthy or excellent as a means to temper our personal attitudes and behaviors. We refer to these responses as acts of submission and temperance. Clearly, these virtues identify us to the work of the Holy Spirit in our lives.

This is why it is vital that, as Christians, we connect to our environment to ensure order. After all, if I am out of order in my environment, I can be assured that nothing will be in order. Whether it is my inward state or my outward atmosphere, I must be in order to ensure order.

Obviously, there must be personal discipline to make certain that I can properly discern my environment. Keep in mind, I must interact with my environment to properly discern what is going on around me. The tendency is for people to ignore, adjust, or try to change those aspects of one's state to maintain personal reality.

People's attempts to control reality will eventually cause the environment to spin out of control. For example, there are four ways in which people try to control their reality. The first way some people deal with reality is from an intellectual arena where all matters are reasoned out. However, such individuals fail to connect with their senses;

therefore, they fail to come under the Spirit. This will cause the fruit of indifference towards reality. Eventually, all unresolved issues will become a tidal wave that has the potential of swallowing these people in utter hopelessness.

There are those who operate in the senses but fail to come to a place of temperance. Therefore, they may be open to the spiritual but fail to come to truth, since it will be obvious that they lack the necessary discipline to properly discern their environments. The lack of discipline will cause these individuals to become unrealistic and unreasonable in their environments as they try to control their realities. Eventually, these people will display the fruit of skepticism towards all reality, making them ineffective at properly interacting with it.

Some people deal in images. In other words, these people operate partially in each arena of the intellect and the senses. However, their senses are used to confirm how they intellectually perceive themselves and life around them. These people will only reason with what will bow down to their images of themselves and life. Ultimately, they will refuse to let reality prove contrary to their way of thinking. The fruit of their attitude is cruelty.

Other people deal with only certain aspects of truth while adjusting their senses to create a certain atmosphere that will be in compliance with their ways of thinking. In a way, these people control the spirit of an environment to ensure their ideas of truth. This is their way of controlling reality. Such reality will lack balance in which to discern matters, as well as dimension that ensures a realistic perspective. The fruit of this reality is harshness.

As you consider how people strive to maintain their particular reality, you can begin to see how they will play mental and emotional games with others. As we consider the world around us, we realize that the essence of life is discovered in relationships, and not in tangible things, power, or prestige. However, the pursuit of happiness in relationships often ends in failure because people are looking to those in their lives to create an environment that is conducive to their particular happiness. When this happiness is missing, these people attempt to take matters into their own hands as a means to order their worlds in such a way that they will experience this happiness. These attempts are nothing more than games. These games point to selfishness that is reacting to that which does not serve its purpose. Games are deceptive and will create a false reality.[1]

There are three types of games that people play. One involves conning people as to what the real issues of a matter are. To affectively con, these people will comply outwardly while maintaining the right to their personal realities. The goal of conning is to gain a person's confidence in order to influence him or her to agree or see it according to the con's reality.

---

[1] Psalm 119:128

The second type of game involves flattery. Flattery feeds off of pride. It appears to be in agreement when, in reality, it is striving to get the one who is being flattered to bow down to its desired reality. In this game, the one being flattered perceives that the one flattering not only sees his or her worth, but is also impressed with it. It all comes down to feeling good about self.

Many people try to flatter God with promises and bargains as to what they will do if God just does it their way this one time. Amazingly, most people forget their bargain once the crisis is over. However, God has not forgotten. Flattery may present a picture of glorious intentions, but, as the saying goes, the road to hell is paved with good intentions.

The third way people attempt to get others to come into agreement with their realities is through control and manipulation. In many cases, this is where people try to rationalize with others about their particular realities through different attempts. Such attempts are nothing more than perverting reality. Perversion simply means that one is adding to something or taking away from it.

Each one of these games does not represent the truth. Truth brings clarity and liberty in matters that are shrouded in confusion. Even though people perceive that their particular realities will produce a desired affect, the reality is that chaos is the byproduct of such attempts.

Obviously, the problem with these different realities is that the environment will be out of order. There must be personal order to ensure that a person can properly discern his or her surroundings. Truth is what will guarantee order. Keep in mind, we each must be able to truthfully interact with our environments to properly discern and confront what is going on around us to bring any kind of resolution in relationships or matters.

Surely, people will agree that life is chaotic, but, if there is no real stake as to what is true and real, it will prove to be more than chaotic. It will prove to be devastating and destructive.

Clearly, we must learn to properly interact with our environments. Therefore, it is important to discern our environments. In a sense, this is where we can take some of our lives back from the uncertain waves of life and determine the attitude and quality of it. It is at the point of order that we can begin to determine what will influence us.

That which influences us is what will define the people we become. Granted, we cannot control the waves of life, but we can determine what influences us and how we will respond to it. Such influences will establish the basis from which we will regard life.

People who are angry about life have failed to take responsibility for how it is influencing them. They are angry that they cannot change or influence life. Once again, they must face that they are not God and that they are at the mercy of this unpredictable ocean called "life." Instead of being on a journey to discover life, they are at the mercy of the waves and storms that roll across the ocean of humanity because they are not in any real vessel.

As Christians, we know there is one sure ark ordained by God, Jesus Christ.[2] But, there are some believers still sitting in the life rafts of their own strength, trying to paddle through the waves and storms of life. There are some who are floating around God's provision, but they have not left what they are used to in order to discover real deliverance. There are others who are struggling against being saved, consecrated, and sanctified unto God because they are still clinging to the world in some way, thinking they can bring both together. The final group is comprised of those who are in the world's luxury liner. However, this liner is compared to the Titanic. This great liner is going down, but many individuals who are on it are not willing to lose their present lives in order to secure their future lives in Christ. Therefore, they live in denial as they continue to partake of the corrupt fruit of the world.

Are you hid in the ark of Jesus or are you on another type of vessel, trying to ride out the different waves of life? As you can see, on the ocean of life, it is a matter of sinking into the miry depths of despair, desolation, and death, or learning how to ride in the flow of the Holy Spirit.

---

[2] Colossians 3:3

9

POINT OF RELIANCE

Life will always reveal a person's place of dependency. The point of dependency will determine a person's character. It is easy to discern a person's point of reliance by the attitude that he or she displays towards life. In fact, there are four attitudes that can be seen in people.

The first attitude is the one where people are going to make life happen on their terms. They are busy using their strength to control, manipulate, and adjust people and reality to submit to their concepts of life. Obviously, the point of reliance is on their personal strength.

Personal strength becomes the platform on which all rebellion will operate. After all, this attitude concludes that all opposition can be subdued along the way. This type of strength invades every aspect of these people's attitudes and perspectives. The momentum of this strength turns into frustration and anger when it fails to bring matters of life under control. It will cause these individuals to become hard in the matters of life. Ultimately, the happenings of life will erode personal strength, leaving these people weary of life. Zechariah 4:6 gives this insight, "...Not by might, nor by power, but by my Spirit, saith the LORD of hosts."

The second attitude comes out of idolatry. These are the people who wait for life to come to them. They are waiting for the right environments or circumstances that will serve their purposes, and then they will determine the direction of their life. These individuals are actually waiting for something about life to catch their fancy or attention. Since they are fleshly in their preferences, they live on the wave of excitement or sensationalism. They want life to make them feel alive, rather than discovering life in order to find out what it means to live it.

As you consider these people's direction, you will realize it is all very self-serving. In fact, anything can appeal to their fancy causing them to go with whatever flow will bring the most excitement. For example, these are the people who will try everything from alcohol, drugs, religion, to God to see what will keep them flying high on their emotional wave. As a result, these people prove to be vulnerable, quick to fall into traps that leave them empty, disillusioned, skeptical about life, and angry.

Obviously, the point of reliance is self. Life must revolve around self before self will make any real moves towards it. Life will pass such people by, leaving them unable to discover its true meaning. Jesus made this statement in Matthew 16:25-26, "For whosoever will save his life shall lose it; and whosoever will lose his life for my sake shall find it. For what is a man profited, if he shall gain the whole world, and lose his own soul? Or what shall a man give in exchange for his soul?" Life will never come to such people. However, temptation, sin, false hope, and disillusionment will find them, causing spiritual ruin.

The third attitude can be seen in those who float through life. They act as if they do not care about life. However, this is a façade to hide anger and rebellion. At the core of this attitude is unbelief. These people portray this attitude because they desire their particular take on life, which is nothing more than a fantasy. These individuals feel life should be handed to them, but they have already realized that the people in their environments will not bow down or produce the life they think they deserve. These people can display a great deal of complacency.

As you contend with these people, you discover that they have no intention of taking accountability for their attitude. They are closed down emotionally in order to remain clueless about the reality around them. They resent any truth that might intrude into their unrealistic realities. The harsh reality is that nothing will make these people happy. They will remain miserable because they refuse to grow up and face life.

However, even in their pessimistic attitude, they continue to look to worldly means or people for some spark of happiness, only to become angry and depressed since they are closed to the real essence of life. It takes faith to receive that which is good. Since they lack faith, there is no means by which to be receptive. Everything becomes tainted in the cesspool of unbelief.

The first group of people is motivated by self-sufficiency. In this self-sufficiency, they are going to come out on top. The second group of people is motivated by selfishness. In other words, everything must be about them. Ultimately, everything they partake of must make them feel good about self and life. The third group of people is actually drowning in their small cesspool of their personal worlds. They are miserable because self is consuming them in every way.

The final group is made up of people who seek to find their life in Jesus. Seeking our lives puts our pursuit for life in perspective. First of all, we each will determine the quality of our personal life by how we respond to the life God has for us. Obviously, this life is not going to be obtained by any personal strength because it is found outside of personal control and manipulation. Since we need to be seeking out this life, it is obvious that it will not just happen to find us. We must first seek it out as a means to find it outside of all selfish designs. Apparently, this life is not always obvious to the physical eye; therefore, our understanding of what we perceive life to be must change in order to recognize true life. This brings us to the final realization, which is that life will not somehow cross a person's path while he or she is floating through his or her present reality. It will not just be handed to someone. Such a life takes initiative, diligence, and the desire to find it.

Looking for this life means I have a responsibility to find it. To find my life in Christ, I must make sure that I have the right attitude. The first three attitudes are fleshly and worldly. The last attitude will display wisdom, sobriety, and godly determination.

This brings me to my need to interact with my environment. The quality of life depends on our relationships. However, most relationships fall in disarray, causing chaos in our worlds. But, the one relationship that must be in order is our relationship with God. If we do not discern a matter from the vantage point of His Spirit and truth, we will not come out with the right perspective. It is from the vantage point of a living relationship with God that we can face life, confront reality, and find resolution.

Obviously, the quality of our life is based on the strength of our relationships, beginning with God. Without a right relationship with God, our other relationships will lack some type of substance such as strength, character, purity, and commitment. Clearly, relationships are a matter of the heart, and the heart will determine the quality of a person's life. This is why Jesus warned people that life does not consist of the abundance of the things they possess.[1]

Solomon, one of the wisest men that ever lived, made this statement, "Keep thy heart with all diligence; for out of it are the issues of life" (Proverbs 4:23). We are to guard and preserve our hearts because the matters of life find their origins or springboards in the heart. Obviously, the spirit and attitudes of life are determined by the heart condition. Therefore, life finds its source in the type of heart we maintain before God.

The prophet, Jeremiah tells us that the heart is deceitful above all things and desperately wicked.[2] Jesus made reference to this fact in His discourse about the heart in Matthew 15:17-20. What an indictment of the inward disposition of man. There is no way man can reform or change the heart. It seems so hopeless unless you receive the words of Ezekiel by faith, "A new heart also will I give you, and a new spirit will I put within you; and I will take away the stony heart out of your flesh, and I will give you an heart of flesh" (Ezekiel 36:26).

As you consider Ezekiel 14:3-6, you find out why the heart is untrustworthy. Ezekiel tells us that the heart is where we set up our idols. These idols serve as the source that puts iniquity constantly before our face, as well as make us estranged from our God. God will have no part of any idols. To do away with the influence of the idols, they must not only be brought down and destroyed, but the platforms (hearts) torn up and purged by the fires of judgment.[3]

As you study Ezekiel 36:26, you will see that an idolatrous heart has become stony towards God; therefore, it is not just a matter of purging the heart. As a result, God must give us a fleshly heart that is capable of responding to Him.

---

[1] Luke 12:15
[2] Jeremiah 17:9-10
[3] Exodus 23:24; 34:13-14

In fact, Jesus told a parable about a sower and his seed that reveals the three unreceptive heart conditions.[4] The first heart is a hard heart that is unable to avail itself for the seed to take root. It is in this precarious condition that Satan will rob the heart of the seed of the Gospel, preventing it from taking root.

The second heart is a stony heart. The seed of the Gospel may find a bit of space to grow, but it will eventually hit the rocky obstacle of the self-life. Since the seed cannot take root, Satan will eventually kill any hope of spiritual maturity and fruit.

The third heart condition is the worldly heart. It is full of the attractions of the world that will choke out and eventually destroy the Word of God from having its way in a person's spiritual life. Obviously, these three hearts must be changed to become receptive to the life of the Gospel, Jesus Christ. Without the life of Jesus, Christianity becomes a dead-letter religion.

Obviously, we must have a new heart to ensure there is no more hardness of heart as the stony aspects of our attitudes are torn up by a new-birth experience. As we give way to the new hearts, all the influences of the world will be rooted out of our ways of thinking. As the Apostle Paul declared, we become new creations as the old passes away to give way to the new life that is being established in us.[5]

What a glorious new heart we will possess as born-again believers! It will be a heart inclined towards God, open to His work, receptive of His will, and desirous to walk in His ways. It is a heart that will no longer serve as a springboard from which sin operates. Rather, it will find its origin in the love of God and will be brought forth to maturity, as it bears eternal fruit. Consider the following table on the next page.

---

[4] Matthew 13:1-23
[5] Matthew 15:16-19; John 3:3, 5: 2 Corinthians 5:17

Attitude Towards Life	Point of Reliance	Type of Heart	Affect Of the Seed
Makes life happen on their terms	Personal Strength	Hard Heart	Unable to take root
Waits for life to come to them.	Self (How something makes self feel.)	Stony Heart	Is unable to come to any type of maturity.
Floats through life.	High Opinion of self	Worldly Heart (The best the world has to offer.)	The things of God are drowned out and lost in the midst of the enticements of the world.
Seeks life	God (Must find Him)	Open, Receptive Heart	Takes root and brings forth maturity and fruit.

Obviously, the heart attitude must be examined. The way we consider the attitude of our heart is by inspecting its desires. Jesus stated, "For where your treasure is, there will your heart be also" (Matthew 6:21). Treasures have to do with our affections. Whatever or whoever possesses the main focus of our affections will also reveal our points of adoration and reliance.

As you follow affections, they will lead you to agenda, emphasis, and priorities. What is your agenda? If self lies at the source of one's agenda, then most likely it will be to ensure his or her particular reality. Since the person's reality must be about self, then his or her emphasis will be focused on personal happiness. It is from this basis that priorities will be established.

Agendas, emphasis, and priorities will determine the spirit that people will operate within. However, it is important that one realizes emphasis serves as a point of attitude. The attitude is determined by the focus of the heart. Agenda serves as a breeding ground for the emphasis, but emphasis will reinforce agenda. This environment will eventually reflect itself in what will be lifted up or glorified in a person's life as his or her priorities.

Clearly, there is only One who deserves adoration and must serve as our source of reliance and that is Jesus Christ. However, self can cleverly hide our self-serving agendas behind religious garb. It will taint the things of God as well as give people a false sense about their so-called "goodness". This is why the prophet Jeremiah stated that the heart is deceitful and wicked in Jeremiah 17:7-9. King David also recognized the untrustworthy state of his heart and asked God to, "Search me, O God, and know my heart; try me, and know my thoughts; And see if there be any wicked way in me, and lead me in the way everlasting" (Psalms 139:23-24).

As we struggle with the issues of life, we must come to terms with our heart conditions if the matters of life are to ever be resolved. After all, all unresolved issues exist because of how people perceive life due to their heart attitudes and their relationships with God.

Obviously, the issues of life are not many, but they become confusing as people lose their way in their struggles to conquer and control life. Such an attempt leads them away from the real source and center of all life, God. The further people get away from God, the more confusing and overwhelming life becomes.

God must not only be the center of our life, but He must be the One who possesses our hearts. Our agendas should be to please Him, our emphasis should be to do His will, and our priorities should be to glorify Him. Our lives must begin with God, our walks must be in line with Him, and our activities should end with Him. Such a life constitutes a God-centered life that will ensure maturity and fruitfulness on our part.

It is only in maturity and the evidence of eternal fruits that we can be assured that we are gaining the very life of Christ. After all, at the center of God's work, will, and heart for His children rests the revelation of His Son. It was Jesus who died on the cross to light man's way back to God. It was Jesus' redemption that allows each of us to know reconciliation with God. It is Jesus' life in us that identifies us with the eternal and abundant life that is being offered to all who will come to Him by faith.

Although the life in us is not our life, it is obvious that we are responsible to keep, guard, and preserve the purity of our hearts towards Jesus' life. Satan is forever trying to rob, kill, or destroy this purity with the influences of self and the world. As Jesus said, "Blessed are the pure in heart; for they shall see God" (Matthew 5:8). We need a heart that can not only hear the voice of our precious Shepherd, but will also be able to see the majesty of our God.

In challenges, I am reminded of how important it is for us to see God. He is our perspective, or vantage point of hope. To consider life from the vantage point of self is to become lost in the misery of hopelessness and depression. To regard life from the vantage point of God is not only the only means by which to discover life, but to gain it.

Job brought this out after his grave ordeal that caused him to curse the day, as well as voice his regret for the day he was born.[6] As previously stated, he could not see through his misery. He could not gain understanding in the darkness that engulfed him. Through it all, he hung on to the faithful character of his God. At the end of his ordeal, he saw the light. It was not the light of healing or understanding, but the light that came with a greater revelation of his God. Hence comes his incredible statement, "I have heard of thee by the hearing of the ear, but now mine eye seeth thee" (Job 42:5).

Obviously, Job gained a greater vantage point after his season of great suffering. God is behind all matters of life. He is the One who guides us through the challenges of life and He is the One who is found at the end of the issues of life. Consider the all-encompassing reality of God, "And when all things shall be subdued unto him, then shall the Son also himself be subject unto him that put all things under him, that God may be all in all" (1 Corinthians 15:28).

Are you gaining the life you have in Christ in order to discover what it means for God to be your sole point of reliance, the all in all for your life?

---

[6] Job 3:2-3

10

GAINING LIFE

Consider the following table concerning what affects your life and how you may respond.

Type of Response	Type of Pain	Type of Games	Determines Spirit
Quality of Relationships	Physical Pain (Mourning)	Conning Others Avoid Confrontation	Agenda (Focus/ Affections)
React	Emotional Pain (Suffering)	Flattery (Maintain personal reality)	Emphasis (Attitude towards life)
Interact	Mental Pain (Anguish)	Compliance (Keep the Peace)	Priorities (How you will approach life.)

As you consider what the Word of God states about life, you have to realize that, even though it is a gift, it must be regarded in a right way. Discovering life requires one to choose to find it in the midst of all of its counterfeits. Self will tell you life is found when it is being rightfully exalted. The world claims life is gain through all of its riches, pleasures, and practices. Religion declares that life is obtained through certain religious beliefs or activities. We could go on and on about the different claims about finding and experiencing life. However, each of these counterfeits leaves people with unresolved issues. Life definitely proves to be more than religion, riches, pleasures, activities, and food.[1] There is only one place to find life and that is in a relationship with the Living God.

The Apostle Paul summarized life in this way, "For to me to live is Christ, and to die is gain" (Philippians 1:21). Until we find life in Christ, we remain miserably lost. We may be pursuing various avenues, but we are still miserably lost. We will become dissatisfied with the life that self

---

[1] Matthew 6:25-33; Luke 8:14; 12:23

promotes. The type of life the world promotes leaves us with an empty vacuum, while man's religion always leaves us disillusioned. However, to live is realized when we seek out, find, receive, and enter into actually inheriting the life God has provided. In light of Christ's redemption, He is now offering this life to everyone, and will freely give it to those who believe Him.

Consider the different aspects of the life of Christ. To gain His life, we must first lose our present life. It is through the death of the self-life that we gain the life of Jesus. It is at this point that we pass from death to life. It is from this place that we begin to possess or inherit His life.

As we consider the prospect of seeking out this life, we realize that there is some point where we deem that our present way of living does not constitute life. In other words, there is no life to be found in it. This is when we begin to seek out life. Needless to say, most people end on various detours. For example, many have tried religion to only become disillusioned with man's interpretation through tradition or rules. It all seems to become hopeless as life appears to be illusive, harsh, and temporary.

It is in such despair that God finds us. I know this to be true for my own life. Once that God finds us, we can begin to find Him. He is infinite and beyond our finite comprehension. But we can know Him in a personal way if we seek to find Him with all of our hearts.[2]

Once we find Him, we can begin to receive the life He desires to give us. God can only give life to those who are humble and receptive of it. John put it in this way, "But as many as received him, to them gave he power to become the sons of God, even to them that believe on his name" (John 1:12).

Once we receive His life, we have the power to enter into this life. God's life is like a gate, door, or veil. These entryways point to Jesus' redemption as the gate, His life as the door, and the place of communion and rest as the veil.[3] Each of these entrances represents a greater revelation of the life we can have in our Lord.

As we begin to enter into the life of God, we will start inheriting it. Life is meant to be experienced. It can be tasted, seen, heard, touched, and smelled. After all, the life of God is living; it is the life of Jesus. Every one of our senses can encounter His life and know it is real and alive. Once we begin to embrace this life by faith, we will begin to obtain and possess it. The Apostle Paul was running the race to apprehend this life and to be apprehended by it. His whole focus was to possess the prize of the high calling this life empowered him to reach in Jesus.[4]

We must now consider how this life will manifest itself. Jesus gives us insight into how His life will become apparent in believers' lives, "But seek ye first the kingdom of God, and his righteousness, and all these

---

[2] Jeremiah 29:13
[3] Matthew 7:13-14; John 10:9; Hebrews 10:19-21
[4] Psalm 34:8; 2 Corinthians 2:15-16; Philippians 3:12-14; 1 John 1:1

Challenging the Christian Life

things shall be added unto you" (Matthew 6:33). God's kingdom is realized in Jesus, and Jesus serves as the essence of righteousness in our lives.[5] His righteousness becomes active and evident at the point of our faith.

Romans 4:11, 22-23 talks about how righteousness was imputed or reckoned to Abraham because of his unfeigned faith in God. Romans 4:24 goes on to say this about believers, "But for us also, to whom it shall be imputed, if we believe on him that raised up Jesus, our Lord, from the dead." The Christian life is a matter of righteousness.

Righteousness is a disposition. In other words, it is right standing before God. Right standing points to the fact that one is not only doing right, but he or she is being right in what he or she is doing. Obviously, the right spirit must be present that will express itself in a right attitude. This attitude will be obvious in how one conducts his or her affairs in every aspect of his or her life.

Job was considered a righteous man. God actually pointed him out to Satan because of his right standing before Him. There were four qualities acknowledged about Job's character. He was perfect in his attitude about the things of God, upright before God in his approach to the matters of life, displayed the fear of the Lord in his conduct, and hated evil.[6]

It is important to point out that we cannot be perfect as Jesus was in His sinless state, but we can be brought to perfection or maturity in our attitude towards God. For such perfection to be brought forth, we must be upright in our approach and humble in our conduct. We must hate evil.

In comparing the self-centered life with the disposition of right standing before God, the differences are obvious. Right standing begins with the foundation of righteousness. It always starts from the basis of truth. Truth is turned on as a searchlight in regards to the person's standing before God. The main goal of the person is to ensure he or she is upright in his or her life before God. Such a perspective causes a person to be God-centered rather than self-centered. Those who maintain a self-centered life are more concerned about preserving the concept of self than they are about being upright before God. Although self might give the impression it desires righteousness, it is nothing more than a façade or mask that is hiding a wrong spirit.

A righteous disposition allows a person to approach life from the perspective of personal accountability. In other words, these people will take responsibility for their dispositions, attitudes, and conduct. They will not allow selfishness to justify away any moral deviation in their perspective, approach, and lifestyle. All aspects of their lives must be consistent with the life of Jesus that is being worked in them by the Holy Ghost.

---

[5] Mark 1:14-15; Luke 17:20-21; 1 Corinthians 1:30
[6] Job 1:1, 8

To preserve self, selfish people must maintain and guard their high opinion of self. After all, self cannot afford to be wrong and vulnerable. Such a state implies weakness. Self with its pride cannot appear weak if it is going to maintain its arrogant, self-sufficient, or confident presentation of itself. Therefore, self refuses to be wrong, thereby, not taking any accountability. When found to be wrong, self will justify, ignore, or delude itself to maintain its innocence in the matter.

Right standing before God points to godly actions. God's Spirit, character, and Word inspire these people's actions. The Apostle Paul made this statement, "For bodily exercise profiteth little, but godliness is profitable unto all things, having promise of the life that now is, and that which is to come" (1Timothy 4:8). The Apostle Peter says that believers have been given all things that pertain unto life and godliness through the knowledge of Jesus who has called us to glory and virtue.[7]

The Apostle Paul reveals what we must do to ensure godliness, "Teaching us that, denying ungodliness and worldly lusts, we should live soberly, righteously, and godly, in this present world" (Titus 2:12). Notice how we must deny ungodliness and worldly lusts at every point. It is not just enough to deny ungodly practices and lust, but we must replace it with the right type of living. This requires us to be sober in attitude, righteous in disposition, and godly in conduct. Galatians 5:17 tells us how the flesh lusts against the Spirit. The Apostle Paul goes on to say what the works of the flesh are, and ends with the warning that those who walk by such works will not inherit the kingdom of God.[8]

When we talk about the disposition of right standing before God, we are talking about the state of holiness. Holiness points to separation from the unholy in order to be separated unto the holy. It is in the state of holiness that man is perfected or brought to maturity. He will be upright in attitude towards the matters of life. He will guard against evil influences and alliances. He will test his spirit in matters of service and conduct. He will bring the members of his body under subjection to ensure that he will make honorable decisions in regard to his life and responsibility. Ultimately, the way in which he walks will be disciplined as it is being perfected or matured in the ways of God.

Sadly, Christians are failing to understand their need to be perfected or matured in the ways of God. This was the problem with the children of Israel. They witnessed God's power, but they failed to let the reality of God discipline them according to His ways. Hebrews 3:10 makes this statement, "Wherefore, I was grieved with that generation, and said, They do always err in their heart, and they have not known my ways."

Obviously, the children of Israel were erring in their heart about their God. People err in their hearts about God because they really do not know Him. How can you test your life if you do not know the one that you must come into agreement with?

---

[7] 2 Peter 1:3
[8] Galatians 5:18-21

There are Christians who clearly do not know their God. As a result, they are erring in their hearts about what is pleasing and acceptable to Him. They may be hiding behind His love and grace, but they have no real personal sense of who He is.

We must know the character of our God if we are to understand His ways. God will not move outside of who He is. Everything He does will line up to His character. Since He is a holy God, all things must be considered from a state of holiness. Ultimately, it will prove to be righteous before God, upright in attitude, and right in conduct.

The only way we can begin to know our God is in a relationship. However, healthy relationships must start from a correct premise. All relationships start from the premise of position. For example, if you desire friendship with someone, you must start from the premise of what it means to be a friend.

The Apostle Paul told us what position we must start from to gain the right perspective about the matters of life, "And hath raised us up together, and made us sit together in heavenly places in Christ Jesus" (Ephesians 2:6). The position is a heavenly position. Therefore, our premise is not from the perspective of earth, but it must be towards and from heaven itself. After all, we have been raised up in position to consider the issues of life and the matters of this present world from such a view.

Think about this prospect for a moment. If we would consider all the issues of life from the heavenly perspective, our lives would be powerfully affected and changed. Would not our attitudes, personalities, and lifestyles reflect such a powerful influence? Obviously, heaven must influence every aspect of our lives if we are going to develop and maintain an inward state of holiness before God.

What position are you starting from in your relationship with God? It must humbly reach upward to ensure you are being influenced, touched, and affected by heaven in the character and conduct of your life.

11

REACHING OUR POTENTIAL

We have been discussing what it means to gain the life of Christ. We can only gain it from a heavenly premise. We have been positionally placed in the heavenlies in order to consider all matters of life from the heights of God. All issues of life must be considered in light of the character of Christ. Once a matter has been disciplined and sanctified through the Person of Jesus, then a person can begin to develop His mind.

When we talk about being placed in heavenly places with Christ, we are talking about the vantage point from which we must consider our life. Too many Christians are earth-bound. Their vantage point is that of self, the world, or religion. Self perverts the matters of life, while the world defiles it and religion can kill it with all of its dead-letter rhetoric. Obviously, such a vantage point implies affections that can easily become inordinate in their emphasis.

Christians often remain immature in their lives before God because they do not understand their position in Christ. Yet, the Word clearly tells believers that they are in Christ and He is in them. In Christ the believer is hidden, while Christ in the believer becomes his or her point of heavenly wisdom, godly righteousness, the essence of sanctification, and complete redemption.[1]

The reason our position in Christ is so important is because this is the vantage point from which the Father regards us. He does not regard us in light of our human best, consider our failures in regards to our human frailties, or overlook our weaknesses out of love. In His holy state, out of love for humanity and in light of His desire towards us, He provided the way in which He could accept each of us. He can only consider each person from the vantage point of what His Son accomplished on the cross. However, each of us must be hid in Jesus, and He must be in us to ensure that the Father sees us from this point.

It is from the vantage point of Jesus as our Savior, Redeemer, and Lord that the mark of heavenly ownership will be realized in our lives. This is why we are sealed with the Holy Spirit. This heavenly seal serves as an endowment to identify us with a heavenly inheritance.[2]

It is from the vantage point of our heavenly position in Jesus that we can realize our potential. Our potential is to reflect the glory of Jesus.

---

[1] 1 Corinthians 1:30; Colossians 3:3
[2] Ephesians 1:11-14

This reflection will come through our personality. Most people want to control personality through rules. However, personality is an expression of our disposition. As Christians, we must have the liberty to reflect Jesus according to our particular personality. Any form of dictate in this arena will become a point of bondage. Bondage of this nature encourages people to become robots in their actions. Jesus is not reflected through such actions, but through our personalities that will determine how we express ourselves in a matter.

Jesus was lowly in disposition and meek in attitude.[3] Due to His mind, He reflected this state in His compassion towards others. His mind not only determined His conduct, but also the spirit in which He expressed a matter. It was His spirit that confirmed the validity of His actions. When people watched Jesus in action, they saw the heart of the Father. When they heard Jesus, they heard the voice of God. When Jesus touched them in His benevolence, they felt the touch of heaven. Jesus summarized it best to Philip, "...He that hath seen me hath seen the Father;..." (John 14:9b)

The Apostle Paul made this statement, "For in him dwelleth all the fullness of the Godhead bodily" (Colossians 2:9). The issue is who or what are we expressing in the life that God has given us? Our disposition determines who we become, but our reflection is based on who we allow ourselves to become. For example, disposition is influenced by our environment. We do not have a say over what affects our environments, but we do determine the attitude and approach we will have towards those things that challenge our atmospheres. Reflection will be established by what we come into agreement with. Therefore, what we agree with will determine what we allow ourselves to become. We ultimately reflect what we are in unity or agreement with. As man, Jesus was in total agreement with the Father. Thus, He clearly reflected the Father in His person. This agreement determined how Jesus' very person would be expressed to others.

It is important to understand how our dispositions and personalities operate. Our dispositions must be upright or operating from a holy state. From a state of holiness, our personalities will reflect our points of agreement. In such a state we will have agreement with Jesus, thereby, reflecting His glory to the world. If we are reflecting His glory, we will be reaching our potentials in His kingdom. Remember, because of sin, men fall short of reflecting the glory of God.[4] Jesus reestablished the means on the cross in which man could once again be brought into communion with God.

Jesus stated that He is the way, truth, and life to the Father. Jesus became the place of reconciliation. At this place, man could once again be in communion with God. Such communion points to agreement. The more I commune with God, the more I will reflect the glory of the Lord.

---

[3] Matthew 11:28-29
[4] Romans 3:23; 2 Corinthians 3:18

This was made apparent in Moses' life. He was in the presence of God for forty days and nights. When he came down from his place of communion with God, his face reflected God's glory.[5]

As you can see, it is all about influence and agreement. Sadly, many people are influenced by the philosophies and lusts of the world and come into agreement with the spirit and practices of the world. The Apostle Paul stated that Satan is the god of this world and the spirit of this world works disobedience towards God in those who come into agreement with it. James tells us that those who are friends of the world are enemies of God. In fact, people are committing spiritual harlotry if they have come into agreement with the world. Paul instructs us to come out and be separate from that which is unclean. In other words, take responsibility for what we allow to influence our life.[6]

Most Christians never get to the point where they understand their positions in Christ. They allow outside forces to define their positions in this present life. As they allow the lusts of the world to influence them; they simply reflect the selfish disposition that plagues man. If they come into agreement with the spirit of the world, they reflect the self-serving darkness of the world. If man's religion becomes their conscience, they will reflect the false light of self-righteousness. Clearly, sin, wrong influences, and unholy agreement mars man's potential to reflect the beauty and glory of his Creator.

It is vital that we take accountability for what or how something influences our inward environment to ensure an upright disposition. We must take responsibility for what we come into agreement with. After all, we will reflect such agreement to others. This is why, as Christians, we must cease to be irresponsible for our view and attitudes towards God and life. It is from the platform of disposition and agreement that all the issues of life will be regarded and handled. If we are of the right disposition and in agreement with our Creator, we will consider all matters from the heavenly vantage point of our position in Christ.

The Word of God speaks about such a vantage point,

> Doth the eagle mount up at thy command, and make her nest on high? She dwelleth and abideth on the rock, upon the crag of the rock, and the strong place. From thence she seeketh the prey, and her eyes behold afar off (Job 39:27-29).

The eagle is a good example of what it means to see from this heavenly vantage. Eagles soar on the current of the wind. Christians must learn to walk after the Spirit in order for the Spirit to lead them to the currents of God that will take them beyond this world, giving them a heavenly perspective. It is from this perspective that believers will abide on the Rock of God as they find protection in the crag of the rock, Jesus. This will serve as their strong place and it is from this perspective that they

---

[5] John 14:6; 2 Corinthians 3:7-13; 5:18-19; Ephesians 2:13-16; Colossians 1:20
[6] 2 Corinthians 4:3-4; 6:14-18; Ephesians 2:2-3; Colossians 2:8; James 4:4

can behold afar off. It is from this vantage point that Christians are able to powerfully interact with those in their environments.

The question is who or what are you reflecting to others? Is it the glory of Jesus, the foolishness of self, the ignorance of the world, the false light of religion, the darkness of Satan, or the very glory of your Creator? Such a reflection will reveal whether you have the mind of Christ or are being conformed to this present world.

12

TRANSFORMING THE MIND

Reflecting the glory of Jesus entails having His mind. We have already mentioned how the mind of Christ expresses itself. It revealed that He was lowly in disposition and meek in attitude. A lowly disposition points to humility, while meekness manifests itself in being under control. Jesus was in subjection to the will of the Father due to His humble disposition. Subjection to the Father made Jesus meek, meaning that all of His strength was under control. He did nothing outside of the Father's plan. Obviously, as man, Jesus' vantage point was heaven. Everything He did came from the throne room of heaven. There was total agreement or oneness between Him and the Father.[1]

We are told to have the mind of Jesus.[2] This involves becoming one with Him in total agreement. As previously stated, our countenance will reflect what we have come into agreement with in our way of thinking. This is why we must consider what is influencing our disposition because it will determine what we will come into agreement with.

Agreement will determine how we express the life in us. Keep in mind, since life is living, we will express the essence of this life in our personality. When it comes to influences, there are only two real sources of influence in our lives. These two sources will determine who we allow ourselves to become in the scheme of life. Obviously, this shows us that the quality of our lives is our choice and personal responsibility.

We respond to the different influences of life in two ways. We will either conform to its way of thinking or we will allow our way of thinking to be transformed. The Apostle Paul summarized it in this way, "And be not conformed to this world, but be ye transformed by the renewing of your mind, that ye may prove what is that good, and acceptable, and perfect, will of God" (Romans 12:2).

The influences of life will either conform us to this present world's way of thinking or it will transform our way of thinking to understand that which is good, acceptable, and perfect according to the will of God. Anyone can conform. They simply outwardly comply with a matter to give an appearance, while transformation results in a complete change in a person's way of thinking. It is the change that will be enduring and reflected to others.

---

[1] Matthew 11:28-29; John 5:19-20, 30; 10:30; Philippians 2:5-8
[2] Philippians 2:5

There are three ways a person is conformed to this world's way of thinking. They are conditioned, indoctrinated, or come into an "appearance" of agreement through compliance. These three ways find their avenue through different influences. For example, family and culture will condition us in our lifestyles. As we give way to these conditionings, we become unfulfilled as we sense that these influences have no real regard to who we are. Since our lifestyles reflect our family or culture, we can find no purpose in our life, except to fulfill something or someone else's idea of life. Such conditioning will leave people frustrated, angry, and rebellious.

Indoctrination is done through such mediums as religion, entertainment, and education. Indoctrination is the means by which to program individuals into a particular reality. When the matters of life challenge these people, they will automatically think in accordance to their indoctrination. Obviously, this is a limited, biased, and perverted perception. However, people who have been indoctrinated do not see any other reality. Eventually, their perverted reality will fail them and bring them to an identity crisis. Some become more deluded as they convince themselves that their particular indoctrinated concepts are true. However, others become disillusioned towards their particular source of hope and reliance and dissatisfied with their concept of life. They recognize something is clearly missing in their life. What is missing is the reality of God. But, in many such cases these people cannot discern between their indoctrination about God and the Person of God that has been clearly outlined in Scripture and will be confirmed and maintained by the Holy Spirit in all wisdom and revelation.

The third type of avenue is done in the name of peace. It encourages the concept of compliance. Compliance is nothing more than playing the games of others. Compliance is the means to control or manipulate personal realities. For example, I play your game to keep the so-called "peace" between us. But, in reality, I do not want to confront you or be considered the bad guy. I am simply complying to maintain my own particular reality about myself and my world, while encouraging you in your particular fantasy. It is a way of keeping you quiet so you will not invade my particular space. In this game playing, I will appeal to your pride so that you will give way to my reality at certain points. I will cater to your emotions so that you can feel good about self and, in turn, promote my personal well-being. In such a reality, everyone appears to win. However, according to the Bible, everyone is really losing. The reason is because truth is missing in these false ways. Without truth, no one will win, be set free, or saved from their wretched realities.[3]

Such compliance cleverly maintains a fragile peace that lacks real substance. In this fragile peace everybody will be happy in their particular realities. However, the lustful appetites are enlarging, insecurities are escalating, and self is becoming more tyrannical in its

---

[3] John 8:32-36

demands to be considered and worshipped whenever it sees fit. Ultimately, such an environment creates discontentment and uncertainty.

As you consider the power behind these influences, you begin to see that conforming to the world's way of thinking simply reinforces perverted views of life, results in condemnation because the perverted worldview remains intact, and becomes indifferent as the conscience becomes seared and deluded in its perception about the issues of life. Obviously, influences define us and will either challenge our perception or delude us into a reality that is unrealistic and far from the center of what is true.

Due to the powerful influence of the world, Paul does not call for rehabilitation of the mind, but for transformation. Most people are into reforming their minds in order to properly conform and perform to what is required. However, transformation implies a complete change taking place that will transfigure the very thinking and reflection of a person. It works from the same concept of metamorphoses where the caterpillar changes into a butterfly

Obviously, every aspect of our thinking must be completely transfigured. Instead of possessing a selfish way of thinking that is bent towards conforming to the things of the world that serves its purpose, it will take on a new attitude. As a new attitude is developed, the behavior of a person (who he and she is) will change, causing the person (what he or she expresses) to become renewed by the power of the Spirit. As the mind is being transformed into the very attitude of Christ, the person's disposition or state will be transfigured by the life of Christ being worked in him or her. This will change what a person intends to be. In this case, the person intends to be all that his or her Creator has designed him or her to be.

Once a person is being influenced by the mind of Christ, he or she is able to come into agreement with God's purpose for his or her life. In agreement, true communion takes place. As a person gets to know the character of God, he or she will have a sense of how to please God. The Apostle Paul brought this out in Romans 12:2c, "...that ye may prove what is that good, and acceptable, and perfect, will of God."

There are many people serving God, but they have no real inclination as to what will please Him. They have not proven what is good, acceptable, or perfect in regard to God's will. These particular people's activities may look religious and appeal to others' pride, while making them feel good about themselves, as a means to bring some type of recognition to their person. Obviously, the person is being glorified in such an arena and not God. The Apostle Paul made this statement, "That no flesh should glory in his presence" (1 Corinthians 1:29).

The problem with self is that it is about self, for self, and because of self that the person is reacting and responding to his or her environment. Its attitude and actions toward God is to cause God to become impressed with self. However, God is never impressed with the perverted, self-serving attempts of self. Self must be out of the way before a person can truly know God. When self is not reigning, a person has the ability to come to terms with what will please God.

If a person has the mind of Christ, then clearly, he or she will reflect Christ in attitude and conduct. Such a person will become an expression of Jesus, bringing glory to God and fulfilling his or her purpose.

As we can see, the mind must be transformed. To renew the mind is clearly the work of the Spirit. But, how can we encourage such a work in our own lives? It will come down to the matter of faith.

13

RECKONING A MATTER AS SO

For the last two chapters we have been talking about our positions in Christ and the need for our minds to be transformed into His mind. Eternal life is given to us by grace, but the abundant, victorious life is only realized when it is being worked in us by the power of the Holy Spirit.

Eternal life is always being offered to mankind, but it is God's desire to work within believers the abundance of the life of Christ. Sadly, many Christians think of the Christian life as being handed to them. The fact that eternal life is being offered to us is not the same as handing it to us. Most people think of being handed something according to their particular interpretations of it. God offers eternal life but it must be received in our heart by faith in accordance to what He says.[1]

When you study the concept of faith, it becomes an avenue by which something can be imputed or reckoned to us. Due to faith in God's saving work of grace on the cross, righteousness can be imputed or reckoned to us.[3] As you consider the concept of the Christian life, it is a matter of reckoning it as so.

For example, we must reckon that we have a heavenly position in Christ. To reckon a matter begins with knowing a matter is so. Knowing comes from a premise of what we already recognize as being true. Once a matter is known, then we must believe it is true. Belief graduates to the stage of counting it as true. To count something as true activates faith as it applies the truth to one's way of thinking and being. If something is true, there is no room for debate. Therefore, the concept of reckoning is that a matter will come out the same, no matter what angle you approach it from. It works from the same concepts as mathematics. Two plus two equals four, no matter from what position you approach it. Obviously, there is much power and authority in reckoning a matter as true.

To count a matter as true takes determination. Once a matter is reckoned as true, it is put to the test through application. This is why faith without application (works of obedience) is considered dead.[4] There may be a mental agreement, but if there is no change to a person's way of thinking, it is conformation, not transformation.

---

[1] Romans 10:17
[3] Romans 4:1-13
[4] James 2:14-26

Active faith will change or transform a person's approach to a matter. The mind will come into agreement for the purpose of changing direction. As the direction is changed, the behavior will begin to adjust to the new focus. As behavior adjusts, affections will change their momentum to realign to the focus. The focus will bring us into agreement with God's perspective about a matter. This is a summation of the process of transformation. It seems simple enough, but how many of you could implement it into your lives?

We must first reckon our position in Christ before we can reckon our status in Him. After all, I must first have the heavenly vantage point to accept my status within His kingdom. Status will, in turn, compliment or ensure the right vantage point. Since our vantage point as Christians is heavenly, it allows me to understand what I need to prepare myself to separate *unto*—the holy in light of the eternal—in order to separate *from* that which is defiled and temporary.

Let us follow the reckoning process from the point of position to the reality of status. Positionally, we will start from Ephesians 2:6, "And hath raised us up together, and made us sit together in heavenly places in Christ Jesus." God's Word has told us that we have been raised up together to sit in heavenly places in Christ. As a believer, I must reckon this as so.

Since I have counted myself in heavenly places, I now know that, positionally, I have a heavenly vantage point. Now that I have counted myself in this position, I must apply it. Colossians 3:1-3 tells me how to apply this promise as a truth. "If ye, then, be <u>risen</u> with Christ, seek those things which are above, where Christ sitteth on the right hand of God. Set your affection on things above, not on things on the earth. For ye are dead, and your life is hidden with Christ in God." (Emphasis added)

My initial response to my position is to seek those things which are above. The essence of my life is found in heaven. Therefore, I must seek the perspective from the heavenly vantage point. This will discipline my pursuits or inclinations.

Then, I must set my affections on things above. Once I discipline my pursuits, my affections will naturally follow the direction of my new found focus. Since my focus is heavenward, my affections or tendencies will now be set on the things of heaven. Set is also a discipline. However, I cannot set my affections on that which is above unless my focus has been placed there as my source of reliance and confidence.

This will bring me to my status—I am dead in Christ. If I am dead in Christ, then I am hidden in His life. The status of being dead in Christ was clearly outlined by the Apostle Paul in Romans 6. When you follow the process of reckoning a matter as so, remember, you first begin from the premise of knowing it is true. It is true because God said it.[5] Once you know a matter is true, you believe it by applying it to your walk. This

---

[5] Romans 10:17

means walking it out as if you are dead to the self-life and this present world.

Application of or obedience to a matter takes you to the next stage—counting it as so. You cannot count a matter as so unless you are practicing it. Practicing something ensures you are not a hypocrite. After all, hypocrites are all talk and no show. They are simply pretending a matter is true when, in reality, they do not believe it enough to walk it out. Counting a matter as so, allows it to be confirmed by the Spirit of God. All things will be confirmed in the Spirit by knowledge, wisdom, and revelation that is Scripturally maintained in intent and truth. We need to walk after such knowledge to ensure the Spirit will lead us into wisdom that will produce revelation.[6] It is at the point of revelation that a matter that has been reckoned as truth becomes personal reality. Personal reality means that it has become my personal truth that will forever impact the way I approach and respond to an issue of life.

As we follow the progression of realizing our status of death, we can begin to see that we know we are dead in Christ because we have been baptized into Jesus Christ. There are a couple of different baptisms. However, I believe this baptism has to do with being baptized into His Body. The Apostle Paul gave us insight into this baptism

> For as the body is one, and hath many members, and all the members of that one body, being many are one body, so also is Christ. For by one Spirit are we all baptized into one body, whether we be Jews or Gentiles, whether we be bond or free; and have been all made to drink into one Spirit (1 Corinthians 12:12-13).

Baptism points to total identification. As members of His Body, we do not stand alone, rather we stand as a whole Body identified by the head or leadership of Christ and the life of Christ that is pulsating through each of us. Since Christ died for our sins, total identification with Him in His death means that we also stand dead to the influences and consequences of our sins. They no longer have any reign over us. Obviously, we must know that the status of death identifies us with Christ.

Once we know we are dead in Christ, we can also believe that we are buried with Him in His death. Burial represents complete separation from the old life. Now that we know we have been separated from the old life, we can know the third part of our status as being dead in light of resurrection. In Christ, we also have been raised up in newness of life.[7]

As the Apostle Paul stated, since we have been planted together in the likeness of his death, we shall be also in the likeness of his resurrection. Such identification points to the fact that we have been crucified with Jesus so that the body of sin might be destroyed. Destruction of the influence and hold of sin on our lives will ensure that

---

[6] Romans 6:3-4; 8:1, 14-18

[7] Romans 6:4

we no longer serve sin. The Apostle Paul instructs us to not let sin reign in our mortal bodies by obeying its lust.[8] Since we know this, how do we graduate to the second stage of reckoning it as so? Actually, we find that answer in Colossians 3:5, "Mortify, therefore, your members which are upon the earth: fornication, uncleanness, inordinate affection, evil concupiscence, and covetousness (which is idolatry)."

We must put anything to death that would attract, justify, or give way to the works of the flesh. It is up to us to put these temptations down once they stand up to challenge our pursuits. We must reckon ourselves raised into a new life to ensure that a separation unto God will occur. Separation unto God will ensure that we will live unto Him. But we must first reckon ourselves dead to sin to be separated from that which would entangle us into its destructive web. After all, such things bring the wrath of God upon us.[9]

Mortifying the pursuits of the flesh is just the beginning. The next challenge will come from the platform of our affections. We must put the matters of the flesh off. In other words, the old ways of the flesh rise up from within and we must put them off as we would dirty clothes to ensure that they do not become platforms from which the works of the flesh can operate.[10] Consider what these things are, "But now ye also put off all these: anger, wrath, malice, blasphemy, filthy communication out of your mouth. Lie not one to another, seeing that ye have put off the old man with his deeds" (Colossians 3:8-9).

Affections must be disciplined to ensure their focus remains upright. This allows me to remember that the deeds of the old man have been put off in order to put on the new man. It is as that new man is put on that each of us are renewed in the knowledge according to the One who created us. It is in this renewed state that we can begin to put on that which will compliment the attitude of the new man. We will put on that which is holy, merciful, kind, humble in disposition, meek in attitude, longsuffering, faithful, forgiving, and loving. Obviously, the new man is the life of Jesus being realized in us in attitude, conduct, and lifestyle. Since it is holy, it is upright. Due to mercy, it is compassionate as well as gentle, kind, considerate, patient, and full of grace. It is from this premise that the very peace of God will rule in our hearts.[11]

As you can see, reckoning means something will become a living reality to us. We will no longer be instruments of unrighteousness since sin no longer has any dominion over us. Now that we have been freed from the influences, affects, and activities of sin upon our lives, we now can be servants of righteousness, operating within a state of holiness.[12]

---

[8] Romans 6:5-6, 12
[9] Roman 6:10; Colossians 3:6
[10] Colossians 3:8
[11] Colossians 3:12-15
[12] Romans 6:12-13, 19

Being dead in Christ ensures the guidance of His wisdom, the influence of His righteousness, the working of His sanctification, and the fullness of His redemption being realized in our lives. Sadly, such a reality is missing in many Christians' lives. They live in defeat because the truths of the Bible have never been made a living reality to them.

However, the Word of God is true. It is living and full of the power of His Spirit. But it must be received by faith. Faith knows a matter is true because it is His Word; therefore, it counts it as so and responds in obedience. At the point of obedience, the Spirit of God will faithfully make His Words as life and truth to our spirits.[13]

Reckoning a spiritual matter as true allows the Holy Spirit to transform the mind about all matters that concern life in God's kingdom. The question is, have you applied unfeigned faith to all spiritual matters regarding your life in Christ? If not, God's Word will never become living, thereby transforming your mind. Without the transformed mind, you will never become a living witness in the kingdom of God.

---

[13] John 6:63; Romans 10:17; Hebrews 4:12; 11:6

14

A LIVING MEMORIAL TO GOD

We have waded through much in order to come to terms with the concept of life. Clearly, most people are trying to survive the challenges of life while becoming disillusioned, skeptical, and overburdened by it all. Some live in denial about it, others go into total delusion to maintain some type of fantasy or hope, and others resort to rebellion, anger, and despair.

Life seems hopeless unless we look beyond this present world. Life seems to mock us unless we are willing to consider that which we cannot see. Life is so unfair unless we choose to believe that there is more to life than we can experience in this present world of darkness.

Searching for life will bring us to one conclusion, that there must be a God who is not only the source to real life, but holds the purpose for our very beings.[1] After all, if there is no God, we are the most miserable of people. If there is no way to escape the mockery of this cycle that is referred to as life, we are the most hopeless of people. If there is no solution to our plights, we remain the most wretched creatures in this universe.

I have struggled with the issues of life to only find resolution and hope in the blessed redemption of Jesus Christ. However, in my search to understand life in light of Jesus, I discovered that life is more than believing His redemption, it is a matter of experiencing the beauty of His life in a personal way.

As you may have gathered, this book is about what I have discovered about the life of Christ. Discovering that my potential is to reflect Him to this lost world was humbling enough, but I also had to realize that I was to serve as a living witness to His work in my life.

The first disciples were empowered from above to become living witnesses of Jesus' redemption to a lost world.[2] These people turned the upside-down world right side up with the power of deliverance from its hopeless plight, the promise of life that exceeds beyond this present world, and the blessed hope of experiencing the fullness of it in the next world.

---

[1] Acts 17:28
[2] Acts 1:8

As I considered my life, I had to ask myself if I had become a living witness to the life Jesus promised us in His redemption. It is eternal, but it is empowered by His Spirit. It possesses resurrection power that will one day raise up each blood-bought saint in a new incorruptible body. As my present body gives way to the working of physical death, I remind myself that, in spite of the weakness that plagues my flesh and the death that works in my body, I possess resurrection power because of Jesus' redemption. It is from this perspective that I sincerely want my faith in the reality of Christ to mark my life with this resurrection power as it did the cloud of witnesses of old. After all, they accepted greater suffering to be ensured of a greater resurrection.[3] Such a reality reminds me that I must testify of this resurrection power to others who live a life that is based on a false or void hope.

Hence, enters the realistic evaluation and judgment in regard to my personal life before Christ. Does the light of Jesus' life shine in the midst of the death working in my body to draw people to the One who was lifted up on a cross on their behalf? I cannot tell you how many times I have asked God to enable me to finish this course by running across the finish line and not just being content to crawl across it. After all, life carries a toll with it and I want the scars I carry from this present existence to mark my life with death to the self-life, rather than scars of rebellion because I fought and struggled against the promised life of God.

The Word of God also tells me I am a living epistle. As a witness, my life is empowered by the Spirit to testify of the work of Christ in my life. As a living epistle, I carry the living words of Jesus' life in my conduct.[4] These words have been written by the Spirit of the Living God upon a fleshly heart that is able to respond in spirit and truth. I must be reckoning these words in order to be assured that they are living and real to those who see me in the challenges of life. After all, these words have been written in my heart by the Holy Spirit who brought knowledge, wisdom, and revelation of them to my very being.

These words are powerful because they are living. They are transforming because they have become my reality, inner strength, and abiding hope. They are life itself because they belong to the One who is the giver of all life.

Clearly, my life must reflect the life of Jesus for me to be able to testify of His impact and importance upon who I have become in this hopeless world. His mind must be seen in my attitudes and conduct before others. People who see His mind in my character and being will be stirred up in their hopelessness, attracted in their spiritual dullness, and given a glimpse of hope in their darkness.

This brings me to the final aspect of my life. It must serve as a living memorial to God. As we have already discussed, the life that I now live

---

[3] John 5:21,24-29; 11:25-26; 1 Corinthians 15:40-53; Hebrews 10:15-16
[4] 2 Corinthians 3:2-3

Challenging the Christian Life

by faith in the Son of God must become a visible, bold witness of His redemption. It must serve as a living epistle that can be clearly seen and read by all who come in contact with me. In summation, they must see the very mind of Christ.

However, to be a witness I must suffer death to the self-life. After all, witness means "martyr". Death must mark my life. It is I that no longer lives, but it is Christ in me and His life that is coming forth in power. As a living epistle, I must give way to the cross so that the words that come forth through my attitude and conduct are according to the life and mind of Christ. The old ways that marked my previous life and existence must cease so that my Lord can increase in my life in greater measure. Now that death marks my life, I can presently serve as a living memorial to the ongoing reality of God and His Gospel.

One person's action was singled out by Jesus and identified as serving as a true memorial to the Gospel. It was Jesus' final week leading to Calvary. He was at Simon the leper's house for a feast. In came Mary, the sister of Lazarus. She was the one who sat at Jesus' feet while her sister, Martha, frantically served Him. She brought with her an alabaster box of very precious ointment, pouring it upon Jesus' head.[5] She was greatly criticized for her action, but Jesus made this statement, "For in that she hath poured this ointment on my body, she did it for my burial. Verily I say unto you, Wherever this gospel shall be preached in the whole world, there shall also this, that this woman hath done, be told for a memorial of her" (Matthew 26:12-13).

As I considered Mary's action I realized that there were three points of significance to her action. The first one was identification. She was anointing Jesus for His burial. The Gospel is that Jesus died for our sins, was buried, and rose three days later.[6] Mary was becoming identified with Jesus in His death, burial, and resurrection.

The second point is that it was sacrificial. It cost her something to anoint Jesus. There is some speculation that Mary may have been saving this for her personal burial. Regardless of her reason for having this expensive ointment, God put it aside for this point in time. It would designate Jesus as the sacrificial Lamb who would die on our behalf. He was being set apart for His death.

Finally, due to her identification with Jesus and the sacrifice she poured upon Him, her action made her life a memorial. As a memorial she would point people back to Jesus and His Gospel. Her life would serve as a reminder of a time that forever changed the course for those who would believe in the redemptive work of the cross. Although her life became a memorial that night over 20 centuries ago, she continues to serve as a living memorial to the ongoing reality of God and His work.

As I considered the essence of my life through the years, I realized that I truly wanted my life to count for something. Granted, there are

---

[5] John 12:3-7
[6] 1 Corinthians 15:3-4

those who have impacted history in some way, as well as others who have left stunning masterpieces behind for others to study and admire. There are those who have accomplished great feats. However, as you consider all of these accomplishments, you realize that all identification with such accomplishments will be burned up in judgment.[7] Only that which has impacted lives for eternity will remain.

It was from the premise of eternity that I began to consider how I could make life count. After all, I was given the gift of life to not only experience it, but to make it count for something. Obviously, my life must be touched by eternity and, in turn, it must touch eternity in order to become the expression of its source, the gift it was intended to be, and the purpose it was designed to fulfill.

It was only by becoming a witness to the source and power behind my life that I could begin to become a living epistle of His greatness. It would be out of the revelation of the Lord's greatness that sacrifice would come forth, establishing my life as a living memorial of the character and work of my Creator. It is only by becoming a living memorial to my God that I can be assured that I have found the essence of life and fulfill my reason for being in this present world.

Was I willing to live a life consecrated totally unto God to ensure that my life would become a living memorial to God? As I once again considered the cloud of witnesses found in Hebrews 11, I could not help but realize how these people's lives spoke volumes about their Creator.[8] They were witnesses of His greatness and faithfulness. They carried His living words in their hearts and by faith they allowed God to take them through challenges that would serve as a memorial to the testimony, declaration, and victory that they had in Him. Their lives became such a living memorial that the world was not worthy to even witness their faith.[9] Can you imagine the depth they had in God, the unwavering confidence that found its strength in the immovable Rock of ages, and the hope they had knowing that the promise of a greater resurrection awaited them?

There is no way that I can bring this book to a conclusion unless I end with the reality of God. All life started with God's handiwork, all life will be maintained by His intervention, and life as we know it will end according to His plan and purpose. However, there is life beyond this world. This life will be realized in the presence, power, and glory of God.

The question is what do you want your life to say about your short journey through this world? I have no concern about what this world will say about me, but I do care about what the corridors of heaven will declare about my journey. Will they declare that the gift of life I possess became the means by which to invest the life of Jesus in others or will they declare I wasted the gift of life on the wasteland of selfishness and the altars of the idolatrous world that abounds around me?

---

[7] 2 Peter 3:10-12
[8] Hebrews 12:1
[9] Hebrews 11:38

Challenging the Christian Life

Life is clearly a choice. In my innermost being I am accountable for the quality of my life and I take responsibility for the attitudes and actions of my life. In taking accountability and responsibility for my life, I actually make the same choice every day. I choose God and His life and work. I choose the essence of His life, His Son Jesus Christ. I choose His way of life, that of righteousness. I choose the fullness of His life that is not only abundant, but also eternal. As a result, I one day hope to offer this life back to my Creator as a living memorial of His love, faithfulness, and majesty.

In closing, consider the words of the Lord and consider the daily choices of your life:

> I call heaven and earth to record this day against you, that I have set before you life and death, blessing and cursing; therefore, choose life, that both thou and thy seed may live. (Deuteronomy 30:19, emphasis added.)

PRESENTATION OF THE GOSPEL

Book Two

Copyright © 2006 by Rayola Kelley

INTRODUCTION

I tried to avoid the inevitable task of writing a book about the Gospel for our Discipleship Course. I reasoned that I had properly dealt with this important subject throughout the course, as well as in my other books. However, due to the times in which we live, it is impossible to ignore how the Gospel is misrepresented, twisted, and devalued. All too often, if the Gospel is presented at all, we find that it is merely tacked on as an after thought or watered down to avoid insulting anyone. The fact is that the Gospel of Jesus Christ is being reduced to a "feel-good" and culturally acceptable bit of dogma. Too often, it is presented with a sugar coating that robs it of its real power or treated as an insignificant burden that is vaguely alluded to. The impression is often given that the Gospel is too outdated for today's sophisticated society.

The truth is that the Gospel rests at the core of the Christian life. Without a proper presentation of it, people will not see the kingdom of God. In fact, those who have based their entire religious experiences on one encounter with the Gospel through a single prayer are going to be shocked when they realize that Jesus will most likely not recognize them on judgment day.

This book is long overdue. Of all the spiritual books available today, few properly deal with the subject of the real Gospel. Most of the Christian world assumes that one simple encounter with the Gospel ensures eternal life. However, the Word of God presents a different picture. As you approach God's Word in regards to the Gospel, you will see that behind its simplicity is an ongoing revelation of man's plight and God's intervention. These ongoing revelations reveal that the power of the Gospel will never fade with time or cultural changes, the depth of the Gospel will never be reached in a person's fleeting lifetime, and the purpose of it will never be realized until it is unfolded in eternity.

My prayer is that Christians will put aside their comfortable concepts about this subject and open themselves up to the power, depth, and revelation of the Gospel. In so doing, the Christian walk will become more understandable as sin is properly confronted in light of the manifestation of the life of Jesus Christ and His redemption on the cross.

1

WHAT IS THE GOSPEL?

When you ask Christians what the Gospel is, few are able to respond according to the Scriptures. I have spent years instructing those I have been entrusted with as to what constitutes the Gospel of Jesus Christ. Although it is a simple message, its meaning and purpose are far-reaching and eternal in nature.

I have learned over the years that people cannot understand the work of redemption unless they grow in an understanding of the Gospel. My first encounter with the Gospel was vague. I had belonged to a cult that spoke of a gospel, but never defined it; therefore, it lacked substance and contrast. To me, the gospel implied spiritual truth. After I became a Christian, I realized that the true Gospel is a fact surrounded by eternal truths and examples. It can be defined and observed from different angles, but it will always remain consistent. Obviously, my former cult could not define the Gospel because it did not possess the real Gospel. This cult treated their particular gospel as if it was spiritual, but indescribable, and wonderful, yet illusive.

When I initially became a Christian, I was more aware of the fruits of the Gospel, rather than the actual message. I witnessed peace and contentment in those who had embraced this message. I knew these people possessed something I desired. I was eventually given a small glimpse of the Gospel in relationship to my sin and need for salvation. Later I learned that the word "gospel" means "good news." But what constitutes the good news of the Bible? As believers, we have a tendency to take so much for granted when it comes to God that we fail to come to an understanding about the ways, truths, and heart of God.

It was during my process of maturing in the knowledge of the Lord that I came to an understanding of the depth of my spiritual plight. It was in light of my inability to save myself that I began to discover the purpose of the Gospel. Sometimes, I became overwhelmed by the implications of what the Gospel meant for every lost, struggling sinner, as well as the new convert. It proved to be truly the best of news for any person who found him or herself struggling with the serious issues of life and death.

Sadly, most people stay with their vague concept of the Gospel. They have, in some cases, reduced this message to simply mean a prayer that has no real, up-front meaning. Some associate the Gospel with God's love. The reason for this is due to John 3:16, "For God so loved the world, that he gave his only begotten son, that whosoever believeth in him should not perish, but have everlasting life."

John 3:16 is a beautiful introduction that lays a foundation for the Gospel. It reveals the motive behind the Gospel, as well as gives a summary of God's intention towards us. It is vital that the love of God is brought to the forefront to set up the premise of His commitment to save each of us, for His heart is for us to possess eternal life.

The Scripture in John gives us the indication that something is wrong. Out of love, God solved the problem by sending His only begotten Son. The problem is that many hide behind this love and they assume or hope that all will go well for them on judgment day because God so loved them. However, this love is often defined according to the world's definition of love, causing it to lose its effectiveness and, thereby, hindering the person's ability to come to terms with the problem that the Gospel of John is alluding to.

God's love is a commitment to ensure our spiritual well-being. He so loved every soul that He gave His only Son to provide the means of securing and ensuring a state of spiritual bliss. This well-being hinges on us receiving eternal life. Without this life in us, we will perish in our present miserable state and experience complete ruin and devastation.

The idea of perishing should cause us to question why God gave His Son. Why are people perishing, and what exactly constitutes eternal life? Eternal implies it is a life that will last forever. However, what does eternal life mean for my present life? We all must physically die; therefore, in what way will a person perish? Obviously, even though John 3:16 is a beautiful Scripture, it does not really explain the crux of the problem. We know that we are perishing in our present state, but we do not know why.

Those who hide behind a perverted perception of God's love sense there must be more than just the idea of accepting the fact that God loves them so much that He gave the ultimate sacrifice. No matter how sentimental we get about God's love, we must acknowledge there is a separation between God and man. This separation means people are actually perishing in their present state. To avoid perishing each one of us must receive life itself.

At different times, people can also sense that there is a void in their lives, but they are afraid to scripturally explore the responsibilities or possibilities that the real Gospel holds. They fail to realize that they are spiritually separated from God. In fact, God's solution involves reconciliation. His Son is the means to bring that reconciliation between God and man by providing eternal life to all those who will believe.[1] Once again we are confronted with the question of why there is a separation between man and God. After all, most people believe in God and have had some religious influence.

Sadly, many cling to their ignorance about the subject of God's love, eternal life, and the harsh reality of perishing while living in uncertainty. After all, they must one day stand before God and answer to Him. But

---

[1] John 14:6; 2 Corinthians 5:18-19; Colossians 1:20-21

what if the Gospel is more than the "sinner's prayer" which has become a magic term, concept, or reaction towards God's love? What if the Gospel is a door to a changed life that leads to righteousness and holiness?

Clearly, John 3:16 serves as a powerful introduction to the Gospel and begins to prepare the environment in which the Gospel can be preached or explained. As you continue the search for this answer, you begin to realize the New Testament is also full of references to and explanations of the Gospel. However, is there a simple summary of it that can be found in Scripture to take away any possible vagueness or debate that may be left in wondering minds? The answer is yes. The Apostle Paul gives such a summary of the Gospel in 1 Corinthians 15:1-4,

> Moreover, brethren, I declare unto you the gospel which I preached unto you, which also ye have received, and wherein ye stand; By which also ye are saved, if ye keep in memory what I preached unto you, unless ye have believed in vain. For I delivered unto you first of all that which I also received, how that Christ died for our sins according to the scriptures; And that he was buried, and that he rose again the third day according to the scriptures.

The Apostle Paul gives us a powerful summation of not only what the Gospel entails, but how the Gospel must be presented and how man must respond to it. He gives a brief description of the message of the Gospel. The summation of the message in this section of Scripture shows us why Jesus had to die on the cross for us—because of sin. It shows us the reality of our plight— that of death and the grave. It reveals the hope found in the Gospel—Jesus' resurrection.

The Apostle Paul once again verifies that Scripture or the written Word has confirmed the Gospel. In other words, it has been clearly established in Scripture and as well as by the testimony of others whose lives were changed by it. He also reminded the Corinthians of its impact and message. Let us now consider these different aspects of the Gospel.

It Must Be Preached

The Gospel must be preached, not taught. We can teach about the Gospel, but for it to make an impact on others, we must preach it. What is the difference between preaching and teaching? Preaching means proclaiming and exhorting. It is the means of trying to reach through people's spiritual dullness to stir their souls. In a way, it is like waking someone up from a coma so that the individual can recognize his or her plight in order to embrace the solution. Its main purpose is to bring a person to a decision about whether or not he or she will accept the proclamation or exhortation as fact, receive and believe it as truth, and embrace it as a way of life.

Teaching involves reasoning with the intellect in order to bring a person to a conclusion about a matter. In the spiritual realm, anointed teaching enlarges a person's capacity to receive truths into his or her spirit. Once the person has come to an understanding, it is up to him or her to act upon it. Acting upon the truth will produce wisdom.

This brings us to why the Gospel is preached. The reality and challenge of the Gospel must first spiritually awaken man to his real condition before he can receive the hope of it. Unless the Gospel first awakens a person, he or she will remain blind to his or her spiritual condition and God's truths. Therefore, the Gospel is always associated with preaching and not teaching. Such a fact is important as one strives to come to terms with this message. The fact that the Gospel can and has been incorrectly presented is a frightening prospect. It means that people are being allowed to remain in their states of spiritual dullness and death.

The Apostle Paul made reference twice to the fact that he was the one who preached the Gospel to the Corinthians. Mark 16:15 commissions every believer to preach the Gospel. The Gospel is what opens the door to the kingdom of heaven, while teaching or discipling establishes the life of Christ within the believer.[2] Jesus preached to and taught the crowds, while discipling His followers.

The Gospel serves as a door into the spiritual life with God. A powerful preacher will always bring people back to some aspect of the Gospel as he or she proclaims, exhorts, and contends for souls in his or her messages. The Gospel is meant to awaken people to consider or examine their spiritual plight so that they can receive what God has for them. It is when individuals become recipients of this life in God that they will personally discover the good news that is found within the message of the Gospel.

Since the true Gospel brings people to a decisive moment where they must make a decision, many reject it. They do not like being brought to a decision about what is true. Hence, enter various presentations of the Gospel that will not insult, challenge, or cause discomfort. Such presentations are fraudulent lies and represent the greatest type of tragedy in the Church. Those who proclaim another gospel to keep people happy or deluded will stand accursed and those who accept such false messages will remain condemned.[3]

Man's Response

The Gospel must first awaken man before he can properly respond to it. This is why there should be sobriety in the churches in regards to the true Gospel being properly preached. I cannot tell you how many Christians do not understand the real implications of what Jesus did on behalf of mankind. Many people talk about God's love or the deep emotional and religious experiences they have had, but they do not

---

[2] Matthew 11:1; 28:18-20; Luke 20:1
[3] Galatians 1:6-9

seem to understand forgiveness or redemption. Yet, at the heart of the Gospel is forgiveness towards man and redemption of his soul. It is vital that the Gospel be preached so it can penetrate man's spiritual dullness and awaken him to his urgent need to respond to it.

How must people respond to the Gospel once they are awakened to it? There are three responses associated with the Gospel: believe, receive, and stand. For example, an individual has a choice as to what he or she will do with the Gospel. A person can disregard it or choose to believe it. To believe the Gospel, the individual must believe each aspect of it as it is presented to him or her. There are three main elements in the Gospel: The problem, the provision, and the solution. In order to believe the Gospel, man must recognize his problem, acknowledge the provision, and become identified with the solution according to God's plan and purpose.

Once people choose to accept the reality of Gospel, they must receive it as truth. In other words, they must apply it as truth to every aspect of their lives. This means that it becomes a point of conscience, change, and obedience. It is truth that will compel individuals in their focus, discipline them in their pursuits, and guard them in their conduct. This shows us that the Gospel does not just serve as a pivotal point of change, but becomes a motivating factor of change and conduct in a person's life as he or she seeks God.

Once the Gospel is clearly established, it becomes an immovable foundation that one will stand upon. As you study the Gospel, you will find that it contains the Rock of Ages. It is upon this Rock that people discover unwavering confidence, power, and authority. It is at this point that the Gospel becomes a stake that cannot be moved by time, adversity, or weariness. However, in order to stand, people must keep the Gospel alive, powerful, and real.

Therefore, Paul stated that we must remember what the Gospel is all about. If we forget, we will become lost in the chaos and uncertainty of life. When the Gospel is not being preached, people will forget what their Christian life is all about. The message will eventually become vain or considered a silly fable. In fact, life will cease to be about the good news of God and become a religious pursuit that is nothing more than a self-centered, small-minded, and pathetic exercise in futility. This brings us to the purpose of the Gospel.

Salvation

How important is the Gospel? The good news of the Gospel is that man can be saved from his spiritual plight of oppression and his state of death. Today, the Gospel is treated as if it is obsolete or outdated. In other words, man no longer needs to be saved. He has figured out how to get to God on his own merits. Sadly, this is what various people in Christendom are implying. I want to make a statement at this point. If the gospel that is being preached in different churches appears to be obsolete, it is because it is not the Gospel of the Bible. The Gospel of the New Testament has never lost its ability to save, but, obviously, man has lost sight of the true Gospel. The Apostle Paul was concerned about people believing other gospels that have no power to save.[4] As I consider the current presentation of the Gospel, I can see where it has been demoted in many ways, stripping it of its ability to impact men and women in their spiritual dullness and ignorance so that they might be saved.

How important is it for people to believe the true Gospel? It is the difference between eternal life and death. When something involves life and death, it is an issue that must not be taken lightly. The real challenge for many is that there is only one true Gospel. This Gospel stands separate from all other gospels. Granted, the other gospels may seem religious, appeal to our self-righteous conscience, honor our social reforms, justify some of our fleshly appetites, and feed our pride. They may run parallel to the real Gospel, but they have been adjusted to fit the weak, fragile, and worldly desires of people who want to appear religious. However, the one difference between the counterfeit gospels and the true Gospel of the Bible is that these counterfeits cannot save. They only placate, dull, delude, and destroy.

The Message

This brings us to the message of the Gospel. The Gospel is made up of three distinct realities: sin, the Person of Jesus, and His redemption. In order for something to be good news, a person must be cognizant of the bad news that is plaguing him or her. The bad news that many people refuse to face is that they have a problem. It is called sin. Sin is not a matter of doing what is wrong, but it is a matter of who we are. We have an independent and selfish disposition that comes from the first man, Adam. When Adam rebelled in the Garden of Eden, we were all made slaves to sin and death was passed upon all of us.[5] Because of this disposition, we are inclined to sin and we possess a tendency to justify it and make it right in our own eyes. As a result, death reigns in us as darkness invades and deludes our souls.

Sin is rebellion against or independence from God who is the author of life. It is the essence of self that freely reigns in the fallen disposition. It is important to point out that this self-serving independence does not deny there is a God. This attitude simply has no regard towards God one way or the other unless it is challenged. However, this inward independence will oppose God's sovereign reign, making people lawless in their ways. The fallen disposition of man wants to call the shots, have its own way, do things according to its terms, and determine its own reality or truth right down to who God is and will be in its midst. Even if

---

[4] 2 Corinthians 11:1-4
[5] Romans 5:12, 19

each of us wanted to do right by God, our self-serving motives would condemn us, our selfish attitudes would expose us, and our indifferent actions would tell on us.

After honestly examining the depth of his own depravity in Romans 7, the Apostle Paul concluded the utter hopelessness that sin creates in every one of us who have not received God's solution when he declared, "O wretched man that I am! Who shall deliver me from the body of this death?" (Romans 7:24).

Sin is a terminal disease of the soul that results in death or separation from that which constitutes real life. This real life only comes from God. Since God is holy, sin separates a person from God and the life He has prepared for him or her. Therefore, the person will never reach his or her potential to discover the real meaning and satisfaction that comes from the gift of life that God wants to give each of us.[6]

The bad news gets even worse when people begin to realize they cannot change the diagnosis. It does not matter if they change their lifestyles or try to think positively. The death sentence remains in place. Each individual has a spiritual cancer in them that cannot be placated or done away with through any personal attempts. Eventually, this disease will bring utter devastation and destruction to the person.[7]

Sadly, the bad news goes down hill from there. Death to most people represents finality. It is true that death in any form symbolizes finality to the present life as we know it. However, death also serves as a door to a different existence. For example, physical death is just a door to eternity.

When God formed man, He made him to live for eternity by giving him the breath of His Spirit.[8] Death in regards to our lives before God is a spiritual death or separation from God. Separation from God means the breath or Spirit of God is missing, ensuring a state of spiritual death that will express itself in the ruin of a person's spiritual well-being. In our unregenerate state, we actually live and walk in a state of death due to our separation from God. We walk in its darkness, give way to its useless works, and remain content in our indifference to righteousness. This death is not temporary, but will last forever. Daniel 12:2 addresses this very subject, "And many of them that sleep in the dust of the earth shall awake, some to everlasting life, and some to shame and everlasting contempt."

Each of us are in a hopeless state. The more we struggle against it, the more we become aware of it. We may want to change, but we find ourselves falling back into old patterns and cycles. We may want to go a different way, but our feet will automatically walk down a path of denial, despair, delusion, and destruction.

This is where the Gospel or the good news comes in. Granted, none of us can do anything in our power to change or prevent the death

---

[6] Isaiah 64:6; Romans 3:10, 23
[7] Romans 5:12; 6:23
[8] Genesis 2:7; 3:22-24

sentence, but nothing is impossible with God. God, who wants us to know Him and reside in His abiding love, provided a solution for us.[9] The Apostle Paul summarized this solution in this way, "For I delivered unto you first of all that which I also received, how that Christ died for our sins according to the scriptures (1 Corinthians 15:3).

Jesus Christ is the solution to man's spiritual plight. People initially get caught up with what Jesus did for them. He died on the cross for our sins. In other words, He became a substitute for each of us on the cross, and paid in full the death sentence that hung over everyone's head. The Apostle Paul made this statement, "For he hath made him to be sin for us, who knew no sin; that we might be made the righteousness of God in him" (2 Corinthians 5:21).

However, the real key to Jesus' success in rescuing us from our spiritual plight does not rest solely on what He did, but also in who He is. Granted, Jesus died for us, but there have been many others in the past who have given nobly of their lives and means for others. What makes Jesus different from these other heroes is who He is. It is because of who Jesus is that He is able to secure salvation for those who come to Him in faith.

Sadly, many people never come to terms with who Jesus is. They get caught up with His love, devotion, and sacrifice, but they never get caught up with His Person, attitude, and character. They never come to terms with His true identity. It is at the point of Jesus' identity that the Gospel takes on the eternal dimension that makes it powerful and profound, capable of producing growth and maturity.

Jesus is the reason the Gospel never grows old or becomes obsolete. He is the actual light in the Gospel, and, as people grow in the knowledge of who He is, the Gospel becomes more real, alive, and eternal.[10] If Jesus is properly presented, the Gospel will be upheld as people are constantly reminded of their need for Him in every aspect of their lives. However, if the Jesus of the Bible is missing, the Gospel is rendered powerless and useless to save and change a person.

Jesus died for our sins as the sinless Lamb of God. Those sins were taken to the grave with Him. This brings us to the final part of the Gospel--Jesus rose from the grave three days later. Without the resurrection, our faith in Jesus would be in vain. Once again, Jesus rose from the grave because of who He is.[11] It is the resurrection of Jesus Christ that sets Him apart from all erroneous beliefs and religious leaders. It is His empty tomb and resurrection that confirm our faith in what He did. It is His resurrection that allowed the Apostle Paul to make this declaration, "Death is swallowed up in victory. O death, where is thy sting? O grave, where is thy victory?" (1 Corinthians 15:54b-55).

---

[9] Matthew 19:23-26
[10] John 1:4-5; 2 Corinthians 4:3-6
[11] John 1:29; 2:19-22; 1 Corinthians 15:14

In the Apostle Paul's summation of the Gospel in 1 Corinthians 15:1-4, he talked about believing and receiving. People must believe the message of the Gospel. In other words, they must believe by faith that Jesus died on the cross in their place, that their sins were laid to rest in the grave, and that He was raised to prove victory over the consequence of sin—spiritual death. This was confirmed in Romans 10:9-10,

> That if thou shalt confess with thy mouth the Lord Jesus, and shalt believe in thine heart that God hath raised him from the dead, thou shalt be saved. For with the heart man believeth unto righteousness; and with the mouth confession is made unto salvation.

Notice in Romans, how one must confess that Jesus is Lord. The term 'Lord' has many implications. In fact, it gives us a small glimpse into Jesus' identity and the position He must hold in our lives. We must confess, acknowledge, or make a mental assent that He is Lord. However, belief must take place in the heart and not the mind. It is not a matter of intellectual understanding, but a matter of knowing in one's innermost being that Jesus did rise from the grave and that He must be Lord of one's life.

Once the Gospel becomes a truth, the person will be able to receive the Person of Jesus as God's provision. At this time, he or she is born again of water (the Word of God) and of His Spirit. To be born again means that God puts a new heart in you that will be inclined towards Him and His righteousness. He will give you a new spirit that will change your tendency to give into the ways of sin as well as justify it. This new spirit is His Spirit. Once again, God's very breath will flow in our lives. Our bodies actually become temples of the Holy Ghost as His Spirit seals us until the day of redemption. In the end, we will have a new disposition, making us new creations in Christ. However, this new disposition must be worked within, through, and out of our lives through submission to the Holy Spirit, obedience to the Word, and communion with the Father.[12]

The real means of coming to terms with the Gospel in a greater way comes down to discovering Jesus in His teachings, Person, and glory. As you will see, the Gospel will be presented in light of who Jesus is throughout this book. The beauty, power, authority, and life of the Gospel can only be realized as one discovers the wonder, power, authority, and life of Jesus.

The question is, have you received the true Gospel, or have you settled for some prayer or religious exercise in regards to your salvation? Do not settle for anything but the true Gospel. Allow it to open up the kingdom of God to you so that you are able to discover the real power and light of that which is sure, eternal, and glorious.

---

[12] Ezekiel 36:26-27; John 3:3, 5; Romans 8:1, 4, 9-14; 10:17; 13:14; 1 Corinthians 6:19-20; 2 Corinthians 5:17; Ephesians 1:13-14; Philippians 2:5, 12; James 1:21-25; 1 Peter 1:23

2

PREPARATION FOR THE GOSPEL

As you study the Gospel of Jesus Christ, you will realize that it is made up of the bad news surrounding man's spiritual plight and the good news of God's intervention on behalf of sinful, condemned man. If you take the bad news out of the Gospel, you have no need for the good news of God. If you change or do away with the true hope of the Gospel, which is summarized in the Person and work of Jesus Christ, you make it an ineffective gospel, leaving man in a hopeless state of delusion, despair, and destruction.

The reason I say this is because, in the many different presentations of the Gospel, the bad news is being alleviated or watered down and/or the hope of the good news is being changed, adjusted, or redefined to fit the preference of the crowds. In either case, such presentations cease to be the Gospel that saves and become an appalling, "politically correct" gospel that is causing greater spiritual dullness and certain spiritual ruin among the people.

The real hope of the Gospel rests with the Person and work of Jesus Christ. However, you cannot consider the Gospel without considering the powerful message that Jesus preached. After all, Jesus serves as the only hope or main substance in the Gospel. Therefore, how did He present this message? We must study the four Gospels to answer this question.

To understand the good news in light of Jesus' preaching, you must keep in mind that the preaching of the Gospel was for the purpose of saving man. Although Jesus never makes a distinct reference to Himself as the way to salvation when it came to the preaching of the Gospel, He does explain what it means for people to receive the salvation that has been made available in this message. In other words, Jesus clarifies what it will mean to receive Him as the Way, the Truth, and the Life.[1]

---

[1] John 14:6

Preparing for the Gospel

The preaching done by Jesus in the Gospels was for the purpose of preparing people to believe and receive the Gospel. Keep in mind, the good news of the Gospel is that Jesus, the Promised One or the Messiah, died on the cross to redeem man from the dictates of sin and the state of death. The Apostle Paul made reference to this in Acts 17:3, "Opening and alleging, that Christ must needs have suffered, and risen again from the dead; and that this Jesus, whom I preach unto you, is Christ." Since Jesus had not yet paid the price for man's sins, His preaching of the Gospel was a means of introducing and preparing people to recognize the way of redemption. As a result, before its conception as the saving Gospel, Jesus and others initially prepared people for this message as they introduced the Gospel of the kingdom, the Gospel of the kingdom of God, or the Gospel of the kingdom of heaven.[2]

As you study the Gospel of the kingdom, you will realize that the good news of the kingdom is that the kingdom of God was near or at hand. There has been a distinction made between the kingdom of God and the kingdom of heaven. In my studies, the kingdom of heaven is made in reference to the work of God being done on this earth within man, while the kingdom of God embraces every aspect of His will, work, and intervention on earth and in heaven. Fenelon made reference to this when he stated that the kingdom of God had to do with the will of God.[3] Jesus also made reference to this when He made this statement in regards to acceptable prayer, "Thy kingdom come. Thy will be done in earth, as it is in heaven" (Matthew 6:10). For God's will to be realized in man, man's will must come into total subjection to and in agreement with God's will.

What is God's will? Jesus answered this question in John 6:40, "And this is the will of him that sent me, that every one which seeth the Son, and believeth on him, may have everlasting life: and I will raise him up at the last day." Believing a matter involves the will of man. He must choose to believe. Therefore, believing results in action. With this in mind man's will or inner resolve will line up with God's will when he believes that Jesus is the only way to eternal life. Such belief will maintain the confidence that Jesus will raise that person up in everlasting life on the last day.

Since Jesus made His entrance as man twenty centuries ago, the Father's will was at hand to reveal His heart and purpose for man. It was also His will that men believe and receive Jesus as Savior and Lord to realize the power and liberty of His will in their lives.

---

[2] Matthew 4:23; 9:35; Mark 1:14-15
[3] Royal Way of the Cross; pgs. 135-136

In Luke 16:16, Jesus made this statement, "The law and the prophets were until John: since that time the kingdom of God is preached, and every man presseth into it." This Scripture signifies that a new dispensation was coming forth.[4] In this case, the kingdom of God was being revealed to man with the intent of it being realized in him. The unveiling of God's kingdom in man would signify a new dispensation or age.

Jesus confirmed this in Luke 17:20b-21, "The kingdom of God cometh not with observation: Neither shall they say, Lo here! or, lo there! for, behold the kingdom of God is within you." For the kingdom of God to be realized within the individual, man's will had to become subjected to the reign of the immortal King of heaven to ensure His indwelling presence.[5]

At the time that the Gospel of the kingdom of heaven was being preached, it was considered the acceptable year of the Lord. According to Matthew Henry's commentary, the term, "the acceptable year of the Lord" pointed to the year of release or redemption when all the Jewish servants were set free to choose whether or not they wanted to secure their former life or abandon all to serve their master.[6] The preaching of the Gospel of heaven signified the acceptable time for God to reach out to man, with a means of reconciling him back into a relationship with Him. The Apostle Paul confirmed God's intention in 2 Corinthians 6:2, For he saith, I have heard thee in a time accepted, and in the day of salvation have I succoured thee: behold, now is the accepted time; behold, now is the day of salvation." Jesus stepped into time and history as Man to secure salvation on the cross. Therefore, the kingdom of God was at hand and was ready to be ushered in on a personal level.

The Gospel of the kingdom of God implied a new king being ordained, a heavenly kingdom being established among men, a new life being offered, and a new inheritance ready to be embraced and experienced. For this kingdom to be brought forth within the hearts of men, Jesus was crowned with a crown of thorns. The door to this kingdom was actually opened by His death, while a resurrected life was secured for all who would pay homage to Him as Lord and Savior. There would also be available a new inheritance that would make people kings and priests by the means of adoption into a heavenly family. This new inheritance would be brought forth in a new covenant established by the shedding of Jesus' blood.[7]

This new kingdom would be a spiritual kingdom that could not be observed by the physical eye.[8] As Jesus stated in John 18:36, "My

---

[4] Ephesians 1:10; 3:2
[5] 1 Timothy 1:17
[6] Deuteronomy 15; Luke 4:19
[7] Matthew 27:29; John 1:12; Hebrews 9:14-17: Romans 8:15; Hebrews 8:6-13; 12:24: 13:20; Revelation 1:6
[8] Luke 17:20

kingdom is not of this world: if my kingdom were of this world, then would my servants fight, that I should not be delivered to the Jews: but now is my kingdom not from hence."

The Apostle Paul stated that the kingdom of God was not meat and drink, but righteousness, peace, and joy in the Holy Ghost.[9] In 1 Corinthians 4:20, he stated that the kingdom of God would not be realized in word, but in power. In 1 Thessalonians 1:5, he made this statement, "For the gospel came not unto you in word only, but also in power, and in the Holy Ghost, and in much assurance; as ye know what manner of men we were among you for your sake."

The Gospel has power, and it is because of this power that the kingdom of God grows in a miraculous way. As people come to Jesus in sincere faith, this spiritual kingdom would be realized in their lives, and, in turn, many would boldly declare it to others.[10]

The Recipients

Who will receive the Gospel? The Gospel is available to everyone, but there is only a certain group of people who will be receptive to it. These are the people Jesus came for. We are told about the spiritual condition of those whom He targeted when preaching the Gospel of the kingdom. He preached to the poor in spirit.[11] This is why He said, "Blessed are the poor in spirit: for their's is the kingdom of heaven" (Matthew 5:3). The word "poor" means cringing beggar.[12]

Jesus explained that those who were poor in spirit were ready to be receptive to the Gospel. He brought this contrast out in Matthew 9:12-13, "But when Jesus heard that, he said unto them, They that be whole need not a physician, but they that are sick. But go ye and learn what that meaneth, I will have mercy, and not sacrifice: for I am not come to call the righteous, but sinners to repentance." The poor were those who recognized that they were in need of God's intervention.

Luke 5:17 gives us the contrast to those who did not consider themselves to be poor; therefore, they proved to be unreceptive to God's healing, reconciliation, and restoration, "And it came to pass on a certain day, as he was teaching, that there were Pharisees and doctors of the law sitting by, which were come out of every town of Galilee, and Judea, and Jerusalem: and the power of the Lord was present to heal them." The power was available to heal those who were religious, but they did not see their need for Jesus. They were blinded by their self-righteousness.

Everyone is spiritually lost, but not every person recognizes his or her plight. Those who are needy in spirit and aware of their sinful

---

[9] Romans 14:17
[10] Matthew 13:31-33; Acts 2:47
[11] Matthew 11:5; Luke 4:18; 7:22
[12] Strong's Exhaustive Concordance #4434

condition are humble enough to consider the answer and receive the solution. Therefore, the Gospel of the kingdom is able to penetrate the poor in spirit with hope.

The right inward condition brings us to the necessary response for people to embrace the hope of the Gospel. The acceptable response is found in true repentance. John the Baptist baptized in the wilderness preaching, "... the baptism of repentance for the remission of sins" (Mark 1:4). Baptism is a form of identification. Obviously, repentance was to bring people into a place of identification for the purpose of having their sins properly dealt with.

Jesus' proclamation was similar to John's, "Repent: for the kingdom of heaven is at hand" (Matthew 4:17). In Luke 13:3 and 5, Jesus told people to repent or perish. The Apostle Peter declared that it is not God's will that any perish, but that all come to repentance.[13] Scripture tells us that the disciples, "...went out, and preached that men should repent" (Mark 6:12).

The preparation of the Gospel had to do with preparing oneself to see the need to change in order to receive salvation. Jesus came to save, but this salvation could only take place if a person would change his or her direction to embrace the essence of life. True repentance begins with a step of faith as people choose to believe the message. As they turn in a new direction to face the reality of sin in light of God, change becomes inevitable. Even John the Baptist talked of the fruits fit for repentance.[14]

John the Baptist came forth preaching repentance and baptizing people after their confessions of sin.[15] Water baptism is a form of identification, but true repentance is the prelude to embracing and becoming identified with the light and hope of the Gospel. Repentance requires one to turn from darkness to embrace the light of God. In other words, a person ceases from the way and direction he or she is traveling to turn around and face the glorious light of God. Such repentance involves humility and brokenness. Humility is the ability to come into agreement or identification with that which is contrary, while brokenness means a person is now pliable. Humility occurs when a person receives a sense of God's holiness and love. Brokenness occurs when one begins to see the reality of his or her sin and what it did to Jesus on the cross.

Today, the normal presentation of repentance is nothing more than an outward remorse for the shame or consequences of sin. However, true repentance occurs when a person has a deep sense of his or her sin and what it actually cost God. As my friend, Jeannette, states, salvation truly goes back to true repentance.

---

[13] 2 Peter 3:9
[14] Matthew 3:8
[15] Matthew 3:2-6

Paris Reidhead, in his book, *Finding the Reality of God,* referred to the different tenses of salvation. For example, repentance is considered the perfect tense of salvation, while justification the past tense, sanctification the present tense, and glorification the future tense. As you consider the manifestation of each of these stages of salvation, repentance does represent the perfect tense of it because it prepares a person to embrace the salvation brought forth by our Lord's grace through faith. It is also obvious that justification declares the gift of salvation has been received, sanctification reminds us that the work of salvation is presently being worked in us by the Holy Spirit, and glorification points to the future where our salvation will be fully realized in eternity.

The reason that repentance is the perfect tense of salvation is because the fruit of it in our lives is that of the compelling love of God that is constantly being shed abroad in our hearts by the Holy Spirit to respond to the holy ways of God. When Christians do not possess love for others, it is because they do not really love God. They do not really love God because they have never come to terms with the depth of their depravity. When people merely have an emotional stirring about sin, rather than a gut-wrenching reality about their sinful condition, they fail to realize how far Jesus had to come to reach them in their lost state. In fact, they feel superior as they lose sight of the fact that all stand equal at the foot of the cross, in need of forgiveness and restoration. Jesus brought this out when He asked Peter which debtor would love the most. Peter answered, "...I suppose that he, to whom he forgave most" (Luke 7:43).

As long as a person stays on the same broad path of self and the world, there is no hope for him or her to be saved. A person must repent. This means turning in direction, becoming changed in heart, and realigning his or her attitude in order to agree with God's evaluation of his or her condition. Such agreement allows one to receive the hope of salvation.

There cannot be remission of sin without true repentance. Once again, the remission of sin points to the Gospel. Remitting sins means to release from penalty or to pardon.[16] Such a release could not take place until Jesus redeemed man or ransomed him back from the harsh taskmaster of sin. Jesus made this statement, "Even as the Son of man came not to be ministered unto, but to minister, and to give his life a ransom for many." When sins are properly dealt with, fruits will come forth. These fruits are nothing more than a radically changed life that will ultimately reflect Jesus.

---

[16] Webster New Collegiate Dictionary

The Commission

Some religious people act as if the Gospel plays a minor role in Christianity. This is a dangerous perception. The fact that preaching the Gospel is the commission given to every believer confirms the importance of it. Preaching the message was not an option for Jesus and His disciples. Jesus is our example. He initially started out preaching the good news concerning the kingdom of God before He completed His mission on the cross. Jesus made this statement, "I must preach the kingdom of God to other cities also: for therefore am I sent" (Luke 4:43). Jesus preached, not only in cities, but also in synagogues. [17]

Likewise, the Son of God sends us out to preach the Gospel. [18] We read His commission in Mark 16:15, "Go ye into all the world, and preach the gospel to every creature." Since Jesus was not silent about the Gospel, we must not hide it behind a lot of religious activities or platitudes. We must be ready to share the Gospel with those whom God brings into our midst

One of the signs of the end days has to do with the Gospel being preached to the entire world. The good news will serve as a witness unto all nations as to Jesus' true identity, thereby validating His work of redemption, along with the power that follows those who proclaim it. Healing, gifts, and the miraculous follow the preaching of the Gospel. [19] This is why on judgment day there will be no excuse for why people have not received the gift of God. It has been made known and available, as well as confirmed as being true. If people do not possess the Gospel, it is because they have gone the way of unbelief, denial, and rejection.

Jesus must be lifted up above the world's activities, philosophies, and religions. People must see Him before they sense there is a need to respond to the hope of God. Once He is properly lifted up, people can be convicted by the Spirit and drawn by the Father. [20] Clearly, the proclamation of the Gospel lifts Jesus up above man's best attempts, religious counterfeits, and the world's many false hopes as the only solution for the downhill destruction of man.

The Gospel brings us to a humbling reality about salvation. It is a total work of the Godhead. The Father draws, the Spirit convicts, and Jesus invites and saves. The responsibility of man is to believe the Gospel, then likewise preach it in simplicity and with sincerity. [21]

There can be no power in preaching this message unless the Person of Jesus Christ is being lifted up, allowing the heart to be stirred by the Spirit to consider, believe, and receive God's incredible hope and provision. There can be no conviction unless the message of sin, Jesus'

---

[17] Mark 3:14; 16:15; Luke 4:44; 9:2
[18] John 17:18
[19] Matthew 9:35; 24:14; Mark 13:10; 16:15-18
[20] John 6:44; 12:32; 16:7-13
[21] Luke 9:56; John 6:44; 16:7-13

costly sacrifice, and the hope of eternal life has truly humbled an individual and brought him or her to the foot of the cross, seeking and receiving God's mercy, grace, forgiveness, and reconciliation.

This brings us to the memorial that is referred to every time the Gospel is preached.

The Memorial of the Gospel

Jesus was less than a week away from His ordeal on the cross. He was in Bethany, at Simon the leper's house, avoiding the religious leaders. Even though a traumatic time was at hand, the disciples were feasting. Mary, the sister of Lazarus and Martha, enters the room. She was that Mary who had taken time to sit at the feet of Jesus to the distress of her busy sister, Martha. She was carrying an alabaster box of expensive ointment of spikenard. She broke the box and anointed Him, wiping His feet with her hair. Her sacrificial action served as a platform for the disciples of Jesus, especially Judas Iscariot, to exalt personal self-righteousness. Jesus informed them that she was preparing Him for His burial.[22]

In Matthew 26:13, Jesus made this statement about Mary's actions, "Verily I say unto you, Wheresoever this gospel shall be preached in the whole world, there shall also this, that this woman hath done, be told for a memorial of her." One would wonder why her action was to serve as a memorial. I believe that it has to do with the fact that she was anointing Him beforehand for His burial. Keep in mind that they did not have time to properly prepare Jesus for His burial after His death on the cross because the Sabbath was at hand. Mary Magdalene, Mary the mother of James, and Salome brought the sweet spices to anoint Him after the Sabbath. But, what did they find? An empty tomb![23] Mary's' action pointed to the Gospel. Anointing Him for burial pointed to the fact that He would give up His life on the cross. However, for her to do it beforehand signified an empty grave that pointed to His resurrection.

Each time we consider or preach the Gospel, we indirectly refer to Mary's one action of sacrifice that set up the premise of Jesus' death by which the Gospel would be brought forth in power and victory in the midst of sorrow, fear, and uncertainty.

Christians have another memorial to commemorate the Gospel. It is called communion. Taking of the bread reminds us that Jesus' body was broken for us so that His blood could freely flow from his veins for the purpose of healing and restoration. Partaking of the cup points to the fact that His blood was shed for us to redeem our souls and reconcile us back into a new covenant and relationship with the Father.[24]

---

[22] Luke 10:38-42; John 11:1-2; 12:1-8
[23] Mark 16:1
[24] 1 Corinthians 11:23-34

It is hard to say how many Christians soberly partake of these two elements. The lack of sobriety and humility would imply that communion is nothing more than a ritual, rather than a remembrance or memorial to the time our faith was clearly established and justified by the sacrificial offering of the Son of God.

The truth is that we have such memorials established within our Christian life so we will not forget that we have been bought with a price.[25] As Christians, we have no right to live unto ourselves, to heap the world upon all of our lusts, or justify ungodly lifestyles. We are here to please, serve, and honor God with the fruits of righteousness and peace.

Have you embraced the Gospel by repenting of your ways and practices? Do you soberly consider the memorials that remind you of what Jesus did on your behalf due to the fact you stood as a doomed sinner without hope? What have you done with the presentation of the Gospel of the kingdom?

---

[25] 1 Corinthians 6:20; 7:23

3

THE GOSPEL IN ACTION

Jesus had been crucified and buried. Judas Iscariot had betrayed Jesus and hung himself. Jesus' other disciples had been tested in the afflictions of fear as they scattered in the night, placed in the depths of sorrow as they mourned, and landed in a pit of hopelessness as they saw their futures snatched from them. John, the beloved, had stood at the cross of Jesus and watched as all hope seemed to die. However, the grave could not hold Jesus; He rose three days later. His resurrection turned sorrow into joy, mourning into laughter, and despair into hope.[1] Thomas had initially doubted Jesus' resurrection, only to stand before the risen Lord to declare the ultimate reality, "My Lord and my God" (John 20:28).

These disciples had given up much to follow Jesus including families, homes, and careers. They had witnessed great miracles and heard the proclamations of others as they testified to the identity of Jesus. They had been part of sharing the Gospel of the kingdom of God.[2] The Gospel of the kingdom had prepared the people to receive the Gospel that would come forth from Jesus' redemptive work on the cross.

Now that Jesus had redeemed man, the next stage was to preach the Gospel of Jesus Christ that had been secured on the cross, or, was it? Jesus had initially sent these disciples to preach the Gospel of the kingdom. As they preached, power followed them to confirm the message in the form of miracles and deliverance.[3] However, Jesus made this statement in John 14:12, "Verily, verily, I say unto you, he that believeth on me, the works that I do shall he do also; and greater works than these shall he do; because I go unto my Father." Jesus made it quite clear that He had to go to the Father before they could do greater works.

Jesus went on to explain the significance of His going away in John 16:7, "Nevertheless I tell you the truth; It is expedient for you that I go away: for if I go not away, the Comforter will not come unto you; but if I depart, I will send him unto you."

Interestingly, upon His ascension, Jesus did not instruct the disciples to preach the Gospel. Rather, He told them to tarry in Jerusalem until they had been endued with power from on high.[4] These men had been

---

[1] Matthew 26:47-58; 27:1-5; John 19:25-27; 20:11-29
[2] Matthew 19:28-30; Luke 9:2
[3] Luke 10:17-20
[4] Luke 24:49

with Jesus for over three years. They had sat under His teachings. They had witnessed miracles. Yet, none of these things had empowered them. Granted, power had followed them when they preached the Gospel of the kingdom, but now they needed power on a personal level. Therefore, before they could carry on Jesus' ministry, they had to wait for the power from above to come upon them.

Acts 1:8 explains what this power constituted and what it would accomplish, "But ye shall receive power, after that the Holy Ghost is come upon you: and ye shall be witnesses unto me both in Jerusalem, and all Judea and Samaria, and unto the uttermost part of the earth." The power was that of the Holy Ghost. Once the Holy Ghost came upon them, they were to serve as witnesses to Jesus' death, burial, and resurrection.

Obviously, without the Holy Ghost, the Gospel would lack the power to impact people's lives. Sadly, the Holy Ghost is missing from much of the preaching today. Granted, there may be educated orators who can expound on the Gospel or debate it, but without the power of heaven, it will not penetrate people's darkened minds. Many people may have the Gospel down pat in words or formulas, but without the power of the Holy Ghost, there is no revelation of one's need to be saved. Religious leaders may have various degrees in theology and religious understanding, but without the Holy Ghost, it is all dead letters and useless to the hearers. There may be zealous evangelists who go door-to-door with their pat formulas that enable them to appeal to the emotions and logic of people. These means may cause people to say a prayer in regards to salvation, but, until the Holy Ghost impacts the heart, the message they heard remains a passing fancy or a logical fact, rather than a revelation from heaven.[5]

Jesus' disciples were not educated men. Even though Jesus had taught them for three years, He still needed to open their understanding so that they could comprehend the Scriptures in relationship to Him. Without the touch of heaven upon carnal minds, religious truths become controllable theology or doctrine that will feed the intellectual arrogance of man, rather than edify his spirit and soul.[6]

Today, the Gospel has been reduced to a fine art, rather than being inspired by the Holy Ghost. It is a doctrine, rather than a reality that is meant to grow with each new revelation of Jesus Christ. It is a formula that is often presented with fleshly zeal and pleading, but lacks conviction of sin, the need for repentance, the reality of salvation, and the desire to change one's direction, attitude, and life.

The Holy Ghost must be present in every evangelistic movement. It is not enough to evangelize and assume or hope the Holy Ghost will honor such attempts. As Christians, we are instructed to walk by the Spirit and be led by the Spirit. The importance of the Holy Ghost is

---

[5] John 16:7-13; 2 Corinthians 3:6; 4:2-6; 1 Thessalonians 1:5
[6] Luke 24:44-48; 1 Corinthians 8:1-2

brought out by the fact that blasphemy of Him is considered the only unpardonable sin. "Blasphemy" means to defame, speak evil of, or revile.[7] I often wonder how close some Christians are, in their ignorance and/or abuses of the Holy Ghost, to actually blaspheming Him.

William Law explains that the reason the blasphemy of the Holy Ghost is the unpardonable sin is not because He is more important than the Father and the Son. It is because the significance of the third Person of the Godhead rests with His work. He works within the human heart. His work signifies the last and highest manifestation of the Godhead in and to fallen man. To blaspheme the Holy Ghost is rebellion against the last and highest dispensation of God to bring forth the full redemption of man. Obviously, after the work of the Spirit, there remains no further or higher power of redemption by which God can reach the soul and spirit of man.[8]

Out of ignorance, more and more Christians are relying upon their own personal programs, strengths, and knowledge to proclaim the Gospel, rather than upon the Holy Ghost. Their testimony and preaching fall short. At best, it appeals to the intellect or the emotions, but without the Holy Ghost, there is no power to penetrate the spiritual ignorance and darkness that engulf people's minds and enslave their hearts. Many Christians fail to realize that the Holy Ghost must prepare the hearer and empower the one proclaiming before there can be any impact into the recesses of the soul to awaken a person to his or her spiritual plight and destination.

As I have studied the book of Acts, I realize that the contrast between the New Church and the present Church is obvious. There is a great gulf between the New Church that was aflame with the Holy Ghost and the present institutional Church, especially in the free world. For example, much of the organized Church in America takes pride in what it knows, the doctrine it adheres to, and its various programs that attract numbers and increases revenue. These different ploys used by the modern organized Church are nothing more than a smoke screen that hides the fact that many such organizations lack genuine power from heaven.

The Holy Ghost has lifted off of most of the organized Church. Today, there appears to be extremes in the institutional Church. There are local churches like Sardis in Revelation 3:1-6 that are dead because the Holy Ghost is clearly missing. The other extreme is a combination of Pergamos and Thyatira. These churches display a spiritual mixture of Christianity that consists of idolatry and paganism. This mixture produces spiritual fornication. The extreme combination of the spiritually dead and spiritual fornication produces the lukewarm works that can be observed in the church at Laodicea.[9]

---

[7] Strong's Exhaustive Concordance; #987
[8] The Power of the Spirit; pg. 109
[9] Revelation 2:12-24; 3:1-6, 14-18

Most people think that being lukewarm is being devoid of religious activities. This is not true. The people at Laodicea did works, but they were neither hot nor cold. Being "spiritually lukewarm" means that you are indifferent to God. The passion of the Spirit is missing, along with the disciplines of truth. Sadly, the Laodiceans perceived that God was with them because they were blessed in a material way. Such a condition is frightening because they were not even aware of their true spiritual plight.

Being lukewarm towards God is a dangerous condition. It is like Samson. He was entrusted with strength, but he betrayed his vow as a Nazarite by revealing the visible sign of this vow—his long hair. Samson was so indifferent because of unholy compromise and practices, that when his hair was cut, the Spirit of the Lord departed from him without his knowledge.[10] To reiterate, the Spirit has departed from most of the practices of the organized Church, but how many of those who enter the doors of these lifeless or counterfeit assemblies even realize it?

The Christians of Laodicea were blind to their spiritual condition. They had confidence in their worldly status, but not in God. They had works, but they were not aflame with the Holy Ghost. As a result, Jesus told them that they needed to zealously repent.[11]

The history of the Church that was recorded in Acts shows us that the Holy Ghost must be present before any attempts or inroads are made. Believers waited in the upper room in a state of prayer and agreement until the Spirit came upon them. This not only fulfilled a prophecy in Joel 2:28, but it also made John the Baptist's words about Jesus come alive, "I indeed baptize you with water unto repentance: but he that cometh after me is mightier than I, whose shoes I am not worthy to bear: he shall baptize you with the Holy Ghost, and with fire" (Matthew 3:11).

We know the event in the upper room as Pentecost. Pentecost shows us that the spiritual condition of people must be right before the Spirit will come upon a person or a group. There must be preparation in prayer and agreement in Christ Jesus to ensure the presence of the Holy Ghost.

Another example that we are given in regards to Pentecost is that we must not do anything outside of the inspiration, direction, and leading of the Spirit. To do something outside of the Spirit means to do something in our own strength. As the Apostle Paul reminded us in 2 Corinthians 3:5, "Not that we are sufficient of ourselves to think anything of ourselves; but our sufficiency is of God."

The first preaching done in Acts was under the power of the Holy Ghost. In this first proclamation in Acts 2:15-40, the Gospel of Jesus Christ is clearly presented. Interestingly, Peter speaks up front about the Holy Ghost being poured out on God's servants in his first presentation

---

[10] Judges 16:17-20
[11] Revelation 3:19

of this powerful message. He then begins to present his case about Jesus of Nazareth, whose identity was proven or confirmed to the Jews by miracles, wonders, and signs. As Peter pointed out, according to the Scriptures, Jesus, the Christ, was delivered up to be crucified and slain, but rose from the grave.

Peter's presentation of Jesus constantly reaffirmed both His identity and His death and resurrection. You can see Peter contending for souls, not in zeal or with intellectual deliberation, but in the simplicity and power of the Holy Ghost. The results are obvious. About three thousand souls were saved and added to the Church (body of believers).

Acts 2:47 declares, "And the Lord added to the church daily such as should be saved." Salvation is the work of God, not the attempts of man. The Father draws, the Spirit convicts, and the Son invites and saves. Man must be empowered, directed, and anointed by the Spirit for the glorious Gospel to be imparted to lost, blinded souls. It is the Spirit who bears witness of this salvation on earth, along with the Word and the blood of Jesus.[12]

There is nothing that makes me cringe more than man taking credit for the salvation of souls. If man perceives that he has personally saved anyone, such a soul still remains miserably lost. If God has truly saved a soul, but man takes credit for it, he has just touched the glory of God. As the Apostle Paul stated, "That, according as it is written, He that glorieth, let him glory in the Lord" (1 Corinthians 1:31). It is God alone who has the ability to save souls. Man is only an instrument in the scheme of things. As Romans 10:14-15 states,

> How then shall they call on him in whom they have not believed? and how shall they believe in him of whom they have not heard? and how shall they hear without a preacher? And how shall they preach, except they be sent? as it is written, How beautiful are the feet of them that preach the gospel of peace, and bring glad tidings of good things.

A person must be sent to preach the Gospel. This brings us back to the work of the Holy Ghost. He directed the steps of the Apostle Paul in taking the Gospel to the Gentile world. Obviously, the Holy Ghost had to go before the disciples. Interestingly, the disciples were surprised at the people that the Spirit of God would touch with this powerful, life-changing message. However, it was obvious that the power of the Gospel contained a flame that could set hearts alive with saving faith and resurrection power.

As you study the acts of the Holy Ghost in the history and building of the Church, you realize that it was His power, His flame, and His anointing that made the Gospel real to the seeking heart. In Acts 4:8, Peter and John were set in the midst of the religious leadership. The leadership demanded to know by what name or authority these two men had healed a lame man in the temple. You wonder if Peter remembered

---

[12] John 3:3 & 5; 7:36-39; 1 Peter 1:23; 1 John 2:20, 27; 5:6-8

the words of Jesus, "But when they shall lead you, and deliver you up, take no thought beforehand what ye shall speak, neither do ye premeditate: but whatsoever shall be given you in that hour, that speak ye: for it is not ye that speak, but the Holy Ghost" (Mark 13:11).

As Peter stood before them, he was filled with the Holy Ghost. In power, he declared Jesus Christ of Nazareth, the one whom they had crucified and God had raised from the dead. It was in the name of Jesus Christ that the impotent man, standing before them, had found his life completely restored. As Peter had previously said to the lame man, "Silver and gold have I none; but such as I have give I thee: In the name of Jesus Christ of Nazareth rise up and walk" (Acts 3:6).

Peter also told the religious leaders that Jesus was the Stone that the builders had rejected. Jesus was the foundation and cornerstone of true faith. These men, in their religious self-righteousness, had rejected the very foundation of their spiritual lives and the cornerstone of all truth. Then, Peter made this incredible declaration about Jesus, "Neither is there salvation in any other: for there is none other name under heaven given among men, whereby we must be saved" (Acts 4:12).

In Acts 5, we see quick retribution to those who dare lie to the Holy Ghost. It is in this text that the Holy Ghost is identified as God. A couple by the name of Ananias and Sapphira lied to God's servants about a commitment they had made in regards to the giving of money for a possession. Peter rebuked Ananias, revealing that he had lied to the Holy Ghost. It is amazing how people perceive that all they must do is deceive man and they will get away with ungodly schemes. However, the Holy Ghost knows the truth. He is the third Person of the Godhead and nothing is hidden from Him. As Peter declared in Acts 5:4b, "Thou hast not lied unto men, but unto God." Both the husband and wife lost their lives over this incident, and the fear of God came upon the Church.[13]

The power of God was so evident in God's servants, such as Peter, that even his shadow could result in healing and restoration. Although persecuted, imprisoned, and threatened, these followers of Jesus could not keep silent about the testimony that burned in their very beings. There is no way of telling how many times they declared the same, unchanging truth about Jesus. However, we do know one fact about them; they had the seal, power, and confirmation of the Holy Ghost with them. When they proclaimed the Gospel, it would cut to the heart of even those who refused to believe. In the end, they turned the world upside down with the preaching of the Gospel.[14]

In Acts 7, we can observe the power of the Holy Ghost in the life of a man named Stephen. It was said of Stephen that he was a man full of faith and the Holy Ghost. As a result, he did great wonders and miracles among the people. Those opposed to his message were not able to resist the wisdom and the spirit by which he spoke. He was an

---

[13] Acts 5:1-11
[14] Acts 5:15, 17:6; 18-33

outspoken man who caused a stir that found him standing before the Jewish council on the charges of blasphemy.[15]

Stephen rehearsed the history of Israel before the council. He reminded them of the covenant of circumcision and the history of Joseph, Moses, and the house of God. Then, he accused them of being stiff-necked and uncircumcised in the heart for they had received the Law, but had not kept it. They were cut to the heart and began to gnash at him. But he, being full of the Holy Ghost, looked up to heaven and saw the glory of God and Jesus standing on the right hand of God.[16]

Jesus' position is of utmost importance in this incident. He was standing, not sitting, as various Scriptures refer to Him as sitting on the right hand of the Father.[17] Why was He standing in this particular incident? Stephen declares what he sees, "Behold, I see the heavens opened, and the Son of man standing on the right hand of God" (Acts 7:56). Stephen clearly established Jesus' identity, equal with the Father, and standing at the place of the throne as the Son of Man. This declaration resulted in his demise. Stephen was the first martyr of the Church. No doubt, Jesus stood up to receive Stephen as this servant kneeled down, asked for pardon for his persecutors and killers, and fell asleep in physical death, only to be spiritually awakened in the presence of his faithful and precious Lord.

One man who witnessed his death was a man named Saul. He took it upon himself to silence the testimony of those who dared to declare Jesus and His salvation. On the road to Damascus, he encountered this Jesus. It not only changed Saul's direction, but his purpose. Saul became Paul. He became the voice who would proclaim the Gospel to the Gentile world.

Paul could not be deterred from preaching the Gospel. Beaten, imprisoned, and mocked, his voice would not be silenced. He once described the challenge, as well as the hope of presenting the Gospel in this way,

> We are troubled on every side, yet not distressed; we are perplexed, but not in despair; Persecuted, but not forsaken; cast down, but not destroyed; Always bearing about in the body the dying of the Lord Jesus, that the life also of Jesus might be made manifest in our body (2 Corinthians 4:8-10).

Following Paul through Acts is an incredible journey. You can see how the presentation of the Gospel can prove to be versatile. The Apostle Paul would aim it towards the people he witnessed to. For example, he gave a different testimony to the Gentiles than what he testified to the Jews. In Acts 22, Paul related to a Jewish crowd how he was educated in the Law of his fathers, but how his focus and zeal changed when he met Jesus of Nazareth. In his testimony to the

---

[15] Acts 6:5; 11-15
[16] Acts 7
[17] Hebrews 1:3; 8:1; 10:12-13

Gentiles, he made reference to his Jewish roots, but he did not emphasize them. He talked about how he persecuted people for believing in Jesus, and how his encounter with Jesus made him realize his error and caused him to embrace Jesus as his Lord and Savior.[18]

You can also see how Paul used the cultural customs or practices of people to relate the Gospel to them. For example, in Acts 17, he used the altar to the unknown God to introduce the one true God to the people of Athens. He made this statement in 1 Corinthians 9:22-23, "To the weak became I as weak, that I might gain the weak: I am made all things to all men, that I might by all means save some. And this I do for the gospel's sake, that I might be partaker thereof with you."

The Apostle Paul boldly proclaimed the Gospel. He was a man led by the Spirit.[19] His boldness and authority came because he was submitted to the guidance of the Spirit. His message impacted people because his preaching was empowered by the Spirit. In his preaching, you can actually identify five different responses to the Gospel.

The first response is indifference. You can see this in Gallio. He was not interested in spiritual matters and wanted no part of the debate. There are those like Felix who are procrastinators toward the Gospel. Such people hope that reality will change to avoid facing the harsh truth and future consequences of their lifestyles. Such people may tremble at the possibilities of judgment, but they will never repent. Then, there are people like Festus who rationalize away all spiritual truths in light of worldly philosophies and reasoning. In fact, he thought Paul to be mad. You also have those like Agrippa who would not allow himself to be persuaded to embrace the Gospel, regardless of what he understood about spiritual truths. After all, if he believed, he would have to come into agreement with God about all matters. Finally, you have those like Lydia, Justus, and Crispus. These are people who believed the Gospel. No doubt, they had receptive hearts towards God. An open heart allows the Father to draw such people to Jesus as the Son of God, while the Holy Ghost reveals their need for the Lord's salvation.[20]

As you study the acts of the Holy Ghost, you cannot help but notice that Philip was sent to witness to an Ethiopian and, then, was caught away by the Spirit. Peter was sent to a Gentile by the name of Cornelius, so he and his household could hear about Jesus. The Holy Ghost honored the incident by coming down on Cornelius and his household.[21]

There are many such incidents of the Spirit's involvement in furthering the Gospel and impacting the hearts of men with this life-changing message. We must not ignore the examples we have been given. We must not think that we can effectively proclaim the message or serve God without the leading and preparation of His Spirit. We must not

---

[18] Acts 24:10-24; 26:2-23
[19] Acts 16:6-11
[20] Acts 16:13-15; 18:7-8, 12-16; 24:11-26; 25:13-27
[21] Acts 8:26-39; 10

allow formulas, methods, or intellectual reasoning to replace the power of the Holy Ghost in the Gospel because, if we do, we will strip it of its power to save.

What about you? What is your response to the Gospel? Are you carrying out your commission? If so, are you carrying it out in your own strength or in the power of the Holy Ghost? The type of impact it makes upon people will tell on you. After all, the Gospel did turn the world upside down so that God could turn it right side up with the glorious revelation of His Son.

4

THE POWER OF THE GOSPEL

We have been introduced to the preparation for the Gospel in the four Gospels, as well as to the power and authority behind the Gospel in Acts. It is time to consider what the Apostle Paul said about the Gospel in his letters. Paul simply confirmed what has already been said about this incredible message, while elaborating on its effect and purpose in regard to the souls of men.

I have been asked why the Apostle Paul's letters are not in chronological order. As I studied the Gospel in the Pauline Epistles, I began to realize that there was a powerful presentation of the Gospel immerging that unveils an incredible, complete picture of its power and purpose. There is a clear order in these letters in which the Gospel is being presented. This order verifies that both the Bible and those who penned it were inspired.

Paul introduced the Gospel in the letter to the Romans in this way, "For I am not ashamed of the gospel of Christ: for it is the power of God unto salvation to everyone that believeth; to the Jew first, and also to the Greek" (Romans 1:16). Paul established up front that he was not ashamed of the Gospel of Christ. Notice how he is distinguishing it from the Gospel of the kingdom by referring to it as the Gospel of Christ. Jesus paid the price of redemption on the cross. The good news now pointed directly to Him as the Savior of the world.[1] In fact, He is the only door by which one can enter the kingdom of God.

The Apostle Paul also stated that he was not ashamed of the Gospel. His need to stipulate his attitude towards the Gospel was necessary. After all, he had been called to be an apostle, separated unto the Gospel of God. Separation in this manner points to consecration. As you study the representations of the different offerings found in Leviticus chapters 1-6, you realize that the separation of Paul unto the Gospel was like that of a burnt offering.

A burnt offering was consumed for the purpose of consecration unto God. All that was left of the offering was the smoke that served as a sweet savor to God.[2] Smoke is symbolic of holiness, for all had been

---

[1] 1 John 4:15
[2] Leviticus 1

Challenging the Christian Life

purged by fire, and what was left was considered holy and acceptable to God. Perhaps, this is why the Apostle Paul penned this popular Scripture, "I beseech you therefore, brethren, by the mercies of God, that ye present your bodies a living sacrifice, holy, acceptable unto God, which is your reasonable service (Romans 12:1).

Paul's attitude of boldness towards the Gospel is clearly reflected in his other epistles. His different references to the life-changing message reflected its focus, reality, position, purpose, benefits, and hope throughout his epistles. For example, in his letter to the Corinthians, Paul declared that he did not want to know anything among them, except Christ and Him crucified. His desire in Galatians was that, even though he lived, it was not his life that was being manifested, but the life of Jesus being lived in and through him. In the letter to the Ephesians, he reminded believers that they have been raised up to sit in heavenly places together in Christ.[3] In Philippians, he summarized his life in this way, "For me to live is Christ, and to die is gain" (Philippians 1:21).

In the letter to the Colossians, we are told that all the treasures of wisdom and knowledge are hidden in Christ. The letter to the Thessalonians reveals that the goal of the work of God was to establish the hearts of believers, blameless in holiness before God and at the coming of our Lord.[4]

Paul lived for and by the Gospel. He knew its power and was consumed by its reality. His life was dedicated to it and taken up by preaching it. As we study Paul's progression through his letters in relationship to the Gospel, we cannot help but note where the Gospel will bring those who embrace it in spirit and truth. They will experience the power of its salvation.

In Acts, the power of the preaching of the Gospel was directly associated with the Holy Spirit. However, in the letter to the Romans, Paul made reference to the evidence of this power in the Gospel, "And declared to be the Son of God with power, according to the spirit of holiness, by the resurrection of the dead" (Romans 1:4). Clearly, the source behind the power of the Gospel is the Holy Spirit, but the evidence of this power will be found in the resurrection of a new life. In other words, death will not be able to hold believers any more than it could hold Jesus.

Jesus was declared to be the Son of God. This made Him equal to God the Father. His heavenly identity was proven by the resurrection from the dead. The resurrection power found in the Son will also raise His people up on the last day.[5] Keep in mind, the victory of the Gospel will be fully realized in resurrection power, and Jesus' life in us, as believers, is the essence of this victory. Jesus confirmed this about

---

[3] 1 Corinthians 2:2; Galatians 2:20; Ephesians 2:6
[4] Colossians 2:3; 1 Thessalonians 3:13
[5] John 5:21-29; 6:38-40, 44

Himself, "I am the resurrection, and the life: he that believeth in me, though he were dead, yet shall he live" (John 11:25).

The Apostle Paul also introduced Jesus as the Son, the Christ, and our Lord, who was made of the seed of David according to the flesh.[6] This introduction pointed to the prophetic Scriptures about Jesus. What can we learn about Jesus as the Son of God? Psalm 2:7 states, "I will declare the decree the LORD hath said unto me, Thou art my son, this day have I begotten thee." The word "begotten" means to bring forth.[7]

The Apostle John explained this concept of Jesus as the begotten Son in this way, "No man hath seen God at anytime; the only begotten Son, which is in the bosom of the Father, he hath declared him" (John 1:18). Jesus was brought forth through human form to secure salvation. To confirm His work, the Father had to establish Jesus' identity. Twice He introduced Jesus as His Son, once at Jesus' water baptism and, again, at the Mount of Transfiguration.

The Father's testimony of Jesus at His water baptism was to clearly identify Him. However, it was also established the second time when His disciples were told to hear Him on the Mount of Transfiguration. It takes two consistent testimonies to confirm a truth according to the Law of Moses.[8]

The second point of Jesus' identity is that He is the Christ or the Anointed One. It is the anointing that breaks the yoke off of people.[9] Jesus actually quoted Isaiah 61:1-2 in reference to His anointing,

> The Spirit of the Lord is upon me, because he hath anointed me to preach the gospel to the poor; he hath sent me to heal the brokenhearted, to preach deliverance to the captives, and recovering of sight to the blind, to set at liberty them that are bruised, To preach the acceptable year of the Lord (Luke 4:18-19).

Paul also said of Jesus, He is our Lord. This has a powerful implication. As you study the concept of lord, there are many rulers. However, there is only one Lord who is Jehovah, God, and Master. Jesus is King, but we know Him as the Lord Jesus Christ. There is a difference between kings and lords. Kings rule kingdoms, but lords rule individuals. Therefore, there is only one true Lord who can reign over the spiritual lives of a people. The Apostle Paul identifies Jesus as this Lord.[10] Isaiah 43:10-11 gives us insight into the nature of our Lord, "I am he: before me there was no God formed, neither shall there be after me. I, even I, am the LORD, and beside me there is no savior."

---

[6] Romans 1:3
[7] Strong's Exhaustive Concordance, *# 3205*
[8] Matthew 18:16; Luke 9:28-36; John 1:31-34
[9] Isaiah 10:27
[10] 1 Corinthians 8:4-6

To confirm Jesus' identity, we see Paul associating the power to the Godhead in the book of Romans.[11] At the core of sin and rebellion is idolatry. People, in their independence from God, are choosing to bow down to other gods and walk in the ways of darkness. These gods can be self, the world, man, governments, belief systems, and religion.

Idolatry simply means that people are worshipping the creation rather than the Creator. The exaltation of the earth is especially being promoted through the New Age. The New Age is humanistic in origin and exalts the earth over the welfare of man. Granted, man is destroying the earth, but not because he fails to live in spiritual harmony with it. Rather, it is because man will not properly honor the Creator. Worshipping the creation is a blatant affront against the Creator who is being declared by His creation. Such idolatry produces paganism, immorality, and indifference. It is when men give into a sinful, abominable environment that eventually the earth will literally spew them out.[12]

There is only one true God. Within the essence or working of God are three Persons, God the Father, the Son, and the Holy Ghost. Each Person has the same nature or attributes of deity being expressed in oneness of complete agreement through their person, power, and glory. Since they have the same nature, they not only operate as one, but they also equal one God. These three Persons together are referred to as LORD and God in the Old Testament. In the New Testament, they are referred to as the Godhead. However, the New Testament also beautifully establishes these three Persons' distinct responsibilities on behalf of man's salvation. For example, the Father draws men to His Son, the Son invites them to the wells of salvation to save them, and the Holy Spirit convicts them of their need for salvation.

The Apostle Paul gave us insight into the Godhead in this way, "For the invisible things of him from creation of the world are clearly seen, being understood by the things that are made, even his eternal power and Godhead; so that they are without excuse" (Romans 1:20). Regardless of our intellectual conclusions about the essence of God, creation reveals the reality of the Godhead along with the eternal power associated with the Creator of the universe. There will be no excuse when people fail to believe in the one true God. Everyone who refuses to believe will stand condemned in their sins, unbelief, and darkness before the Righteous Judge of all.[13]

The Apostle Paul was also establishing Jesus as the Son of Man by declaring that He was made of the seed of David, according to the flesh. Consideration of this statement will take us back to Isaiah. In Isaiah 11:1-2, the prophet prophesied that the rod would come forth out of the stem of Jesse, King David's father, and that it will be on this man (the rod) that

---

[11] Romans 1:20
[12] Leviticus 18:24-25; Romans 1:20-26
[13] John 5:22-, 30

the Spirit of the LORD shall rest. John the Baptist in John 1:32-34 gave this testimony about Jesus,

> And John bore record, saying, I saw the Spirit descending from heaven like a dove, and it abode on him. And I knew him not; but he that sent me to baptize with water, the same said unto me, Upon whom thou shalt see the Spirit descending, and remaining on him, the same is he who baptizeth with the Holy Ghost. And I saw, and bore record that this is the Son of God.

In Isaiah 9:6-7, Jesus is identified as the one upon whose shoulders the government shall be. His government will increase, and peace shall have no end upon the throne of David and within the kingdom He establishes. Jesus is clearly the One whom Scriptures spoke of as being the Messiah and King. His identity was confirmed by many witnesses and miracles, and the Spirit continues to seal His identity in the hearts of those who choose to believe, love, and follow Him.

Jesus was declared to be the Son of God with power, according to the Spirit of holiness. His resurrection confirmed Him to be the Son of God. He was also clearly established according to that which was holy. This brings us to an important theme of the Bible, holiness. The Holy Spirit is the essence of holiness. As the Spirit of holiness, He will ensure all matters are in line with the holy character of God.

The theme of holiness in the Bible also reminds us of why Jesus came. Hebrews 12:14 instructs believers to, "Follow peace with all men, and holiness, without which no man shall see the Lord." Paul established the importance of holiness when he made reference to this subject in his initial introduction to this epistle. As you study the book of Romans, you realize that Paul is about to bring a real contrast between a holy God and the sinful state of man.

Jesus came because man could not please God nor make himself acceptable to Him. In his sinful condition, man practices ungodliness, handles the things of God in unrighteousness, and walks in the ways of death. As a result, we read this warning, "For the wrath of God is revealed from heaven against all ungodliness and unrighteousness of men, who hold the truth in unrighteousness" (Romans 1:18).

The case that Paul presents in Romans about our sinful condition is of the utmost importance. Many people, including those who call themselves Christians, hold to an amoral perception about life. Amoral means that everything is relative. In other words, there is nothing good or bad. There is no absolute standard to righteousness; therefore, there is no real distinction between what is right or wrong. Man is no different than an animal that is subject to appetites or instincts that he has no control over. Ultimately, in this environment, people choose their own moral codes. Some of these codes are good, but they blind men to their need for a Savior. As the Bible says, these people do what is right in their own eyes.[14]

---

[14] Judges 21:25

Sadly, this amoral environment has found its way into Christianity. As you study the reasons for Christians maintaining this perception, you will realize that they become susceptible to it as they continue to hold to agnostic attitudes that have been influenced by worldly philosophies. Worldly perception promotes humanistic philosophies in various ways, from evolution to psychology. These philosophies maintain this amoral view as it undermines or spoils the work of holiness.[15] For example, in the 1970s, the world was promoting the concept that says, "You're okay, I'm okay." This amoral view allowed people to think there was some good in them.

The problem with most people, including Christians, is that they cannot accept that there is nothing good in them that is redeemable. God did not provide a way for salvation because man had something of worth in him, but because man could not change his hopeless plight.

This amoral view has manifested itself in various ways. You have those who think they are okay because they are not bad people. Such individuals are blinded by their personal righteousness. However, Scripture clearly states that man's best is as filthy rags to God.[16]

You have Christians who stand behind this idea of goodness, while advocating a worldly lifestyle. I had one Christian woman tell me that her daughter was "good". To me, if a person has to make such a comment, it is to hide a matter, rather than define it. I knew this person's daughter. Her so-called Christianity was an outward show. She had no real inclination towards spiritual matters, and there was no fruit in her life that identified her to Jesus. In fact, she had no personal testimony of Jesus.

Every time her mother made that statement, I would cringe. The incident of the rich young ruler would come to mind. He came to Jesus to ask about eternal life. He called Him "Good Master". Jesus clarified the term "good" by saying that only God is good.

There is a difference between being good and possessing the virtue of goodness. Only God who is good can bring forth goodness in our lives. This was brought out in Job's life. He was considered a righteous man. His righteousness was based on upright living. However, when God revealed Himself to Job, Job had to repent before God. Job's action shows us that even saints must repent. The question of man's plight is not based on what he does, but on who he is. At the core of man is his heart. Proverbs tells us that the issues of life come out of the heart. Jeremiah declared that the stony heart of man is full of deceitfulness and wickedness. Jesus stated that all sin originates with the heart. Therefore, no man can be considered good. Goodness is part of the fruit of the Spirit and not a state or disposition that man can personally develop or lay claim to.[17]

---

[15] Colossians 2:8
[16] Isaiah 64:6
[17] Proverbs 4:23; Jeremiah 17:9-10; Matthew 19:16-17; Galatians 5:22-23

Goodness is associated with what is moral, beneficial, and is considered well or acceptable. God is holy; therefore, He alone determines what is moral, beneficial, and pleasing. When people fail to line up with Him, they become amoral in their ways of thinking. In fact, they will determine the moral code of their lives, subtly exalting themselves as God.

As believers, we must line up with God's evaluations of a matter to ensure a right standing before Him. However, due to an amoral view, many Christians have developed their own moral codes that benefit their personal lifestyles and please their religious consciences. As a result, many have an appearance or form of righteousness, but they are denying the source and power behind it.[18]

There was a man who was considered decent in our community. Those who knew him referred to him as good "old Joe". His religious background included being a member of a cult, although he did not practice the cult's beliefs. However, he was still considered a good man, and, when Jesus was presented to him, he saw no need to consider Him in any other light other than a name he occasionally invoked. The last time I saw this man, he was singing in a Christian church choir. One can only wonder if he received Jesus or if the Christians were trying to convert him by allowing him to sing with them. Perhaps, they figured he was okay. The harsh reality is, if this man fails to see his need for Jesus, he will end up in hell with all of his goodness being exposed as filthy rags in light of a holy God.

Jesus came for sinners. Every individual born in the human race becomes a slave to sin, identifying him or her as a sinner. This is why Jesus stated that He came to die for the world. However, the most deluded sinners see themselves as being good or acceptable. For example, the Pharisees were sinners, but they could not see their sin because of their self-righteousness. As a result, Jesus referred to them as white tombs that housed dead men's bones.[19]

White tombs are prevalent in religion. Religious people fill their lives with the knowledge of God. They spend time doing good things to silence their religious conscience. They harbor this knowledge and these works as the assurance that they are okay, when, in fact, they are dead because the Spirit of the living God is missing.

Today, the amoral view is being disguised by tacking Jesus on to religious activities and doctrines. This view is being justified by so-called "goodness" that is determined at a personal level, rather than from a heavenly perspective. Christians are showing tolerance towards sin, coming into unholy alliances with the world, mishandling the things of God, and shunning those who challenge their worldly, liberal reality.

The case that the Apostle Paul presents against man in the book of Romans is undeniable as to how God views man in his unregenerate

---

[18] 2 Timothy 2:5
[19] Matthew 23:26-29

condition. This epistle reveals why man stands condemned and is subject to God's wrath. In Romans 1, Paul showed the progression of how this amoral view of life operates. It begins with ingratitude and vain imaginations.

Vain imaginations create a reality separate from God, producing delusion. Delusion is spiritual ignorance towards God. It is in ignorance that man gives way to paying homage to the things of creation. As man gives way to idolatry and worships some part of creation rather than God, he begins to change the glory or majesty of God that is evident in creation. God ceases to be God in the man's mind. He ceases to be holy or insists on righteousness. He is now demoted to being in a controllable box of doctrine or theology.[20]

In idolatry, God gives people over to their lusts. This is a form of judgment or separation. Now, they will taste the vanity and bitterness of their fleshly desire and worldly pursuits. If they do not repent, their delusions will give way to a reprobate mind. Such a mind will not retain the true God in its understanding, as the person worships a god of his or her own making.

The Gospel has no power to penetrate a reprobate mind. Such a mind is unable to respond to the message. There will be no conviction or point of reasoning. The reason for this unteachable condition is because of the mind's perverted perception. It is unable to discern what is true. Sin often becomes good to these people, while truth and righteousness become evil.[21]

As you follow Paul through the first seven chapters of Romans, you begin to see how sin works and its effects on people's perceptions and lives. It begins with an uncircumcised heart. It proves that it is void of any righteousness and, therefore, the condition and acts associated with it are condemned by the Law. Such a sinful disposition came through Adam and has reigned ever since, making people servants to its whims, deceptions, and ways. Man may want to do that which is right, but sin defiles even his motives, proving that there is no good thing that dwells in the flesh. After all, the pride of flesh desires to take credit for any goodness. It is in competition with God and has no intention of casting crowns or rewards at the feet of Jesus. Paul came to one conclusion as he faced the harsh reality and effects of sin upon man, "O wretched man that I am! who shall deliver me from the body of this death?" (Romans 7:24).

The Apostle Paul also made this statement, "In the day when God shall judge the secrets of men by Jesus Christ according to my gospel" (Romans 2:16). The secrets of men will be judged by the Gospel. It is in the heart that people can say there is no God and erect altars to other gods. It is in the mind that people reject and mock His truths. It is in the soul that God is replaced with the things of the world. Ultimately, those

---

[20] Romans 1:26-28
[21] Isaiah 5:20

who tread such a spiritual path will reject the one true God by not believing what He says about Himself and their spiritual conditions. Then, in the secret chambers of their beings and minds, they deny or justify the bad news concerning their sin, thereby, doing away with their need for salvation.

In the book of Romans Paul clearly presented the case of man's need for God's intervention in order to reveal how man is to respond to the Gospel—by faith. He makes this powerful statement, "For therein is the righteousness of God revealed from faith to faith: as it is written, "The just shall live by faith" (Romans 1:17).

Righteousness or that which is right is revealed from faith to faith. Faith is a matter of believing what has been said. For example, the Gospel states that I am a sinner and that the wages of sin is death. Faith would take such a statement as truth, allowing the Holy Ghost to convict of sin. The Gospel says that you must believe in the Person of Jesus and what He did on the cross to save you. Faith would believe this to be true and receive Jesus as the solution. From that point on, faith would inspire how one would respond to God's Word. Each time the individual responds to God and His Word by faith with obedience, it is reckoned as righteousness. The righteousness of the Law will be fulfilled; therefore, God is able to meet the person through promises, answered prayers, and revelations.[22]

Faith comes by hearing and hearing by the Word of God. As one approaches God's Word to hear and submit to it in obedience, he or she will come under the leading of the Holy Ghost. The Holy Ghost brings us into an intimate relationship of communion with the Father. It is in this relationship that one realizes his or her status as a child of God.[23]

Faith is ongoing. It produces godly conduct as it responds in simplicity and obedience to the Word. Believing the Word allows God to meet us, entrusting us with a greater revelation of Jesus. It is revelation that enlarges our faith to receive more insight about God, allowing the mind to be transformed by the Holy Spirit.[24]

As you study faith in Romans, you will see that it is not a New Testament doctrine. Faith existed before Abraham entered into the covenant with God. It was Abraham's faith that justified him before God, reckoning him as righteous. This virtue existed before the Law of Moses. The Law could only condemn, never justify. The Law left people hopeless, while faith left people reckoned as standing upright before God.[25]

The true spiritual heritage of God's people cannot be traced back to the Law, but to faith. Abraham was the example of true faith. He knew God as his portion, believed God in the times of testing, and followed the

---

[22] Romans 3:10, 6:23; 8:4; 1 John 1:8 & 10
[23] Romans 8:13-17; 10:17
[24] Romans 12:2
[25] Romans 3:28; 4:23, 17-19

leading of God without knowing where he was going. This is the legacy of faith.[26]

Faith results in salvation because it believes every part of the Gospel.[27] The message becomes a truth that changes one's life and direction. It justifies a person before God, causing him or her to stand righteous in Christ and righteous because of God. The Apostle Paul put it this way, "For if by one man's' offense (Adam) death reigned by one; much more they which receive abundance of grace and of the gift of righteousness shall reign in life by one, Jesus Christ" (Romans 5:17, parenthesis added).

Righteousness is imparted as a gift and act of God. The gift proves that we cannot earn such righteousness; it is imputed to us as we believe God's Word. The act of God points to grace. All that comes from God to us is an act of grace. The Gospel not only declares God's love and desires to redeem His people, but it is an act of grace on His part to do so.

The Apostle Paul spoke of this grace in his other epistles. His presentation of grace throughout his letters is wondrous. We will be dealing with this subject in greater measure in later chapters. However, there is one Scripture I would like to bring out on this subject, at this time, "Moreover the law entered, that the offence might abound. But where sin abounded, grace did much more abound" (Romans 5:20).

Many people talk about the ability of grace to abound where sin once reigned. But one must know that the term *abound* is used in the past tense and not the present tense. This means where sin once abounded, grace now abounds. Grace cannot be given until there is repentance. Grace begins at the point of a person facing God, confronting what personal sin did to Him, and repenting. Repentance brings a person to the foot of the cross, allowing grace to flow downward in the form of cleansing, forgiveness, reconciliation, and restoration to bring forth a new life.

Belief in the Gospel will produce a life or walk that is upright. We see the Apostle Paul advocating this life through the book of Romans. The Spirit will lead people who embrace the Gospel. They will see themselves as vessels of God. Such individuals will know Him by believing the Word. Although grafted in the Vine, these people will not assume or take for granted their position in Christ. The love that motivates them will be pure as they prefer others to self, fulfilling the Law. They will put on the character of Christ, instead of making provision for the lust of the flesh. They will make sure that all they do is of faith, and not a manifestation of sin and unbelief. They will give way to the sanctifying work of the Holy Spirit.[28]

---

[26] Hebrews 11:8-10
[27] 1 Peter 1:9
[28] Romans 9:19-23; 10:17; 11:17-23; 12:9-17; 13:8-13; 14:23; 15:16

The Apostle Paul started with the power of the Gospel in this epistle. In Romans 16:25-26, he ended with the same theme,

> Now to him that is of power to stablish you according to my gospel, and the preaching of Jesus Christ, according to the revelation of the mystery, which was kept secret since the world began, But now is made manifest and by the scriptures of the prophesy, according to the commandments of the everlasting God, made known to all nations for the obedience of faith.

Have you experienced the power of the Gospel through faith, or does it still remain a mystery? It is not enough to have an intellectual knowledge of the Gospel. It must be a heart revelation that has changed your life, attitude, and direction, ultimately lining you up to the holy character of God.

5

THE GOSPEL AND CARNALITY

In the book of Romans, the Apostle Paul explained the power of the Gospel. It can penetrate the dark minds of those lost in hopelessness and despair with the reality of the Son of God. However, there is one source that strips the Gospel of its power in a person's life—sin. Unhindered and unrepentant sin always expresses itself in idolatry. Idolatry is a product of unbelief that finds its logic and reinforcement in vain imaginations. Vain imaginations will manifest an attitude that disregards God in attitude, behavior, and practice. The inward knowledge of the invisible Godhead that is present in the conscience is eventually seared, leaving the person with the inability to retain knowledge of the true God.[1]

People who do not retain the knowledge of God have no foundation from which the Spirit of God can work to bring conviction of sin and the need for salvation. As a result, they are unable to respond to the true Gospel. The reality of salvation will mock them, the revelation of Jesus will be far from them, and hope will elude them as a curtain of darkness, fear, and delusion engulfs their hearts and minds.

In the book of I Corinthians, the Apostle Paul contended with another type of spiritual condition—carnality. A carnal Christian is one who has experienced the illumination of light to the heart and mind about Jesus, but the mentality and practices of the world remain intact. Such a mentality results in religious practices that are fleshly. The Apostle Paul gave this instruction in regards to the world in Romans 12:2, "And be not conformed to this world: but be ye transformed by the renewing of your mind, that ye may prove what is that good, and acceptable, and perfect, will of God."

Carnal Christians may have a new heart, but the Spirit and the Word of God have not yet transformed their mind. In other words, they do not possess the mind of Christ. As a result, the philosophies and practices of the world are still influencing the mind. When you take the things of God and combine them with the world, it creates a mentality that majors in religious intellectual pursuits. Such a mentality will eventually see itself as being wise about spiritual matters. It will operate in deception as it is

---

[1] Romans 1:28

unable to properly discern anything that is spiritual.[2] Ultimately, it changes the focus or emphasis of a matter.

An intellectual pursuit in the things of God creates a dangerous mixture. It will cause people to depend on what they know about God, rather then in the reality that they must know Him in an intimate way. Such an intellectual pursuit sets people up to fall into the trap of ever learning in light of worldly wisdom, but never able to come to the knowledge of that which is unseen, spiritual, and true.[3]

Worldly wisdom is opposite of the mind of Christ, which expresses itself in humility and submission. The world's wisdom sees itself as wise in the things of life. It sees the unchangeable truths of God as obsolete, narrow-minded, and foolish in light of present-day knowledge and circumstances. Worldly wisdom is attracted to God's wisdom, but it simply tacks it onto philosophies that come from the influences of the world, defiling the wisdom from above. The world's wisdom sees itself as superior to the simplicity of the Gospel and the truths of God. It sees itself as reasonable in light of worldly tolerance. It considers itself noble because it is capable of embracing the beliefs of others without being judgmental and critical. As far as it is concerned, it has a well-balanced picture of all that is in the world and of the world. However, Jesus is clearly missing.[4] As the Apostle Paul warned in Colossians 2:8, "Beware lest any man spoil you through philosophy and vain deceit, after the tradition of men, after the rudiments of the world, and not after Christ."

As the philosophies of the world rule in the minds of Christians, the Gospel is often adjusted to fit into the times, allowing for so-called "open-mindedness." Open-mindedness of this nature is perceived as having the ability to attach the world to its wisdom and tolerance in the name of Christian love and benevolence.

However, worldly wisdom becomes shocked at intolerance towards sins that are a product of paganism and sees it as weak and bigoted. It becomes insulted by the absolutes of the Word and will consider them metaphoric, obsolete, or base. It despises the simplicity of the cross of Jesus and only glories in that which feeds the arrogance of the mind. It wants to remain happy and content in its lost state of delusion.

When you combine carnality and the Gospel, you end up with a social gospel that is more interesting in reforming society than in transforming individuals into the likeness of Jesus. The social gospel does not necessarily reject the cross of Christ; rather, it tacks it on for credibility, while cleverly changing the focus or emphasis of a matter. The social gospel is a very popular gospel in the "politically correct" environment of America as it advocates the Marxist practices of "social justice."

---

[2] 1 Corinthians 2:14; Philippians 2:5; Colossians 2:8
[3] 2 Timothy 3:7; Hebrews 4:2; 11:6
[4] 1 Corinthians 1:26-28

The social gospel also can fade into the cultural gospel that implements Christ into the moral code or ethics of a country's culture. There are many in America who purport this "good ole boy" gospel with patriotic fervor, which arouses the same type of sentiment that can be associated with the concept that the "good ole boy" gospel is as American as apple pie and baseball.

The attitudes vary in this social gospel depending on the emphasis. For some, the gospel becomes a political matter, rather than an issue of the heart. In some cases, the social gospel regards pagan practices as a matter of free expression, rather than the superstition and sensual, unholy practices ascribed to it by the Bible. This gospel also tolerates unscriptural beliefs, as they are simply considered a personal preference or a means to enlarge cultural understanding and tolerance, rather than the means to confuse and defile the truth. Abominations that result in the judgment of God are simply regarded as an alternative lifestyle. Such a gospel in its various presentations sounds good to many people. It may uphold good deeds and decency while justifying indulgence in the things of the world. It may also encourage moral change without calling practices sinful. It can be quite critical towards a society out of control, but this gospel lacks the cross. Without the cross of Jesus, the true Gospel is rendered useless.[5]

In Christendom, the social gospel hides behind God's love while taking comfort and pride in seeing the "good" of man. Needless to say, the presentation of God's love is not scriptural. There is no good in man, and God's precious love has been perverted by the world's idea of love. The world's idea of love has no real accountability or sacrifice. It is very fragile because it is self-serving. In most cases, it is nothing more than fickle sentiment, an impulsive passion, a form of lust, or a temporary feeling of sympathy or emotional charity.

God's love is translated as a commitment or moral obligation to be right before God and to do right by others. It does not display tolerance towards sin, rather it shows long-suffering towards man to give him time for repentance. It is morally committed to man in such a way that it becomes sacrificial.[6] God's love desires not only the best for each of us, but it desires to see us embrace the best that He has to offer. The best of God would ensure that we would reach our potential and experience the complete life in Him.

The Apostle Paul did everything he could to maintain the integrity of the Gospel. At the heart of this integrity is the simplicity of the cross. Paul made this statement in 1 Corinthians 1:17, "For Christ sent me not to baptize, but to preach the gospel: not with wisdom of words, lest the cross of Christ should be made of none effect." The Corinthians were forty miles from Athens, where there was much emphasis on

---

[5] 1 Corinthians 1:17
[6] Mark 12:29-31; John 3:16-19; 14:15; 15:12-14; 1 Corinthians 13; 2 Peter 3:9

knowledge.[7] On top of the worldly knowledge and philosophies, judaizing teachers from Jerusalem were also adding their religious emphasis and debates to the mixing pot.

The Corinthians had a smorgasbord of intellectual and religious influences to choose from in the midst of commercial activity and financial success.[8] But, as Paul reminded them in 1 Corinthians 5:6b, "Know ye not that a little leaven leaveneth the whole lump?"

In the culture that was present in Corinth, Paul addressed both the intellectual emphasis of the Greeks and the Jewish influence of religious practices and rituals, "But we preach Christ crucified, unto the Jews a stumbling block, and unto the Greeks foolishness" (1 Corinthians 1:23). The Jews constantly tripped over Jesus with their religious laws and ceremonies. This stumbling was due to the fact that Jesus was a fulfillment of prophecies and the Law. Therefore, they could not get around Him, no matter how hard they tried.

The Greeks thought the preaching of the cross was absolute foolishness. It never allowed for the superiority or arrogance found in worldly knowledge.[9] It implied regression in intellectual emphases and pursuits in order to embrace the truths of God in their sincere, simple forms.

It was clear in Paul's day that the intellectual people who prided themselves in the philosophies of the world thought that the Gospel of Jesus was beneath them. Arrogance in this arena will not humble itself enough to realize that the simplicity of God's truths may be considered foolish to the intellect, but, to God, they constitute pure wisdom, as they stood strong and immovable.[10] The Apostle Paul gave this instruction, "Let no man deceive himself. If any man among you seemeth to be wise in this world, let him become a fool, that he may be wise" (1 Corinthians 3:18).

Another aspect of carnality is that it results in schisms in the Body. Schisms simply mean that there is not one source by which to judge matters. In the case of the Corinthians, the right emphasis and focus were missing. Carnality relies on the logic of the flesh to determine what is important in life. For example, the Corinthians majored in who baptized them in water, rather than in the foundation of their faith, Jesus Christ. Rather than identifying themselves to the head of the Body, Jesus, they were associating themselves with men such as Paul and Apollo. Such associations caused feelings of superiority and division in the Body.[11]

The Corinthians also took pride in their status and gifts, rather than walk in sobriety about such matters. Once again, attitudes of superiority and exaltation were going on among the members according to the gifts

---

[7] See Acts 17:16-34 to get a sense of Athens.
[8] Smith's Bible Dictionary
[9] 1 Corinthians 8:1-2
[10] 1 Corinthians 1:24-25
[11] 1 Corinthians 3; Colossians 1:18

Challenging the Christian Life

they operated in, as well as to their position in the Body of believers. Because of the financial status of some, there were both abuses and neglect in practices such as communion.[12]

The Apostle Paul wanted to impart meat to the Corinthians, but their carnality would only allow for the milk or doctrine of the Word. Carnality keeps Christians in spiritual diapers. They have no means by which to discern spiritual matters. Their focus is limited to outward practices, rather than the unseen realm of the spirit. In such a condition, outward performance becomes important. Instead of personal works being refined and made priceless in the fire of God, they will be destroyed, because they are mixed with the stubble of self, the fragile hay of the world, and the wood of personal works and self-effort.[13]

To address carnality, the Apostle Paul explained how our Christian life was and will actually be perfected in Jesus Christ. His summary of this life is found in 1 Corinthians 1:30: "But of him are ye in Christ Jesus, who of God is made unto us wisdom, and righteousness, and sanctification, and redemption." Carnality explores all possibilities to establish perfection. However, the perfected or sanctified life can only be found in the reality of Jesus Christ as it consumes the old life or ways of the flesh.

Paul confirmed this up front in 1 Corinthians 1:2, "Unto the church of God which is at Corinth to them that are sanctified in Christ Jesus, called to be saints, with all that in every place call upon the name of Jesus Christ our Lord, both theirs and ours." The Godhead brings forth a perfected or sanctified life in the Christian. The Father places us in the position of sanctification. Jesus serves as the place of sanctification, while the Spirit sanctifies us for the work of God. Therefore, the wisdom of the world will not make us wiser to do the work of God nor will dead-letter religion make us more righteous.

The Apostle Paul explained how Christ is that place of wisdom, righteousness, sanctification, and redemption. In the area of worldly wisdom, Paul displayed the demonstration of the Spirit and of power. It is the Spirit that reveals the wisdom of God, for it is shrouded in mystery. Only those who stand in faith in the Son of God will be entrusted with the power and revelation hidden in the mysteries of God.

Righteousness belongs to God. As Christians, we need to awaken to the integrity of it in attitude and practice to separate ourselves from that which is fleshly.[14] Once again, righteousness is only reckoned to Christians at the point of faith. However, carnality lacks strong or true faith. Faith results in obedience and godly conduct as it responds to the leading of the Holy Ghost. The Apostle Paul summarized it this way, "For we are his workmanship, created in Christ Jesus unto good works, which

---

[12] 1 Corinthians 11:23-34; 12:12-27; 14:33
[13] 1 Corinthians 3:1-3, 12-15
[14] 1 Corinthians 15:33-34

God hath before ordained that we should walk in them" (Ephesians 2:10).

Christ is our point of sanctification or perfection. Paul made this declaration, "And such were some of you: but ye are washed, but ye are sanctified, but ye are justified in the name of the Lord Jesus, and by the Spirit of our God" (1 Corinthians 6:11).

Part of the place and work of sanctification has to do with us being holy temples.[15] We cannot allow ourselves to be defiled by the deception and practices of carnality. We must choose to have faith in place of worldly logic and reason. We must choose confidence in God over religious activities. We must choose to believe the Word of God regardless of our personal conclusions and feelings. Obviously, the work of sanctification can only occur when we make the right choices.

Jesus is our redemption. He became the Passover Lamb, our substitute on the cross.[16] The Apostle Paul made this statement, "For he hath made him to be sin for us, who knew no sin; that we might be made the righteousness of God in him" (2 Corinthians 5:21). Jesus' redemption was complete. In Him we find a complete life. This life is surrounded by His wisdom, realized in His righteousness, and perfected in His sanctification.

Redemption reminds us that we have been bought with a price. In fact, we have been redeemed back from sin with its various taskmasters and influences. Since we do not belong to ourselves, we need to purge or separate ourselves from the old to take on the new.[17]

The victory of the cross rests in the Victor. Jesus rose from the grave. He is the one who took the sting out of death and the victory out of the grave. All that each of us as believers do in our lives, must find its source or origins at the point of the reality of Jesus; His work, who He is, and who He must become for His life to be established in us.[18] This is why Paul was adamant in preaching the Gospel. In 1 Corinthians 9:16, he made this statement, "For though I preach the gospel, I have nothing to glory of: for necessity is laid upon me; yea, woe is unto me, if I preach not the gospel."

Jesus' resurrection is proof of His victory over death and it ensures the believer's confidence in His redemption. It is one of the principle doctrines of Christ.[19] Resurrection is another aspect of the Gospel that is under attack. Interestingly, many pagan beliefs ascribe to the belief of the resurrection. In Paul's day, pagans were actually baptizing for the dead in light of their belief of resurrection. The apostle pointed this out to make a point about resurrection.[20] Even the pagans were wise enough to

---

[15] 1 Corinthians 3:16-17
[16] 1 Corinthians 5:7-8
[17] 1 Corinthians 5:7; 6:20; 7:23
[18] 1 Corinthians 15:47-58
[19] Hebrews 6:1-2
[20] 1 Corinthians 15:29

believe there was life after death. Apparently, some Christians were refusing to believe there would be a resurrection, while others were debating about it.

Such a debate was not unusual. For example, in Jesus' day, the Sadducees did not believe in the resurrection. It was the main point of contention between them and the Pharisees. Although Job, David, Isaiah, and Daniel talked about resurrection, somehow these religious people explained it away. They even confronted Jesus over this matter in relationship to marriage. Jesus' reply was quite clear in Matthew 22:30, "For in the resurrection they neither marry, nor are given in marriage, but are as the angels of God in heaven." In lay terms, it means there will be no marriage in heaven, for we will be as angels—resurrected in new glorified bodies. Such a body will function totally contrary to our present body of fleshly functions such as marriage and worldly activities, which include desires, attractions, and sexual relationships. [21]

Today, we not only have the influence of unbelievers who outright reject resurrection, but we also have beliefs that have subtly replaced resurrection. For instance, we have the New Age belief of reincarnation. Reincarnation has people entrapped in an endless cycle of birth, death, and rebirth. Dave Hunt points out the diversity of this belief according to cultures. For example, in the western world, it has replaced Hebrews 9:27, which states that it is appointed for men to die once, then face judgment.

In the East, reincarnation is viewed as punishment. To those who live under the hopelessness of it, it becomes a burden too great to bear. In order to bear it, they have developed Yoga as an escape from this endless cycle.[22] Yoga is a means for one to enter an altered state of consciousness. The problem with Yoga is that it actually yokes or links a person to seducing spirits.

This brings us to another source behind reincarnation—Satan. There are familiar spirits in operation in the world. These spirits are familiarized with past lives. People who are open to the spiritual realm, ignorant of God's ways, or are desperate to find some kind of closure about those who are dead are open to the deceptive practices of these entities. As a result, there are people who believe they are a reincarnation of someone who once lived. In other cases, people seek mediums to speak to the dead to bring resolution or fortunetellers to give them an edge on their life. It is not unusual for some kind of counterfeit proof or spiritual experience to confirm whatever erroneous conclusions or predictions have been given. However, such practices are inspired by the wrong spirit to keep people from coming to the light of the Gospel.[23]

---

[21] Job 19:25-27; Psalm 17:15; Isaiah 26:19; Daniel 12:2; 1 Corinthians 15:39-52
[22] Occult Invasion, Dave Hunt, © 1998, pgs. 227-228
[23] Deuteronomy 18:9-15; 1 Samuel 28:3-8; Isaiah 8:19; 19:3-4; 29:4; 47:13-14; 2 Corinthians 4:3-4

These practices are clearly denounced by God in His Word. In fact, demonic activities have escalated to alarming proportions. Sadly, many Christians innocently fall into these deceptive traps because they do not know who God is or what His Word states about such matters. They also lack discernment. Therefore, subtle forms of witchcraft are prevalent in the professing Church and are also being blatantly practiced in the name of Jesus.

Another belief that undermines resurrection is purgatory. According to L. H. Lehmann, a former Roman Catholic priest, the concept of purgatory is no different than reincarnation.[24] Purgatory is the place where people experience an indefinite period of expiation and suffering in another world before the disembodied spirits can be sufficiently purified to enter into eternal bliss.

Obviously, deliverance to the Catholics is acquired through great suffering. You can see this emphasis throughout the movie *The Passion*. The main emphasis of Jesus' plight was placed on His suffering. However, His suffering was not what redeemed man from the consequences of sin. It was the shedding of His blood. Jesus was the sacrifice that fulfilled every major offering in the Old Testament. As a result, His redemption was complete. However, He was not man's sacrifice, but God's sacrifice. Abraham prophetically pointed this out to his son Isaac on Mount Moriah. No man could provide a sacrifice that would properly address the harsh realities of sin. Therefore, God sent His only begotten Son to become the sin offering for man.[25]

As you study the Jewish sacrifice, it was not tortured before it was sacrificed. The throat was simply cut in order for the blood to be shed to make atonement for sin. Needless to say, Jesus' throat was not cut. The reality of Jesus' type of physical suffering is that it was the means by which His blood would be allowed to flow from His body as a payment for our sins. He was put on the altar of the cross, where He was offered up to God as the sin offering on behalf of all men. The reason we are healed by His stripes is because the blood of Jesus flowed from those stripes. The problem with putting such emphasis on Jesus' suffering is that it appeals to the emotional senses such as sympathy and sentiment, but it will have no impact on the spirit.

In this fleshly arena, our understanding of Jesus' journey to Calvary becomes an emotional experience, rather than a choice of faith in the will area where we will embrace salvation. We walk by faith, not according to our different senses. Our hope does not rest in what Jesus experienced on His way to Calvary, but it rests on what He accomplished on the cross—the redemption of our souls. Sadly, in many cases, He is made into a suffering, honorable martyr, rather than the obedient, sacrificial

---

[24] Out of the Labyrinth, L. H. Lehmann, pg. 50
[25] Genesis 22:7-8; John 3:15-18; 2 Corinthians 5:7; Hebrews 9:12-23

Lamb of God who willingly offered up His body as a sin offering to take away the sins of the world.[26]

Jesus clearly established that His work of redemption on the cross was complete when He declared, "It is finished" (John 19:30b). The idea that any person must continue to suffer after death to enter into some type of nothingness or an eternal bliss undermines Jesus' very declaration and work. Hence comes the warning from Hebrews 10:38-39, "Now the just shall live by faith: but if any man draw back, my soul shall have no pleasure in him. But we are not of them who draw back into perdition; but of them that believe to the saving of the soul." How can we believe that any form of perdition awaits us if we have embraced the complete work of Jesus on the cross? To not fully receive Jesus' redemption is to draw back from it in unbelief.

In His book *A Woman Rides the Beast,* author Dave Hunt writes how the Catholic Church teaches that Christ's salvation must be received in partial installments along with man's good works.[27] Here we see Jesus' redemption plus man's attempts to obtain salvation. It is amazing that Jesus' suffering is exalted to the highest pinnacle of honor, but it is not enough to secure salvation for these lost souls. Even in this particular text, it is clear Jesus' suffering does not pay the price for our redemption. Scripture confirms the correct perception of His redemptive work. It clearly states that it was His blood that paid the full payment for our sins.[28]

Jesus confirmed this full payment by rising from the dead. His resurrection was the ultimate proof that everything He said about Himself and His death and burial was true. Notice how the true Gospel is not made up of Jesus' suffering, but of His death, burial, and resurrection. Granted, suffering was a prelude to and a product of the cross. However, Jesus' main reason for coming was to die for us in order to redeem us.[29]

Unlike Roman Catholicism, the Christian's symbol is an empty cross. This cross declares the victory of Jesus' finished work. It stands silent because redemption was fully secured by the Author of eternal life. As the Apostle Paul clearly stipulated, we are saved by grace and not by any personal works.[30]

To downplay the complete work of redemption of Jesus is an affront against the faith that was first delivered to the saints. In fact, there is a heretical belief that maintains that Jesus' death on the cross was not sufficient to secure our salvation. This heresy claims that He had to also die spiritually and continue to suffer in hell at the hands of Satan for three days to make our redemption complete. For Jesus to spiritually die would

---

[26] John 1:29; 10:18; Ephesians 2:13, 16; Colossians 1:13-14; Hebrews 9:12-23, 10:10, 18-19; 13:10-13

[27] A Woman Rides the Beast, Dave Hunt, © 1994, pg. 485

[28] Hebrews 9:22-28; 10:10

[29] Matthew 12:39-40; Luke 9:56

[30] Ephesians 2:8-9; Hebrews 5:8-9

mean that He would cease to be the eternal God of Scripture. As God, He is a Spirit and must be worshipped in spirit and truth.

My understanding of Jesus is that, while His body was physically in the grave, He was preaching to the captives. It was in His flesh, on the cross, that Jesus defeated Satan, not in hell.[31] Obviously, Christ was not put at the mercy of Satan in hell, nor was He made to suffer according to his whims. Do I understand all the implications behind Jesus' absence from His body for three days and nights? No, I do not. Rather, I choose to believe the Word of God in its presentation instead of establishing beliefs to explain such mysteries. It concerns me that so-called Bible "teachers" would advocate such unscriptural nonsense.

Jude made a comment about contending for the true faith in his epistle, "Beloved, when I gave all diligence to write unto you of the common salvation, it was needful for me to write unto you, and exhort you that ye should earnestly contend for the faith which was once delivered unto the saints" (Jude 3). The true faith is under attack by unscriptural and erroneous beliefs. To undermine any part of the Gospel is to change the face of the redemption and the hope we have in Jesus Christ.

Apparently, Paul's apostleship was under attack in Corinth. In 2 Corinthians, Paul revealed his heart as a minister. You can see through this letter how the Gospel impacted his life. In 2 Corinthians 1, it worked both compassion and comfort in him. Chapter 2 reveals how the life of Jesus in the believer serves as a fragrance for God's glory, as well as edification to the saved and a challenge to the unsaved. In chapter 3, it shows that the purpose of this life is to reveal the glory of the Lord.

In chapter 4 of 2 Corinthians, Paul brought out how the Gospel is hidden from those who are perishing, but the light of Jesus still shines through adversity. Although the adversity may be great in its present state, it will be considered minor in light of eternity. The reality of this life is that the outward man may be perishing, but the inward man is renewed day by day.[32]

In 2 Corinthians 5, we learn that we are to walk by faith. Genuine faith will lead us into the presence of the Lord. It is in this chapter that we learn the results of the Gospel—reconciliation. Everything Jesus did was to reconcile us back into a relationship with God. Reconciliation means there is peace between God and man.

Chapter 6 calls for separation from the unholy to embrace the promise of being children of God. In the next chapter, Paul called Christians to cleanse themselves from all filthiness of the flesh and spirit, perfecting holiness in the fear of God. After all, fear of God will produce

---

[31] John 4:24; Acts 2:27, 31-32; 13:35-37; Ephesians 4:8-10; Hebrews 2:14-15; 1 Peter 3:18-22
[32] 2 Corinthians 4

Challenging the Christian Life

godly sorrow towards sin, resulting in repentance that will lead to salvation.[33]

In 2 Corinthians 8:9, we have this incredible promise, "For ye know the grace of our Lord Jesus Christ, that, though he was rich, yet for your sakes he became poor, that ye through his poverty might be rich." The Gospel is marked by benevolence. The blessings that come from heaven are not meant to be heaped upon ourselves, but used to bless others. We read about this benevolence in 2 Corinthians 9. Paul concluded the chapter by thanking God for the unspeakable gift of Jesus.

Although, Paul was greatly criticized for his speech and appearance, he reminded them that he came a far distance to preach the Gospel of Christ to them. He did not come to glory in his looks or personal accomplishment, but in the Lord.[34]

The problem with carnality is that it will be vulnerable to another Jesus, a wrong spirit, and a different Gospel. In its arrogance, it could very well replace the simplicity of Jesus with that which appears new, refreshing, and more spiritual. Since it is superficial and immature, it often proves to be susceptible to accept the false light of Satan, receive deceitful workers who transform themselves into apostles, and embrace false ministers who transform themselves into the ministers of righteousness. Carnality will be drawn to these counterfeits in the name of new revelations, outward reformation, so-called "revival," or "greater truths."[35]

In 2 Corinthians 12, Paul related a personal testimony of how he found that Jesus' grace was sufficient in the times of weakness. In fact, Jesus' strength is made perfect in personal weakness. Therefore, Paul learned to glory in his infirmities so that the power of Christ could rest upon him.

The Apostle Paul concluded his second epistle by challenging the Corinthians to examine themselves to see if they are in the faith. Although the Corinthians may have seen themselves as being wise, the truth of Jesus will stand when all that is unholy falls into the abyss of judgment.[36]

The second epistle to the Corinthians ends with this desire, "The grace of the Lord Jesus Christ, and the love of God, and the communion of the Holy Ghost, be with you all. Amen" (2 Corinthians 13:14). Notice how the Apostle Paul associated grace with Jesus, love with the Father, and communion with the Holy Ghost. It is true that we begin with the grace of God that was manifested in Jesus, and grow in the Father's love, but this is to bring us into a place of true communion by way of the Holy Ghost.

---

[33] 2 Corinthians 7:1, 10
[34] 2 Corinthians 10:10-14, 17
[35] 1 Corinthians 11:3-4; 12-16
[36] 2 Corinthians 13:5, 8

Examine the quality of your faith. What is it relying upon for life, purpose, and salvation? Do you have carnality mixed in your life before God? If so, you may have failed to properly mix faith in your God into your walk. Hebrews 4:2 gives us this warning, "For unto us was the gospel preached, as well as unto them: but the word preached did not profit them, not being mixed with faith in them that heard it."

Consider also whether you are attracted to a social gospel that allows you to toy with the world while you hide behind a religious cloak. God knows the truth, as do those who walk by the Spirit. Eventually, your carnality will bring you to spiritual bankruptcy. If this describes you, my advice is simple, repent in godly sorrow. Quit settling for the milk of the Word and begin to desire the meat of God's will. At first, the meat will overwhelm you, but continue to partake of it until it becomes your only nourishment and source of spiritual growth.

6

THE PERVERTED GOSPEL

The Apostle Paul was carrying what I call a big stick in Galatians. As I read this letter, I feel the sting of that stick coming down upon those he is challenging. At times, I find myself shaking in my shoes in sobriety. His approach is anything but meekness and joy. He is thoroughly upset with the Galatians. His tone is one of rebuke and admonition. Obviously, he is not about to cater, reason, placate, or sweetly contend with them. His warnings are decisive, and his declarations clear. It reminds me of what Jude said in his epistle, "And of some have compassion, making a difference: And others save with fear, pulling them out of the fire; hating even the garment spotted by the flesh" (Jude 22-23).

What brought on Paul's attitude and approach in this letter? Was it some grave sin or rejection of the things of God? No, Paul's attitude towards the Galatians had to do with their perversion of the Gospel. In fact, Paul actually puts forth a curse on anyone who would dare to pervert the Gospel, including an angel from heaven.[1] He summarized his opinions about the Galatians in Galatians 3:1, "O foolish Galatians who hath bewitched you, that ye should not obey the truth, before whose eyes Jesus Christ hath been evidently set forth, crucified among you?"

Paul not only put forth a curse to those who perverted the Gospel, but he referred to those who adhered to such a gospel as foolish and being bewitched. To be bewitched is to be maligning something or to become fascinated by a false representation of something.[2] The Body of believers of Rome was contending with idolatry that changed the glory of God to embrace another god. The Corinthians were tacking the things of God onto a mixture of fleshly practices and worldly philosophies. However, the Galatians were taking the things of God and perverting them to establish personal salvation and righteousness outside of Jesus.

Perverting something means to add to it or take away from it. Nevertheless, perversion of any type changes the spirit or intent of something. The Galatians were actually adding on to the Gospel. In other words, it was Jesus plus something to bring about salvation or righteousness. This is not only a blatant attack or dismissal of Jesus' character and work on the cross, but it strips the Gospel of its true power to save.

---

[1] Galatians 1:6-9
[2] Strong's Exhaustive Concordance, #940

The problem with perverting something is that it causes confusion because, in most cases, you can actually find that the Word of God makes reference to the religious practice or belief that is in question. However, as you examine the subject, you will find the emphasis or reference has been changed to promote personal agendas or exaltation. Perversion in any form will actually rob something of both its purity and its simplicity. Therefore, it confuses the purpose or issue of something, causing that which is pure to become defiled, and that which is simple to lose its focus and authority.

This brings us to how the Galatians were handling or presenting the Gospel. The book of Romans shows how people mishandle the things of God, stripping the Gospel of its power due to unchanged worldly attitudes. Corinthians exposes how man adjusts the things of God to suit his personal pursuits by tacking on the Gospel to worldly understanding. However, Galatians will reveal how man perverts the things of God, especially the Gospel to suit his own religious agenda.

Let's again consider what affects the power of the Gospel to save. In Romans, Paul revealed how sin, with its worldly attitudes and associations, causes people to become unresponsive towards the Gospel. Corinthians shows how carnality, with its intellectual arrogance and worldly influences, renders the Gospel ineffective. However, Galatians shows how perversion will actually frustrate the grace of God.[3]

How important is the work of grace in salvation? The Apostle Paul gave this insight in Ephesians 2:8, "For by grace are ye saved though faith; and that not of yourselves: it is the gift of God." If the grace of God is not present in your life, you are still dead in your sins.

The Apostle Paul presented the work of grace throughout his epistles. Today, grace is either being abused or frustrated, but few in Christendom seem to understand how it works. People's ignorance about grace is a product of not understanding the nature of God and how sin has personally affronted His character and cost Him His only begotten Son. For example, grace abounds at the point of repentance, never at the point of practicing sin. It meets us in our weakness, never in our arrogance. We can only acquire this grace through faith that properly responds to God, never through good works. We have been called into this grace, and it is by grace that we are partakers of all that God has for us. In other words, everything that is good and worthwhile comes from God, which is a matter of His grace. It is not a product of personal attempts or goodness.[4]

We live in a dispensation of grace. This dispensation does not allow us to live as we choose, but to experience God's mercy in our lives and to know His faithfulness in our times of need. After all, God's longsuffering towards us is not for the purpose of hiding behind some

---

[3] Galatians 2:21

[4] Romans 5:20; 1 Corinthians 10:30; 2 Corinthians 12:9; Galatians 1:6; Ephesians 2:8-9; James 1:17

concept of grace, but to give us time to repent, so that, out of grace, He can intervene on our behalf.[5] We are reminded that mercy is a form of grace, but mercy allows God to show His grace. Hebrews 4:16 confirms this, "Let us therefore come boldly unto the throne of grace, that we may obtain mercy, and find grace to help in time of need."

We are justified by grace; therefore, we need to be strong in it.[6] Being strong in grace means it is something we reside in, not something we try to hide behind. The people who hide behind grace do so because it is simply a concept that will cover up their inconsistencies and ungodly practices before God. However, those who stand strong in grace realize it comes down to a Person. Grace can only be understood in light of Jesus Christ. John 1:14 states, "And the Word was made flesh, and dwelt among us, (and we beheld his glory, the glory as of the only begotten of the Father,) full of grace and truth."

If you do not know the real Jesus and embrace His work, grace will remain elusive. It is in the fullness of Jesus that we begin to understand the perpetual, ongoing work of grace in our lives. As John 1:16 says about Jesus, "And of his fullness have all we received, and grace for grace."

How were the Galatians frustrating the grace of God? What were they adding to the Gospel to pervert it? Surprisingly, the answer is the Law. This may sound confusing since the Law is from God. We know that the Law is a moral standard that has been established among humanity. The Apostle Paul said that the Law was holy, just, and good. Therefore, how could the Law pervert the Gospel and frustrate the grace of God? It is vital that these questions be answered.

There is much confusion over the Law. This confusion has caused two extremes to operate in the Church. One extreme is known as antinomianism. Antinomianism is the belief that Christians are liberated from observing any aspect of the Law when God's grace is active. In this case, grace is cheapened and becomes a right that allows any Christian to do as he or she wants, under the guise of God's grace. However, Scripture clearly shows this is an incorrect conclusion.

Keep in mind, the Law embraced every aspect of the Jewish lifestyle. As we are about to see in Galatians, the Apostle Paul was addressing the part of the Law that dealt with rituals (statutes) such as circumcision. However, the part of the Law that deals with moral obligations (commandments) before God and towards others is very much in place, and must be adhered to in ensuring right standing before God and righteous conduct towards others. Righteous conduct serves as a means to reflect a holy lifestyle. In fact, grace only reigns in our life through righteousness. Paul confirmed this in Romans 5:21, "That as sin hath reigned unto death, even so might grace reign through righteousness unto eternal life by Jesus Christ our Lord."

---

[5] Ephesians 3:2; 2 Peter 3:9
[6] Romans 3:24; Titus 3:7

There is also an exaltation of the Law that is unscriptural. For example, well-meaning evangelists are exalting the commandments as a means to promote salvation. Granted, we are responsible to keep the moral commandments of the Law, but the problem with this emphasis is that it is scripturally incorrect. We are told to preach the Gospel, not expound on the commandments. It is Jesus who saves, not the commandments. The Gospel identifies man's problem as sin. In this case, it is not just a matter of what we do, but who we are. We are in a fallen condition due to a disposition that prefers and embraces independence outside of God's reign. Therefore, people can outwardly keep the commandments, but still end up in hell.

The Gospel points to our disposition as being a problem and lifts up Jesus as the sole solution to man's entire plight. It is as the Father draws the individual to the solution of His Son that the Spirit of God will bring conviction to the sin-laden soul, revealing his or her need for Jesus. Although I have no problem with upholding the commandments as the standard of God's righteousness, I have long realized that they are powerless to bring conviction and result in salvation. Granted, they show us that we have a sin problem. However, these commandments have no means by which to penetrate the spiritual blindness of man to reveal it is not just a sin problem that can be remedied by refraining from certain actions, but it is a disposition that can only be changed when one is born again from above. Therefore, solely presenting the commandments simply brings a contrast that often leaves man hopelessly condemned and in much despair.[7]

There is also Replacement theology. This is where the rituals of the Law, such as the Jewish feasts, are being exalted as a means for Christians to secure the spiritual or complete life they desire. Although Jesus is cleverly tacked on to this theology, His means of salvation is subtly being replaced by man adhering to the rituals of the Law, rather than trusting in His work of redemption.

Replacement theology expounds the belief that the Church has replaced Israel. Supposedly, by associating with Jewish celebrations and practices, believers can begin to rightfully claim their Jewish heritage. In spite of the fact that God has not finished fulfilling His promises or plans concerning the people of Israel, many in the Church are ignoring or doing away with National Israel. Granted, the Jewish heritage is rich, but the main purpose for its practices and rituals was to point to Jesus. Our heritage as Christians is not traced back to the Law through Moses, but to the heritage of faith that Abraham established before the Law.

In a recent interview on a Christian program, a man was advocating how we need to come back to our Jewish roots. He stated that we were all the children of Abraham. There is some Scriptural merit to what this person was saying, and it sounded good. However, there was something missing in his presentation—Jesus Christ. Christians have one

---

[7] John 1: 4-5; 3:616-21; 12:32; 16:7-13; Romans 7:12, 14

commission—to preach the Gospel. In many cases, people simply use Christ to promote religious causes that do not have anything to do with salvation or the real heart of God for His people. In fact, these causes replace the simplicity of the Gospel.

It is easy to know what a person's real agenda is up front. Those who have an agenda other than Christ and Him crucified cover up their real goals with religious terms and rhetoric. Their words may sound harmless enough and come across as a wonderful gesture or ideology, but the emphasis is all wrong. As Christians, we need to discern by listening to what is really being promoted. For example, if a person does not begin with the presentation of Jesus, he or she will not end with Him. If a person starts out with Jesus, but takes a detour away from Him to exalt a different cause, belief, or agenda, Jesus will clearly be missing in the end. In many cases, Jesus is merely tacked on to the end of some promotion of personal agendas for credibility. However, preaching Jesus means you begin with Him and you will continue to lift Him up, thereby ending with Him. It is Jesus who will draw people to Himself when He is properly lifted up.[8] When Jesus is missing from any part of the presentation, the presenter is nothing more than a salesperson who is trying to promote some religious cause or agenda under the guise of Christianity. If Jesus is missing, the Holy Spirit will be missing. If the Spirit is missing, there is no real conviction taking place and there will be no protection against being deceived by counterfeits.

Let us consider what this guest on the show was saying in light of the Word of God. First of all, I believe this man was a Gentile. He was claiming Jewish roots because of his association with Abraham. What do we need to understand about Jewish roots? In Jesus' day, the Jews were quite impressed with their Jewish roots. They saw this identification as a point of deliverance and prestige. However, consider what John the Baptist said about the root of the tree that was associated with the religious system of the Jews, "And now also the axe is laid unto the root of the trees; therefore every tree which bringeth not forth good fruit is hewn down and cast into the fire" (Matthew 3:10). God laid an axe to the root of the old way to bring forth a new way. The old way was established in a system of rituals and beliefs. In many cases, it produced legalistic, self-righteous people who crucified Jesus when He challenged their religious system.[9]

The new way God established was not a belief system. Rather, He grew and established a Vine in the midst of His people. As Christians, it would not be a matter of being identified to a root system; rather, it would be a matter of abiding in the Vine, or the Person of Jesus Christ. The Christian's history and lineage begins with the cross of Jesus. Everything about the history of the Jewish nation before the redemption of Jesus, pointed to this one reality. Obviously, the reason Christians are trying to

---

[8] John 12:32; Acts 5:42
[9] Matthew 3:7-10; Luke 3:7-9; John 11:46-48

reconnect to a root system that was judged by God is because they do not know their place in Christ. The reason they do not know their place in Christ is because they are not abiding in Him. It is by having a right relationship with the Vine that will not only bring satisfaction to our inner man, but will also allow the necessary fruits to be produced in our lives that will spare us from being cut off and cast into the fire.[10]

It is true that, as Christians, we are identified as children of Abraham. However, as Gentiles, our identification to Abraham is strictly a spiritual association based on faith and not a biological one. As Paul stated, there is no distinction between Jews and Greeks when it comes to one's life and heritage in Christ.[11] To emphasize that we are the children of Abraham without putting it in the right context is a grave mishandling of the truth and intent of the Word.

Once again, let us consider how the Jews considered their biological association with Abraham. Many of the Jews saw this association as children of Abraham as their ticket to God. John the Baptist made this statement to the Jews, "And think not to say within yourselves, We have Abraham to our father; for I say unto you, that God is able of these stones to raise up children unto Abraham" (Matthew 3:9). Paul counted his Jewish roots and lineage as dung in light of gaining Christ. The apostles of the new Church never promoted their Jewish roots. Rather, they preached and taught Christ. Although Jesus was a Jew in His humanity, His biological lineage simply identified Him as the Messiah. However, our salvation was secured because He is God who came in the flesh.[12]

It is vital to point out that Abraham did not die for us, rather he serves as an example of true faith. When you study his life, you will realize that his faith was accounted to him for righteousness because he believed God. His belief in God was unshakeable because he understood his real heritage and promise. This man, who was a friend of God, knew that God was his heritage and that his ultimate promise was to dwell forever in a city that was made by the hands of God.[13]

In light of our identification to Abraham on the basis of faith, it is obvious that the emphasis must never be put on Christians being children of Abraham; rather, it should be put on the blessed reality that each of us are children of God. Keep in mind, God can rise up biological seed unto Abraham, but it takes faith to make a person a child of God. The Apostle Paul confirmed this in Galatians 3:26, "For ye are all the children of God by faith in Christ Jesus."

Our status as God's children cost Him His Son. It was His will that we be placed in this eternal heritage. We are related by the blood of Jesus, established in His kingdom by the same type of faith Abraham

---

[10] John 15:1-8; Romans 11:17--22
[11] Galatians 3:7
[12] Acts 5:42; Philippians 3:2-8
[13] Genesis 15:1; Romans 4:2-3, 11-13; Hebrews 11:8-10; James 2:23;

displayed, and placed in a Body and spiritual family that is bound together by One Spirit and the love of God.[14]

Genuine faith will always lead us back to the work of redemption that Jesus secured on the cross. Abraham's faith in God reminds us that our heritage is God. This faith is rich because it looks beyond this world to embrace the unseen blessings and life of God in confidence and expectation.[15]

The Galatians' emphasis on the Law seemed innocent and harmless enough, but the Apostle Paul clearly denounced this emphasis as perverting the Gospel. As you listen to some of the people who get caught up with these different practices, you will hear about how it made them feel or that they felt it added to their personal or spiritual worth before God. Obviously, these testimonies show how these people are emotionally caught up with the idea or the practice, but it is obvious that they are not caught up with the Person of Jesus.

To actually put into practice such things as the Jewish holy days and feasts was to resurrect beggarly elements whose main purpose was to simply cast a shadow of the reflection of the true light that would come into the world, Jesus Christ. These elements were not to become a means or ends of salvation in and of themselves.[16]

The Apostle Paul pronounced a curse upon those who advocated such a perversion, no matter how religious or righteous it may seem. To accurse someone seems harsh, but Paul was justified. After all, the Law curses those who fail to adhere to it. This is brought out in Galatians 3:10, "For as many as are of the works of the law are under the curse: for it is written, Cursed is every one that continueth not in the things which are written in the book of the law to do them." If a person breaks one statute of the Law, he or she is guilty of breaking the whole Law.[17]

I've observed how people pick and choose what laws they will comply with. For example, in the case of the Galatians, the conflict was over circumcision, but, today, it could be the Sabbath or the laws pertaining to dress or food.[18] However, there are also statutes surrounding different practices concerning the priesthood and sacrifices that are not practiced for various reasons. Yet, if these people fail to keep the Law at one point, they break the whole Law.

Those who insist on coming under the Law stand cursed because of it. They are not able to keep every bit of it in intent or practice; therefore, they stand condemned because of it. Since the Law cannot justify man in his sinful state, Christ had to redeem each of us from the curse of the

---

[14] John 1:12-13; Romans 5:2-5; 8:15-17; Ephesians 4:4-6; Colossians 1:7; Hebrews 10:10, 18-22
[15] Genesis 15:1; Romans 4:1-14; Hebrews 11:8-16
[16] John 1:1-9; Galatians 4:9-11; Colossians 2:14-17
[17] James 2:10
[18] Galatians 2:2-5

Law by being made a curse for us. He became this curse by hanging on the cross.[19]

When people preach another gospel, they are subject to the only means by which they can be judged—the Law. Romans 8:2 tells us there are only two laws in operation—the law of sin and death and the law of the Spirit of life in Christ Jesus. The Law does not address the things of the Spirit. Therefore, to come under the Law means one is under the law of sin and death. Each person will be declared a sinner, or one who offends God in principle and deed by transgressing His Law. The wages of those sins is death.[20] Therefore, a person who preaches another gospel will stand accursed by the only means of judgment available—the Holy Law of God.

As you study the Law, you begin to understand that the Law was brought forth to point men to their need for Jesus. Paul referred to it as a schoolmaster. The Law revealed and identified the extent of sin and how it abounded in our lives. Without the Law, there was no standard by which men could be rightfully judged as transgressors, justly condemned in their state of sin, as well as stripped of their self-sufficiency to make the error of their ways right in their own power. If the Law was absent, the bad news would be missing and, without the bad news, the good news would never be recognized and received.[21] It is the recognition of sin and its consequences that produces the openness to see the solution being offered through God's intervention.

Without God's intervention, each of us would remain under a death sentence or on death row. We would continue to be under a legal debt or obligation to God that would require our deaths because of our sins or offenses against Him. We would stand guilty without any recourse, except for a possible act that could only be taken outside of ourselves. In other words, we each need to be pardoned.[22]

God provided an advocate who would not only stand on our behalf, but who could pay the price for our sins and satisfy the judgment that was passed down on all men through Adam. It is on the basis of the intercession and substitution of the advocate that God gives the condemned person a pardon. This pardon comes by way of Jesus' death on the cross. However, we can only receive pardon by faith. The pardon that is appropriated is an act of grace on God's part. Once we receive this pardon, we will stand justified in God's sight.[23]

The Apostle John told us that Moses gave the Law, but grace and truth came by Jesus Christ. Jesus became the fulfillment or completion of the purpose or intent of the Law. In other words, He satisfied it in every aspect. Those who embrace Jesus as the solution stand in His

---

[19] Galatians 3:11, 4:9-11
[20] Romans 6:23; Galatians 5:22-23
[21] Romans 4:15; 5:20-21; Galatians 3:24
[22] Romans 4:4-5
[23] Romans 5:1-2, 12, 15-18; 1 John 1:1-2

righteousness. The righteousness of Christ fulfills the Law in the believer's life. Since they are dead in Christ, they are not subject to another law, that of the Spirit; therefore, they are no longer subject to the holy Law of God.[24]

The Apostle Paul made some challenging statements to the Galatians about perverting the Gospel with the Law. He asked them, "Are ye so foolish? Having begun in the Spirit, are ye now made perfect by the flesh?" (Galatians 3:2) The true Gospel is the work of the Spirit. These people started out believing the true Gospel, but then they began trying to make themselves acceptable in the flesh by adhering to the Law.

As Paul clearly warned, those who do the work of the flesh will not inherit the kingdom of God. He asked them if they received the Spirit by the works of the Law or by the hearing of faith.[25] As he stated in Galatians 3:12, "And the law is not of faith: but, The man that doeth them shall live in them."

The Apostle Paul's questions were a reality check. He clearly stipulated that the flesh could only reap corruption, while those who sow to the Spirit would reap everlasting life. The fruits of our lives reveal what we are sowing. Man can only respond to the Law in a fleshly or carnal way. He can attempt to conform outwardly in the flesh to its rules, but he will not be transformed in the inner man by the Holy Ghost.

As Scripture points out, in the new covenant, God will give believers a new heart and a new spirit. It will be the new spirit within them that will cause individuals to walk in His statutes and keep His judgments. Hebrews 8:10 and 10:15-16 confirm this. However, the statues and judgments we will adhere to will line up to the righteous intent or purpose of the Law, which have been summarized in the Ten Commandments. Adhering to these commandments will not be a matter of duty or conscience, but a natural response of the new disposition that reigns in believers through the indwelling presence of the Spirit.

It is vital that people recognize that they are unable to keep God's statutes and judgments in their own power. Such attempts are sowing in vanity. Therefore, those who sow to the flesh become self-righteous and deluded in their attempts, while those who sow in the Spirit have the liberty to experience the life that God has for them.[26]

This brings us to another fruit of the Gospel—liberty in Christ. Paul assured the Galatians that the Gospel was not from man. In other words, he did not receive it from man, nor was he taught the Gospel by man. It came by the revelation of Jesus Christ. Obviously, to preach the Gospel, Jesus had to be revealed to Paul by the Spirit.[27]

---

[24] Matthew 5:17; John 1:17; Romans 6:3-8; 8:4; 10:4
[25] Galatians 3:3: 5:19-21
[26] Galatians 6:7-8
[27] Galatians: 1:11-12, 16

Since the Law could only condemn, it ultimately left man oppressed and hopeless. However, where the Spirit is, there is liberty.[28] The liberty of the Spirit does not grant man freedom to do as he desires. Rather, liberty in the Spirit means a person can now freely discover his or her life in Jesus.

It is in Christ that a person can fulfill the Law in one word—love. When Christ is our reality, the love of God will be shed abroad in our hearts. His love will compel or constrain us to be righteous before Him and do right by others. Righteousness is accounted to us because of our faith, but faith also walks hand in hand with love.[29] As the Apostle Paul stated, "For in Jesus Christ neither circumcision availeth any thing, nor uncircumcision; but faith which worketh by love" (Galatians 5:6).

It is liberty in Christ that allows us to walk in unfeigned faith and respond in the love of God. God's love is pure; therefore, it is able to fulfill the Law in spirit, attitude, and godly practice. Without the liberty to discover this incredible life in Christ, our faith will be tarnished and our love full of hypocrisy as we simply play the religious game.[30]

The Apostle Paul brought a contrast between the bondage of the Law and liberty wrought by grace. He related the promises of God to Isaac who was wrought by the Spirit in a miraculous way according to God's will and the bondage of the Law to Abraham's son, Ishmael. Ishmael was born because of fleshly attempts. His mother was a bondmaid, subject to Abraham's wife Sarah. Abraham had to send Ishmael away because he had no part in the promises of God.[31] This is true for the flesh. It is a product of sin and, therefore, subject to its dictates and bondage, as well as being accountable to the Law. The flesh and its works have no part in God's kingdom or His promises.

The attempt of the Galatians to make themselves righteous before God through the rituals of the Law was an affront to the grace of Jesus. No man could satisfy the Law through his own meritorious efforts. As individuals strive to adhere to the Law to please God, they become more condemned by it and begin to fall out of grace. This makes Jesus' work on the cross of no affect in a person's salvation.[32] In other words, His redemption carries no real meaning or purpose for them. It has simply been tacked on to justify the present delusion or to establish a false credibility.

Jesus was the only one who could fulfill the Law so that man would no longer stand condemned by it. In Christ, believers stand righteous, no longer subject to the condemnation of the Law, but heirs to the promises

---

[28] 2 Corinthians 3:17-18
[29] Romans 5:5;
[30] Romans 13:8-10
[31] Genesis 21:9-12; Galatians 4:22-31
[32] Galatians 5:4

of God. In fact, Jesus blotted out the handwriting of ordinances that were against each of His followers by way of the cross.[33]

The Apostle Paul stressed in Galatians the liberty found in Christ. He contended with Peter over the place the Law had in the salvation of man. He had asked Peter why he supported the impression that Gentiles should live or conduct themselves like Jews when he lived like a Gentile.[34]

The Church leaders in Acts 15 had already addressed the subject of the Law in relationship to Gentiles. No doubt, the debate was heated. However, the leaders were reminded that the Law was a yoke that neither their fathers nor they could bear. After the debate, this is what came down from the leaders to the new Church, "Wherefore my sentence is, that we trouble not them, which from among the Gentiles are turned to God: But that we write unto them, that they abstain from pollutions of idols, and from fornication, and from things strangled, and from blood" (Acts 15:19-20). Once again, we must note that the Gentiles were being called to a moral responsibility in their conduct before God and towards others.

People are forever trying to put their religious causes and doctrines on others. Apparently, faith in Christ's redemption is not enough to these people. In their minds, you might have to be part of a particular denomination, theology, practices, or preference before they will consider you saved. And, if you dare defy their beliefs, they become harsh and judgmental towards you.

These causes and doctrines may be backed up with Scripture, but they do not constitute salvation. Jesus alone saves; therefore, a person's salvation hinges on what he or she is doing with Jesus. All of these causes and doctrines are nothing but detours away from the eternal into the fleshly realm, where certain religious emphases become sacred cows. Obviously, grace is cast off and Jesus and His work are rendered useless in a person's life.

The truth is that each of us must fight to maintain our liberty in Christ. There are so many perverted presentations of the Gospel in the world. They are religious and can be backed up with Scriptures taken out of context, but they pervert the real character and work of Jesus. For instance, some emphasize repentance in light of personal righteousness, rather than coming to Jesus who is the place of righteousness. In other arenas, personal holiness is exalted. This is where holiness is worked out on a personal level by maintaining certain beliefs and practices, rather than finding one's life in Christ who serves as the essence of true sanctification. Each perverted gospel subtly replaces Jesus with man's best attempts to make himself righteous or holy before God. Yet, Isaiah 64:6 tells us that the best man has to offer is filthy rags before God.

---

[33] Colossians 2:14
[34] Galatians 2:14

Since liberty in Jesus is always being threatened by man's best religious attempts, the Apostle Paul gave this instruction, "Stand fast therefore in the liberty wherewith Christ hath made us free, and be not entangled again with the yoke of bondage" (Galatians 5:1). It is up to us to stand fast in the liberty of Christ. We must deny ourselves the right to come out noble or superior in our religious ways and accept the evaluation of God concerning our sinful condition. We must become crucified to the world as we put to death the works and influence of the flesh. Such death will ensure that we do not nullify the work of the cross or hinder the Spirit of God in our lives.[35]

Have you fallen for a perverted presentation of the Gospel? A good way to examine yourself is to consider whether you have the liberty to discover your true life in Jesus and the fruit of the Spirit. If you discover bondage in this area, you have come under a yoke that you cannot bear and which will ultimately judge and condemn you. Exchange any burdensome, religious yoke for Christ's easy yoke of love and obedience.[36] You will not only find liberty, but you will experience godly discipline and confidence in your life before Him.

---

[35] Galatians 5:16-26; 6:14
[36] Matthew 11:28-30

7

THE INHERITANCE OF THE GOSPEL

The Apostle Paul had been dealing with the enemies of the Gospel—sin, carnality, and perversion. He was ready to present the reality of the Gospel in the rest of his epistles. This reality is not complicated, but simple. It is not hidden to the pure in heart, but it also has the promise that it will become a reality to those who walk by faith. It is important to understand this because God has not hidden the reality of His kingdom from us. He has done all He can to make known this mystery to all who desire to see it by allowing it to be hung on the cross.

The reality of the Gospel is the life of Jesus being made manifest in our dispositions, attitudes, and conduct. As you study the reality of the Gospel through Paul's eyes, you will see a glorious picture of the position the Gospel secures for those who believe, along with the power behind it and the revelation of the light of the life that it possesses.

As we have seen in Paul's first three epistles, our attitudes in regard to our life or position in Jesus will determine our approach towards the Gospel. If we fail to approach the Gospel with the right attitude, it will strip the Gospel of its power to save. When the Gospel has been stripped of its power, the revelation of Jesus will be missing. In fact, this is how Satan blinds unbelievers to the light of the Gospel and robs believers of truly embracing a complete, abundant life. As Jesus said in John 10:10b, "The thief cometh not, but for to steal, and to kill, and to destroy: I am come that they might have life, and that they might have it more abundantly."

The question is how does one come to terms with this life in Christ? The answer is found in the concept of inheritance. The Apostle Paul outlined the inheritance of the Gospel in his epistle to the Ephesians. This inheritance is glorious and is summarized in Ephesians 1:13-14,

> In whom ye also trusted, after that ye heard the word of truth, the gospel of your salvation: in whom also, after that ye believed, ye were sealed with that Holy Spirit of promise, Which is the earnest of our inheritance until the redemption of the purchased possession, unto the praise of his glory.

The Holy Spirit is the believer's earnest payment from God towards his or her inheritance. He serves as the advancement to secure this inheritance until redemption is fully realized in our lives. This inheritance is not earthly, but spiritual. The Apostle Paul clearly stipulated this in Ephesians 1:3, "Blessed be the God and Father of our Lord Jesus Christ, who hath blessed us with all spiritual blessings in heavenly places in Christ."

As previously pointed out, the Holy Spirit is not obvious in most of the activities surrounding the work of redemption. However, He is a part of the complete package of salvation. He is the one who works this salvation in, through, and out of believers' lives as they submit to Him. Sadly, most Christians think they have arrived at the completion of redemption based upon the concept or experience of salvation, rather than recognizing that the Holy Spirit has been given as a means to make salvation a reality.

The Holy Ghost is often abused, ignored, and rejected by much of the Church as to having any significant part in believers experiencing the full, complete life in Christ. Christians do not see Him as the earnest payment that must be evident in their lives to ensure securing the full redemption. This spiritual pledge does not silently rest in some account, but must be actively working in and through our lives. After all, He has been given as a seal out of good faith by God to distinguish those who would receive this complete inheritance in the future. Ultimately, believers are being set apart for the purpose and glory of God. Therefore, the Holy Spirit is working on behalf of believers to prepare them for their glorious inheritance. This work is referred to throughout the epistle to the Ephesians.

The work of the Holy Spirit begins with position. As believers, we are actually seated in high places in Jesus. This implies that, positionally, we are above the workings, influence, dominion, and condemnation of the world and its spirit.[1] In God's eyes, we are already spiritually seated in heavenly places, regardless of where we are located physically. This heavenly position identifies us with the heavenly inheritance we have in Jesus.

It is in our identification in and with Jesus that we are reminded that we were chosen before the foundation of the world as a means to represent and manifest Him to the world. To effectively manifest His life, we must be holy and without blemish, displaying love for Him in devotion and faithful service.[2]

The identification in Jesus reveals the type of relationship we are to have with the Father. Ephesians 1:5 sates, "Having predestinated us unto the adoption of children by Jesus Christ to himself, according to the good pleasure of his will." We have been adopted into a new family.[3] However, this adoption was secured through Jesus' redemption. We are now related to the Father because of the blood of Jesus that provided a way for us to obtain forgiveness for our sins. This redemption was done according to the unseen riches found in His grace.

---

[1] Ephesians 2:2-3
[2] Ephesians 1:4
[3] John 1:12; Romans 8:15-17; Ephesians 3:14-16

Our adoption into God's kingdom was according to the good pleasure of His will. But what is His will? Most people struggle with God's will, but the Word tells us what God's will is. John 6:39-40 reveals three aspects about God's will,

> And this is the Father's will which hath sent me, that of all which he hath given me I should lose nothing, but should raise it up again at the last day. And this is the will of him that sent me, that every one which seeth the Son, and believeth on him, may have everlasting life: and I will raise him up at the last day.

God's will is simple. He wants Jesus to preserve those things He has entrusted to Him, to ensure salvation to those who see and believe on Him, and to raise the believers up at the last day. Obviously, Jesus is the central focus. He carries the burden to preserve, save, and maintain all that the Father has given Him. Hence, enters Jesus' invitation of coming unto Him. As our all in all, Jesus is found in all things as He fills all things up with His grace and life, for He alone represents the wells of salvation. Each well possesses the Living Water of the Spirit that brings forth the different treasures and blessings of the Son of God's divine attributes and anointed work, along with the fullness of His redemption.[4] For those in Christ, the Father's will points to a rich heritage, a fulfilling present, and a glorious future.

Man has no part in this redemption. He can only submit to the Holy Ghost to fully realize his inheritance.[5] It is his submission to the Spirit of God that allows him to discover the unseen riches of Christ. It is the Holy Ghost who gives believers wisdom from above to recognize the nuggets of God in His Word and ways. It is the Spirit of God who unveils the mysteries of Christ in Scripture.

These mysteries are based on the eternal nature of Christ. We can know Him in part, but only the Spirit can unveil the depths of Him in order to reveal greater mysteries of His character. In fact, the Spirit is the One who leads us into all truth about Jesus. He is the only teacher who can make the Word of God alive with the reality of Christ. This is why Jesus said that His words were spirit and life. No man can gain life from the Word unless the Holy Ghost enlightens his spiritual eyes to see the Lord in the Scriptures.[6]

Jesus is the essence of our inheritance. He has shown His power through His resurrection. He sits on the right hand of the Father in heavenly places, proving Himself to be above all other powers. In fact, He has put all things under His feet and has been made head over all, including the Church.[7]

---

[4] Isaiah 12:3; John 4:14; 6:35; 7:37-39; Ephesians 4:10; Colossians 3:11
[5] Ephesians 2:8-9
[6] John 6:63; 14:16-18; 16:7-14; 1 John 2:27, 3:24; 5:6
[7] Ephesians 1:19-22; Hebrews 6:4-6

It is from Jesus, as the head of the Church, that the Holy Spirit places believers in His Body for the purpose of edification. It is from the point of fitting each saint in the Body that His work begins to make believers into God's actual workmanship, for the purpose of good works. Since each believer was chosen from the foundation of the world, he or she has been ordained to walk in good works that will bring glory to God. As you can see, good works do not save us, but we have been saved unto good works for the glory of God. In other words, salvation is not the product of good works, but true salvation will be the source that inspires good works in those who truly believe.[8]

As believers, we have been reconciled unto God and are no longer estranged from Him. We are now fellow citizens in His household. Our lives are established on the foundation or teachings of apostles and prophets who were inspired and led by the Holy Ghost. However, these teachings must line up to and be supported by the chief cornerstone, Jesus Christ.[9]

Today, the establishment and edification of the Church are being threatened by another gospel. This gospel is known as Kingdom Dominion. Kingdom Dominion is about man establishing the kingdom of Christ on earth, rather than the King of kings bringing it forth in His power and glory. This movement has its own heretical breed of apostles and prophets. Instead of reaffirming the foundation set down by the prophets and apostles of old, this new breed of religious heretics is redefining the foundation, thereby, presenting another Jesus. Their emphasis is that man has the ability to work himself into a state of immortality. Once again, we see where man's attempts are trying to replace Jesus' death on the cross. These individuals are trying to work themselves into an immortal state without putting all their reliance on Jesus by humbly coming to the cross, in need of forgiveness of sin and redemption from the dictates of sin.

As you study the heretical belief of Kingdom Dominion, you will find that, at the core of it, is the rejection of the literal return of Jesus.[10] Supposedly, He will return to earth through the Manifested Sons of God who work themselves into this state of immortality while they secure a physical kingdom or dominion for Him on earth.

How can people do away with the blessed hope? These heretical wolves have cleverly indoctrinated people with religious and popular terminology that has been changed to suit their agendas. Through so-called "revelations", these false apostles and prophets are also redefining the call of the Church to preach the Gospel. The new call is for an aggressive army to come forth to take the world for Jesus. This new aggressive army is blindly and erroneously trying to take control of the

---

[8] Ephesians 1:4; 2:10; 4:12-13
[9] Ephesians 2:15-16, 19-21
[10] Acts 1:9-11; 1 Thessalonians 4:13-18; Revelation 1:7

Challenging the Christian Life

heavens with "warring tongues." They are also striving to gain control of different areas through territorial praying.

These people are not only trying to gain control of the heavens, but they are also trying to gain full control of the Church. They are cleverly replacing Jesus' leadership as both the head and Lord of His body with the idea of coverings. People now need coverings over them that come in the form of religious leaders or organizations to guide them. These coverings often hide sin and rebellion towards the authority of God. As you consider such a covering, the logic behind it is not only unscriptural, but it is not practical. It either places man over Jesus, cleverly replacing His leadership in the person's life, or it places man between the person and Jesus as some type of mediator who must interpret or discern all spiritual matters. According to the Apostle Paul in 1 Timothy 2:5, there is only one mediator between men and God, and that is the man Christ Jesus. To place flawed man above another individual will make the leader the guiding factor in the person's life, instead of the Holy Ghost. There is only one acceptable covering according to Isaiah 30:1, and that is the Holy Ghost. Any other covering is considered wicked or deceptive and will be removed or destroyed by God.[11]

Godly leaders will always point to Jesus as the only true Shepherd of His people. Those who point to any other leadership are imposters of the worse type. Jeremiah is clear that to look to man or rely upon him in such a capacity is to stand cursed. The reason is because the leadership of Jesus has been cleverly replaced with the weak arm of man.[12]

The various practices and claims that are involved with this heretical movement of Kingdom Dominion are many. Sadly, many unsuspecting Christians are getting caught up with it, thinking it is a new thing from God. In reality, it is not a new thing; it is simply an old lie of Satan's that has been covered up with acceptable terminology and falsehood.

The extreme version of this kingdom movement is not only radical, but also militant and dangerous. Those who blindly follow the agenda of this movement label themselves with such titles as "Joel's Army" and they will have no qualms about physically killing the true servants of God who oppose them. Of course, they will do it in the name of God.[13] They will see their actions as righteous and those who oppose them as ungodly hindrances in ushering in the kingdom of Christ.

The Bible is clear that man has no part in salvation, except receiving or rejecting it. It is an act of God's grace. For people to experience salvation, they must give way to the work of the Holy Ghost. He is the One who enables believers to discover the mystery of Christ that is hidden in Scripture, veiled from human eyes, beyond intellectual reasoning, and made useless by worldly philosophies and man's religion.

---

[11] Isaiah 25:7; Colossians 1:18
[12] Jeremiah 17:5
[13] John 16:2

The Holy Spirit's goal is to build a Church that is in love with the Jesus of the Bible and will be adorned in His humility. It is love for the true Jesus of the Bible that will bring forth unity in His Body. This brings us to another movement—ecumenism.

Ecumenism's goal is to bring all religions together under one auspice, regardless of differences in regard to Jesus' identity, sin, or the work of redemption. This ecumenical movement promotes the idea of a gospel of peace. However, Scripture is clear about true peace. True peace can only be found in a relationship with God. This peace is possible because of what Jesus did on the cross. Outside of the cross of Jesus, there is no agreement with God, and there can be no unity or peace with those who belong to the true Body of Jesus.[14]

Needless to say, the gospel of peace is very attractive. Countless Christians are being swept into this façade. Many of the Protestant Churches have joined ranks with unscriptural, liberal, religious organizations in order to bring about this peace. They have compromised with sin to fit into the world's ways of doing and thinking to ensure political correctness. In their attempts to appear loving and reasonable, they are fulfilling the prophecy of the establishment of a one-world religious system that will be ruled by the antichrist who will appear as a man of peace.[15]

Once again, the true Gospel is being replaced with man's philosophies and compromised for something that is a façade, rather than a reality. One must not forget Paul's warnings about false peace in 1 Thessalonians 5:3, "For when they shall say, Peace and safety; then sudden destruction cometh upon them, as travail upon a woman with child; and they shall not escape."

Christians need to remember that personal peace and unity among believers can only be found at the point of the head of the Body, Jesus. Jesus is the only true Prince of Peace. He is the One who gives peace that is beyond the world's comprehension. It is at the place of Jesus as head and Lord that the one true Spirit can move, baptize, and perfect the saints. Out of this perfection, the one true faith will be realized, the one true God worshipped, and the Father glorified.[16]

When it comes to fitting the saints into the Body, it has nothing to do with personal abilities or intelligence, but with the perfect will of God. It is His good pleasure to save, sanctify, and bring each believer forth in resurrection power. It is His desire to fill us with His fullness in such a way that every aspect of our lives will be filled with the glorious life of His Son.[17]

In order to ensure our inheritance, we must put off the old life with its disposition, attitudes, and ways. We must cease from giving way to the

---

[14] Ephesians 1:7, 10, 2:13-17; 3:17-19; 4:14-16
[15] Revelation 6:2
[16] Isaiah 9:6; John 14:27; Ephesians 4:3-6
[17] Ephesians 1:6, 23

practice of darkness and begin to desire the light of Jesus' life and ways. We must seek to edify other believers in the ways of God, and, above all else, we must avoid grieving the Holy Spirit.[18]

So much of what is being done in the name of God, Christ, or the Holy Spirit, is grievous to the Holy Ghost. It is not of Him, but a product of man's attempts. It is not from Him, rather it is motivated by wicked, self-serving agendas. It is not about Jesus; rather, it is the promotion of a counterfeit messiah. Clearly, the true Gospel is missing and being replaced by religious rhetoric that has no truth or purpose.

Sadly, many in the Church are being deceived by these various presentations. They are coming under the tentacles of the spiritual darkness that is engulfing much of the organized church. As a result, the unfruitful works of these heretical teachings are not being reproved and exposed.[19] Instead, they are making inroads into the Church, resulting in spiritual dullness in the Body and preventing believers from discerning truth and righteousness from that which is heretical.

The true Church is in a fierce battle for truth. However, many in Christendom are weak. The foundation has been eroded, the cornerstone reshaped, and the Spirit of God replaced. The true Jesus is not being lifted up. As a result, there is no order or harmony in homes or churches. Religion is becoming more "spiritual," but it remains self-serving and vulnerable to another spirit. A whole generation is becoming indifferent because there is no distinction between right and wrong. The Church is becoming powerless and lost in the midst of man's various uninspired doctrines, movements, and entertainment.

Sadly, much of the Church stands naked, stripped of its armor, and unable to withstand the attacks of the devil and the onslaught of the powers and rulers of darkness. Without power and authority, many will not be able to stand in the midst of wickedness. Although there are those in the organized Church that claim they have the armor in place, it is clearly missing. The belt of truth has become tarnished with compromise and the breastplate of righteousness weak with worldliness. The feet are becoming lame and tormented because the power of the Gospel is absent, while the shield of faith has been rendered into a pretty paper shield of pseudo-faiths that blow away with every wind of doctrine. The helmet of salvation is no longer in place. It has been put aside to accept the false security of man's coverings or latest attempts to make himself righteous, holy, or immortal. The sword has been rendered useless, dissected in many pieces in the name of intellectual and religious pursuits for truth and replaced with man's watered-down Bible versions, traditions, and theology.[20]

Today, the elite in the religious world believe they know the mystery of God. However, what they fail to realize is that the mystery has nothing

---

[18] Ephesians 4:22-30
[19] Ephesians 5:6-13
[20] Ephesians 6:10-17

to do with intellectual pursuits, new revelations, greater truths, cemented theology, or spiritual insight. As stated, the mystery of God has been revealed in part. The mystery remains the same throughout each generation. It is summarized in Jesus Christ and His redemption. Man must see this mystery through the convicting power of the Holy Spirit and receive it by faith to ensure his spiritual inheritance.

Jesus is eternal; therefore, there is no way we will know Him in His fullness. We will simply catch glimpses of Him in His Word as the Holy Ghost uncovers Him. But, what glorious glimpses they will be! Such glimpses will contain spiritual riches that one will never be able to describe, for they can only be experienced in the recesses of one's heart and soul. The Apostle Paul put it best, "That in the ages to come he might shew the exceeding riches of his grace in his kindness towards us through Christ Jesus" (Ephesians 2:7).

Saints will be discovering the riches of Christ in His glory for ages to come. How can we possibly think that our inheritance is earthly and temporary? How can we believe that unity can take place by ignoring our spiritual heritage of the cross, the unchanging reality of Jesus, and the promise of His coming as King of kings to reign? How could we believe that there is no need for the edifying and perfecting work of the Spirit or that we do not need the evidence of Him as our pledge in regards to our inheritance? Obviously, many have become spiritually dull by false movements, deluded by a promise of false peace and unity, and blinded by their own arrogance.

The Apostle Paul told us that our inheritance begins with the earnest payment of the Spirit and will be realized in full when our redemption is truly revealed in resurrection power. Meanwhile, we positionally sit in heavenly places with Jesus, above all that would try to claim us for the works of darkness. We have the Spirit of God who seals us and the unseen riches of heaven that are available because of our status as His children. We also have the opportunity to experience the fullness of Christ's abundant life in our journey through this present world.

The question is, have you become identified with the inheritance of the Gospel or are you waiting for it? You need to realize that, as a saint, you presently possess the seal of this inheritance. However, you must experience the life of Jesus by putting off the old and submitting to the work of the Holy Ghost to possess and manifest the new.

8

FELLOWSHIP OF THE GOSPEL

In Ephesians, we learned about the spiritual inheritance that is associated with the true Gospel of Jesus. In Philippians, we will discover the purpose of the Gospel—fellowship. The Apostle Paul made this statement, "For your fellowship in the gospel from the first day until now" (Philippians 1:5). Fellowship in this text means partnership, participation, communication, and communion.[1] Such fellowship points to agreement.

The Gospel of Jesus is a place of partnership. Such a partnership begins with man and God. As the Apostle Paul stated in 1 Corinthians 3:9, "For we are labourers together with God: ye are God's husbandry, ye are God's building." The salvation of man's soul is a joint effort in the harvest field. Man proclaims the good news and the Holy Spirit imparts it into man's soul as truth.

The partnership between God and His servants is valuable. Those who preach the Gospel must live by the Gospel. Other believers prayerfully and financially maintain servants of God on the mission fields of the world such as the Apostle Paul. Although Paul occasionally worked at his trade, it was for the purpose of being an example.

It is the Church's responsibility to show support in the furtherance of the Gospel and encouragement of the brethren. The new Church in Acts displayed this sacrificial support. A good example of the Church showing support was the Corinthians. They liberally helped other members of the Body. This benevolence often served as an active example of the power of the Gospel. In the case of those at Philippi, they not only helped other brethren, but they also supported Paul in his ordeal.[2]

Obviously, the Philippians shared a special partnership with Paul. To share in this way points to identity. In Ephesians, we see identity through inheritance; but, in Philippians, we see identity through fellowship. Without fellowship there is no agreement. Agreement encourages communication and produces communion. Communion represents intimacy. For Christians, this intimacy occurs in the spirit. It actually allows people to enter into one's plight and circumstances.

The Apostle Paul was in prison. He had lived an active life for Jesus. However, it resulted in persecution and suffering.[3] Paul had endured

---

[1] Stong's Exhaustive Concordance, #2842
[2] Acts 4:32-37; 1 Corinthians 9:14; 2 Corinthians 9:13; Philippians 4:16-18
[3] Philippians 1:12

much for the sake of the Gospel. I am sure he fought times of depression, but he found comfort in the fruits of his labor. He had established churches that held fast to Jesus and supported him in his times of persecution. His heart must have leaped for joy seeing the faithfulness of God reach out to him through those he had served. He said of the Philippians that their gifts to him through Epaphroditus were a sacrifice that emitted a sweet smell to God that was acceptable and pleasing to Him.[4]

Fellowship in the Spirit entails being "like-minded." Like-mindedness points to the direction of affections.[5] Christians have agreement and are like-minded when their affections are directed toward Christ. Their focus is on the same source and they are heading in the same direction. They do not think outside of the one who holds their affections. This is why Paul instructed Christians to set their affections on things above.[6] He made this statement in Romans 15:5, "Now the God of patience and consolation grant you to be like-minded one toward another according to Christ Jesus." Obviously, our point of agreement begins with the object of our love and devotion.

In order to establish the right perspective, Paul talked about the mind of Jesus. His mind was single towards the Father. All of His love and devotion were focused on doing the will of the Father. He did nothing outside of the Father's will. His goal was to glorify Him.[7]

The Apostle Paul maintained that we must have the same mind as Christ. Our hearts must be single in devotion to Him, while our minds are fixed on doing His will. We must do everything in lowliness of mind, allowing others to be honored and exalted.[8]

Jesus' mind or attitude allowed Him to become identified with man. He gave up His glory as God and took on the disposition of a servant. This was necessary so that He could become a servant to the Father and to man. He then allowed Himself to be fashioned as a man. It is as man that He humbled Himself as the Lamb of God and became a sin offering for us. As He humbled Himself to embrace the cross, He was lifted up as our only solution.[9]

Identification and fellowship are a glorious reality of the Gospel. Jesus became identified with man's plight so that man could once again fellowship with God in glorious communion. The Apostle John talked about the fellowship that is available because of what Jesus did on the cross. "If we say that we have fellowship with him (God), and walk in darkness, we lie, and do not the truth: But if we walk in the light, as he is in the light, we have fellowship one with another, and the blood of Jesus

---

[4] Psalm 15:5; Philippians 2:2, 20; 4:16-18
[5] Strong's Exhaustive Concordance, #5426
[6] Colossians 3:2-3
[7] Matthew 26:36-42; John 5:19, 10:17-18; Philippians 2:5-8
[8] Philippians 2:1-5
[9] John 1:29; Philippians 2:6-8

Christ his Son cleanseth us from all sin" (1 John 1:6-7, parenthesis added).

Fellowship results in an upright life. Godly living ensures fellowship between those who belong to Jesus. Such fellowship finds its common ground at the point of love and devotion towards Him. It also keeps His people upright as Jesus' light reveals sin, causing each believer to seek forgiveness, cleansing, and restoration when necessary.

To share in fellowship means that one is also a partaker of Jesus' grace. Communion represents a table where one partakes of Jesus as the bread to maintain his or her spiritual life. It means coming to this table daily for the Living Water that He alone uncaps in our very being. Obviously, as we walk through this world, we must daily come to this table of abundance to spiritually rest and be nourished and refreshed.[10]

What does it take to come into a place of abiding fellowship? The answer is suffering. Identification and fellowship in the kingdom of God entail suffering. It is suffering that makes us more pliable in the hands of God. Otherwise, our self-sufficiency will cause resistance to His ways. Our independence will try to find ways around His work. Our rebellion will oppose Him as we harden our hearts towards Him.

Without suffering, there is no way that we are able to identify or enter in with those who are suffering. As our example, Jesus encountered suffering so that He would understand the discipline of obedience and become perfected in His humanity. As a result, He became the author of eternal salvation for those who obey Him.[11]

Jesus' commanded His followers to deny self, pick up their crosses, and follow Him. Personal suffering comes through self-denial. However, if the personal cross is not properly applied, the old man insists on becoming a suffering martyr. It is at the point of personal suffering that many Christians perceive that they are paying the price in their Christian life. Such a conclusion is untrue. Suffering that comes through sacrificial love, devotion, and obedience to God is not only a point of identification with our Lord, it is our reasonable service.[12]

Godless perceptions of suffering became a breeding ground for another gospel. It is known as altruism. Altruism expresses itself as an unselfish regard or devotion to the welfare of others, even at the expense of personal well-being. Although altruism appears to be Christian in displaying admirable qualities of sacrifice for the benefit of others, it overemphasizes self-denial, while nobly promoting its selfless sacrifice and devotion. Up front, it seems meritorious, glorious, and very religious. However, when you peek behind the cloak it exalts the idea of self-sacrifice, but lacks the cross of Jesus and true faith. Confidence is put in man denying himself of any real pleasure and sacrificing all for the sake of his devotion to others, rather than possessing the Person of Jesus.

---

[10] John 6:35; 7:36-38
[11] 2 Corinthians 1:3-7; Hebrews 5:8-9
[12] Matthew 16:24; Romans 12:1-2

Such an emphasis on man's sacrifice is idolatrous and humanistic. As the Apostle Paul declared, you can show incredible faith and give of yourself sacrificially, but if you do not have the real love of God motivating you, it means nothing in the scheme of things.[13] Ultimately, such attempts subtly exalt the so-called "goodness" of man, while demoting the harsh reality of sin and the cross of Jesus.

As Jesus stated, no one is good but God; therefore, goodness can only come from God.[14] It is as man gives way to God that God's goodness can be expressed through man to others. Such goodness will not exalt man, but God.

For the Christian, the cross of Jesus is not just about self-denial and sacrifice. Rather, it represents the great exchange. The Gospel is a powerful revelation of this great exchange. The exchange is nothing more than putting off the old man in order to put on the new man. Jesus' cross represents the place of exchange, while the daily application of the personal cross serves as the means of working the new man into His followers.[15]

People, who get caught up in a life of denying themselves for the benefits of others, including their religious beliefs, do not understand the real purpose behind the Christian life. Christians are not here to promote self-denial or sacrifice. As believers, we are here to worship and bring glory to God. God is glorified when Jesus is being reflected in our lives. Therefore, the purpose of self-denial and the application of the cross is not to make us glorious martyrs on the altars of religion so that others can admire our devotion to Jesus. Rather, denial of and death to self are to bring forth the new man so that Jesus can be lifted up as the means of salvation and God can be glorified.

For religious people to establish personal righteousness in self-denial and sacrificial giving simply reflects their best attempts to make themselves acceptable to God. Their endeavor to apply the cross does not constitute death to the old man. Rather, it makes this rebellious entity a martyr who will be exalted and complimented for being noble. Such attempts make these people's lives extreme, unrealistic, morbid, and unattractive to others. These individuals will often reflect a life that is empty as well as absent of joy and peace. They actually become burdened under the harsh taskmasters of useless, religious exercises that rob them of the abundant life, rather than their life being defined in light of Jesus.

The Apostle Paul understood the aspect of suffering associated with the Gospel. When Jesus told His disciples to daily pick up a personal cross and follow Him, it had nothing to do with sacrifice, but with being willing to experience whatever personal loss was necessary to gain his or her life in Jesus. Personal loss can be a valuable avenue that allows a

---

[13] 1 Corinthians 13:1-3
[14] Matthew 19:16-17; Romans 3:10, 12
[15] Romans 6:2-8; 13:14; Ephesians 4:22-32; Colossians 3:5-17

believer to gain the real and eternal riches of heaven.[16] Gaining such a life would prove to be contrary to the former life. It speaks of struggle and death. The Apostle Paul not only understood this identity and fellowship, but summarized it in this way, "That I may know him, and the power of his resurrection and the fellowship of his sufferings, being made conformable unto his death" (Philippians 3:10).

In Philippians 2, Paul talked about what Jesus gave up and endured to become identified with us on the cross at Calvary to secure redemption. In Philippians 3, he talked about what he willingly lost in order to possess Christ. In fact, he counted all things loss to gain the excellence of the knowledge of Christ. His whole focus was to win Jesus. He considered his rich heritage as a Pharisee loss. He regarded his Roman citizenship as a means that gave him certain privileges. However, in light of his heavenly citizenship, it was all dung. He realized that his fleshly circumcision had no significance in light of those who were circumcised in heart, for they were the ones who worshipped God in spirit and always rejoiced in the reality of Jesus. Obviously, Paul's past life and the present world held no meaning, purpose, or worth to him.

The Apostle Paul wanted to experience the power of Jesus' resurrection in the midst of a dying world. He wanted to fellowship in His sufferings so that he could be glorified with Him.[17] He wanted to be made conformable unto his death so that he could declare with certainty, "I live; yet not I, but Christ liveth in me" (Galatians 2:20b).

Paul had his sights on one goal, to apprehend Christ and to be apprehended by Him. His whole heart was to possess Jesus and be possessed by Him. He knew that Jesus was the real prize and that the life he was being called to was not of this world. It was a life that had no earthly designs, no fleshly significance, and no worldly attachments. It was Jesus alone who stood in Paul's sights. He was consumed and compelled in his constant pursuit to become identified with Jesus and to fellowship with Him.

In Paul's mind, he knew that all the suffering in his present age was worth it. He made this statement in 2 Corinthians 4:10-11, "Always bearing about in the body the dying of the Lord Jesus, that the life also of Jesus might be made manifest in our body. For we which live are always delivered unto death for Jesus' sake, that the life also of Jesus might be made manifest in our mortal flesh."

It was the reality of Jesus that made Paul rejoice. He rejoiced in his weakness, for he knew Jesus' strength would be realized. He rejoiced in his prison chains, for he knew the liberty he had in Christ. Clearly, he knew the joy of his suffering, for Christ was being formed in him. He understood the joy of dying to his old life, for he would experience the

---

[16] Luke 9:23-24; Philippians 1:21-23; 3:7-8
[17] Romans 8:17; Galatians 6:14

power of Jesus' resurrection.[18] This is why he was able to declare, "Rejoice in the Lord always: and again I say, Rejoice" (Philippians 4:4).

The Apostle Paul lived, walked, breathed, and pursued the reality of the Gospel. He knew there was a glorious fellowship in it that could not be realized at any other point or in any other way except in Jesus. Is it any wonder that he said, "For I determined not to know any thing among you, save Jesus Christ, and him crucified" (1 Corinthians 2:2).

My heart has been to experience the reality of the Gospel as Paul did, but am I willing to pay the price of suffering? How much of a value am I willing to put on coming into a place of true fellowship with Jesus? Do I have the sobriety of a King David who said, "I will surely buy it of thee at a price: neither will I offer burnt offerings unto the LORD my God of that which doth cost me nothing" (2 Samuel 24:24). Although salvation is free, knowing Jesus is not. I must be willing to pay the price of what I value about this present life and world to possess the inheritance of the next world.

Am I like Solomon who declared in Proverbs 23:23, "Buy the truth, and sell it not; also wisdom, and instruction, and understanding?" Am I willing to allow my foundations to be shaken, my present reality challenged down to its last abyss, and my dreams shattered in millions of pieces so I can accept, believe, receive, value, and love the truth of Jesus above all else?[19]

I can nobly declare such things, but is it in my heart to possess this reality? Has this reality invaded every fiber of my being? Is it my consuming reality or a passing fancy or fad that temporarily holds my attention, only to give way to selfish affections that lead me elsewhere in other pursuits?

The Apostle Paul had gained Christ. He was willing to suffer any loss and experience any opposition to know fellowship with his Lord. In his fellowship of the Gospel, he did learn how to rejoice. He worried about nothing for he knew with confidence who would hear his requests. Even though he experienced adversity, he knew real peace because he kept Jesus in center focus in his heart and mind. He practiced what he learned. He received both the good and the challenging aspects of his life in Christ with gratitude. Paul had learned to hear the Spirit and see the reality of heaven. As a result, he learned to be content in whatever state he found himself. He knew where his strength came from, as well as who supplied all of his needs. He was a man who knew the depth of joy in the midst of suffering, as well as the abiding presence of peace in the midst of great loss.[20]

Paul also struggled with and wept over those who were the enemies of the cross. Apparently, these enemies claimed to be part of the Church. However, Paul instructed the Philippians to mark them. He distinguished

---

[18] 2 Corinthians 12:9-11
[19] Hebrews 12:26-27
[20] Philippians 3:6-11, 13, 19

these enemies in three ways: their god is their belly, glory is their shame, and they mind earthly things. Obviously, these people were idolatrous in their pursuits and worship. What were they worshipping? From what I perceive, they were worshipping their fleshly appetites. Such pursuits can become lustful, greedy, obsessive, gluttonous, and empty. Perhaps this is why Paul instructed the Philippians to let all things be done in moderation.[21]

The next insight to these enemies of the cross is that their glory is their shame or reproach. Such people are glorying in things other than God. Many are glorying in self, riches, or abilities. However, to glory in anything but God will end in shame or reproach.

This brings us to why they were idolatrous and glorying in that which had no significance other than to bring destruction to their souls. They minded earthly things. In other words, their affections belonged to the things of this world. They were attached to the things of this earth.

Is there a gospel that promotes such a pursuit? The answer is yes. There is a gospel that encourages people to actually become an enemy of the cross. Keep in mind, the purpose of the cross of Christ became a point of identification and fellowship with God.

Jesus became identified with us so that we could be made into the righteousness of God. He was lifted on a cross so that He could become the ladder between man and God. As a ladder He would bring reconciliation and restoration to a relationship that was lost in the Garden of Eden.[22] Therefore, those who serve as enemies of the cross would promote that which cost nothing. They would promote a gospel that compliments the fleshly appetites, rather than a call for self-denial and crucifixion to embrace the new, powerful life of Jesus. The gospel that fits into this category is what I refer to as the "Hollywood Gospel."

The Hollywood Gospel is nothing but a gospel of fantasy. This gospel attracts people on the basis that God wants them to be happy, prosperous, and free from problems. It presents the idea of a good or perfect life. At the core of this self-serving gospel is self-esteem. In fact, self-esteem is at the core of many of the popular heretical gospels. Christianity simply becomes a means by which self can be realize as one benefits on an earthly plane, rather than discover God and His eternal perspective.

The fantasy gospel offers romantic notions about the Christian walk, sensationalism in regards to the supernatural life, and a comfortable religion that allows one to enjoy both the world and God's blessings without personal cost or loss. However, this gospel makes people indifferent to the purpose of the cross—identification and fellowship.

The baby boomer generation was quite smitten with this gospel, but, amazingly, it holds little attraction to this present generation. The present generation has seen the vanity of such a fantasy. In fact, they have

---

[21] Phil. 3:18-19; 4:5
[22] 2 Corinthians 5:18-21

become victims of it. They have been inundated with things in place of personal relationships and investments. They are surrounded by things, but are miserable and lost in all of it. In fact, they are quite bored with it. Romantic notions have turned into lust, sensationalism has become reality television, the supernatural has turned into an attraction to the occult, and the comfortable religion is considered a farce.

As a result, the Hollywood Gospel has lost much of its original glory, but it has conditioned much of the Church to pursue and embrace the world, coming under its spirit. Today, people are running to movies where Jesus' death is sensationalized, rather than to the Bible where His life, examples, death, burial, and resurrection are realized through faith, obedience, and application. It is clear that the Church has been conditioned to prefer the world's presentations and methods to the reality of the cross.

Since the Hollywood Gospel has lost its original luster, it has given way to the latest craze or fad in the kingdom of God—the gospel of personal fulfillment. Instead of unbelievers being considered lost, they are now regarded as the "unchurched". Such a term implies that people's salvation does not hinge on being found by God through His grace and forgiveness of sin, but on the fact that they are not going to some type of church.

Since people are "unchurched", all that needs to be done is find the means to attract them to the churches by appealing to that which is unfulfilled. Supposedly, the worldly church experience will stir them up, and then they will be attracted to what is being offered. Hence, enters the seeker-friendly churches. In the case of the seeker-friendly churches, popular attractions of the world are employed such as entertainment, coffee, and a McDonalds type of environment to attract "unchurched" people into their corridors. The difference between the Hollywood version of the Gospel and the newest version is that the Hollywood Gospel pursued the good life, while the seeker-friendly churches are setting up an environment where one can feel fulfilled and good about him or herself.

Since the goal is to simply get people into church to expose them to Christ, every harsh truth of sin, self-denial, and death has been watered down. The purpose for such fluff is to establish an environment where people will not be offended, convicted, or challenged. As a result, people of the world are flocking into these churches, but not to do business with God. They are coming to have some type of religious experience that will make them feel good about themselves and life. The tragedy behind this fantasy is that it simply makes people comfortable in their dead spiritual state so they can happily slide into the abyss of hell. The end result of such a gospel for all involved is destruction. This gospel clearly serves as an enemy of the real Gospel. Such a gospel lulls people to sleep, preventing unsuspecting victims from seeing their need for salvation or their ultimate destruction.

Challenging the Christian Life

To add Christianity to an earthly perspective and preference means that true faith in the Son of God has not been properly applied. Hebrews 4:2 talks about this condition, "For unto us was the gospel preached, as well as unto them: but the word preached did not profit them, not being mixed with faith in them that heard it." The people in this Scripture reference were the children of Israel. They had misdirected faith that caused them to be idolatrous and rebellious. As a result, they never entered into the rest that can be found in the promises of God.

Many people put faith in what God can give or do. In such cases, the Christian life ceases to be about redemption, but about identifying the so-called "goodness" that is found in people and experiencing the fullness of this present world. In fact, much of the Christian life in America is viewed as being a spiritual Disneyland. Eventually, this Disneyland gives way to disillusionment about true Christianity when reality collides with such a delusion.

The true Gospel is not realized in the good life, but in fellowship found in suffering for the sake of knowing and possessing Jesus. The true attraction to Christianity is not found in this world's methods and philosophies, rather it is found when Jesus is truly being lifted up as God's only solution for what ails us. Granted, Jesus will not draw the "unchurched" people to His nail-pierced hands, but He will draw those who are lost and seeking the solution to their lost, empty lives.[23]

It is time we do away with unrealistic gospels and believe the Word of God. After all, Jesus never promised such fantasies. He actually guaranteed tribulation. The Apostle Paul stated that we must die to live, and we must suffer in order to reign and be glorified with our Lord. He also stated that all who live godly in Christ will suffer persecution.[24] Acts 14:22 summarizes the harsh reality of the Christian life in this way, "Confirming the souls of the disciples, and exhorting them to continue in the faith, and that we must through much tribulation enter into the kingdom of God."

Perhaps, you have come to the idea of Christ because of a morbid presentation of self-denial or the Hollywood version of the Gospel. You have seen it as a way of being righteous or a means of escape, rather than a life that must be embraced in spirit and truth. Maybe you wanted to feel good about something and felt that the latest gospel would add something to your life, but now you are empty.

The Gospel is not about finding personal righteousness or happiness in this world, but about finding the heavenly promise of Jesus Christ in the midst of that which is temporary and stands condemned. The Christian life is not about being a glorious martyr or having a good life. Rather, it is about discovering real life in Christ. This life is not about what you can do for God or what He can do for you. Rather, it is about

---

[23] John 12:32
[24] John 16:33; Romans 8:17; 2 Timothy 2:11-12; 3:12

allowing God to have His way in your life so that you can discover and obtain an eternal inheritance.

If you have bought any of these counterfeit versions of Christianity, turn from the delusion and the disillusionment of it to the real Jesus. Make Him your focus and pursue Him with everything in you. As the Word says, He will be found by you.[25]

---

[25] Jeremiah 29:13

9

THE HOPE OF THE GOSPEL

We have been considering the reality of the Gospel in Paul's letters. The reality of the Gospel brings us to the truth and work of the Gospel in our Christian lives. Believing the Gospel is what opens up the door to eternal life for each of us. However, discovering its power in our lives is what produces the abundant or complete life. The abundant life has to do with discovering our position or place in Christ.

The full life is brought out in Paul's epistles. For example, in the letter to the Romans, we are baptized into Jesus and buried with Him in His death. This ensures that we will be raised up in newness of life. In Corinthians, Jesus serves as our wisdom, righteousness, sanctification, and redemption, implying that we stand complete in this incredible life. Galatians shows that we have liberty in Christ, giving us the means to discover the new life. In Ephesians, we are seated in high places with Him, allowing us a different perspective of this promised life in light of an eternal inheritance. In Philippians, our conversations, lives, and citizenships are in heaven, changing our purpose in regard to this life. However, Colossians presents the summary of the Christian life, "To whom God would make known what is the riches of the glory of this mystery among the Gentiles; which is Christ in you, the hope of glory" (Colossians 1:27).[1] Positionally, we are in Christ, capable of discovering our lives in Him. Jesus in us is the One who is actually establishing His life through the presence of the Holy Ghost.

The letter to the Colossians shows how the Gospel produces hope in light of Christ in us. In fact, the Apostle Paul made reference to this in Colossians 1:5, "For the hope which is laid up for you in heaven, whereof ye heard before in the word of truth of the gospel." The Christian life is full of hope. The hope that is laid up in heaven is found in Jesus who sits on the right side of the Father. He is the light of truth in the Gospel. However, this hope is only realized when the life of Jesus is being formed in us.[2]

Positionally, we must discover our life in Christ. This life is rich, full, and satisfying. However, positionally, Christ in us ensures the means by which we can discover this life and obtain our inheritance. Ephesians

---

[1] Romans 6:1-5; 1 Corinthians 1:30; Galatians 5:1; Ephesians 2:6
[2] John 14:6; Acts 2:33; Hebrews 8:1

confirmed that this life is present through the abiding presence of the Holy Spirit.[3]

What significance does the glory of Jesus play in our lives? In Romans, we are told that sin has caused us to fall short of the glory of God. Many people think that falling short has to do with doing right. However, falling short of the glory of God means that we are failing to reach our potential. Man's original potential was to reflect God's glory. Because of sin, that potential has been marred. As a result, man is reflecting the essence of a selfish disposition, while representing the interest and influence of the god of this world, Satan.[4]

We must be restored to a state where we once again reflect the glory of God. In the Christian life, this means reflecting Jesus Christ. In order to be brought to this state, we must go through a process that involves suffering. We talked about suffering in regards to identification and fellowship, but it is also a necessary process to possess His glory. Romans tells us that we must suffer with Him in order to be glorified with Him. Corinthians informs us that we must be partakers of Christ's sufferings to bring consolation to others. The Apostle Paul instructs believers in Galatians to only glory in the cross of Christ, while he told Timothy that those who suffer with Him will reign with Him.[5]

The glory of Jesus must be experienced on a personal level. Corinthians tells us that the glory of Jesus must be reflected in us. In Ephesians, glory is associated with our inheritance, and, in Philippians, it is related to riches that are found in Christ Jesus. In Colossians, this glory is clearly revealed as being the person of Jesus Christ.[6]

Glory is associated with dignity, honor, praise, worship, and exaltation.[7] This brings us to Paul's presentation of Jesus in Colossians. The hope of the Gospel is the Person of Jesus. Therefore, the hope of the Good News is associated with Jesus being honored in a way that He is worthy of. As Paul stated in Philippians 2:9-10, "Wherefore God also hath highly exalted him, and given him a name which is above every name: That at the name of Jesus every knee should bow, of things in heaven, and things in earth, and things under the earth." He must be exalted in our lives.

If we exalt Jesus in our lives, His glory will begin to be realized and manifested in and through us. It is the glory of Christ in believers that attracts wandering souls to the Gospel.[8] The reason this glory has this affect is because of what it reveals about Jesus. In fact, this glory gives us insight into the Person of Jesus. It is because of who He is that He deserves honor, adoration, praise, worship, and admiration.

---

[3] Ephesians 1:9-14
[4] John 8:44; Romans 3:23; Ephesians 2:2-3;
[5] Romans 8:17; 2 Corinthians 1:3-9; Galatians 6:14
[6] 2 Corinthians 3:18; Ephesians 1:17-18; Philippians 1:27
[7] Strong's Exhaustive Concordance; #1391 & 2744
[8] John 12:32

We were told in Philippians that Jesus had to give up His original capacity or majesty to take on the disposition of a servant and to be fashioned as a man.[9] The Apostle John gave us this insight about Jesus' glory in John 1:14, "And the Word was made flesh, and dwelt among us, (and we beheld his glory, the glory as of the only begotten of the Father,) full of grace and truth." John witnessed the unveiling of Jesus' glory on the Mount of Transfiguration.[10]

The reality of this glory is that such honor is due to only one entity—God. The Apostle Paul clearly presented Jesus as God Incarnate, God in the Flesh, or the second Person of the Godhead in Colossians. The first presentation of Jesus in Colossians is as the Son of God. Paul informed us as believers, that the Father has made us fit to be partakers of the inheritance of saints. He is the One who has delivered us from the power of darkness and translated us into the kingdom of his dear Son.[11]

In Colossians 1:15, Paul stated that Jesus is the image of the invisible God. As the Son, Jesus is equal with the Father in nature, power, and authority. Therefore, Jesus was not simply a visible reflection of God in His humanity, but He also possessed the very nature of God. He had to take on the body of man to become the Lamb of God that would take away the sin of the world, while maintaining His deity.[12]

God, taking on flesh while maintaining His deity, is the mystery that Paul is talking about in Ephesians and Colossians. This mystery cannot be understood on an intellectual level. In fact, to try to understand it causes people to go into unbelief. Unbelief in this arena often turns into heresy as people try to explain the mystery on an intellectual level in order to make sense out it.

Today, there are cults which deny the deity of Christ, yet claim to be "Christian." They have reasoned His deity away in their intellectual conclusions. Ultimately, Jesus is stripped of His power and authority. Of course, such people reason that Jesus is simply a reflection of God and that He has been given all power and authority. It is true that Jesus gave up His power and authority as God. His example in His humanity simply shows us that all power and authority come from God. As servants we must come under the authority of God to receive authority to overcome and power to stand.

The idea that Jesus is simply a reflection of God may sound logical, but it is not consistent with Scripture. For example, as Christians, we are to reflect Jesus. We have been endued with power from above and given authority, but we still do not have the means to save anyone, nor do we receive worship that only God can lay claim to. Jesus not only receives

---

[9] Philippians 2:6-7
[10] Matthew 17:1-9
[11] Colossians 1:12-13
[12] John 1:29; 5:17-18

worship from men and angels, but He is able to save because of who He is, God Incarnate.[13]

It is important to realize that, as an obedient servant, Jesus subjected all of His authority as God to the Father, and, as Man, He limited His power according to the will of the Father. However, all power in heaven and earth was given back to Him as man to carry out His commission.[14]

It is the Holy Ghost who reveals the mystery of Jesus as God Incarnate to the hearts of men. But, before He can reveal this incredible mystery about God becoming man, man must choose to believe the witness of Jesus that the Word clearly outlines. Without the application of faith, the Holy Ghost will not be able to confirm this mystery as a reality.[15]

Sadly, the mystery about Jesus remains unknown to those who refuse to believe the record that has been given about Jesus' identity. Such people possess another Jesus, and have been brought under an antichrist spirit. Even though they claim that Jesus saves, they are presenting a Jesus who has no authority with the Father or power to save man from his hopeless plight.[16]

As Man, Jesus subjected Himself to various temptations, rejection, and, finally, death on the cross. The subjection to the cross was the means of redeeming man back from the claims, works, and consequences of sin. However, as God, He proved victorious over death by His resurrection. God is accredited for raising Jesus, but, as you study Scripture, Jesus said He would raise Himself. Scripture also states that the Father and the Spirit raised Him. Once again, this points to the Godhead. All three persons of the Godhead were involved in Jesus' resurrection.[17]

Paul confirmed Jesus' deity in Colossians in a couple of ways. The first way is that he told us that all things were created by Him.[18] The concept of creation immediately takes us back to Genesis 1:1, "In the beginning God created the heaven and the earth." The Apostle John made reference to Jesus being the Creator in John 1:1-3. He had created everything that is in heaven and earth. This includes all that is visible and invisible, whether they are thrones, dominions, principalities, or powers.

Since Jesus is the Creator, it is by Him that all things exist.[19] The Apostle Paul talked about the Creator in this way, "For in him we live, and move, and have our being" (Acts 17:28a).

---

[13] Matthew 4:10; 28:18-20; Luke 24:49; 2 Corinthians 3:18
[14] Matthew 28:18
[15] Ephesians 1:17-18; Colossians 1:26-27
[16] 1 John 5:11-13
[17] John 2:19-22; 1 Corinthians 15:15; Galatians 1:1
[18] John 1:29; Colossians 1:15
[19] Colossians 1:16-17

Paul also verified that Jesus was before all things. The Apostle John told us that, as the Word, Jesus existed in the beginning, He was with God, and He is God.[20] John the Baptist, who was physically older than Jesus by at least six months, stated this of Jesus, "He that cometh after me is preferred before me: for he was before me" (John 1:15c).

Jesus said of Himself in John 8:58, "Verily, verily, I say unto you, Before Abraham was, I am." Obviously, Jesus existed before His incarnate state.

The Apostle Paul stated this about Jesus, "For in him dwelleth all the fulness of the Godhead bodily" (Colossians 2:9)." When you look up "Godhead" in the *Strong's Exhaustive Concordance,* it means divinity.[21] Therefore, Jesus possessed the fullness of divinity in bodily form. He was not just a visible expression of God in bodily form, but He possessed the very nature of God, the fullness of deity. In fact, Paul told us that it pleased the Father that in Jesus should all the fullness dwell.[22]

It is at the point of embracing the mystery of God that hearts will be comforted and knitted together in love. Paul reminded us that it is in Christ that all the treasures of wisdom and knowledge are hidden. Believers are complete in Him, who is not only the head of all principalities and power, but also the head of the Body of believers. Jesus is the firstborn from the dead that, in all things, He might have preeminence. Once again, "head" implies that He is our source of inspiration and function. "Firstborn" points to His resurrection in a glorified body. As our preeminence, Jesus must rank first in our life and serve as our foremost influence.[23] Such preeminence points to Him being God, for only God can rightfully hold this position in a person's life.

It is also in this letter that the apostle makes mention of the philosophies of the world.[24] These philosophies subtly replace the truth of Jesus. When the truth is compromised or done away with, the very image of Christ will be changed or adjusted to fit the philosophy. As you study the philosophies of the world, you can discover one common denominator. They are humanistic in nature. In other words, they exalt man's wisdom over God's wisdom.

There are many humanistic philosophies that I have already made reference to, such as the New Age belief that exalts creation over the Creator. Another good example of worldly philosophies is humanism. This popular belief is at the core of all humanistic philosophies, such as the theory of evolution. This belief judges the worth of a person on the basis of what he or she can offer to society. The Church has rejected many of these humanistic philosophies. However, there is one worldly philosophy the Church has erroneously embraced—psychology.

---

[20] John 1:1
[21] # 2320
[22] Colossians 1:19
[23] Strong's Exhaustive Concordance, *#4409*
[24] Colossians 2:8

Psychology has become a sacred cow in the Church. This demonically-inspired and worldly philosophy has been exalted over the wisdom of God and negates the final authority of the Word. It has replaced the Counselor (Jesus) with man's understanding and made His counseling guide (the Bible) obsolete and ineffective to address present day problems. Instead of people being brought back to the Word for counseling and instruction, they are sent to psychologists who help them realize their godless attitudes and sins are not their fault. After all, these people just lack self-esteem and, if they could see their personal worth, they would change their ways.

According to psychology, sin is no longer sin. The blame for moral breakdowns has been shifted back on to parents, society, or "bad breaks," alleviating a person of responsibility and accountability. Sin is now considered hereditary problem or a disease, but not a preference of selfishness or a choice of rebellion and independence from God's rule and authority.

It is God's unshakeable truth, not psychology that sets people free of what ails them. The truth is that it is true humility before God, brokenness over sin, and sincere repentance that will restore man's sanity and peace of mind in a world of hopelessness and darkness. This is why truth strips away all cloaks to reveal sin. It shakes all faulty foundations, challenges all wrong ways of thinking, exposes selfish motives, demands self-denial, exalts the way of the cross, and results in obedience to the Word of God. In fact, we are sanctified through the truth of God's Word.[25]

The truth leads us back to Jesus for forgiveness, reconciliation, and restoration with God. And, what we discover is that what really ails people emotionally and spiritually is that they are not at peace with God because their sin has broken fellowship with Him.[26]

Psychology, at best, tacks Jesus on, but it ultimately transfers Jesus to the background as it declares His Word to be obsolete or ineffective. Ultimately, it becomes the final authority and solution to man's behavior and spiritual state in many Christian camps.

Although many Christians try to justify the existences of psychology in the Church, they refuse to admit that it is humanistic by nature. It is therefore, unholy by nature and will defile that which is holy.[27] Even though these people can point to popular counselors and psychologists as a good indication to this philosophy's worth, they fail to realize that many of these individuals are not popular because of their degrees in psychology. Rather, their attraction is the fact they use common sense with the practical experiences of life and manage to cut through people's delusions and foolishness. Common sense is attractive at any level, but it must not be mistaken for psychology or the wisdom of God.

---

[25] John 8:32; 15:22, 17:17; Hebrews 4:12
[26] John 14:6; Colossians 1:20-21
[27] 2 Corinthians 6:14-18

Christians must also keep in mind that it was psychology that was used to put Christians in Russian prisons. Today, psychologists are used in court to deem someone sane or insane in a commission of a crime. They are often the final authority to a person's ability to function in this world. As the world becomes more skeptical towards Christian's values, who or what will ultimately be used to determine if certain values constitute sanity? Is the Church content to leave such matters in the hands of that which is godless and contrary to the Word's evaluation?

This brings us to the shadow that was cast in the Old Testament. So much of the world's philosophies and ways make Jesus a shadow that is vague. The Apostle Paul made this statement about Jesus, "Which are a shadow of things to come; but the body is of Christ" (Colossians 2:17). The Jewish tabernacle, furnishings, feasts, and rituals were a shadow of things to come. A shadow cannot be cast unless light is present to cast an image. Therefore, the light that cast the shadow in the Old Testament was revealing something that was already existing and real. But what were the light and the image that was being outlined by the shadows of the Old Testament? John confirms that Jesus is the light, while Paul verifies that He is also the image.[28]

1 John 1:5 tells us that God is light. Once again, we see that Paul is pointing to Jesus as God Incarnate. For years, the Jews were waiting for the visible appearance of the image, but, when He did come, they rejected Him.[29] Jesus did not come in the way they expected Him. Instead of coming as a Victorious King, He came as a sacrifice that would be offered up on the cross in humility.

Today, many people have kept Jesus as the shadow. He is not real, nor is He reigning. He is a concept at best, a doctrine that is in flux due to convenience, or concrete theology that keeps Him in a comfortable box. But, as a shadow, Jesus has no dimension. He is treated as a mere force or a puppet that can be controlled, but not as the Living God who deserves to be glorified.

Other people are maintaining the shadows of the Old Testament, while tacking Jesus on to their rituals. In such cases, the shadows are being exalted and pursued, while Jesus, the image, remains obscure. The Apostle Paul made this statement about Jesus, "Blotting out the handwriting of ordinances that was against us, which was contrary to us, and took it out of the way, nailing it to his cross" (Colossians 2:14). Christ nailed all the ordinances to the cross. As a result, He remains standing as the fulfillment of every shadow that was cast in the Old Testament. After all, a shadow cannot die on the cross for you. Christ serving as the fulfillment of the shadows of the old is also clearly upheld in the Gospels.

When Jesus was on the Mount of Transfiguration, He stood with Moses, the great lawgiver, and Elijah, the great prophet. We see that the flesh of Jesus parted to reveal His glory as God. It was after Jesus' glory

---

[28] John 1:4-5, 9
[29] John 1:10-11

was revealed, and the Father introduced Him as His Son, that Moses (the Law) and Elijah (prophecies) gave way to Jesus Christ. After all, He would fulfill the Law and the words of the prophets; therefore, He alone stood before His disciples. No one can claim such preeminence unless He is God.[30]

It is because Jesus is who He is that He is able to save us to the uttermost. It is through His blood that we obtain forgiveness of sins, find peace, and experience reconciliation.[31] The Apostle Paul gave us insight into the final product of Jesus' death, "In the body of his flesh through death, to present you holy and unblameable and unreproveable in his sight" (Colossians 1:22). The blood of Jesus cleanses us from sin, making us stand free of accusation. His blood has purged us so that we can stand faultless before God. Because of His blood, we have been made near to God by way of an everlasting covenant.[32]

The blood of Jesus is also under attack. The first way it is being attacked is through modern translations. The mention of the blood of Jesus is being alleviated in many of these new translations, along with other fundamental beliefs of the Christian faith. Such alleviation may be acceptable to our politically correct society, but it does not change the fact that, without the shedding of blood, there is no remission of sins.[33] Without the remission of sins, there will be no forgiveness. Without forgiveness, there cannot be any reconciliation between man and God.

The twisting or redefining of God in many of these translations has concerned me. As I was struggling over this issue, I remembered that the purpose of these translations was to help people to understand the Bible. Although the intentions may have been good, these translations have taken the inspiration and mystery out of the Bible. In other words, people think they now understand the mysteries of the Bible; therefore, they do not need to dig, seek, meditate, study, or challenge themselves to come to a greater knowledge of Jesus. Since they assume they understand the Word because they have this easy-reading bible, they do not see a need for the inspiration of the Holy Spirit to bring revelation or expose the depths of the mysteries of God. However, without the Holy Spirit, the Word remains lifeless and ineffective.

The end product is that many Christians have become increasingly ignorant about the character of God and His ways as they major in man-made doctrine and theology and minor in biblical principles and eternal truths. They are not partaking of or assimilating the Word. Rather, they are just fitting it into their intellectual arrogance. As a result, there is a famine of the true Word of God developing in our country. Even though we are a nation that has many Bibles, we are suffering spiritual malnutrition as we become more indifferent to the Spirit and truth of God.

---

[30] Matthew 5:17-18; Romans 10:4
[31] Colossians 1:14, 20; Hebrews 7:25
[32] Hebrews 9:22; 1 John 1:7
[33] Hebrew 9:22

This alleviation of Jesus' blood produces a bloodless religion. If you take away the sacrifice of Jesus, He becomes merely one of the New Age way-showers, rather than The Way to obtain eternal life. He is redefined as a good man, a great prophet, and a noble martyr, but not the Lamb of God who came to take away the sin of the world.[34]

What is sad about the alleviation of Jesus' blood from Scripture is that many Christians are not concerned. They are not outraged that a fundamental truth of the Christian faith is being discarded in books that are promoted as the inspired Word of God. In fact, they eagerly buy these so-called bibles and defend their erroneous presentations with zeal.

Another affront to the blood of Jesus is the counterfeit bloodline. Satan has counterfeited everything of God. The blood of Jesus is no exception. What many fail to realize is that the blood of Jesus represents the place of defeat for Satan. He hates the blood of Jesus.

A former witch told me that there was a red circle painted on the floor at the entrance inside the door of her coven. This mark represented the blood of Jesus. Every time the members walked through the door, they had to stomp on this red mark. One day, she asked what the significance was of this activity. She was gravely disciplined for it. After she became a Christian, she asked me why the blood of Jesus was so important. I suddenly realized what emphasis Satan was putting on the blood among his own followers. Sadly, he understands the significance of the blood more than most Christians.

In some so-called Christian camps, the reference to Jesus' blood is used as a type of magic wand to control their reality in the area of power and authority, rather than as the payment for our sins. It is important to point out that the blood of Jesus was not unique in itself. Granted, it was not tainted by the mark of death that has been passed down upon all men from Adam. Besides being void of the mark of death, the important aspect about the blood is the fact that it came from the veins of the sinless Lamb of God, God Incarnate that makes it valuable. He allowed His blood to be shed for us to buy us back from the bondage of sin. When our lives are marked by His sacrifice, His blood serves as a mark of ownership in our lives. Satan cannot intrude into that ownership without God's permission.[35]

The sacrifice of Jesus dealt a deadly blow to Satan's kingdom. No doubt, this foe undermines it from every angle. Hence, enters the counterfeit bloodline that supposedly belongs to the Messiah. The idea of this belief found its origins in the gnostic gospels such as the Gospel of Thomas and the Gospel of Mary. It is gaining popularity through the fictitious book, *The DaVinci Code* by Dan Brown. However, this belief about a messianic bloodline is not new. It is part of the belief systems found in Gnosticism and secret societies such as the Freemasons and

---

[34] John 1:29; 14:6
[35] 1 Corinthians 6:20; Hebrews 10:1-10

cults such as Mormonism. Until recently, this so-called "bloodline" remained hidden from public view and fell into the category of the mystery of iniquity, which the Bible claims will be revealed in the end days.[36] Now, it is blatantly being presented from various media resources. Books, as well as recent documentaries, have exposed this mystery in great detail. Granted, the beliefs may vary according to the organization, but the core of it remains intact.

The belief is that Jesus did not die on the cross, but was taken by His followers when He was put in the grave. Supposedly, He was taken to Europe where He married Mary Magdalene. They had children. Their offspring makes up this bloodline. This bloodline apparently made up the royalty bloodline of France. Secret societies have guarded the so-called "integrity" of this bloodline that still exists and will eventually be revealed to the world. Their attempts have resulted in occult practices, conspiracies, murders, and secret involvement in world events, but, meanwhile, society is being conditioned to accept the counterfeit through the media blitz and promotion of this belief.

Obviously, this belief demotes Jesus to mere man, thus, alleviating Him as being God, as well as His resurrection that serves as the proof of His deity. Clearly, this heretical belief does away with the true Gospel. Paul said it best in Romans 10:9-10,

> That if thou shalt confess with thy mouth the Lord Jesus, and shalt believe in thine heart that God hath raised him for the dead, thou shalt be saved. For with the heart man believeth unto righteousness; and with the mouth confession is made unto salvation.

The purpose of this bloodline is to bring forth a one-world leader. Since this leader will be of this bloodline, his lineage supposedly can be traced back to Jesus Christ; therefore, he will be able to take his rightful place as the long-awaited Messiah. Such a concept points to the antichrist who will make his appearance in the last days.

To Christians who understand the fundamental beliefs of their faith, this seems totally absurd. However, it is gaining momentum, even among those who call themselves Christians because they have no sure foundation. Many Christians have a combination of beliefs that cause them to be like corks on the seas of change, religion, and heresy. As a result, they are tossed to and fro, as they are carried about with every wind of doctrine that comes out of the deception of man and the seduction of the kingdom of darkness.[37]

The real issue of salvation comes down to whom we perceive Jesus to be. Jesus even made reference to this reality in Matthew 16. Much of man's understanding of Jesus is based on whom others perceive Him to be. However, when we stand before Him, He will ask us individually, "Who do you say I am?" It is not enough to have some Jesus; you must

---

[36] 2 Thessalonians 2:7-9
[37] Ephesians 4:14; 1Timothy 4:1

believe and possess the Jesus of the Bible. If you do not, you are still under condemnation.

What about you? Are you distinguished by the glory of Jesus in you, or do you hide behind popular religious movements? Does the glory that you display belong to you, the world, or Satan? The religious rhetoric must be stopped. It is important that all those who refer to Jesus as Lord and Savior believe what He said and are reflecting Him in the midst of darkness, ignorance, and delusion.

10

THE ASSURANCE OF THE GOSPEL

We have been considering the Apostle Paul's presentation of the Gospel throughout his epistles. His presentation created a picture of the Gospel that expounded its power to save and change man. For example, Romans reveals the power of the Gospel in regard to sin and salvation. Corinthians points to the power associated with the Gospel in regards to a new creation. In Galatians, we see its power in light of liberty from the bondage of the Law. Ephesians shows us the power of the Gospel in reference to the realization of our inheritance.[1] Philippians reminds us that the power of the Gospel is associated with a heavenly prize and citizenship that is discovered through loss and suffering. Colossians shows us how the power of this message is connected with the glory of Jesus Christ. In Thessalonians, we are about to learn that the power of the Gospel produces assurance.

The Apostle Paul said this about the assurance found in the Gospel, "For our gospel came not unto you in word only, but also in power, and in the Holy Ghost, and in much assurance; as you know what manner of men we were among you for your sake" (1 Thessalonians 1:5). Paul had not presented the Gospel to the Thessalonians in a way that would be pleasing to man or with flattering words designed to con them, but in a manner that confirmed its integrity. The apostle knew that the real power of the Gospel rests in God.

The word "assurance" in the Scripture in Thessalonians means entire confidence.[2] Here again, we see the complete life found in the Gospel. It is abundant, full, and satisfying. If people fail to experience this satisfaction, the fault does not rest with God and His provision, but with man and his unwillingness to respond in genuine faith.

Assurance and confidence are associated with faith. Faith finds its basis in hope. In hope, there is expectation. We are instructed to walk by faith in the hope of the unknown in order to discover the expectation for our lives in light of the unseen. This is the essence of faith. It takes us step by step into the complete life we have in God. As we take steps of faith, it is accounted to us as righteousness. It is in righteousness that we

---

[1] 1 Corinthians 4:19; Galatians 5:1; Ephesians 1:19
[2] Strong's Exhaustive Concordance, #4136

find quietness and assurance where God can meet us with His grace or favor. In fact, we have access by faith to experience His grace. Therefore, discovering this life can only come by faith.[3]

There must be the right environment to develop this assurance. Most Christians begin with a fleshly confidence. They have confidence in what they know, instead of whom they know. This confidence is based on a limited understanding of sin and Christ. However, this understanding allows for the assurance of forgiveness of sin and a promise of a new life. Without the assurance of forgiveness, people would not be able to approach God with confidence.[4]

As spiritual maturity grows, confidence is shifted from head knowledge to heart revelation. As the Apostle Paul stated in Colossians 2:2, "That their hearts might be comforted, being knit together in love, and unto all riches of the full assurance of understanding, to the acknowledgment of the mystery of God, and of the Father, and of Christ." As the mystery of God is revealed by the Holy Ghost, the person begins to catch glimpses of the power that works through the Gospel to save souls, change lives, and bring peace to the tormented soul. It is an incredible revelation that brings such confidence to those who stand upright before God. They become more assured that, on judgment day, they will not be ashamed of the faith that they put in their God.[5]

The Apostle Paul confirmed that the Gospel did not come in mere words, but in power and in the Holy Ghost. His words in regard to the Gospel stirred the Thessalonians up to consider the hard facts and God's glorious provision. However, it was the power of God in the Gospel that shook their foundations. It was the Holy Ghost who stripped away the veil from their hearts, allowing them to see the reality of the Gospel.[6]

The Thessalonians had formerly served idols, but they had turned in repentance to the one true Living God to serve Him. However, the Gospel was received with many afflictions. These people were suffering much persecution because of their faith. Although it had to be overwhelming at times, they discovered the joy of the Holy Ghost. Because of their testimony in their affliction, these people were serving as examples to others. They had shown faith, love, and patience in their ordeal.[7]

Persecution serves as a fire of separation. It often proves that the life of Christ is discovered through purifying fires of suffering, rather than in times of great blessing. Believers become more identified with Christ as their faith is tested, their character refined, and their confidence established in Him.

---

[3] Isaiah 32:17; Romans 5:2; Hebrews 11:1, 6
[4] Hebrews 10:22
[5] Romans 1:16; 9:33; 10:11
[6] 2 Corinthians 3:14-18; 1 Thessalonians 1:5
[7] 1 Thessalonians 1:3, 6, 9

The Thessalonians had assurance because of the Gospel. This assurance would give them peace and hope during their ordeal. But what was this assurance? The assurance of the Gospel contained two promises for the Thessalonians: 1) that believers would be delivered from God's wrath to come, and 2) that Jesus is coming back.[8]

It is important for Christians to realize that God will deliver them from His anger, but they will not be spared from tribulation. Anger is associated with God's fierce judgment, while tribulation is associated with the world we live in. For example, Satan, the god of this world, will buffet us in our lives. Those who belong to the world will hate us, and they will attempt to silence us through persecution. The Thessalonians were living examples of this reality. They were drinking from the bitter cup of persecution, while discovering the preciousness of their Lord.[9]

The Apostle Paul wanted them to realize that this tribulation was not of God. Such tribulation will last for a season, but the judgment against the ungodly will last for eternity. Although the Thessalonians tasted the bitter cup of tribulation, they would not partake of the wrath of God because of what Jesus did on the cross. To be spared from such wrath is the assurance that is found in the Gospel.

Today, this assurance is being undermined by the presentation of the false gospel of Universalism. This belief states that, in the end, the whole world will be restored and saved. Granted, Jesus died for the whole world, but the provision of salvation requires a personal response. Therefore, the Word clearly refutes this false presentation. It is appointed for man to die once, then judgment. Judgment brings one to a decision. It points to a separation unto eternal life or separation into everlasting damnation.[10]

A similar belief is that all Jews will be saved in the end. Once again, the Bible refutes this. Zechariah 13:6-9 tells us that only a third of the Jews will be saved in the time of great tribulation. This prophecy clearly refutes that the Jews will be saved on the basis of their lineage. God made a promise to the great patriarch Abraham in regards to establishing a people or nation. However, it was in God's plan to establish this nation for the purpose of bringing forth the Messiah and an everlasting kingdom. This kingdom would be established on the basis of faith, not lineage, religious affiliations, or practices. Faith was the spiritual legacy that Abraham left for all who would believe God about Jesus Christ. Granted, God is not finished with the nation of Israel. He will restore this nation and the Messiah, the King of kings, will reign over the whole world from Jerusalem. But, when it comes to salvation, there is no distinction as to whether a person is Jew or Greek in God's sight. Each

---

[8] 1 Thessalonians 1:10; 2:14-16, 19
[9] John 16:33; 2 Corinthians 4:4; 1 Thessalonians 1:10
[10] Hebrews 9:27

person must receive Jesus Christ as his or her personal Savior and Lord.[11]

The early Church was made up of Jews. This proves that the Jews have as much of an opportunity to come out from under the bondage of the Law as well as the judgment and oppression that has exploited them for centuries as the Gentiles have in coming out from under their spiritual darkness of paganism and idolatry. Salvation is an individual choice and is not based on association or class, but on identification of redemption wrought by Jesus' blood.

We will all stand before the Great Judge, Jesus Christ. There are two types of judgment: the judgment seat of Christ for believers and the Great White Throne of judgment for those who refuse God's provision of Christ. The Christian will be judged according to works done in his or her body. This judgment will determine positions and rewards in the kingdom of God. For the unbeliever, the Law will judge them. We already know that the Law can only condemn, not justify. We see a contrast between these two types of judgments in Matthew 25 when Jesus separates the sheep from the goats. The sheep will inherit eternal life, and the goats will be cast into everlasting fire and punishment.[12]

Advocating Universalism in any manner denies that a person must receive God's provision of Jesus Christ on a personal level, by faith, to ensure salvation. Therefore, personal faith in the Lord Jesus as the only way, gate, door, and entrance to heaven is done away with and replaced with a false assurance that will be exposed by the wrath of God in the day of judgment. Sadly, it will be too late for these people to believe what the Word says about the impending judgment awaiting those who do not believe what God says about matters concerning life and death. Even the wicked Felix trembled at the concept of righteousness, temperance, and judgment to come. Although it appeared that he remained a fool and died in his sins, he at least could see his chance to get it right before the holy God, in order to rest in this present life, and not in some false hope that would fail him when he entered eternity.[13]

Jesus coming back is another part of the assurance we have from the glorious Gospel. The epistle to the Thessalonians showed the impending wrath of God, but it also presented Jesus as the returning King, Bridegroom, and Judge. To those who do not expect Him, He will come as a thief in the night, leaving the unprepared in a state of hopelessness and uncertainty.[14]

Jesus coming back was the blessed assurance that served as a great comfort to the Thessalonians in their time of persecution. The believer's hope does not rest in this present life, but in the next world. This blessed hope will be fully realized when Jesus comes back for His

---

[11] Zechariah 14:9-21; Romans 10:9-10 Galatians 3:5-9, 27-28
[12] Matthew 25:29-46; 2 Corinthians 5:10; Revelation 20:10-15
[13] Matthew 7:13-14; John 10:7-11; 14:6; Acts 24:24-26
[14] 1 Thessalonians 5:1-3

bride. In fact, the Apostle Paul described this scene in 1 Thessalonians 4:13-18. It will be a glorious scene, as the dead in Christ will be raised first, then those who are alive will be caught up together to meet Jesus in the air. This blessed hope can be found throughout Paul's epistles. It is as though it is the motivating factor behind upright living, sobriety in service, and keeping a watchful, discerning eye on the times in which we live.

The Apostle Paul made various references to this blessed event to remind and encourage believers as to where their real hope rests. In 1 Corinthians, Paul instructed people to take communion until Jesus comes. In 1 Corinthians 15:51-54, he also declared that those who believe will be changed in the twinkling of an eye as the corruptible gives way to the incorruptible. He also makes reference to this event in Ephesians by referring to the time that Jesus' Church will be presented to Him without spot and wrinkle. In Colossians, the apostle talked about Jesus' appearing, and, in 2 Thessalonians, he speaks of Jesus' coming at a time in which He will be glorified in His saints. The apostle called Jesus, God our Savior in reference to His appearing in Titus.[15]

As stated in a previous chapter, Jesus coming back for His Body is under attack. Some in the Church believe that Jesus is not bodily coming back in the clouds. These people actually believe He is coming back through the Manifested Sons of God who have obtained immortality through personal holiness. Supposedly, these people will usher in His kingdom. However, the Word is clear. As Jesus ascended in the clouds, heavenly messengers told His disciples that He would come back in the same manner as He departed.[16]

Jesus talked about His physical return. He said that mankind would see Him coming in the clouds of heaven with power and great glory. At that time, He will send His angels to gather the elect. Obviously, it will be the King of kings who will set up His kingdom and not man. In fact, Jesus will come when the world is in great turmoil. There will be a falling away from the truth. Great signs and wonders, along with a false hope of peace, will seduce people into falling for the counterfeit and coming into the one-world religious, economic, and political system.[17]

Believers who maintain their testimony of Jesus will be persecuted and killed for their faith.[18] The word, "remain" in 1 Thessalonians 4:15 refers to those who survive or are left.[19] Jesus even posed this question in Luke 18:8, "Nevertheless when the Son of man cometh, shall he find faith on the earth?"

The Apostle John also informed us that every eye shall see Him when He comes back in the clouds. The prophet Zechariah states that

---

[15] 1 Corinthians 11:26; Ephesians 5:26-27; Colossians 3:4; Titus 3:4
[16] Acts 1:9-11
[17] 1 Thessalonians 5:3; 2 Thessalonians 2:3-11
[18] Matthew 24:30-31
[19] Strong's Exhaustive Concordance, #4035

the inhabitants of Jerusalem will look upon the One whom they have pierced, and they will mourn for Him as one mourns for his only son.[20]

The significance of Jesus coming back has been lost in the various debates surrounding His coming. These debates are known as the different views on the Rapture or the quickly taking out of the saints as described in 1 Thessalonians 4:13-18. The debate is not whether Jesus is coming back. Rather, it surrounds what His Church will experience before He comes for His bride. These debates have validity to them. They point to the fact that Jesus is coming back. However, Christians must be careful as to what they emphasize. This debate has nothing to do with ensuring the salvation of a person, but it can become a cause.

Too much emphasis on when Jesus will come can drown out the real assurance every Christian needs to focus on when it comes to the essence of their real hope: Jesus is coming back for His Church. Although the signs Jesus talked about in the Gospels are important as far as preparing and warning us about the events that will lead up to His coming, they are not meant to become a point of debate or contention in the Body of Believers. In fact, every past generation has experienced these signs in some form, and each generation has been instructed to watch for Jesus. The real hope does not rest on who is right about when the Rapture will occur, rather it points to the main event of Jesus returning. As Jesus stated, no man can know the exact time of His coming, but people can be aware of the events leading up to and the closeness of His coming. The purpose for knowing the times in which we live is that one will be ready and watching for His coming.

God clearly defined this hope for me when I asked Him which theology about the "Rapture" was correct to stop the debate in my own soul. I will never forget His simple answer: "All you need to know is I am coming back." It does not matter what we, as believers, experience in this present world, as long as our focus remains steadfast towards heaven and our faith is established on the Rock. By ensuring our life is clearly established in Him, we will be ready for His appearance.

Another debate about Jesus' coming is that He has already come back to earth. One of the beliefs that advocate this is known as preterism. Preterism is the eschatological belief that all Bible prophecy is history. Those who hold to this belief consider most of the Bible as being allegorical or symbolic, especially when it involves the end days. There are two groups operating under the guise of preterism. The "Full Preterists" believe that Jesus actually returned in a spiritual sense in 70 AD and that all prophesy stopped at this point. The "Partial Preterists" believe in the Second Coming, but do not believe in a literal Millennium, the antichrist, or the Battle of Armageddon.

We have already discussed how Jesus is coming back. Obviously, He has not come for His bride. But we must not negate the events that lead up to His coming, victory, and rule. The Bible is clear that we must

---

[20] Zechariahs 12:10; Revelation 1:7

rightly divide the Word. The main issue is how we approach the Word. Do we approach it to believe what it says, knowing only the Holy Spirit can bring revelation to it or do we approach it with our own personal theologies and place Scriptures in such a way that they confirm or verify our theologies? Sadly, most people approach the Bible from the latter perspective. As a result, we have so many theories about the Word that it is hard to recognize what is the pure Word of God. We must get back to the basics of what the Bible says and choose to believe it as true. [21]

The Thessalonians felt their tribulation signaled the time that would usher in Jesus' coming. Some were sitting around waiting for Him to come back to deliver them out of their present situation. The Apostle Paul contended with them over this matter. This attitude can be presently observed in some Christians. In their mind, He is coming back, so what is the use? Some are actually living for themselves as they heap the world upon their lusts. Some have fled to other parts of the world as they wait for America to fall in fulfillment of prophecies surrounding the end-day Babylon. Some are hiding in secluded places trying to avoid the tribulation that will engulf the whole world. These attempts are for the purpose of preserving life, rather than the sacrificial offering up for the sake of Jesus and the Gospel. As Jesus warned, those who try to save their life as they know it will ultimately lose it. Such activities will cause believers to be indifferent to reality, disobedient to their commission, and insensitive to the leading of the Spirit. As true servants of God, we must be occupying wherever the Holy Ghost leads us until Jesus comes.[22]

As you study the environment to which Jesus is coming back, you will not only see indifference, but scoffers. Jesus spoke of the time He would return, and He detailed birth pangs and spoke of the persecution of the saints and fearful signs in the sky. In His warnings, He instructed His disciples to be aware of the day they lived in by watching the signs and being in prayer.[23] In Luke 21:19, Jesus told them to possess their souls in patience.

Every generation has been looking for Jesus, believing that current events were signaling His imminent return. The generation of WWI just knew that Jesus' coming was near because of the great tribulation that encompassed the world. A certain cult even used this time to predict His Second Advent. The greatest generation, as it has been called, witnessed WWII and the atomic bomb. No doubt, there were those who just knew the world would not survive. Since then, we have witnessed various skirmishes and wars in different parts of the world: the Korean and Vietnam conflicts, along with Afghanistan and two confrontations with Iraq. The latest war on terrorism is a present-day war that is engulfing the whole world.

---

[21] John 16:13-14; Romans 10:17; 1 Timothy 2:15; 1 John 2:27
[22] Matthew 16:25; Luke 19:13; Galatians 5:16
[23] Matthew 24:4-13, 26-31

As the world has grown increasingly worse, each new generation predicts His coming. These claims have produced scoffers, even among Christians. The truth is, we do not know the exact day or hour Jesus is coming back. Each new generation simply means we are a generation closer to His entrance upon the world scene. Each major world event often points to the fulfillment of prophecies that confirm that His coming is drawing near. It is not up to believers to prove a point about His coming in regards to the unbelief of others, but it is vital that we be ready for His coming by guarding our hearts against skepticism and unbelief in these precarious days. We do this by continually looking up and knowing that our redemption draws near, whether it is through the door of physical death or by being taken up in the clouds with our Lord.[24]

Another aspect of assurance is found in sanctification. It is God's heart to wholly sanctify us. 1 Thessalonians 5:23 states, "And the very God of peace sanctify you wholly; and I pray God your whole spirit and soul and body be preserved blameless unto the coming of our Lord Jesus Christ." God is the one who sanctifies or sets us apart for His purpose.

All three Persons of the Godhead are involved with the work of sanctification. For example, the Father places a believer positionally in the place of sanctification. This designates the individual for His work to be brought forth. Jesus serves as the place of sanctification for the believer. It is in His name or authority that the Holy Spirit does the work of sanctification through the washing of the Word.

The Word of God serves as a washing machine that cleanses us from the ways of unrighteousness. Obedience to the Word brings us to the will of God. It is God's will that serves as the point of sanctification. The purpose of sanctification is to bring us to spiritual maturity or perfection before God. Therefore, the peace of God is associated with the work of sanctification. It implies confidence to meet with God in sweet fellowship, assurance of not being ashamed when He comes, and the authority to maintain one's testimony in the midst of wickedness.[25]

Sanctification is a necessary means to prepare God's people for His work and return. The Apostle Paul talked about sanctification throughout His epistles. Believers have been chosen before the foundation of the world to be holy and without blame before the Lord in love. They must be perfected and prepared unto every good work to be fit for the Master's use and glory.[26]

The truth of sanctification has also been undermined by different belief systems. The reason for this confusion is that people fail to realize two major factors about sanctification. First, man has no holiness in

---

[24] Matthew 24:36, 43-44; Luke 21:28, 34-36; 2 Peter 3:3-5
[25] John 17:17; Romans 15:16; 1 Corinthians 1:2, 30; 6:11; Ephesians 5:26; 1 Thessalonians 4:3-4; 2 Thessalonians 2:13; 1 Timothy 4:5; 1 Peter 1:2; Jude 1
[26] Ephesians 1:4; 2:10; Philippians 1:6; 2 Timothy 2:21; Titus 2:14

himself nor does he have the means to obtain it. He is a wretched sinner whose only real hope rests in God's intervention. Secondly, the work of sanctification is totally done by God. Man must consecrate or separate himself from the unholy and walk in the holiness established in his life, but God is the one who sets him apart for His purpose and glory.

Today, there are those who believe they can obtain this state of holiness outside of God. Such a belief not only shows ignorance towards God, but a blind arrogance towards the wretched condition of man. These people live in denial about their inability to please God in their own power.

The other erroneous belief about sanctification is that a person automatically arrives at this state once he or she is born again. There is a difference between being positionally sanctified in Christ and being sanctified by the Holy Ghost. God must first designate us for sanctification. In other words, He puts His ownership on us. However, the Holy Ghost must bring a person to the state of holiness. The state of holiness begins when a Christian begins to separate him or herself from the unholy in order to submit to the work of the Holy Ghost. It is only as a Christian gives way to the Spirit that the work of sanctification is accomplished in and through him or her.

People who believe they are the ones who bring themselves to a state of sanctification are very self-righteous and harsh. Those who believe they have automatically arrived at this place of maturity display a false confidence and often remain shallow and judgmental.

The Apostle Paul gave this instruction in 1 Thessalonians 5:19-21, "Quench not the Spirit. Despise not prophesyings. Prove all things; hold fast that which is good." We must not quench the work of the Spirit in our lives. Quenching the Spirit prevents the work of sanctification. Without this work, we remain inconsistent and hypocritical in our walk and claims.

The Holy Ghost is a promise of the Father. Jesus talked about the fact that the Holy Ghost will show His people things to come. Such revelation points to prophecy about future events. This unveiling of events is for the purpose of preparation, which will enable His people to withstand in those times, as well as possess the readiness to stand against the attacks of the enemy. Therefore, we need to prove all things and not speculate or judge on the basis of our own vain imaginations. We are to hold fast to that which is true and morally upright.[27]

There is also assurance in the Gospel because it is true. The Apostle Paul dealt with the issue of truth in light of the end-times. People were trying to frighten the Thessalonians about Jesus' coming. Like Jesus, he warned people that many would be deceived. In fact, God would send a delusion to test the hearts of people.[28]

Part of the delusion will be counterfeit signs and wonders. Such signs and wonders will create a false reality through experience. Most

---

[27] John 16:13; Acts 1:4-8;
[28] Matthew 24:4-5; 2 Thessalonians 2:3

people do not know how to discern the supernatural. They often judge their encounters with the supernatural according to the flesh, rather than discern the spirit behind them. They perceive that, since it is supernatural, it must be from God. However, Satan operates in the supernatural. He counterfeits the things of God. In 2 Thessalonians 2, there is a harsh warning that lying signs and wonders will surround the son of perdition.

These counterfeit signs bring us to another area that is presently undermining the true Gospel. Over a decade ago, there was a push for unity through signs and wonders. Consider the emphasis. It was not on Jesus, but on the supernatural. This movement began to inspire and embrace various supernatural phenomena such as the "laughing revival." People started seeking after the supernatural, rather than the Person of Jesus. Any time people seek after the supernatural, they open themselves up to the kingdom of darkness. As a result, Satan's kingdom found inroads into the Church through the emphasis of the supernatural. Out of this influence has come works of darkness such as pride and division in the Body.

Such a pursuit for signs is not unusual. In Jesus' day, religious people sought after a sign. Granted, miracles confirmed Jesus' identity. However, these people were not interested in Jesus' identity or the truth. The pursuit for such signs and wonders swept through a generation of people during Jesus' days. Like King Herod, who wanted to see Jesus do a miracle as a means of entertainment, many of these people were simply seeking after miracles to be entertained or provoked in some kind of emotional or spiritual way.[29]

Jesus stated that only a wicked generation seeks after a sign. Paul concurred with Jesus when he pointed out that those who will be caught up with these lying signs and wonders will do so because they are operating in the deception of unrighteousness. Miracles never inspire true faith; they simply confirm it.[30] People who seek after signs are not seeking to believe Jesus. They have no intention of coming to terms with who He is. They are simply impressed with the benefits He offers or the supernatural events that are attributed to Him.

Another theme that came out of the modern church as a result of all the supernatural hoopla was revival. Although revival has been at the heart of the Church, major prophecies about revival started to come forth. One of those prophecies is that there will be a world-wide revival before Jesus returns for His Church. Does the Scripture back up such a concept? According to Jesus, many will be deceived in the end-days. Paul did not mention a revival in 2 Thessalonians. Rather, he stated that there will be a falling away from the truth before the son of perdition is revealed. He also warned that God is sending a strong delusion.[31] What

---

[29] Matthew 12:39; Luke 23:7-11; 2 Thessalonians 2:9-10
[30] Hebrews 2:1-4
[31] Matthew 24:4-5, 23-24; 2 Thessalonians 2:3-11

will this delusion look like? Will it look like a counterfeit revival that many will be swept away with because they do not love the truth?

Revival is a personal matter. In other words, it begins in the contrite heart.[32] Revival does not occur because the Church clamors after it. There are no methods or activities that will cause it to happen. It happens when the environment of man's being becomes repentant and pliable before God. Such an inward environment allows God to move upon the individual with the convicting power of the Holy Ghost.

Few people realize that revival has nothing to do with numbers of people, but with the purging fire of the Holy Ghost. Revival means that God is raising His broken-hearted people out of the filth of their sin, raising His dull repentant people out of the delusion of their fleshly compromise, and removing the indifference of deaf ears with personal cries for mercy. Revival will not occur unless people are willing to face the fact that they are unresponsive to God in their lives because they are either dead in sin, in a spiritual coma because of compromise, or spiritually asleep because of indifference.

Most people are caught up with the idea of revival. They think this move of God has to do with power, miracles, and more people added to the church rolls rather than man getting right with God to enable him to once again properly respond to Him. The fact that there is a sense for the need of revival in the Church, even among all of the religious activities, should give us a wake-up call that something is missing from all of these movements. The question is, will there be such a revelation in the Church of its true condition that it will create a revival that actually changes the face of the Church as we know it?

I have no doubt there is revival going on in the individual hearts of God's people throughout the world. However, many of Jesus' sheep have been confused about what is going on in Christendom. They feel leanness in their spirits, but they cannot put their fingers on it. They are going to church, but they come out with a greater emptiness. They are singing the songs, but they feel as if they are only going through the motions. They hear preaching, but it causes emptiness, rather than nourishment to the soul. This confusion has caused God's people to honestly seek out the missing ingredient. The problem is, they are not hearing their Shepherd's voice. What does it mean for Jesus' sheep to hear His voice? It means that they are hearing unadulterated truth being preached and taught.

I have personally experienced having a whole group of sheep threaten mutiny when they heard a different voice than Jesus'. Sadly, the voice of Jesus is becoming weaker in the midst of endless religious and church activities and erroneous movements. As a result, the sheep are becoming restless and beginning to leave the dry water holes, the infested presentations of the wolves, and the hireling shepherds. These

---

[32] Isaiah 57:15

Challenging the Christian Life

sheep are being scattered, but they do know the voice of their Shepherd, and, in due time, they will be found by Him.[33]

Sheep are truth seekers. Truth seekers are those who seek to know the truth. It is easy to say that each of us prefers the truth, but truth will challenge any fantasy or lie we may harbor about God or ourselves. Sadly, many will not love the truth enough to recognize or reject the delusion that God is sending in the world to test the hearts of those who claim to belong to Him. These deluded individuals will ultimately expose themselves. After all, they would have to confess sin, acknowledge their unrighteousness, and humble themselves before the throne of God. Due to their preference for darkness, these people will not receive a love for the truth. When the delusion comes, they will fall for it. The end result is that they will be taken out with the tide of deception for the purpose of damnation.[34]

Believers have much to be thankful for. We have a Lord who is coming back for us. We have been given a Gospel that saves, changes, and gives us assurance. We have the Word of God that serves as a lamp that will light the path of our walks of faith. We have the Holy Ghost who will do the work of God, as He brings us to perfection in Christ. We have it all, yet we are dissatisfied. We are dissatisfied because we want to have life on our terms, to possess the world according to personal agendas, and to control God's intervention in our lives. Do you fit any of these categories? If you do, it is because you have failed to experience, by faith, the power and assurance of the Gospel of Jesus Christ.

---

[33] John 10:1-18
[34] John 3:19-21; 2 Thessalonians 2:3-12

11

THE GLORIOUS GOSPEL

The Apostle Paul made this statement in 1 Timothy 1:11, "According to the glorious gospel of the blessed God, which was committed to my trust." Paul saw the Gospel as glorious, worthy of recognition, and honorable. He recognized that it was committed to his trust, making this life-saving message a privilege and a responsibility that he could not take lightly. He knew that Jesus enabled him to be a minister of the Gospel. He was thankful that his Lord considered him in such a light.

Why did Paul consider the Gospel glorious? We can see his unwavering commitment towards this message. As we consider his epistles to Timothy, we will see that Paul considered this simple message glorious because he truly understood the intent and power of it.

As you follow the Apostle Paul's train of thought, you begin to taste a bit of his appreciation for the Gospel. He begins with his testimony of how he was a blasphemer and a persecutor of those who believed in Jesus. Although he was sincere about his religious zeal in destroying the new belief or the Way, he was sincerely wrong. He came face to face with how wrong he was on the road to Damascus when he encountered Christ.[1] It was at this point that Paul caught a glimpse of the extent of his sin. No doubt, the awareness of his spirit and deeds grew as he matured in Jesus. Paul's conclusions of his past pursuits and the essence of his life were that he was a chief of sinners.

The Apostle Paul was not trying to be noble when he declared that he was a chief of sinners. Rather, he was a man who, in spite of his misguided religious zeal and deeds, met the fulfillment of all of his hopes. When he realized that he had ironically opposed with zealous ignorance and cruelty the very Messiah for whom he had been watching, he found himself at a point of great shame. Here was a Pharisee who expounded on the hope of the Messiah, but had ignorantly opposed Him and the furtherance of his Messiah's kingdom in the lives of men.

In many cases, such a realization would cause utter despair. However, Paul met the real Jesus. In spite of the harsh reality of his blasphemy, Paul actually found grace being extended to him. Grace in this text points to mercy that refrains from judgment, while offering undeserved forgiveness and redemption.

---

[1] Acts 9

The Apostle Paul recognized that Jesus had come into the world for such as him. The greater the sin, the more precious Jesus' redemption becomes to a person.² Paul not only recognized his serious sin against the Son of God, but also that he was a sinner. In other words, it was not just a matter of what Paul did, but the essence of who he was. In his fallen condition of sin and ignorance towards God, he was bent on doing things his way. In his religious zeal, he assumed that he could not be wrong about his conclusions. He was thoroughly sold out to his way of thinking.

A person who is sold out to his or her own way of thinking is blinded by the light of personal righteousness. The Apostle Paul learned that his "religious light" was really darkness that blinded him to the truth. However, when he encountered the light of the world, his light or understanding was consumed by total darkness. Instead of seeing, he became blinded by the light. Based on his blindness, how great was Paul's inner darkness? Thus, he described himself as being the chief of sinners.³

When Paul encountered Christ on the road to Damascus, he came face to face with how wrong he was. He then realized the extent of his inner darkness and he sought mercy from Jesus and found it. People who have worldly remorse are too noble to seek mercy. They try to do penance by showing how sorrowful they are. However, this remorse comes from pride that refuses to humble itself and seek forgiveness.

The Apostle Paul was humbled by the revelation of Christ in light of his own depraved self. In fact, the more the light is revealed in our darkness, the greater the revelation of Jesus. Paul experienced Jesus as the eternal King who would not only deserve to reign in his heart as Lord, but who would reign forever from the throne of heaven. He knew Him as immortal, always existing, invisible to the naked eye, but glorious to the spiritual eye. Paul knew Jesus as the only wise God who deserved to be honored and glorified forever.⁴

It is also in the first letter to Timothy that Paul presented Jesus as the Mediator between God and man. Unlike the first chapter in 1 Timothy, where we see Jesus as God Incarnate, the Son of God, the second chapter reveals Jesus as the Son of Man who stands as mediator. The second Person of the Godhead is still fully man, but now dwells in a glorified body. This reality is also a part of the great mystery. The fact that Jesus kept His humanity is significant. It is as man that He stands in the gap as our High Priest, Intercessor, and Advocate.⁵

Jesus standing in the gap reminds me of a Scripture in Ezekiel 22:30, "And I sought for a man among them, that should make up the hedge, and stand in the gap before me for the land, that I should not

---

² Luke 7:42-48
³ 1 Timothy 1:15
⁴ 1 Timothy 1:17; 6:15-16
⁵ 1 Corinthians 15:49-54; 1 Timothy 1:17; 2:5; Hebrews 7:22-26; 1 John 2:1-2

destroy it: but I found none." Keep in mind that Daniel lived during this time, but he could not stand in the gap to prevent judgment upon Israel. Ezekiel was a godly priest, but he could not stand in the gap. Eventually, God would send forth a man who could stand in the gap. His name is Jesus Christ.

Sadly, Jesus as our sole Mediator is under attack. There is a belief that Jesus is not the only Mediator between man and God, but that He shares this position with His biological mother, Mary. Mary is actually presented as the mediator between Jesus and man. Those who believe this see her as being more compassionate and approachable than Jesus. However, this is unscriptural. Mary confessed that God was her Savior. In other words, she needed intervention and salvation for she also was part of the Adamic race.[6] The Gospels proved that Jesus was very approachable. After all, He was the One so many sought after for mercy and healing.

Jesus clearly dealt with the exaltation of Mary before it ever occurred by bringing a clear contrast of what must be considered important in the kingdom of God. At one point, the women were declaring blessings towards the one who had bore Him and from whom He had nursed. He made this statement in Luke 11:28, "Yea rather, blessed are they that hear the word of God, and keep it."

When Jesus spoke about the family of God, He did not exalt His mother into a place of importance. In fact, He established who would make up this heavenly family, "For whosoever shall do the will of my Father who is in heaven, the same is my brother, and sister, and mother" (Matthew 12:50). In both incidents, Jesus clarified what must be honored and considered as important in the lives of His followers—obedience to the will of God.

Although Mary was recognized in Scripture as being blessed for being considered and used by God, she was never exalted to an idolatrous position as mediator. After Acts 1:14, Mary is never mentioned again. No doubt, she had influence on the new Church, but she quietly receded into the background as Jesus, the Son of the Living God, was preached and exalted by the apostles. We do not know where her grave is located. Clearly, this prevents any idolatrous worship of her. Peter, John, and Paul do not mention her. After all, she never died for our sins. She was simply a vessel of God who was touched by the miraculous to accomplish the impossible task of bringing forth the Messiah. Therefore, the idolatrous regard that is unjustly shown to her is born out of vain imaginations and speculations influenced by paganism.

Jesus, not Mary, is sitting on the right hand of the Father. The harsh reality of mankind is that there is no one of the Adamic race worthy enough to stand in the gap in this capacity. Scripture clearly shows us that Jesus does not share His position as Mediator with any other entity or being. The Father sent the man Christ Jesus to close the gap between

---

[6] Luke 1:47; Romans 6:23

Challenging the Christian Life

God and man through reconciliation on the cross, and now, as man, Jesus is able to stand in the gap as our Mediator in heaven due to the fact He is also God. As God, He is able to represent the heart of God to His people while maintaining the integrity of God's holiness and judgments. As a man who was tempted in every way, but was without sin, He can best represent man's plight before the throne as Priest. As our substitute on the cross, He is able to stand as our Advocate in the courts of heaven. Therefore, He alone is worthy to be honored as the only Mediator between God and man.[7]

The Apostle Paul made another reference to Jesus as the Son of Man in his second epistle. He says of Him that He was of the seed of David that was raised from the dead. As man, He did not remain in the grave. As God, He rose from that grave, proving victorious. His death on the cross paid a ransom for all men, exalting Him as the Savior of all men.[8]

It is because of Jesus' divinity and humanity that He is able to represent the Father's heart before men as well as man's hopeless plight in the courts of heaven. As a result, He is able to save man to the uttermost. But, if you strip Him of any part of His character or work, you will end up with another Jesus who is powerless to save you from the wrath of God that will come upon all disobedience and unbelief.[9]

In 1 Timothy 3:16, the Apostle Paul made this statement, "And without controversy great is the mystery of godliness: God was manifest in the flesh, justified in the Spirit, seen of angels, preached unto the Gentiles, believed on in the world, received up into glory." The apostle referred to the mystery of godliness. This mystery is revealed as Jesus Christ. Once again, Paul stressed that Jesus is God manifest in the flesh, justified or verified to be the Promised One (the Messiah), seen of angels, preached unto the Gentiles, believed by man, and received up to glory by the Father. Jesus is our example of godliness. His life must be manifested in us in such a way that it can be seen and observed by others. For example, we must be sealed and anointed by the Spirit to make an impact. The unseen world must be capable of recognizing to whom we belong. Our commission to preach the Gospel so heirs of salvation will believe remains unchangeable. In the end, we will also be received up into glory.

However, in the latter days, this mystery of godliness will be greatly threatened. For many, it will remain a mystery as they develop their own form of godliness. Paul warned of this condition in 2 Timothy 3:5, "Having a form of godliness, but denying the power thereof: from such turn away." Godliness will become a matter of outward show rather than a revelation of inward righteousness. Inward righteousness is established

---

[7] 2 Corinthians 5:18-19; Ephesians 2:14-18; Hebrews 4:14-16; 7:23-27; 8:1, 6; 1 John 2:1-2; Revelations 5:4-14

[8] 1 Timothy 2:6; 4:10; 2 Timothy 2:8

[9] Ephesians 2:2; 1 Thessalonians 5:9

by the manifestation of Christ in a person's life by the Holy Ghost. However, there are wolves who are advocating a form of godliness that is devoid of power. False presentations of godliness will cover up heretical teachings. The Word is clear. We must turn away from such people and not follow them down a path to judgment.

Obviously, Paul's instruction about godly leadership to Timothy was necessary. Leadership will determine the character of a body of believers. We see the breakdown of the Church because of faulty leadership. The problem is that many leaders are being chosen according to worldly evaluation. Godly leadership is often being compromised as so-called "leaders" are being exalted because of money and worldly influence.

We see this compromise trickling downward. For example, the exaltation of worldly vanity for the sake of outward show becomes a poor substitute for the inner beauty of godliness in a woman's life. Novices are often exalted to fill positions, placate egos, and to keep the show going. Godly conduct is replaced with outward facades or religious masks that cover wrong dispositions, wicked emphases, and shameful conduct.[10]

We know that the condition of many in the end of the last days will be the product of seducing spirits and a worldly gospel that is nothing more than doctrines of demons.[11] "Positive Confession" is an example of such a worldly gospel. A worldly gospel justifies pursuing after the world in the name of blessings. Such blessings supposedly serve as a verification of personal godliness. This type of gospel prefers temporary material riches to heavenly blessings and treasures.

The Apostle Paul addressed a worldly emphasis when it comes to godliness. He called those who suppose that the idea of worldly gain is godliness, perverse and corrupt in their minds, being destitute of truth. After all, we bring nothing into this world and we will take nothing with us into the next life. Our needs, such as food and raiment are few. To possess our needs should bring personal contentment towards the One who provides us with all of our needs, according to His riches in glory that are found in Christ Jesus.[12] Paul brought this out when he stated, "Not that I speak in respect of want: for I have learned, in whatsoever state I am, therewith to be content. (Philippians 4:11).

The desire to be rich in this world serves as a temptation and a snare to those who love money. This is why the Apostle Paul charged those who are rich in this world to not be high-minded or trust the uncertainty of such riches. He reminded believers that those who do well financially are to be rich in good works, always ready to distribute their blessings among the needy and to communicate the heart of Christ in all matters.

---

[10] 1 Timothy 2:9-10; 3:1-13; 4:1
[11] 1 Timothy 4:1
[12] Philippians 4:19; 1 Timothy 6:3-8

Such giving is a way of storing up a good foundation against the challenging times to come, as one truly lays hold on eternal life.[13]

Worldly emphasis in riches will undermine true faith. It will pervert faith as it changes the glory of God. Those in the "Positive Confession" movement try to change reality with their words. They believe they can positively confess something into existence by using God's promises to arm-wrestle Him into submitting to their wishes and fleshly whims. Most of these confessions are centered on a person getting his or her way about a matter or obtaining worldly goods that they can heap upon themselves since they are God's children and worthy of such blessings. But, what happens when blessings elude them? Instead of recognizing that their perception of God is wrong, they look within to find a breach in their life where faith or sin is concerned. Sadly, many of these people end up in utter despair and walk away from any association with God.

The Apostle Paul addressed unfeigned or sincere faith in his second epistle to Timothy. Sincere faith is based on the knowledge of God. If we know God, we will not give in to the fear that often plagues people. This fear undermines the power to overcome and will cause mistrust and confusion regarding God's commitment toward His people.[14]

Therefore, the believer's testimony does not rest on the ability to say certain words, but on the unchanging character of God. God is committed to our spiritual well-being. The Gospel verifies this. However, we must recognize that the power of our testimony hinges on us partaking of the afflictions of the Gospel according to the power of God that works through it. It is in identification with the Gospel that we begin to recognize that He has called us for a holy calling. Such a calling is not manifested through personal works, but according to His own purpose and grace, which were given to us in Christ Jesus.[15]

Jesus Christ abolished death, thereby, bringing life and immortality to light through the Gospel. As a result, Paul was able to give this incredible testimony in 2 Timothy 1:12, "For the which cause I also suffer these things: nevertheless I am not ashamed: for I know whom I have believed, and am persuaded that he is able to keep that which I have committed unto him against that day."

How does one establish a testimony on the immovable Rock that actually embraces suffering with assurance? The apostle gave us insight into the answer to this question. We must begin with faith. Contrast is brought out between believers and those who hold to another gospel, such as the worldly gospel. For example, "Positive Confessors" who put their confidence in vain words become void of sound doctrine. Their faith rests in their words. This subtle shift from faith in God to faith in the power of words originates in the occult and is promoted by such cults as Unity and Christian Science. Because of this worldly emphasis, those

---

[13] 1 Timothy 6:9-10, 17-19
[14] 2 Timothy 1:5, 7
[15] 2 Timothy 1:8-9

who practice such a gospel may have a form of godliness, but they deny its power. They may be ever learning about Jesus, but they will never be able to come to the knowledge of who He really is.

Emphasis has to do with pursuits. The "Positive Confessors" have put their trust in what they see. Their emphasis is to fulfill their lust; therefore, they heap to themselves teachers who will tickle their itching ears with fables.[16]

On the contrary, true believers hold fast to sound words in faith and love, which find their origin in Jesus Christ. It is His words that can change one's personal reality. As He declared in John 6:63, "It is the spirit that quickeneth; the flesh profiteth nothing: the words that I speak unto you, they are spirit, and they are life." Jesus' words are always in line with His righteous character and the Father's perfect will and plan.

Since Jesus' words carry life, we are told to study the Word to show ourselves approved unto God. After all, Scripture is for the purpose of instruction in righteousness.[17] This brings us to another aspect that undermines the Gospel—wrong presentations concerning righteousness.

Intellectual arrogance has replaced righteousness in many people's lives. In fact, Christians are seeking knowledge about spiritual matters, rather than seeking the truth about God. They believe that, since they know certain spiritual things or they can quote certain Scriptures, they must be righteous. The Apostle Paul warned about the dead-end of knowledge that lacks the revelation of Jesus, "Ever learning, and never able to come to the knowledge of the truth" (2 Timothy 3:7).

Righteousness is not a matter of knowing, but of being upright before God. It implies that God is having His way in our lives. The only way that God can have His way in our lives is by us obeying the Word. As we obey the Word, it becomes a living sword that will cut away, expose, and reveal our hearts. Sadly, many either adjust the Word to line up to their personal perceptions of God and righteousness, or they use the powerful sword as a form of judgment against others. Instead of the Word being a personal surgical tool for self-examination and maturity, it is used as a harsh sword of destruction upon those who fail to adjust to the personal conclusions or lifestyles of the self-righteous.[18]

The Word must not be used as a means to get our way with God or to expound our superior knowledge over others. If we properly study and apply His Word, we will be workmen who will not be ashamed before God because we have rightly divided His word of truth. Properly dividing, applying, and obeying the Word of Truth will bring us to perfection in our walk. A righteous walk will manifest itself in good works.[19]

The Apostle Paul told us that this walk is developed as we endure as a good soldier of Jesus Christ. Believers will guard their lives against the

---

[16] 2 Timothy 4:3-4
[17] 2 Timothy 2:15; 3:16
[18] Hebrews 4:12; James 1:22-25
[19] 2 Timothy 2:15; 3:16-17

entanglements of the world. Instead of pursuing the world in the name of blessings, they will depart from iniquity, flee youthful lusts, and purge themselves from ungodly influences. They will actually prepare themselves to become sanctified vessels, fit for the Master's use by following after righteousness, faith, charity, and peace.[20]

The Apostle Paul experienced heartache over the issues of the world. He spoke of Demas. Apparently, this individual was under Paul's auspice, but he forsook Paul and departed because he loved this present world. No doubt, Paul struggled with why people could turn their back on the glorious Gospel. How could they be enlightened by salvation, taste of the heavenly gift of Jesus and His grace along with the good Word of God, and partake of the Holy Ghost, only to go back to the pig trough of the world? The Apostle Peter eventually answered such a question. He related such people to those who have eyes full of adultery and hearts that have been exercised with covetousness. They have forsaken the right way because they love the wages of unrighteousness. In fact, they are wells without the refreshing water of the Holy Ghost. Without the power of the Spirit, people are carried away with vanity and the lusts of the flesh. Ultimately, they will fail to pay the price to know and possess Jesus Christ.[21]

The Apostle Paul understood that the glory in the glorious Gospel was Jesus Christ. His ultimate desire was to receive the crown of righteousness from his righteous Lord. In confidence, he knew he would receive it because he had fought a good fight as a soldier of Christ. He had finished the course by never taking his eyes off of the One he desired to apprehend, and he kept the faith unfeigned in Christ that was first delivered to him in the Gospel. It was in this confidence that Paul recognized that God had delivered him out of the mouth of the lion, Satan. He also declared that the Lord would deliver him from every evil work and would preserve him unto His heavenly kingdom.[22]

What kind of testimony do you have about Jesus? Does it manifest the glorious reality of what Christ did and is doing in your life, or is it lifeless because Christ is missing or being replaced with man's leadership, denominational preference, popular theology, or personal opinions?

---

[20] 2 Timothy 2:3-4, 19-22
[21] John 7:36-39; 2 Timothy 4:10; Hebrews 5:4-5; 2 Peter 2:14-22
[22] Philippians 3:12; 2 Timothy 4:7-8, 17-18; 1 Peter 5:8

12

THE DISCIPLINES OF THE GOSPEL

Embracing the true Gospel will produce an inward discipline. The manifestation of this discipline is the new man. How does this new man express himself? Titus 1:1 gives us insight into the first type of discipline that is manifested in a person's life due to the power of the Gospel—godliness. The first Scripture in the first chapter of Titus states, "Paul, a servant of God, and an apostle of Jesus Christ, according to the faith of God's elect, and the acknowledging of the truth which is after godliness."

Holiness is a state that is established with separation from the profane, while righteousness is a disposition that is developed through faith and obedience in regard to the matters of God. However, godliness is the product of a holy state and a righteous attitude before God. Godliness is displayed in the ways we think and conduct ourselves. Our actions will display the attitude and ways of God. In fact, that which does not originate, or is inspired and sincerely expressive of God, is ungodly, regardless of how religious or pious it may be. Godliness is strictly associated and identified with God.

The Apostle Paul confirmed how godliness expresses itself by bringing a clear contrast between the ungodly and the godly. To the godly, all things are pure, but, to the ungodly, all things are defiled. Even though the ungodly may profess God, their works deny Him. These works show that they are abominable and idolatrous in nature.[1] They are contrary to the character and will of God; therefore, they are disobedient to the intent and truth of the Word. Ultimately, these good works are regarded as reprobate or worthless to God.

Paul is the only writer who firmly dealt with the condition of being a reprobate. He shows that there are three areas of people's lives that can become reprobate. The apostle talks about a reprobate mind in Romans 1:28. Such a mind no longer retains the knowledge of the true God because it has replaced the glory of God with another god. He then talks about a reprobate faith that does not possess the true Jesus. In fact, such a faith rests in some form of idolatry.[2]

---

[1] Titus 1:15-16
[2] 2 Corinthians 13:5-7

In Titus, Paul dealt with reprobate works. The small epistle proves to us that not just any old work will do when it comes to our lives before God. Even though we may do good works for Christ, they must be in line with His will in order to be approved of God. Such works that are not approved become a source of iniquity; therefore, failing to bring glory and honor to God.[3] This is why Jesus made this statement in Matthew 5:16, "Let your light so shine before men, that they may see your good works, and glorify your Father which is in heaven." Therefore, for works to be accepted by God, they must be an extension of His character, will, and heart, and not from any other source. Ultimately, acceptable works will glorify God.

Godliness cannot be faked, for it is based on a God who never lies, a Lord and Savior who will return for those who are ready, and a regenerated life that has been brought forth through cleansing and change. It is a life that proves to be consistent and blameless behind closed doors.

A blameless life occurs when a person has denied ungodliness and worldly lust. Godliness lives soberly because it knows that the great God and Savior, Jesus, will appear. Godliness will always manifest itself in good works that will ultimately honor God.[4] A person who is godly lives righteously because he or she understands the significance of the redemption that took place on his or her behalf.

Those who insist on godliness become sanctified people set apart for His purpose. Such a life stands confident because it has been justified by grace and made an heir by hope.[5] As Paul stated, "This is a faithful saying, and these things I will that thou affirm constantly, that they which have believed in God might be careful to maintain good works. These things are good and profitable unto men" (Titus 3:8).

One of the attacks against the Gospel is the idea that man can make himself acceptable to God by works. Once again, we are saved by grace through faith. Therefore, good works do not save us. Rather, we are saved unto good works. This is brought out in Paul's writings. Acceptable works are works that are being done through us by the Holy Ghost.[6] Good works are simply fruits of salvation, not the source of it.

The next discipline of the Gospel is love. We love God because He first loved us. We encounter this love at the cross where we can choose to become bondservants to our loving, dedicated Master and Lord. Such love begins with loving God. This love will express itself in a moral obligation to do right towards others in spite of the circumstances.[7]

---

[3] Matthew 7:21-23
[4] Titus 2:12-14; 3:5, 8
[5] Titus 2:12
[6] Ephesians 2:8-10; Philippians 1:6; Colossians 1:9-10; 2 Timothy 2:21; 3:16-17
[7] Mark 12:29-31; 1 John 4:19

We see this love being brought to the forefront by Paul when he appealed to Philemon's moral obligation towards a runaway slave.[8] The slave, Onesimus, committed his life to Jesus under Paul's auspice. Up until this runaway servant became a believer, he remained a slave to sin, treacherous and untrustworthy, even towards his godly Christian master.

No doubt Philemon was kind and just towards his servants, but Onesimus' actions reveal that he refused to submit to even righteous authority. Apparently, he could not accept his lot in life as a slave; therefore, he could not humble himself before his master as a trustworthy servant. His insubordination was a manifestation of sin. The problem with being a slave to sin is that you will defy and run away from the real liberty found in being a bondservant to Jesus.

A bondservant is a slave out of love. Totally committed, such a slave consecrates his or her whole life to one purpose, serving the master. Philemon was such a slave to Jesus. As a result, Paul was appealing to this man to show his servant, Onesimus, mercy and restoration. He was asking Philemon to prove his devotion to Jesus by showing the sacrificial, forgiving side of love.

The Apostle Paul was also ready to show his moral obligation on behalf of the new convert. He was ready to pay for any wrong this man may have done to Philemon.[9] Clearly, Jesus' words are being applied in practical ways, "By this shall all men know that ye are my disciples, if ye have love one to another" (John 13:35).

The next discipline of the Gospel is faith that results in obedience. We have already talked about faith, but few realize that it is actually a discipline. We are told in 2 Corinthians 5:7 that we are to walk or live by faith. Faith shows itself through obedience that results in good works. In fact, it is tested and refined in the fires of temptation or trials.[10] Faith is a choice and requires us to discipline our thoughts, feelings, and ways, in order to believe and obey what the Word says. Usually, people immediately give in to self. Therefore, faith requires the discipline of denying self up front for the purpose of obeying in the right spirit in light of truth.

Hebrews and James talk about faith. Faith is a glorious gift of God to those who have a heart to receive. It is living, active, and possesses an enduring hope in the things that are not seen. Sincere faith comes to God based on who He is, as well as from the confident knowledge that He is the rewarder of all who diligently seek Him. Sincere faith naturally expresses itself in good works. This eternal virtue moves in fear of God, goes where it is called, and condemns the world as those who possess faith become heirs of righteousness. Due to faith being counted as righteousness to God's servants, their prayers reach the throne of God, and they even sometimes find themselves being counted as God's

---

[8] Philemon 5-15
[9] Philemon 16-19
[10] James 2:17-26; 1 Peter 1:6-9

friend. Faith is patient, confident, and lives on after death. It will choose to suffer affliction, rather than partake of pleasure for a season. It esteems the reproach of Christ greater than the riches of this world. In fact, God has chosen the poor of this world to be rich in faith and heirs of the kingdom of God. Faith also strives in the midst of tribulations, and it will suffer loss to obtain a better resurrection. In the end, it causes the saint to become so separate from the world that the world ceases to be worthy to witness its operation and blessings.[11]

When people lack true faith, they will test God as their hearts become hard towards truth.[12] Unbelief will cause such people to neglect or make light of salvation, as they walk in ignorance towards God and the gift He has so freely offered.[13]

How could a person neglect such a gift of life after he or she was enlightened concerning Jesus and tasted of this heavenly gift and the Word of God, along with the powers of the world to come? How could people neglect salvation after being made partakers of the Holy Ghost?[14] It is simple; they have never entered into that rest in God because of unbelief. Rest in God is associated with Jesus Christ. Jesus invited all of those who labor to come to Him and He would give them rest. However, there were a couple of disciplines that were stipulated in regard to this rest, "Take my yoke upon you, and learn of me" (Matthew 11:29a). We must come under His yoke. Jesus' yoke is that of truth, and it will discipline our walk. It is in a disciplined walk that one will learn of the character, ways, and will of Jesus.

Hebrews tells us why we need to learn about Jesus. He is the brightness of glory, the expressed image of God. He upholds all things by the word of His power. However, to secure our redemption, He became lower than the angels as He was fashioned as a man. As the Son of God, the Father said this to Him, "Thy throne, O God, is forever and ever: a scepter of righteousness is the scepter of thy kingdom" (Hebrews 1:8). After He purged our sins on the cross, He rose from the grave to bring reconciliation between man and God and sat down on the right hand of the Majesty on high. His work was accomplished on earth, for, through death, He destroyed the authority of the devil, who had the power of death.[15]

In heaven, Jesus as man would serve as the High Priest and Advocate. He would intercede for us and remind the courts of heaven that He served as our substitute on the cross when we fall into sin. He would also open the way for us to boldly come to the throne of grace to obtain mercy and find grace in time of need. His work would be complete

---

[11] 1 Corinthians 13:13; Hebrews 11; James 2:5, 14-26; 5:11-18
[12] Hebrews 3:8-19
[13] Strong's Exhaustive Concordance, #272
[14] Hebrews 2:3; 6:4-6
[15] Hebrews 1:2-3; 2:6-10, 14-17; 8:1

in both this world and in the heavenlies. As Hebrews 7:25 tells us, Jesus, as our Intercessor, is able to save us to the uttermost.

The next discipline that will come out of a changed life is wisdom. The wisest man, Solomon, stated that we should seek after and value wisdom. James tells us that if we lack wisdom, we are to ask for it. There are two types of wisdom in operation: God's wisdom and man's wisdom. God's wisdom comes from above, while man's wisdom comes from the world. We need to consider both forms of wisdom to rightly discern the wisdom that we are operating within.

God's wisdom contains another discipline—the fear of the Lord. In God's wisdom, we want to please Him because we fear and love Him in a proper way. The world's wisdom lacks the fear of God, but fears consequences. Therefore, godly fear will give in to God, while unholy fear will try to find ways around responsibilities to avoid consequences. True wisdom produces sobriety, while worldly wisdom results in irresponsibility and game playing.

Wisdom of any form will eventually cause man to be found foolish. God's wisdom brings a contrast to man's ways, exposing his foolishness. The wisdom of the world produces that which is foolish, such as strife and jealousy, as a person gives way to every evil work.[16]

For Christians, the exposure of their foolishness will produce repentance. However, the pride of man that motivates his wisdom will not allow the person to be exposed for a fool. Such wisdom will live in denial and deception, causing the heart to become hard towards truth.

Once wisdom declares us to be a fool, we are humbled by it. Humility, for the Christian, allows wisdom to silence our pride as we become broken by the foolishness of our fleshly ways. However, man's wisdom must maintain its pride. In order for pride to keep its dignity at the point of foolishness, pride will resort to worldly remorse and fake nobility. In other words, it will adjust outwardly to fit an image of brokenness, while refusing to be wrong in heart and contrite in spirit.[17]

Now that we are at the state of some type of humility, we are open to learn the lessons of wisdom. Wisdom is knowledge that has been applied in practical ways. Godly wisdom is always ready for instruction. It desires the necessary change to become more like Jesus. In fact, godly wisdom will not be content until it has been challenged and changed by the blessed revelations of Jesus. These revelations are applied with the intent of disciplining the walk of the believer to ensure godliness. Application of these life-changing insights makes Jesus the Christian's reality.

Man's wisdom is different. It simply wants to feed its intellectual arrogance. This type of wisdom perceives that whatever it knows or concludes is reality. The reality of the mind and the reality that surrounds us are diverse. The reality of the mind is nothing more than self-delusion.

---

[16] James 3:14-16
[17] Psalms 34:18; 51:17; Hebrews 12:16-17; James 3:13-16

Challenging the Christian Life

Self-delusion makes us indifferent to the reality around us. Such "wisdom" not only causes us to look foolish to those around us, but clueless as well.

The Apostle Paul told us that Jesus is the essence of all wisdom. James actually described the wisdom of Jesus, "But the wisdom that is from above is first pure, then peaceable, gentle, and easy to be entreated, full of mercy and good fruits, without partiality, and without hypocrisy" (James 3:17). To have the wisdom of Christ means that one must have the mind of Christ. Jesus was pure, He advocated peace with the Father, and He was kind and meek towards others. He was ready to hear heart cries and show mercy and love in the form of compassion. He had no prejudices; therefore, He could be trusted. His trustworthiness ensured that His words were real, His actions genuine, and His dealings with people a product of integrity.

Today, the wisdom from above has been replaced with man's doctrines and theology. This intellectual preference has created a type of self-righteousness that is both blind and judgmental. The idolatrous emphasis of religious knowledge has caused man to worship his conclusions and approach things based on what He knows, rather than by the leading of the Spirit.

When the Holy Spirit is missing from any equation, many well-meaning people will miss the life, truth, and instruction of Jesus' words and ways. Even though these people may quote the Word, they will still lack revelation that changes and establishes authority in their lives. Sadly, this worldly pursuit for intelligence in the religious world has made cemeteries out of seminaries, and whitewashed sepulchers out of pastors and teachers.[18] There is no life to be found in either arena. These people fulfill Paul's prophesy about the perilous times surrounding the end-days, when he stated, "Ever learning, and never able to come to the knowledge of the truth" (2 Timothy 3:7).

Another discipline of the Gospel is sanctification. The first epistle of Peter brings out the work of sanctification. Peter reminds believers that they were elected because God foreknew who would truly come to Him. This did not keep God from reaching out to every person, but it clearly confirms that God is all-knowing, and is never caught off guard by events or the decisions of men.[19]

The Spirit does the work of sanctification as man obeys. This obedience is the product of the redemption secured by the blood of Christ. It is realized as the powerful life of Jesus is manifested through the believer. Needless to say, this life is accomplished by faith that will be tested and strengthened by fiery tests. Faith that is matured in the fires will endure until the appearing of Jesus.[20]

---

[18] Matthew 23:24-29; John 16:13
[19] 1 Peter 1:2
[20] 1 Peter 1:2-9

Sanctification is the work of holiness. The work of holiness that comes out of our lives will be realized through separation from the world and ungodliness. Such separation involves girding up the mind and no longer fashioning it after the former lust that operated in ignorance towards God. Once the former lusts are put off, one can be distinct in his or her conversation. The problem in America today is that there is no distinction between the visible Church and the world.

This is a grave tragedy. Peter was clear that believers should be strangers and pilgrims in this world. Separation from the world is made evident when such foreigners abstain from fleshly lusts. After all, as Christians, we must hate evil, do good, seek the peace of God, and pursue it. He also tells us that that, as believers, we are a holy priesthood that is to offer up spiritual sacrifices that are acceptable to Jesus. It is according to Jesus, who is the Cornerstone that saints stand as lively stones that comprise a chosen generation, a royal priesthood, a holy nation, and a peculiar people who will bring forth the praises of Jesus as they walk in His glorious light.[21]

Distinction from the world will bring the persecution upon those who truly follow Jesus. Such people can only stand and withstand affliction because they have sanctified the Lord in their hearts. Therefore, persecution will cause confidence because the eyes of the Lord are on the righteous, and His ears are open to their prayers. As a result, those persecuted for the sake of Christ will discover the faithfulness of God, along with true happiness as they become identified with Jesus and bring glory to God.[22]

Christians cannot be priests without being clothed in humility. They cannot be co-laborers with God without learning to cast personal burdens upon Him. They cannot be victorious soldiers unless they are sober, vigilant, and steadfast in their faith and aware of their enemy, Satan.[23]

Peter showed us in his first epistle that we must come to a holy state before we can become godly in our conduct. In his second epistle, he spoke of what it takes to ensure godliness. One of the themes of 2 Peter is remembrance. Remembrance is about having the right focus. In 2 Peter 1, Peter wrote about becoming barren and unfruitful in the knowledge of Jesus.

To be barren and unfruitful in the knowledge of Jesus implies that a person has failed to apply what he or she knows as being true and right to his or her life or walk before God. Of course, this means that godly wisdom is lacking. Peter shows how our knowledge of Christ is line upon line. In this case, it begins with the diligence to apply godly virtues to one's way of life. To apply something takes faith that will establish character. Character is able to take knowledge and properly apply it to

---

[21] 1 Peter 2:5-9; 3:11
[22] 1 Peter 3:11-15; 4:13-19
[23] 1 Peter 5:5-9

the disciplines of the Christian walk. Once the proper disciplines are in place, patience can operate, producing godliness. Godly conversation becomes an open avenue by which God can express His love through us to others.[24]

The reason Christians become barren in their knowledge is because they forget their humble beginnings at the cross. To be barren means there is no life. To kill the life of Christ in us means that we have become indifferent to the reality of, not only who Christ is, but also what He did for us. As Peter stated, to forget is to become blind to the fact that we have been purged from sins.[25]

It is up to believers to make their callings and elections sure by remembering that Jesus is who He says He is. Peter reminded us of His encounter with Jesus on the Mount of Transfiguration to confirm this point. Jesus' humanity gave way to His glory. It was while the glory of the only begotten of the Father was being unveiled that the Father introduced Him as His Son. The three witnesses were told not to share the event until after Jesus' resurrection and ascension. We know that the Gospels describe this event, but we also see that both Peter and John make reference to this event in their letters.[26]

Peter was an eyewitness of Jesus Christ, but He knew of the sure word of prophecy. Jesus came forth as the promised light that shines in the darkness of sin. He now serves as the dawn to the lost who are seeking Him and becomes the day star that arises within the hearts of those who are born again of Water and Spirit.[27]

Jesus' first advent was not merely an event, but a planned occurrence. It was prophesied by the Holy Ghost through men, subject to His leading. This sure prophecy was to establish His people on the immovable Rock, so they could become like Noah, whose very righteousness brought the flood of judgment upon the world. These prophecies were also given to establish the Lots of the world, who being so vexed by sin, that God would be able to deliver them from judgment. He wanted these prophecies to warn men so they would avoid becoming wells without the water of the Holy Ghost, carried about with lusts, false doctrines of men, and seducing doctrines of demons. He wanted to prepare His people for the time of great judgment on the earth.[28]

The truth is that all things will dissolve except that which is godly. As believers, we must be diligent in our lives to display holy conversation or godliness. We must shun counterfeits and pursue after that which is real, glorious, and eternal. We must come to the place of holiness where we

---

[24] 2 Peter 1:5-8
[25] 2 Peter 1:8-9
[26] 2 Peter 1:16-18
[27] 2 Peter 1:19
[28] 2 Peter 1:20-21; 2:4-17

are at peace with God and stand blameless and without spot before our precious Lord.[29]

We must grow in the knowledge of Jesus. This requires us to operate in the disciplines established by the powerful Gospel and the life it brings forth. We must check our focus. We must never forget the humble beginnings of the cross and the call for repentance from sin.[30] We must have our faces set heavenward and our awareness fined-tuned to the impending judgment. As saints, we must always be prepared to meet Jesus in the state of holiness, with the attitude of righteousness, and within the confines of godliness.

The question we must consider is, is my knowledge of Jesus barren or is it growing with greater revelations? Is my life akin to the world or is it the expression of God's virtuous character? These questions must be honestly answered to ensure our preparation to meet Jesus in His majesty and judgment.

---

[29] 2 Peter 3:10-14
[30] 2 Peter 3:9, 17-18

13

THE PRODUCT OF THE GOSPEL

The Gospel's main purpose is to deliver us from the bondage of sin and its consequences. At the core of the Gospel is the truth. Truth not only liberates, but it changes lives. Obviously, changed lives begin with a personal encounter with the essence of all truth, Jesus Christ. The Apostle John begins his first epistle with this very introduction of how Jesus who, from the very beginning, was heard, seen, observed, and touched by mere man. In Him, eternal life was manifested. It was the life that John declared to others.[1]

The product of the Gospel is eternal life. Jesus clearly established in John 5:26 and 14:6 that He is life itself. Again, His life in us is eternal, and it has the power to change us and raise us up on that last day. This life will bear witness of who He is. Such a life is not hidden, for joy is evident and the light of God is present in sweet fellowship.[2]

To encounter Jesus means that one has encountered the Rock of ages. No one person can get around this Rock that looms in history as a point of conflict, confusion, separation, hope, and life. Perhaps the initial encounter for many started with a realization of a Savior who obeyed the Father, a Lord who was committed to His servants, and a God who so loved that He offered up the ultimate sacrifice for our redemption. However, this eternal life begins for each believer, there has to be the realization of sin. Man wants to ignore, deny, or do away with sin. But, without the reality of sin, we deceive ourselves about our spiritual condition and our spiritual destination. If sin is not brought to the forefront of what ails all people, man will continue to create a false reality that makes him indifferent to his need for God.

Without the awareness of sin, there is no need to confess it. The main reason for confessing sin is for the purpose of seeking forgiveness and reconciliation with a Holy God, who has no part with or in any sin. If any of us fail to recognize the problem of sin in our dispositions, attitudes, and conduct, we make God a liar. After all, He stated that we have all sinned. Sin causes separation between Him and us. To close

---

[1] John 8:31-36; 1 John 1:1-2
[2] 1 John 1:3-7

that gap, He sent His Son to die for us. If we refuse to see the gap caused by our sin, it just proves that the truth of His Word is not in us.[3]

The Word of God clearly verifies our sinful disposition, but it takes faith to believe the Word and apply its truths to our lives. To disregard the Word is to walk in denial about our spiritual conditions, to remain ignorant about God, and to remain in darkness to the ways of death and destruction in our lives.

There are two main issues about the Gospel that we must have the correct understanding of in our minds and hearts: our hopeless condition that we have already considered and the identity of Jesus. Jesus is the light of the Gospel. To walk in the light of the Gospel means to walk in light of Jesus' character, example, teaching, and ways. John made this statement, "He that saith he abideth in him ought himself also to walk, even as he walked" (1 John 2:6).

To walk as Jesus walked means, first of all, that He must be the source in which we abide. In essence, He must become our all in all. After all, He is the incredible Vine that ensures every aspect of our well-being. However, to experience this well-being, we must be fully connected to His life. This means there must be an intimate relationship or fellowship with Him. Such fellowship points to agreement. As the Vine moves, those abiding in Him will move in unity. As the Vine freely gives all that is present in His life, His branches must freely receive by faith to ensure growth and maturity. As a result, the fruit that comes forth will be sweet to those who are searching, sour to those who are rebellious, bitter to those who are in denial, salty to those who are struggling and wounded, and a sweet fragrance to God who will be glorified.[4]

For Jesus to be such a Vine, we must know Him for who He is. John told us in the first verse of His epistle that Jesus is the Word of life. The word "Word" takes us back to the Gospel of John that declared that the Word not only existed from the very beginning, but that the Living Word is God.[5]

John also revealed that Jesus is our advocate who serves as a propitiation for our sins. As our advocate, He not only stood in the gap on our behalf, but He also satisfied the judgment of the Law upon sin for each of us. To satisfy the judgment on sin, He was required to die on a cross in our place. But, praise God, He arose from the grave to serve as our living advocate in the courts of heaven.

As we consider Jesus' role as our advocate, we have to come to terms with why He was successful in that position. After all, He paid a price we could not pay. The key to His success lies with who He is.[6] The Apostle John clearly outlined who Jesus is. It is vital that we see John's presentation of Jesus in his epistle.

---

[3] Romans 3:23; 1 John 1:7-10
[4] Matthew 5:12; 15:1-10; John 15:1-8; 2 Corinthians 2:15-16; 1 John 1:6-7
[5] John 1:1
[6] 1 John 2:12

We must, first of all, know Jesus as the Christ. The word "the" is very important in this text. It is singular. Jesus is the only true Christ. As the Christ, He is the promised Messiah and God's Anointed One. As the Messiah, we are reminded that He is the Son of Man. In other words, His lineage can be traced back to King David. He came to set the oppressed free through His anointing. "Anointing" means He was ordained, commissioned, or set apart for a special mission. The mission of Christ was to set the spiritually oppressed free. Once they were free, they could freely embrace Him as King, Lord, Master, and Ruler of their hearts, thereby establishing the kingdom of God from within as well as on the earth.[7]

Jesus is the only One who holds this position. In fact, He warned us that many would come claiming the position of the Messiah, but we are not to believe or follow them. True to His warning, today there are many running around claiming this special anointing on their life. Yet, if a person is truly born of Spirit and water, he or she will have the anointing of the Holy Spirit in his or her life. There are no exceptions in God's kingdom. We all have been born into the Adamic race; therefore, no one person can claim elitism in the kingdom of God.[8]

The anointing of the Holy Ghost may manifest itself differently in people's lives. This difference does not determine the level of importance of a person in the kingdom of God, for God is no respecter of persons. He enables His people according to their positions or responsibilities in His kingdom to do His bidding and to fulfill His plan. However, the main problem is that, either the anointing of the Holy Ghost is stifled because He is being grieved or quenched by ignorance and unbelief, or this anointing is abused or counterfeited by a wrong spirit such as the antichrist spirit.[9]

This brings us to another attack against the Gospel. There is a concept that says, because we are children of God, partakers of Jesus' divine nature, and we have this anointing, we are little gods or christs. The Word is clear that there is only one God by nature and there is only one Messiah or Anointed One. To be children of God or partakers of His divine nature does not make us divine. To partake of His divine nature simply means we are becoming identified with Him as we adhere to His Word; thereby, allowing His life to be formed in us. To be adopted as the children of God points to a new disposition, complete identification, and an eternal inheritance, and not to a whole new nature.[10]

To be anointed by God means we are vessels in which the work of Christ can be accomplished. The power of anointing is solely based on the sovereignty and work of the Spirit in accordance with God's perfect

---

[7] Matthew 1:17; 6:10; Luke 4:18-19; 1 John 2:22-23
[8] Matthew 24:23-24; John 3:3, 5; 1 Corinthians 6:19; 1 John 2:20, 27
[9] Acts 10:34; Ephesians 4:30; 1 Thessalonians 5:19; 1 John 2:22-23, 27
[10] Isaiah 44:6; Romans 8:15-17; 2 Peter 1:4-8

plan.[11] However, man must be an open, available, and willing vessel for the Holy Ghost to work through. Today, there are many imposters who claim this anointing. If they possess any power, it is from Satan. The way to test these people is simple. Is Jesus being glorified or is man being lifted up as the one who has a corner on this anointing? Sadly, many people are ignorantly following these imposters. In some cases, their followers have such perverted loyalties that they would willingly persecute those who oppose the imposter or die for him or her.

When individuals are being anointed for a specific work, they simply serve as an extension of Jesus. For example, these people are His mouth as they proclaim Him as the solution to all that spiritually, emotionally, and physically ails man. They serve as His ears that will hear the cries of the lost, eyes that will see the pain of the outcast, and hands of compassion that will be willing to touch lives with God's mercy, grace, and love.

However, the imposters who lay claim to a "special anointing" outside of what has already been made available to all of those who believe upon the Lord Jesus Christ are motivated by an antichrist spirit. Their goal is to become a substitute Christ in their followers' lives. They are not looking to make followers of Jesus. Rather, they want people to follow them. These people are doing Satan's bidding, leading people away from the redemptive work of Jesus Christ. They are not only under a different spirit, but they subtly replace Christ with themselves, as they preach another gospel.

The second issue about Christ's identity comes down to His nature. Once again, an antichrist spirit is busy changing the glory of Jesus from God in the flesh to simply being a person who was serving as a mere reflection of God. Jesus gave up His glory or capacity as God to become man. He never ceased to be God, but He did give that up which distinguished Him as God—His power and authority. He then functioned contrary to His sovereignty in the status of a servant in His humanity. As stated, God in the flesh is the glorious mystery Paul often made reference to. Can man in his mere intellectual understanding come to terms with the mystery of God being fully man while maintaining His deity? The answer is no. This is why man must first accept it by faith upon hearing this truth about Jesus. It is only as one receives a truth by faith that the Holy Ghost can make it revelation to the soul of man. It is only at the point of revelation that man is enabled to come to an understanding of this reality.

Jesus was presented as God in the flesh from different angles throughout the New Testament. However, the most blatant presentations are found in the Gospel of John, Colossians, and 1 Timothy. In John 1:1, Jesus was presented as the Word that always existed as God. Then, in John 1:14, John declared that the Word became flesh. Jesus, in John 17:5 mentioned the glory He shared with the Father before the world

---

[11] 1 Corinthians 12:7-11

ever existed. In Colossians 1:15-18 and 2:9 the Apostle Paul clearly identified Jesus as Creator and the manifestation of complete deity in bodily form. In 1 Timothy 3:16, Paul stated, "And without controversy great is the mystery of godliness: <u>God was manifest in the flesh</u> ..." (Emphasis added).

As pointed out in previous chapters, the Apostle Paul addressed Jesus as God in various ways throughout his epistles. He stated that Jesus was God by nature in Philippians and. in 1 Timothy, Paul also referred to Jesus as eternal, immortal, invisible, and the only wise God. In Titus, Jesus is referred to as God and Savior. The other epistles continued this presentation. Hebrews addresses Jesus as God. The writer of Hebrews also stated this about Jesus' unchangeable, eternal character, "Jesus Christ the same yesterday, and today, and for ever" (Hebrews 13:8). Jude declared that Jesus is the only wise God and Savior.[12] Clearly, Jesus was referred to as both God and man throughout Scriptures. Obviously, Jesus' manhood is not always a controversial issue, but in many cases His deity is.

John told us that a person who denies that Jesus Christ came in the flesh is of the spirit of the antichrist. His statement concerning Jesus would seem to be a no-brainer. It appears as if John was saying that people must not reject the idea that Jesus came in the flesh. What is John really saying? Since it is a historical fact that a man named Jesus lived and walked upon this earth, most people would not reject such an idea. However, you need to understand what John was saying in light of the premises he has already established about Jesus. John had already stipulated that Jesus is God by nature. Therefore, in his first epistle, he was stating that, if individuals deny that Jesus Christ, who is God by nature, actually came in the flesh, they clearly are not of God, but are of the antichrist spirit.[13] A person who is under such a spirit will accept a counterfeit Jesus who will be incapable of saving him or her. Sadly, such controversy should not exist among those who have called upon the name of Jesus, but it does.

Those who cannot see Jesus' deity being unveiled in human form have often been blinded by intellectual arrogance. This condition happens when people approach the Bible from the point of intellectual deduction, rather than child-like faith. As they try to explain the mystery of Christ based on their limited and perverted intellects, they can only logically come to one conclusion—that such a Jesus is an imposter and a liar. He cannot be both God and man.

Intellectual deduction of this matter sets up a frame of reference that will actually blind these people to the mystery that is unveiled throughout the Bible. Although we clearly have Scriptures that declare Jesus to be God, these people will not see these declarations, or they will twist them according to their own beliefs.

---

[12] Philippians 2:6; 1 Timothy 1:17; Titus 2:13; Hebrews 1:8; Jude 25
[13] 1 John 4:2-3; 2 John 7

Those who do not recognize Jesus for who He is do not know the one true God. Jesus brought this fact out in John 8. He told the Jews that, if they knew the Father, they would know Him.[14] If you do not know the true God of heaven, there is no basis on which to test what you do know. Jesus will become a concept that will be fit into religious beliefs, causing such people to come under an antichrist spirit. The biggest goal of this counterfeit spirit is to deny the true God of heaven by stripping Him of His glory, work, and plan in the hearts and minds of people.

There is another point of controversy over Jesus' deity. There are people who believe that Jesus is God, but they do not believe in the Godhead. They believe that Jesus and the Father are the same entity and that there is only one Person who makes up the Godhead. The Bible clearly distinguishes the fact that the Father and the Son are two distinct Persons. After all, Jesus would not seek or talk to Himself in prayer. If the Father were not another person, Jesus would simply make reference to Himself, rather than to the Father. If the Father were not distinct from Jesus, He would have not introduced Jesus as His Son at His baptism and on the Mount of Transfiguration.[15]

Jesus was always referring to the Person of Father as being distinct. Paul also confirmed this in 1 Corinthians 8:6, "But to us there is but one God, the Father, of whom are all things, and we in him; and one Lord Jesus Christ, by whom are all things, and we by him." Paul was stipulating that there are two distinct Persons. There is only one God, the Father, and there is only one Lord Jesus Christ. If you consider what Paul was saying, He was not saying there is one God who is the Father and who is Lord. He was saying there is only one Person who is God, the Father, and only one Person who is the Lord Jesus Christ.

The Apostle John identified the three Persons of the Godhead in His epistle, showing that they are distinct Persons. He made this statement in 1 John 5:7, "For there are three that bear record in heaven, the Father, The Word, and the Holy Ghost: and these three are one." We know according to John 1 that the Word is Jesus Christ.

It is important that we see Jesus in His deity, as well as know Him in His humanity. If Jesus were not divine by nature, He could have never secured our redemption. Therefore, He is the Savior of the world because, as the Man, He died on the cross in our place, and, as God, He rose from the grave to secure both redemption and life for those who trust Him.

John stated that Jesus is the Savior of the world. The word "the" once again points to singular. If you study the concept of Savior, you will see that position is only allotted to God. Once again, as Savior, Jesus' deity is being verified. Jesus does not share the responsibility of salvation with any other person or source. He alone saves. The problem is that many cults agree that Jesus is Savior, but add, in a subtle way,

---

[14] John 8:19, 38, 42, 47, 54-55
[15] Matthew 3:17; 17:5; John 1:18; 8:28-29, 38; 11:41-42

that He is not enough. In other words, His work of redemption on the cross was not finished.[16]

For these cults, it is Jesus plus something. For example, many beliefs maintain that salvation hinges on Jesus plus doctrine or denomination. In other cases, it is Jesus plus works, the Law, or traditions. For some, it is their leader plus Jesus or the latest movement that has Jesus tacked on for credibility. One belief maintains that Jesus shares His position as Redeemer with His biological mother, Mary. Yet, Mary was not deity or eternal in nature. She was simply a vessel that God used to bring forth His Son. This vessel of God did not die for mankind, nor does she have any means by which to redeem man. She has not risen from the dead to prove victory over death. Neither is she omnipresent, omniscient, or omnipotent to answer prayer or change the reality of life. Again, all such exaltations of her are unscriptural and misguided. Jesus alone is Savior. He is the way to God, the truth about God, and the eternal life that can only come from God.[17]

Although Jesus is mentioned in these cults or movements, He is never exalted as the only way to a relationship with God, the only source of redemption, and the only means to reconciliation. Therefore, whoever advocates a different way is offering a counterfeit that will not be able to save. It is also easy to identify these people. They do not have a real testimony of Jesus. Rather, they exalt their leader, denomination, movement, or doctrine.

The final aspect of Jesus is that He is the Son of God. Most cults will declare that Jesus is the Son of God, while denying what it means. The title Son of God carries a lot of meaning with it. Up front, this term means that Jesus was equal with the Father, as well as a total reflection of God in His humanity.[18] However, the meaning of it includes Jesus' position as the Messiah, His divine nature that identifies Him as God, and His responsibility as Savior. If any of these aspects are missing from the presentation of Jesus, such people do not believe or know Jesus as the only begotten Son of God.

Once again, we come to the harsh reality that many people possess a different Jesus. As a result, they are offering another gospel to their hearers. Sadly, ignorance of God has caused many to chase after wolves, thieves, or hireling shepherds.[20] Each person who falls into these heretical traps proves that he or she did not know God in the first place. The reason people do not know God is because they are not seeking to know Him; therefore, they do not have a relationship with Him.

An individual who has a relationship with God will know the true God and will recognize heresy and flee from it. Such a relationship with God

---

[16] Isaiah 43:11; 45:15, 22; John 19:30; Titus 2:13; 3:4, 6; Jude 24-25; 1 John 4:14

[17] John 14:6; Galatians 4:4-5; 1 Timothy 2:5-6

[18] John 5:17-18; 14:9; Colossians 2:9; 1 John

[20] Matthew 7:15; Acts 20:29; John 10:1, 8, 12-13;

begins when an individual has truly been born again. To be born again means that a person has been born into the kingdom of God and has been adopted into the family of God. The new life that comes out of this birth is the total work and will of God and not any attempts of man.[21]

John brought out the manifestations of this new life in his first epistle. Many people talk about a sinner's prayer, but few ever talk about the fact that they indeed have been born again with a new life. This new life means a new disposition or inclination. As John stated, whosoever is born of God will not walk in sin. Those born of Spirit and water will have a new disposition that will no longer be inclined towards sin, but will be inclined towards God.[22]

Another manifestation of a relationship with God is our walk. If we are developing a relationship with God, we will be walking in the light. The light will reveal any sin in our lives, ensuring forgiveness and fellowship with God and others.[23]

The third manifestation of a relationship with God is that we will walk as Jesus walked. To walk as Jesus involves self-denial with the intent of obeying. Jesus' whole purpose or mind was to obey, please, and glorify the Father. In order to do this, He became a Servant of man, in total subjection to the Father, and submissive to the cross. As a result, people can possess eternal life.[24]

The final aspect of a relationship with God is separation from the world. If one is a friend of the world, he or she is an enemy of God. Only those who are born again and desire God will find the means to replace any love for the world with indifference. Those who love the world will be devoid of the love of the Father. Since they belong to the world, they will serve it. People can only serve one master at a time, and John was clear that only those who do the will of God will abide forever in His kingdom.[25]

The final evidence of eternal life is the presence of godly fruits. One of the fruits of eternal life is joy. This joy is complete because it has the confidence that God is God. In His last night with the disciples, Jesus told them that He had spoken of the things to come so that their joy might remain. In his epistle, John told believers that he was writing these things so their joy may be full or complete.[26] In God's kingdom, it is not what we intellectually understand that brings us joy. Rather, it is what we receive by faith that will bring such confidence and delight to our spirits.

The most predominate fruit of eternal life is love. This love is greatly lacking in much of what is called Christianity. Godly love is a moral obligation to do right, regardless of differences in beliefs. It manifests itself in benevolence. Today, there is hardness of heart and lack of God's

---

[21] John 1:12-13; 3:3, 5; 10:5, 8, 12; Romans 8:14-17
[22] 1 John 3:9-10
[23] 1 John 1:5-7, 9
[24] Philippians 2:5-8; 1 John 2:6
[25] Matthew 6:24; James 4:4 1 John 2:15-17
[26] John 15:11; Galatians 5:22; 1 John 1:4

love in these heretical movements. This hardness is arrogance, and it is militant and self-serving. Instead of being sacrificial, it will sacrifice those who do not live up to the standards that are being advocated. The lack of godly love is the biggest proof that Jesus is missing from the equation. The commandment Jesus left with His Church is to love one another as He has loved us. It is the presence of this love that distinguishes His true disciples from those who are just playing a religious game in the name of Jesus. This love cannot be faked when the chips are down or when a person is being tested in the midst of rejection and persecution.[27]

A true Christian cannot say that he or she loves God, but refuse to obey Him. Believers cannot claim this love if they are clinging to the right to hate any brother who might offend them. Contradictions of this nature prove that one is a hypocrite who does not have the capacity to love God. After all, the love of God is obedient and shows no partiality or wickedness towards others, regardless of offenses. A person who disobeys or hates his brother is walking in the darkness of personal self-delusion.[28]

God is love. Love expresses itself in doing right by others, regardless of circumstances. If a person hates his or her brother, he or she is devoid of eternal life. If a person truly loves his or her brother, he or she will not shut up his compassion towards others' needs. Benevolent people become responsible and willing to sacrifice in order to lift the burden of their less fortunate brothers or sisters in a time of need. Therefore, God's love is not only a verbal expression, but it is active as it shows itself in deeds and in truth.[29]

If you have a relationship with God, you will develop an upright disposition that will express itself in the virtue of righteousness before God. John is clear that whosoever abides in sin is of the devil and has not seen or known Jesus. Jesus is the essence of righteousness in every Christian; therefore, we must do what is right, just as He would do it. Righteousness is a product of the love of God. You cannot be right before God unless you are doing right by others. You cannot do right by others unless the love of God is motivating you.[30]

The final fruit of eternal life is overcoming. The Apostle John gave us a clear picture of overcoming. He actually revealed how those at different stages of maturity will be overcomers in the midst of different challenges. If a person is born of God, he or she will overcome the world in the knowledge that he or she is forgiven, as well as in realizing the commitment of the Father. It is the love of the Father that preserves His growing children in the midst of the influence of the world, enabling them to grow in the knowledge of Jesus. Young people will overcome Satan

---

[27] John 13:34-35;
[28] Matthew 5:43-48; Romans 12:9, 17-21; 1 John 2:9-11; 3:14-18; 5:2-3; 2 John 5-6
[29] 1 John 3:15-18; 4:7-8
[30] 1 Corinthians 1:30; 1 John 3:7-9; 3 John 11

when the Word of God abides in them. The more mature believers will naturally respond in godliness to all matters. They will display the life of Jesus with humility and perfection of character.[31]

Overcoming is a mark of the Christian life. The new life possesses the revelation of Jesus, the power of the Spirit, and the love of the Father. It expresses itself in joy, love, and righteousness. The problem today is the same that John was contending with in his day. This problem is that of Gnosticism.[32]

Gnosticism is a philosophy that exalts inner knowledge of hidden truths. This religious knowledge is considered a spark of divinity in humans, but it cannot be obtained by the masses. Only the elite "knower" (the Gnostic) can know these deep truths. Gnostics hide behind Christian terminology, while advocating that their mystic experiences verify these deep truths. Therefore, the Word of God is being replaced by spiritual experiences. Since knowledge is being exalted, these mystic experiences become the person's reality. This will make a person indifferent to the deeds he or she does in his or her body.

This indifference to reality translates into the concept that, since man is intellectually obtaining the right level of spirituality in his soul area, it matters little what he is doing in the body. He stands superior in his spiritual insight, making everything else inferior to his understandings and experiences. Therefore, evil deeds simply reveal that the body is evil, while insight into these hidden truths proves that the soul remains good. The truth is, the body is simply the manifestation of the soul of man. Jesus confirmed this in His teachings.

The Apostle John was confronting this belief in his first epistle at every point. This belief was threatening the true Gospel and making inroads into the new Church. John outlined how eternal life will express itself in a Christian's attitude towards sin and God and in daily conduct.

Sadly, Gnosticism is making great inroads into today's Church. Many Christians are falling into this trap of intellectual spiritualism. Since these people's understanding is intellectual, it creates a reality that is indifferent to the fruits of their life. Because such people intellectually see themselves as okay or righteous, they are blinded to their true fruits. These people display self-righteousness towards others and hypocrisy in their practices. Obviously, reality is missing in their lives, as there is a separation from the thought processes of the soul and the outward conduct of the body.

Jesus said that we would know people by their fruits.[33] However, people who operate in this indifference between body and soul become deluded about their spiritual condition because they refuse to test their personal fruits. They allow their intellectual understanding of God and self to determine how they perceive their Christian walk, rather than

---

[31] 1 John 2:12-14; 3:1; 5:4
[32] 1 John 2:27; 3:1; 5:20
[33] Matthew 7:16-20

examine their fruits to see if the Spirit of God is even present in their lives.

The Apostle John's presentation of eternal life was very black and white. It is a life that has been established in a relationship with God and is being clearly displayed in an upright disposition and a fruitful life. This life cannot be hidden because it is the expression and extension of Jesus Himself. It is not a life that others will have to guess about. Rather, it is a life that will identify the individual with Christ and distinguish the person's testimony and ways from the world.

People who lack the evidence of this life must go back to the beginning of their encounters with Jesus to see if they truly possess eternal life. If the life of Jesus is not present, they must examine their relationships with God to see whether they have replaced Jesus with other religious sources. If the life does not display the mind of Christ, a person must go back to the place where he or she hindered or killed the work of the Son of God through unholy alliances or intellectual and religious idolatry and pursuits.

We cannot assume or hope that this eternal life is present within us. Rather, we must come to terms with whether it is evident in our lives. We must honestly examine our fruits. In order to do this, we must connect the soul (motivations and attitudes) to the body (activities) and honestly evaluate whether or not our lives are the expressions of the life of Jesus. This honest evaluation is not introspection. After all, this life is not the product of or an expression of our best self. Rather, this life is the expression of Jesus Christ. People must see Jesus in us and not the old man clothed in religious or self-righteous garb.

Do you possess and reflect the life of Jesus? Resolve this issue, for it is a life and death matter.

14

THE PURPOSE OF THE GOSPEL

In the epistle of Jude, we see where Jude wanted to write about the common salvation that was, no doubt, brought forth by the preaching of the Gospel. However, the conditions of his time called for him to exhort the brethren and earnestly contend for the faith that was once delivered to the saints.[1]

As you read this small epistle, you realize that contending for the faith is no insignificant matter. Jude talked about the judgment of the angels that fell from their first estate, along with Sodom and Gomorrah and the contention over Moses' body between Michael the archangel and the devil. He made reference to Cain and Balaam's selfish, covetous ways. Then, he talked about the attitude that should be shown towards those who are falling into the traps of damnation. As believers, we must be discreet about how we respond. In some cases, we must have compassion, while in others we must fearfully pull such souls out of the fire.[2]

What faith was Jude talking about? The Apostle Paul gave us a glimpse into what constitutes the faith of every Christian, "Examine yourselves, whether ye be in the faith; prove your own selves. Know ye not your own selves, how that Jesus Christ is in you, except ye be reprobates?" (2 Corinthians 13:5). The faith that was first delivered to the Church was the revelation of Jesus Christ dwelling within the believer.

The revelation of Jesus is the power behind the Gospel. The purpose of the Gospel is to cause us to walk this incredible life out by faith in the Son of God. The message of redemption serves as a platform for coming into a greater knowledge of Jesus. We see this in Paul's preaching. He talked about preaching Christ. No doubt, the Gospel message served as a springboard to establish the foundation of Jesus upon which all spiritual growth takes place. Paul stated that he kept the faith. In other words, he forever kept Jesus as the focus of His life and pursuits. As a

---

[1] Jude 3
[2] Jude 7-11, 22-23

result, he never swayed from the hope of glory that became the essence of his earthly purpose and his heavenly hope and vision.[3]

There are many counterfeit faiths that are inspired by weak or false gospels. These pseudo-faiths put their confidence in sources other than the Jesus of the Bible. These sources may sound religious, look moral, come across as righteous, and even make reference to Jesus, but they lack a testimony of the one and only Jesus of the Bible. For example, people put their confidence in a sinner's prayer, but their intellectual understanding is never translated into a faith in the Person of Jesus that finds its way into the heart of the person. Without the heart revelation there will be no evidence of genuine faith in the person's life.

Some people put their confidence in religious rituals such as the Eucharist. These people believe they are literally receiving Jesus by partaking of a wafer. Their faith is being subtly transferred away from receiving the Son of God by faith, to receiving an object in Jesus' stead. Jesus talked about eating of His body and drinking of His blood in John 6:53-58. However, Jesus was not talking about literally partaking of His body or drinking of His blood. Such a task would be impossible since His corruptible body gave way to a new incorruptible body.[4] In these verses in John, Jesus was talking about receiving Him by faith. This was brought out in previous Scripture verses in John 6:35-40. Jesus talked about being the bread of life. To receive Him as this bread, people needed to believe on Him. If they believe Him about spiritual matters, they will inherit everlasting life, and He will raise them up at the last day.

Faith in or believing on Jesus is the means by which we partake of Him. We are choosing to believe Him by believing His Word. If we believe His Word, we will obey it. Each time we apply His Word to our lives and conduct, we will experience the reality of His life being established in us by the sanctifying work of the Holy Ghost. To drink of His blood simply points to being part of the covenant that was established by His blood. It is His blood that ensures forgiveness and reconciliation with God.[5]

Another gospel that is gaining popularity is the Mystical Gospel, which is another form of Gnosticism. Like Gnosticism, mysticism is the pursuit for insight into mysteries of God that will transcend ordinary human knowledge. In this gospel, people miss the true intent of Christianity—knowing the Person of Jesus. These people are not seeking Jesus, but some kind of spiritual revelation that will give them a corner on God through mystical insights or experiences.

In this gospel, people put their confidence in so called "prophecies" and "unseen experiences" of spiritual ecstasy. Many Christians innocently fall into this gospel by majoring in spiritual insights that come by way of excessive prayer and fasting. However, Christianity is

---

[3] 2 Corinthians 5:7; Galatians 2:20; Philippians 3:12-14; 2 Timothy 1:12; 4:17
[4] John 1:12-13; 20:16-17; 1 Corinthians 15:47-54
[5] Ephesians 2:13; Hebrews 10:19-21; 1 John 1:7

practical. Although it affects our spiritual condition, it expresses itself in outward, practical obedience in our daily lives.

Christians who fall into the Mystical Gospel may glory in their spiritual insights and prophecies, but they fail to obey the Word in practical terms. They often become so spiritually minded, they are no earthly good to those around them. They become self-righteous towards others and inconsistent and hypocritical in their everyday practices.

The Christian life always deals in reality for the purpose of effectively walking this life out by faith and ministering to others. The Gospel of Jesus has the Holy Spirit behind it, which points to the unseen and spiritual. The Spirit also deals with the truth that every person is a sinner in need of God's salvation and intervention. This salvation is not some great mystery, for a child can embrace it. God's love, mercy, grace, longsuffering, and holiness are not great mysteries, but can be experienced through simple, child-like faith. The only mystery one can discover is a greater revelation of Jesus. However, this ongoing revelation of Jesus is not experienced on some mystical plane of bliss, but in the confines of trusting Him with the details of life and obeying His Word. The unveiling of Jesus in a greater measure will not reveal unknown mysteries about Him. Rather, it brings greater dimension to what already has been revealed about Him in Scripture. Keep in mind, Jesus is eternal; therefore, dimension points to the unveiling of the depths of His character, not the revelation of something new or unknown.

The Mystical Gospel allows people to divorce themselves from reality and from practical Christianity in order to operate in an area that has no boundaries. This gospel is akin to the New Age and often operates in the metaphysical arena. In the Mystical Gospel, anything goes because there is no standard of truth by which to test knowledge or experiences. In fact, there is a fine line between the spiritual reality of God and the experiences encountered in mysticism. Mysticism opens people up to superstition and the occult; therefore, innocent people step over the line into the kingdom of darkness. They end up worshipping experiences, while becoming elite or separate from others because of their so-called "great" insights. The end result of this gospel is a person becoming deluded by the false light of Satan.[6]

To leave genuine faith behind means to forget the purpose of the Gospel. In today's world, it is easy to forget the true Gospel of Jesus Christ because this message is under attack. Sadly, many Christians are blind to how the Gospel is being rendered ineffective. Much of the organized Church is indifferent to the fruit that it is producing—spiritual dullness. This dullness is present because of unholy alliances with the world. In fact, much of the Church has been clearly organized to outwardly comply, conform, reform, and perform to some type of code, but not to believe or obey the Word of God in such matters as sin,

---

[6] 2 Corinthians 11:14

Challenging the Christian Life

repentance, self-denial, death to the old man, regeneration, holiness, and righteousness.

Sadly, Jesus Christ, the fullness of God in bodily form, has been reduced to a sentimental concept in different ways. To the worldly mentality, He is represented by an image of a "good old boy," given the honor of a good guy, the admiration of a successful CEO, and the position of a Santa Claus who is here for our benefit. Although these worldly attitudes can be found among the world's perception of Jesus, the religious people have also added their own religious touches to Jesus. For example, He is simply a great prophet, an angel, the spirit brother of Lucifer, a wonderful teacher, and/or a loving, tolerant Savior who died for us because He saw personal worth in us. As a result, the light in the Gospel has been clothed in various disguises, preventing people from seeing the darkness that freely reigns in their lives. The results are devastating and have eternal consequences.

When Jesus was confronting Peter about His identity, He did not ask Peter if he believed in Him. Rather, He asked Peter, "Who do people say that I am?"[7] The reality is that our first initial understanding of Jesus is based on what others say about Him. For me, in my initial encounter with Jesus, He was not presented according to the Word of God. My understanding of Him was nothing more than a vague concept. Any emotion regarding Him was stirred up at Christmas when I thought of Jesus being a babe in a manger. How sweet and romantic it all seemed!

Although, in my younger years, I remember attending church on Easter, it held no meaning. Easter was about dressing up in a cute dress, as well as wearing a hat and white gloves. I realize this scenario is dating me, but Easter held no other meaning to me except that the Easter bunny left me a basket of goodies.

Christmas and Easter are mentioned here because these two holidays are the only perceptions many people have of Jesus. His birth and death are historical facts about the truth He did exist, He did come, and He did impact history. But, when people maintain Jesus as a historical fact alone, they remain indifferent to the fact that He is a present reality that must be confronted.

On these two holidays, people may regard Him with sentimentality, but by doing so, He has no dimension or meaning behind His character and life. For example, on Christmas, He remains a sweet baby in the manger who never really becomes the Man who turned the whole world upside down. On Easter, many admire Him because He became a martyr on a cross, but they never see Him as the risen Lord. These presentations of Jesus are nothing more than emotional hogwash. The question is, why are the birth and death of Jesus significant to mankind? After all, there have been many babies born and many martyred heroes. What is the difference when it comes to Jesus? If this question is not

---

[7] Matthew 16:13-14

properly answered, Jesus will remain a sentimental notion. I discovered this in my personal search for truth and purpose.

It was only when I had a real encounter with Jesus that I began to realize that He was more than a vague notion or a fleeting emotion at Christmas time. Although, my understanding of Him was limited at my salvation experience, I realized that He was a living Person.

In my Christian journey, I have found that the greatest obstacle for most people in their faith is that they never get past the initial presentation of Jesus. In other words, they never grow in the knowledge of who He is and must be in their lives. In such cases, Jesus remains a historical fact, a sentimental notion, or a fantasy that simply existed.

Since my born-again experience, I pondered many times Jesus' question to Peter about His identity. My initial understanding came from others. However, they were wrong about Him. Obviously, man's ability and credibility to get Jesus right went out the back door for me. I concluded that I simply could not trust other's presentation of Jesus even if they were right. I had to be able to answer the question for myself to ensure a faith that could stand in crisis and withstand any attack. After all, Jesus personally asked Peter, "But whom say ye that I am?" (Matthew 16:15).

Peter's answer was short, "Thou art the Christ, the Son of the living God" (Matthew 16:16).

Jesus' response was very revealing, "Blessed art thou Simon Barjona: for flesh and blood hath not revealed it unto thee, but my Father which is in heaven" (Matthew 16:17). Jesus will not be understood from an intellectual level. Man's intelligence is fleshly and cannot receive spiritual truths.[8] The most man can do with spiritual truths is reduce them to some controllable concept, doctrine, or theology.

Clearly, the Son of God will never be understood from the premise of man's teachings. Granted, godly pastors and teachers may give us a foundation upon which to ponder and consider the Person of Jesus. However, this understanding will become dead-letter if the hearers fail to possess a heart revelation. Doctrine, theology, or traditions may give us some knowledge of Jesus, but there must be spirit and life to these insights before they will change the inner man.

It is the Spirit of God who makes the Word powerful and brings forth life that will change one's disposition. Where there is spirit and life, people come to the knowledge of Christ, who is the summary of truth.[9] He becomes real, alive, and powerful, ceasing to be just an idea. Therefore, knowledge of God alone does not constitute knowing Him.

Throughout Paul's epistles, he talked about revelation and knowledge of Jesus. Peter also made reference to the knowledge of Jesus.[10] People rarely graduate from their initial understanding of Jesus

---

[8] 1 Corinthians 2:14
[9] John 6:63; 8:31-36; 14:6
[10] Ephesians 1:17; Philippians 3:8; 1 Timothy 2:4; 2 Peter 1:8; 3:18

to a personal knowledge of Him that has come from the throne room of God. Such people may dazzle you with their scriptural understanding of Jesus, but they will lack the authority that comes from knowing Him in an intimate way.

It took me seven years to realize that intellectual knowledge of Jesus was not the same as knowing Him. I had become impressed with my intellectual understanding of Him, instead of becoming caught up with an ongoing revelation of the One Isaiah referred to as Wonderful, Counselor, The mighty God, The everlasting Father, and The Prince of Peace.[11]

As you study the reality of Jesus, you realize that the Gospel begins with His redemption. Redemption is the door through which one discovers the mystery of God Incarnate in His humanity and in His glory. Each new revelation of the Son of God enlarges our perspectives to embrace more of God's infinite character. Each glimpse takes us out of our comfort zones to discover new territories, where exploring the depth of His incredible character goes beyond our worldly intelligence. In fact, each revelation is simple, but profound in the possibilities of discovering that which is veiled from mortal eyes. Possibilities attached to the unveiling of the eternal are what will enrich our lives with a bit of heaven. The Apostle Paul summarized it in this manner, "That in the ages to come he might shew the exceeding riches of his grace in his kindness toward us through Christ Jesus" (Ephesians 2:7).

As believers, we must never be content to live off of present knowledge or yesterday's revelations of Jesus. We must desire to come higher in our lives in Him in order to be entrusted with greater revelations. The test of each revelation is to walk it out by faith to make it a reality. Each time an aspect of Jesus becomes reality, we are enlarged to receive more. Enlargement of this spectrum allows the Holy Ghost to go deeper within our souls and spirits to tap into the deep wells of salvation. These wells represent different aspects of Jesus' character, examples, and work of redemption. Each well brings forth Living Water that allows God's faithfulness to express itself afresh every day in His mercy and compassion. It is the means by which we can discover how the flow of His grace is ready to bring more grace to us in our times of need and growth.[12]

Do you have a heart revelation of Jesus or only an intellectual concept or a romantic notion of Him? It is not enough to cling to that which never challenges your perception of Jesus and your walk before Him. Never settle for the familiar, but strive to embrace the incredible, regardless of what it costs you. Seek to know Him in greater ways. However, remember that enlargement can mean your foundation and understanding of God will be shaken. Sometimes, in our innocence or immaturity, we may not realize that seeing Jesus in a new light may not

---

[11] Isaiah 9:6
[12] Isaiah 12:3; Lamentations 3:22-23; John 4:13-14; 7:37-39; 16:13

be wonderful or sentimental, but frightening. Whether it is wonderful or frightening, our goal as Christians must remain consistent. We must grow in the knowledge of Jesus! We must see Jesus!

15

REVELATION OF THE GOSPEL

The other night, I was sharing with my Bible Study group the frightening reality that is prevalent in the Church in America. The pure Gospel is hard to find in the midst of all the religious claims and activities that are going on in the name of Jesus. Today, people are supposedly chasing after God, rather than seeking Him. They have to be driven by some type of spiritual purpose, rather than led by the Holy Ghost. God is not lost; He is simply obscured by the domination of self and the influence of the world. It is up to us to push through those things that obscure Him in our lives, so we can see Him in a greater measure.

There are people in the Church talking about greater anointing. Such a claim is false and has the backing of the kingdom of darkness behind it. In fact, if the truth is really faced, the Holy Ghost, who anoints God's people, is clearly missing from such claims and activities.

There are claims of new revelations. Apparently, God is doing a new thing. However, there are no new revelations, just repackaged lies of Satan that appeal to the pride of man. The new thing that was prophesized in the Old Testament pointed to the unveiling of Christ in the New Testament and in the lives of His saints. The new thing God would do for His people was to give them a new heart and spirit, so they could be part of a new covenant that would be established by the blood of Jesus.[1]

The tragedy of the different versions of the "Americanized" Gospel is that they have been exported throughout the world. One of God's servants shared that as he was wrestling over the oppression of the Church in China, that God actually revealed to him that He kept this Body of believers in this precarious position to keep these believers pure from the perversion that sweeps through much of the Church in the free world. If this is true, we as believers in the free world, are obviously miserably failing God.

This very thought came to me as I witnessed via video one of the first evangelistic meetings held in Romania. It was held outdoors in the dead of winter. In America, few, if any, would show up to such an occasion, unless it was an entertaining event such as the Superbowl.

---

[1] Isaiah 43:18-19; Ezekiel 36:26-27

The question is how many people would show up to such a meeting after the government had banished God from every aspect of these people's lives for seventy years? Amazingly, over 60,000 people attended the meeting. I actually saw the picture of these people who crowded together in the streets. The line of these poor souls went for miles. The picture also revealed the hollow eyes of the people who were the closest. Their eyes haunt me even to this day.

As I watched the evangelistic presentation, I was ashamed of what was being presented to these poor souls who were hungry and thirsty for what was real and pure. It was nothing but a sham. Granted, God used it to heal and save people, but crumbs were being presented in the name of American entertainment and emotional hype. In my book, the so-called evangelist did not know what the Gospel was. He was simply parroting what he had heard and seen.

In another video, I watched Russians hurriedly file down through a narrow flight of stairs of a crowded stadium in response to an invitation to receive Christ. I watched as people were helped over an eight-foot drop from the stands so they could run to the platform to receive this extraordinary gift of eternal life. However, at the time, I was wondering what version was actually being presented to them. Was it the pure Gospel or was it the watered-down gospel of "easy believism" that could embrace any of the popular versions that have invaded the hearts and minds of many people in the Church world?

I have also wrestled over the short-term missionaries that have gone overseas. No doubt some are genuine, but many are arrogant and see it as an opportunity to feel good about their Christianity at the expense of needy people. Instead of seeing it as a calling or an honor to be able to minister to such people, they have an opposite perception. There is no real calling or heart for these people, just a fanciful notion about their personal worth or work in the kingdom of heaven. Their investment is temporary, and it may leave them with some sobriety, but few come away with the understanding of the cost of sacrifice in order to be truly entrusted with such a high calling in God's kingdom.

It is obvious that such people are not only devoid of the authority to present the real Gospel, but they have also left a warped presentation of America behind. Sadly, many of these poor souls see Americans as being the solution to their problems instead of the Lord Jesus Christ. Granted, we have the means to lift many of the burdens of these people and should do so where God directs, but we are not their solution or necessarily a realistic example of genuine Christianity or service in the kingdom of God.

As I watch bigger church buildings being built in the honor of man and his worldly attempts, I cannot help but think of the genuine missionaries who are struggling in poverty and experiencing persecution throughout the world. The Church in America is creating a McDonald's type of atmosphere with its abundance, while the true ministers of the Gospel are often being sacrificed on the altars of persecution and poverty. No doubt the rewards of these godly ministers of the Gospel will be great, but how does God look at a Church that gives Him the crumbs of indifference, while it feasts at the table of abundance and worldliness? How much will those who make up the "so-called" church of Jesus answer for on judgment day?

As you study these perverted gospels and pseudo-faiths, you realize that the real Jesus of the Bible and His redemption are clearly missing from their presentations. In other words, the light is going out of the worldly visible church. It is being rendered ineffective by defilement and compromise. Without the right Jesus, there will be a wrong spirit in operation. Without the right spirit, the Word of God will become defiled and perverted. Obviously, the Body of Christ needs a revelation of the Jesus of the Bible that will bring it back to the center of truth. Without truth, there is no means by which to test religious environments and influences. However, to have this revelation, believers must get back to the Word of God. They must make the decision to believe what the Word says and obey it. The revelation of Jesus must not cease because of familiarity or what is comfortable, but it must be ongoing as Christians seek to grow in the knowledge of the Son of God. Saints must be constantly enlarged in their perceptions of Jesus to receive all that God has for them.

We see this enlargement as it occurred in the Apostle John's life. The Apostle John was part of the inner core of Jesus' disciples. He witnessed Jesus' glory on the Mount of Transfiguration, as well as His miracles. After Jesus' ascension, John was on the cutting edge of establishing local fellowships and influencing the Body of Believers. As a result of his faith, he had suffered for the sake of Christ. He said this about his own situation, "I John, who also am your brother, and companion in tribulation, and in the kingdom and patience of Jesus Christ, was in the isle that is called Patmos, for the word of God, and for the testimony of Jesus Christ" (Revelation 1:9).

John had been an eyewitness of Jesus. He had been identified with Jesus as well as used to display the power of the Holy Ghost. Humility, wisdom, and authority must have marked his years of preaching, teaching, and suffering. Clearly, this man knew Jesus. However, in the Book of Revelation, Jesus was unveiled in greater ways to John.

The greater revelation of Jesus caused John to fall at His feet as if dead. Jesus was revealed to John in such a way that there was no familiarity, only a sense of fear and awe. John was not seeing an old friend, but someone who was unfamiliar. The new revelation of Jesus caused John to fall on his face in fear.

The message of the Gospel initially introduces Jesus as our Savior, Redeemer, Master, and Lord. However, the ultimate goal of the Gospel is that you receive even greater revelations of Jesus. Granted, some revelations will encourage you and others will challenge you, but some will make you fall on your face to seek mercy. It is only fitting that the Word of God ends with a revelation of Jesus that will challenge people to enlarge their perceptions of Him and reconsider the place He has in their lives.

It is important that we remember and consider the Gospel in light of these revelations because it causes us to understand, in greater measures, the extent of God's love and redemption. The more we understand about the depths of Jesus' character and work, the more we become aware of the grace that provided us with salvation.

What revelations did John receive about Jesus? The first revelations were nothing new to John. They were in reference to the Gospel, as well as Jesus' abiding presence and work on behalf of His people. The first unveiling of Jesus is that He is the faithful witness, as well as the first begotten from the dead. He was faithful because He carried out the plan of salvation according to the will of the Father.[2]

"Witness" in this text implies martyr and record.[3] Jesus became a sacrifice in order to establish a record or living testimony of eternal life. In 1 John 5:8-13, John clearly brought out this truth. Christians now serve as martyrs or living testimonies of His life. The Apostle Paul referred to believers as living epistles that are read by men.[4]

Jesus' faithful testimony is followed by the reality of His resurrection. Once again, we are reminded of the victory and hope of the Gospel. Without Jesus' resurrection, the preaching of the Gospel, along with our faith, would be in vain. In fact, we would still be in a state of death and condemnation.[5]

The next part of this revelation is that Jesus is the Prince of the kings of the earth. Although Jesus was called the King of the Jews, the Jews rejected His leadership. His title of King points to His Second Advent when He will come back and will rule as King of kings and Lord of lords.[6]

Finally, we are reminded of the covenant established by Jesus' blood. We have been washed of our sins in His blood. We now can walk in forgiveness, be restored in wholeness of life, be reconciled back to God as His children, and made heirs of an eternal kingdom where we will be considered kings and priests.[7]

The next revelation John received of Jesus pointed to the blessed hope. He is coming back, and every eye will witness this event. Not only will every person have to acknowledge Him for who He is, but the Jews will also wail because of Him. It will be a time of great sorrow, fear, and judgment. As John stated, "Even so, Amen" (Revelation 1:7).

In the revelation that follows the reality of the Gospel and the promise of His coming, Jesus is clearly unveiled as God. In Revelation, Jesus made reference to Himself at least four times with this

---

[2] Revelation 1:5
[3] Strong's Exhaustive Concordance of the Bible, #3144
[4] 2 Corinthians 3:1-3
[5] 1 Corinthians 15:14-15; Revelation 1:5
[6] Revelation 1:7; 19:11-16
[7] Hebrews 1010-22; Revelation 1:6

introduction, "I am Alpha and Omega."[8] Alpha means He is the beginning. Everything starts with Him; therefore, we are reminded of Genesis 1:1, "In the beginning God..."

As the Omega, He is the ending or the last of all things. He is the end of the Law. He is the door that ends life as we know it, but He becomes an entrance into the promised, eternal, and abundant life. In Him, all saints meet with death to their self-life in order to come forth in His life. In the end, He will be standing. In the end, He will have the final say.[9]

As the Alpha and Omega, Jesus is declaring His eternal existence. He is the Alpha, the beginning, the first of all creation. He is the Omega, the end, last in all matters. These terms point back to the prophet Isaiah. Isaiah 44:6 stated, "Thus saith the LORD the King of Israel, and his redeemer the LORD of hosts; I am the first, and I am the last; and beside me there is no God." It is interesting to note that there are two persons of the Godhead being mentioned here. First, it is the LORD who is the King of Israel. No doubt this points to the Father, whom Israel acknowledges to be Lord and God. The word "and" is a word that implies connection to a matter as well as conjunction with a matter. We not only have the LORD who is king, but we also have the Redeemer who is the LORD of hosts. The New Testament identifies our redeemer to be the second Person of the Godhead, Jesus Christ.[10]

God alone deserves our worship. Jesus established this fact in the wilderness when He made this statement to Satan, "Get thee behind me, Satan: for it is written, Thou shalt worship the Lord thy God, and him only shalt thou serve" (Luke 4:8). However, Jesus openly received the worship of others. Once again, such worship points to the fact that Jesus is God in the flesh, worthy of all adoration and honor. In Revelation 4:8-11, we see the Lord God Almighty who was and is and is to come, who lives for ever and ever, being worshipped by those around the throne.

It is important to note that John made this reference about Jesus in Revelation 1:8, "I am Alpha and Omega, the beginning and the ending saith the Lord, who is, and who was, and who is to come, the Almighty." Jesus is declared to be the Almighty in this Scripture. Clearly, this term is being used in relationship to Jesus and His majesty as deity.

In Revelation 5, the worship continued around the throne, the identity of the One who lives forever and ever was unveiled. This chapter began with John weeping over the fact that there was no man in heaven or on earth who was worthy to open the book that would loose the seals. He was told not to weep for the Lion of the tribe of Judah had prevailed; therefore, He was able to open the book.

As John looked, he beheld, in the midst of the throne, a Lamb. This Lamb appeared as if He had been slain. We know this Lamb to be

---

[8] Revelation 1:8, 21:6, 11; 22:13
[9] John 10:7-9; Romans 6:3-11; 10:4
[10] John 8:41; 1 Corinthians 1:30; Ephesians 1:7

Jesus. Those around the throne sang a new song, saying, "Thou art worthy to take the book, and to open the seals thereof: for thou wast slain, and hast redeemed us to God by thy blood out of every kindred, and tongue, and people, and nation" (Revelation 5:9). The Lamb is worthy to receive power, riches, wisdom, strength, honor, glory, and blessing. He is worthy of worship, for He sits on the throne forever and ever. Jesus came as the Lamb of God who would redeem His people from sin and death. Since Jesus is considered our redeemer and worshipped by both man on earth and those around the throne, we know He is God. As God Incarnate, He alone could satisfy judgment on sin and redeem or buy back His lost sheep.[11]

These revelations were already instilled into the heart of the Apostle John. In his gospel, John had declared Jesus as the Lamb of God and the Word who was not only God, but who had become flesh. John knew that Jesus is King and that He was worshipped by those in heaven and those on the earth.[12] Therefore, what revelation of Jesus caused John to fall on his face as if dead?

The revelation of Jesus that caused John to fall on his face is found in Revelation 1:13-16. Jesus did not come to John as a mere Servant. Rather, He came to Him clothed in a garment with a golden girdle, implying authority. John did not see a Jesus who was a humble Savior. Rather, He saw Him with white hair like wool and eyes that were as a flame of fire, pointing to separation and holiness. He did not see Him as a Lamb ready to be offered up. Rather, he saw His feet like fine brass that burned in a furnace, implying wrath. Instead of hearing Jesus in the capacity of a Master, His voice sounded as many waters, pointing to purification and power. Rather than contending for souls with compassion, hope, and truth, out of His mouth came a sharp two-edged sword, inferring judgment. Instead of His glory being veiled by humanity, his countenance was as the sun shines, revealing His strength.

Amazingly, there is a similar revelation about Jesus in the Old Testament in the book of Daniel. Daniel 7:9 made this declaration, "I beheld till the thrones were cast down, and the Ancient of days did sit, whose garment was white as snow, and the hair of his head like the pure wool: his throne was like the fiery flame, and his wheels as burning fire." Daniel went on to identify the One who sits down as the Son of man. We know the Son of man to be Jesus Christ. We see in this Scripture along with Daniel 7:22 that Jesus is referred to as the Ancient of days. "Ancient" points to something that is old in light of existence, but it also means venerable or one who deserves to be recognized or worshipped.[13]

Obviously, in John's revelation of the Son of God, Jesus was on a mission. It is Daniel who summarized that Jesus' mission is one of

---

[11] Revelation 5:6, 11-14
[12] John 1:1, 14; Revelation 5:13-14
[13] Strong's Exhaustive Concordance of the Bible, #6268

judgment. Daniel 7:10 gave us this insight around Jesus' throne, "A fiery stream issued and came forth from before him: thousand thousands ministered unto him, and ten thousand times ten thousand stood before him: the judgment was set, and the books were opened." Jesus confirmed that the Father judges no man, but has committed all judgment unto Him.[14]

The Apostle John began to unveil Jesus as the ultimate judge. Although He was once dead, it is Jesus who lives forevermore. It is Jesus who possesses the keys of hell and of death. It is Jesus who will remove the candlestick from the churches who fail to repent of their ungodly works, attitudes, alliances, and ways. It is Jesus who will be coming back with the armies of heaven to take revenge. He will be clearly identified, for on His vesture and on His thigh, a name is written: KING OF KINGS AND LORD OF LORDS. Out of His mouth will issue a sharp, two-edged sword. He will smite the nations in judgment. He will rule with a rod of iron, and He will tread the winepress of the fierceness of the wrath of Almighty God.[15]

Jesus will prevail as King and Lord. Satan will be bound up for a thousand years. During those thousand years, there will be peace because all rebellion will be quickly squelched. The knowledge of God will be everywhere. After the thousand years, the great white throne judgment will take place. Those who were not part of the first resurrection will be raised to face the Judge whom they refused as Lord and Savior. These are the people who rejected the real Gospel and will be missing from the Book of Life. From here, they will be cast into the Lake of fire.[16]

The Apostle John elaborated on the different aspects of Jesus. He is the Redeemer of His Bride. His Bride will be distinguished when she partakes of the marriage supper of the Lamb. He is the light of heaven that will never grow dim. His face will be clearly seen, and His name will forever be on the foreheads of those who belong to Him. He will reign forever and ever. Jesus' declaration in Revelation 1 was reiterated in the last chapter of Revelation, "I am Alpha and Omega, the beginning and the end, the first and the last" (Revelation 22:13).

Jesus is the ongoing revelation of the Gospel. The power of the Gospel is to spare us from tasting of the judgment and to deliver us from the wrath of God. This message enables us to see Jesus in a greater light. It is the light of Jesus that brings contrast and allows us to honestly examine our lives and source of faith.

Sadly, few people see Jesus outside of their comfort zones. There are various reasons for this state of affairs. For example, the Gospel has been watered down in such a way that there is no room in which to discover the Jesus of the Bible. Rather than people being challenged in

---

[14] John 5:22
[15] Jude 14-15; Revelation 1:20, 2-3:19; 19:14-16
[16] Isaiah 11:9; Habakkuk 2:14; Revelation 20

their concepts about Jesus, they hold on to their familiarity of Him. As a result, they quench the revelation of the Spirit.

A. W. Tozer stated that the real obligation of the Church is not to spread the Gospel, but to be spiritually worthy to spread it.[17] Today, many zealots are making converts to their way of thinking, rather than to Jesus. As already mentioned, weak or erroneous presentations of the Gospel and of Jesus are being passed on to others. Such weaknesses are compounded as people come into unholy alliances and under a wrong spirit after being constantly exposed to other gospels. Ultimately, they will embrace another Jesus. The implications of the results are frightening. People will have a hard time wading through the counterfeits to come to the true knowledge of Jesus Christ.

Today, what often passes as Christianity is nothing more than a fad that has been embraced by religious people and cults alike. However, the Christian life is not just associated with the concepts of true Christianity that save a person. True Christianity is the total identification with the real Person of Jesus Christ that ensures salvation. It is the Jesus of the Bible who serves as eternal life to those who receive Him as God's provision.

It is not enough to hear the Gospel; we must receive the light of that Gospel. It is not enough to quote the Gospel; we must walk in the light of this incredible message. It is not enough to preach the Gospel; we must live the Gospel in the resurrection power and authority of the Son of God.

Jesus Christ must graduate from the romantic position of Savior and become Lord of our life. He must cease from being a mere prophet and become the Son of God. He must be allowed to leave the manger as a baby and become the Lamb of God who died on the cross as our personal substitute. He must not just be sentimentally adored as a sacrifice on the cross; He must be recognized and worshipped as the One who has risen from the grave and now sits on the right hand of the Father. He must not remain just an expression of God's love, but He must become the motivating reason for doing what is right and coming to a place of holiness before God. As the Apostle Paul pointed out, Jesus must become our all in all.[18]

What will your answer be when Jesus asks you "Who do you say I am?" Your answer will reveal your life before God. The truth of the matter is that Jesus must become your all in all. He must be what you begin with and what you end with. He must fill every area of your life with His disposition, attitude, and ways. In order for Him to fill every area of your life and take His rightful place, you must continually accept the invitation that is in compliance with John 7:37-38. This invitation is found in Revelation 22:17, "Come. And let him that heareth say, Come. And let him that is athrist come. And whosoever will, let him take the water of life freely."

---

[17] Tozer on Christian leadership, (Devotional) August 1
[18] Ephesians 1:23; Colossians 3:11

Challenging the Christian Life

Have your heard the invitation? Have you accepted this invitation by coming to Jesus Christ, the Alpha and the Omega?

FOR THE PURPOSE OF EDIFICATION

Book Three

Copyright © 2006 by Rayola Kelley

INTRODUCTION

My reason for writing this book is to bring a balanced presentation of the gifts of the Spirit. Such a desire was born out of the reality that the discipleship group I was overseeing did not have a proper perspective of them. This aspiration to make sure that each of these disciples properly understood the gifts was in compliance with 1 Corinthians 12:1, "Now concerning spiritual gifts, brethren, I would not have you ignorant."

During the preparation for this project, I discovered that the gifts were part of a bigger picture that is often overlooked and rarely emphasized. The result of this limited picture was that gifts have become the main focal point, while their purpose or significance in the kingdom of God was totally ignored. This has caused much speculation, debate, and abuse in this area.

I began to consider the gifts in light of their purpose. They have one main function and that is to bring the Church to maturity or perfection. I also found there were other avenues that God had designed to bring the Body to maturity. Like the gifts of the Spirit, these avenues were either shrouded in debate or ignored altogether. The final result was that balanced presentations of these subjects, along with spiritual maturity, were often missing in the Body of believers.

In fact, balance is greatly missing in much of the Church because many people fail to see the larger presentation of a matter. They focus on individual parts or pieces of the depiction rather than the picture as a whole. This focus may establish theology about these subjects, but it rarely produces proper and godly practices that end in believers or a body becoming spiritually mature. What is the purpose of gifts? They are for the purpose of edification.

My prayer for this book is that it brings some balance to the controversial subjects that surround edification. I also hope that it will give hungry and thirsty Christians a sense of how far the Church has removed itself from fundamental truths that were established to bring much needed growth to believers. If one person gains a glimpse of the glorious vision of what God had in mind when Jesus died on the cross to purchase a peculiar Bride for Himself, all the time, energy, and struggles that went into writing this book will be well worth it.

1

EDIFICATION

As I tackled this project with the goal of explaining the gifts of the Spirit to bring a balanced perspective, the concept of edification repeatedly surfaced. The main purpose for certain positions and gifts in the Body of Christ is for its edification. An honest study of these gifts in light of edification will actually change how the gifts are viewed. There is clearly a broader perspective behind their purpose.

Today, debates rage over positions and gifts, but the reason God established them and gave them to the Church is never discussed at length. Granted, these positions and gifts, outside of God's reasoning for them, not only cause abuse, but also fear, ignorance, and heated debates. God did not give positions and gifts for the fun of it so people could debate, ignore, or test their personal spirituality. He gave them for the work of edification.

What is edification? A careful study of this word reveals that it has a very clear function in the Church. According to *Strong's Concordance*, this word points to building some type of structure. One might ask what structure is being constructed. Ephesians 4 and Colossians 1 make reference to Jesus' Body or Church. Peter described this spiritual structure in this way, "Ye also, as lively stones, are built as a spiritual house, an holy priesthood, to offer up spiritual sacrifices, acceptable to God by Jesus Christ" (1 Peter 2:5). The Apostle Peter clearly pointed out that there is quite a building project taking place in the kingdom of God. This process started over two millennia ago and continues today.

The writer of Hebrews also brought out this concept of building in Hebrews 3:3-6. He pointed out that Moses was faithful in his house, that the one who builds the house has more honor than the structure, and that God builds all things. Hebrews 3:6 gave this analogy, "But Christ as a son over his own house; whose house are we, if we hold fast the confidence and the rejoicing of the hope firm unto the end."

The house that is being constructed is made up of living stones or people. The Apostle Paul clearly brought this out in Romans 12:4-5, 1 Corinthians 12:12-28, and Ephesians 4:13-16.

Many Christians believe that building Christ's kingdom means building bigger church buildings. However, Jesus said in John 18:36, "My kingdom is not of this world."

The Apostle Paul made this statement in Romans 14:17, "For the kingdom of God is not meat and drink; but righteousness, and peace, and joy in the Holy Ghost." We can see that the kingdom of God is not made evident by the things that can be seen, but by that which is unseen. It is ongoing and universal in nature, and the reality of this kingdom is distinguished by the manifestation of Jesus' life in His followers.

Every structure has a design, a foundation, and a builder behind it. This spiritual building is no exception. The Father lovingly designed this spiritual structure, the Son supplied the payment for it on the cross, and the Holy Spirit is the builder.

Scripture also shows us that Jesus is the foundation and the cornerstone of this building, while Christians are the stones. The Holy Spirit is the One who properly places each stone upon the foundation, in compliance with the Cornerstone and according to the Father's eternal design.[1]

Each stone (Christian) has its place in this building, no matter how great or small the stone is. There is no bias or prejudice towards the significance that is placed upon each person in Jesus' Church. In fact, lively stones that are considered least by others are exalted by God to show the importance of every stone in this incredible building.[2]

As Peter stated, this is a spiritual house. This stipulates that it is not of an earthly nature, but has an eternal and heavenly function in this world. The function of this spiritual house is two-fold. First, is to serve as a holy priesthood. Priests are meant to minister to both God and man. We see that they are to offer up spiritual sacrifices acceptable to God through Jesus Christ.

Hebrews 13:15-16 gave us insight into these sacrifices, "By him, therefore, let us offer the sacrifice of praise to God continually, that is, the fruit of our lips giving thanks to his name. But to do good and to communicate forget not, for with such sacrifices God is well pleased." These Scripture verses tell us that we minister to God with praise and to others by doing good.

Sacrifices also had to have an altar. In the Old Testament tabernacle and temple, the main altar was the Altar of Burnt Offering. This was located in the outer court of the holy structure. God established this tabernacle in order to abide in the midst of Israel. Today Christians serve as the tabernacle or temple of God, and the cross of Christ serves as the altar. Like the tabernacle of old, God desires to abide in the midst of the temple or, in this case, the Christian.[3]

The greater the abiding presence of God, the more distinct and holy His people will become in the midst of the world. This is the second purpose for this spiritual house—to serve as a distinct priesthood, holy nation, and peculiar people in the midst of a dark, lost world. Such a

---

[1] 1 Corinthians 3:11; 1 Peter 1:19-20; 2:5-8
[2] 1 Corinthians 12:22-26
[3] Exodus 25:8; 1 Corinthians 3:16; Hebrews 13:10-12

Challenging the Christian Life

distinction will show forth the praises of Him who has called us out of darkness into His marvelous light to be His followers.[4]

God's main desire is to establish a spiritual house that will bring Him glory, but this house must be constructed. Christians are to serve as the stones, not the builders. In other words, Christians do not determine where they will fit in this building, nor will they place other stones into this structure. It is solely the Holy Spirit's responsibility to construct this house.

This is why Christians' perception must reach beyond doctrinal or theological views in order to embrace God's heart. His heart is simple; He wants to have a spiritual house for Himself. God's desire is often hindered because of ignorance, fear, and theological beliefs. When these culprits are on the scene, Christians cease to become the lively stones that make up this structure. At this point, Christians try to become both the designer and the builder of their spiritual lives, as well as the lives of others. This state of affairs can change the face of the Church, rendering it powerless or ineffective.

Anytime man interferes with spiritual matters, the holy becomes profane, and the vision ceases to be heavenly and becomes earthly. In the case of edification, we see where man determines spiritual practices according to theological comfort zones and emphasis, rather than the design of God. Therefore, the means of edification have become a great debate, rather than godly practices that build up the Church.

The final product is that Christians are failing to serve as stones that compliment the rest of the structure. It is not unusual to see some Christians taking on the role of the Holy Spirit to determine the direction of the Church. Christians, who are trying to be the Holy Ghost, reveal that they have lost sight of the fact that edification is not about personal beliefs, but it is the means God uses to bring believers to maturity.

The real work of edification is always about the other person being nurtured in a spiritual way and serves as a mandate to all believers. According to the Apostle Paul, all things must be done for edification; therefore, believers must avoid being caught up with things that do not edify.[5]

This proves that edification is not a matter of personal preference, but a sober responsibility of each Christian. Christians must be part of the building, rightly placed, and used by the Holy Spirit to edify others. However, to be personally part of the building, there must be self-denial and application of the cross.

The one identification mark of the Church is Jesus Christ. It must reflect His life, power, and authority. To accomplish this, Christians must become Christ-centered by coming into submission to the Holy Spirit and not self-centered nor man-centered.

---

[4] 1 Peter 2:9
[5] John 15:8-14; Romans 14:19; 1 Corinthians 8:1; 14:26

The Holy Spirit does the work of edification through three avenues—positions, grace, and gifts. The Apostle Paul also talked about believers having the necessary authority and power to do the work of edification in the Body.[6] Both authority and power in this text point to positions. There have been five positions established to do the work of edification within the Church.

The number five points to grace. All work done by God within people's lives and the Church is an act of grace. Grace points not only to undeserved gifts of God, but also to an inward establishment of godliness within believers that reaches outward to others. The grace of God is meant to produce a humble attitude that results in discipline and sacrificial actions that will impact and benefit others.

The Word of God also points out that the Holy Spirit gives the necessary gifts to build the Church. The controversy surrounding gifts has practically nullified the work of edification altogether in the Church. As a result, the Body is not being built up by the power of the Spirit, but torn down by man's religious arrogance and fear.

The Apostle Paul explained the purpose of edification in Ephesians 4:13-16 as well as gave us a clear picture of how it works. Edification is to bring unity to the body. Unity of this nature comes through the knowledge and revelation of the Son of God through the Holy Ghost. This shows us that proper edification is built upon the knowledge of Jesus Christ that will produce unity in the Body.

Today there are many different Christ's being presented, and, as a result, there is no common ground or foundation. Instead of the visible Church being founded on the truth of Jesus and growing up into Him in all things, it is advocating unity at the cost of truth. This not only redefines Jesus, but also eliminates the means by which to test spiritual matters, since the real foundation will be blatantly missing.

These different "Christs" are causing many to be tossed to and fro and carried about with every wind of doctrine. This is one reason why the Church appears fragmented and vulnerable to spiritual defeat.[7] The Son of God must be perfected in a Christian before he or she can experience Jesus' fullness in his or her life. This means that certain aspects of Jesus' character or life has become a reality to and in the believer. The reality of Jesus is what constitutes real edification and unity in the Body of Christ. Such perfecting cannot be done without the love of God. Everything must be motivated and done with His love or it will fall short of edifying a person.

This brings us to another aspect of edification; it is not always pleasant. The love of God is the motivation behind true ministers of the Gospel. This commitment has one goal and that is to see a person become mature in his or her life in God. This commitment may take on various forms. For example, it may show compassion to the hurting,

---

[6] 2 Corinthians 10:8; 13:10
[7] Ephesians 4:14

while aggressively contending for the faith. This may mean confronting and dealing with rebellion and iniquity which rarely makes a person feel good about self or life in general. However, spiritual maturity rarely takes place without challenges, failures, and purification brought on by the various challenges of life itself along with consequences and truth.

Truth can serve as a harsh reality check to those who are hiding or justifying sin. It is meant to instruct, reprove, and correct in righteousness. When we study some of the gifts, you will begin to see that edification has a sharp edge that exposes and confronts spiritual deviation.

Another aspect of edification is that it is an ongoing work until the last lively stone is put into place. Until then, the Church is being brought to perfection or maturity. This shows us that the Church will never be completed until the Holy Spirit finishes the work, and Jesus comes for His bride.

In understanding that edification will continue until completion of the structure, one will have to conclude that the different avenues that have been established for this work will continue as well. This means that the avenues of positions and gifts will not cease until the spiritual building is finished.

Have you allowed yourself to be placed in the Body of Christ by the Holy Spirit? Are you following after that which edifies, or are you advocating that which quenches the work of the Holy Spirit?[8] Make sure you understand edification before you continue reading in order to keep this information in the proper perspective.

---

[8] Romans 14:19; 1 Thessalonians 5:19

2

THE GIVER

Once believers are exposed to the gifts, they have a tendency to pursue the gifts rather than the Giver of those gifts. Gifts do not set a person apart as a means to verify their importance in the kingdom of God, but are a medium by which God has chosen to build up the whole Body. To improperly use or over-emphasize gifts not only encourages a lopsided presentation of them, but it can cause misinformed, zealous believers to open themselves up to another spirit.

The lopsided presentation or emphasis on gifts is a product of immaturity and a misguided understanding of the Holy Spirit. This immaturity has caused many abuses of the gifts and has conditioned people to embrace that which proves contrary to the Spirit of God.

The Holy Ghost is the third person of the Godhead. He is God by nature and represents the presence and sanctifying work of God among believers of Jesus Christ. He leads to all truth and must be allowed to guide and lead each individual in order to accomplish the work of holiness or separation unto God.[1]

The Apostle Paul confirmed that the work of the Holy Spirit is spiritual; therefore, the natural man cannot understand, receive, or know His work because it must be spiritually discerned. Since the work of the Holy Spirit is supernatural, many become receptive to anything that is supernatural. This is dangerous because Satan's works are also supernatural and serve as counterfeits to the Holy Ghost and His work. Therefore, it is important to test the spirit behind any supernatural move or act to ensure that the Holy Spirit is behind it.[2] Sadly, few know how to test the spirit. Subsequently, leaders and Christians either reject the Spirit's work or accept the wrong spirit because they are afraid to quench any type of supernatural workings, fearing that they would be quenching the Holy Spirit. These extremes have caused much confusion and debate over the Holy Spirit and His work.

E. Stanley Jones, in his devotion *The Way*, made this comment about the first group, "The almost entire absence of emphasis on the Spirit has impoverished the main stream of Christianity. It often degenerates into a humanistic striving to be good."

---

[1] Acts 5:3-4; Romans 15:16; John 16:13
[2] 1 Corinthians 2:14; 1 John 4:1

The other group abuses the Holy Spirit, along with His gifts, because they do not know His character. They live in fear that they are quenching His work. This ignorance has allowed Satan to effectively counterfeit the Holy Spirit and His works in the midst of many Christians and congregations. This has caused destructive spiritual mixtures that profane the holy. Therefore, it is vital that people who desire to experience the Holy Spirit in a greater measure understand His character.

The character of the Holy Spirit can be realized in His work and the many symbols that point to Him. In Genesis 1:2, He moved upon the face of the earth to bring order through recreation. In all of His workings, there will be order and not chaos. In many of these meetings where the supernatural is working, order is missing, and it seems like there are no boundaries to the different manifestations. Therefore, much is being embraced as originating from the Spirit of God, when it is nothing but a counterfeit. The truth is that legitimate moves of God will not operate outside of the character of the Holy Ghost. His very character demands a clear order and reverent conduct.

In Genesis 2:6, the Holy Spirit was symbolized by the mist that went up from the earth that revived that which was unproductive. We see this similar example of His work in the spiritual birth. He is the breath of God that brings life to a lifeless soul, as well as the Living Water that cleanses and brings restoration to the parched soul.[3]

In Genesis 8:8, He was the dove sent forth by Noah (a type of Father God) from the ark (a type of Jesus) to explore the condition of the terrain (a type of man's heart).[4] In the case of the Church, the Holy Spirit can only move and land upon that which is prepared and holy. He is gentle and can easily be quenched, causing Him to quickly withdraw.[5] He tests the spiritual temperature of God's Church and determines if the Church is prepared for His move and work. If He encounters sin, that which is fleshly, or the wrong spirit, He will lift and return to the Father until He is sent again to test the terrain. After all, it is God's heart to move upon His people in a powerful way. It is during such a move that He will sovereignly meet people in their spiritual plights as He distributes gifts, comforts, and reveals the heart of God to the searching, humble heart.

We see the third person of the Godhead descending like a dove after the baptism of Jesus Christ at the River Jordan. The Holy Ghost always illuminates the reality of Jesus in the midst of His Body, the Church. In fact, His main responsibility is to lead a person into the truth about the

---

[3] John 3:3-6; 7:37-39

[4] There are many types in the Old Testament. These types serve as an example or representation of someone or something. The greatest type is the tabernacle, which serves as one of the greatest revelations of Jesus Christ— His nature, purpose, and ministry.

[5] 1 Thessalonians 5:19

Son of God.[6] If Jesus is not being lifted up in a meeting or movement, the Holy Spirit will be absent as well.

In Genesis 8:1, the Holy Spirit was represented by the powerful wind that passed over the earth to push back judgment in order to bring forth the promises of God and a new beginning for man. All men stand condemned because of sin, but if any man gives way to the reality of Christ, the Holy Spirit comes in to push back judgment and bring forth new life. He then serves as the seal in the lives of believers, making them heirs to an eternal inheritance.[7]

Jesus also referred to the Holy Spirit as the wind that man couldn't explain or control in John 3:7-8. As already mentioned, He is the very breath of God in a new creation's life. But He is also ascribed as being the wind. He came as a rushing wind on the day of Pentecost that not only stirred up the fire that had been slowly burning in the hearts of Jesus' followers, but He also caused it to spread as they became powerful witnesses of the Gospel.[8]

Genesis 24 presents the trustworthy servant (a type of the Holy Ghost) sent out by Abraham (a type of Father God) to find a bride (a type of Church) for his son, Isaac (a type of Jesus, the Son of Man). In this powerful story, we can learn that the Holy Spirit does not represent or promote Himself. He acts in accordance with the Father, and His main goal is to find a bride, adorn her with jewels, woo her to the Son, and lead her back to dwell with her bridegroom. This picture shows that He will not act outside of God's design, and He will always glorify Jesus, not Himself. If a person rejects His overtures, the Holy Ghost will be released from all responsibilities, but He will be greatly grieved.[9]

In the building of the tabernacle, we see at least three representations of the Holy Spirit. His character can be observed in Bezaleel, a man from the tribe of Judah. It was out of the tribe of Judah that Jesus would come forth, and it is because of the Holy Spirit that Jesus is made a reality to His followers.

Bezaleel is the man who was filled with the wisdom, understanding, and knowledge to build the tabernacle. The Holy Spirit is the essence of all knowledge, understanding, wisdom, and revelation among Jesus' followers. He resides in the temple of man and, as a result, He can make the Church a living, active reality that is able to express the very image of Christ to the world. He is the One who makes a dead soul alive unto God by regenerating the person.[10] He places each believer in the Body and makes the head, Jesus Christ, a passion that cannot be quenched, a reality that cannot be denied, and the very source of a person's heartbeat.

---

[6] Matthew 3:16; John 16:13-14
[7] Ephesians 1:11-14
[8] Acts 2:2-7
[9] Ephesians 4:30
[10] Exodus 35:30-31; Ephesians 1:17; 1 Corinthians 3:16; Titus 3:5

Bezaleel's helper, Aholiab, points to the work of the Holy Ghost among the believers, specifically the gifts of the Spirit. Aholiab was from the tribe of Dan, which means "judge." The gifts not only edify, but also serve as a type of judgment to bring separation from that which is unholy. God often uses the gifts as a means to instruct, exhort, and warn in order to bring such separation.[11]

Author and teacher, Ruth Specter Lascelle, pointed out certain aspects about Bezaleel and Aholiab. Bezaleel was from Judah. Judah was the leading camp when Israel was traveling through the wilderness, while Dan, Aholiab's tribe, was the last camp of Israel. We are to follow after the Spirit, be led by the Spirit, and walk in the Spirit. Clearly, as believers, He is to be in front of us, in our midst, and surrounding us. As part of the first and last, these two men stand as representatives of the complete camp. Lascelle pointed out that the gifts of the Holy Spirit (followed after Jesus' ascension) and the "ministry" gifts go together with Jesus (the head).[12] The completion of this combination of these works and gifts points to the edification and perfecting of the whole Body.

The next representatives of the Holy Spirit in the work of the tabernacle are the anointing oil and spices.[13] Oil represents the anointing of the Holy Spirit, while the spices symbolize His work through Christ and the believer.[14] There are five ingredients in this anointing oil, which point to the work of grace. Bezaleel originally prepared this oil, showing that only the Holy Spirit can combine the right ingredients in man's life and in the Church to make both holy and acceptable to God.[15] This oil was used to set people, objects, sacrifices, and places apart for God's use and glory.

How well do you know the character of the Holy Spirit? Is He simply a doctrine that you control or a comfortable concept that never challenges your ignorance about Him and His work? It is vital that you allow the Spirit to shake you as He did those in the upper room, so you can personally experience the third person of the Godhead in an intimate, powerful way.

---

[11] Exodus 35:34-35

[12] A Dwelling Place for God by Ruth Specter Lascelle; © 1990 by Hyman Israel Specter, Van Nuys CA.

[13] Exodus 30:23-25; Luke 4:18-19

[14] A Dwelling Place for God; pages 343-345

[15] Exodus 31:11; 37:29

Receiving the Promise

There are many misconceptions about how a person receives the Holy Spirit. Many believe if they want more of the Holy Spirit, they must personally seek Him out. There is no Scripture to back up this concept.

The Word clearly states that the Holy Spirit is a gift that cannot be earned and a promise that must be given.[16] Jesus Christ is the one who gives the Holy Spirit to the believer as a gift, while the Father provides the promise by sending Him forth to do a work among believers.

There are two distinct ways by which Jesus gives the Holy Spirit. The first act occurs when a believer is born again. We see Jesus giving His disciples the Holy Spirit before He ascended to heaven.[17] This was the example of the born-again experience, but this only occurred after Gethsemane and Calvary. In other words, spiritual birth is marked by self-denial and death (the cross of Christ) to ensure life. This birth implies that the presence of God is within the spirit of man.

The next distinct act happened at Pentecost. The disciples had the Spirit, but they were told to wait until they were endued with power from on high.[18] They waited for seven days for the Father's promise of the Spirit. On the seventh day, Jesus took the promise and made Him the gift with which He baptized the believers with Living Water from above. This Water would subdue all residues of self and empower His followers to live righteous lives, as well as serve as bold witnesses for His kingdom.

E. Stanley Jones explained the difference between the new birth and the fullness of the Holy Spirit, "Before Pentecost the disciples had the Holy Spirit, but after Pentecost the Holy Spirit had them."[19]

It was at Pentecost that the Presence of God from within connected with the power from on high to raise each believer up to testify of the new life from within with power and authority. These people became living epistles of God's love that was displayed on the cross. They spoke with authority because they carried with them the mark of death and displayed power because of the resurrected life that pulsated through their very being.

This brings us back to the subject of how we can receive this power. Do we seek the Holy Spirit to receive a greater measure of Him? Scripture is very clear that we are not to seek out the Holy Spirit because He is not here to give Himself to us. He is a promise from the Father; therefore, we must ask the Father for more of the Spirit of the Living God. Luke 11:13 confirmed this, "If ye then, being evil, know how to give

---

[16] Luke 24:49; Acts 1:4; 8:17-20
[17] John 20:22:23
[18] Luke 24:48-49; Acts 1:4-8
[19] The Way, E. Stanley Jones, devotional, pg. 274

Challenging the Christian Life

good gifts unto your children: how much more shall your heavenly Father give the Holy Spirit to them that ask him?

The Father desires us to ask Him for His Holy Spirit, but our motives must be right. We must not ask the Father for the Holy Ghost so that we can have gifts that will bring us recognition, but so that we can have the power to bring Him glory. After all, the Holy Spirit's main motive is to shed love abroad in the believer's heart towards God and others. His intent is to bring glory to God, and His goal is to lift Jesus above the world, fleshly desires, and Satan's designs to serve as an invitation to the seeking, despairing heart.

The Father waits for us to ask Him for the Holy Spirit, while Jesus waits for us to come to Him, so that He can give us more of the Spirit to fulfill His many promises to His Bride. The ring in the parable of the Prodigal Son represents the Holy Spirit. This ring is a seal that shows that one belongs to a particular household. For the Christian, he or she belongs to the kingdom of God, and the seal of the Holy Spirit guarantees each one an eternal inheritance.[20]

Interestingly, the early Christian writers referred to the filling of the Holy Spirit as the Lord's seal. They believed that the born-again experience was where the new Christian became the possession of the Lord. But, the sealing of Christians was like putting a brand on them just as a man might brand the sheep that were already His.[21]

This reminds us that the whole goal of the Holy Ghost is to exalt Jesus in everything. When a believer comes to Jesus, seeking to possess Him in a greater reality, he or she receives a greater measure of the Holy Ghost. Jesus confirmed this in John 7:37-39,

> Jesus stood and cried, saying, If any man thirst, let him <u>come unto me</u>, and drink. He that believeth on me as the scripture hath said, out of his belly shall flow rivers of living water. (But this spake he of the Spirit, which they that believe on him should receive: for the Holy Ghost was not yet given; because that Jesus was not yet glorified.) (Emphasis added)

When was the last time you asked the Father for more of the Spirit, so that you can live a life pleasing to Him? When did you last come to Jesus, seeking more of Him, only to be given more of the Holy Ghost? Do not seek the Spirit for more of His abiding presence and power. Rather, believe what the Word says and respond in simple child-life faith, knowing God wants you to have more of the presence of His Spirit in your life.

---

[20] Luke 15:22; Ephesians 1:11-14

[21] Deeper Experiences of Famous Christians, James Gilchrist Lawson, © 2000 by Barbour Publishing, Inc.

3

THE DESIGN

The Body of Christ is meant to function as a fine-tuned organism, void of division. To ensure unity in this Body, there is only one body, one Spirit, one calling, one Lord, one faith, one baptism, and one God. This Body has one head, is established on one immovable foundation, and is lined up to one cornerstone, Jesus Christ.[1]

Five positions were instituted to line the Church up to the leadership of Jesus and establish it on the right foundation—apostles, prophets, evangelists, pastors, and teachers. The Apostle Paul made reference to all of these positions in Ephesians 4:11 and to some of them in 1 Corinthians 12:28.

It is important to put these positions in the right perspective because there has been much erroneous teaching and abuse about this subject, especially in the areas of apostles and prophets. Much of this violation has to do with Ephesians 2:20, "And are built upon the foundation of the apostles and prophets, Jesus Christ himself being the chief corner stone."

This Scripture shows that the apostles and prophets initially established the foundation of the Church, but it was always in line with the Person of Jesus Christ. Everything these individuals established as foundational truths and everything they instructed and maintained in written epistles was in line with the spirit, character, example, and teachings of Jesus Christ. Not only were these teachings to serve as immovable truths, but they also contained within them great treasures that could be discovered by those who were sincere and child-like in heart.[2]

Once these treasures were uncovered, they would reveal a greater revelation of Jesus Christ. It is important to point out that the apostles and prophets who initially laid the foundation were not establishing new revelations. Rather, they were embellishing on a revelation that had been hidden until unveiled in Jesus Christ. This is why Jesus Christ is the only spiritual foundation and cornerstone.[3] Every teaching must be founded in Him and be in line with His character and example.

---

[1] Matthew 21:42-44; Ephesians 4:3-6; 1 Corinthians 3:11; Colossians 1:15-18
[2] Colossians 2:2-3
[3] 1 Corinthians 3:11; Ephesians 1:17; 2:20

Challenging the Christian Life

In his book *Will the Real Heretics Please Stand Up*, David W. Bercot explained how the early Church maintained pure doctrine. The new Church had to contend with many counterfeit epistles or letters. Apparently, it was the early Christians who depended on the guidance of the Holy Spirit to determine which letters were genuine. Once the New Testament was in place, the attitude of the believers from that point on was that there would be no special doctrinal revelations beyond the foundation that was established by the prophecies of the Old Testament prophets and the teachings of the first apostles and prophets.

For the first three centuries, Christians maintained this strong stand in regards to any other presentations of doctrine. This strong stand protected the purity of truth and doctrines as well as maintained the intent of the Word. Since the channel had been preserved in relationship to purity of God's Word, people could be led to a greater revelation of Jesus Christ.

The doctrinal wall of protection began to especially erode away in the fourth century when the pursuit for purity of doctrine and separation from the world changed to unifying the different religious beliefs under one "Christian" auspice. This concept sounded wonderful to the Christians who had suffered various types of persecution for over two centuries, but, in the end, it robbed the Church of its authority and power.

I have no doubt that, in the fourth century, this new zeal over having a "Christian" world, blinded well-meaning Christians to the harsh reality that Christians were not meant to come into unity with the world, but to attract lost souls out of it to Jesus Christ. As one of the illustrations found in *Encyclopedia of Sermon Illustrations* pointed out: "If the church joins the world, there is no need for the world to join the church." Today, we see this same trend to bring the world under a "Christian" umbrella even though history proves it to be disastrous.

We see where Christians today are more politically minded than spiritually inclined in their pursuits for personal holiness. As a result, there is no distinction between the world and the Church. Christians are busy trying to change governments, laws, and policies rather than contending for souls in order to see changed hearts and lives. In fact, they are in the business of conforming people to a moral standard, instead of upholding that which transforms the carnal mind in its enmity against God.[4]

The early Christians failed to realize the danger of unity with this unholy combination. It meant compromising truth and implementing a leadership that would establish perverted doctrines. Initially, these leaders were not given the titles of apostles and prophets in the first couple of centuries, but they were placed into the same type of positions in order to redefine the foundation laid by the first apostles.

As the walls of protection crumbled, the Church became open to the creeds of men to redefine foundational truths and doctrines, often

---

[4] Romans 8:7-8; 12:1-2

exceeding the norm or negating the authority of the written Word. As men's traditions and superstitions invaded the Church, issues such as holiness, repentance, faith, and grace were redefined, causing many to become blind to the spirit or complete counsel of Scripture. As they became blind to foundational truths, they lost sight of the real Jesus.

This breakdown caused men to become reliant on man to interpret the Word rather than on the Holy Spirit. Such alliance put basic truths and doctrinal issues into the arena of intellectual pursuits, endless debates, and higher criticism. Men began to debate the legitimacy of some of the New Testament books, while embracing certain gospels or epistles that corresponded to their beliefs. What started out as an attempt to bring unity ended in division, denominations, and disillusioned people. Instead of people becoming followers of Jesus, they became followers of a person and preferred beliefs, making them promoters of men's traditions rather than fulfilling their commission to preach the Gospel of Jesus Christ.

Through the years, these traditions and so-called "revelations" have been added to the religious state of the Church. Different denominations and cults have mushroomed, drowning out the simplicity of Christ and watering down the Gospel. These beliefs have become the final authority to what many believe.

In this last century, the Church has seen the rise of countless self-proclaimed apostles and prophets. These positions have been exalted as ranks, making the people who hold such titles the final authority. These people are claiming to have new revelations that cleverly undermine the foundational truths and doctrines of Christianity. They have subtly changed the face of Christianity by presenting another Jesus, promoting another gospel, and operating under another spirit. They have accomplished this by exalting a few "elite" men as the anointed ones or messiahs.[5]

These self-proclaimed leaders advocate faith in man and encourage blind allegiance to their leadership, as these imposters are often exalted as God in the eyes of their followers. They are arrogant, demanding, and have become rich at the expense of their blind subjects.

The victims of this movement are the local bodies of believers. Many unsuspecting Christians have lost their heavenly vision as they became lost in a maze of expensive mega-churches. This has caused many to accept counterfeits as they became caught up with the fleshly hypes and different religious movements that are ecumenical in nature. This ecumenism is a means of trying to unify the true, universal Church under the auspices of the new breed of apostles and prophets. Sadly, this unity is moving the Church into the heretical, dangerous one-world religion that has been prophesied in the Word of God.

---

[5] 2 Corinthians 11:1-11

It is important to point out that the New Testament apostles and prophets were placed in a position and not in leadership roles. Positions determine responsibility and imply an official capacity. For example, the official capacity of apostles and prophets was to establish the Church on the right foundation and ensure all growth was in line with Jesus Christ. Their activities were not to exceed the norm of their official capacity, such as taking over the leadership of the local bodies. Keep in mind, many apostles traveled from place to place to establish or edify the different local bodies. Once the local churches were in place, these apostles continued to instruct through epistles, while working among other bodies of believers. We see this in the lives of Paul and Peter.

Leadership of local bodies was given to individuals who worked within the local church and were recognized by their godliness and spiritual wisdom. These believers had to fit strict criteria. They were individuals who were often financially poor, but were rich in faith and the knowledge of Jesus Christ. They were meek and lowly in spirit and knew how to count the cost. The reason for this is because these pillars were the first to be targeted when persecution raised its fist against local churches. They were believers who had to be dead to the world and alive unto God. They cared only for the reality of Jesus and being faithful to the sheep that were entrusted to them. These saints were referred to as elders (bishops) and deacons, not apostles and prophets.[6]

These leaders of the New Testament Church ensured accountability on a local level, but those of the local body also held them accountable. We clearly see this in the instruction the Apostle Paul gave Timothy in 1 Timothy 5:19-20. Sadly, today these leadership positions are either being compromised, abused for personal gain and exaltation, or whittled down to a title with no real meaning or responsibility in the Church.

This undermining of leadership has caused the Church to become vulnerable to wolves in sheep's clothing. I have no doubt many of these wolves are masquerading as ministers (apostles and prophets) of righteousness to steal sheep away from the local bodies.[7]

The main goal of these wolves is financial gain. They are making merchandise of people's souls with vain words and promises.[8] Their foolish covetousness will bring greater damnation on them. In the meantime, the sheep are being isolated, wounded, and, in some cases, destroyed by these wolves. As unsuspecting people support these wolves, the real work of God is overlooked and greatly hindered. In short, these wolves are robbing from the real servants of God.

The positions and gifts were given for the edification of the Body and not for the promotion of a few self-appointed leaders. Godly leaders are humble servants who do not merchandise God or His sheep for personal prestige and gain. They are not trying to sell any goods for personal gain;

---

[6] See 1 Timothy 3:1-13; 5:17-20; Titus 1:5-9; James 2:5
[7] Matthew 7:15; Acts 29:29
[8] See John 2:16; 2 Peter 2:3

rather, their heart desire is to exemplify the Person of Jesus in attitude and actions. They are not trying to promote the Gospel with enticing words or worldly means, but "in power and with the Holy Ghost."[9]

These counterfeits require that a distinction be made by believers between false leaders and the positions that were established for the benefit and growth of the Church. As you examine this distinction, ask yourself if you have bought the lies from any of the many wolves that are parading around in the name of God.

---

[9] 1 Thessalonians 1:5

4

THE POSITIONS

Positions in the kingdom of God do not point to rank; rather, they represent an act of placing a person in a proper order to fulfill God's purpose or design. This concept is made obvious when one considers how every Christian is not only personally placed within the Body of Christ, but placed by God in Christ. We also know that the placing of individuals is not an attempt by God to exalt a few over the masses because God is no respecter of persons. In fact, His order within the Body of Christ exalts members that seem insignificant in the scheme of things to equal footing and importance in His kingdom.[1]

This equality is due to the fact that everyone is a sinner and stands equally in need of forgiveness and salvation. Such equality does away with superiority and elitism, the very attitudes that cause competition, division, and resentment among people.

This brings us back to who is the greatest in the kingdom of God? Is greatness in God's sight the same as in the world? Sadly, many Christians consider greatness in light of the world and not according to Scripture.

The world determines greatness based on titles and degrees. It matters little to most people if the person fits the title in practical skills as long as the degrees, certificates, and education confirm that the person has rights to declare such honors.

In the kingdom of God, greatness is not determined by position, but by attitude and action. According to Jesus, the greatest in the kingdom of God is a servant of all.[2] A servant is humble in attitude, submissive in action, and obedient in practice. He or she has given up rights and given way to a worthy authority. Servants are not here to serve their personal pursuits, but those of their master.

The disposition of servitude and a sincere and sacrificial love for the Master is what sets all great leaders apart in God's kingdom. These leaders have no personal agendas outside of Christ and Him crucified.[3] They stand for truth, contend for one true faith, and are singular in vision. They are led by the Spirit, compelled by godly love, and heaven bound. They are sojourners who are crucified to the world and possess one

---

[1] Acts 10:34; 1 Corinthians 1:30; 12:23-24
[2] Matthew 20:25-27
[3] 1 Corinthians 2:2

main goal of finishing the course to gain and possess the ultimate reward of heaven, Jesus Himself.

Today there are many claiming titles in the kingdom of heaven, but few can rightfully lay claim to them. These counterfeits lack the disposition and fruits that would confirm that they are legitimate.

This brings us to the subject of the positions that were established for the purpose of properly building the Church. Those who will ultimately possess greatness in God's kingdom will not do so on the basis of these positions, but because they have a disposition of a real servant. Individuals who declare their legitimacy based on titles alone are those who are fraudulent in their claims. Those who are frauds will lack the heart and attitude of a servant and will be void of the life of Christ. It is the life of Christ that serves as the light within the soul of man. If this light is present, it will reveal the mind of Christ. If this light is absent, it reveals that the person is self-serving and a servant of the kingdom of darkness.

With this in mind, let us now consider the positions that were established for the Church's benefit.

Apostles

According to *Strong's Exhaustive Concordance*, "apostle" means an official delegate, ambassador of Christ, or sent out one. As an official representative of the kingdom God, this individual is commissioned to take one consistent message to each kingdom, country, or nation that he or she is sent to. The message is known as the Gospel, the power of God unto salvation.[4]

As you can see, the implications of a modern-day apostle are not to redefine or establish a new foundation, but to officially represent the King of kings and the Lord of lords wherever he or she may go. Usually, these people start new local churches wherever they are called. Once a work is started, these servants must ensure that Christ is the foundation and cornerstone to every life that is being placed within the local church or body for the work and glory of God. After all, each member makes up a lively priesthood, a spiritual house.[5]

Because of the confusion and misuse of the word apostle, the Church has devised another term that would embrace the work of the apostle—missionary. A missionary is sent to other places to represent Jesus as ambassadors. These people's responsibilities may vary according to the needs of those around them, but like the first apostles, they can find themselves establishing local bodies through preaching, teaching, contending for souls and truth, and serving as a light in dark places.

---

[4] Romans 1:16
[5] 1 Peter 2:5

The work of the apostle or missionary may last only a season. The Holy Spirit may move these servants on to another work or change their present status by redefining their work according to the needs and the direction of the new church. These servants of God must be capable of showing love, flexibility, patience, and obedience to any change of direction in God's work. As a result, their greatest contribution to the kingdom of God often becomes their example of devotion, sacrifice, and sincerity to do God's bidding wherever they are planted.

Prophets

These people are known to operate in two areas—foretelling (warning others of future events) and forthtelling (preaching and exhortation). The apostles establish the local church, but prophets are responsible to guard the spirit of the new church and maintain it in righteousness.

The problem with this position is that many wolves have hid behind the position of prophet.[6] The reason this position is so attractive is because of the prophetic implications. Even though the position of prophet has a greater responsibility than foretelling future events, many people are drawn to the prophetic and can be easily deceived by false prophets.

Although the greatest Prophet of history, Jesus Christ, pretty much covered the last days in an extensive way, these modern-day false prophets are running around with a word for every person, city, nation, and country operating as fortunetellers, rather than foretelling according to the Spirit of God. Many of their words are generic and fleshly. This is important to note because a genuine prophet will give prophecies that can be tested by specific details and will not have to be stretched in any fashion to make it appear genuine like the counterfeits do. The genuine prophet will always point people to Jesus Christ and never exalt self as the only legitimate voice of God that people must trust.

On the other hand, false prophets may call people to repentance and holiness, but never to Jesus Christ. They subtly exalt themselves to the place of a religious expert and eventually take center stage as "the anointed one" or "messiah".

The false prophet ultimately fails to fulfill this position because the main concern of genuine prophets is to prepare others for the coming of Jesus. These dedicated servants are to make the path straight for the Holy Spirit to move freely to unveil Christ to seeking hearts. This is where preaching, warning, and exhortation will become the tools they use to contend for the spiritual growth and wholeness of the Church.

In order to prepare His people, God gives prophets discernment. They will discern the spirit or intent behind leaders, doctrines, and movements. They will display sensitivity to the Spirit and will only speak under His inspiration. As a result, they are able to take up the sword of

---

[6] Matthew 7:15-16

the Word and impart it with power and authority. As the sword becomes powerful and living, the motives and intents of others will be exposed.

Since darkness resents light according to the religious counterfeit, godly prophets are unpopular. They will insist on purity, rather than popularity and money. They will reprove sin, stand against heresy, silence foolishness, and take an axe to all roots and practices of idolatry. They will prove to be bold for truth, as well as relentless soldiers of the cross, and will have a no-nonsense approach towards all deception. As a result, prophets are unattractive to the religious masses and travel a lonely road of separation like Jeremiah and John the Baptist.

Because of the skepticism caused by false prophets, the Church, once again, has given these people another name—watchmen. We see this term was used in the case of the prophet, Ezekiel.[7] God also made a reference between the righteous watchmen and the false prophets in Hosea 9:8.

It is important to note that the prophet is not always obvious. He or she might be the unassuming person sitting next to you in the pew. Like the prophet Amos, a true prophet can only respond when God calls him or her, and God might only call the individual once to warn His Body of heresy, trouble, or pending judgment. The initial response by most to a true prophet of God is to ignore, discredit, or silence his or her voice instead of testing the warning or exhortation. If you discover a person is a false prophet, contend with the person. But, if you find the saying or warning of the prophet is true, respond in humility, submission, and obedience or judgment will follow.

Evangelist

When we think of an evangelist, we envision a person who is preaching fire and damnation behind pulpits, in tents, and on the streets. Granted, an evangelist reaches out to the unsaved, but the individual who holds this position is also responsible for the edification of the Church.

Apostles establish new churches upon the right foundation and line them up to the Cornerstone. The prophets guard the Church against heresy and call members to scriptural accountability. But the evangelists are responsible for challenging and enlarging the vision of the Church.

Christianity is a spiritual kingdom existing within worldly kingdoms and nations. As a result, Christians are called to be separate from the world. Believers who live separate from the world ensure a powerful testimony that enables them to carry out their commission—to preach the Gospel and make new converts followers of Christ. This commission serves as the Church's vision in the world. It is supernatural and heavenly, as well as laying at the heart of God and the Church's purpose for being in the world.

---

[7] Ezekiel 3:17; 33:7

A church without this vision becomes like the Dead Sea, where much fresh water is taken in, but none of it is given out. This type of church will be good at taking from the resources of others, but it fails to become a conduit from which the Living Water flows to others. This condition causes stagnation, which produces spiritual dullness. Spiritual dullness translates to indifference to souls and a slumbering local church that will fail to carry out its commission.

This is where the evangelist becomes part of the edification of the body. He or she must stir the church out of its spiritual slumber to once again consider the purpose for being in the world—to preach the Gospel and make disciples of Jesus. This stirring means a renewing or reviving of the church. In order to accomplish this, the evangelist has to be empowered with the Holy Spirit and must shake the church out of its comfort zone with inspired preaching from the throne room of God. The main call of the evangelist will not be for Christians to fulfill their commission, but to repent for failing to do so.

The absence of the Church's heavenly vision displays disobedience and a lack of godly love. It takes the love of God to properly respond to the commission. Once the Church repents of its wicked ways of unbelief and of being lukewarm and adheres to the commission, it is being obedient to the Word of God. Therefore, the evangelist must revive not only the vision, but also a love for God. This is why he or she must have the inspiration of the Holy Spirit. Only the Spirit of God can cause repentance that will translate into a fire of revival and fervor that will not only cause the church to rise up in boldness, but fan the fire of devotion and boldness.

Sadly, evangelists are becoming a rare breed in America. In the 1800's and early 1900's, evangelists held meetings that lasted for weeks. This allowed the evangelist to tear down idolatry, root-out disobedience, and properly challenge people in order to build up the local church. It gave time for the Holy Spirit to prepare, move, break, restore, and save souls. It encouraged both the saved and the unsaved to do business with God until the person knew God's will and direction for his or her life.

These meetings were eventually cut down from weeks to days and, finally, to a few meetings a week. Apparently, the church became too busy to commit to weeks of intense spiritual examination. The reasons vary, but one of the biggest reasons, besides a loss of vision and the instant society mentality, is entertainment.

Evangelistic meetings used to be the main attraction in town for believers, but now believers can be exposed to all the Christian influences they need via radio and television. They can sit and partake of various religious themes and be professionally entertained at the same time. They can become emotionally hyped without getting real about what is going on in their hearts and lives. They can tack a religious cloak on and deem all is good without coming to repentance. They can walk in a religious fantasy, while ignoring their commission.

The main difference between these two avenues of evangelistic meetings and religious entertainment is the personal touch. People can be indifferent to personal spiritual problems because there is no accountability when it comes to the media. After all, the Holy Spirit wants to personally meet with the individual to expose hidden problems and sins as well as encourage and build up. These different medias allow for the religious conscience to be soothed while hiding sins beneath a religious cloak. This atmosphere encourages a feel-good religion without any substance or power behind it.

God uses man to be an extension of His heart, voice, hands, and feet. There is something about a personal touch and encounter that encourages and allows healing and restoration to take place in a weary soul.

Another reason the evangelist is becoming a dying breed in America is because of the attitude of some church leaders towards this position. I had one pastor tell me he did not need an evangelist to come to his church because he was all his church needed. The doors of his church are now closed, silently mocking his high evaluation of himself and his blatant disregard for the Word of God. The Bible clearly states that evangelists are part of God's plan of edification for the Body, and true leaders of God will not brush such a reality to the side.

An international evangelist gave me another aspect of the challenges that buffet evangelists. He stated that most leaders of churches, especially in America, are only interested in numbers and not souls. He shared with me that, if an evangelist failed to get the numbers of people up to the altar, he or she was not asked back.

This has placed evangelists in a competitive role, rather than a contender for souls. Evangelists have to resort to manipulative and controlling practices to get people to the altars, whether their repentance or rededication is sincere or not.

I remember attending an evangelistic meeting where I never heard one word preached from the Word, but instead witnessed a variety of manipulative approaches by the evangelist to get people to respond to his call for them to come to the altar. I became repulsed by his methods and left the meeting early.

Much of the evangelism going on is pleasing to the ears, stirring up emotions, and entertaining, but the power of the Spirit and Gospel is missing. It stirs up the flesh, rather than the spirit. It sets self aflame with good feelings, rather than obtaining a heavenly vision that burns for lost souls.

The apostle, prophet, and evangelist are not permanent positions within the local church. People who hold these positions either travel or have their responsibilities redefined by the condition or needs of the local body of believers. People who hold these positions must be flexible and sojourners at heart. They are often hidden in obscurity, ready to respond to God's call to be broken vessels and poured out like wine for the benefits of others and the glory of God.

Challenging the Christian Life

Now that we have considered the versatile positions of the Church, let us examine the two permanent positions found in the local bodies.

5

A SERVANT OF ALL

While the positions of apostles, prophets, and evangelists can be temporary, changing, or even obscure to the rest of the body, the last two positions in Ephesians 4:11 remain constant within the Body of Christ. This brings us down to the responsibility these last two positions hold and why they are constant and visible. The apostle establishes the local church, the prophet guards and maintains the body of believers, and the evangelist protects and revives the vision of the body, while the pastor leads and the teacher instructs.

When we think of a pastor, we automatically think of a preacher who stands behind a pulpit and delivers a weekly message on Sunday. However, a pastor's responsibilities are more far reaching than just preaching. This is clearly established by the meaning of pastor—a shepherd.[1]

Spiritual shepherds are mentioned in both the Old and New Testaments, and both point to the one great shepherd of mankind, Jesus Christ. Psalm 23:1, Isaiah 40:11, and John 10 confirm that the Lord desires to be our shepherd. His heart and desire for His followers comprise a beautiful picture of the total abandonment and commitment of a shepherd towards the welfare of his sheep.

For example, a committed shepherd will not lead his sheep to muddy waters, to barren waste lands, or into danger. He does everything to protect his sheep against predators, irritants such as fleas, and emotional stress such as fears. His goal is to bring his flock to still waters that revive, and green pastures that nourish.

This is a vision of a true shepherd. But today that vision is not prevalent. Many pastors in the Church appear as if they are failing to live up to this example. Some give the impression they have lost their heart or vision for shepherding. This makes a pastor a hireling shepherd or a self-centered wolf that is posing as a shepherd.

Shepherds who are void of heart and vision, lack the commitment to properly lead Jesus' sheep. Ezekiel 34 reveals the attitudes and works of both the hireling shepherds and those who are wolves.

The first thing the prophet Ezekiel said about these shepherds is that they feed themselves rather than the sheep. We see this today as pastors or leaders are more interested in bigger buildings, kingdoms, and numbers, rather than individual sheep. Most of the pursuits of these

---

[1] Strong's Exhaustive Concordance of the Bible, # 4166

worldly shepherds include money, prestige, and power instead of souls. Instead of leading the sheep to fresh water, they allow them to partake of muddy water (fleshly doctrine), stagnant water (dead-lettered doctrine), and poisoned water (blatant heresy). Instead of leading them to green pastures, they lead them to a spiritually barren wasteland where the sheep struggle to live, causing spiritual malnutrition, weakness, and death. Instead of protecting them, they allow the wolves to come in to devour the innocent lambs and to take down the vulnerable and wounded sheep. This is a classic example of the shepherds feeding their own self-serving purposes at the expense of the flock.

The second quality that Ezekiel brought out about a false shepherd is that he does not take care of the wounded sheep.[2] I have been in churches where the wounded fall through the cracks of indifference, neglect, and statistics. In other words, the shepherd does not personally know the sheep. How can a pastor help a wounded soul unless he takes the time and energy to become personally involved with every individual who sits under his or her leadership?

This brings us to the mega-churches. They may appear impressive to the world and try to accommodate many people by having various pastors and programs. However, the wounded are being swallowed up by too much business that has been developed in the name of God. This business is supposedly for the purpose of maintaining a religious kingdom. The meaning of Church has ceased to be that of a living body; rather, it has been rendered an unfeeling organization where many leaders only goal is to see the masses flock in, instead of ensuring the individual is among the flock feeding on the Word of God.

Sadly, when the wounded sheep succumb to their open wounds and become missing, it goes unnoticed. Jesus said this in regard to the one missing sheep in Luke 15:4, "What man of you, having an hundred sheep, if he lose one of them, doth not leave the ninety and nine in the wilderness, and go after that which is lost, until he find it?"

One must keep in mind that a legitimate shepherd cares about every one of his sheep because he has personally invested in each one of them. Jesus is the one who purchased the sheep that sit in the church buildings throughout the world, not the earthly pastors. This is why souls are often treated as commodities by pastors. After all, what is one lost soul compared to the ninety-nine that are tithing, loyal, and visibly participating in the building of the pastor's personal kingdom?

Any time a pastor is without the heart of Jesus, he or she will lack the vision to see the worth of every soul who walks through the door of the church. I know that many pastors start out right, but with the worldly demands of maintaining physical growth and keeping up with the competition, the vision of souls can be choked out. Pastors must maintain the heart of Christ to ensure that the heavenly vision remains intact.

---

[2] Ezekiel 34:4

Because shepherds are neither properly feeding the real sheep of Jesus nor having personal relationships with them, the sheep are being scattered as they search for personal leadership, pure water (the Word), and green pastures (nourishment). As the sheep scatter, they become prey to predators. According to a figure I heard back in the 1980s, 80 percent of the kingdoms of the cults were made up of people who used to attend Christian churches. This simply means that the sheep looked elsewhere because the leadership or the body failed to do their part. Granted, some sheep are rebellious and will go their own way regardless of the investment, but the figure of 80 percent is an indictment against Christian leadership and the Body. Both have failed in some way, and both need to come back to Scripture and examine their attitudes, examples, and responsibilities to see where failure occurred.

Ezekiel 34:6 revealed where the failure occurred, "...and none did search or seek after them." Let me summarize the lacking ingredient that would produce such a response—the love of God.

Godly love is what causes one to make the proper investment in souls. This love compels a person to care for and seek after the one lost sheep. "Agape" love enables shepherds and believers to recognize and become identified with the wounded sheep, and it is this love that sets the Church apart from worldly indifference and self-serving kingdoms.

The love of God also produces a right attitude in the shepherd. A shepherd is also referred to as an elder, bishop, or overseer. Peter instructs these shepherds to feed the flock of God, not by harshness, but with a willing heart. They are not to feed them with financial gain in mind, but because they have the mind or determination to please the Shepherd that gave His life for the sheep. He also instructed them not to be superior in attitude, but an example of true leadership.[3] This leadership would come from an attitude of servitude, which expresses itself in meekness and lowliness.

This brings us down to the commission of the shepherd. It is quite simple. It is not to build big churches, establish great kingdoms, or have a great following. It is to simply feed God's sheep.

When Jesus told Peter that He would be part of the building of His Church, Peter probably envisioned great things for himself because of his pride. This pride set him up for great failure as he denied Jesus three times in the hour of his testing. The denial of Jesus put up a mirror that revealed his depravity as his pride received a fatal blow.

When Jesus met with Peter after His resurrection, He asked Peter the same thing three times in order to rid Peter of misconceptions, allowing him to recognize his true responsibility. "Simon, son of Jonas lovest thou me more than these?"[4] I believe every true shepherd must go back to this simple question for, if the love is not there, they should step down from their position until the love once again abounds in their

---

[3] John 10:1-16; 1 Peter 5:1-4
[4] John 21:15-19

Challenging the Christian Life

hearts. If they are representing Jesus without His heart of commitment, they are not only betraying their position and high calling, but they are betraying Jesus and His sheep.

Once a shepherd can truly answer as Peter, "Yea Lord; thou knowest that I love thee," they will again grasp the importance of their position.[5] Once they properly perceive the motive behind their high calling, their commission will clearly be defined, their vision exalted to a heavenly perspective and hope, and their hearts in tune with the true Shepherd and Bishop of people's souls.[6] From this point, they will be able to hear the same instructions Jesus gave Peter—to feed His lambs, sheep, and flock.[7]

As I studied the writings and lives of the Apostle Paul and the Apostle Peter, I can see how their hearts and visions varied. They both established the Church, but Peter was a pastor and shepherd at heart. He understood the importance of this position like no other person in his situation, due to his experiences surrounding the cross and the calling of Jesus.

This is why Peter's warnings to pastors are as sobering as Ezekiel's. Ezekiel pronounced a "woe" on irresponsible shepherds and declared that God would seek His sheep and bind them up. He would also be against the false shepherds; He would take the flock away from them and feed the shepherds with judgment.[8]

Peter warned the shepherds who have been entrusted with Jesus' sheep to treat them properly, so that when the chief Shepherd appears, they would receive a crown of glory that would never fade.[9] Obviously, there will be some type of judgment rendered towards shepherds.

It amazes me that some pastors appear to be flippant about their positions. Many act as if their position is a profession or equivalent to the CEO of a big company. Instead of being a humble servant to God's flock and a committed lover of Jesus Christ, such a pastor will merchandise souls and the things of God.

This reminds me of an incident with a pastor of a large church. He asked me what he needed to beware of in his position. I considered his responsibilities, staff, and grandiose goals. I looked at him and told him that his biggest challenge was not to leave his first love.[10]

It is easy to get caught up with good works and leave Jesus behind. Pastors have to guard their hearts and consider their ways to make sure they do not leave the source of their life, purpose, and strength behind. They must not forget that the sheep entrusted to them do not belong to them, and that, one day, they will give an account for the general spiritual

---

[5] Ibid
[6] 1 Peter 2:25
[7] John 21:15-19
[8] Ezekiel 34:2, 10
[9] 1 Peter 5:1-4
[10] Revelation 2:4

condition of their flocks, as well as the sheep who are missing due to neglect, business, and worldliness on their parts.

I pray that every wayward pastor who has lost his or her vision will come back to the Chief Shepherd to renew and restore his or her life, calling, and commission. Restoration of the pastor's vision is necessary to prevent any further scattering of the sheep. A revived vision will allow the servant of God to be available to those sheep who are trying to find their way home. They will have the stamina to withstand the wolves, swine, and goats of their congregations, avoiding wounds and defeat. This vision will remind them to whom their allegiance must be directed towards, and what their responsibility is to Jesus' flock.

Teachers

The position of teacher in the Church is vital for edification. Without both the proper leadership of pastors and the instruction of teachers, the Church becomes subject to failure, destruction, and death. Each of these five positions is vital to the complete edification of the Body, but pastors and teachers are the positions that ensure the growth and well-being of the Body. For example, apostles appeal to the spiritual needs of people, prophets appeal to the spiritual condition of people, and evangelists appeal to the vision of people, while shepherds appeal to the hearts of people and teachers appeal to the understanding of people. We see how all five positions result in what would be considered a complete picture of edification, but it is clear that pastors and teachers meet the Body at its point of personal needs and growth.

Teachers in Jesus' day were referred to as masters and rabbis. Another meaning for "teacher" was doctor.[11] The concept behind this position demanded respect from the pupils. But, the greatest reason for adhering to people placed in this position by God is because they directly influence a person's eternal destiny.

Today, the term teacher does not hold the same significance as it did in Jesus' day. In many cases, teaching is simply a position that needs to be filled, rather than a position that has been ordained by God. As we consider the idea of teaching in the kingdom of God, there are various goals to meet in order to ensure the integrity of this position.

Scriptural teaching points to discipline in every facet of life. It helps a person understand the path of righteousness, points him or her to walk in the ways of God's character, and instructs the individual in what it means to fear God and do His will.[12] Godly teaching is meant to get down into the spirit of man in order to change his perception, purpose, and direction.

Great teachers do not tell people how to think through indoctrination. Rather, they give them the tools that will challenge their ways of thinking.

---

[11] Strong's Exhaustive Concordance of the Bible, #1320
[12] Psalm 25:4, 8; 27:11; 143:10

These teachers want to enlarge people's ability to consider the possibilities of a matter. It is not just a matter of enlarging their ability to explore outside of the normal, intellectual boxes that many operate within, but it also is about enlarging one's world in regard to a matter.

Teaching in the kingdom of God must get down into a person's spirit to become life. For teaching to become a source of life and discovery, it must be manna from the throne room of God. This means it will be living, powerful, anointed, and inspired by the Holy Spirit. It will enable man to realize that spiritual truths cannot just be perceived as facts, intellectual conclusions, or doctrines. But they are to serve as milk, bread, meat, and life to the soul.

The real challenge for godly teachers is that they must do everything within their means to cause their students to exceed them in spiritual insight. In order to instruct students to come higher, these teachers must be experienced spiritual mountain climbers. They must know how to enlarge their pupils enough that their pupils can develop personal skills that will take them higher in Christ. After all, a teacher cannot lead students where they have never been, and students are only as good as their teacher.

Teachers shape minds by the type of emphasis or pursuits they uphold in their instructions. For example, my emphasis, as a servant of God, is a relationship with God. Valuable experiences have grown out of this pursuit. These experiences have given me authority in my teachings. Often, my emphasis will bring people back to this reality, but only the Spirit of God can impart it into a person's spirit to bring forth life.

The real authority and power of godly teachers becomes evident when they are serving as a conduit for the Holy Spirit to stir up the pupil with the anointed, pure Word of God. This will inspire the student to explore the possibilities of a greater reality of Christ. Such inspiration means the pupil's flame to discover truths beyond present understanding must be fanned into a fire. This fire will cause him or her to pursue every bit of information presented, to reach and travel beyond present understanding.

Godly teachers encounter challenges because of how their students value or perceive truth. Students can fall into four categories. Some are like sponges. They soak everything up, but, because there is no commitment to comprehend the information in a personal way, they quickly dry out and change eludes them. Others are like the Dead Sea. They take much in, but the information never gets down to the heart to produce revelation and change. Then, you have those who take information in, but are like sieves. It all quickly flows through and out because there is no real foundation for any of it to rest upon.

The final group is made up of those who desire and seek after truth. They are not happy with facts, doctrine, or opinions. They want God's words to become life and substance to their souls. As a result, they see the Word as a gold mine and are forever seeking out nuggets that will make them grow in the knowledge of Jesus Christ.

Today, spiritual truths have been summarized into intellectual and doctrinal pursuits. People get excited about learning new facts and doctrines or confirming firmly held doctrines, but there seems no concern or desire to personally encounter Jesus in their pursuits.

I realize that students may not always give a good presentation of their teacher's commitment or emphasis, but, as a teacher, I want my students to have a basic understanding of godly principles. I realize that students determine how much depth of truth will reach into their souls and spirits. But every student still must understand basic foundational truths that will serve as a good foundation from which they have the abilities to explore the mysteries of God.

The question I must ask when I see Christians who lack this vital foundation is: What is their teacher's main emphasis? Paul warned of teachers who taught things that tickled fleshly ears, promoted the Law, and were a means to financial gain. Peter warned about teachers teaching damnable heresies, as well as people who would wrest Scriptures to their own destruction.[13] The warnings of false teachers and the destruction they wrought are manifold, but it is also clear about these imposters' final end—a greater condemnation.[14]

It is important, in each of the five positions, that the people who hold them are actually called to them. They must be inspired and led by the Holy Spirit as they do the work of edification in the Body. As Ephesians 4:12-13 stated about the ultimate goal of these positions, "For the perfecting of the saints, for the work of the ministry, for the edifying of the body of Christ: Till we all come in the <u>unity</u> of the <u>faith</u>, and of the <u>knowledge</u> of the Son of God, unto a perfect man, unto the measure of the stature of the fullness of Christ." (Emphasis added)

These two Scripture verses tell us that servitude in God's kingdom is about perfecting saints so they can do the work of ministry for the building up of the Body. Godly edification produces unity in faith according to the knowledge of Christ. This type of edification causes a person to embrace the fullness of Christ so he or she can manifest Him to the Church and in the dark world.

Are you called to any of these positions? If so, are you being faithful to the leading of the Holy Spirit and the heart of Christ to bring people to spiritual maturity according to your calling and God's plan?

My main hope for all believers is that our Lord, Shepherd, and Savior will find His leadership faithful when He comes for His precious sheep.

---

[13] 1 Timothy 1:7; 4:1; 2 Timothy 4:3; Titus 1:11; 2 Peter 2:1; 3:18-16
[14] James 3:1

6

THE GIFTS OF GRACE

In Romans 12:6-8, we discover seven gifts that are to bring Christians to maturity. These gifts are not only for the edification of the Body, but they also are a means by which to reach out to the unsaved to touch their lives with the reality of Jesus. These gifts are given according to grace and point to what some would consider natural abilities. However, God is the one who disperses them throughout the Body of believers.

To ensure these gifts are brought forth, the Apostle Paul set up the type of atmosphere that will allow them to manifest themselves in ministering the life of Christ to others. The first responsibility to secure and operate in these gifts is that a believer must present his or her body as a living sacrifice.[1]

The presentation of our bodies is for the purpose of consecration. Before consecration can take place, one must deny self, pick up the cross, and follow Jesus. Once the self-life is out of the way, a person can present his or her body to be set apart for God's use.

This separation allows the Holy Spirit to do the work of sanctification by transforming the mind of the person so that he or she can rightly discern what will be regarded as the good, acceptable, and perfect will of God. This transformed mind points to the mind of Christ. After all, He had one focus, purpose, and function—to do the will of the Father.[2]

The problem is that, until the mind is transformed, believers play guessing games as to what is pleasing to God. The usual test of such matters includes the following: 1) it has a religious tone to it; 2) it makes the individual feel good about self; and 3) it is a point of recognition of personal piousness.

Every blood-bought saint must have the same focus as Jesus in order to keep everything in perspective. As long as our minds are directed towards the so-called "goodness" of self, instead of the will of God, we will think more highly of ourselves than we ought to.[4]

Grace reminds us that we have no power to save ourselves; therefore, it was accomplished outside of any personal goodness. We know this is true because Jesus secured our redemption on the cross. Our responsibility is to respond to this grace with the measure of faith

---

[1] Romans 12:1
[2] Philippians 2:5-11
[4] Romans 12:3

allotted to us. This shows us that even the faith that we have available to properly respond to this work of grace comes from God.[5]

Grace is God's part in spiritual matters, but faith is man's response. Without the act of grace, man has no avenue by which to respond because he stands hopeless in his spiritual plight. Without faith responding to grace, God has no means by which to show His favor to a person. This is brought out in Romans 5:21, "That as sin hath reigned unto death, even so might grace reign through righteousness unto eternal life by Jesus Christ, our Lord." Faith is accounted to believers for righteousness when it comes to their state and actions as being righteous.[6] It is only at the point of righteousness that God's grace can reign in and through our lives.

Even the measure of faith is an act of grace. This measure of faith to respond properly to God's work and plan entails steps of obedience. As a person responds out of faith in obedience, the Holy Spirit meets the person in order to impart spiritual insight concerning the proper attitude toward and use of his or her gifts for the glory of God and the edification of others. Each time a person responds to the opportunity to exercise one of these gifts, he or she is enlarged to operate in the gift in greater measure. Such an attitude and approach point to being faithful before God concerning those things that He has entrusted to each of us. Christians who fail to be faithful with the gifts He has given them will not be entrusted with more, and their impact in lives will be non-existent or minimal.[7]

The atmosphere the Apostle Paul established in Romans 12 reveals that self must be out of the way to ensure that people will properly handle these gifts. Once the individuals are in the right disposition, God can effectively use them in any gift. These gifts are meant to be a natural extension of the working of His grace in their lives towards others. The purpose for these spiritual gifts is to bring Him glory.

I have broken these gifts down into two categories: gifts of servitude and gifts of benevolence. The reason for breaking down these gifts into two categories is because Jesus left us two distinct examples: servitude and suffering.[8] Once again, we are reminded that all true leaders in the kingdom of God are to be servants of all. Keep in mind that godly leaders are defined by God's grace that should be displayed in them by the attitude of servitude. Therefore, grace will be evident in their actions and attitudes towards those they are overseeing or ministering to. The four gifts that fall into the first category are prophecy, teaching, exhortation, and ruling.

Godly suffering occurs in two forms: persecution and entering into the sufferings with others. The second type of suffering is also known as

---

[5] Ibid
[6] Romans 4:3; 5:1-2
[7] Luke 12:8; 16:10-12
[8] John 13:5-17; 1 Peter 2:19-25

compassion, which always produces benevolent acts. These acts are often sacrificial in nature as well as serve as a means of man extending grace to others in practical ways. The three gifts that fall into the second category are ministry, giving, and mercy.

It is important to point out that each of these gifts possesses boundaries that bring discipline to them in order to ensure their proper use. Therefore, we must consider the gift in light of its discipline.

The first gifts we will consider are the gifts of servitude. These gifts find their authority and power within the attitude of servitude. Such gifts are brought under the leading of the Holy Spirit. Sensitivity to the Spirit results in a person showing discretion in regards to these gifts of grace. Without the right attitude and sensitivity, these gifts can become arrogant, hard, and indifferent.

The first gift in this category is prophecy. Prophecy has a couple of different meanings, but, since we are dealing with personal gifts, the correct meaning would imply an inspired speaker or preacher.

It is not enough to have the ability to be charismatic or to effectively speak or preach. For God to use any gift for His purpose, it must be prompted by the Holy Spirit. Therefore, prophecy, in this text, means an inspired speaker and preacher who only speaks according to the unction of the Holy Spirit. This would mean that the speaker would be imparting living manna from the throne of God.

Inspirational speaking of this caliber manifests authority, boldness, and power. It will penetrate the souls of man, "...piercing even to the dividing asunder of soul and spirit, and of the joints and marrow, and is a discerner of the thoughts and intents of the heart," powerfully impacting the hearers" (Hebrews 4:12). We can witness this natural ability to pierce and separate in action through Spirit-led pastors and evangelists.

The boundary or discipline of the gift of prophecy is that it must be done according to the proportion of faith. The hearers, not the preacher, will determine the proportion of faith in which this gift is exercised. For example, a preacher who is being led by the Spirit will have a sense of where his or her hearers are spiritually. This will dictate the emphasis of the person's message.

The next gift is teaching. This gift is self-explanatory, but, once again, a teacher must wait before God as to the type of manna that must be offered to the hearers. The purpose of teaching is to instruct others, but the boundary of this gift implies that it goes beyond just instructing others. The goal of teaching, in this text, points to providing the necessary tools to the recipients so they can, in turn, instruct others.

Good teachers inspire curiosity to explore beyond comfortable truths and doctrines. Committed teachers want to see their students exceed their instructions and reach greater heights of understanding and maturity. Sadly, much of teaching simply deals with the facts. Believers are busy feeding their minds with facts. As a result, many people become like the Dead Sea. Information is poured into them, but it is never imparted elsewhere, resulting in spiritual stagnation.

Every Christian should be quick to instruct, whether it is through teaching, sharing, or being a visible example of God's grace and love. The problem is that much of what believers understand is not living, which means there is no heavenly vision and inspiration behind it.

Teaching which lacks heavenly vision and inspiration will lack the power to impact lives and bring forth changes. After all, powerful teachings not only stir up curiosity, but they challenge intellectual comfort zones, spiritual complacency, and personal piousness.

According to *Strong's Concordance,* "exhortation" means to call near, invite, invoke, implore, console, comfort, desire, interact, and pray. This definition not only shows servitude, but benevolence. Those who exhort will preach the Gospel, invite people to fellowship with God through Jesus, and invoke them to be holy and upright. An exhorter will implore people to repent of their sins, console those who are suffering, and comfort those who are sorrowful.

The desire of godly exhortation is to see people love, serve, and follow Jesus. This means exhorters must interact with people in meekness and humility, as well as earnestly intercede in prayer for them.

When you combine all of these ingredients of exhortation, you have an individual who will, "contend for the faith which was once delivered unto the saints" (Jude 3). To contend or wrestle for the faith of others can be an intense, thankless, and drawn-out process. This is why those with the gift of exhortation need to keep eternity in focus to maintain a right attitude and perspective.

However, it is vital that those with the gift of exhortation wait for the Spirit's leading. They must show discretion. The hearer must be prepared, as well as the one who is exhorting. The goal of exhortation is to prepare others to contend for the faith. The Church needs leaders who will have compassion on Jesus' sheep, but will also contend with sheep who are erring with the intent to pull them out of the fire of destruction.[9]

The final gift in the category of servitude is the ruler. To be a ruler means to preside, practice, maintain, or be over. It points to someone who can be an effective administrator.[10]

This individual has the natural abilities to lead. However, to be an effective leader in the kingdom of God, he or she must know how to follow. A ruler who is not submissive, teachable, and humble will not be a powerful leader in God's kingdom. A leader who has not truly been humbled by the Lordship of Jesus is not open to instruction and will lack healthy fear to keep this position in proper perspective.

Real leaders in the kingdom of God lead more by example than words. This is why they must have the attitude of a servant and the actions of a trustworthy leader who is truly representative of Jesus Christ.

---

[9] James 5:19-20; Jude 22-23
[10] Strong's Exhaustive Concordance, # 4291

The boundary established for the ruler in God's kingdom is that he or she must rule with diligence. According to *Strong's Concordance*, "diligence" means speed, dispatched, earnest, and eager. Godly leaders must be speedy in seeking God's wisdom in confronting problems that affect the local body. They must be able to wisely disperse responsibilities to others to bring about spiritual growth and be quick to stop discord or destruction among Christians. They must be earnest about their responsibilities and eager to serve as God's mouth, heart, hands, and feet. They must practice meekness and maintain purity of heart and leadership in all spiritual matters.

Now that we have looked at the gifts of servitude, ask the Lord which gift or gifts He has entrusted to you. Once your gift or gifts are established, ask Him to give you grace to display the attitude of a student, the example of a follower of Jesus, and the ability to properly use these abilities. Keep in mind that these gifts are meant to edify each member of the body, to become living witnesses to those who are perishing and to bring glory to God.

7

GIFTS OF BENEVOLENCE

At the heart of God is benevolence. Due to His great act of benevolence displayed on the cross for each of us, He expects His people to display the same attitude that will produce sacrificial actions.

Benevolence is as much of an attitude as it is an action. The attitude that is expressed most in benevolence is selflessness. This is important because real benevolence is going to sacrificially cost something. If an individual is indifferent or self-serving, he or she will fall short of showing benevolence.

This is obvious when you consider that the greatest act of benevolence in the history of man came from Jesus. He gave up the glories of heaven, became both servant and man to become identified with humanity. He walked among people to personally touch them. He entered in at every point of human suffering to minister to hurting and lost souls. He made the ultimate sacrifice to redeem mankind. He clearly defined benevolence through His acts of kindness. His actions revealed that our good will was at the heart of His attitude and service.

The motivation behind benevolence is love. This love is not an emotional love that shows sympathy. Sympathy is superficial and lasts only as long as the emotion. Such an emotion is self-serving and always causes the sympathizer to feel good about self. It prides itself in its emotional involvement, but lacks both substance and action. It claims the glory without paying the price.

Benevolence is empathy. This means a person will actually enter in with the individual at the point of his or her plight. It is selfless because it is compelled by the sacrificial love of God to take moral responsibility for the welfare of others. It is not conscious of its actions or sacrifices; therefore, its kindness is natural, unconditional, and generous. It is not seeking to receive personal rewards, nor is it after personal glory or recognition because it is devoid of selfish motives and personal agendas. A good example of this benevolence is found in the actions of the Good Samaritan in Luke 10.

True benevolence will test the character of a person. Many people think they are benevolent when, in reality, they fail the test of benevolence when they are required to go the extra mile. They give up before they pay the ultimate price or finish the course. They stop at a few good acts by convincing themselves they did their part. They become agitated if a person's needs supersede their good-will. They become angry when they don't get the desired response from their actions.

Benevolence is not a feeling or an emotion that has been stirred up by some emotional ploy. It is a commitment that is ready to act with sensitivity. It is quick to recognize the plight of others because the heart is tender, open, and available to enter in with people in practical ways. In fact, the earmark of Christianity is benevolence.

It is genuine benevolence that sets the real Church apart and attracts people to the kingdom of God. Sadly, this virtue is missing. Christians in America appear to have lost sight of what constitutes benevolence. They give enough to soothe their religious conscience, while they heap the things of the world upon themselves. Some give to get back, while others give to impersonal organizations to avoid personal involvement with needy people. Yet, God calls His people to become personally identified with others in their plights to ensure blessings and avoid judgment and spiritual poverty.

It is important to point out that blessings are not the same as spiritual treasures and riches. Blessings often have to do with the outer man and point to worldly riches, while spiritual treasures have to do with the inward man and the unseen riches of heaven. The Apostle Paul reveals that Jesus Christ is the real treasure of the Christian. Therefore, a person's riches come down to how much of Christ he or she possesses.[1]

Most people prefer blessings that will personally minister to the outer man, but fail to consider treasure that will not rot, but will ensure godly character, substance, and satisfaction to the inner man. We get a glimpse of this in Hebrews 11 where it talks about people experiencing blessings as they subdued kingdoms, obtained promises, escaped the edge of the sword, and received their dead, but, "others were tortured, not accepting deliverance that they might obtain a better resurrection" (Hebrews 11:35). The latter group was denying physical blessings in order to pursue heavenly treasure.

This is why the Apostle Paul instructed Christians to set their affections on things above.[2] If believers are seeking after heavenly treasures, they will not be part of the "bless me" club of America. Ultimately, they will become more caught up with Jesus than with the world.

Due to the emphasis on worldly blessings, many American Christians appear as if they are preparing to stay here on earth, rather than abide forever with Jesus. Instead of being sojourners, many have put roots down in this world that will prove to be devoid of benevolence.

Godly-inspired benevolence has a touch of heaven and is beyond this world's comprehension. All benevolent deeds are acts as well as gifts of grace that point to the example of Jesus Christ. This is why this virtue will go the extra mile without complaining, give without expecting

---

[1] Philippians 3:10-14; Colossians 2:2-3
[2] Colossians 3:2

anything in return, and go on to the next opportunity of service without remembering the deeds of yesterday.

It is important to realize that, without the touch and reality of heaven, people with these gifts will not be able to fully operate in them. They will fall short along the way. This is why we must remember that these seven gifts are an act of grace from God. Therefore, they must find their real source in God's love and their real inspiration and power in submission to the work of the Holy Spirit.

This brings us to the last three gifts of grace. The number three represents entirety or completeness. In these last gifts, we can see the position and attitude behind true benevolence and how it points to the effective ministry of Jesus Christ as the Servant to servants.

The gift of ministry points to position. According to *Srong's Concordance,* this word means one who attends, aids, offers official service, and brings relief. Another word for minister is "deacon". Therefore, ministry points to a true servant who is ready to attend any need, aid in any project, and offer any point of service where needed and who will ultimately bring much needed relief.

This is why the Bible refers to believers or saints as ministers. Our whole mission in life is to learn to minister in order to inspire reconciliation. But this reconciliation cannot take place unless ministry has a touch from heaven. It must be done in much patience, affliction, necessity, and distress.[3] People must see that godly ministry goes beyond good deeds to embrace gentleness. It speaks of a sacrifice that is supernatural in nature.

As believers, we must learn such ministry at the feet of Jesus. Very few people learn to wait at His feet while the Lord ministers to them. They miss the satisfaction that comes from abiding in Him. After all, Jesus is our Vine and we must not move until He does. This example shows us that Jesus is not after ministry, but after our hearts, attention, and senses.

In Luke 10:38-42, we see Martha serving Jesus, while Mary sat at His feet. From all appearances, Martha was proving her worth, while Mary was selfishly enjoying the presence of Jesus. When Martha became upset over Mary's apparent lack of service, she pointed it out to Jesus. Jesus' words would have seemed strange if you didn't understand the importance of waiting before Him, "Martha, Martha, thou are careful and troubled about many things: But one thing is needful: and Mary hath chosen that good part, which shall not be taken away from her."

As you can see, the boundary for ministry is to wait for the expected time. Waiting prepares people for God's appointed time and purpose. It is a way of renewing the strength so a person can go the extra distance, reviving the vision so he or she can effectively count the cost, and being given the power to finish the course for the glory of God.[4]

---

[3] 2 Corinthians 3:6; 5:18: 6:4
[4] Isaiah 40:31

Since Mary took the time to sit at the feet of Jesus, she, in turn, had been prepared to minister to Jesus at a very important time in His life. We see this incident in John 12:3-7. Mary was the one who anointed Jesus ahead of time for His burial. This ointment was very costly to Mary, but she humbly offered it to Him as she anointed His feet with it and then wiped His feet with her hair. The smell of this ointment not only filled the room, but also reached the throne room of God. Her very act now serves as a memorial to others.[5]

The key to the length of waiting must rest solely with the presence of God and the leading of His Spirit. If His presence is present, a minister must sit in preparation and expectation and wait until the Holy Spirit moves. We see this same scenario with the Israelites. They only moved when the cloud moved and waited when the cloud abided in their midst.[6]

The effectiveness of a minister will be determined by how much he or she learns the lesson of waiting in expectation for the time when God calls him or her forth to do His bidding.

This brings us to the second gift of benevolence. The virtue that is consistent in this second gift is giving. Righteous giving is ready to give out of its needs, share what it has without reservation, and impart without conditions. This shows that giving is generous in nature.

We see this generosity in Israel. A call went out to the children of Israel to willingly bring God an offering to establish the tabernacle, a dwelling place for Him.[7] According to Exodus 36:3-7, the children of Israel brought so many offerings that they had to be constrained to stop. The problem today is that much of the Church must be compelled to give, and it is usually done by emotional manipulation. This type of giving lacks genuine commitment, making it temporary and conditional.

The reason that the people of Israel freely gave was because they realized God had given them everything they possessed. After all, they were slaves in Egypt; therefore, they were glad to adhere to God's call.

The problem with some of the Church is that its vision is not eternal and its hearing has become dulled by fleshly and worldly pursuits. Giving has ceased to be a valuable calling of the whole Body, in spite of the fact that every possession comes from God. For the Body of Christ, the act of giving should be a natural response to show appreciation towards God who has given His Church everything. This type of benevolence shows reliance on God to continue to give according to people's needs and His eternal plan.

We can see this total reliance on God with the widow and her mites. She gave it all to God, showing faith in God to be her provider. Jesus actually pointed her out as giving more than all who gave that day because, "...they did cast in of their abundance, but she of her want did cast in all that she had even all her living" (Mark 12:44)

---

[5] Leviticus 2:2, 9, 16; 2 Corinthians 2:15-16; Matthew 26:12-13
[6] Exodus 13:21-22
[7] Exodus 25:1 & 2

The widow gave all back to God and now serves as our example. This proves that acceptable giving will actually cost the individual in such a way that it ultimately makes the person needy and dependent towards God. Giving of this nature is done in faith, but it is this type of giving that God can honor and multiply. It is in the multiplication that we see the touch of heaven.

We see this multiplication factor in the feeding of the five thousand in John 6. Jesus could have made stones into bread, but, instead, He took a lunch of a young boy and multiplied it. Consider this boy's situation. It happened to be his lunch, yet he gave it up. As a result, Jesus fed thousands with it. This clearly shows us that God wants to be a co-laborer with us in this harvest field, but we first must faithfully offer everything back to Him that He has entrusted to us.

The reason so much eludes the American Church today is because many will not trust God with that which He has entrusted to them. They hoard temporary goods to ensure an uncertain future and heap upon themselves the things of life, only to experience the vanity of the world. Even though they have been entrusted with much, they will give very little to God. As a result, He cannot multiply it in order to impact others in a powerful way.

The boundary for the gift of giving is simplicity. Simplicity points to giving that is not self-serving, but is pure, faithful, and liberal. This shows that acceptable giving must be done with the right motive—to impact others with the intention of bringing glory to God.

The main purpose of giving must be to bring glory to God. This motive will allow His followers to get beyond earthly concerns and be generous about eternal matters that will exalt and honor the Lord.

Giving is at the heart of God's love. As Jesus pointed out with the widow and her mites, it is not what we give that shows our devotion, but what we give out of our own personal need. We see this very attitude in the new Church in Acts 2:44 and 4:32-37.

The new Church was so giving that there were none among them who lacked. Some sold houses and lands to ensure the Body was properly taken care of. Is it any wonder that many were added to the Church by such examples of benevolence?

We can never out give God, but are we willing to give above the required, acceptable, or normal idea of giving? Are we willing to give in such a way that the world could actually see a contrast as God multiplied it for His glory?

Much of the Church lacks the benevolence that comes out of the love of God, but those who have a gift of giving must understand how it works. It will mean nothing unless all is generously offered to God, so He can touch it for His work and glory. Those with this gift must realize that they are to serve as conduits for the Holy Spirit to distribute God's goodness to others through faithful, sacrificial giving. This type of giving is distinct because it will speak of something beyond this world that is powerful and life changing.

The keys to this giving are the love of God, the power of the Spirit, and faithfulness to the blessings, gifts, and means that God has provided, regardless of how small or great.

The final gift in this category is mercy. Lamentations 3:22-23 states, "It is of the LORD'S mercies that we are not consumed because his compassions fail not. They are new every morning: great is thy faithfulness." Mercy points to the act of restraint from judgment that produces compassion. Compassion is the ability to enter in which actually is the truest form of grace in action.

Jesus showed us this mercy when He took on the form of a servant and was fashioned as a man. He was tempted in all areas and tasted the harshness of life, the hatred of man, and the darkness of death. He entered into people's plights such as the woman at the well, the woman caught in idolatry, and Zacchaeus. He touched lives, thereby, changing these people's plight and often their eternal destination. He still impacts the world today as the High Priest. As man, He understands the temptation and struggles that often besets man, but, as God, He knows the heart of God. Because of this combination, He is able to bring both together into reconciliation.[8]

As our High Priest, Jesus' intercession still gives us glimpses into how this mercy still works on our behalf before the throne of God. It is beyond human means because it is unable to turn the other cheek in humiliation or persecution unless self is out of the way and the Spirit of God is serving as a person's strength. It cannot go the extra mile unless compelled to do so by the love of God.

Mercy without the power of the Holy Spirit turns into sympathy and, without the love of God as the motive, it turns into self-pity. Ultimately, sympathy produces self-righteousness that will judge, while self-pity makes a person into an insipid martyr who justifies sin, anger, and resentment.

God's mercy does not consider offenses, for His love covers a multitude of sins, and His compassions never fail. His heart is the same towards all as He seeks out the one lost sheep.[9]

This is the face of mercy. It is truly a gift from heaven because man is devoid of any personal virtue that comes close to this gift. Granted, people often have high opinions about their love and hospitality. But, when tested, these characteristically lack the heavenly touch, perseverance, and sacrifice that are so prevalent in the gift of mercy.

The boundary of this gift is cheerfulness. Cheerfulness, in this text, is a willingness to go the extra distance. It is prompted by undivided devotion, not begrudging about costly sacrifice and is overjoyed when it comes to giving all for the glory of God.

---

[8] 2 Corinthians 5:18-20; 1 Timothy 2:5
[9] Luke 15:1-10; 1 Peter 4:8

The gifts of benevolence are indeed a picture of God's sacrificial love coming forth through grace. His grace serves as an extended helping hand towards those who are lost, weary, alone, and afraid.

Ask the Lord what benevolent gifts He has entrusted to you. Once He reveals what the gift or gifts may be, ask Him to give you the love, heavenly vision, and grace to properly operate in the gift or gifts for His glory.

8

SUPERNATURAL GIFTS

The next categories of gifts that will be discussed create the most controversy. This controversy has not only nullified the part these gifts play in spiritual maturity, but it has undermined the concept of edification.

The Holy Spirit, not the will of man, controls these gifts. This means they are supernatural in nature and are given according to the will of the Spirit.

Many are aware of the debate that argues whether or not these gifts ceased after the initial growth of the new Church. This argument is based on 1 Corinthians 13:8-10. These Scriptures are interpreted as saying that the gifts of the Holy Spirit were done away with because perfection had arrived; therefore, there was no longer any need for them. I could agree with this conclusion except it does not remain consistent with the work and purpose of the Spirit that has been clearly displayed throughout the complete counsel of God.

There are a couple of important points we must look at according to the intent behind the instruction concerning these gifts, and not according to the intellectual evaluation of man that is limited, denominational, and often biased. The Apostle Paul is clear to point out that man only knows in part. If you study the nine gifts of the Spirit, you will see that they actually are designed to bring understanding where man's inability and frailties keep him from seeing beyond the flesh into the spiritual realm. These gifts operate on a temporary basis for they only come as the Spirit wills.[1] In other words, they are not constant or always present like the gifts of grace that are found in Romans 12.

These supernatural gifts work beyond man's limited knowledge and not only open him up to the supernatural, but also reveal the heart and mind of God. Even though Scripture points out that man sees through a glass darkly, he often believes he understands all he needs to grasp in order to arrive at a right conclusion. After all, he has looked at all the angles, logically thought it out in his mind, and found the Scriptures to confirm his conclusions. But, as the Apostle Paul echoed in Scripture, "man knows only in part."[2] Therefore, spiritual gifts that cannot be controlled by man are given not only to show that man can only see in

---

[1] 1 Corinthians 12:11
[2] 1 Corinthians 13:9, 12

part, but also to show that his reliance must be on the Holy Spirit to effectively minister to others in the Church.

The second point we must examine in light of this debate is what constitutes perfection. Apparently, these gifts will be in operation until that which is perfect comes. For these gifts to cease early in the Church age would mean that the appointed perfection came into the midst of the early Church and completed its work. But what work is that? The Church has not reached a state of perfection; therefore, what could be considered perfect?

Some believe that the Word of God represents that perfection, but there is nowhere in Scripture that such a theory is verified. Scripture clearly states that the work of perfection for the Church will continue until the coming of Jesus Christ. We know scripturally that the only person or source that is considered perfect is the Person of Jesus Christ.[3]

Jesus has not come, and it is clear that the Church is operating in a limited fashion in spite of the intellectual or doctrinal resources that might be available to it. Therefore, one must conclude that the gifts are still in operation and available to help edify believers in their imperfection and limitations. In fact, the Church will be in the stage of being brought to perfection or maturity until the Bridegroom comes for her.

Due to the controversy over these supernatural gifts, the Holy Spirit has been quenched or grieved in this area. Since part of the development of the Church involves the correct application of gifts for the benefit or profit of the whole Body, this living organism has greatly suffered.[4]

The Apostle Paul made it clear in his epistles that the leadership positions and gifts were for the main purpose of making the Church into a fine-tuned body that works in harmony.[5] He called for all of the members of this Body to be servants and to have unity according to godly love, a right foundation, and a right spirit.

In order to bring forth this harmony, there is only one Spirit who distributes the diverse gifts among the different members of the Body for its growth. There is also one Lord who oversees the different aspects of ministries within the Church to ensure order; and there is only one God who knows how to work maturity through these various operations into the soul of the Body.[6]

This formidable leadership of the Godhead over the Church is to ensure the Body operates according to Spirit and truth and not the flesh. The positions and gifts have a spiritual nature to them that are capable of bringing believers higher in their relationships with God and empowering the Church with authority to carry out its commission. It also has a

---

[3] Philippians 1:6
[4] 1 Corinthians 12:7
[5] Romans 12:3-8; Ephesians 4:4-16
[6] 1 Corinthians 12:4-6

heavenly vision to walk in confidence and the strength to stand as the salt and light in this dark world.

Sadly, the Church's prideful debate over this subject has demoted the gifts to a fleshly arena. They have been placed in Satan's camp by ignorance, fear, or ungodly exaltation that discredits and often mocks their purpose in the Body.

Once again, we must remind ourselves of the instructions found In Ephesians 4:4-16. We are told that the Church was given the necessary tools for the purpose of edifying or building this Body up into a healthy representation of Jesus Christ. Every position and gift has one purpose and goal in mind. That goal is to bring the whole Body together "in the unity of the faith, and the knowledge of the Son of God, unto a perfect man unto the measure of the stature of the fullness of Christ" (Ephesians 4:13).

After studying the attitude and status of the modern Church, it is apparent that many of its members have lost sight of the spiritual birth, nature, and function of the Body. They have reduced the Church into a worldly organization that is bound by denomination and not the love of God. Much of this Body puts faith in their intellectual understanding and interpretation of Scripture, rather than allowing the Spirit of the Living God, to lead them into all truth.[7]

It is time to get rid of our intellectual interpretation of the Word and come back to square A. The truth is the new struggling Church of the first three centuries after Christ's ascension proved to be powerful because Scripture was not a matter of doctrinal interpretation, but of truths that needed to be upheld in spirit and practical obedience.

As I compare the spiritual condition of the young, New Testament Church to our modern-day Church, especially in places such as America where worldly abundance and self-sufficiency have been in operation, I can see a diverse difference. Much of the visible Church of today, with its entire intellectual prowess, is weak, worldly, and ineffective. As part of this Body, I have come to recognize that all of our pursuit for truths according to higher learning and denominational influences has made us expert debaters of the Word rather than lovers of it. We are not richer for our theological understandings and differences. We are poorer for them. In fact, we are missing the simplicity behind the order and function of the Body of Christ. Unlike the young Church, many in the modern-day Church would not be able to stand. They do not know how to hear the voice of God and adhere to the Holy Spirit's leading. As a result, it appears as if much of the present-day Body has closed down the avenues in which the Holy Spirit operates.

In the Church's attempt to fit all beliefs into personal comfort zones and denominational preferences, it has succumbed to unbelief as its different members pick and choose to interpret certain areas of the Bible away with higher education or denominational creeds. Not only have

---

[7] John 16:13

many in the Church ceased to believe the truths of the Bible, but many have also become religious fools and scoffers of those truths that do not fit into their nice little doctrinal boxes. In such unbelief, people develop hard hearts as their ways of religion ultimately become empty and useless to them in a world designed to exalt man and his knowledge over the so-called "fables" of the Bible.[8]

The Church must come back to center because it has lost its way. It is no better for its endless education or theological debates. It is not more powerful because of its divisions or more respected because of its incessant demand of being right about certain spiritual matters. The Church needs to cease being a parasite that feeds on the pride or ignorance of others to prove a senseless spiritual point. Rather, it needs to regain the heavenly vision of how each member is meant to function for the benefit of the whole Body for the glory of God.

I have often wondered what the Apostle Paul would say about the Church in America. Would he accuse the Church of being bewitched like the Galatians, carnal like the Corinthians, or unrealistic like the Thessalonians? Would he compare much of the Body to the church of Ephesus that had much work, but no love? Maybe he would show the Body that most of it possesses wrong doctrine like Pergamum, is committing spiritual harlotry like Thyatira, is dead like Sardis, or lukewarm like Laodicea.

On the other hand, how would our present-day religious leaders respond to the Apostle Paul if he confronted them? Would he be able to commend some, while rebuking many others?

What is your attitude towards the supernatural gifts? Have you closed down this spiritual avenue because of theology? Are you confused because of the debate over it? Are you open to these gifts even though you don't understand them, or is your understanding of them correct?

I believe this issue has to be resolved because the Church in America is coming into a time of great spiritual darkness and all of our theology, denominational beliefs, and spiritual knowledge will not prepare or enable us to withstand it. Only the Holy Spirit will be able to instruct, warn, and lead us through it. But, how many of us are prepared to hear what the Spirit is truly saying in these days?[9]

---

[8] Hebrews 3:7-19
[9] John 16:13c

9

DIVERSITY OF GIFTS

While studying the supernatural gifts in 1 Corinthians 12 and 14, I recognized the working of the Godhead in the function of both the Body and the gifts. When considering the Body, the Holy Spirit baptizes each member into it. The Body is being molded into the image of the Son and will serve as His extension in this lost world. Based on God the Father's design and plan, each member is set into the Body, with the intent of tempering this living organism together. This work of the Godhead is to ensure edification and unification of the whole Body.[1]

We see the Godhead working within the area of gifts as well. As we will see, the Lord administers these gifts to ensure order in the Body and the Father determines how they will operate in the Body to ensure their integrity. However, it is the Spirit who distributes the gifts. These different gifts actually serve as a manifestation of the Holy Spirit in the Body.[2]

There are nine supernatural gifts. It has been interesting to observe the numbers used in positions and gifts. These numbers show the consistent order and work of God. Remember that there are five positions that point to grace, seven gifts of grace that symbolize perfection, and now we have nine supernatural gifts. The number "nine" points to the work of the Holy Spirit. We see this number in the fruit of the Spirit.[3] Nine also is a number of "finality." The Holy Spirit's work is complete and will bring forth perfection or maturity.

The Holy Spirit is the one who gives these gifts according to His will for the profit of man and the Church.[4] In fact, man has nothing to do with these gifts except to allow the Holy Spirit to use him as a vessel in which to express Himself.

Once again, we are reminded that there are differences of administrations, but the same Lord. Administration points to aid, service, or servant.[5] These gifts are to aid or serve the Body in accordance with the attitude and example of the Son of God, who is not only the head of the Body, but is Lord over it. As Jesus said, "If I then, your Lord and Master, have washed your feet; ye also ought to wash one another's

---

[1] 1 Corinthians 12:12-13, 18, 24, 27
[2] 1 Corinthians 12:4, 7
[3] Galatians 5:22-23
[4] 1 Corinthians 12:7, 11
[5] 1 Corinthians 12:5

feet. For I have given you an example, that ye should do as I have done to you" (John 13:14-15).

1 Corinthians 12:6 told us there are also diversities of operations, but it is the same God who works all in all. This refers to God the Father. (See 1 Corinthians 8:6.) Philippians 1:6 states, "Being confident of this very thing, that he which hath begun a good work in you will perform it until the day of Jesus Christ."

Diversity of operations points to effect, power, and work. God the Father wants to produce a certain effect with these gifts. In order to do this, the power must be available to work this effect or result within the body. This effect will not only be in accordance with His will and eternal plan, but it will bring Him glory.

These three divisions of gifts show that there are three main purposes behind these gifts that will result in edification. They will serve as an expression of the Spirit, honor the leadership of Jesus, and glorify the Father.

The number "three" points to the Godhead and completeness. We can begin to see that the gifts are not only meant to edify, but to unify the Body and make it complete. After all, without the presence and power of the Spirit, the leadership of Jesus, and the work of the Father, there is no completion. The Body would be nothing more than an empty shell.[6]

Another number three can be found in the division of the nine gifts. Harold Horton, in his book entitled *The Gifts of the Spirit,* broke these gifts down into three categories.[7] They are gifts of revelation, gifts of power, and gifts of inspiration.

The gifts of revelation point to those areas of truths, problems, or sins that must be supernaturally uncovered by the Holy Spirit. His purpose for using these gifts is to bring to light hindrances, struggles, or works of darkness in order to instruct, exhort, encourage, or warn. These gifts become the means by which to express not only God's awareness of a person's spiritual condition or plight, but also His infinite insight into all matters. Although, at times, people may convince themselves that He does not know or really care about them, nothing is hidden from our omniscient God. He uses these gifts to bring this reality to the forefront. The gifts that fall into the category of revelation are word of wisdom, word of knowledge, and discerning of spirits.

The gifts of power involve the supernatural intervention of God. In these gifts, God's power is often displayed in a miraculous way. However, these gifts work within two boundaries: man's faith and God's sovereign will. They are often used for confirmation or to bring glory to God. Gifts that fall into this category are faith, healing, and miracles.

The gifts of inspiration are considered the vocal gifts and are used as a means for God to be heard. They are the gifts of prophecy, tongues, and interpretation of tongues. The Holy Spirit must inspire the vessel or

---

[6] See Ezekiel 37:1-10

[7] © 1934

person to speak forth what He gives him or her, but the vessel must willfully submit as the instrument.

Inspirational gifts usually occur during worship when God's people are praising Him. After all, He inhabits the praises of His people.[8] These gifts also have strict guidelines set down in 1 Corinthians 14 to prevent chaos and confusion. Chaos and confusion occur when these gifts are being improperly used or abused for personal vainglory or spiritualism.

By keeping in mind, the different functions of these gifts, one will be more realistic about them, instead of fearful and superstitious. Each of these gifts is God's means of working within the Body and is beyond or outside of man's realm. They are clearly supernatural and are meant to bring the awe of God and awareness of His commitment back into the midst of man.

Sadly, the gifts of inspiration have caused the great controversy that has resulted in many ignoring or abusing these gifts. As a result, these nine supernatural gifts have been brought down into the arena of unbelief and debates, discrediting or closing down this vital avenue of edification.

Consider your attitude towards these gifts. Are you open or closed to them? Are you ignorant about them, or do you show prejudicial opposition when confronted with their use? Make sure your attitudes line up with the Word of God and not denominational preference and indoctrination.

---

[8] Psalm 22:3

10

WORD OF WISDOM

Before we can consider the gift of wisdom, we must have a proper perspective about godly wisdom. James 3:17 states, "But the wisdom that is above is first pure, then peaceable, gentle, and easy to be intreated, full of mercy and good fruits, without partiality and without hypocrisy." All godly wisdom comes from God and manifests itself in godliness. Its goal is to obtain peace with God, be gentle in response, and be quick to listen and learn. It is full of mercy that results in compassion and forgiveness. It is neither biased nor insincere.

Godly wisdom has a touch of heaven that is simple in presentation. This wisdom is developed as a person submits to God and becomes obedient to His ways and Word. It is fine-tuned as righteousness wins over temptation, arrogance gives way to humility, conceit yields to godly instruction, foolishness submits to sobriety, and knowledge is applied in godly ways.[1]

This wisdom is founded on the fear of God; therefore, its warnings are heeded and its instructions obeyed. It has the power to deliver because it teaches discretion and makes one vigilant. It rewards because it enables a person to walk in liberty, to embrace life, and to discover its treasures.

This wisdom can be summarized in two words—Jesus Christ. "But of him are ye in Christ Jesus: who of God is made unto us wisdom..." (1 Corinthians 1:30). Wisdom will be manifested in a person's life through the manifestation of Jesus Christ. His very nature expounds wisdom and expresses itself through His attitude and responses towards others.

God's wisdom is quite different from man's wisdom. James 3:14-16 describes the wisdom of man,

> But if ye have bitter envying and strife in your hearts, glory not, and lie not against the truth. This wisdom descendeth not from above, but is earthly, sensual, devilish. For where envying and strife are, there is confusion and every evil work.

We can see man's wisdom is self-serving and competitive. It will produce jealousy and strife when it finds itself being challenged or not properly recognized. It often walks in confusion because it is hypocritical and unrealistic. This wisdom is not only earthly and sensual, but will display a demonic influence that will complicate, pervert, and defile truth.

---

[1] Proverbs 1

Godly wisdom is often established or developed through obedience. However, the wisdom that is given by the Holy Spirit for the purpose of edification is a gift that is meant to address a particular situation in the life of an individual or in the conduct of the Body. This gift can edify a person to whom it is directed, but it has the capacity of edifying the whole body because it always has a point of godly instruction.

The word of wisdom actually gives insight into the mysteries and mind of God concerning a matter. It not only serves as a point of instruction, but can also be a means of encouraging, exhorting, or warning. Ultimately, it will line up to God's character and evaluation of a situation to ensure a right spirit or intent in a matter.

It is important to understand that godly wisdom will take the lessons, failures, and practices of the past and consider them in light of present attitudes and actions to reveal future consequences. Wisdom that is properly heeded has the capability of changing a person's mind or perception about past and present actions, keeping him or her from future destruction.

The gift of the word of wisdom takes in the above scenario in regards to a person or even a body of believers. For example, Elijah brought a word of wisdom to King Ahab in regards to the murder of Naboth as a means to obtain his vineyard. Elijah uncovered the sins committed towards Naboth, and then he rebuked Ahab for his present attitude. We see a point of instruction when Ahab was informed that his idolatry caused his present situation, which was described by Elijah as selling himself to work wickedness in God's sight. Because of the past sin and the present practice of evil, future judgment was pronounced upon Ahab.[2]

Ahab repented and changed his mind and his practices. Because he adhered to Elijah and humbled himself before God, God put off the judgment until the days of his son. In spite of his wickedness, Ahab responded wisely to Elijah's tough, but wise rebuke and warning. This reminds us that if wisdom is heeded, it has the capacity of producing wise decisions or acts that change future events.

In one incident, the Lord revealed that one of the young women in our Bible Study group was harboring destructive plans. As the Holy Spirit was bringing it to the light, He showed me the struggles of her past that had brought her to the present situation and the future consequences if she did not abort her present plans.

Upon confronting her, I shared with her that the Holy Spirit had revealed the destructive patterns of her past and her present delusion and where it was leading her. In the confrontation, the Lord continued to reveal the core of her struggles so we could properly instruct and minister to her in order to bring her to a correct perspective. Praise God for His faithfulness because she aborted her plans; thereby, ceasing her present practices and avoiding devastating consequences.

---

[2] I Kings 21:17-29

In another situation, I had been working with a man who was trying to save his marriage. I had only heard his side and realized that his wife had her own version. After a few weeks of his prompting, she agreed to meet with both of us. Just before the meeting, the Holy Spirit gave me a word of wisdom concerning what was really going on in their marriage. Within seconds, He showed me the man's cruel mind games, the wife's battle to keep her sanity, and the inevitable end of their marriage if the man did not get a reality check about his cruelty and repent of his attitude and practices.

In our meeting, I explained what had been revealed to me. The wife was surprised at the insight, while her husband sat in a daze. I spent the next couple of hours trying to instruct the man in the ways of righteousness, while ministering to the battered wife. Sadly, the husband never recognized the mind games he was playing, but the wife felt a tremendous relief because she sensed God really understood her difficult plight. Needless to say, their marriage ended in divorce.

In another incident, a young man listened to his father cover up his past practices by justifying his present attitudes and activities with the Word of God. The Holy Spirit unveiled the intent or spirit behind his father, prompting the young man to challenge his father's perspective with the complete counsel of God's Word. Although his father maintained his right to practice wickedness, it silenced him for the rest of the night.

Another point of wisdom is that it always leads back to the character and mind of God. As wisdom is upheld, God's character is unveiled or glorified. In my experiences with the word of wisdom, I have come out with a greater sense of who God is.

God is aware of the history behind something and He knows the future, but He operates in the present. Godly wisdom brings the past and the present together to produce discretion as a means to change future results. Many times, we fail to realize that so much of the future is determined by the present. We see this in the case of King Josiah in 2 Chronicles 34. King Josiah was considered a righteous king, but even in his righteousness he never realized how far away Israel had fallen from Jehovah God until Hilkiah, the priest, found the book of the Law. When the king heard the words of the Law, he tore his clothes in fear, humility, and repentance. He could see that the past actions of Israel demanded the wrath of God. He sent trusted men to Huldah, a prophetess, to inquire of the Lord.

The Lord assured the men, through the prophetess, that He would bring destruction upon Israel. But, because the king's heart was tender and he had humbled himself before Him, it would not happen in his lifetime.

Godly wisdom can change the future by changing the face of the present. God contends with the present in order to prolong or change the future. This is the main purpose behind the word of wisdom in the Body. It is to avoid experiencing the consequences for foolishness in the future.

This virtue of wisdom reminds me of how God introduced Himself to Moses, "I AM THAT I AM" (Exodus 3:14). God is the God of the present who works to bring the lessons of the past and the possibilities of the future together. This has the capacity of changing a person's present reality by enlarging his or her perception of Jehovah God. Every time I encounter and adhere to God's wisdom, I can almost hear His declaration, "I AM THAT I AM," and I know that if I line up to His unchanging reality or truth, He will change the focus of my life and my present reality.

Many Christians have unknowingly operated in the gift of wisdom. God uses the unsuspecting vessels to show His faithfulness to reach out to those with a searching, struggling heart. Ask the Lord if this is a gift that He would like to entrust to you. If He affirms it, give Him permission to use you in the area of His incredible wisdom. This gift will not only edify the Church, but it will also build you up as you grow in the knowledge of the Lord Jesus Christ.

11

WORD OF KNOWLEDGE

Many people confuse the word of wisdom, the word of knowledge, and prophecy with each other. It appears that they are similar; therefore, they are hard to distinguish from one another. However, these gifts are quite different from each other. Although the word of knowledge can appear to spill over into other gifts such as the word of wisdom and prophecy, it still stands distinct from the others.

According to *Strong's Concordance*, "knowledge" means to perceive, resolve, and understand. Perception points to the concept that the light comes in to reveal a matter, bringing understanding that will produce resolution and action.

The Apostle Paul told us that we can only see or perceive through a glass darkly.[1] Because of our flesh, we can only see shadows or outlines of something. This causes points of darkness and confusion that will leave a person struggling with unresolved issues. It can cause anger, sorrow, and despair.

The Holy Spirit uses the word of knowledge to bring understanding of a situation to a person who is struggling in his or her life. This gift can also reveal sin and corruption in the Church for spiritual correction. Therefore, it can be used to encourage, reprove, rebuke, warn of pending judgment, intercede, and challenge a person in the area of salvation.

Unlike the word of wisdom that brings the past and future together in light of present-day decisions, the word of knowledge strictly operates in the present. The purpose for the word of knowledge is not to reveal the intent of something, but to identify with the person in his or her present plight, for the purpose of ministering, edifying, or contending for the faith.

Personal identification usually points to the edification of one person, but, in the area of the word of knowledge, it can be given to the entire body. It is God's way of saying to a believer or a body of believers, "You are (presently here)..." and bringing a situation to light in order to produce some type of ministry. Knowledge that is put into practice becomes wisdom.

We see the great prophet, Elisha, operating with this gift. In 2 Kings 5:20-27, Elisha's servant gave way to personal greed and pursued after Naaman to benefit from his offer to bestow Elisha with many gifts after

---

[1] 1 Corinthians 13:12

his miraculous healing in the Jordan River. The prophet had turned his offer down, but his servant saw an opportunity to capitalize on God's miracle. Although he thought he was being wise and discreet, God showed Elisha what he had done. When the servant stood before his master, Elisha asked him where he came from. I believe the prophet was giving his servant a chance to come clean, but, instead, he lied to his master. This probably sealed his doom as Elisha exposed his sinful actions and pronounced judgment upon him.

In 2 Kings 6:9-12, Elisha warned the king of Israel a couple of times about the destructive plans of the enemy. This supernatural protection that was in operation on behalf of Israel gained the attention of the king of the opposing side as he felt the betrayal came from within his own camp. Upon confronting his men, they assured him the information came from Elisha, the prophet, to the king of Israel who had also shown great wisdom by adhering to his warnings.

People have a tendency to wear masks to cover up various aspects of their personal lives. They silently struggle with issues that are swallowing them up in hopelessness. The Holy Spirit simply unmasks the person in order to bring correction, prevent consequences, or offer encouragement to stir up faith to receive His comfort and hope.

My friend, who has operated in the word of knowledge for years, sees pictures of where a person is spiritually. She has seen into the soul of a person in the areas of struggles, discouragement, and sin. On one occasion, the Lord revealed to her that a person was making plans that were destructive. She confronted her and the woman confessed to it, along with the battle that had been raging in her soul.

In another situation, the Lord showed my friend that a person was experiencing a deep loneliness that served as a deep ache in her soul. She shared the insight and encouraged the woman in the Lord.

Another lady had gone through terrible situations in her life. My friend, who was not even aware of this person's plight, came into the room and told her the Lord was going to cause her wounds to become badges of valor.

There was another individual who was having a problem with her aging father as he was becoming more difficult to handle. The Lord showed my friend that he had a tremendous amount of fear.

Another friend who operates in the gift of knowledge actually feels what the person is feeling, especially in the area of physical ailments. It is not unusual for her to feel some kind of pain or physical hindrance just before a meeting. She has to discern if the pain belongs to her or if it must be called out in the meeting. If she discerns that it must be called out, she knows God intends to heal the person. This personal identification in the word of knowledge is meant to actually stir up the faith of the recipient, as he or she must come forward in faith to receive the healing.

This brings us to another important aspect of the word of knowledge—what to do with it. A person must ask God what he or she is supposed to do with the knowledge He has entrusted to him or her. For my friend in the previous paragraphs, she knew that, once the ailment was properly discerned, she had the responsibility to call it out. However, in some cases, God may not want the information to be revealed as much as He wants the person to intercede in prayer.

In one situation, a saint was awakened in the middle of the night. She had a burden for a missionary friend. She was aware that the person was in some kind of grave danger. She interceded for her until the burden lifted. Later, she discovered that her friend was in a life-or-death situation due to political unrest in the country.

Unlike wisdom, certain knowledge should be kept hidden until the Holy Spirit gives permission to speak it. Some knowledge may be kept hidden from certain people while it is revealed to others around them in order to bring proper guidance. This is why people with this gift need to seek God's wisdom in how to properly exercise it and ensure the integrity of it.

In one situation, a woman was in a marital crisis. The Lord not only revealed what her husband was doing, but also lined out every step she was to take in order to counteract his destructive actions. As a result, to her husband's utter amazement, the woman kept one step ahead of her husband's evil plans and actions.

As you can see, this type of knowledge is beyond human comprehension. It is supernatural and reveals how our all-knowing God uses it for the edification of the Church and for His glorification.

Have you benefited from this gift in the past? Perhaps He has or is entrusting it to you for the purpose of edification?

12

DISCERNING OF SPIRITS

Discerning of spirits is a gift that is shrouded in misunderstanding and confusion. For example, people who have this gift are usually accused of being judgmental or suspicious. People who are judgmental and suspicious often think that they are discerning. This confusion has caused those with the gift of discerning of spirits to close down their gift while allowing those with a critical spirit to freely reign under the guise of wisdom and discernment.

Therefore, it is important to understand the difference between judgmentalism and discernment. Discernment is the ability to detect a spiritual reality with senses other than vision. It is the ability to grasp or comprehend something that is obscure. According to my secular dictionary, man's judgment is nothing but an opinion that is held as an ultimate authority to a matter.[1]

The *Strong's Concordance* presents judgment as a determination, decision, or a decree for or against something. If the decision goes against something, it becomes the law that will accuse, condemn, or judge.[2]

As you compare discernment with man's judgment, you will see that they are on opposite poles. For example, discernment involves testing the spirits, while man's judgment is based on what he hears and sees. Discernment evaluates the fruits of something, while judgment comes down to personal likes and dislikes. Discernment makes a righteous judgment in accordance with Jesus' words, "Judge not according to the appearance, but judge righteous judgment," while judgment comes down to how something makes a person feel.[3] Discernment deals with the unseen world, while judgment evaluates according to earthly, fleshly things. Discernment discerns what is real, while judgment determines its own reality. Discernment is done for the sole purpose of the protection of souls, while judgment is to exalt and protect self. Discernment is spiritual in nature, while judgmentalism is personal in nature. Discernment sees into the unseen world, while judgmentalism has a critical eye that looks

---

[1] Webster's New Collegiate Dictionary, © 1976 by G. & C. Merriam Co.
[2] #2919 and 2020
[3] John 7:24

for and focuses on any discrepancy to justify personal ungodly attitudes, accusations, and criticism.

The Holy Spirit is behind discernment, while the natural man is behind judgmentalism. The intention of judging is to find and condemn what are considered unacceptable attitudes and actions. In most cases, it is the means to judge those considered inferior or too human for self-righteous people to accept. Discernment, on the other hand, is for the purpose of separating and distinguishing the spiritual from the natural.

Consider the following diagram and determine if you are truly discerning or whether you have a critical spirit.

DISCERNMENT	JUDGMENT
Test the Spirit.	Consider things according to what one hears and sees.
Evaluate the Fruits	Evaluates according to personal likes and dislikes.
Makes a righteous judgment.	Comes down to how something makes a person feel.
Deals with the unseen world.	Deals in the earthly, freshly realm.
Shows you what is real.	Determines what is reality according to its own personal preferences.
Protect souls and desires to properly minister to others	Protects self and has a critical eye.
Spiritual in nature.	Is carnal, fleshly, and personal in nature.
Holy Spirit is behind discernment and distinguishes spirit from natural.	The flesh is behind judgmentalism and will find fault and error.

It is important to point out that man's judgment consists of this combination:

Pride + vision and hearing = cement opinions

Man often judges according to religious or self-righteous opinions that are considered doctrine. These opinions are nothing more than personal theology, but they determine how a person will look at people and handle the pure doctrine of Jesus.

The combination for spirit is as follows:

Attitude +doctrine + fruits = spirit

Our attitude towards God and the doctrine we adhere to will influence the type of fruit our lives produce. The fruit reveals our disposition and will determine how we respond to that which opposes us. Judgmental pride sets up the attitude or prevailing mood, while spirit determines the environment or state of a matter. For example, if our attitude is that of arrogance, we will most likely hold to doctrine tightly and exalt it as the final authority. We will also have a critical, narrow-minded, and unteachable disposition.

Hebrews 5:13-14 gives us this insight about discernment, "...for everyone that useth milk is unskillful in the word of righteousness; for he is a babe. But strong meat belongeth to them that are of full age, even those who by reason of use have their senses exercised to discern both good and evil." Hebrews shows us that discernment is found among those who are matured in their relationships with God and in their skills with the Word of God.

Discerning good and evil is a process that entails a person testing the spirit as he or she considers the disposition and fruits in light of the Word of God. However, the gift of discerning of spirits is opposite. In other words, when a person has this gift, he or she immediately knows something is wrong in an environment when he or she walks into a room or meeting. This revelation will set many signals off in the person who will immediately be put on guard. This will lead them to discern what is amiss in the environment.

Such discernment is not based on the person's personal perception, but an awareness of the spirit or environment behind leaders, churches, movements, and teachings.

Environment also represents foundation and practices. Wrong environments are dangerous, and not only will they harbor a wrong spirit, but they will establish a person on shifting sands of delusion and destruction.

Jesus uncovered the spirit behind Peter when he rebuked Him about going to the cross. "Get thee behind me, Satan. Thou art an offense unto me; for thou savorest not the things that are of God, but those that are of men" (Matthew 16:23).

We see the Apostle Peter revealing the motive behind the deceitful practices of Ananias and Sapphira in Acts 5:3-4,

> But Peter said, Ananias, why hath Satan filled thine heart to lie to the Holy Ghost and to keep back part of the price of the land? While it remained, was it not thine own? And after it was sold, was it not in thine own power? Why hast thou conceived this thing in thine heart? Thou hast not lied unto men, but unto God.

The gift of discerning spirits helps in deliverance by revealing the works of demonic spirits in a person. It helps discover and expose Satan's ministers as well as checks the plans of Satan. It exposes error and discerns miracles inspired by demons.

I have witnessed the value of this gift. I remember a woman with a bad spirit came into one of our meetings. My co-laborer warned me that she was there to gain attention and to find an inroad into the ministry. She actually saw herself as superior and was looking for a ministry to be exalted as a leader. As a result, I was able to avoid her traps and stopped her in her plans.

In another situation, we attended a church that had a wrong environment. The Holy Spirit immediately identified it as idolatry. As my friend observed the pastor, she recognized how the leader was trying to manipulate people out of their money for a fancy vacation.

We have walked out of meetings where both the spirit and teaching were wrong. In such cases, our spirits were grieved and we felt repulsed at the abuse of the Word. Likewise, sorrow filled us as we watched the sheep willingly embrace error on their way to the slaughter.

In one case, we ministered in a church in which both the spirit and environment were erroneous. After the meeting, my co-laborer, Jeannette, got deathly ill. It took some intense prayer for the wrong spirit and heaviness to lift from her, leaving her weak but able to recover from her ordeal.

Sadly, people with this gift are often abused by the people they are to protect. Many do not want their beliefs, leaders, and churches to be challenged. They would rather live in their delusion than face the fact that they have been duped because of the ignorance and pride in their own lives. The unreceptive attitudes of others cause those with the gift of discerning of spirits to either flee the situation or be driven to prayer until God gives them direction.

If you have this gift, take heart and make sure you are not closing it down. Give God permission to show you what is going on in the spiritual realm for your protection as well as those you care about. Be available to not only warn others, but also to pray for their deliverance from the tentacles of Satan.

13

GIFT OF FAITH

The gift of faith belongs to the gifts of power. Jesus said that genuine faith has the ability to move mountains.[1] The real power in godly faith does not lie in the concept of faith, but in its ability to trust in the character of God, thereby, letting Him be God in matters. It is God who holds the power, while faith serves as a means or conduit by which God can show Himself mightily in and through a person.

According to *Vine's Expository Dictionary of Biblical Words,* faith is a firm persuasion or conviction based on what a person hears. This is why faith comes by hearing and hearing by the Word of God, not by some method or practice.[2] It is active and will produce action, whether it is obedience, upright conduct, or a miraculous intervention from God. It is a firm confidence and child-like trust that will believe what God says because of who He is.

God gives all genuine faith; therefore, it comes from the outside of man and not from within. In other words, it cannot be conjured up by any personal attempts, faked, or spoken into being, no matter how sincere or fervent a person may be. It is not an idea, but an active walk that makes it an experience rather than an intellectual concept.

Romans 12:3 states that God is the One who gives us a measure of faith. Granted, a person chooses to believe a matter is true. In other words, he or she chooses to believe the Word of God is true. Such a choice is a matter of faith, but it finds its origins in the character of God or in His Word. Therefore, this measure of faith prepares and enables a person to take a step of obedience. Each step of obedience enlarges the person to be entrusted with greater measures of faith, allowing him or her to take larger steps of obedience before God. This is why the Christian life is considered a walk of faith, because what is not done by faith in the Christian life is considered sin.[3]

Hebrews 11:6 says that it is impossible to please God without this active faith. Real faith results in action because faith without action is dead and useless in the Christian life.[4] It is responsive to the Word of God. It simply chooses to believe everything God says as absolute truth.

---

[1] Matthew 17:20
[2] Romans 10:17
[3] Romans 14:23; 2 Corinthians 5:7
[4] See James 2

It diligently seeks to know God and His will and way in order to respond properly in matters.

The faith walk is not a blind walk because it is based on the reality and character of a living, unchangeable God. It is a walk that is meek in its response, sober in its responsibilities, and confident in its actions. Ultimately, it allows God to fulfill His plan in and through a person's life.

The real measure of the faith a person possesses is determined by how much a person allows God to be God in challenging situations. The more confidence a person has in the character of God in the midst of testing, trials, and losses, the greater the potential for God to show Himself in a powerful way, bringing glory to Him. In fact, it is in the challenging times of life that faith is both tested and refined.[5]

Faith allows God to show His faithfulness to, in, and through a person. God's faithfulness greatly edifies the individual, while it has the potential to inspire and edify those who witness it in the lives of others. It is God's faithfulness that makes a person's testimony grow. This has been obvious in my own life.

After a four-year absence from people that I had worked and ministered with in the harvest field in the state of Washington, I was able to share with them the incredible faithfulness of God that I had experienced in those years. It was as if I had lived some of Hebrews 11 and could declare how God met me at every bend, turn, challenge, and crisis in my life. As I recounted God's numerous acts of intervention, the recipients were being strengthened in their own faith.

I shared with them the message of Psalm 89:1, "I will sing of the mercies of the LORD for ever: with my mouth will I make known thy faithfulness to all generations." I realize that this has been my consistent declaration about God for all the years I have known Him. Granted, I have failed to recognize it in the past and can easily take it for granted in the present, but I know His faithfulness has kept me in spite of my periods of faithlessness before Him.[6]

People have a tendency to get caught up in the idea of God's power, but powerful testimonies are based on the character and integrity that He shows through His faithfulness. Every intervention, no matter how great or how small, is because of God's incredible faithfulness to deliver, reconcile, and restore His people.

Sadly, many people try to brainwash themselves about having faith, or they try to conjure it up in order to get God to move. Real faith is not a means by which to get God to move, but an avenue that encourages and allows God to move according to His will and purpose in and through His people.

Pseudo faiths are always based on man's design and not God's will. People often see faith as a magic wand or a means of controlling and

---

[5] 1 Peter 1:6-7
[6] See 2 Timothy 2:11-13

manipulating God in a matter. Needless to say, these faiths undermine the faith that was first delivered to the saints.[7]

These pseudo faiths have perverted the gift of faith, opening a dangerous door to the occult. It has caused people to spiritualize faith by making it into a method or formula in wicked attempts to control God and obtain worldly blessings and success.

This demonically inspired faith is not only worldly, but also impulsive and morbid. People who are under the influence of this heretical faith make impulsive decisions that are based on emotional fervor to do something noble and spiritual for God. God is put to a foolish test every time the flesh is involved in the concept or operation of faith, setting the person up as a fool. Once the person is deemed a fool, the individual will resort to becoming a silent, suffering martyr for God. This whole scenario is not only unfair to God, but it becomes morbid as this person believes he or she is suffering for the sake of Christ when, in reality, he or she is reaping the consequence of his or her religious foolishness.[8]

People need to test their responses. They need to discern if the flesh is driving them or if the Holy Spirit is leading them. This can easily be accomplished by testing everything with the Word of God.

There was an incident where a woman felt God was calling her into ministry. She immediately quit her job, bought clothes, and began to sit around waiting for the call. It never came and she fell into unbelief. If she had only studied the lives of Jesus and Paul, she would have recognized that there was a time of preparation before the fulfillment of her call could materialize. Such preparation does not call for drastic change in lifestyle, but learning to be faithful with what is already in front of you until the proper doors open.

In another situation, a man felt God was calling him to a higher life in God. He quit his job and started becoming very spiritual, but all he managed to do was put a burden on his family that brought them close to bankruptcy. In the process, the man lost respect and became a mockery and reproach to the Gospel.

People who are being driven will be impulsive in their decisions and pursuits. These sincere, but fleshly individuals will not only get ahead of God, but will become lost in their endeavors.

People who are being led by the Holy Spirit will be prepared to walk a matter out according to God's timing. They will learn discipline as they wait for the proper doors to open. They will be tested in their faithfulness to God as they deal with the drudgeries of life. Ultimately, they will be ready to walk this life out under the leading of the Holy Ghost.

With this in mind, we can consider the gift of faith. It is not impulsive, but tempered by the understanding that God is about to do something extraordinary that is contrary to man's way of thinking and doing. For example, a friend had the assurance from God that He was going to

---

[7] Jude 3
[8] Galatians 6:7-8; 1 Peter 4:15-17

move her family to our area where she would be actively involved with this ministry. This was not an emotional sentiment or an impulsive feeling based on desire, but an abiding truth that was already a reality to her. Needless to say, many did not share in her confidence. In fact, she was often criticized and mocked, but this conviction remained strong and steady.

She began to prepare for the move as projects were finished around the house. She even looked for housing in the area. I will never forget that the first house she looked at she immediately knew it was the house God had in mind for her and her family.

To make a long story short, almost two years after she had received the initial revelation from God, she and her family moved into the house the Lord had revealed was hers. There were various steps of faith that were taken by her and her family in those two years. The gift of faith that God gave her not only enabled her to endure skepticism and sustained her through uncertain times, but she continued to take what seemed like ridiculous steps, allowing God to fulfill His purpose in her life.

The gift of faith is actually opposite from the measure of faith. When God gives us the measure of faith, it is to enable us to take steps of obedience to enlarge us to receive what He has for us. On the other hand, the gift of faith immediately enlarges the individual so the person can be receptive to God's plan or promise, as he or she begins to respond accordingly in expectation of a future event.

It is important to point out that people must be prepared to even receive from God. One of the problems people have is recognizing what God has for them. This failure to recognize God's provision is due largely to the fact that people think in grandiose terms while God sovereignly operates in practical ways.[9] As people are looking for the miraculous to happen, God is quietly operating from a different angle. As a result, people miss what God is doing and become disillusioned in their spiritual lives.

The gift of faith enlarges a person enough so that he or she can immediately act upon it and eventually receive from God. It is in such cases as these that this gift has been known to result in healings and miracles.

For example, a person with the gift of healing may feel led to pray for a person's healing. As he or she steps out in obedience to the Holy Ghost's leading, God immediately gives the intended recipient the gift of faith in order to receive the healing.

This is why God's sovereign will and man's faith are the two boundaries that all gifts of power work within. It must be God's will to ensure something takes place and man's ability to respond according to obedience or in preparation to receive God's blessings or promises by faith.

---

[9] Jeremiah 45:5

The gift of faith makes a person wide open for God to do the impossible. The Holy Spirit has given both Jeannette and me this gift at different times to accomplish some amazing feats through us. In one incident, we had the opportunity to go to Georgia for a free promotional package for our book and her art. Immediately, we both knew that God wanted us to go, but we didn't have the money for the airline tickets. The unwavering knowing in our spirits about the matter was nothing more than the gift of faith. In response to the gift of faith, we began to inquire about the cost of airline tickets. Although the money was not there, we were not deterred from knocking on doors until the right one miraculously opened.

One day, Jeannette was led to call a most unlikely individual and ask him and his wife to pray about the Georgia trip. The next morning, when we entered our office, we were greeted with a phone call from this man. He informed us that the airlines had informed him that very morning that he had accumulated enough mileage plus in all of his traveling, that he was donating half of them to us so we could fly to Georgia.

Faith allows God to show Himself in powerful and unsuspected ways. It is not amazing that God does the miraculous, but He always does things in a surprising manner. Therefore, you never know how and when He will do something. However, you can be sure of one thing. If God truly said it, it is already a reality.

This is why, in our faith walk, we occasionally remind Him, "God, you said..." We know without a doubt He will do what He has declared.

It is important to keep faith in perspective. There are many pseudo faiths being presented that will prevent the growth of real faith or sabotage the gift of faith within the Body.

If you have been given the gift of faith, respond according to God's leading. Avoid getting ahead of Him and knock on all doors, trusting that He will open the right one at the right time. Even though you will be assured of seeing God move in some incredible ways, know that the most sustaining reality is that He is faithful!

14

HEALING AND MIRACLES

When people think of healing and miracles, they are reminded of power that is operating in the supernatural that will produce the miraculous. Sadly, many people chase after this power by pursuing after the gifts of healing and miracles.

There are some major reasons why people pursue the supernatural, and one of the reasons is sensationalism. Power of the supernatural not only serves as a means to attract people to the unexplainable, but it also entertains them as well.

Jesus encountered this same attitude in His lifetime. Sensationalism was prevalent in the Roman Empire. They went to great lengths to entertain the people. Not only did they lull them spiritually asleep and cause their fleshly appetites to become insatiable, but they also caused them to operate in an unrealistic world.

When Jesus encountered Herod on the last trek of His journey to Calvary, Herod was interested in what He could do, and not in His identity, guilt, or innocence. Luke 23:8 reveals this attitude, "And when Herod saw Jesus he was exceedingly glad; for he was desirous to see him for a long time, because he had heard many things of him; and he hoped to have seen some miracle done by him." When Jesus did not perform a miracle for Herod, he and his men treated Him with contempt, mocked Him, and arrayed Him with a beautiful robe.[1]

Self-serving pursuits into the supernatural often set people up as they put God to a foolish test and bring a reproach on Him. When people are in the flesh, they can be foolish and make impulsive, fleshly declarations about Him that are not according to His will. Such people who operate in this manner will often become a Herod in attitude as their pursuit turns into contempt and mockery towards the One who refuses to perform according to their whims.

It is easy to put God to a foolish test, thinking that surely, He will not allow believers to look foolish and bring doubt upon His character. The truth is that God will not keep people from looking foolish to protect His reputation. He will allow the foolish to pay the price of their arrogance to teach them valuable lessons.

The overemphasis of the supernatural is due, in part, because God's people make the mistake of putting faith in what He can do instead of

---

[1] Luke 23:11

who He is. In fact, people transpose their own ideas of what they would do if they were all-powerful onto God. They forget God's power is just one aspect of His character. He is so much more, and all of His attributes contribute to His intervention in people's lives. Therefore, His intervention is not based on His ability to do great things, but on His great character to work the impossible in a situation that will cause spiritual growth for His followers and bring Him glory.

Due to the American mindset, the combination of power, attraction, and entertainment plays quite nicely into these types of religious pursuits. The difference is that God is tacked on, giving such pursuits a noble, religious quality, while covering up a fleshly, demonic hype that often proves to serve as a wicked covering in which these people hide their sin.

Another reason that the gifts of healing and miracles are sought after is because they supposedly confirm the person's spiritual authority and claims. Mark 16:17-18 states,

> And these signs shall follow them that believe; In my name shall they cast out devils; they shall speak with new tongues; They shall take up serpents; and if they drink any deadly thing, it shall not hurt them; they shall lay hands on the sick, and they shall recover.

The Scriptures in Mark are in relation to the preaching of the Gospel. They state that certain signs will follow those who believe. In other words, these signs will be a natural result of those who believe the Gospel and, in turn, preach it to others. These signs are meant to confirm the message, not the vessel.[2]

This brings us back to the real test of signs and wonders. Is the person preaching the true Gospel, and what spirit is in operation? The Holy Spirit will always lift up Jesus, while another spirit will direct people away from the only way to heaven, causing him or her to put his or her reliance elsewhere.

There is no place in Scripture where signs and wonders serve as proof of someone's validity other than Christ. In fact, people who stress the supernatural over Jesus Christ and the Christian's commission to preach the Gospel and make followers of Christ reveal they are of another spirit.

Jesus made this statement about those who seek after signs and wonders in Matthew 16:4, "A wicked and adulterous generation seeketh after a sign; and there shall no sign be given unto it, but the sign of the prophet, Jonah." Jesus clearly revealed that only those who are wicked and adulterous (spiritual harlotry) seek after signs, rather than the reality of God.

It is important to test the spirit behind signs and wonders. In the end days, there will be many signs and wonders, but they will be counterfeits

---

[2] See Mark 16:20

along with the ones who perform them.[3] Matthew 24:24 gives us this warning, "For there shall arise false Christs, and false prophets, and shall show great signs and wonders, insomuch that, if it were possible, they shall deceive the very elect." Christians should never seek after signs and wonders. Rather, they need to seek God and know that He is the source of all truth and spiritual life.

Let us now consider the gift of healing.

Gift of Healing

The gift of healing is totally an intervention on God's part that is marked by His sovereignty. On the other hand, man's part in the gift of healing involves the measure of faith and not the gift of faith. The gift of healing will be an act of obedience on the part of the person to pray for healing.

This is why the gift of healing is a separate gift from the gift of faith. Many people believe that the person who is praying for the healing of someone is operating in a gift of faith when, in reality, it is nothing more than a step of obedience. At times God has been known to give the gift of faith to the recipient to receive the healing, but the gifts of faith and healing work independently from each other.

This is why people who feel they have the gift of healing must discern if they are being pushed, driven by impulsive feelings, or are clearly being led by the Holy Spirit to pray for a person's healing. It is easy to discern if a person is being pushed or driven by overwhelming emotions, zeal, or sentiment because he or she will have a sense of infallibility. This person will actually perceive that this sentiment is the gift of faith and will see it as a means to accomplish anything as long as that feeling remains.

Now, notice where the focus is. It is not on God's purpose or greatness, but on the person who possesses the infallible feeling. This person does not realize that God is clearly missing, and that he or she is operating according to emotional zeal or fervor that is setting him or her up for disaster. This fervor is fleshly and operates on an earthly plane of sentiment and it will ultimately put God to a foolish test.

The Apostle Paul Warned us of such zeal in Romans 10:2, "For I bear them record that they have a zeal for God, but not according to knowledge." Obviously, people who operate on this level do not understand the character, way, and will of God.

Christians who understand and properly operate in any of the gifts of power will know that it has nothing to do with them. They are just the vessels through which God's power will flow. They do not have a sense of infallibility when operating in the gift, but an awareness of how great, powerful, and faithful God is. In fact, they will often feel small, insignificant, and powerless, causing them to fling themselves on God to allow Him do His bidding through them.

---

[3] 2 Thessalonians 2:9-10

Believers who properly operate in the gift of healing have admitted feeling reluctant, sober, or afraid to pray for a person's healing because they felt no power within themselves to do anything. The reason for this is because the Holy Spirit is leading them, and they are simply being obedient to be used as a conduit or instrument of the Holy Ghost.

In one incident, my friend was asked to pray for an individual whom she was not fond of. This person had liver cancer and definitely needed God to step on the scene. My friend reluctantly obeyed and prayed for her. The lady was healed and God received the glory.

I often instruct people who feel led to pray for someone's healing to use discretion when approaching the individual. It is unwise to tell the person anything other than that God has impressed them to pray for him or her. The reason for this discretion is that one is never sure what God wants to accomplish until the Holy Spirit reveals it. The healing might not be obvious, or it may be something other than what can be perceived with the eyes. The healing may be spiritual rather than physical, and it may encompass various things.

There are three types of healings found in the Word. The greatest of these healings is spiritual healing.

Jesus came to bring spiritual healing. Although He healed many physical ailments, His greatest desire was to make people spiritually whole. It is important to point out that He healed many physical ailments, but it was only the people's response of faith in Him that made them whole.

For example, the woman with the issue of blood displayed the gift of faith as she pressed through to touch the hem of Jesus' garment. Jesus had the power to heal her physically, but, because of her faith, He made this statement to her, "Daughter be of good comfort; thy faith hath made thee whole" (Matthew 9:20-22). As you can see, her physical healing was not the same as her being made spiritually whole.

This woman's healing went beyond the physical into the spiritual realm. Physical healing may change the physical quality of a person's life, but it does not make him or her spiritually whole. People can be healed physically, but be spiritually lost. The key to spiritual healing is that faith not only reaches out to Jesus, but it touches Him in such a way that it connects to the very heart and goal of God—reconciliation and restoration.

Luke 4:18 talks about spiritual healing,
> The Spirit of the Lord is upon me, because he hath anointed me to preach the gospel to the poor, he hath sent me to heal the broken-hearted, to preach deliverance to the captives, and recovering of sight to the blind, to set at liberty them that are bruised.

Jesus presented five different spiritual conditions in this verse that not only needed to be addressed, but healed. These spiritual conditions are the result of the fallen disposition of man and sin that can only be dealt with on a spiritual level. Poverty of any type causes oppression and mental anguish, while a broken heart is hard to bear. Oppression can break a person's spirit, while spiritual blindness can cause hopelessness. Spiritual bruising or contusions can cause unexpected pain caused by memories, soreness of the emotions, and other problems.

Jesus was anointed to address these conditions and managed to deal with the source of them on the cross. This was brought out in Isaiah 53:4-5. Isaiah 53:4 reveals how Jesus bore the fruits of spiritual poverty, broken hearts, captivity, blindness, and bruising by taking on our griefs and carrying our sorrows. Isaiah 53:5 refers to the source of these griefs and sorrows—transgression and iniquities. These spiritual ailments caused enmity with God that caused separation. Jesus not only addressed these ailments, but He brought healing and peace on the cross. Isaiah 53:5 summarizes it in this manner, "...and with his stripes we are healed."

One of the problems surrounding healing is that most Christians think in terms of physical healing and not spiritual. Isaiah 6:10 shows the need for spiritual healing, "Make the heart of this people fat, and make their ears heavy, and shut their eyes; lest they see with their eyes, and hear with their ears, and understand with their heart, and convert, and be healed." Many people believe that God does not want them physically sick when, in reality, God's heart is to see them spiritually healed or saved. Physical sickness lasts only for a season compared to a spiritual healing that will last an eternity.

This brings us to physical healings. There is an erroneous belief that physical ailments are a result of sin and a lack of faith. Granted, sin such as unforgiveness can cause physical problems, but not all ailments are a result of sin or unbelief.

Jesus made this quite clear in John 9:2-6 when his disciples asked Him who sinned to make the man blind, the man or his parents. Jesus answered, "Neither hath this man sinned, nor his parents: but that the works of God should be made manifest in him."

This Scripture verse clearly shows that not all physical ailments are associated with man's fallen condition; rather, it could be marked with God's eternal purpose. God actually uses physical challenges to manifest His work in and through people. This could mean a lot of different things. For instance, God can use physical challenges to do a deep work in a person's soul like He did with Job. Job came out knowing God in greater ways.[4]

I have seen this in various cases such as that of Joni Erickson Tada. God could have healed her, but, instead, He showed her that He manifests His glory through her physical weakness in a greater measure, enabling her to minister to others.

It is important to point out that Jesus did not heal everyone. At the pool of Bethesda, many sick people were waiting for the miraculous to

---

[4] Job 42:1-6

happen. Jesus only healed one man out of many.[5] This, once again, reminds us that God does not heal people for the sake of healing, but that He operates according to an eternal plan and purpose.

Sometime physical ailments are caused by spiritual oppression, as in the case of the daughter of Abraham in Luke 13:10-16. This is why a person who operates in this gift must not assume anything until the Holy Spirit reveals the type of healing and the source behind the affliction. It might require spiritual deliverance.

The third type of healing is physical death. If a person is a saint, physical death is the ultimate healing. 2 Corinthians 5:8 states, "We are confident, I say, and willing rather to be absent from the body, and to be present with the Lord."

Psalm 116:15 gives us God's perspective on the death of a saint, "Precious in the sight of the LORD is the death of his saints!" People enter the door of physical death through accidents, catastrophes, and physical illness. It is God's way of ushering the saint into His everlasting presence.

Christians need to remember that we are simply passing through this world and our destination is of an eternal nature.[6] This world is simply a place of testing, training, and preparation for that which will be everlasting.

Each person is preparing for heaven or hell according to the path they are traveling.[7] This is why saints must hold lightly to the things of earth and trust God with all obstacles, including physical ailments. They need to realize that each challenge prepares each of them for that blessed time when they will enter through the door of physical death and embrace the Lord in everlasting joy and adoration.

Has the Holy Spirit used you in this gift? Be wise and discerning as to His leading. Never allow yourself to be pushed or driven by emotional fervor, putting God to a foolish test and bringing a reproach on your character and testimony.

Gift of Miracles

Some Christians express surprise that gifts of healing and miracles are separate. It is true that healing is a miracle, but miracles encompass the rest of God's supernatural intervention on behalf of man.

One of the challenges that occurs in the area of miracles is that many Christians have an improper perception about them. Therefore, it is important to establish what constitutes a miracle. We know it is supernatural in nature. In other words, it works outside of what is natural. It supersedes physical laws, the elements of nature, and man's abilities.

---

[5] John 5:1-16
[6] 1 Peter 2:11
[7] Matthew 7:13-14

The perception that many have of miracles comes down to such acts as the parting of the Red Sea, the calming of the storms, causing the sun to stand still, and the feeding of the 5,000. These miracles definitely stand out, but what many fail to realize is that these miracles were in *proportion to the need or situation.*[8]

For example, it was more practical to part the Red Sea for thousands to cross over than to enable each of them to walk on water as Jesus did with Peter. Since there were 5,000 people to feed, God simply fed them by multiplying some fish and bread, rather than pouring manna out of heaven as He did for the children of Israel. Therefore, providing the needs of one person who has no other means is just as much of a miracle as the feeding of the 5,000 because it is beyond personal abilities to solve the problem.

God works in practical and personal ways. When God performs a miracle, He might be meeting a need, moving an obstacle, straightening out crooked paths, or pushing back storms and enemies. He meets people right where they are.

I encountered God's miraculous intervention in the way of healing. The Lord was calling us to minister in the Seattle, Washington area. I had injured my knee when I was in the Navy. It served as my barometer, warning me of impending weather change. I had briefly mentioned to God how the weather in Washington would have a tremendous affect on my injured knee. A couple of weeks later, I was in a prayer meeting with some friends. One friend just reached over and began to pray for me. Suddenly, the power of God came down through my head and shot down to my knee. Within seconds, it lifted, but my knee was completely healed.

It struck me that God touches our lives when we are either at a point of desperate need or not expecting it at all. I had not specifically asked Him to heal my knee, and my friend was not praying for my knee. However, God sovereignly stepped on the scene during a time of intercession and showed His grace and power in an unexpected way.

In my walk with God, I have experienced and been part of many miracles. I have watched God step on the scene and heal and restore lives and relationships as well as save people from inevitable destruction. I learned that any willing vessel that has child-like faith and is humble, broken, or prayerful can serve as a conduit through which His miracles can occur.

An evangelist shared a personal experience where he had witnessed a man collapsing and dying of a heart attack in one of the major airports in America. At the time, the evangelist was with other godly men waiting for a flight. One of them suggested they all pray for God to intervene and resurrect the man. The evangelist admitted that he reluctantly placed his small finger on the man in front of him as some of the others fervently prayed. Within seconds breath came back into the man, and he was restored back to life.

---

[8] Exodus 14:13-22; Joshua 10:12-14; John 6:1-21

Challenging the Christian Life

We often forget how the fervent prayers of Elijah ended a three-year drought and that Jesus asked the Father to honor His requests such as the feeding of the 5,000 and the resurrection of the dead.[9] We forget the miraculous because we fail to see the practical side of God's intervention. This failure is due to our expectations of the miraculous that are often sensational and self-serving in nature. As a result, many unbelieving or skeptical people chalk God's miracles up to coincidence.

It is important to stress that God does not exploit His power to entertain people, nor does He toy with people in order to impress or control them. He does not do the miraculous to prove Himself. Rather, He does the miraculous because of Who He is. Anytime God intervenes on behalf of man, it becomes a touch of the supernatural, which makes it a miracle.

People's motives to witness or be part of miracles are often fleshly and worldly. They want God to prove Himself, defend His reputation, or back up their claims with some supernatural act. God will do none of these. God does the miraculous because it ultimately fulfills His purpose or brings glory to Him.

Jesus made this clear in the raising of Lazarus in John 11. He was informed that Lazarus was sick and He needed to come to heal him. Jesus purposely tarried a couple of days after declaring, "This sickness is not unto death, but for the glory of God that the Son of God might be glorified in it" (John 11:4).

God never steps outside of His character, will, purpose, or promises. Granted, He does the unexpected to surprise you at times. The unexpected gives you a sense that it is not only a matter of showing you how aware He is of you, but that it brings such pleasure to His heart when your response is that of child-like excitement and adoration.

There are three facts you need to remember at all times about God's intervention on behalf of man.

1) God has nothing to prove because He is God. He is not on some pride trip as man would be in His position, but rather He is silently and patiently working behind the scenes to bring about a desired end.

2) His goal is not to straighten up men, but rather to save them.[10] When we think of power, we think in terms of getting people to see it our way. I have been guilty of this emphasis. In the past, I have used my prayers to try to stir God up to line people up by causing them to see it my way. Eventually, He showed me how self-serving my emphasis was. After all, it is not a matter of getting people to agree with me, but believing in their hearts the truth about His provision of Jesus. Sadly, our pride causes us to not only miss the heart of God, but to fail to become part of His work and harvest.

---

[9] Mark 6:41; James 5:17-18
[10] Luke 9:56

3) God could create a solution out of the dust or air, but He wants to take what is available and multiply it. The key to multiplication in the kingdom of God is being faithful with what God has given you and offering it to Him in faith like the boy who offered his lunch in John 6. This small lunch was multiplied to feed 5,000.[11] We often consider God's intervention in light of the unseen or abundance instead of realizing that God can take something we often consider small or insignificant and multiply it, bringing Him glory.

This brings us to the greatest miracle—the salvation of man's soul. We often look for miracles outside of what God accomplishes in the humble heart of the repentant man. The concept of the salvation of man points to something beyond personal abilities. Jesus clearly brought this out when His disciples asked Him who could be saved. He said, "With men this is impossible, but with God all things are possible" (Matthew 19:26).

If you have truly received God's provision of salvation through Jesus Christ, you need to realize that you are a walking miracle. Every believer is a living testimony not only of God's commitment, but also His ability to do the impossible on behalf of man.

If you are a Christian, you also need to realize that you have been a part of the miraculous. God is still in the business of miracles. Take this time and consider the ways in which God has touched your life in practical, but miraculous ways. Begin to bring honor and glory to the One who is worthy of all praise and worship.

---

[11] John 6:9

15

GIFT OF PROPHECY

The inspirational gifts are found at the core of the conflict over the gifts of the Spirit. It is as though the debate over these gifts, especially the gift of tongues, has brought into question the validity of the other gifts of the Spirit. Amazingly, it is what Scripture said in regard to the gift of tongues that made me consider and study the gifts of the Spirit in an unbiased way.

1 Corinthians 14:39 instructs, "Wherefore, brethren, covet to prophesy, and forbid not to speak with tongues." This Scripture showed me that believers must covet the best of the gifts. For example, in the category of the gifts of revelation, wisdom would be the most desired, while, in the gifts of power, faith ranks in importance, but prophecy should be coveted in the gifts of inspiration. Once again, I could see no indication that the Church was to overlook or ignore them.

After I realized that I was being instructed to covet certain gifts, I was also being told not to forbid tongues. I had a choice. I could ignore this Scripture, and hold on to denominational beliefs and teachings about these gifts, which would bring me into disobedience to the Word of God, or, I could accept what it said and seek out God's perspective on them. Needless to say, I chose the latter.

As I pondered the controversy centered on the inspirational gifts, I started to see the real core surrounding the validity of the gifts. It actually comes down to control.

Christians have unknowingly operated in the gifts of revelation and power, and it is easy to accredit these occurrences to intellectual wisdom, insight, blessings, or coincidence. However, a person cannot consider the inspirational gifts in light of the normal, especially the gift of tongues. If the inspirational gifts are valid for today, they speak of something outside of the control of man, making them supernatural in nature.

Man fears what he cannot control or understand. This is clearly seen in how people respond to the gift of tongues. For example, they can ascribe prophecy to imagination and interpretation of tongues as part of the show, but what do you do with those frightening tongues that can throw people into confusion and cause one to sweat as he or she hears something he or she cannot control or understand. In the scheme of things, one has to either do away with all the gifts, even though it is clear we have need of such insights that come from wisdom, knowledge, and faith, deem such practices as fanaticism and, therefore, from Satan, or consider the possibilities that the Bible is true and these gifts are still available and in operation. The problem with the gift of tongues is that it proves there are things outside of man's understanding and control that must be accepted on the basis of faith and obedience.

This inability to control makes one feel vulnerable to the supernatural. The abuses in the area of the inspirational gifts have not helped people's fears, doubts, and debates about the gifts of the Spirit.

The inspirational gifts are the most abused of the nine gifts. It is not unusual to see people step over the line into the fleshly and demonic in these gifts. Once individuals begin operating with fleshly hype or under the influence of a demonic spirit, chaos takes over that can border between fanaticism and insanity. Such chaotic actions will bring a reproach to Christianity, as well as drive others away in fear and skepticism.

I believe this is why there are some stringent guidelines surrounding the inspirational gifts. These guidelines not only guard against the counterfeits, but they establish boundaries to ensure the integrity of these gifts. For example, there should not be more than three messages of prophecy and tongues in each meeting. Each prophecy must be confirmed by the Word of God and by fulfillment of it. The tongues must be interpreted for the edification of those present.[1]

After being in meetings where these gifts were abused, I could see the necessity of such boundaries. People treat spiritual matters as if there are no boundaries or rules and as if anything goes, as long as it appears to be spiritual or supernatural.

In one meeting, fleshly hype began to replace the moving of the Holy Spirit. I watched the pastor as concern and sternness came over his countenance. The next Sunday, the pastor took the opportunity to instruct people and warn them that chaotic behavior would not be tolerated. It is important that, if gifts are in operation, the leadership must be alert, discerning, and quick to instruct as to the gifts' proper use to ensure order.

This brings us back to the subject of control. If these gifts are of God, how do you control them? You cannot unless you happen to be the vessel that refuses to vocalize the inspiration that is being given to you. It is not up to man to control God. It is simply his responsibility to test all messages, and, if they are of God, he needs to receive them, regardless of the method or the vessel God may use.

It is not unusual to see people try to dictate to God according to their understanding and comfort zones. These people test things according to how something makes them feel. If they feel uncomfortable, they automatically deem it as erroneous and close down. They never get to the stage where they actually test the message according to the spirit and Word.

---

[1] Deuteronomy 18:20-22; 1 Corinthians 14:27-33

As a result, many miss valuable insight, encouragement, and warnings. They not only close themselves down to the possibilities of God speaking directly to them in this unusual manner, but they forbid the practice of these gifts, such as tongues, coming into opposition of Scripture.

This brings us to the other aspect of the inspirational gifts—understanding God's use of them. People cannot understand why God uses a method that appears foolish and insignificant to them to get His point across. 1 Corinthians 1:27-29 explains why God uses such methods,

> But God hath chosen the foolish things of the world to confound the wise; and God hath chosen the weak things of the world to confound the things which are mighty; And base things of the world, and things which are despised, hath God chosen, yea, and things which are not, to bring to nought things that are, That no flesh should glory in his presence.

We are not meant to understand the reason of God, but we do have a responsibility to embrace what is of God by faith. The gifts of the Spirit are meant to bring God's perspective to a matter and the gift of prophecy is no exception.

Prophecy is the one consistent work of the Holy Spirit that can be found in the five positions, the gifts of grace, and the gifts of the Spirit. In the case of prophecy in the relationship to the five positions established for the Church, the prophet is meant to guard the spiritual well-being of the Body. This may mean forthtelling to bring instruction or foretelling in order to warn. In the gifts of grace, prophecy often points to an inspired preacher who only speaks according to the spiritual condition of the hearers.

The gift of prophecy can operate within both the boundaries of forth-telling or foretelling. It implies one is definitely speaking on behalf of someone else. In this atmosphere, a person is speaking on behalf of God.

In forth-telling, it is often used as a means to encourage or exhort the body or a person. In foretelling, it serves as a means of warning with the intention to tear down with truth with the intent to build up in godliness. This gift deals with the present in order to confirm or change the direction of a person or local body by pointing to future promises or consequences.

As you study the importance of the gift of prophecy, you will realize that one of the responsibilities of the Holy Spirit is to show us things to come.[2] Obviously, if we close down the avenue of gifts, we will prevent the Holy Spirit from preparing us for the future. Without preparation, we will not be able to stand, withstand, and endure to the end.

As pointed out, there are different emphases of these gifts. The word of wisdom emphasizes God as the great I Am; therefore, one must

---

[2] John 16:13

line up to His instructions, while the word of knowledge deals with the present by stating, "You are (here)." The gift of faith will declare, "God, you said," while the gift of prophecy has God declaring: "I will (carry this out)."

Prophecy is often confused with the gifts of the word of wisdom and the word of knowledge, but each gift is designed to address and change different aspects of the person (or body of believers). For example, the word of wisdom is directed at the person's perception and is meant to change how a person perceives reality, especially in the area of God. The word of knowledge meets a person in his or her present situation with the intention of changing present reality. The gift of prophecy is meant to minister to the whole body or man with the intent of establishing or changing the person or body's direction or inward environment.

We see this in the case of Israel. Many times God exposed the Israelites' rebellious and idolatrous condition in order to warn them of future judgment. God's goal was to bring them to repentance in hopes of postponing or warding any judgment off. As we know, they did not heed Him; therefore, they had to drink the bitter dregs of their folly.

One must point out the encouragement that was intermingled with the pronouncement of judgment upon Israel. Although the judgments would be carried out, God promised them that, one day, He would restore national Israel and that their king would rule over them. I have read accounts of how the Jewish people have clung to these promises in trying times because they know if God said it, He will do it.

I have witnessed this in my own life and heard various testimonies of God's integrity to His Word. I remember an incident where God promised a woman that He would save her husband. Her husband later died and she felt betrayed because she had not witnessed any conversion. It was not until five years later that she learned from a stranger who was trying to touch base with her husband that God had fulfilled this promise. As they compared notes, the woman learned that this man had caught a ride with her husband. The Lord had prompted him to share the Gospel. As a result, he had led this woman's husband to Christ the very night he was killed in a car accident.

Prophecies can have conditions that one must meet before they can be fulfilled. My co-laborer, Jeannette, prophesied over a man concerning his potential in the kingdom of God, but it carried a condition. Before God could make him this godly man, he had to get into the Word of God. The man failed to do his part and today remains in the same pigpen of hopelessness.

It is also important that people do not become impulsive or presumptuous about a prophecy. In one situation, a man was given a personal prophecy that he decided to bring about in his own strength. He packed up his family and went in search of the fulfillment of it, only to become disillusioned and financially close to ruin. Prophecies are brought forth when the right environment or timing are in place, such as in the case of Jesus' birth.

Regardless of how spiritual a prophecy may sound, it must be properly tested. Prophecies often confirm what you already know to be true in your spirit. For example, if a person brings a prophecy to you, it will be in accordance to what God has already shown you.

In one incident, a man brought a prophecy of judgment upon me. Immediately, I knew it was not of God, because it failed three important criteria that are clearly brought out by the Old Testament prophets.

1) It was out of order. God has an order when He pronounces any type of judgment. He will first always expose sin and call for repentance before He pronounces judgment. This person did not expose any sin, nor did he call for repentance. God's heart is to always bring reconciliation, not judgment.[3] Repentance will change a person's direction, thwart judgment, and bring reconciliation. Therefore, a prophecy that lacks both order and God's heart is not from Him.

2) There was no confirmation in my spirit. God uses such gifts as prophecy to confirm something that He has already laid on a person's heart. At the time of this man's so-called "prophesy", God was not convicting me of sin, nor was He calling me to repentance.

3) The person's spirit was wrong. I sensed the prophecy this man was giving me was more about his own jealousies and personal arrogance than it was about me. He did not seem concerned for me spiritually, and almost appeared to glory in the perspective that I was coming down. This is not a spirit of meekness and compassion. It is God's will to bring everyone to repentance in order to avoid judgment. Therefore, He does not glory in bringing people down, nor should His followers. In fact, they should tremble at such prospects, for they could fall in the same traps and experience the same judgments.[4]

If a prophecy is of God, it is not up to individuals to fulfill it. People must wait on God to bring it about. Believers' responsibility in such times is to be faithful stewards with what they have been entrusted with until God brings forth the prophecy. Also, prophecies that have conditions will not be fulfilled until the person meets them. This is why learning to be faithful on a daily basis in your life before God ensures that all godly prophecies will be brought about for God's glory.

Prophecies can also be improperly exalted in ways that will not only result in abuse, but will be idolatrous in nature. I know of a woman who kept all of her prophecies in a notebook and would refer to them as if they were the Bible. It was as if her whole life hinged on and operated according to these prophecies. Christians must never operate according to prophecies or promises, but according to the leading of the Spirit and the righteous instructions and boundaries of the Word of God.

---

[3] Luke 9:56; 2 Corinthians 5:18-19
[4] 1 Corinthians 10:12; 2 Timothy 2:24-26

Over the years, I have received various prophecies. I have put them on the shelf and continued with the work that was before me. Prophecies can be abstract; therefore, they can be fulfilled without a person even knowing it until he or she looks back. It was only years later that I realized that most of these prophecies were fulfilled without me even realizing it.

In one prophecy, I was told that I would have a time of pinnacle where I would move into my gift without sweat. It was not until three years later, when I heard that part of the prophecy, that I realized it had been fulfilled in an unusual way. I had been moving into a certain gift without any effort or sweat for over a year. The most amazing part of this time was that it took place at our office that was located in a building called the "Pinnacle Building." This showed me that the fulfillment of valid prophecies simply confirmed that I was on the right path and to continue to walk in that direction.

This brings us to the issue of personal prophecies. Do they exist? Yes, they do, but there are a lot of abuses and misunderstandings in this area. There are numerous people running around claiming to be prophets with a personal prophecy for anyone they encounter. Many of these people are nothing more than fortune-tellers who use Christ as their authority, a familiar spirit as their source, vain imaginations as their glass ball, and empty promises as a means to feed the flesh and pride of those who believe them.

Today, there are a lot of false prophecies floating around. Sadly, many people have believed them, causing devastation and unbelief in their life.

One man received various prophecies that he would marry a well-known woman. This man clung to this prophecy because it fed his fantasy. But realistically, this woman would have never given this man the time of day. Life basically passed this man by as he held on to the fantasy, rather than face reality and live his life for God, entrusting Him with the events of his life.

All prophecies must be tested. Each prophecy must have the evidence of the Spirit of God by upholding the Word of God. If a prophecy is contrary to God's character or His Word, it must be rejected.

This is why prophecies must be put on the shelf until God brings them forth. People who try to fulfill their own prophecies or cling to false prophecies will be made to look the part of a fool, rather than obedient servants of God. If a prophecy is false, a person does not want to cling to it regardless of how it might serve his or her purpose because it is not of God. Rather, the prophecy is a lie that will result in disillusionment.

God does keep His word. He is able to move heaven and earth, but it is on His terms, not ours. We also must make sure a prophecy is from God and refuse to believe or toy with anything that would give us false hope or lead us down a path of delusion.

When godly prophecy is maintained in purity and integrity, it will serve as a vital part of the Church's edification. This is why 1

Thessalonians 5:20 instructs, "Despise not prophesyings." According to *Strong's Exhaustive Concordance*, the word "prophesying," in this Scripture, points to prediction. In this text, we see the Church must not despise foretelling. Predictions from God can be quite unnerving for those who are not used to them, but they must be embraced to ensure preparation.

Two days before Jesus was offered up on the cross, He predicted the events that would lead up to the end of the age. His reason for this was not to scare people, but to encourage them to be spiritually ready to stand, endure, and patiently wait in confidence for His return.[5]

As Jesus shared hard truths about the days of great tribulation, encouragement was interwoven within the darkness. The hope surrounding these events is that it will bring the Light of the world back in His glory as His Body is ushered into His presence to be with Him forever.

The Church must not despise prophesies. Instead, they need to be discerned because they might be from God. This might serve as His means to warn and prepare His Body or Church for what is about to come upon it.

Is this one of the predominate gifts you operate in? If so, walk in integrity of heart and in the disposition of humility and sobriety. If God gives you a prophecy, be faithful to deliver it in meekness according to His perfect timing and trust God to confirm it.

---

[5] Matthew 24, Mark 13, Luke 21

16

TONGUES AND INTERPRETATION

The next inspirational gift is the gift of tongues. You cannot properly present this gift unless you do so in light of the gift of interpretation.

As previously stated, the gift of tongues is what creates the greatest controversy over the gifts of the Spirit. The reason for this conflict surrounds three issues: 1) control, (2) the Baptism of the Holy Spirit, and (3) the difference between the gift of tongues and the prayer language.

People who encounter the gift of tongues can perceive it as a frightening situation. The strange language initially gives the impression of chaos or insanity to unsuspecting Christians.

I remember taking a friend to an Assembly of God Church. I was aware that the gifts had been in operation in the past, but it seemed minimal. During worship, a person received a message in tongues. As she was speaking forth in this strange language, my concern immediately went out to my friend who never had witnessed the manifestation of the Spirit.

My thought was, "Oh brother, she will probably run out of this church and never look back." Amazingly, she stayed and heard the interpretation of it and remained for the rest of the service. After church, I questioned her. She admitted that her initial response when she heard the strange language was to flee, but the Lord spoke to her and told her that the message was for her.

I can recall that the interpretation of the tongue was that of encouragement, but I had no idea that He was personally reaching out to my friend to minister to her during a difficult and trying time. He not only edified her, but He made me more aware of just how faithful He is to reach out to His people in the most unexpected ways.

My friend actually shared her experience with others and the next Sunday there were more people at church to witness this unusual manifestation. But, true to His sovereign nature, nothing happened. Once again, God confirmed to me that He is not a performer nor does He move just to prove a point to others.

As I have watched people struggle over the gifts of the Holy Spirit, I have wondered why God uses such controversial means to speak forth His truths to His Body, especially the gift of tongues. As I have observed the manifestation of tongues, it struck me that, when this gift manifests, it quickly catches people's attention. When a message comes forth in tongues, it is as if everything stops in great anticipation and everyone's senses are tuned into the very voice of God in readiness to receive from Him.

This is why it is sad that many ignorantly quench this gift because of the need to control even that which is spiritual. Granted, there has been much abuse in the area of the inspirational gifts, but the Church must not do away with a valid work of the Holy Spirit because man has perverted it.

In Christianity, the key to spiritual growth does not lie in personal control, but in personal surrender to the work of the Holy Spirit. The use and reception of gifts is a matter of faith and not a point of personal control or intellectual debate. Instead of believers grieving the Holy Spirit because they limit His work in their midst, they must choose to become discerning and receptive in order to protect His liberty to move as He wills in order to ensure spiritual edification and growth.

The second issue that clouds the gift of tongues is the baptism of the Holy Spirit. Due to the many misconceptions about this subject, it is important to understand this baptism in order to keep it in the proper perspective and avoid unnecessary debates and abuses. For example, there is a debate that the born-again experience is the same as the baptism of the Holy Spirit. If we consider the Scriptures, we will see that there appears to be a distinction between these two experiences.

In John 20:22, we see Jesus giving the Holy Ghost to His disciples before He ascended, "And when he had said this, he breathed on them, and saith unto them, Receive ye the Holy Ghost."

In Luke 24:49, He gave His disciples this promise, "And, behold, I send the promise of my Father upon you: but tarry ye in the city of Jerusalem, until ye be endued with power from on high."

Acts 1:8 states, "But ye shall receive power, after that the Holy Ghost is come upon you: and ye shall be witnesses unto me both in Jerusalem, and in all Judea, and in Samaria, and unto the uttermost part of the earth."

These Scriptures appear to give the impression that the reception of the Holy Ghost upon salvation and the Baptism of the Holy Ghost are two distinct experiences. Keep in mind that the Holy Ghost is referred to as both a gift and promise. He would be given to the believer as a gift upon salvation and a promise upon baptism. The fact that these experiences also end in two different results also implies they are distinct. For example, salvation is the product of the born-again experience where the Spirit of God becomes a resident within the spirit of man. The baptism of the Holy Spirit is an experience that empowers the person to be a bold witness on behalf of Jesus Christ and what He did on the cross for lost man.

As I studied the early Church, I recognized these two experiences were treated as distinct. In fact, the normal practice of the new Church was that, after water baptism (confession of faith), hands were laid upon the individual to receive the Baptism of the Holy Spirit. According to the information, the laying on of hands for the Baptism of the Holy Ghost was strictly observed for the first 200 years and eventually became a ritual that lost its meaning as it was only allotted to the so-called elite leaders. As a result, it ceased to be a promise to be obtained, but became an unfeeling religious exercise that lost its real purpose or significance.[1] Today, the laying on of hands to receive the Holy Spirit is acknowledged by some in the American Church and is still practiced by those in other countries where adherence to the Word of God is observed in child-like faith and obedience.

I personally believe that, when the power of the Holy Spirit touches His residing presence from within, He becomes the Rivers of Living Water that Jesus made reference to. As the Living Water, He breaks forth from deep within to break down any dams of self, rid of all debris, and bring forth newness of life in power and authority. I believe Scripture confirms this. Jesus said in John 7:37-39, "If any man thirst, let him come unto me, and drink. He that believeth on me, as the scripture hath said, out of his belly shall flow rivers of living water. (But this spake he of the Spirit....)."

John the Baptist made this statement about Jesus in Matthew 3:11, "I indeed baptize you with water unto repentance: but he that cometh after me is mightier than I, whose shoes I am not worthy to bear: he shall baptize you with the Holy Ghost, and with fire."

John the Baptist had been baptizing men in water in light of repentance. In this Scripture verse, he is pointing to a baptism that is solely done by Jesus and is of greater purpose. E. Stanley Jones stated that John's baptism was to get rid of something, while Jesus' baptism is to get possession of the lives of people. He pointed out that water baptism unto repentance died while the baptism of the Holy Spirit lives on. John the Baptist challenged and irritated the religious realm, while Jesus inspired His sheep.[2]

It must be noted that the water baptism that is practiced today is not a sign of repentance, but of identification. The sign of repentance is no longer water baptism, but a changed life.

The controversy over the Baptism of the Holy Spirit escalates when it comes to the evidence of this baptism. Acts 19:6 states, "And when Paul had laid his hands upon them; the Holy Ghost came on them; and they spake with tongues, and prophesied."

It is maintained by a majority of those who believe in the manifestation of the Holy Ghost that the main evidence of this spiritual baptism is speaking in tongues. They back this up with Scriptures such as Acts 2:3-4 and 10:44-48.

---

[1] Deeper Experiences of Famous Christians; by James Gilchrist Lawson; © 2000 by Barbour Publishing, Inc. pg. 47

[2] The Way; Daily devotion, pg. 271

This belief often insults those who don't agree with teachings surrounding the Baptism of the Holy Ghost. Obviously, Scripture shows that tongues are evidence of this baptism, but I personally don't believe it is the only evidence. Acts 19:6 also states that the people prophesied as well. We also see that prophecy was the visible evidence manifested after the Spirit of God came upon King Saul in 1 Samuel 10:6 and 19:19-24.

Scripture proves to me that tongues are just one of the signs and not the only sign. Paul reinforced my conclusion by asking the question in 1 Corinthians 12:30, whether all would speak with tongues? I have witnessed in my own life that this baptism brought forth boldness to proclaim my testimony as well as significant change in my life. The Word of God also became more illuminated and personal to me.

I have also operated in other gifts before I ever spoke in a strange tongue, which brings me to an important question. Can a person display the manifestation of the Spirit without first being baptized with the Holy Ghost?

It is up to each person to explore the Scripture and seek God's perspective on this matter. The truth is that God wants to empower us, not only to victoriously live the Christian life, but to be bold in our witnessing and effective ministers in His kingdom.

As previously stated, the Holy Spirit serves as both a gift and a promise.[3] As a gift, He is given to those upon salvation as a seal to an eternal inheritance and, as a promise, He enables believers to carry out their commission and reach their potential in Christ.

As I have observed the emotional debate over the Baptism of the Holy Ghost and speaking in tongues, I wonder what serves as the greatest point of conflict. It seems both issues are debated with great intensity, but I have to admit it is hard to discern between beliefs driven by pride, ignorance justified by fear, and anger reinforced by the need to control and understand the move and work of God. When you listen to this debate, it becomes obvious that few are seeking for the truth and many are trying to maintain tight reins on their present theology.

No Christian should let the influence of religion and the flesh determine these issues. The responsibility of every Christian is to seek God's perspective through the unbiased study of Scripture and allow Him to establish the proper perception.

The truth about the Holy Spirit is that we need to be constantly filled up with Him.[4] It matters little if we have never experienced His fullness or whether we have; we need to strive to experience the Living Water on a daily basis. My suggestion in this matter is that Christians adhere to Luke 11:13, "If ye then, being evil, know how to give good gifts unto your children: how much more shall your heavenly Father give the Holy Spirit to them that ask Him?" (Emphasis added.)

---

[3] Acts 2:38-39
[4] Ephesians 5:18

The third issue that causes confusion in this area is the difference between the prayer language and the gift of tongues. The Apostle Paul dealt with these two subjects in 1 Corinthians 14:1-6.

Many Christians believe that the gift of tongues and the unknown prayer language are the same. This is a misconception. Just because a person may have a prayer language does not mean he or she has the gift of tongues.

I have never operated in the gift of tongues, but I do have a prayer language. Once again, we are reminded by Paul's own words in 1 Corinthians 12:29-30 that not everyone would possess the same gifts, which includes the gift of tongues. Upon questioning those who operate in this gift, they admit that their prayer language is not the same as the tongue they speak with when the gift comes upon them. This would make sense because a person has control over his or her prayer language, but the gift of tongues would be totally controlled by the Spirit of God. This means the person could utter only that which the Holy Spirit is inspiring.

The gift of tongues and the prayer language also differ according to whom they edify. For example, the gift of tongues must be interpreted which will edify the whole body, while the prayer language mainly edifies the one who prays in it.

There have been situations where people have heard others pray in their native tongue, thereby, being greatly edified. For example, a pastor, through an interpreter, asked a couple of American missionaries who were working in his area to pray for him to be baptized with the Holy Spirit. They laid hands upon him and prayed for him. Within a short time, he began to pray in another tongue. To the missionaries' surprise, his tongue was English. The Lord used this pastor in his new prayer language to thank the missionaries for their faithful obedience to come to the mission field, and then he began to pray for America.

In another situation, foreign visitors to America were greatly troubled by events surrounding Christians in their native country. When the invitation went out for people to come to the altar to unload their burdens, these Christians went forward to intercede. As they kneeled down by an American, they could hear the person praying in another tongue. To their surprise, the person was praying in their native language. The Lord spoke to them through that person. Prophetically they were told that He was about to resolve the trouble and for them to take heart. They not only walked away edified, but rejoicing. True to His Word, God took care of this matter in a miraculous way, confirming the message in tongues.

There are many stories about people being ministered to through another person's prayer language. Therefore, this prayer language not only edifies the person who prays in it, but it can touch other people as well.

The prayer language often serves as a shortcut to bring a person past self and personal understanding right into the throne room of God where His will and purpose will be upheld in prayer. Once the person's understanding is out of the way, the Spirit will have the liberty to pray through the person. This is why the prayer language has the ability to offer up unhindered praise, stand in the gap to ensure deliverance, and be used in intercession.

In my own case, I recognize that my personal understanding will often cause repetition of praise, thanksgiving, and requests. By praying in my prayer language all personal boundaries can be quickly brought down as I turn my tongue over to the Spirit. It is from this premise that I can begin to soar in an eternal perspective, bringing edification to my spirit.

The prayer language is great in intercession. The Lord woke a woman up in the middle of the night with a burden for a missionary friend in Africa. She had no idea what was going on, but she sensed the situation was dangerous. The woman began to intercede in her prayer language and continued to do so until the burden lifted. She learned later that the night she was called into intercession for her friend was the night guerrilla fighters took control of the community her friend was ministering in. There were not only bullets flying around, but there was also a possibility of great emotional harm. Throughout the frightening ordeal, God protected the missionary.

Romans 8:26-27 tells us we do not know how to pray, but the Holy Spirit makes intercession for the saints according to the will of God. These intercessions can come out in groanings that cannot be uttered.

This brings us to another aspect of this debate: What does it mean to pray in the Spirit? The Apostle Paul made this statement in Ephesians 6:18, "Praying always with all prayer and supplications in the Spirit, and watching thereunto with all perseverance and supplication for all saints."

I had one individual become furious with me because she had spent hours praying for her family, but it was with her own understanding. She claimed she had been praying in the Spirit. I could not agree with her because of what the Apostle Paul said about this issue in 1 Corinthians 14:14, "For if I pray in an unknown tongue, my spirit prayeth, but my understanding is unfruitful."

As I have studied Scripture, I have not found any other description of praying in the spirit except in this verse, where a person does not understand what is being said. I really do not care if a person agrees or disagrees with my findings, because scriptural understanding should not be a matter of who is right or wrong, but rather the willingness to line up with God's Word about a subject.

The Apostle Paul went on to say, "I will pray with the spirit, and I will pray with the understanding also" (1 Corinthians 14:15). Again, Paul made a distinction between praying with the Spirit and praying with understanding.

However, the Holy Spirit can impact prayers in three ways: 1) He can *inspire* a person to pray for something specific; 2) He can *lead* an individual to pray because of a burden; or 3) He can *anoint* a person in his or her prayers to bring about a desired result. If the Holy Spirit is involved in our prayers in any way, we can be assured that they will have power before the throne and will hit the mark.

Now that the distinction between the prayer language and the gift of tongues has been discussed, it is time to consider how the gift of tongues operates. According to the Apostle Paul in 1 Corinthians 14:22, the gift of tongues initially serves as a sign to them who do not believe. The fact that tongues serve as a sign to unbelievers is confirmed by what Mark 16:17 stated, "And these signs shall follow them that believe: In my name shall they cast out devils; they shall speak with new tongues."

This confirmation was evident on the day of Pentecost. Those in the upper room were given many different tongues, and, as a result, the Gospel touched many people of different languages.[5]

When the gift of tongues is in proper operation within the Body, it can have words of knowledge, wisdom (revelation), or prophecy that will reveal the mysteries of God.[6]

This means God may be instructing, warning, encouraging, or giving direction to a person or the body through this gift. This is why this gift must not be forbidden as long as it is inspired by the right spirit and within scriptural boundaries.

1 Corinthians 14:27-28 clearly states that there must not be more than three messages in tongues in a meeting, and it must be interpreted. In fact, the person who speaks in tongues is instructed to pray for the interpretation of it.[7]

This brings us to another point of conflict. There is so much suspicion in regards to this gift. Skeptics have a tendency to question the validity of a tongue that is interpreted by the same person. On the other hand, I have sensed in a couple of incidents where both tongues and interpretation were staged between two different people. This proves that everything must be discerned on the basis of spirit, and not according to one's feelings or beliefs.

Are you personally open to this gift? Does God want to use you in this area or are you unwilling to even go there because of concrete doctrine, fear, or ignorance?

Gift of Interpretation

The gift of interpretation is the gift that verifies the gift of tongues and ensures that the whole body will be edified. The gift of tongues may get our attention, but interpretation is like turning on the light to bring understanding and enlightenment to people.

The gift of interpretation is not a true form of translation that is word for word of a message, but the means of conveying the spirit, intent, and meaning behind the message. For instance, there was a message in

---

[5] Acts 2
[6] 1 Corinthians 14:1, 6
[7] 1 Corinthians 14:13

tongues and interpretation in a church I was attending. The actual message of tongues was short, but the interpretation was lengthy. The pastor who interpreted the message reminded the congregation that interpretation was not a word for word translation.

This is the one inspirational gift I operate in the most. I can tell you from experience that to operate in one of the inspirational gifts is like stepping off of a cliff and hoping God will be there to meet you.

In my first experience of interpretation of tongues, I missed the opportunity because of fear and inexperience. There was a message in tongues and I felt heat rushing up my body. Four words ran across my mind like a ticker tape. I asked God for more words to ensure I was receiving the interpretation, but the four same words kept running across my mind.

I struggled in the silence as I wrestled with this new experience. I did not want to open my mouth and speak only four words and then be left up in the air, looking like an immature fool. After much silence, a prophecy came forth, allowing me to justify my silence and fear as well as let off a sigh of relief that I had remained quiet. Just as I was about to pat myself on the back for restraint, another person opened her mouth and the same four words that had run across my mind came out in boldness and authority.

The woman who was overseeing the meeting took time out to instruct us about gifts. To this day, I appreciate her sensitivity to the struggle and her willingness to share her experiences in the area of gifts to bring proper instruction.

In my years of being a Christian, I have only met two other individuals besides the instructor who took time out of the meeting to properly instruct the saints about this subject. Today I still consider these people gems.

There are so many people who secretly struggle with the gifts, especially the inspirational gifts. These gifts require a measure of faith to step out in obedience to participate in something strange and uncomfortable. The possibilities of looking foolish in the process can be overwhelming to the inexperienced and uncertain vessel.

I don't know how many times I have wrestled over the gift of interpretation. I have wondered if it is my imagination, yet I never know what I am going to say past the four words that I am initially given. Out of faith, I open my mouth and speak what I see until the words cease.

I remember when, in one interpretation, I was clipping along as I was speaking forth the combination of words and pictures. All of a sudden, the words came to an abrupt end as if I stopped in the middle of a sentence. Of course, it was not the middle of the sentence, but my momentum was still at high speed. I realize God used that situation to show me that it was not my imagination, but a true manifestation of His Spirit.

I have even argued with God about the gift of interpretation. In a firm voice, He put me in my place when He said, "I can take it away from you." I realize that not only would I be burying a gift, but I also was failing God and His Body. I quickly repented.

Over the years, I have learned to wait for a few seconds before giving the interpretation as a means to confirm to me whether or not I have the interpretation. Even after years of experience, I still have some anxiety when God gives me the interpretation of a tongue. However, as I talk to others who operate in these different gifts, I have discovered this anxiety is not unusual when it comes to the function of these gifts.

I have also found the gift of interpretation can be used in interpreting visions or dreams and explaining mysteries or hidden treasure that can be found in parables or proverbs. We see this ability to interpret visions and dreams in the lives of Joseph and Daniel.[7] In my own situation, I have been used in the interpretation of visions and dreams and, always in a state of awe, I have watched some come true.

Do you have the gift of interpretation or are you closing it down because of fear and the lack of instruction? Be willing to open yourself up and take the step of faith and allow the Holy Spirit the freedom to minister to the Body through you.

---

[7] Genesis 40:5; Daniel 2:4; Proverbs 1:6

17

THE CHALLENGE

As I struggle with my conclusion to this book, I have to recognize that God did establish an incredible pattern to bring about edification in the Body. This pattern has been carefully laid out and recorded, yet His Body debates and quibbles over how to interpret it. As a result, much of the Body picks and chooses according to indoctrination and not scriptural instruction.

2 Timothy 3:16 tells us **all** Scripture is inspired and given to establish doctrine, and it is to be used for personal reproof, correction, and instruction in righteousness. Yet, how many Christians consider all Scriptures as being from God and the only means of substantiating righteous attitudes, pure doctrine, and godly lifestyles? Sadly, the percentage of Christians that approach the Bible with the correct perspective is dangerously low.

Much of the scriptural debate that is going on is not a matter of standing for truth, but a platform on which religious pride is exalted, ignorance is covered by a cloak of religious zeal, and fear is hidden behind skepticism and theological discussion. I do not have a problem when people admit they do not understand certain aspects of the Bible. My main complaint rests with people who change, ignore, or do away with Bible truths because of pride, fear, or ignorance.

It is up to each person to make a choice. Either the entire Bible is true or none of it is true. It is not up to mere man to determine what is acceptable in it or try to justify it by influencing others to follow in his spiritual causes. It is one thing to admit personal challenges over a scriptural teaching, but it is another matter to stand in the way of other people seeking out God's perspective.

When will the Body of Christ learn that God's truths do not come down to what is considered popular or accepted theology of man any more than God's works must be considered in light of what is comfortable? God's truths and works never will come down to man's fleshly or religious perspective, but to what God wants to accomplish in and through His people. This work has an eternal purpose that mere man is unable to grasp except by faith.

Subsequently, the debate in the Church does not find its origins in doctrine, but in unbelief. Many Christians have allowed others to define their beliefs. These assumed beliefs are nothing more than idolatrous in nature and, wherever idolatry exists, there is unbelief towards the real truths of God.

God has clearly established a pattern and avenues by which the Body is to be edified. The first pattern is found in the leadership in Ephesians 4:11. This leadership is to serve as a visible expression of Jesus' disposition—servitude and total commitment to the building of His kingdom for the glory of God.

In Romans 12:5-8, we see a diverse Body that is to be a physical extension of Christ as it serves in humility and reaches out in benevolence. This extension of Jesus is not only for the edification of the Body to bring it to maturity, but it is also to reach out to the lost in example, sensitivity, and sacrificial ways.

This brings us to the gifts of the Spirit found in 1 Corinthians 12 and 14. These are the gifts that have been done away with in so many different denominations. They are treated as if they hinge or depend on man when the Scripture states that these gifts are a manifestation of the Holy Spirit.

The Holy Spirit's main responsibility is to lift Jesus up, but He does have one area in which He manifests His sovereignty and supernatural works—the supernatural gifts. These gifts are either being denounced, accredited to Satan, or they are being abused in such a way that they give the Holy Spirit a spiritual black eye.

My scriptural understanding is that the Church needs the intervention and work of all three Persons of the Godhead. Each person of the Godhead is necessary, and to do away with any work or manifestation of them is to do away with the complete work of salvation and edification.

2 Corinthians 13:14 states, "The grace of the Lord Jesus Christ, and the love of God, and the communion of the Holy Ghost, be with you all. Amen." In this verse, we are reminded that Christ's death on the cross was an act of grace that secures our salvation.

As we consider the love of God, we know this is in reference to the love of the Father, "Behold, what manner of love the Father hath bestowed upon us, that we should be called the sons of God: therefore the world knoweth us not, because it knew him not" (1 John 3:1).

Jesus' death on the cross established a new covenant wherein God's people would be known as children of God. This would point to an intimate relationship with God, but this relationship is only made possible by the communion of the Holy Ghost.

The Holy Spirit reproves, seals, guides, and sanctifies. He is the One who moves upon, in, and through God's people. He is the one who unites and edifies the Body of Christ. He is the one who ensures the sacrifice of praise and opens the door of worship for sweet communion. Yet, few know the third Person of the Godhead enough to be able to discern His presence, work, and manifestation.

As a result of this lack of intimacy with the Holy Spirit, there are two extremes: 1) Those who do away with His work; therefore, keeping Him abstract instead of personal and, 2) those who accredit everything supernatural and spiritual to Him, making Him appear foolish and ridiculous.

There is a proper balance when it comes to the Person of the Holy Spirit and His work, but that balance can only be found in the Word of God. Sadly, it is often explained away. People, who cling to doctrines will close down, ignore, or abuse those areas of the Bible instead of seeking to know God's perspective about His Spirit and the work He does.

Each individual will be responsible for how he or she handles the third person of the Godhead. Each will be held accountable if he or she buries any of His gifts or grieves, quenches, or rejects Him.

This brings us back to the gifts of the Spirit. As you study these gifts, you cannot help but notice that the Holy Spirit remains true to form in them. We see through these gifts that the Holy Spirit is powerful, but remains a quiet servant as God's plans, heart, and intent are revealed to the Body. He remains gentle as faith is given, discernment is added, and wisdom is unveiled. He gives way as Christ is exalted in worship and moves in the body as its members are warned, encouraged, instructed, and ministered to.

It is easy to declare that these gifts have ceased until a person encounters their operation. It is convenient to ignore them until there is a testimony of their importance. It is justifiable to accredit them to other sources besides the third Person of the Godhead until one comes face to face with their supernatural ability to change lives.

To close down this avenue of edification is a great loss for the Church. In spite of the abuses, I have seen the Holy Ghost manifest Himself, and, in doing so, I have witnessed obstacles fleeing, hearts changed, and heaven revealed.

As I weigh the pros and cons of these different means of edification, I have concluded that I would rather risk and confront the improper use of them than close down the means by which God's Spirit can move.

I want to encourage believers to put aside pet theologies and seek God's face about this matter. My desire for this search is not to prove a point, but my desire is that Christians will find their proper place in the Body of Christ and be used effectively in the work of edification.

I believe that it is vital for the days we live in that every blood-bought saint is in his or her proper position in the Body and operating with the gift or gifts the Holy Spirit wants to allocate to him or her. It is of little concern to me what position or gift a believer has, but what does matter to me is that the Church will properly function in a powerful way for the glory of God.

The question is how does one find his or her place in the Body of Christ? It is simple. Go to the Father and ask Him to give you the life He has for you. This means asking for more of His life, which means you will be asking Him for more of His Spirit. Ask Him to also equip you to be effective in the Church and to give you boldness to work in the harvest field. Once the Father gives you more of His life, make sure you go to Jesus daily to ask to be filled up with His Living Water.

The power and anointing of the Holy Spirit are vital, especially as darkness is about to engulf this world. The Church needs to be healthy so that it can serve as the salt of the earth and the light of the world in order to penetrate the darkness for the sake of searching souls.

The question is will you seek the reality of this powerful life? Will you accept the challenge to put aside religious boundaries and seek the life and perspective of God about all matters? After all, how you handle God's truths comes down to whether or not you want to possess everything He has for you in spite of what you personally believe or perceive.

WHATEVER HAPPENED TO THE CHURCH?

Book Four

Copyright © 2008 by Rayola Kelley

INTRODUCTION

One of the questions that many Christians struggle with is, "Whatever happened to the Church?" This haunts many of God's saints as they find themselves searching for some type of sanity in Christendom. As they go from one church to another, they seem to find broken cisterns of man's religion and influence, poison waters of heresy, stagnant pools that are lifeless, and the endless mixture of worldly influences and perversion taking center stage in many of the attitudes and practices that are going on in the name of Christianity.

In this book I am going to attempt to answer this question. To be perfectly honest with you, I have also struggled with this issue. As I have waded through the many challenges that seem to plague the Christian Church, I have been accused of being too negative or even as being against the Church. Such accusations are false. However, what I have discovered is that what is now considered to be the Church has been cleverly redefined according to worldly or erroneous attitudes and mindsets that are firmly in place, causing confusion for many in the Christian realm. Even though Scripture is clear about the makeup of the Church that Jesus died for, it appears as if many within Christendom have been conditioned by a counterfeit presentation.

My desire is to establish the real meaning of the Church in light of how it has been cleverly redefined. In so doing, I hope to set the seeking heart free from the torment and struggle that is going on among so many of God's people.

Keep in mind that we are about to take a journey through the struggles of the Church. These struggles are not new. What many saints are experiencing now also challenged the new Church. What the watchmen contended with in the first centuries of the Church, and throughout its history, happens to be the very same issues the present day watchmen are trying to expose, warn against, and bring proper instruction about to God's people. Granted, these issues may have been repackaged to fit our modern-day palates of higher criticism, the psychology of the world, and the endless bombardment of useless entertainment and humanistic philosophies, but the issues remain the same.

Challenging the Christian Life

Although some people might consider this book discouraging, they will also discover that the Church that Jesus Christ died for stills exists. It may be hidden, discarded, persecuted, rejected, and mocked, but it is still very much alive, even in the midst of the great darkness that is engulfing the present age.

Let us now begin this journey to discover the true face of the blood-bought Church of the Lord Jesus Christ.

Part I
LAYING A FOUNDATION

1

WHAT IS THE CHURCH?

My initial religious exposure and influence came from a cult. Although this cult appeared to have attractive presentations in its various stands regarding family and moral issues, it was all simply a front that had no spirit or life. This was obvious, as I had to constantly face the harsh reality of the besetting sins that confronted my family and me. These constant struggles were shrouded by unrealistic religious standards and demands that, all too often, exposed hypocrisy in the lives of my family and the other cult members that I was personally acquainted with. It was clear that the standards of this cult did not empower its members or provide a sustaining anchor that would bring lasting hope.

I never thought much about whether the religion of my cult was genuine. In my younger years, I was not really concerned about such issues. However, I would learn that such matters would eventually be challenged, tested, or even shaken.[1] Such challenges would sometimes penetrate the indifference of my immaturity to cause me to consider if there was some type of absolute truth to matters of life and death that surrounded the issue of God that I needed to discover for myself.

When I was a teenager, I encountered such a challenge. My mother was talking about religious matters to my stepfather's mother, who I also fondly considered to be my grandmother. Since I was in the vicinity, I was listening to what was being said. My mother, who was doubtful about the cult because of unanswered questions and suspicions, was sharing some of her feelings. My grandmother made a statement that penetrated both my mother and me. She stated that the true Church was not made up of buildings, denominations, or organized religious systems. Rather, it was actually made up of people.

---

[1] Hebrews 12:27

The idea that the real Church was made up of people went into my spirit. It seemed strange because I had always identified "church" as a "building" that promoted religious beliefs and practices. However, the idea that the Church was not made up of lifeless buildings or indifferent doctrines made sense to my spirit.

As I look back upon that time, I realize my indifferent spirit was actually being stirred by the definition of the true Church. This challenge started a small fascination in me concerning the possibilities of God and His real Church. The fact that His Church was actually comprised of people who somehow understood what it meant to believe, love, and serve Him made God appear less indifferent. In a way, it served as a key that would slowly unlock a door that would lead me to the salvation of my soul.

When I became a Christian, one of my goals was to understand the real makeup of the Church that Jesus died for. Obviously, this very Church had to be established in Spirit and truth. I wanted to see if what my grandmother had originally said about the Church was true. If it was true, I sensed that so much of the indifference or vagueness that caused me to see God as impersonal was not only incorrect, but it was a product of the religious state of ignorance that was clearly in operation in the cult that was influencing my family and me.

Such a revelation about my misconceptions about God being indifferent caused me to realize how personal He can be if allowed, and how He desires to meet with His people and be involve with their welfare. It would also mean that He does not use the means of buildings, denominations, and even doctrines to identify and meet with those who belong to Him.

It is from this premise that I am approaching the subject of what makes up the true Church. It is important that we identify what is actually considered the true Body of Christ for the purpose of understanding what has happened to it in the twenty centuries since it was born and brought forth with Spirit and truth. If we fail to start from the proper premise, we will never understand the identity crisis that the Church has been struggling with throughout the years.

This identity crisis is nothing new. In fact, in many cases, it has served as the refining fires that have caused the true Church to come forth with distinction, purpose, and renewed commitment and vision. In such testing, the real Church has always emerged distinct, peculiar, and separate from what is considered normal and acceptable by the masses.

Such separation is the real key behind resolving the identity crisis that is shaking many within the Church. The true Church must understand its authority, purpose, and power if it is going to come back to its roots and the place that God has designed for it in His kingdom.

Once we, as believers, understand the design that God unveiled in Scripture in regard to His true Church, we will understand what it will take for it to be established according to the heavenly design. Once the Church is reestablished or realigned according to God's design, this entity will understand what it will take to function in light of His plan. This means the Church will take its rightful place in His kingdom.

In studying the Scriptures about the Church of Christ, I found that my grandmother was correct. We are told that those who truly believe in the Lord Jesus Christ for their salvation make up His Church.[2] Clearly, God meant the Church to be a living organism.

The Church would serve as the Body of Christ, while Jesus served as the Head of the Church. As the Head, all life and functions of the Body would originate or come from Him. In this Body, God would individually place each member by way of baptism of the Holy Spirit, for we are told that the Holy Spirit is the One who baptizes each member into this incredible Body. The members of this entity would be equal in importance, distinct in their places and function to ensure the effectual working of the whole Body. Obviously, God is the One who will temper this Body together for His use and glory.[3]

The Church would serve as a living building. We know that God is building this house, but He has placed Christ, as a Son, over it. A house reminds us that it is meant to be a dwelling place. The Word of God makes it clear who will dwell in this incredible house when it speaks of each believer as being a temple of the Holy Spirit. Clearly, the Church will be serving as a residence for God in the midst of this world.[4]

This brings us to the activities that must take place in this spiritual house of God. The Apostle Peter is the one who gave us insight into this matter. He first described believers as lively stones that have been used to build up a spiritual house. As a spiritual house, we as believers will be subject to the Spirit and not to the ways of the flesh or the world. Peter went on to stipulate that the Church not only represents a spiritual house, but it also comprises a holy priesthood. Each believer is also a priest. As priests of this spiritual house, we are to offer spiritual sacrifices, acceptable to God by Jesus Christ.[5]

The Apostle Peter also informed us that we are a chosen generation, a royal priesthood, and a holy nation of peculiar or special people that belong to God. As a chosen generation, we have been marked and set apart to represent God in this world. As a royal priesthood, we are reminded that, as part as the building of the Church, we have royal ties to an eternal King and kingdom, and we are here to represent God to man and man to God. Of course, as priests, we perform devoted service in God's house and to His people under the ever watchful, caring auspice of our High Priest: Jesus Christ.[6]

The Church is also a holy nation. This again points to separation. We may be in the midst of this world with its many kingdoms and nations, but

---

[2] Ephesians 4:11-16; Colossians 1:18
[3] 1 Corinthians 12:12-26
[4] 1 Corinthians 3:9, 16-17; 6:19-20; Hebrews 3:4-6
[5] 1 Peter 2:5
[6] Hebrews 7:17-28; 1 Peter 2:9

Challenging the Christian Life

we are not part of it. We have a separate king, law, mission, and lifestyle that we live in accordance to, which will also bring us into agreement with the intent and purpose of our King. As a result, we will stand distinct from the rest of the world.

The Church would become the harvest field of God. As His field, we must be cultivated. The Father is the true husbandman of our lives. He must, through the working of the Spirit, plough up the fallow ground of our hearts so that the seed of His Word can take root. He allows the north wind of trials to challenge our faith, but He also sends the gentle south breezes to bring forth new life. Under His watchful eyes, each season of regenerating, growing, purging, harvesting, and dying to the former beauty gives way to a deeper work in our hearts.[7]

As believers, we experience a deeper work during each cycle of these different spiritual seasons. In the springtime, the life of Christ is established in us in greater ways, unfolding a beauty that is virtuous and lasting. In the summer, the heat will purge that which is not of God, as bits of the flesh and pride wither under the penetrating heat of trials. In spite of the challenge of each season, the harvest is eventually reaped. However, the fruits that come forth must be the extension of the Vine of Jesus Christ.[8]

It is God's desire to take the barren wilderness of man's heart and soul and make it into a wondrous garden. In this garden, we, as believers, are being planted as trees by the rivers of water. As His saints, we will be established in righteousness for the purpose of bringing forth acceptable fruit.[9]

In this garden are a variety of flowers. These flowers point to us as His saints, reflecting the glory of our Lord as the fragrance of His life in us reaches the throne of God. Although the outward beauty of our flesh will eventually fade, as the inward beauty will be constantly renewed and established by the working of the Holy Spirit. It is in this garden of our hearts that sweet communion takes place.[10]

Once the husbandman has established His garden in our inner man, we must pull up our sleeves and put our shoulders to the plough. God is calling us to be co-laborers with Him in the harvest field of humanity. His whole goal for working in the harvest field of our lives is to bring forth fruit. This fruit points to the very life of Christ being multiplied in others.

The Apostle Paul talked about how some servants plant the seeds of Jesus' life through the preaching of the Gospel and how others water the seeds through the work of making disciples. The key to being fruit-

---

[7] Song of Solomon 4:16; Jeremiah 4:3-4; Matthew 13:1-23; 1 Corinthians 6:9
[8] John 15:1
[9] Psalms 1:3; Proverbs 11:30; Song of Solomon 4:12, 16
[10] Psalms 103:14-1; Isaiah 58:11; 2 Corinthians 2:15-16; 3:18; 4:16; James 4:14; 1 Peter 1:24

bearing Christians is that others will become attracted to Jesus by the fruit of our lives.[11]

There is a debate over who is the Bride of Christ. Some believe it will be Israel, while others believe it is the Church. Jesus told the disciples that He was preparing a place for them.[12] According to the culture at that time, those who were espoused were considered married. However, the bridegroom had to first prepare a place for his bride before the marriage could be consummated. It was the father of the bridegroom who decided when this place was acceptable for the bridegroom to bring his bride home.

It is obvious that, as the heavenly matchmaker, the Holy Spirit has sought out those who will become part of the Body. He has wooed all who have been drawn to the Son by exalting Him, leading saints into all truth about His character and commitment. He has been sanctifying them with the linen clothes of righteousness.[13]

The debate over this issue of the Bride of Christ may prove to be unprofitable. The marriage supper of the Lamb will take place. Clearly, the Church is the Body; therefore, the Body is going to be where the Head is. Right now the Head is not physically present, but, one day, Jesus is going to come for His Church. Whether He comes in the capacity of the Head or the Bridegroom, we, as believers, will be raised up with resurrection power to meet Him in the air.[14]

We know that, as Jesus' Body, His Word is cleansing us. We also know that only those wearing the proper garments will attend this most important supper.[15] Whether we are at the wedding supper of the Lamb because we are His Body or because we are part of the Bride, or both positions are intertwined together will probably seem immaterial when we are actually in His presence. We will simply rejoice because, as our Head, we will clearly be united with Him once and for all. And, if Israel solely serves as the Bride, we will be rejoicing that all matters have been completed according to the covenant and plan of the Father.

Obviously, the Church must humbly submit to this glorious preparation that must take place. All weddings have invitations and the marriage supper of the Lamb is no exception. There is an invitation that has gone out, and each person needs to accept it. Hear the invitation, "And the Spirit and the bride say, Come. And let him that heareth say, Come. And let him that is athirst come. And whosoever will, let him take the water of life freely" (Revelation 22:17).

Those of the Church must daily come to the source of life to be refilled, refreshed, and renewed. They must come to Jesus and partake of the Living Water that will constantly spring up into eternal life. As part

---

[11] Luke 9:62; John 15:5-8; 1 Corinthians 3:6-8; Galatians 5:22-23
[12] John 14:1-3
[13] John 16:13-14; Romans 15:16
[14] 1 Thessalonians 4:13-18; Revelation 19:7-10.
[15] Matthew 22:10-14; Ephesians 5:26-27

of the Body, we must each sit at the table of communion and partake of the divine nature of Jesus to be established in His life by faith. We must come to be washed by the water of the Word and cleansed from all unrighteousness by His blood.[16]

Today many of God's sheep are being scattered because they cannot hear the voice of the Shepherd. They desire to come to the Living Water, but they encounter dry wells and muddied water. There are many invitations, but the tender voice and signature of the Spirit is missing. Therefore, the sheep continue to seek for the Shepherd who will lead them up the paths of righteousness to the still waters that renew and the green pastures that they are able to feed upon.[17]

This brings us to what distinguishes the real Church of Jesus from the counterfeits. It is alive. It is not an indifferent building, system, denomination, or doctrine. It is a living organism. It lives because of the Spirit that inspires and leads and the liberating truth that establishes it upon the immovable Rock. After all, it is the Spirit who leads believers to all truth about Jesus, who will show the Church the things to come for preparation, and who serves as the true teacher to the Body.[18] Although the flame of life might appear weak in some of the Church and the resolve of some to cling to the Rock may be questionable, the Church lives. It has the eternal flame within it and the eternal Rock of ages to keep it.

The Church lives, and, one day, this extraordinary Body will be brought forth in the unhindered glory of the One who purchased her. There will be no doubt about her existence, witness, flame, or foundation. Her existence will be unveiled in His glory, her witness will be confirmed in a future reign with her Lord, her flame will become a consuming fire in light of His judgment, and her foundation will be standing when all others crumble as shifting sand beneath the storms of God's wrath.

The question is are you part of this living organism? If not, you need to receive the life of Jesus. You do this by humbling yourself before God, and saying a heart-felt prayer similar to this one.

Lord Jesus, You are the Son of the Living God, the Christ. You came in the flesh to meet all of us in our sinful, hopeless plight. In fact, You have invited all of us to come to You to receive Your life. I know I am a sinner separated from You, but I know You gave Your life so that I could live. I now come to You in need of forgiveness and salvation. Forgive me for my sins and have mercy upon my soul. Show me Your grace by giving me the gift of eternal life. By faith I accept Your pardon, in order to receive Your life, knowing that from this day forth I am a new creature,

---

[16] John 4:10-14; 7:37-39; Ephesians 5:26; 2 Peter 1:3-4
[17] Psalm 23:1-3; John 10:1-11
[18] John 16:13; 1 John 2:27

walking away from the old towards the new to receive all that You have for me. Amen.

2

A BIT OF HISTORY

As my family and friends know, I am not a professional historian. However, I believe one has to understand history in order to realistically evaluate the present with the intention of making sound decisions in light of the future. Therefore, it is important to consider the history of the Church in order to understand what has happened to it over the past two thousand years.

In order to think about the history of the Church, we need to regard it from the perspective of what has influenced or challenged it over the years. Obviously, we are not going to be caught up with dates, but with events or incidents that have challenged or changed its state.

This brings us to what must always be kept in mind in order to understand what happened to the Church, and that is the environment or disposition of the Church. Environment will determine the weaknesses and strengths of something. For example, the Church was persecuted off and on for the first two hundred years. After years of persecution, the believers were weary. Although much of the Church had been refined through the persecution, its members wanted some relief or deliverance from the unpredictable waves of persecution that would come upon them. When Constantine supposedly had his vision that inspired him to make the whole known world Christian, the believers saw it as an answer to prayer. After all, the members were weary of withstanding the attacks from religion and the world.

However, Constantine was a test and not an answer to prayer. The Christian life is not legislated through declarations or laws, nor does it exist through some type of force or association, such as we see in the case of extreme, violent Islam practices. Rather, Christians are born again from above. Such individuals must be drawn by the Father, hear and receive the invitation of the Son, and be convicted by the Holy Spirit about their need for salvation due to sin.[1] As one can see, this is a spiritual preparation that is done from above and not from worldly, fleshly, or legal attempts that come from man's best attempts to right the wrongs of the present world according to his personal take on matters.

Sadly, we see the same attempts taking place today. There are Christians who are trying to stop the moral decline of this nation through political avenues. However, this is clearly the world's way and not God's. We can see this in the case of Babylon. The Israelites were told they

---

[1] John 3:3, 5; 6:44; 7:37; 16:7-11

needed to make their homes in godless Babylon because they would be in exile for 70 years. However, they were to pray for peace for the city in which they were held captive. As Christians, we are told to pray for the leaders that we may also lead a quiet and peaceable life in all godliness and honesty. Clearly, as Christians, we do not have a mandate to become political activists. Don't get me wrong, we have a voice in the voting booth, but we need to be realistic about where our power and influence will rest. It will be on bended knees in our prayer closets, humbly seeking forgiveness and mercy for the wretched state of this nation and the professing Church.[2]

Many in America also believe we are a Christian nation that God will somehow preserve and honor. This is not true. Keep in mind that God allowed His city, Jerusalem, and His temple to be destroyed because of sin. Granted, people such as Daniel and Ezekiel survived, but they were taken into captivity to serve foreign leaders.[3]

It is true that much of America is founded upon Judeo-Christian principles, which also makes it more accountable to the spiritual condition to which it succumbs. However, just because the establishment of our nation's foundation was influenced by those who understood that God's blessings were necessary for this nation to survive does not make it Christian. The identifying mark of Christianity that must be seen is meant to identify individuals to the unseen kingdom of God. Granted, leaders set a tone for the moral attitude of a nation and the people are to maintain the integrity of it, but the term "Christian" describes individuals.

The mark that sets Christians apart and identifies them with the kingdom of God is the seal of the Holy Spirit. This seal identifies each of us as believers to an actual inheritance and endowment that will only be fully realized in light of the fullness of redemption and eternity. Since the Holy Spirit is the identifying mark, we must recognize that He can only be discerned spiritually, not recognized from the basis of the natural man.[4]

This brings us back to what happened to the Church in the fourth century. It was simple. Under the auspice of Constantine, it was organized into a religious system. This may not seem like a terrible blow to the Church, but, in a way, it was the beginning of the Church experiencing an identity crisis. In fact, the seeds that were planted ultimately produce what we now know as the Roman Catholic Church.

The Church that Jesus died for was to function according to its Head, Jesus, and was to be led by the Holy Spirit in all spiritual matters. The members of this Body were to be fitted together by the Spirit according to the eternal plan of the Father. The idea of organizing this Body would appear to be quite logical to bring order. However, the order of the true Body of Christ was and is dependent upon it being in sync with the Head in its functions and responsibilities. If the Body is acting contrary to the

---

[2] 2 Chronicles 7:14; Jeremiah 25:11; 29:4-7; 1 Timothy 2:2-3
[3] Deuteronomy 28:36-37;
[4] 1 Corinthians 2:11-14; Ephesians 1:11-14; 1 John 2:20

Head, it will eventually discover that it is out of order, and it will become sick with ineffectiveness.

The question is how do you organize a living Body whose very life and functions are dependent on the Head and Spirit? You don't. All you can do is ensure the order of the present surroundings in order to establish a certain environment in which the Body can be properly influenced in the right way.

When man organizes a matter, it is often to control it in order to influence it according to his agendas. Clearly, such organization is meant to influence the minds of those who come under the auspice of such an association. In other words, such organizations will end up setting the premise of how people will perceive, evaluate, or judge a matter.

Until the fourth century, the Church may have faced persecution, but the members understood that they were an extension of the Head. They worshipped in one accord in places such as homes and catacombs. They would come together to partake of God's Word and commune together. They edified one another, as well as tarried before God in prayer. Such meetings were personal. After all, when one member of the Body suffered, the whole Body shared in that member's suffering. This is why the Apostle Paul talked about weeping with those who weep and rejoicing with those who were rejoicing.[5]

When you consider that many Christians start from the premise of an organized church, you can begin to understand why the real identity of the Church is shrouded in confusion. Granted, we as Christians may know intellectually that the Church of Jesus is made up of blood-bought saints, but such understanding does not serve as the premise by which we naturally judge a matter. Without the right premise from which to evaluate the real makeup of the Church, we, as believers, will never possess a true revelation of it in our spirit.

It is important for us to understand that, when the Church comes under the auspice of man, whether it is through an organized effort or system, it becomes disconnected from the Head. Without this vital connection, the Body cannot function, and it will eventually lose all sense of its heavenly identity and inner life.

When you consider the apostles of the new Church, their main goal was to connect each member to the headship of Christ. The Apostle Paul instructed the Corinthian believers to follow him as he followed Christ. The Apostle Peter wrote to the Christians, reminding them of their humble beginnings. He told the pastors to humbly feed the sheep in light of facing the Chief Shepherd when He appears for His Body.[6]

If you are a Christian, the question is, are you connected to the Head? Is your life and purpose being inspired and motivated by love and devotion towards Jesus Christ? If it isn't, you are most likely feeling restless in your soul. You will sense something is missing, but you

---

[5] Romans 12:15-16; 1 Corinthians 12:12, 26-27
[6] 1 Corinthians 11:1; 1 Peter 5:1-4; 2 Peter 1:4-12

cannot quite figure it out. After all, you possibly go to church, pay tithes, and do good works, but none of it is really satisfying. In your mind, you are doing everything you can to be a good Christian, and yet it all appears to be empty. It simply does not make any sense.

Be sure to continue on to the next chapter to discover what could be missing from your spiritual life.

3

WHAT IS MISSING?

In the last chapter, we touched a bit on the history of the Church. It is important to note that the initial challenge for the new Church was to ensure the integrity and completion of God's Word. According to David W. Bercot in his book entitled *Will the Real Heretics Please Stand Up,* the leaders of this new Church had to wade through the heretical writings that were claiming validity and authority with the writings of such godly leaders as John, Peter, and Paul. As a result, the leaders of this new Body had to wade through the endless parade of counterfeit writings and letters. Sadly, the professing Church, which is quite visible and popular today, has embraced some of these very writings that the early fathers of the new Church clearly rejected and labeled as heretical.

These leaders had to become Bereans and test the spirit of these writings to see if they were in agreement with the complete spirit and intent of what had already been established as truth according to Scripture.[1] In order to ensure that the spirit lined up to the truth of God, these writings had to uphold and maintain the character and work of God. In order to make sure that they came into line with the intent of God's examples and plan of redemption, they had to uphold the will and ultimate purpose of God towards His people.

The new Church understood that these counterfeits were after the minds of the vulnerable sheep of God. Once these heretical claims or teachings took the mind into captivity, the heart, with its devotion and affections, would naturally follow. In a sense, these leaders were fighting to maintain the integrity of the faith that was first entrusted to them by the first apostles of the new Church. No doubt, it was an intense battle that they could not and would not lose. After all, the Spirit would identify what He inspired, and the grace of God would give those committed saints entrusted with such a grave responsibility the necessary favor to see this solemn challenge through to the end.[2]

Within the first four centuries the Word of God had been established. In fact, the Church was in agreement with its validity and the type of authority it had to have in its life and function as the Body of Christ. As clearly stated within Scripture, it had to serve as the milk and meat to the

---

[1] Acts 17:10-12
[2] 2 Timothy 2:16; 2 Peter 1:19-21

very growth and survival of the Body.³ It is hard to ignore the statement that Jesus made to Satan in the wilderness during His temptation, "It is written, Man shall not live by bread alone, but by every word that proceedeth out of the mouth of God" (Matthew 4:4b).

When Constantine came on the spiritual scene in A. D. 313, after he supposedly became a Christian, his vision to make his empire Christian, no doubt, appeared to be a Godsend to the battle-weary Body. As persecuted Christians, their sincere desire would be to seek a place of peace and liberty in which they could truly worship God. It seemed simple enough, but such relief usually comes with a price. For example, the children of Israel had to be led out into the barren wilderness to worship God. For the pilgrims that first settled America, they had to give up what little they had in their present lives to pursue a new land of spiritual hope and opportunity to truly worship God. When they finally reached America after weeks of unbearable conditions and terrible storms, half of them lost their lives due to the adverse conditions that confronted them in the new land.

The problem with being offered something that appears to be too good to be true is that the intentions and hopes may be good, but the end results may be devastating. There is always some type of price attached to such presentations. The price attached to the concept that there could be a Christian empire was that it was nothing but a lie that was based on wishful thinking.

No doubt, my statement might surprise some of you. It may seem foreign to you, but the Word of God will bear it out. What many in the professing Church have forgotten is that we, as believers, make up a separate kingdom in this world, just as Israel makes up a separate nation. The Apostle Paul stipulated that we are citizens of heaven. We happen to represent this kingdom in this present world in the official capacity of ambassadors.[4]

The Apostle Peter referred to the Church or Body as a holy nation who was peculiar or special because its members belonged to God. Clearly, those who are members of this Body make up a kingdom that resides in the midst of other nations and kingdoms. This kingdom has one king over it. His name is Jesus Christ. The walls of buildings and the borders of this present world cannot contain this unseen kingdom that is realized in the hearts of believers and is universal in scope.[5]

Jesus said of His kingdom, "My kingdom is not of this world; if my kingdom were of this world, then would my servants fight, that I should not be delivered to the Jews; but now is my kingdom not from here" (John 18:36b). Jesus was not saying that His kingdom was not *in* the world; rather, He was making it quite clear that it was not *of* the world. In other words, it would not belong to the world, be like the world, or have

---

[3] Hebrews 5:11-14
[4] 2 Corinthians 5:20; Philippians 3:20
[5] Mark 4:30-32; Luke 17:20-21; 1 Peter 2:9

any part or agreement with the world. His kingdom would function separately from the nations of the world.

This brings us back to the lie that a nation or a kingdom of the world could be Christian. There may be Christian roots and foundations, which identifies the nation to a spiritual heritage or influence, but there is only one god and ruler that greatly influences the systems of this present world. We know this god and ruler to be Satan, not Jesus. Granted, Jesus is coming back to rule over the nations of the world as King. The knowledge of the Lord will fill the earth at this time, and there will be both a moral and spiritual accountability that will discipline and bring all conduct into order. However, He does not rule over America as king, nor does He rule over any other nation of the world in this capacity, including Israel. Nations can be associated with the Judeo-Christian principles that can be seen in their laws and in honorable practices, but it does not necessarily make them Christian.

It has already been established that the unseen seal of the Spirit identifies believers with heaven. However, Jesus reigning in our hearts as Lord and King is what will visibly identify us with the kingdom of God. Christians are not only subject to Jesus as King in an official capacity, but He is also Lord. This means that they belong to Him and are called to be servants in His household.

With this understanding in mind, we can now begin to explore what happened to the Church. When the beleaguered Christians were willing to come under the auspice of a national leader, I am sure they did not understand the implications of their agreement. They were weary, meaning that their patience had been worn down. Sometimes such weariness will cause people to put down their guard when something that has the appearance of a viable solution is presented to them. We can probably conclude that they did not see themselves as giving up their autonomy under Christ to a worldly government. Perhaps, they saw themselves as simply supporting a Christian leader who was going to ensure their liberty to serve and worship God without fear of persecution.

We also might conclude that these believers did not see themselves as coming into agreement with any aspect of the world. However, Constantine may have been a professing Christian due to his vision, but, according to history, he did not live it. He was involved in immoral and abominable acts, which included the murder of family members. Based on the fruits of his attitude and conduct, we must consider whether he was simply Christian in name or association only.

Since Constantine was a leader over an empire, how would he institute the concept of a Christian nation or empire? After all, there were many pagans in his empire. He also held to some of those questionable religious practices and beliefs that had been part of his old pagan influences and practices. According to E. H. Broadbent, in his book *The Pilgrim Church*, some of these beliefs and practices that Constantine held to can be traced back to the "Old Catholic Church" that was formed by Cyprian in the first part of the third century. Therefore, how would this ruler bring Christian influences together with idolatrous, pagan inspired beliefs and practices, while making them appear dutifully acceptable or a worthy addition to the masses? After all, Christians would consider those who were not of the faith as heathens or pagan in their practices. If there was any religion in the pagans' midst, it would be deemed idolatrous. Like many of the people today who hold to their old ways, such individuals generally do not care what belief others hold to, but they have no intention of giving up their own particular way of thinking or living.

Consider this environment. Constantine did not have an easy task. You cannot convince someone to be a Christian against his or her will. Such people may comply outwardly, while holding onto their old ways inwardly. They may appear honorable, but these individuals are still on their way to hell.

There was a similar situation in Samaria. The Assyrian army came into Israel and brought the people of Israel to their knees in utter defeat. The people of Israel were dispersed throughout the empire while Assyria brought in people from other areas to settle Samaria. These people brought their gods and culture with them. However, the God of Israel was not pleased. He sent lions among them to slay them. The Creator of the universe clearly gained the attention of the inhabitants of Samaria. The inhabitants went to the king of Assyria and asked for the priest of Jehovah to be sent to them to teach them the manner of the God of Israel. As the story goes, a priest came. These people gladly took the information and instituted it into their different forms of idol worship. Needless to say, they defiled the things of God, but, in their minds, it was a way of keeping peace with Him.[6]

For Constantine to maintain the vision he was given by the Christian God, as well as keep his authority and influence upon all the organizations and activities, there had to be some compromise. In such matters as these, what will be compromised? It is simple—the environment. This is when the first organized church came into being. Buildings were built for such an occasion. This allowed control over the religious activities of the masses. But, what would you do with the idolatrous or pagan ways of those who had power and influence? You simply cover them up with what would appear as religious rituals or activities. Although Christianity is about change occurring within, in this type of environment, a person could comply outwardly while maintaining his or her former idols and pagan practices. Perhaps some would even get "good saved," but, nevertheless, there was compromise occurring.

The stronger Christians, no doubt, maintained their level of sincere worship, but there was a mixture developing. There were people who were pagan inwardly with their idols that simply took the God of Christianity and instituted Him into their idolatrous and pagan ways. Sadly, the term "Christian" was also being attached to these practices to keep everyone happy. The problem with attaching the term "Christian" to

---

[6] 2 Kings 17:4-33

an idolatrous or pagan way is that it will eventually begin to desensitize or spiritually dull God's people to what is holy and what is profane.

We can clearly see this taking place in America. The term, "Christian" has been hijacked by many religions. The reason for this is because there is no clarity or distinction as to what really constitutes genuine Christianity. The visible Church is so full of the world that it has lost its edge and distinct identity. As a result, people perceive if you are religious, somewhat moral, and a freedom-loving patriot, that you are a Christian. The truth is such individuals will possess an unholy mixture that may appear religious and decent according to the world, but the only identifying factor of the Christian life is missing. This point of identification is the divine presence and life of Jesus Christ.

When you bring the holy and unholy together, you will compromise the spirit that is in operation in the environment. Most people do not realize that there is a spirit in operation in the world, the church, and the home. This is why we are instructed to test the spirits. We know that the spirit of the world works disobedience in those who are motivated by it. This spirit is not only clearly in operation in the world, but it is very prevalent in many homes as man often operates according to the independence of his own natural spirit. However, for the religious scene, it is the antichrist spirit that operates from a fleshly and worldly platform. This spirit is very religious, but its main work is to become a substitute for the real Jesus by replacing Him with dead religion, worldly and heretical beliefs, and lifeless activities.[7]

The Bible is clear that God has not given us the spirit of the world. He not only gives born-again believers a new heart, but He also gives them His Spirit. The Holy Spirit will have no part in any belief or practice where there is a mixture of the holy with the unholy. He will not move on or in such an environment.

The Spirit of God is within the believer, but He is also the connection between the Head who is sitting on the right hand of God and the Body of believers. In other words, He not only moves within the believer, but He must move upon the believer and the Body as the rivers of Living Water from the throne of God. This is how the Holy Spirit ensures His presence in the midst of His people. He does this for the purpose of building the Body up into the Head. It is through this connection with the throne of God that He fills or refreshes the believer and the Body, as well as brings forth wisdom and revelation.[8]

If the Holy Spirit encounters any compromise or unholy agreement within the environment, He will immediately be quenched. For the Spirit to be quenched means there is no point of communion or edification in which the members of the Church can get their spiritual bearings and come into real fellowship together.

---

[7] Proverbs 25:27-28; Ephesians 2:2; 4:13-16; Colossians 2:2-8; 1 John 4:1
[8] Genesis 1:2; John 7:37-39; 16:13; 1 Corinthians 3:12; Ephesians 1:17; 3:3-5; 4:15-16; 5:18

The Spirit will end up being grieved by the sin of unbelief that will begin to operate in such an atmosphere, as man-influenced beliefs, rituals, experiences, or practices begin to replace the validity of the Word. As a result, He will depart and, since the Holy Spirit is the source of life in the Body of Christ, the heavenly connection and power from above will subtly evaporate out of the environment, leaving a spiritual vacuum.[9]

For those who are truly Christians, this type of environment will eventually cause restlessness in their souls. They sense something is missing, but they cannot always figure out what is absent. Perhaps Christ is being preached, and the buildings might be full of people that never before named the name of Christ. Perhaps there are many religious activities going on, making it all seem quite successful. However, something is missing.

What is missing is the Holy Spirit. According to Isaiah 30:1, He is to serve as our only covering. However, such unholy compromises will bring people under a wicked covering that will prevent the heavenly connection from ever being made. In fact, this covering or veil will blind people to the real Gospel.[10]

Now that the Spirit is missing, what will replace Him and His work in the Church? It is important that we realize every vacant environment or spot in our lives must be filled with something.[11] As you will discover in the next chapter, such an environment places the members of the Body of Christ in a precarious position. It is a position that will not only cause restlessness in the spirit, but will bring them to a dangerous crossroads in which a decision will be required.

---

[9] 1 Samuel 16:14; Romans 10:17; 2 Corinthians 13:14; Ephesians 4:30; 1 Thessalonians 5:19
[10] Isaiah 25:7; 2 Corinthians 4:3-6
[11] Matthew 12:43-45

4

THE REPLACEMENT

What happens when the Holy Spirit is missing from the environment? Once again, we must be reminded that environments influence our attitudes toward God and life. Our attitudes will determine what we expose ourselves to, as well as the agendas and values we develop along the way.

As you consider Christianity, you must realize that it is a way of life that is meant to influence every aspect of our mindsets, attitudes, agendas, and priorities. As a result, it will determine our approach to matters and our conduct in regard to our different responsibilities.

It is vital that we have the connection of heaven, the Holy Spirit, moving within us and upon us. He is the one who informs us of the matters of heaven through wisdom, knowledge, and revelation. He will warn us of things to come in order to prepare us for future events. To ensure and adhere to this connection of heaven means that we must follow after the Spirit in order to do what is right before God, we must be led by the Spirit in order to do what is honorable and reasonable in our Christian conduct, and we must walk in the Spirit to ensure that we are within the will of God in all matters of devotion and service.[1]

When the Holy Spirit is missing from the environment, a believer could basically find him or herself in what could be considered a comfort zone. In this zone, there is nothing that is clearly right or wrong, but there is also nothing really happening in the spiritual realm. As one considers such an environment, there is no real detection that there is something blatantly wrong in one's lifestyle or relationship with God. In fact, the Christian appearance is still intact. However, such a state is referred to as lukewarm. According to the Bible, this is a very dangerous state to be in. There will be no sharpness in which discernment is maintained, fine-tuned, or developed. Without discernment, a believer will not be aware of what is really going on in his or her environment. Without the sharpness of discernment, Christians can actually come into agreement with the unholy without any sense that a terrible error has been made.[2]

The other problem is that it is a natural tendency for the selfish disposition of the old man to rise up its head and subtly gain

---

[1] John 16:13; Ephesians 1:17; 3:3-5; Colossians 2:3; Romans 8:1, 13-14; Galatians 5:16

[2] 1 Corinthians 2:9-14; Revelation 3:14-18

preeminence in such a state, bringing the person under the influence of the spirit of the world. Without discernment, a believer will not even be aware that he or she is sliding into a slime pit of his or her old ways. This is why the Apostle Paul admonished those who are asleep to awake from the influences of darkness upon their lives.[3]

An environment in which the Spirit is missing can be related to the popular example of a pot of water with a frog in it. Of course, in the compromising state of complacency, the believer is the frog. The fire is turned on under the pot, but it is done in such a way that it is slowly being brought to a boil. Since the frog is initially adjusting to the change, it is unaware of the precarious position it is in.

Sadly, the unholy compromise that took place in the fourth century between the man's version of religion and the Church put the Church in a pot of water. Without knowing it, the fire of influence and compromise has been slowly turned up, taking away the discernment and life of the professing Church. It is now important to identify this pot of water. In fact, as you study the big struggle between the professing Church and the watchmen, you will see that this is a common denominator that is brought out in their warnings. The pot is the world.

Any time you add the unholy (the ways and philosophies of the world) to the holy (the ways of God), the end result will be carnal or fleshly. It may be a comfortable compromise for those who are trying to live in peace with the different aspects of the world, but, as believers in the Body of Christ, the real edge has been compromised. That edge is the presence, power, and working of the Spirit. Instead of being distinct, the believer or Church is now giving up his or her connection to the Head to come under the spirit of the world in the name of compromise, tolerance, and self-preservation.[4]

In his book *You Will Receive Power*, William Law stated that the real sin of all sins, or the heresy of all heresies comes down to the influence and power of the worldly spirit. It is not unusual to minimize the agreement or power the spirit of the world has even on believers, but as Law pointed out, it is the great apostasy from God and the life He wants to bring forth in and through His saints. The spirit of the world is not simply a sin that finds its basis in unbelief or idolatry; rather, it represents the essence of the disposition of sin that works in us. Every sin is a branch that finds its source in or influenced by the spirit of the world.[5]

The spirit of the world causes us to replace the best or the excellent goodness and ways of God with what seems right, acceptable, and nominal to the world. However, as Law pointed out, to depart one degree from God's goodness means you are departing into evil. To choose or

---

[3] Ephesians 5:14-17
[4] 2 Corinthians 6:14-18; Ephesians 2:2; James 4:4
[5] pg. 137

embrace any other life but that which comes from God is to choose the ways of death.[6]

The spirit of the world will call for reformation to the self-life, but the Holy Spirit requires us to deny the self-life. The world offers the self-life happiness, but the Spirit and the Word of God reveals that the self-life is void of being satisfied and must be put down in order to discover real life. As Law pointed out in his book, the self-life is the whole essence of our fallen disposition, but denial of self is our capacity to be saved and humility is our savior.[7]

Surely, the Christians of the fourth century had no intention of giving up their edge, but the reality is that the spirit of the world came into the midst of the professing Church. From the basis of this unholy compromise, the world began to influence the mind of the professing Church with each subtle compromise of its idolatrous or pagan beliefs or philosophies.[8]

As the environment of the professing Church changed, the worldview of it began to change as well. In other words, the world was now influencing how the visible Church would view the world around it. The lines between good and evil became blurred.

It is important to point out that every leader of the new Church struggled with this very issue. The Head of the Body, Jesus, warned that, since the world hated Him, it would hate those who are His followers. He than gave this warning in Luke 6:26, "Woe unto you, when all men shall speak well of you! For so did their father to the false prophets." There are those in the professing Church who believe they must keep peace with the world. However, such compromise will bring them into a state of utter sorrow, despair, and judgment. After all, the world will truly hate those who are followers of Jesus because they do not belong to the world, nor will they have any part in it.[9]

When you consider the writings of the New Testament, it is full of admonishment to believers to come out and be separate from the world. James told us that those who love the world are spiritual harlots, and they will find themselves considered enemies of God. The Apostle John warned us the world will pass away, but those who do the will of God will live forever. The Apostle Paul instructed believers to come out and be separate from that which is contrary to the Spirit of God and the leadership of Christ. After all, there can be no such agreement between the Christian and the pagan ways of the world's idolatry, philosophies, and perverted practices. [10]

Finally, there is the soulful reality that some believers not only fail to consecrate themselves totally to God, but they go back to their former

---

[6] Ibid
[7] Ibid, pg. 80
[8] Colossians 2:8
[9] John 7:7; 17:14-16
[10] 2 Corinthians 6:14-18; James 4:4; 1 John 2:15-17

lives that they had in the world. We have the examples of the disciples who were offended by the truth, and, from that time on, they went back and walked no more with Jesus. There was also a man by the name of Demas. He was part of the Apostle Paul's ministry team. His name is recorded in Paul's letters.[11] However, the apostle made this mention of him in his last letter, "For Demas hath forsaken me, having loved this present world, and is departed unto Thessalonica..." (2 Timothy 4:10a).

The world is very alluring when it comes to the self-life, with all of its fleshly appetites. This is the platform the world uses to gain our dependency upon it. It knows how to attract our pride to gain our loyalty and support. Its clever propaganda is designed to convince us that it is the real source of our hope in finding happiness and purpose. The world's false glory gains the attention of our eyes so we will pursue its deceptive beauty, rather than the glories of heaven. As we become entangled in its destructive web, we begin to discover that its seductive ways only lead to emptiness and bondage and that its attractions result in a freefall into utter despair and defeat. The propaganda of the world leaves us depressed and skeptical, while its beauty becomes bitterness to the soul.

The reality of the world is that it has no life to offer. It has a façade, or semblance of life and false promises in regard to an idea or image of life, but there is no real life in any of it. In fact, behind this idea of life, is a vacuum that proves to be dark and hollow. For this reason, the Apostle Paul stated that he was crucified to the world, and it was crucified to him. Obviously, the world had no more power to influence or attract him into its destructive web.[12]

The Apostle Paul's attitude towards the world was the result of him being realistic about the value and worth of the world. He actually counted his activities associated to the flesh, his earthly heritage as a Jew, and his misdirected devotion to the Law as dung. He realized all temporary pleasure, honor, and sacrifice was a complete loss in light of gaining the very treasure of heaven, Jesus Christ.[13] Paul's attitude reminds us of the challenge put forth by Jesus to all of His followers, "For what is a man profited, if he shall gain the whole world, and lose his own soul? Or what shall a man give in exchange for his soul" (Matthew 16:26)?

What is your soul worth to you? What is my soul worth to me? God estimated the cost of our souls and gave His only begotten Son in our place on the cross. Jesus estimated the cost of our souls and offered up His life on our behalf. But we must also personally estimate the worth of our souls. If we value the world, we will sacrifice our souls to possess what is temporary and what already stands judged. On the other hand, the cost to possess our souls for the purpose of presenting our bodies as

---

[11] John 6:66; Colossians 4:14; Philemon 24
[12] Galatians 6:14
[13] Philippians 3:4-8

a living sacrifice, consecrated for the use, purpose, and glory of God will ultimately cost us our identification, agreement, and association with the world. We cannot possess the life of Christ and be in agreement with the spirit of the world at the same time. What is ultimately offered up will be based on the estimation we put on our own personal souls and ideas of life.

The struggle for saints to come out and be separate from the world is not new to God's people. We can see this same struggle in Israel's case. Egypt represented the world to the people of Israel. In the beginning, their presence as a foreign entity in Egypt seemed harmless. As time went on, these foreign people became a threat to Egypt. To control them, they were brought into bondage. The bondage made them slaves to a cruel taskmaster, and, as a result, they began to cry out to God in their oppression.[14]

God sent a deliverer by the name of Moses. Moses had to lead the children of Israel away from Egypt. But, before he could accomplish such a feat, all of the Egyptian's idols had to be humbled before the children of Israel. This was to show them that Jehovah God was the one and only true God of heaven and earth.

Clearly, God had to get a hold of the people's minds so that they could see the contrast between the lifeless idols and empty, pagan practices of the age they lived in to embrace the One who was and is the great I AM.[15] As the great I AM, God was and is the ever-present reality of the past, the present, and the future about the matters of life and death. The great "I AM" points to God as the essence of all wisdom, as He brings the lessons of the past into the present to change the outcome of the future.

The children of Israel had to be totally separated from the influences of Egypt for God to influence their minds and hearts. Behind such influence was the wisdom of the ages. This wisdom's main thrust was and always will be to bring forth God's promises and plan through His people. Since the people of Israel had been chosen out of the world, they needed to become a separate, holy people, consecrated unto Jehovah God for His work and glory.

Although the children of Israel came out of their present world, it did not come out of them. They brought the world with them. In other words, their affections were still tied to the world they had known. This is why they were quick to resort to pagan attitudes and practices when they worshipped the golden calf and complained about the manna that fell short of the variety of tastes they had experienced in Egypt.

Sadly, because of their affections that remained with their former existence, they never really developed reliance upon Jehovah God. Their submission to their former way of thinking resulted in judgment falling upon the generation of adults who came out of Egypt. The "old"

---

[14] Exodus 1:8-14; 2:23-25
[15] Exodus 3:14-15

generation would not enter the Promised Land, and the generation that finally entered the place God had promised to Abraham had no memories of Egypt, or the memories had been dimmed by their years in the wilderness.[16]

The world ceased to be a temptation to the children of Israel. As a result, they could embrace the blessings of God. However, the children of Israel were about to embark into the midst of the alluring seductions of the idols of the present world or age, along with their various unholy practices. Since the children of Israel were born into the Adamic race, these seductions would prove to be effective temptations to their carnal affections and youthful lusts.

God warned the people of Israel about coming into agreement with any aspect of the world. They were told to rid the land of the people that adhered to such profane worship and practices. Most of us should know the rest of the story. The children of Israel became slack in their responsibility to rid the land of any possible temptation or unholy agreement. As a result, they opened a door to the world, and the world came into their midst through the idols and pagan practices of the heathen people. Consider what was said about this open door,

> Know for a certainty that the LORD your God will no more drive out any of these nations from before you; but they shall be snares and traps unto you, and scourges in your sides, and thorns in your eyes, until you perish from off this good land which the LORD your God hath given (Joshua 23:13).

When you consider what is being said here, this open door to the world doomed the kingdom of Israel. It would take hundreds of years before Israel would come down in judgment because of its unholy agreements, but it would spend hundreds of years more in subjection to the heavy yokes and hatred of the world.

The world stands condemned. Therefore, everything that comes into agreement with it, is associated with it, or looks to it is condemned as well. At first, a relationship with the world may seem harmless enough, but it will slowly ensnare a person into its entanglements and trap him or her into its lies. Once a person is entrapped, the world will turn around to scourge a person for foolishly falling into its traps of deception, as well as blind him or her to the despair and depression that is engulfing his or her soul.

A good example of the destruction of the world is Lot's wife. She was taken out of the world (Sodom and Gomorrah) because of her association to Lot, who was vexed by the cities' spiritual condition. However, her affections were still loyal to the world. She looked back at it

---

[16] If you are interested in the spiritual lessons the children of Israel examples teach believers, see the book, *The Victorious Journey* in Volume Six of the foundational series.

as it was being judged and turned into a pillar of salt.[17] Hence enters a very important warning from Jesus in regard to following Him into a service of devotion and worship, "No man, having put his hand to the plough (to follow me), and looking back (to the world), is fit for the kingdom of God" (Luke 9:62b, parentheses added)

Every Christian is called to be completely separate from the world, but few choose to do so. As a result, few are chosen to enter into all that God has made available to His people. Clearly, Christians must choose to completely close that door to the world, which represents their former life. They must recognize that Jesus came to redeem their souls, but the world desires to enslave and destroy their souls. Therefore, they must choose whom they will serve, the God of heaven or the idols of this present world. They must decide who or what will influence their minds, the wisdom of heaven or the foolishness of this present age. They must decide who will claim the loyalty of their affections, the Head of the Church, Jesus Christ, or the god of this present world, Satan.[18]

Every day, Christians must deny self, neglect pride, hate evil, pick up their crosses, and follow Jesus. The world must not only be considered dung to believers, but dead, a vacant tomb of utter destruction that is void of any real hope of life.

What about you? What is your attitude toward the world? Has the door of its influence been completely shut down or is it still defining your life and values?

---

[17] Genesis 19:1-29; 2 Peter 2:6-8
[18] Matthew 6:24

> *Part II*
>
> # THE SHIFT FROM CENTER

5

THE OPEN DOOR

In the fourth century of the new Church, a door was opened that started the professing Church down a precarious path. The door that was opened was to the influences of the world. This allowed the spirit of the world to come into the midst of the Church.

As you follow the first three centuries of the Church, the message was consistent: "Come out from the world and be separate." One of the individuals who contended for the faith of the Christians in the second century was a man named Tertullian. He was born around A.D. 150. Even though Tertullian was fluent in Greek, he wrote most of his works in Latin in order to benefit the growing number of western Christians who only spoke Latin. He often developed Latin terminology to express truths that had been primarily presented in the Greek language. One of the most famous Latin terms that he coined to express the Godhead was the word "trinity."[1]

In Tertullian's writings, the world's influence upon the believers was one of the foremost issues he confronted. Many of the Christians were coming out from under or were still struggling with the strong influence of the Roman Empire. As you consider the rulers of Rome, you see that they emphasized greater entertainment for the masses in order to keep them happy and win their favor. As a result, people gladly sold their votes, as well as their souls to taste the many idolatrous and pagan flavors of this decadent society. One of those flavors included watching Christians' blood spilled in the Roman arenas in the name of sensational entertainment.

---

[1] A Glimpse at Early Christian Life; Tertullian, © 1991 by David W. Bercot, pgs. 1-2

On top of the entertainment was the extravagance of dress and food. Every tempting taste was presented, while the eyes of the people were being enlarged by the covetousness of the surrounding environment. Although the affairs of Rome sometimes challenged these people's unrealistic world of sensationalism, they always had a fix waiting for them around the corner or in the coliseums, where they watched and cheered for their latest hero as he faced death in the name of entertainment. Does this sound familiar?

If you conduct a serious, comparative study of the environment of Rome and the present environment of America, there is basically no difference. Granted, we Americans are a bit more "civilized" about the type of entertainment we will allow, but the same environment exists today. History is simply repeating itself. Like Rome, America is doomed by her own worldly, idolatrous, gluttonous, immoral, and decadent ways.

Meanwhile every true watchman of God will sound the same alarm. The door has been opened wide to the world, the gate of discernment has been let down in the Church, and now the enemy is not only in our midst, but is trying to invade every arena of our lives.

It is important to understand that, when a Christian is saved, he or she is given a new heart or disposition, but he or she still has the same tendencies. These tendencies are based on worldly mindsets and practices. As a result, the mind must be transformed in order to change the attitude.[2] Once the attitude is changed towards the world's influences, the tendencies or habits will also change.

As Christians, we must understand that being saved places us above the world in heavenly places with Christ. But the world is not completely out of us. Because of our initial premise of being a Christian, which is fleshly, we only can know in part. We also see in part because we are still looking through the "glass" of the world.[3] The world includes such influences as religion, culture, worldly relationships, philosophies, and practices. Therefore, much of our understanding is based on what we have been exposed to or have experienced in our flesh. It is from this worldly understanding or view that we naturally interpret what we see or encounter, including our spiritual understanding and experiences.

Since the world initially has a hold of our minds, it will own the lusts, appetites, or desires of our affections. As Christians, we must claim them back and redirect them in the right direction. To change such a perspective is not something that happens overnight. We must constantly discipline our thoughts and affections.[4] In fact, we must do an incredible juggling act between the two opposing kingdoms of darkness and light, which requires integrity and meekness on our part.

As Jesus' Body, we Christians will remain in this world, but we must cease to be part of it, for any agreement with it is spiritual fornication.

---

[2] Ezekiel 36:26-27; Romans 12:2; Hebrews 10:15-17
[3] Ephesians 2:6; 1 Corinthians 13:9, 12
[4] 2 Corinthians 10:3-5; Colossians 3:1-2

Remember the temptations that caused us to fall in the past are still present in the world we live in. Due to our tendencies to justify sin and satisfy our fleshly appetites, it is easy to give way to any old or new temptations that may come our way. This is why the Apostle Paul stated he counted all associations with the world as dung, and he became crucified to the world, and the world to him. He also stressed that he died daily and brought his body into subjection so that he would not be a castaway or reprobate in the end.[5]

Clearly, Paul understood that the world remained his enemy, even in his consecrated life before God. He had to maintain a right attitude at all times towards the world, as well as guard his affections and discipline his involvement and activities. James summarized the struggle in this manner, "But every man is tempted, when he is drawn away of his own lust, and enticed. Then when lust hath conceived, it bringeth forth sin; and sin, when it is finished, bringeth forth death" (James 1:14-15).

By the world being in the midst of the vulnerable Church, it now had the means to, once again, ensnare the Lord's sheep into its destructive web. The ways of the world are cleverly designed to appear as a Christian's solution when his or her spiritual guard is down. Although it is nothing more than a fanciful deception, it begins to wear down a person's resolve to maintain a spiritual and emotional discernment, as well as a physical separation. As he or she becomes more enticed by the possibilities of how the world is able to become his or her solution, it begins to rob the person of discernment. Eventually, with enough enticement, it can kill a person's ability to discern its influence, ultimately destroying any remaining resolve to stand against it.

In the end, the practices of the world will not seem evil to this individual, but logical. The attitude that was once firmly set against it will begin to adjust as it begins to see consecration as fanaticism, rather than one's reasonable service. Once the attitude is changed, it will mock any stand for truth and holiness that will not bend with the changing winds of the world that are blowing through Christendom.

It is clear that, as Christians, our initial attitude towards the world must be totally changed so we can unlearn the idolatrous ways and pagan practices of it. Often, unbeknown to us, these practices still have the power to influence our mindsets, attitudes, and tendencies. To unlearn the ways of the world means to change the value and importance it holds in our lives. To change our value system, we must expose ourselves to and learn the perfect and holy ways of God. Learning who God is will establish a proper attitude towards Him. However, this means getting into the Word of God in order for it to get into us to cleanse and transform the way we look at the world around us. We must seek godly fellowship, flee those things that appeal to youthful

---

[5] 1Corinthians 6:13-16; 9:27; 15:31; 2 Corinthians 10:3-5; Philippians 3:4-8; Colossians 3:1-2

Challenging the Christian Life

lust, and separate ourselves from the vain activities of the world, while pursuing what is righteous.[6]

This brings us back to what happened to the Church. The godly shepherds and watchmen of the Church were forever calling the sheep to come out of the world and be completely separate from all of its influence upon their minds and affections. This was the only way new believers would unlearn the ways of the world in order to implement the righteous ways of God in their attitudes and practices. There had to be an exchange. By separating from the world and unlearning its wicked ways, a person would have the liberty to separate unto God in total consecration.

By Christians separating from the world and unlearning its wicked ways to embrace the life of Jesus, they could develop an excellent spirit like Daniel possessed when he was in Babylon. Babylon was also idolatrous and decadent. However, Daniel had purposed in his heart to be upright before Jehovah God.[7] This allowed him to maintain His life in God in the midst of the idolatrous and unholy. He never came into agreement with it or submitted to the temptation as a means to keep peace with it. Jehovah God was his God and Lord, and he refused to compromise any of his relationship or life in God as a means to "get along" with the present age.

Daniel is one of the many examples in the Word of God that teaches us how to be in the world without becoming part of it. This is the main struggle between the Spirit and the flesh.[8] As Christians, we must not only find Christ in the midst of this confusing mess, but we must maintain a complete separation from it as a means to maintain our spiritual edge and witness in the midst of the world's great darkness.

The fourth-century Church had unknowingly opened the door to the world, which was now subtly coming into the midst of the believers. The Church had not come into agreement with the spirit of the world, but the gate of truth and discernment would be eventually let down, ultimately changing the face of the visible, professing Church.

Once the door to the world opened, the Holy Spirit lifted from such an environment, leaving a vacuum that would be filled by the spirit of the world with its many different influences. How would the world's influences upon the professing Church express itself?

The world operates according to systems. These systems organize people according to agenda, purpose, and vision. Since the world operates according to systems, it would not be hard for it to organize religion into a nice controllable box. Although the world operates according to systems, it is men's influences based upon worldly philosophies and practices within those systems that will determine how people will be organized.

---

[6] Deuteronomy 4:10; 18:9; 2 Timothy 2:15-16, 21-26
[7] Daniel 1:8; 6:3
[8] Galatians 5:16-17

Needless to say, the operations of this system will look very religious. It will claim its authority and rights according to its association with God and His Word. It will also advocate morality in action and goodness towards the brotherhood. However, since it is carnal and not spiritual, it will appeal to the emotions, pride, and decency of people. Such appeal will express itself in good works, but it will lack true spirit and life, making it a counterfeit of true Christianity.

Once the Holy Spirit is missing, man will step into the Spirit's place to serve as a conscience and interpreter of God's Word. It is important to point out that a religious system was very much in operation in Jesus' day. There had been a period of 400 years of silence (meaning there were no direct revelations from God through prophets) between the Old and New Testaments. The voice of God had once again been silenced due to sin and idolatry among His people.

When you study the history of the Jewish people, you can see the traumatic crisis that their faith suffered. There was one upheaval after another in the political and religious realms. In the midst of these constant struggles, a weaker group known as the Pharisees strived to tenaciously hold on to the Jewish Law, although they added various nonessential traditions to it. The name "Pharisee" was taken from a root word meaning "to separate".

On the other hand, there was another faction that added contemporary Grecian ways and customs to religious attitudes and practices. These particular Jews saw no real deliverance for Israel; therefore, they decided to make a covenant with the heathen. They sought out different ways in which to popularize their practices to make them acceptable to both worlds. These individuals became predecessors of the polished, but infidel, Sadducees.[9]

These two groups give us an insight into what happens when the Spirit of God is missing from the equation. The end result is two extremes that operate according to two distinct philosophies. In fact, the two great systems that were vying for the minds of the people during Paul's day were Stoicism and Epicureanism. The philosophy behind Stoicism is to live nobly and death will not matter. The philosophy behind Epicureanism is that all is uncertain, so, therefore, enjoy life to the fullness regardless of the moral implications.[10] Whether we want to admit it or not, most religions that are inspired by those who belong to this present world will fall under the attitude of one or the other of these philosophies.

The fruits easily identified the influences of these two worldly philosophies upon the minds of people. For example, since the Spirit was missing and not inspiring the Pharisees according to the life of God, they

---

[9] The Four Hundred Silent Years; H. A. Ironside; 16th printing 1980; Loizeaux Brothers, Inc. pgs. 32-33

[10] Lectures on Colossians; H. A. Ironside; 15TH printing, May 1978; Published by Loizeaux Brothers, Inc. pg. 73

held the truth in carnal or fleshly ways. These were, and are, the people who adjust the ways of God to their self-righteous conclusions, while neglecting the spiritual aspect or intent of God's ways. These people prove to be judgmental. The other group came into blatant agreement with the world. Their pursuit was according to the popularity of the world. We know that the Sadducees denied even the doctrine of the resurrection from the dead.[11]

There was also a third party that was present during Jesus' day. They were feeble and afflicted. They abhorred the ways of the heathen, while refusing to give way to the legal pretensions of those who were self-righteous and legalistic. They clung to God's Word and the promise of the coming Messiah. They became eventually known as the Essenes.[12] *Smith's Bible Dictionary* describes these three groups by referring to the Pharisees as Formalists, the Sadducees as the Freethinkers, and the Essenes as the Puritans.

In the midst of the struggle to maintain the purity of the Jewish faith during these four hundred years of silence between the Old and New Testaments, a few men of the priesthood, with the last name of Maccabeus, defied the worldly powers to be such as Antiochus. This started a revolution that cost many of the Jews their very lives because they openly refused to submit to the idolatrous ways being thrust upon them from those who were considered uncircumcised.[13]

However, this conflict went on for years, and even developed within the priesthood. Sadly, the door to the world was again opened when one of the religious leaders made a pact with the Roman Empire to bring some semblance of peace to the conflict that raged within the leadership of the Jewish priesthood. Once again, the people of God began to lose their edge due to the reality that the Spirit would not have any part in such an agreement.

When Jesus entered the worldly scene, the Pharisees and Sadducees were forces to be reckoned with. Although two distinct sects, they had influence in the political realm. When you consider Pilate, Jesus was offered as a peace offering to keep a semblance of peace with the religious leadership of the Jewish religion.

Compromising with that which is contrary to maintain some semblance of peace is a pattern that can be easily followed. However, it ultimately leads to destruction. We see this in the case of the end days, many will come under the destructive rule of an anti-Christ reign in the name of peace. This fragile peace will disrupt into utter chaos, death, and ruin.

To answer the question that was posed earlier in this chapter, how would the system of the world express itself through religion? It will

---

[11] Matthew 22:23-33; Hebrews 6:1-2
[12] The Four Hundred Silent Years; pg. 33
[13] Ibid, pgs. 46-47

express itself through carnality that does not properly handle the truth, or it will use the agreement with the world to promote its religious causes.

Can we not see this same state of affairs in today's professing Church? We either see the philosophy of harsh legalism that has no life in it, or we see the liberal philosophies and methods of the world being instituted into Christians' beliefs and practices. Whether we arrogantly refer to one extreme as being conservative and the other as being liberal, the Spirit is missing from both types of systems or philosophies. If the Spirit of God is not present, such religious attitudes and practices must be regarded as carnal.

Carnality is nothing more than man's best attempts to make him or herself acceptable to God. Such attempts are worldly in nature, but they have proven to be a successful means by which to clothe the world in some righteous garb and sell it as a bill of goods to the professing Church.

What does Scripture say about all of this? Isaiah 64:6 tells us that man's best is considered filthy rags to God. The Apostle Paul stated that the wrath of God will be revealed from heaven against those who hold the truth in any type of ungodliness and unrighteousness. We are also reminded that Jesus did not come to reconcile the systems of the world to Himself, but lost man. The world is already condemned, along with those who love and serve it. We also have Jesus' warning that it does not matter what great acts one might do in His name; if they are not according to the will of the Father, they will be considered iniquity.[14]

As you consider the history of God's people, you will realize that the greater the influence of the world upon their minds and hearts, the further away they slid from the center of that which was and remains to be true, pure, and holy. We know the center is God, and, when God is not our reality as believers, we become lost in the emptiness of religious acts and the ridiculousness of man's rules and conclusions.

What about you? Do you sense that much that goes on in Christendom is foolish and void of substance? If you answer yes to these two questions, then you need to know you are not alone. But you also must realize that it is up to each believer individually to come back to center, regardless of the environment, to develop an excellent spirit before God.

---

[14] Matthew 7:21-23; Romans 1:18; Ephesians 2:13-18

6

THE SHIFT IN LEADERSHIP

The world can only organize activities according to its systems. When the world came into the midst of the Church, man began to organize religion. Buildings were built to set up the environment that would control the activities of the professing Church. Leadership had to be defined in order to maintain the control or order that was being put forth. Practices were instituted to cause an appearance of righteous activities. Most of these practices were idolatrous and pagan. However, they were being repackaged and presented in the light of Christian titles and so-called "responsibilities".

When you follow the progression of the world's influence upon the Church, you can clearly see how everything in the true Church was redefined to fit the world's agendas and presentation. Let's face it; the world has been clearly trying to define the Church for centuries, rather than the Body of Christ being defined by the Head (Christ) and Spirit of God. As a result, the face of the visible Church has changed.

It is vital that we follow this progression to understand how Christians now possess a misconception about the real Church of Jesus Christ. The primitive Church was not visible due to persecution. The members did not always have set places where they came together in one accord. They had no recorded membership, other than that their names were written in the Book of Life. They did not stand out in the world as the greatest or most successful religion the world had ever seen; rather, they were to stand apart from the world in their hearts, mindsets, and lifestyle. It would be this distinction, not necessarily verbal claims, which would draw people to Jesus Christ. In such drawing, the simple Gospel would be shared and preached under the anointing, authority, and power of the Spirit.

The new Church had typical struggles. However, the members were clear about their commission and responsibility in light of the world. Their commission was to preach the Gospel and make disciples of Jesus. Their religious responsibility was to remain distinct from the world so that they could maintain their edge, authority, and power. This edge, authority, and power were necessary for them to fulfill their high calling in Christ Jesus in devotion, worship, and service.[1] Although the Church had practices that were clearly ordained in Scripture, its responsibility would

---

[1] James 1:27

also be clear. The members had to keep such practices from losing the simplicity of meaning and the inspirational power and life of the Spirit.

Sadly, man is a creature of habit due to the persuasion of his fleshly disposition and the persuasion of the world; therefore, he is not inclined or disciplined to maintain the connection to heaven. Because of this tendency, practices, such as communion, baptism, and the laying on of hands, were often reduced to lifeless rituals and ceremonies that lost their impact upon hearts and minds.[2]

Since the world came into the midst of the Church, the leadership had to be defined. Up until this point, the leadership of the Church was clearly in place. Jesus was to be the Head of the Body, the Spirit of God was to serve as the covering, and the Word was to serve as the Body's final authority in all manners of truth, righteousness, doctrine, and practices.[3] There were positions stipulated for the purpose of establishing the Body upon the foundation of Jesus according to the Father's design. However, these positions were to be marked by humility before God, as well as submission and servitude to others. In fact, God never called His servants to greater leadership, but to greater servitude. Such leadership would be contrary to the world's idea of greatness. Jesus clearly brought this out to His disciples in Matthew 20:20-28.

These positions of service included apostles, prophets, evangelists, pastors, and teachers.[4] Apostles were sent forth to establish local bodies of believers upon the Person of Jesus Christ. The prophets had the responsibility to guard the spiritual condition of the Body against falsehood. Such individuals would contend for the faith that was first delivered to the saints. The evangelists were to challenge the vision of the Body to ensure that the same fire that inspired the new believers on Pentecost remained alive with the flame of authority, power, and life of the heavenly and the eternal.

Pastors were also to serve as elders in the Body and were to oversee the welfare and maturity of God's sheep. Teachers were to challenge the minds and understanding of these sheep as they partook of the manna from heaven. Such manna would not only become life to the saints, but also strength and confidence that would enable them to embrace the impossible, as well as dare to discover the depths of God's incredible character and truths.

On the local level, the positions of elder (pastor and bishop) and deacon (minister) were set apart to establish, guard, and serve the local bodies. The elder was to impart the Word of God to the sheep. The deacon was to be a servant of the needs of those in the local body, as well as to lift the burdens of ministry from the elders. This allowed the elders to commit themselves to preparation of properly dividing and

---

[2] *Deeper Experiences of Famous Christians;* James Gilchrist Lawson, © 2000 by Barbour Publishing, Inc. pg. 50

[3] 2 Timothy 3:16-17

[4] Ephesians 4:11-12

imparting the truth to God's fold. These servants had to have impeccable character. After all, they were to serve as an extension of Jesus to His flock in example and service.[5]

Needless to say, the leadership of the Church has always been affronted in some way by the religious influences of man and the world. In John's revelation concerning the seven churches of Asia Minor, the Lord made strong statements concerning the deeds and doctrine of the Nicolaitanes. He even told the local bodies of Ephesus and Pergamum that He held hatred towards their activities and influence.[6] But, who were the Nicolaitanes, and what deeds and doctrine were they purporting?

As Christians, we must understand what is always under attack when it comes to the spiritual foundation of our lives. It is easy to think that certain belief systems or doctrines (teachings) are what come under attack. The simple reality is that popular and accepted beliefs may be challenged, and there may be attempts to twist fundamental doctrines to fit personal agendas, but what comes under attack is the integrity of God's truth. Jesus, who is our foundation, serves as the essence of all absolute truth regarding God, the Gospel, and eternal life. However, His truth has no power in the lives of people unless it is unadulterated, and the Spirit is the One who firmly leads believers into understanding the intent of such truth in their lives. This is why the Apostle Paul exhorted believers to love the truth, ensuring the salvation of their very souls.[7]

It is vital that we, as believers, understand the battle that was raging in the midst of these different local bodies in the book of Revelation. We also must keep in mind what happened to the light of the testimony or witness of these seven churches. They have all ceased to burn. In fact, the Muslin faith now claims preeminence where these different local bodies once served as living witnesses in their dark age.

As we consider the Nicolaitanes, we must come to an understanding of whether they represented some religious sect, or if they were a movement on the part of a certain group of people to bring about some type of mixture that had the flavor of Christianity, but was void of the life of Jesus and the Spirit of God. Since there is no indication that it was a sect from historical sources, we might conclude that it was some type of religious movement that was trying to take root in the Church.

Since we don't have much to go on except the few Scriptures that mentioned the Nicolaitanes, we need to consider the text in which they were discussed. The main key possibly rests with the likely meaning behind the name, the references, and the environments that were present. The environment will tell us the possible weakness in the Body that would make it susceptible to become indifferent and possibly influenced by this religious movement.

---

[5] Acts 6:2-7; 1 Timothy 3:2-13; Titus 1:5-14
[6] Revelation 2:6, 15
[7] John 14:6; 1 Corinthians 3:11; 2 Thessalonians 2:10

In Revelation 2:6, the Christians of Ephesus recognized the deeds of the Nicolaitanes. Deeds imply labor, work, or occupation.[8] In the case of Pergamos, there was a doctrine that was being taught. Doctrine has to do with teaching people what is required of them as far as their spiritual responsibilities and conduct in matters. A good example of Christian doctrine is the teachings concerning marriage in Ephesians 5:22-33. It is important to mention that doctrine is meant to influence conduct in light of establishing a right attitude about something. Therefore, this teaching of the Nicolaitanes would not only determine conduct, but influence attitude towards spiritual truths.

The Body of Ephesus hated the deeds of the Nicolaitanes, while the Body of Pergamos allowed the Nicolaitanes in their midst. Clearly, the members of the Pergamos local body were not condemning and separating themselves from their teachings.

In his booklet on this subject, F. W. Grant points out that the Greek meaning of Nicolaitane is what will most likely give us a clue into what those promoting the movement might have been advocating. It means "conquering the people." Apparently, the Greek word which was used for "the people" in this text and our commonly-used term "laity" is derived from the same word, "laos." In Grant's conclusion, this could mean only one thing—that the masses of people (laity) were being put down by those who were now being considered the special class of people, or what we would refer to as the clergy.[9]

As believers, we must immediately recognize that this separation is discarding the makeup and function of the true Body. Instead of having one Head over the Body, certain people are exalted into a position of authority, or covering, over what would be considered the "masses" or the lower class of people. Talk about taking away the importance of each member of the Body of Christ and establishing arrogant elitism in the leadership! Clearly, this is the world's way of distinguishing the value and worth of people in regard to its organization and plans, but it is not God's way. We even have this warning from Peter to the elders concerning the local flocks of God, "Feed the flock of God which is among you, taking the oversight of it, not by constraint but willingly; not for filthy lucre but of a ready mind; Neither as being lords over God's heritage, but being ensamples to the flock" (1 Peter 5:2-3).

The important question is what religious basis would Nicolaitanism use to bring the sheep of God into such bondage? Grant believes the answer lies in the environment that was prevalent. Scripture states that the Body at Pergamum was dwelling where Satan's seat or throne was located. He pointed out that Satan is not in hell; rather, he is reigning from his throne upon the earth. This point is firmly confirmed by such

---

[8] Strong's Exhaustive Concordance of the Bible; James Strong, © 1986 assigned to World Bible Publishers, Inc. #2041

[9] Nicolaitanism (The Rise and Growth of the Clergy), F. W. Grant, Believers Bookshelf Inc., pgs. 5, 9

Challenging the Christian Life

Scriptures as Job 1:6-8. Since Satan is the god of this world, the concept of dwelling where Satan's throne is implies settling down in the world.[10]

Clearly, the temptation for the Church to join the world was intense. With each passing year and generation, the resolve to maintain such a distinction from the world would become less and less. However, the new Church would not blatantly come into agreement with the world. There had to be some type of religious entanglement to bring the members into union or agreement. According to Grant, Satan's clever entanglement involved judaizing the Church.[11]

When you read the New Testament, such an attempt was not new. The Apostle Paul constantly confronted the inroads that Judaism subtly made into the new Church. After all, the logic was easy enough to present to any immature, zealous, or gullible Christian since the Law was of God. It was also God who ordained the rituals established by the Law; therefore, it was logical that it was something the new Church had to become subservient to in order to be identified as God's people. However, Paul was quite adamant that to become subservient to the Law in this fashion was to come back under the influence of the flesh. Christ's death on the cross did away with the ordinances (rituals) of the Law.

Jesus fulfilled every aspect of the Law. He now serves as the end of the Law for righteousness, thereby, serving as the righteousness of the believer. As believers, we are now justified by faith, which is accounted to us as righteousness. To walk according to the flesh would bring a person back under the law of sin and death. In the end, the very Law of God would condemn such an individual, not justify him or her.[12] This is why Paul made this statement in Galatians 3:2b-3, "Received ye the Sprit by the works of the law, or by the hearing of faith? Are ye so foolish? Having begun in the Spirit, are ye now made perfect by the flesh?"

To bring God's people under some type of clergy simply puts them under the traditions of those who have been exalted and given underserved authority to dictate to God's people how they are to believe, act, and express their devotion and worship before Him. Jesus encountered this with the scribes and the Pharisees. The scribes or lawyers of the Law were the ones who classified and arranged the Law's precepts. Clearly, these men would determine the intent or emphasis they wanted to bring out about something. Eventually, their words or conclusions became honored above the Law. The Pharisees were the ones who interpreted or explained the Law to the laity.[13]

The concept of the clergy/laity was clearly in operation during Jesus' day. The spirit or intent of the commandments of God was replaced with

---

[10] Ibid, pg. 3
[11] Ibid, pgs. 6-8
[12] Matthew 5:17-18; Romans 3:28; 5:18; 8:2; 10:4; 1 Corinthians 1:30; Colossians 2:14
[13] Smiths Bible Dictionary; William Smith, Thomas Nelson Publishers

the traditions of the elders. These traditions were nothing more than the doctrines of men. They made converts to the religious system with its ridiculous petty rules and regulations, but not converts to the ways of the God of heaven. Jesus said of such traditions and doctrine that the place they held in people's lives actually put aside God's commandments.

It is important to point out that God's commandments remain in place, but many of the practices or rituals of the Law have been fulfilled in Christ. Traditions established by men become rituals that often change the intent or redefine how the commandments were to be honored. In other words, His commandments have been replaced, as men not only nullify their authority in the lives of God's people, but also reject them in preference to the traditions.[14]

When the world came into the Church, it succeeded in doing what the powers behind its religious systems had failed to do in the past. There was now a union between the Church and the world. The Church had now stepped out of its proper place into the environment of heathen idolatry, bringing it under the subtle influence of Satan. As a result, its leadership would now be redefined to make it subservient to the religious system's ways and agendas.

Since Constantine was emperor, as well as the one who spearheaded this new religious movement in his kingdom, it was obvious that he would become the new leader of this religion. In A. D. 325, he convened the first ecumenical council, called the Council of Nicea. He began to establish his agendas and practices at the expense of truth. Sadly, the Christians played into his design. They honored him as the Bishop of Bishops, while Constantine referred to himself Vicarius Christi or the Vicar of Christ.[15] In fact, Constantine became the Roman Catholic Church's first pope.

Constantine replaced Jesus in the new religion. He was the first ecumenist who tried to bring all the religions of his empire under his auspice, regardless of the wrong spirit or perverted truth behind them. This system was a prelude to the antichrist, one-world system that will take center stage in the last days. Clearly, this setup was nothing more than Nicolaitanism, where the clergy was now exalted in position, power, and influence over the masses. The digression created by this wicked system was even more realized in the Middle Ages. It was during this age of grave darkness upon the world that the bishops of Rome began to claim that they were the sole representatives of Christ upon the earth.[16] Ultimately, they replaced the position and work of the Holy Spirit in the visible Church in order to serve as the religious conscience of the people and the sole interpreters of God's Word.

This unholy union would eventually cause the professing Church to prove itself to be unfaithful to the Lord Jesus Christ. It would cause a

---

[14] Mark 7:1-13
[15] A Woman Rides the Beast; © 1994 by Dave Hunt, pg. 46
[16] Ibid

mixture that would reshape the presentation of the Church in the minds of those who profess the name of Christ. Let us now consider how this has affected the "professing" Church.

Leadership: Nicolaitanism is alive and well in the professing Church. Granted, the names may have changed in relationship to the titles in which it may operate under, but it is alive. For example, it is now the modern-day apostles and prophets that are serving in the same positions that the scribes, Pharisees, and Sadducees held in Jesus' day. These false ministers even boldly declare that they are the covering over the Church, clearly deceiving those who come within their heretical grasp.

The positions of most elders and deacons have been reduced to operating as board members that simply work in a capacity of administration, but do not serve in a spiritual capacity. Sadly, those who hold many of these positions do so because of worldly prestige, and not because they fit the criteria set down in Scripture. Since the professing Church is out of order, the heretical leadership of these various false ministers of righteousness has free reign to fleece the sheep, undermine the Word of God, and purport a different gospel. These false leaders also provide the platform for hireling shepherds and wolves to stand upon in the pulpits, gaining control of the hearts and minds of Jesus' fold.

Identification: The members of the true Church of Jesus Christ have three distinct identifying marks upon their lives. The first is the seal of the Holy Spirit. He identifies the members of the true Church with their eternal inheritance. The second identifying mark is separation. True Christianity entails separating from the world in order to separate unto God for His purpose and will.[17] The third identifying mark is true charity, benevolence, or love.

God's love entails both benevolence and charity. Jesus told His disciples that if they loved Him, they would obey His commandments. The three main commandments that were clearly stipulated by Jesus are fulfilled with one word—love. Love is a commitment to God to be right before Him, an attitude of benevolence and compassion to do right by others, and acts of charity that reveal that the believers have truly become identified to the plight of those who are part of the household of faith. If this love is not present in a person's life, he or she cannot claim to be a true disciple of Jesus.[18]

Thanks to the attitude and influence of the world in the professing Church, the identifying marks have changed. Instead of clearly identifying true believers, the established marks of the visible Church are used to control and judge others. This judgment is now based on denominations, doctrines, and practices. For example, the typical concern of many professing Christians is not whether you are saved, but what denomination (church) you are affiliated with. This will classify or identify you as to whether you have any credibility and worth.

---

[17] Ephesians 1:11-14; James 1:27
[18] Mark 12:29-31; John 13:34-35; 14:15; Romans 13:8-10; Galatians 6:2, 9-10

As you can see, the face of the Church has changed in the minds of many professing Christians. Even though the denomination did not die on the cross to save them, it is still regarded as the source of identification with salvation or truth. Membership to some denomination places you in the "in" church that is often presented as having the best corner on truth. Once again it matters little if a person's name is written in the Book of life, as long as he or she is associated with the acceptable denomination and is jumping through the religious hoops.

The Bible does not make any reference to denominations, but local bodies of believers that find a common ground at the point of foundation (Jesus) and sweet fellowship in the Holy Spirit. As far as doctrine goes, we are to go on to perfection in our lives in Christ. Doctrine will establish us in our lives in Christ, but it does not constitute our lives. To go on to perfection means to become enlightened to the ways of God, taste the heavenly gift of His life, and to be partakers of the Holy Spirit. To be partakers of the heavenly life in this way also points to tasting the good Word of God and the powers of the world or age to come.[38]

As we follow the idolatrous exaltation of denominations and man's doctrines, we can begin to see the digression of the visible Church, along with the worldly view it started to adopt. Denomination immediately associates a person with a particular doctrine. Doctrine will not only distinguish the beliefs that a person might hold to, but certain practices as well. With this in mind, it is clear that denomination has subtly become the way to salvation, doctrine has become the sacred cow that one dares not challenge or touch, and practices according to traditions have become marks that identify a person to a particular "elite" group, making a person or denomination superior to the masses. Jesus clearly rebuked such an attitude of sectarianism in His disciples.[39]

Each of these identifying marks of the worldly religious system not only exalts denomination over the leadership of Christ, doctrine over the Word of God, and traditions over the simple, practical ways of God's love, but it also creates the fruit of schisms in the professing Church. Instead of believers being identified to their common ground of Jesus Christ, they become judgmental as they claim elitism over the masses that are not associated to their particular group. After all, they have the real answer to what is true, honorable, and acceptable to God. Although they classify others according to their denominations, interpret the Word of God through their doctrines, and take pride in their traditions, they have failed to see that such identification simply reveals that they are carnal or fleshly, and not counted as righteous.

The Corinthians had similar associations in their Body. They were classifying the validity of their Christianity and salvation based on those with whom they were associated. Some bragged that they were of Paul, while others took pride in being of Apollos. The Apostle Paul identified

---

[38] Hebrews 6:1-5
[39] Mark 9:38-41

Challenging the Christian Life

such schisms as being associated with envy and strife. Such works are carnal or of the flesh.[40]

It is important for Christians to realize that, if their identification goes back to any other person or source than the Lord Jesus Christ, they are still walking in the ways of the flesh and not according to the Spirit of God. The Holy Spirit has one responsibility. He is to lead believers into all truth about Jesus. It is from the premise of Jesus, that pure doctrine is established. Out of pure doctrine comes godly conduct that will make the believer stand distinct from this world in disposition, attitude, and emphasis.[41]

When you consider what the best man can accomplish according to agreement with the world, it is easy to see how people become boxed in and conditioned by a religious system. Man now provides the spiritual covering. The denomination has become a ceiling that will determine how far a person will go in his or her pursuit of God and service. Doctrine will serve as the idolatrous walls that will decide what a person will believe, as well as how he or she should interpret the Christian life. The practices of these religious boxes produce lifeless traditions that become the platforms that set a standard of self-righteousness. Such self-righteousness is nothing more than religious pride. As a result, many of God's sheep find themselves boxed in by an unseen entity that is lifeless, legalist, indifferent, cruel, and unrealistic.

Experiences: The Christian life is meant to be experienced. However, it must be experienced in two arenas—the Spirit and according to God's truth. The natural man who operates in the flesh, according to the influence of the world, cannot discern the things of the Spirit.[42]

Since the Spirit is missing in most religious activities, there is spiritual leanness in many to discover the spiritual part of Christianity. The problem is that many of these individuals do not seek the truth out in Scripture. We are told in Romans 5:3-5 that experiences are part of the Christian life; but they are in light of the hope that awaits each of us in glory. Such experiences imply some type of trial that has taken place in our lives. Therefore, our understanding of God is disciplined by tribulation that works sobriety, patience that works character, and the assurance of hope that lives in expectation according to the godly love that must be present in our hearts.[43]

What most people are missing is a greater revelation of Jesus Christ that is alive and satisfying to the soul. It is in such revelation that they will experience the life, beauty, and glory of our Lord. Since these people have not learned that, in Christianity, a believer's main desire should be to know, see, and experience Christ in greater measure, they seek out spiritual experiences. The reason for their search is because of the

---

[40] 1 Corinthians 3:1-4; Galatians 5:15-21
[41] John 16:12-15; Romans 6:17; 1 Timothy 4:6-8; Titus 2:10-12; 1 John 2:8-10
[42] 1 Corinthians 2:13-15
[43] Strong Exhaustive Concordance of the Bible, #1382

wrong presentation of spiritual matters and because such experiences are mistakenly associated with the presence and power of the Holy Spirit. However, the spiritual door these individuals walk through is not the door of truth, but the door of the occult.

Sadly, these occult experiences become more real than reality to these people. These experiences work a lot like a drug high. People find themselves always in need of another fix or mystic experience in the spiritual realm. In the end, everything will become subservient to these experiences, including the Word of God.

It is easy to see why the face of the professing Church has changed. It is in an identity crisis. When many people think of the Church of Jesus, they think in terms of a building or a denomination, but not according to the Word of God. They do not see that the Church is made up of people who are not associated with some particular denomination, doctrine, or practice, but who have become truly identified with the person and redemptive work of Jesus Christ.

What about you? Do you need to let your concept of Church go to the wayside in order to allow it to be revolutionized by the Word of God? Remember, Jesus did not die for a particular denomination, doctrine, or tradition. He died for people, for you and me. We must never allow any man, system, doctrine, or tradition to replace or undermine our understanding of His salvation and our assurance because of it.

7

FOUNDATION REDEFINED

It is important to keep in mind that God has always had a people. In the Old Testament, it was a nation that was to represent His character and interests in that particular age of darkness. In today's age, the Lord has a Body or Church to proclaim His message, represent His kingdom, and do His bidding. Each of these entities were to clearly serve as the light in this dark world, bringing contrast and hope.

Every age has its own type of darkness. For the children of Israel, that darkness came in the form of blatant practices of idolatry and paganism. In Jesus' day, the present age was darkened by dead religion and internal power struggles between the different factions of the religious and worldly leaderships. In Paul's case, his particular mission field was darkened by various idols, temples, and philosophies that embraced everything the world offered, but were void of truth.

Each age or transition that the world has gone through had its own flavor of darkness that embraced its own brand of ignorance, unbelief, and deception. In each age, man's ignorance towards God was clouded by the different superstitions that had been thrust upon him by family, culture, and/or religious influences.[1] Each age of darkness added to the next age of delusion. Because of this darkness, man continues to walk in blatant unbelief towards God's Word, often deeming it obsolete or insignificant according to the present "enlightenment" that is in operation in the present age.

Ultimately, man will walk according to his own take on reality. This reality will be based on superstitions and the false light of the present age, but, nevertheless, it is the reality he will strive to bring about and maintain. However, it is all a lie that has blinded him to the real light of this world, Jesus Christ.

This brings us to the present age. How does the professing Church express itself now? Since the world is defining much of the visible Church, Christianity has become a subculture within the different cultures of the world. It has it own language, as well as its own religious traditions and beliefs. It boxes people into its system to be conditioned according to the box's particular light, philosophies, agendas, and ways. Therefore, the professing Church is now part of the world's systems. Since it has

---

[1] The use of the word "man" is in relationship to both male and female.

become an integral part of the present age, the professing Church will ultimately fail to stand distinct in the present darkness.

Like any subculture, the worldly Christianity appears to have its beneficial points that will add to the mosaic of the world with its diverse cultures and practices. However, the organized Church will use the philosophies, measures, and methods of the world to try to attract people to its particular take on life. For example, God's love no longer points to redemption, but to tolerance. Sin is no longer a terminal disease of the soul that has brought man under a death sentence, but it is simply a mistake, a physical illness, or an inherited trait that alleviates a person from any real Scriptural or moral accountability. Since God loves us, He wants us to be happy regardless of the fornication or unholy agreement we may commit in our lives to secure this so-called "happiness".

Needless to say, these are blatant lies, but they are affecting the attitudes of believers. The truth is that God's main desire is that we partake of His holiness so that we are able to see Him.[2] But, these compromising attitudes show us that there is a mixture in operation. They are revealing how worldly the professing Church has become. Sadly, the best each individual can do in this environment is to tack Christ on to all of his or her activities as a way to deceive him or herself about his or her true spiritual condition.

As I have considered the struggles of the professing Church, I have realized that it has always been the same throughout the different transitions that have taken place throughout the ages. The real Church that Jesus died for must come back to center, but, first, it must recognize how the darkness of the present age is affecting it. The struggle to come back to center does not occur without some type of travail taking place within the souls of believers.

As with all travail, it begins with restlessness. The soul is no longer comfortable with what is considered normal in the religious scene. Something is being stirred in the believer. The believer may not understand the stirring, but it has to do with the very life of Christ coming to its fullness in his or her life. His life must be birthed, established, consecrated, or revived in a person, depending upon his or her spiritual status. For example, Christ' life must come forth from the womb of the heart or from the grave of the lifeless soul where the work or regeneration and sanctification has been stifled in some way.

The stirring behind this life is the Holy Spirit. Once the restlessness begins, then the process for this new or renewed life must take place. Life that comes forth in the heart, or innermost being within a person points to a lost soul being saved from the clutches of God's wrath through the new-birth (born-again) experience. However, for the tomb that represents the substitute of lifeless religion, wherein life has been grieved, quenched, or vexed, this new life coming forth points to reformation and/or revival.

---

[2] Hebrews 12:14

For the renewed life to come forth in power and glory, it will take revolution, suffering, persecution, and/or death. As you study the history of God's people, much of the renewal of life came from the premise of reformation.

One of the greatest reformations in Israel occurred during the reign of King Hezekiah.[3] The temple doors had been closed to the life, truth, and ways of God. Hezekiah opened the doors of the temple and called the priests and Levites back into the work of service. Their first order of business was to cleanse themselves so that they could cleanse and sanctify the temple. Hezekiah also called the remainder of the people of Israel back to their former roots by observing the Passover.

Reformation usually begins when there has been personal revival within the one who is spearheading it. Hezekiah had a personal renewal take place in his life. Renewal or revival involves a renewing of vision and purpose. Only the Holy Spirit can revive or renew a vision, while man can only reform what is wrong in order to encourage an environment of revival for others.

Revival involves an awakening to one's spiritual condition. This awakening leads to brokenness that produces humility, repentance, conversion, and consecration. Reformation is the means to reform the beliefs, ways, or practices of a body or group of people that have left their original function or purpose. In Hezekiah's situation, he was trying to reform a nation that belonged to Jehovah God. This involved ridding the land of all idolatrous and abominable practices.

Reformation in the religious arena begins at the point of personal faith. Genuine faith will lead the person back to God and His Word. He or she will choose to believe the Word and will come back to the center in regard to God's truth. It is at the point of this faith that God can revive a person with a greater revelation of Jesus and His redemption. It is important to point out that revival occurs when people truly begin to have a personal revelation of how much their sin truly cost God. At this point, people are broken in their arrogance and self-sufficiency, and, in repentance and desperation, they begin to seek God's mercy.

As we study reformation and revival, people can reform without being spiritually revived. In other words, they can change their minds and practices without spiritual renewal. This is why it is important to understand the difference between these two environments. Reformation can result in personal revival for those who are seeking change in their lives or have tender hearts towards God, but such revival will not necessarily sweep the masses.

However, revivals that are clearly being spearheaded by the Holy Spirit are like great waves that sweep the masses into their powerful grip. The most unlikely people can end up falling on their knees in total repentance, seeking forgiveness, being converted to the righteous ways

---

[3] 2 Kings 18-19; 2 Chronicles 29-31

of God, and total consecrating from their wicked ways in order to be sanctified unto God by His Spirit.

Reformation calls for change, while revival produces brokenness and consecration. Reformation can cause people to see the need to change the face of what is going on in the religious environment, but revival often allows people to feel and smell the very fires of hell nipping at their heals, causing a transformation of the inward environment that is conducive for real revival and total abandonment to God.

This brings us back to the activities of the Church. Throughout the years there have been various reformers such as Martin Luther. These reformers came forth as firebrands in the midst of lifeless religion. The stirring that occurred in these men began at the point of faith in God's Word. They chose to believe simple truths such as "the just shall live by faith" and "that salvation is matter of God's grace and not man's works."[4]

These reformers recognized that they could not reform the Catholic Church; therefore, they had to step outside of the system to bring truth and liberty to the poor burdened souls. Repercussions followed. The Catholic Church set out to persecute and silence these firebrands. However, this religious system could not silence the Word of God. It continued to be the source of liberty for those who sought truth among its pages, even within the midst of grave ignorance, lifeless traditions, and possible persecution.

In our Church history, we also have those who were used to bring forth great tidal waves of revival. There are two fires that can burn through the Church—persecution and the Holy Spirit. The fires of persecution often refine faith among the members of Jesus' Body, bringing much needed cleansing and purging. However, the Spirit is what sets the soul aflame with resolve and passion. The resolve is to ensure that one is right before God, while there is passion to fulfill the calling, vision, or commission out of loving devotion. Those who are associated with the great moves of the Spirit upon the saved and the unsaved alike are men with such names as Whitefield, Edwards, Roberts, and Finney.

Whether in times of reformation or revival, these men had one thing in common—they had stepped outside of the box established by the carnal religious influences of man and the sensual practices of the world to personally encounter God.

At such times the true Church of Jesus had the opportunity to get its bearings. However, there was always controversy that followed the reformers and revivalists. They both posed a threat to the rule, control, and influence of the religious system upon the hearts and minds of the people. In times of such controversy, where the fires of persecution and oppression are fanned in an attempt to try to buffet the reformation of the firebrands or the powerful moving of the Spirit, the true Church of Jesus is often clearly refined and established. In such movements of reformation or revival, the choices are made clear. There are no gray

---

[4] Romans 1:17; Ephesians 2:8-10

areas of worldly compromise or uncertainty. People not only clearly see the difference between man's religion and the Lord's Body, but they realize that there is a cost to be part of the Living Church of Jesus Christ.

Once again, we must come back to how the world influenced the Church. We know that when the Holy Spirit is missing, then an environment will be in place for the shifting of leadership. After all, man now can step into place as the spiritual conscience of others and condition them to embrace the religious box designed by fallen man. In this light, man can now subtly replace the Head as the one who holds the authority over the Church as sovereign leader. In such a place, such a leader will take hold of the minds of the people.

Now that man has taken hold of the minds to influence people's point of view to conform to his way of thinking and attitudes towards God, he can now control their practices and behaviors. In this position, he can replace service to God with service to the cause of the religious system or to worldly inspired leadership. It is at this point that the foundation can be redefined.

According to the Apostle Paul, there is only one foundation upon which we can successfully build our spiritual lives. This foundation is known as the Rock. This Rock serves as the stone that will break us at the point of our independent dispositions, or it will crush us into powder with judgment. Not only is a believer's life firmly established upon this immovable Rock of ages, but also the Spirit of God is building the true Church upon it, as the Lord personally adds living stones to this living organism.[5] We are reminded once again that man has no real part in actually building the Church of Jesus. He may be a vessel that is used to preach the message of salvation, but he does not actually build the house.

As you consider that there is one foundation upon which the Body is established, there should and will be agreement rather than schisms. There is only one true Spirit of God who works in accordance to the plans of heaven; therefore, there should never be debates about what is right and acceptable. Since there is only one hope that is being established within the heart of the Body, there should not be any confusion about what we need to pursue as true followers of Christ.

As the Body is firmly anchored in place by one hope, its calling will be brought forth according to its one Lord or Owner. This one calling will be developed and refined by the one faith that was first delivered to the saints who were baptized into the Body by the Holy Spirit. Such baptism is done according to the plan of the Father, who is above all, through all, and in all through the presence of His Spirit in those who belong to the true Body of the Lord Jesus Christ.[6]

The Apostle Paul clearly identifies that the one true foundation is the Lord Jesus Christ. In the previous chapter of this book, it was presented

---

[5] Matthew 7:24-27; 16:18; 21:42-44; Acts 2:47; 1 Corinthians 3:11; 10:4
[6] Ephesians 4:3-6

how false apostles and prophets are presenting themselves as ministers of righteousness. It was also brought out that there are hireling shepherds and wolves standing behind many pulpits. Such facts will not escape those who are guarding the truth. But it must be noted that such heretics are not only motivated by a wrong spirit of the world, but they are open doors or avenues by which this wrong spirit will seduce others into an unholy agreement to embrace doctrines of devils.[7]

It is important to understand that, in such an environment, the foundation can be redefined without people recognizing the error. As I have already established, the foundation is not a matter of denomination, beliefs, or rituals, but the Person of the Lord Jesus Christ.

When it comes to the one true foundation of every Christian, he or she must realize that true agreement can only be obtained at the point of what has been established as the true common ground for all believers—Jesus. However, the Lord Jesus Christ is not just any "old" Jesus. In other words, He is not a figment of someone's imagination or a faceless person who lived and who those of the religious arena can define in any old way that serves their religious causes or emphasis.

The Jesus I am talking about was clearly unveiled in Scripture through shadows, prophecies, and teachings. This very same Jesus stated that He was the only way to heaven. He also warned that, in the end days, many different "messiahs" would be presented, but, as His followers, we are not to give them any audience or follow them into their different delusions.[8]

Jesus brought out this very important issue with His disciples when He asked them a simple question in Matthew 16:13b, "Who do men say that I, the Son of man, am?" I have dealt with this subject many times. However, we must understand why the visible Church is in its present spiritual condition.

Others always influence our initial understanding of God, Jesus, and life. The tendency, in our limited box of understanding, is to assume that whatever we have been told must be correct. After all, our family, church, or religious leaders have conditioned us in our thinking, and they would not lie to us.

Take it from a former cult member; each of these sources could very well lie to you. The reason for such a lie is because many of these sources have also been blinded to the truth of Jesus Christ by their own ignorance and unbelief. They are operating from an assumption and not from the premise of truth. To confirm this point, the disciples' answer proved that people speculate much about Jesus, but they fail to discover who He is for themselves. "And they said, Some say that thou art John the Baptist; some, Elijah, and others, Jeremiah, or one of the prophets" (Matthew 16:14).

---

[7] 1 Corinthians 3:11; 1 Timothy 4:1-2
[8] Matthew 24:4-5, 23-27; John 14:6; Acts 4:12; Colossians 2:14-17

Let us consider for a moment the environment in which Jesus lived in His humanity. The Jewish people were looking for their Messiah, but many held to the concept that Jesus was John the Baptist or some other prophet that rose from the dead.[9] These people were looking for the Messiah, but, when He stood in front of them, they still did not recognize Him. As a result, they were wrong about who He was.

My family and religion were both wrong about Jesus. Since I believed them, I was wrong as well. My whole foundation was wrong. Therefore, my whole premise on which I regarded God, considered Jesus, and viewed life was wrong! The problem with being wrong in this situation is that it would have cost me my very soul if I had failed to get it right.

In my former perspective, God was a vague concept because the cult I attended had subtly replaced Him. I had a sentimental notion of Jesus as a baby in a manger, otherwise there was confusion. The reason for this confusion was that the only time I took note of Him in a religious way was in regard to how the men of my religion were purported to actually serve as a "Christ" in their families. In fact, they were the ones who would supposedly call their wives from the grave. Therefore, I was encouraged to prepare to marry so I could have my own personal "Christ" that would be sure to not leave me in that terrible place of the grave.

To those who maintain beliefs about Jesus, such a delusional belief on the part of my former cult would seem absolutely ridiculous, but, in all honesty, how do each of us know if our understanding about Jesus is correct? How many of us assume we know Him, but, in reality, we do not have a clue? Jesus is not an intellectual, religious concept that has been rendered lifeless and without dimension by the knowledge and philosophies of religion and the world; rather, He is a revelation of the heart to those who truly believe. He is alive and reigns as Lord and King within the hearts of those who love Him.

Jesus then asked the disciples the next question in Matthew 16:15b, "But who say ye that I am?" Jesus was now making it a personal matter. He in fact, was speaking to each of us. "Who do you say that I am?" Peter answered Him correctly, but it is important to note how Peter received such an understanding. It was not based upon his intellectual or religious understanding. Jesus told Peter that the Father in heaven revealed to Peter His real identity.[10]

The Bible is clear. We must believe the record it has given to us about the true Jesus.[11] Such a record is made revelation to the receptive heart. It is from the correct premise of who Jesus is that the Christian life is clearly founded and established.

---

[9] Matthew 16:14
[10] Matthew 16:17
[11] 1 John 5:9-13

Who is the real Jesus? Peter gave us some insight in his answer in Matthew 16:16b, "Thou art the Christ, the Son of the living God." Peter was acknowledging that Jesus was the Promised One who would come to deliver the Jewish people. However, this deliverance was not to be a physical deliverance from the oppression of the Gentile rulers, but a spiritual deliverance from oppression caused by sin. As the Promised One, He was also the King of the Jews. Instead of reestablishing Israel as a physical kingdom, He came to establish a spiritual kingdom that would live within the hearts of men. As the Messiah, He was anointed to carry out a work that would result in the spiritual healing, reconciliation, and restoration of man back into a relationship with God.

Unlike what I was told by my former cult, Jesus is the only Christ, and, as John 5:21-29 clearly stipulates, He is the One who will call people out of the grave, either unto everlasting life or eternal damnation. This brings us to the second aspect of Jesus. He is the Son of the Living God. As the Messiah, we get insight into His work and mission as man. But, as the Son of the Living God, we get insight into His nature and character. We know that, as the Messiah, He came as man to fulfill His mission as the Lamb of God. However, He is also divine by nature. He has the same nature and status as the Father, making Him equal to Him. However, when He was fashioned as a man in the womb of a woman, He gave up His sovereignty as God, thereby, ceasing to be equal with God[12]

The Apostle John clearly brings Jesus' deity out in the first three verses of the first chapter of his Gospel when he identifies the Living Word as being God. He summarizes this revelation in John 1:14, "And the Word was made flesh, and dwelt among us (and we beheld his glory, the glory as of the only begotten of the Father), full of grace and truth."

The Apostle Paul also summarized Jesus' identity as well as His entrance as man into the world. In 1 Timothy 1:17, Paul described the Lord in this way, "Now unto the King eternal, immortal, invisible, the only wise God, be honor and glory forever and ever. Amen." As King, Jesus has always existed (eternal). He is immortal, exempt from ceasing to exist. He is invisible, because He operates in the unseen world, yet He lives. He is the only wise God who deserves to be honored and glorified forever.

The Apostle Paul summarized Jesus' entrance into this world in 1 Timothy 3:16, "And without controversy great is the mystery of godliness: God was manifest in the flesh, justified in the Spirit, seen of angels, preached unto the Gentiles, believed on in the world, received up into glory." God becoming man was a great mystery of godliness. He was manifested in the flesh, confirmed by the Spirit, witnessed by the host of heaven, preached among those who were considered rejected, believed on by those who were in the world, and received up into glory. Such a mystery can only be unveiled to those who are pure in heart and are

---

[12] John 5:17-18; Philippians 2:5-8

prepared to believe, by faith, the record that the Word of God has clearly set forth about the Son of God.

It is this incredible revelation of Jesus that makes up the true foundation. If we do not believe every aspect of this Scriptural record, we will end up possessing a different Jesus. Such a Jesus will be unable to save us. After all, the Father only recognizes His only begotten Son, not a Jesus who is a figment of someone's imagination. The Father even confirmed Jesus' identity on two different occasions—at His baptism and transfiguration. Both times, he introduced Jesus as His Son, fulfilling a prophecy found in Psalm 2:7.[13] The writer of Hebrews brought this into an interesting focus when he pointed out that the Father even referred to Jesus as God in Hebrews 1:8, "But unto the Son he saith, Thy throne, O God, is forever and ever; a scepter of righteousness is the scepter of thy kingdom."[14]

Today there are many different messiahs being presented. Some presentations are blatant heresy, while others possess some truth. But ninety-nine percent of them strip Jesus of His deity. He may be a great man, but He is not God in the flesh. He may be a great prophet, but He is not God Incarnate. He may be spiritual, but He is only a created being like the angels, rather than the Creator. He is the brother of Lucifer who simply presented a better plan, rather than the only one who could fulfill the plan of redemption. He died on the cross, but He is not compassionate enough to be the sole mediator between God and man; therefore, He needs His biological mother to share such a position with Him.[15] In some cases, Jesus never gets past the manger in Bethlehem to die on the cross. In other cases, He never gets off the cross to prove victory over death in His resurrection. He is forever a baby that can bring sentimental tears to our eyes once a year, or He is always paying the price for our sins because His work on the cross was not enough to secure redemption.

Obviously, the reality behind the organized religions of the world is that they cannot let Jesus be Jesus. They oppose Him in subtle ways so they can define Him according to their purpose and agendas. Most of the religions of the world will not outright reject Christ; rather, they will use Him to attract people to a substitute Jesus that has no power to save their souls. Ultimately, these false religions define the spiritual foundation to fit their particular religious boxes.

The struggle in Christianity is to make sure our lives, as believers, are founded upon the correct Jesus. It has been an incredible journey for me to wade through the many religious presentations of Jesus. There are those confusing the real Christ by presenting a picture-perfect

---

[13] Matthew 3:17; 17:5

[14] If you like to in-depth study about the identity of Jesus, see the author's two books titled, *He Actually Thought it Not* Robbery in Volume Two and *Unmasking the Cult Mentality* in Volume One of her foundation series.

[15] 1 Timothy 2:5-6

presentation of the Jesus of the Bible, but when you strip away the initial image, the real Jesus has been rendered useless by the legalistic propaganda and pagan practices of the religious systems that are hiding behind His name or concept.

Another popular Jesus is the worldly Jesus who is here to make people feel good about themselves, as well as do their bidding. There is the New Age Jesus who is simply one of the way-showers, since all the religious paths supposedly lead to God. There is also the Jesus who is the mystic. This counterfeit has no practical side to His life and ministry, especially since Christianity is nothing more than a mystical experience.

We could go on and on about the different presentations of Jesus that are being offered, but there is only one Jesus that is truly the Son of God. He came by way of a simple virgin, a handmaiden that recognized her own need for a savior. He entered into the world via a manger. He was hidden in obscurity for the first thirty years of His life, became identified to man in the waters of baptism, and was tempted in the wilderness by Satan. In His, ministry He turned the world upside down, was crucified by religion, lifted up on the cross by a political system of the world, and treated like a common criminal by those who were ignorant of Him or feared and hated Him.

This Jesus was both the Christ and the Son of God. Since God promised a deliverer, Jesus stepped out of eternity and took on the likeness of man in order to redeem mankind from the harsh taskmasters of sin and death. As the Lamb of God, He was offered upon the altar of the cross where He paid the price for our sins. As God, He rose three days later from the grave to prove victorious over the sting of sin.

Jesus is fully man and fully God. Today, in His capacity as Man, He serves as our example, High Priest, and Mediator. However, as God, He reminds us of His unchangeable character and His power to save us. As Man, we see the compassion of God in His ways, but, as God, we are reminded that we can only meet God at the points of covenant, forgiveness, atonement, and reconciliation. As Man, He fits the criteria of being the only place in which reconciliation can take place with the Father, but, as God, we are reminded that, one day, He will come back as Judge of all, and He will judge according to His righteousness.

The other aspect of our foundation is that we will be discovering the extent of God's grace for ages to come.[16] We can never possess the complete revelation of Jesus, but we can be full of His life, always being enlarged to receive greater measures of Him.

Is your life founded upon the right Jesus, or will your foundation crumble in the fires of judgment? Is your foundation lifeless due to a mixture of spirit, man's influence, and the world, or is it living because the Holy Spirit is bringing revelation of our Lord's character, life, and ways to your spirit? Only you can answer these questions, but remember that, without the right foundation, you will not stand in the day of adversity and

---

[16] Ephesians 2:7

judgment, nor will God recognize you as belonging to the true Church of Jesus Christ.

8

CORNERSTONE READJUSTED

When man begins to replace the leadership of the Head, the tender conscience of the Spirit, and begins to define the source or purpose behind life in the Body of Christ, he has free rein to redefine the foundation. We know Jesus is the only true foundation to every believer. Therefore, man will redefine Jesus to fit his particular emphasis, doctrine, or religious cause. As Jesus is redefined, He will lose the preeminence He must hold in the lives of His people.[1] Sadly, another Jesus will be presented in His place. However, this Jesus is a counterfeit that will not be recognized by God, the Father, as well as those who make up the true Church of Jesus Christ.

To redefine Jesus means to strip the foundation of eternal life of its stability or authority to stand as a shining beacon. Without the stability, the foundation will eventually collapse. Since every foundation will be shaken, each faulty foundation stands already doomed, and, when the winds of judgment finally come, that which is not firmly established upon the Rock will fall into total ruin.[2]

It is at the points of attempting to replace the foundation or the shaking of it that the visible Church will prove to be vulnerable. After all, the cement (Spirit) that holds the foundation together will be missing, and the truths of Jesus that make up this foundation will be undermined by an unholy mixture. However, the true foundation must be stripped of its stability (authority) before the cornerstone of the Church can be readjusted to fit the purpose and cause of those who are trying to gain power over God's people.

The Bible is clear that Jesus also serves as our cornerstone.[3] It is important to understand how the character, life, ministry, and function of the believer and the Church are all found in Christ. As our Head, He ensures that our lives will function according to the will of God. As our foundation, He establishes us according to the authority of His nature and work of redemption. However, as our cornerstone, He determines how our life will line up to His life, attitude, examples, and teachings.

In my study of cornerstones, I realize that structures are designed according to the cornerstone. Based on the information about the temple

---

[1] Colossians 1:15-19
[2] Matthew 7:24-27; Hebrews 12:27-29
[3] 1 Peter 2:5-8

of Solomon, all the stones were constructed outside of the temple and brought to the building site. These stones were all shaped according to the cornerstone. There is a legend that even Jesus made reference to regarding the cornerstone of the temple of Solomon. It says that the builders did not recognize the cornerstone.[4] It was an odd shape compared to the rest of the stones. Therefore, the builders considered the stone to be a mistake and cast it down into their garbage dump. When they placed all of the stones into their rightful place, they discovered that the odd shaped stone they had discarded was the actual cornerstone. They had to dig it out of the dump in order to complete the temple.

This is how the Church of Jesus is built. It is designed according to His pattern that He clearly laid out in His life and ministry. Sadly, like many of the present builders of the Church, the Jews of Jesus' day refused to recognize Him as the only true spiritual cornerstone, and cast Him into the grave. However, Jesus is the cornerstone of all truth, as well as the cornerstone to which all of the living stones of the Church are designed to line up to. He was not only raised from the grave to prove victorious over death, but He also took His rightful place as the cornerstone of His Church.[5]

As our foundation, Jesus enables us to stand against the storms brought against us by the kingdom of darkness. We are empowered to stand against the attacks aimed at God's truth by standing on the truth of who Jesus is. This is where our authority comes from against the powers of darkness. We will never be moved from who Jesus is, for He will never change.[6]

As our cornerstone, Jesus enables us to withstand the onslaught of heretical and demonic teachings and movements that come against His very life that is being formed within us by the sanctifying work of the Holy Spirit. The foundation of Jesus will affect how we view God, which will influence our attitudes and approach regarding Him. However, as our cornerstone, our lifestyle will be affected. In fact, the life in us must line up to the cornerstone to ensure consistency between our claims, our walk, and our fruits. The cornerstone we line up to will, in turn, affect how we view our lives, responsibilities, and places in the kingdom of God.

The problem for many Christians is that there is no connection between their claims of what they believe (foundation) and the life they live (structure). The lack of such a connection will classify such believers as hypocrites. The reason for the inconsistency is unbelief. It takes faith to connect the foundation of who Jesus is to the structure or life that is being established by the Spirit of God. Since His Word is a matter of truth it must be applied by faith to every aspect of our lives.[7] Application

---

[4] Matthew 21:42
[5] Romans 10:9-10; 1 Peter 2:5-8
[6] Hebrews 13:8
[7] Romans 10:17; Hebrews 11:6

of the truth in this manner is what lines believers up to Jesus as the cornerstone, while ensuring that they are being firmly established upon who He is.

When the connection of faith is missing between the foundation and the structure, you end up with a lopsided structure that is already doomed to collapse. The structure is worthless since it is not being established upon the proper foundation. It is easy to witness this inconsistency. There are those who display religious piousness in the religious realm, but they are not firmly established upon the foundation. Eventually, different aspects of their lives will begin to collapse because there is no real foundation to what they believe or are advocating. Even though some of the structure is intact, it will still prove to be worthless when it comes to withstanding any of the storms that may be blowing through the religious world.

This brings us to the construction of the structure. The true builder of this structure is not man, but God. Granted, man is a co-laborer with God as far as establishing or reinforcing this spiritual structure upon the true foundation of Jesus, but the building must be according to the design of the Father and under the auspice of the ever-abiding, watchful care of the Spirit.[8] Psalm 127:1 tells us that, unless the Lord builds the house, man's labor will be in vain. Philippians 1:6 clearly established that it is God's good or beneficial work that is taking place in us. As a result, the Apostle Paul gave this warning, "But let every man take heed how he buildeth upon it" (1 Corinthians 3:10c).

What is being established in the inward sanctuary of man and within Jesus' Church should be His life. The Apostle Paul confirmed this when he stated, "I am crucified with Christ: nevertheless I live; yet not I, but Christ liveth in me; and the life which I now live in the flesh I live by the faith of the Son of God, who loved me and gave himself for me" (Galatians 2:20).

For the very life of Christ to be established in me, I must line up to the cornerstone. This means I will allow the very attitude of Christ to be developed in my life.[9] The attitude of Christ is one of meekness. Godly meekness will always come into submission to the will and plan of God.

To line up to the cornerstone means I will actually take on the very disposition of Christ. He was lowly or humble.[10] This made Him a servant before the Father, always ready to serve man for the glory of the Father.

Part of lining up to the cornerstone is following the pattern or example that Jesus left His followers. The Apostle John made this statement in 1 John 2:6, "He that saith he abideth in him ought himself also so to walk, even as he walked." Jesus left two major patterns for us to follow. However, we cannot follow these patterns unless we abide in the Vine. Such abiding is how the very life of Christ is imparted to us. As

---

[8] 1 Corinthians 3:9; Hebrews 3:4
[9] Philippians 2:5
[10] Matthew 11:29

His life comes forth, we will develop His mind and take on His disposition. His mind will inspire us, and His disposition will discipline us.

Although I have mentioned these two examples many times before in my teachings and books, we must consider them in light of lining up to the cornerstone. The first example is found in John 13:13-17. The example is that of servitude. Jesus took on the disposition of a servant. In so doing, He permitted Himself to be abased as He allowed Himself to be fashioned as a man.

All of us are servants to something or someone, but the critical issue is who we are serving. If we give in to our natural preferences, we will be serving the spirit or god of this world. However, if we take our life back from the dictates of sin and consecrate it to God, we will serve God. The first type of service, service to Satan, is a matter of just giving way to what is natural, fleshly, convenient, and comfortable. The second type of service involves submission that will bring a person into subjection to God. Godly submission is a powerful form of inward discipline.

True servants are disciplined by their very service. However, Jesus' example calls for inward discipline that truly commits all to God for His glory. As Jesus stated, "The servant is not greater than his lord; neither he that is sent greater than he that sent him. If ye know these things, happy are ye if ye do them" (John 13:16b-17).

Jesus showed us the secret of happiness as His servants. True submission simply comes into deference to that which is worthy for the benefit of the whole.[11] Such submission will ultimately put everyone in the Body on equal footing as they come into line with the cornerstone. After all, each spiritual building brick in our lives, and in the Church, is as important as the cornerstone to complete the whole of the building. If we understand this, we will discover true happiness. After all, we will have the freedom to step over our insipid pride, deny ourselves of personal rights to have life on our terms, and truly follow Jesus into a glorious life.

Godly submission also brings us under the yoke of Christ. The yoke will work the very disposition of Christ in us as it disciplines our walk. His yoke will prove to be easy because it is about doing the will of the Father. It will also bring about spiritual maturity as we continue to understand what it means to grow up in Christ, who is our Head.[12]

The second pattern that Jesus left us can be found in 1 Peter 2:21-22, "For even hereunto were ye called, because Christ also suffered for us, leaving us an example, that ye should follow his steps; Who did no sin, neither was guile found in his mouth." We can clearly see Jesus' mind or attitude in these Scriptures. He was willing to give way to suffering in order to fulfill the will of the Father. He refused to sin, or to open His mouth in defense of His innocence, or rebuke His false accusers. In meekness, He came into obedience as the Lamb of God to be led to the slaughter. This suffering was vital to bring Him forth in

---

[11] Ephesians 5:21
[12] Matthew 11:29-30; Ephesians 4:15

perfection in His humanity as a means to bring about the way of salvation.[13]

Hebrews 5:8-9 gives us this insight, "Though he were a Son, yet learned he obedience by the things which he suffered; And being made perfect, he became the author of eternal salvation unto all them that obey him." Godly meekness allows us to learn obedience. However, true obedience comes with a cost. The first cost is that one must deny self to truly obey. The second cost is coming under the spiritual burden ordained by God to see His plan fulfilled.

Jesus came under the burden of the cross. The burden we are asked to carry is light. It is the burden of love. Love is the only way to fulfill the plan of God. It is what inspires or compels us to walk out the Christian life. It is selfless and sacrificial. It always expresses itself in meekness.[14] In other words, its strengths, passions, and devotion are disciplined by godly meekness. This meekness is the product of being under the control of the Spirit.

Since the world came into the Church, it is hard for believers to understand that, unless their mind is transformed, their attitude and disposition will not be fully regenerated. The Apostle Paul stated that the mind is conformed to this world's way of thinking; therefore, it must be transformed by the renewing of the Spirit.[15]

Due to the influence of the world upon the professing Church's way of thinking, some Christians fail to see the problem that is clearly besetting the Church. Since there are no absolutes about the identity of Jesus as the true spiritual foundation, He can now be adjusted to fit people's particular lifestyles. Therefore, any concept of Him will be brought into submission to cultural preferences, lined up to religious pursuits, and presented according to worldly taste. In essence, He is being tacked on to man's activities, attuned to religious agendas, dressed according to personal preferences, and designed according to worldly, popular images. For example, to the businessman, He is the most successful CEO. To the punk rocker, He is tattooed and dressed according to the taste of those presenting Him. To the surfer, He is presented as the coolest surfer of the present age. To the politician, He is anyone you want to make Him to be since we live in a tolerant society. In summation, He has been blended into every culture and race, stripping Him of all distinction.

Clearly, if the foundation has been redefined, then Jesus, as the cornerstone, can be adjusted to fit the present age. Shamefully, the different presentations of Jesus make Him part of the world and its activities. Even though Jesus stated that He came from above and was not of this world, He is now presented from a worldly premise. Of course,

---

[13] Isaiah 53:7
[14] Matthew 11:29-30; Romans 5:5; 13:8-10; 1 Corinthians 13; 2 Corinthians 5:14-15; Ephesians 4:12-16
[15] Romans 12:2

such unholy adjustments are justified in the name of Christ and for the sake of furthering the Gospel.

When we consider Jesus as our cornerstone, we must realize that our lives are meant to be shaped according to the cornerstone; rather than the cornerstone being adjusted to fit our particular lifestyles. It is important to understand that most people are being allowed to define the Christian life according to a worldly presentation of Christianity. The main reason for this is because there is no true discipleship taking place in many of the Christian churches.

If the foundation is wrong, then there is no means by which to properly disciple a person. True discipleship is what properly lines the person up to Jesus as the cornerstone. However, much of the discipleship involves establishing or reinforcing the foundation of who Jesus is and must be in our lives. Subsequently, Christians' lifestyles will adjust according to their attitudes about life. If they do not have a proper perspective about the Lord, then they will fail to have the right attitude to properly line their lives up to His life, teachings, and examples. For this reason, the Apostle Paul, in essence, told us to work out our salvation in the attitude of fear and trembling.[16]

The other important part about the cornerstone is that it will also determine our reality. Jesus is the essence of truth. If a matter does not line up to Him, then it must be discarded. In order to line up to the truth, as Christians, we must operate in reality to properly test and discern both the spirit and fruits of our personal lives. This reality check is also necessary when it comes to testing the spirit and fruits of our different religious experiences and encounters.

When people adjust the cornerstone to fit their own reality, they are lining up to their own form of darkness or delusion, rather than truth. Jesus best described this state of affairs in John 3:19-20, "And this is the condemnation, that light is come into the world, and men loved darkness rather than light, because their deeds were evil. For everyone that doeth evil hateth the light, neither cometh to the light, lest his deeds should be reproved."

When you consider the lives of those who have erected their own cornerstone, you are able to see that nothing really fits. Not only are their lives not properly in line with truth, but they also are not firmly established upon the foundation. Not only are certain aspects of their lives ready to collapse from the lack of a foundation, but their actual structure also has no real design or order to it. The pillars of their belief systems are crooked from inconsistencies, the walls that fortify their spiritual claims are warped due to hypocrisy, and the floors that make up their source of reliance slant from the mixture of self-sufficiency and man-made religion.

As Christians, our lives are not meant to be attractive to the world, but to stand distinct from it. In order to stand distinct from the world,

---

[16] Philippians 2:12

Christians must understand that their lives are to serve as the standard in which the Lord Jesus Christ is lifted up in distinction above the world. It is from this vantage point that people will be drawn to His character, work, and life.[17]

The only way a Christian can ensure that Jesus is lifted up in this manner is to take on His life so that he or she can reflect His glory from his or her disposition. The Apostle Paul talked about reflecting Jesus' glory. However, he also recognized that he had to cease living his personal life in order to live the life of Christ by faith.[18] I have often told other believers that I do not care to see them; rather, I desire to see Jesus being reflected from their lives.

What kind of life is being established within you? As a believer, it must be the life of Christ. However, His life cannot be established within you unless you are firmly planted upon Him as the foundation and are actively lining your life up to Him as the cornerstone.

---

[17] John 12:32
[18] 2 Corinthians 3:18; Galatians 2:20

9

PERVERTING THE GOSPEL

It is important to follow the breakdown that is occurring in the religious realm. It is obvious why some of the Church of Jesus Christ would suffer an identity crisis. Such breakdowns of this nature occur slowly through small ways. For the professing Church, it started by simply changing the perspective about the Church or Body of Jesus. Instead of being composed of people, now it is often identified by denominational affiliation or some type of religious system or movement.

Once the perspective is changed about the makeup of the Church, then leadership in the Body can be redefined. Man and religion can now subtly replace Jesus as the Head and foundation of His Church, allowing people to adjust the cornerstone of all true religion to their own personal religious realities. The Apostle Paul penned his concerns about this matter in 2 Corinthians 11:3-4,

> But I fear, lest by any means, as the serpent beguiled Eve through his subtilty, so your minds should be corrupted from the simplicity that is in Christ. For if he that cometh preacheth another Jesus, whom we have not preached, or if ye receive another spirit, which ye have not received, or another gospel, which ye have not accepted, ye might well bear with him.

"Bear" in this Scripture means to hold oneself up against.[1]

When the Body of Christ was redefined according to the world, its connection with the Head was lost. Since some of the visible Body was not connected and functioning according to the Head, it began to lose its sense of identity. After all, the Body can only know its identity by being connected to the Head, Jesus Christ.

Since the connection is being lost in the midst of an unholy mixture, another Jesus can be presented. As the real Jesus is slowly compromised as a means to condition the people into complying with the religious box that is being presented, these people are brought under the influence of another spirit. This spirit will be an extension of the worldly spirit in operation, but it will be clothed in religion, thereby, being capable of becoming a religious substitute for Jesus.

Hence enters the affront against the true Gospel of Jesus Christ. The Gospel of Jesus is the power of God unto salvation. Although it is simple

---

[1] Strong's Exhaustive Concordance of the Bible, #430

enough for a child to embrace, it has been clearly ordained by heaven. As the Church of Jesus, believers have been commissioned to preach this message.[2] Note that, as Christians we are to preach it, not devise methods by which we can somehow snatch people out of the kingdom of darkness in order to place them in the kingdom of light. Such activities may be religious and hailed by the organized churches as being successful, but how many are truly saved?

The Gospel is really a place of agreement and exchange. This is why people must receive this message by faith. Each of us must come into agreement with God about our need to be saved from the dictates of sin and its consequences of death upon our souls. This agreement is necessary if we, as believers, are going to exchange our old lives of sin and rebellion for a new life of love, obedience, and service to God.

Such agreement finds it origins at the point of conviction about a person's sin-laden soul in light of the righteousness established by God through Jesus Christ's work of redemption on the cross. This person is able to recognize that, unless his or her sin is properly dealt with by the work of the cross of Jesus, he or she will not be able to be placed in Jesus' righteousness wrought by His redemption. Such identification in Jesus' redemption is the only way to avoid the judgment that remains upon those who are still dead and doomed in their spiritual condition.[3]

Although, we may not initially understand all of the implications of this new life upon our salvation, we have indeed become identified with Jesus in His death as the Lamb of God. This identification places us in the grave where all judgment towards our sins is silent, allowing us to realize, by faith, that resurrection power has now been placed within us to bring forth a new life.[4]

The reality of the Gospel is that the message may start out simple, but along the way it has become confusing for many new converts. Receiving the true Gospel ensures salvation. However, those who subtly add to the Gospel complicate the issue of salvation. Such complication opens a person up to another spirit.

When wrong spirits are in operation, they will always subtract or add to the Gospel to take away any real dependency on Christ that establishes a believer on the true foundation. This child-like dependency will also line him or her up to the real cornerstone. We have seen these subtractions and additions in many different ways. They come by way of association with a particular denomination or adopting certain works.

For example, there are those denominations that claim you must be a member of their particular group to be saved. This is definitely an addition to Jesus' salvation. Even though this particular "church" may purport Christ as Savior, the denomination is subtly claiming the position of Savior, even though it never died for the person.

---

[2] Mark 16:15; Romans 1:16; 1 Corinthians 15:1
[3] 1 Corinthians 1:30; 2 Corinthians 5:21
[4] Romans 6:1-10

With these types of denominations purporting to be Savior, then they will either deny the responsibilities Christians have to uphold biblical righteousness in their lives, or they will go to the other extremes where they advocate the works that will identify followers to their particular philosophies. For example, there is one denomination that states you must be water baptized to be saved. Such claims point to doing some type of works to be saved. However, the Bible states that Jesus alone saves. His salvation is a matter of grace. Granted, such works as water baptism will be a natural, but it will also be an upright response or extension of salvation, but such works are not a prerequisite of it. After all, we are condemned because we do not believe the Gospel, not because we fail to be baptized.[5]

This brings us to the next stage of the breakdown. Now that Jesus has been compromised, and there is another spirit in operation, promoting its own lifeless religion, the Gospel will be cleverly perverted without too much opposition from those who are being influenced by the heretical presentation.

The Apostle Paul talked about the seriousness behind presenting another or perverted Gospel. Those who are foolish enough to do it already stand cursed and will face greater damnation.[6] It is important to understand that all you have to do to pervert the Gospel is to take away from it or add to it. When you take away from the Gospel, you are watering it down in some way, rendering it powerless. If you are adding to it, you are stripping if of its simplicity and the power to save. In both cases the intent or spirit of the Gospel has been changed.[7]

As I read the works of some of the late, great servants of God, the one element I am aware of is how they maintained the integrity of the Gospel. In fact, their presentation of the Gospel has put life into my spirit. It stirs me up to once again consecrate my life. It feeds my soul with a greater sense of who my precious Lord is, and what His redemption means for my life.

In considering some of the popular works of the authors of today, all I can say is that if they do present the Gospel at all, it is so watered down that it has no life or meat to it. It may appeal to my sentiment or pride, but it leaves me empty. In fact, most presentations I have heard sound like flimsy attempts to justify any association or use of Jesus' name because there is no heart or spirit behind it.

My question is simple, "Whatever happened to the Gospel of Jesus Christ?" When did the intent of the Gospel change? As already pointed out, the simplicity of the Gospel has been changed or complicated by the various subtractions and additions of religion. When you change or complicate the simplicity of the Gospel, you are going to frustrate the

---

[5] Mark 16:15-16; Ephesians 2:8-10
[6] Galatians 1:6-9
[7] If you want an in-depth understanding of how the Gospel has been perverted, see the author's book, *The Presentation of the Gospel* in this volume.

grace of God. In other words, you are going to make its very work in your life void.

God's grace makes one statement—that salvation is God showing favor towards man so that he can receive His eternal life. This favor allows man to do right towards God, but such deeds will not make him acceptable to God. Rather, they will simply serve as an extension of, or as evidence that eternal life is present, as well as being established in him.[8]

However, the real problem with the false gospels that are being presented is that there is no life in any of them. In other words, the Holy Spirit is not in them. The Gospel is powerful because of the preparation that is done by the Spirit of God to receive it. He is the one who anoints the vessel that proclaims this simple message. This anointing is what is going to impact the souls of others. He is also the one who prepares people to receive the truth of the Gospel with the conviction of sin, righteousness, and judgment.[9]

In fact, when the Holy Spirit has been present in the presentation of the Gospel, I have witnessed people literally running forward to get matters right with God. There was no need to try to stir people up intellectually or emotionally to compel them to come forward. The Spirit had already laid upon their sin-laden souls the need to do business with God.

There are reasons that the Spirit is missing from much of the evangelistic methods that have been implemented to present the Gospel. The first one is obvious. Any subtraction or addition to the Gospel creates an unholy mixture that the Spirit will not honor. When there is an unholy mixture in regard to the Gospel, the light of the Gospel will be compromised, causing it to become dim. The light of the Gospel is Jesus Christ.[10] When one compromises who He is, the person will strip the Gospel of its power to penetrate the heart.

If the Holy Spirit and the light of Jesus are missing, then there will be a void that must be filled with man's best attempts to get people to give some type of an appearance that salvation is taking place. Obviously, the true Gospel has been replaced with methods that con, logic, plead, or manipulate the person to say some type of prayer of salvation. These methods may appeal to the intellect or the emotions, but they often fail to penetrate down to the spirit of man to awaken him to his dreadful condition of sin and death. In a way, man is responding to the message from the premise of his own darkness of self-delusion and not from the urgency of seeing the need to get things right with a holy God who will one day cease to be longsuffering towards the influence, workings, and activities of sin in his life.[11] Keep in mind that man's darkness will never

---

[8] Romans 3:23; 6:23; Galatians 2:21; Ephesians 2:8-10
[9] John 16:7-11
[10] 2 Corinthians 4:3-6
[11] 2 Peter 3:9

come into agreement with the light of the Gospel. It is only when the light of the Gospel penetrates the darkness of a person's soul that he or she will see the desperate need to seek God's forgiveness, redemption, and reconciliation at the cross of Christ.

The light of Jesus is meant to bring a contrast to our spiritual condition. As you study John the Baptist who prepared the way for the Messiah, the light of the world, you realize that people must first be prepared to receive the Gospel. Such preparation comes with the call to repentance so that sins can be remitted or pardoned by God.[12] If people are going to come to the wells of salvation, they need to be aware that they have a sin problem that must be rectified. This will take the conviction of the Holy Spirit. Therefore, the Holy Spirit convicts of sin, bringing about godly repentance that will cause a person to turn from such sin to receive the gift of life. Once a person repents, then he or she must be converted by the ways of righteousness. It is not enough to turn from old ways unless he or she is ready to be converted by the new ways of righteousness.

I can remember my salvation experience. Months before I received the gift of Jesus' life, I was being prepared to repent. The light of the Gospel began to penetrate my dark, foreboding soul with the reality of my sin. The Holy Spirit was allowing me to feel the weight of my sin upon my soul. The weight became so great that a cloud of depression was consuming me. I suspected that God was an answer to my problem, but my understanding of Him was vague; therefore, He appeared indifferent and far away.

Through a series of events, the Lord led me to some real Christians who knew the solution to my sin problem. The first time some committed Christian women shared Jesus with me, I was so much stirred in my spirit that I even asked her to take me to her church. God's presence and power met me when I entered the doors of their local church. To this day I cannot tell you the message that was delivered during the services, but I can tell you the overwhelming revelation of His love that I experienced.

God's love for me was gently drawing me to the reality of the salvation He had so freely provided for me. I received the loving revelation of His Son's death on the cross as my solution to my sin. When I walked out of that church, the burden of my sin had rolled away. I walked away with a living witness in my heart that I had indeed been delivered from the entanglements of sin and the consequences of eternal separation from God.

When the Gospel message presented is watered down because it is missing the revelation of sin, then a person will not understand what he or she is being saved from.[13] As a result, you have people who have a

---

[12] Mark 1:4, 15; Luke 13:3, 5

[13] If you would like to understand the influence, workings and activities of sin upon your life, see the author, *The Anatomy of Sin* in Volume One of the foundation series.

false hope of being saved from a bad life, unpleasant situations, financial difficulties, or despair, but not from sin. If the person is not being saved from sin, then he or she will fail to understand what he or she is being saved unto.

Salvation is not just a matter of being delivered from sin and death, but it is also about being delivered into a whole new life where one can actually experience the glorious reality of God in a living relationship. Since the Gospel is being watered down in one aspect, it will possess a different emphasis. For example, people who accept these watered-down gospels can perceive that they are being delivered into the life they so desire. Hence enter gospels that are influenced by worldly philosophies. They will socialize you, judaize you, entertain you, and make you feel good about yourself, but they will not save you. There is no place of real agreement between God and the person who possesses such a gospel that will result in true reconciliation. Since the emphasis of these false gospels is wrong, the churches that promote them often become nothing more than religious social clubs.

It is also important to point out that, when you make Christianity a religious activity or a matter of doctrine, rather than a life, Jesus will be rendered into some type of controllable intellectual concept. So when people are encouraged, manipulated, or emotionally twisted like pretzels to accept Jesus as their Savior, it seems like a logical or sentimental thing to do. However, Jesus is a Living Person who needs to be received into the heart as Lord and Savior. [14]

Although you can interchange the two words "accept" and "receive", they can have different emphasis behind them. This is why the King James Version of the Bible uses the word "receive" when it comes to our life in Christ. Intellectually, I can accept any type of concept about Jesus that is cleverly or emotionally presented. However, to receive the life of Christ entails faith that actually believes the Gospel is true and receives His very promise of life as a reality in the heart. The Bible is clear that salvation is a heart revelation and not an intellectual assent. We are born again in the spirit or inner being, not born again in our minds or at the point of our intellects. It is only as our spirit is born again that our mind can begin to be transformed by the life of the Spirit working within our inner man to receive the fullness of God.[15]

When you water down what it means to receive Jesus, people will fail to recognize that the Gospel is not just about understanding a matter, but having a complete change that will manifest itself in a new life. If that new life is not being made evident, a person must examine whether or not he or she received Jesus.

The one abiding truth I have been aware of is that it is the Godhead who saves. The Father draws people to His Son, the Son invites people to come to Him as their Lord and Savior in order to drink of the water that

---

[14] John 1:12
[15] John 3:3, 5; Romans 10:9-10; Romans 12:2

Challenging the Christian Life

will spring up into everlasting life, and the Holy Spirit convicts people of their need to be saved from their sin and God's judgment, unto the righteousness of Jesus.[16]

Since God is the one who saves, He moves in spite of, around, and sometimes through man's different methods and attempts to draw people to the Gospel. In essence, God is always quick to honor the tender heart that truly is seeking some type of solution, in spite of the lifeless and religious attempts of man.

This awareness of God's faithfulness to save even those who might not even realize He is looking for them shows not only His power to save, but also His commitment to save. It is not His will that any of us perish in our sins. He has provided the means by which to save each of us from our dreadful plight. In light of this sobering truth, I am also very much aware that the righteous are scarcely saved.[17]

It is impossible to save ourselves, and God must penetrate our hard hearts of arrogance and unbelief to show us our need for His salvation. It is God's longsuffering that allows for the time of preparation that results in godly repentance. It is His mercy that refrains from judging us in our doomed state of sin and death, and it is His grace that is quick to show us favor in our undeserving state by giving us eternal life. This is the glorious reality, assurance, and hope of the Gospel.

There is only one question left, have you truly received the revelation of the Gospel in your heart? Has the issue of your sin been properly dealt with? Does the revelation of the Gospel continue to change your life? Only you can answer these questions. Remember, salvation is a work of God, but you must receive by faith every aspect of the Gospel message as being true to ensure you have received eternal life.

---

[16] Luke 9:56; John 4:13-14; 6:44; 7:37-39; 16:8-11
[17] 1 Peter 4:17-18; 2 Peter 3:9

10

REPROBATE FAITH

We have been considering how the influence of the world has affected the face of the professing Church. Obviously, the only thing the world can do for the Church is to defile it by changing its identity. It has simply been conformed to a religious image that has no life or substance behind it.

As we follow the digression of the professing Church into its present state, we can see how its concept of its identity would change according to the world's influence. The foundation has been redefined, the cornerstone readjusted, and the Gospel perverted to conform it to the various images that have been set forth by man. Sadly, if believers do not seek the true Church's identity in Scripture, they will become confused by what is nothing more than a worldly presentation. After all, as they look at these different worldly presentations of the Church, it is almost like looking at a mirror, but the mirror has been broken. Although the glass has been put back together by the best attempts of man, it still is perverted. In its overall presentation, this mirror is riddled with cracks that break the continuity of the presentation. In other places, it is fragmented where it fails to make sense and clouded due to abuse and neglect. Therefore, there is no real clear image or presentation of the Church when it comes to the world.

The only place the Church can gain its real identity is from looking at itself through the eyes of the Jesus of the Bible. He is the foundation, the cornerstone, and the only light in the Gospel. He is the one that died on the cross for His Body. As a result, the members of His Body have been seated in high places with Him.[1] Clearly, believers' vantage point will not be earthbound, world-inspired, or man-manipulated. It will be a heavenly vantage point that will keep believers far above the entanglements of the world and the limited, useless attempts of man.

This brings us to the final breakdown of the life of the professing Church. There are what I consider to be sad statements or sayings in the Bible. Every time I come to one of these sayings, my heart is wrenched at the prospect of what is being said. In these sayings, there is sadness, as well as urgency. Most of these statements come in the form of a question. A question calls for personal examination. For example, the first sad statement in the Bible is found in Genesis 3:9, "And the LORD

---

[1] Ephesians 2:6

God called unto Adam, and said unto him, Where art thou?" God knew where Adam was, but Adam had to face that the fellowship between his Creator and him had been broken by his disobedience in the garden. Instead of man walking with God, he would now hide from God as he attempted to cover up the guilt of his sin behind worldly fig leaves of shame and religious cloaks of self-righteousness.[2]

Jesus also made some sad statements to His disciples. Every time I read these statements my heart becomes sorrowful. In fact, I can almost see Him saying it to me when the times are tough or I am giving way to the old man. One of these statements was made after many of His followers turned back to their old ways to never follow Him again. For Adam, he broke fellowship with God, but for Jesus' disciples, His truth insulted them. Since they could not understand the truth Jesus spoke, they became uncertain and judgmental towards Him, and departed. These followers did not realize that the sharpness of Jesus' truths would not only expose their level of dedication, but their motives. Obviously, they were not totally consecrated to serving Him. It was at this time that Jesus asked this penetrating question of His remaining disciples in John 6:67b, "Will ye also go away?"

Jesus asked another sad question that always makes me stop and ponder the warning and urgency of it. It is found in Luke 18:8b: "Nevertheless, when the Son of man cometh, shall he find faith on the earth?"

As you consider the digression of the presentation of the Church due to its union with the world, it is obvious that all matters relating to the kingdom of God have been redefined, readjusted, perverted, and undermined. The pure has been defiled, truth compromised, integrity sacrificed, and true consecration mocked. The Apostle Paul summarized the state of affairs when he made this statement in Titus 1:15-16,

> Unto the pure all things are pure, but unto them that are defiled and unbelieving is nothing pure; but even their mind and conscience is defiled. They profess that they know God, but in works they deny him, being abominable, and disobedient, and unto every good work reprobate.

"Reprobate" is an interesting word. It means unapproved, rejected, worthless, and a castaway.[3] When you study this word, you will realize that something is being cast off or rejected because it is impure. It is not coming from an acceptable origin or premise. In each case, it is coming from something that has already been defiled. In Titus, we see that even good works will be rejected if they come from a wrong premise.

The Apostle Paul also spoke of a reprobate mind in Romans 1:28. We know that we have all been given an inward sense that there is a God. This sense also gives us a semblance of His character.[4] Granted,

---

[2] John 15:22
[3] Strong's Exhaustive Concordance of the Bible; #96
[4] Romans 1:18-20

we may not personally know Him, and we may even refuse to listen to that inner sense, ultimately rejecting that aspect of our conscience altogether. But, on judgment day, there will be no excuse for us not really coming to terms with the true God of heaven.

The Apostle Paul described how people acquire a reprobate mind. First, they refuse to glorify God in their lives. The reason for this is because they are unthankful and caught up with their vain imaginations. These imaginations begin to darken their already foolish hearts with greater delusion. In other words, the foolish heart will justify its wicked attitude. Such an attitude will begin to change the glory of God as it gives way to its idolatrous pursuits and preferences.[5]

As the person gives way to his or her idolatrous ways, God will give him or her over to the lusts of his or her own heart. This is a form of judgment where such individuals will experience the emptiness and bitterness of these useless pursuits, as well as consequences. It also means that their deceitful and rebellious heart will manifest itself in unclean practices as they begin to dishonor their bodies.[6] Dishonoring one's body clearly points to fornication, which involves coming into agreement with the unholy in some way. The Apostle Paul made reference to this in 1 Corinthians 6:18, "Flee fornication. Every sin that a man doeth is without the body; but he that committeth fornication sinneth against his own body."

In this unholy agreement, the person will exchange the truth of God for a lie as he or she begins to worship and serve his or her lusts, pursuits, and/or unholy unions. As these individuals are given over to their wicked master, God will give them up to pursue their vile affections, as even the natural becomes inordinate. It is from this premise that God will give these people over to a reprobate mind that no longer retains any real knowledge of Him.[7]

As we consider the word "reprobate" in the text of a reprobate mind, we can see that a mind that does not retain the knowledge of the true God is worthless. However, remember this mind gave up any real desire to know the true God. It preferred its inordinate lusts and wicked pursuits to honoring the true God of heaven. Therefore, we can see where our minds and our good works can be considered reprobate or useless because of their source or motivation.

This brings us to something else that can also be considered worthless because of its source or motivation. Heed the apostle's words, "Examine yourselves, whether you are in the faith; prove yourselves. Know ye not yourselves how Jesus Christ is in you, except ye be reprobate" (2 Corinthians 13:5).

The Apostle Paul stated that we, as Christians, could be considered worthless or castaways. This was one of the Apostle Paul's personal

---

[5] Romans 1:21-23
[6] Romans 1:24
[7] Romans 1:26-28

concerns as well. He made this statement, "But I keep under my body, and bring it into subjection, lest that by any means, when I have preached to others, I myself should be a castaway" (1 Corinthians 9:27). In 2 Corinthians 13:5, the Apostle Paul brought out that the test of our worth will be based on whether we are in the true faith.

In the last three decades, I have seen the presentation of faith change many times. Today, much of the faith that is being presented is unscriptural and worthless. For me, the big struggle has been to come to terms with genuine faith.[8] After all, there is only one true faith. It was clearly first delivered to the saints. This faith has not changed; therefore, there are no new revelations concerning it. In fact, we are told to contend for the faith that was first delivered to the saints.[9] "Contend" means to struggle for something in order to maintain a proper grip on it.[10] It could be related to a wrestling match.

There are so many pseudo faiths that have blown through Christendom. Sadly, I have watched people being swept away by these ridiculous winds.[11] However, the Bible is clear about what constitutes genuine faith. To make sure we start from the right premise, we must understand what faith is.

To describe faith, words such as believe, persuasion, conviction, trust, assurance, and faithfulness are used. Faith involves a choice of the will. I must choose to believe a matter is true. The reason I choose to believe a matter is true is because I am persuaded by a sincere conviction. This conviction will cause me to put my confidence or trust in it. I will be able to be assured about my confidence because the character of faithfulness is clearly present to confirm my trust.

This brings me to the first issue of my faith. What must I choose to believe to be true? Romans 10:17 gives me the bases on which our confidence or trust as believers will begin. "So, then, faith cometh by hearing, and hearing by the word of God." The source of any believer's faith is founded on what the Word of God says. Why is the Word of God so important? It is a record of who God is and His dealings with man. We must choose to believe that God's Word is true and faithful in order to embrace its testimonies.

All unbelief in a person's life begins at the same point. He or she justifies away, ignores, or refuses to believe the Word of God about a matter, thereby, failing to obey it. Romans 14:23b tells us that whatsoever does not originate from or respond according to genuine faith will be considered sin. When King David was confronted by the prophet Nathan concerning his sins of adultery and murder, this

---

[8] If you would like to know about what the author discovered about faith, see her book titled, *In Search of Real Faith* in Volume Two of the foundation series.
[9] Ephesians 4:5; Jude 3
[10] Strong's Exhaustive Concordance of the Bible, #1864
[11] Ephesians 4:14

statement was made, "Wherefore hast thou despised the commandment of the LORD, to do evil in his sight..." (2 Samuel 12:9a)? King David was the man that expounded on the need and importance of loving the commandments of God, and yet he failed to believe and apply them to his own life when he found himself in temptation. In fact, once he fell into the cesspool of sin, his deeds led to the murder of one of his devoted soldiers. God said of David's actions that they showed that he was actually despising, disesteeming, disdaining, or scorning His commandments at that point in his life.[12]

Sadly, the authority and power of God's Word has been replaced by man's traditions and religious activities that include such things as good works and coming back under the covenant of the Old Testament Law. Instead of the Word being used to discern a matter, it is often interpreted according to the doctrine or theology of man. Therefore, it is adjusted to fit man's personal understanding or preference towards a spiritual truth or issue. The key to true faith is that it approaches the Word to believe it, not to debate or adjust it according to personal preferences, understanding, or doctrine. The world will defile the things of God, but man always perverts it. He is forever adding to it or taking away from it.

Faith comes down to where we are putting our reliance or confidence. In many cases, man is putting his faith in what he understands or perceives about God. This type of individual actually perceives and professes him or herself as being wise, but the reality is that he or she is foolish for putting his or her confidence in that which has no spirit or truth. Such a premise is nothing more than perversion. In fact, it is a way to frustrate the grace of God because such individuals are failing to recognize the complete work of redemption that was accomplished on the cross. As the Apostle Paul declared in Romans 5:21, "That as sin hath reigned unto death, even so might grace reign through righteousness unto eternal life by Jesus Christ, our Lord." Once again, as believers, we are reminded that faith is reckoned or counted to us as righteousness.[13]

One of the most blatant examples of this perversion can be found among those who do not believe Jesus is God in the flesh. They have come to this conclusion based on their own vain, perverted, and logical evaluation and/or on information that has been twisted to fit their conclusions. As a result, they have changed the glory of God that was manifested in the flesh and made Him into a mere man that did a sacrificial deed. Obviously, these people do not believe the record given concerning Jesus Christ. They clearly have not approached the Bible to believe it; rather, they have approached it to debate, refute, and reject whatever does not fit into their perverted concept about Jesus Christ.

Faith entails being persuaded that something is legitimate. In other words, we, as believers, are being persuaded that the Word of God is

---

[12] Strong's Exhaustive Concordance of the Bible, #959
[13] Romans 1:22; 4:9; Galatians 2:21

truth. The Apostle Paul clearly brings this out in 2 Timothy 1:12, "For which cause I also suffer these things; nevertheless, I am not ashamed; for I know whom I have believed and am persuaded that he is able to keep that which I have committed unto him against that day."

One of the fruits I have grown to appreciate about genuine faith is that it enables me to face reality. There is not much I like about the reality that constantly confronts me. Over the years, I have discovered that the source of my confidence is going to determine how I confront the many issues of life.[14] These issues can include such unpleasant challenges as bothersome troubles, losses, and death.

Genuine faith strictly finds its source in God. One of the principle doctrines of Christ is faith towards God. Notice, genuine faith is directed at God. Scriptures clearly reveals to us that we are identified to the spiritual seed of Abraham based on this faith. It is this faith that also identifies us to the great cloud of witness mentioned in Hebrews 12:1. We are told that we are given a measure of faith.[15] This measure of faith allows us to take steps of obedience in light of who God is.

When you consider the faith of many in the professing Church, their confidence is not in God. The main push behind their misdirected faith is not to walk by faith through the trials of life in confidence of God; rather, it is a means to change their reality so that they do not have to be tested in the fiery ovens of adversity.[16] For some, they have put their confidence in their words. They try to change reality by claiming or professing their desired reality. Such words lack truth and spirit; therefore, they are idle words. The intent behind such words is selfish and has nothing to do with the will of God. Such words will reveal the treasures that are truly being valued in these people's hearts. Jesus made this statement about idle words in Matthew 12:35-47,

> A good man out of the good treasure of the heart bringeth forth good things, and an evil man out of the evil treasure bringeth forth evil things. But I say unto you that every idle word that men shall speak, they shall give account of it in the day of judgment. For by thy words thou shalt be justified, and by thy words thou shalt be condemned.

Some of these individuals even use God's promises to try to get their way in their particular realities. It is as though they take His promises and beat Him over the head with them until they are fulfilled according to their perspective. However, Hebrews 6:12 gives us this insight about God's promises, "That ye be not slothful, but followers of them who though faith and patience inherit the promises."

Christians who truly understand faith recognize that their faith does not possess any power. Regardless of the methods that are used, faith

---

[14] If you would like to understand the real matters affecting life, see the author's book, *The Issues of Life* in this same volume.

[15] Romans 12:3; Galatians 3:6-9; Hebrews 6:1

[16] 2 Corinthians 5:7; 1 Peter 1:6-8

cannot move God's arm if the prayer, pursuit, or desire is contrary to His character, will, and timing. Therefore, faith does not move God; rather, it personally moves and inspires the believer in confidence, as well as with conviction and diligence, to faithfully obey the Lord until the conditions of the promises are fulfilled.[17]

The main desire of faith is to seek God out in order to do His will. It desires to please God in all that it does. Once faith responds in the proper way, God is able to meet the believer and count his or her action as righteousness. Clearly, genuine faith simply allows God to be God. Genuine faith is often accredited with moving mountains, but, in reality, it allows God the correct environment to move obstacles. Clearly, God desires to confirm and honor genuine faith by doing the miraculous in the lives of His faithful servants.[18]

Faith clearly comes down to a person's real point of confidence. This is why we are told that we cannot please God without faith.[19] Faith chooses to trust God, not according to His power, but according to His character. Faith knows that God does not lie and that He is faithful to those who are His. Even in the darkest time of his life, Job chose to put trust and assurance in God's character and not in his circumstances. His statement confirmed his abiding assurance that he had towards God in Job13:15, "Though he slay me, yet will I trust in him; but I will maintain mine own ways before him." Even if God required his very life, Job would not only trust Him, but he understood that he would be able to maintain or defend his ways before God because they were a matter of sincere faith towards Him.

This brings us back to where people put their reliance. The confusion rests with the fact that people put their reliance on religious things, but it is not in God. They can put their reliance in their denominations, theologies, good works, and religious activities, but all of these pseudo faiths are simply putting confidence in the arm of man. The prophet, Jeremiah had some strong words about such misplaced confidence,

> Thus saith the LORD, Cursed be the man that trusteth in man, and maketh flesh his arm, and whose heart departeth from the LORD. For he shall be like the heath in the desert, and shall not see when good cometh, but shall inhabit the parched places in the wilderness, in a salt land and not inhabited. Blessed is the man who trusteth in the LORD, and whose hope the LORD is. (Jeremiah 17:5-7)

Clearly, there is only one place where we can put our confidence, and that is our Lord Jesus Christ. This brings us back to the warning of the Apostle Paul. If our faith is not in the Lord Jesus Christ of the Bible, we will prove to be reprobates in our Christian life. Therefore, if people's scriptural understanding about spiritual matters is not founded on the

---

[17] James 2:23-26
[18] Matthew 17:20; Romans 3:28; 4:3; Hebrews 11:6; James 5:16: 1 John 5:14
[19] Hebrews 11:6

Person of Jesus, God will reject them as the storms of life expose the fallacy of their foundation. If their conduct does not line up to Jesus as the cornerstone, they will find their ways and works counted as worthless before God. If they are not properly identified to the Head, they will be considered castaways.

For the last twenty centuries, the true Church has had to wade through the many different pseudo faiths that have taken center stage. However, the real Church is able to identify the faith that was first delivered to the saints because it has been clearly unveiled in Scripture. God would never expect us to possess the true faith if He had not outlined it through instructions and examples.

As you study the lives of those found in Hebrews 11, you realize they do make up a great cloud of witnesses. These witnesses show us that walking by faith is not only possible, but also rewarding. In fact, this walk serves as the most natural expression of those who truly love God and want to please Him. As you study this chapter, you can see where active faith inspired these people to risk it all to discover God. They were all seeking God. Abraham not only understood that God was his portion, but he sought the city made by God. In faith towards God's instructions, Noah built an ark, even though he had never seen the rain. Moses refused to enjoy sin for a season so he could be identified with God's people. There were those who sought a better resurrection, regardless of the cost, and there were still others whose faith the world was not even worthy to witness. Truly, these people's faith brought such pleasure to God that He would not share it with an age that would surely mock it.

This brings us to a very important aspect of a life of unfeigned faith. Such a walk is what will bring us into discovering the fullness and majesty of God. Such fullness points to complete satisfaction. Today, people, including professing Christians, are trying to fill the empty vacuum in their souls with activities and things or stuff from the world. Although such things may bring a temporary satisfaction, such satisfaction will not last. As a result, such people move on to other pursuits.

For the Christian who discovers the life that the great cloud of witnesses speaks of, he or she has also discovered the satisfaction that will fill and maintain the soul. It is the life of Christ in each of us, as Christians, that must fill every aspect of our lives with a sense of revelation, awe, and worship. As Scripture states about Jesus, "For in him dwelleth all the fullness of the Godhead bodily...Where there is neither Greek nor Jew, circumcision nor uncircumcision, barbarian, Scythian, bond nor free, but Christ is all, and in all" (Colossians 2:9; 3:11).

The fullness of Christ is the life that unfeigned faith will discover in its walk. It is complete and worth all that it may cost each of us to secure it. For Abraham, it gave him a perspective that reached beyond his present age into eternity. For Noah, it gave him an ark that delivered him through the judgment upon the present age of his day. For Moses, it gave him a point of identification, even in the midst of great slavery to endure the age of great testing in the wilderness. In essence, faith allows saints to discover God in the barren wilderness of the darkness of their present age.

What about your faith or point of reliance? Is it in what you think you know? Perhaps it is in what you do for God? Maybe your point of reliance is in your particular denomination or words or even in using God's promises to get your way concerning the things of this present age? Maybe you think that, by coming back under the Old Testament Law (the deeds and doctrine of the Nicolaitans), it is going to earn God's approval? However, if your faith is not in the true God of the Bible and His provision of Jesus Christ, your whole life could be considered reprobate before Him. What a waste! As believers, we must remember, that on the great day of judgment when all will be stripped from each of us, only the pure gold of unfeigned faith, the refined silver of redemption that has been tried in the fires of testing and separation, and the precious stones of our loving devotion will survive the penetrating fire of His holy judgment upon all of that which has been truly committed to Him by faith.[20]

---

[20] 1 Corinthians 3:12-15; 1 Peter 1:6-9

Part III
THE POWERLESS PULPIT

11

THE PURPOSE

We have considered how the Church has been influenced by the world and how a shift has taken place in the leadership. As a result, the sheep are scattering in every direction in attempts to find waters (preaching and teaching) that have not been muddied with some type of heretical poisons, pastures (fellowships) that are free from the attack of predators, and shepherds who truly possess the heart of Jesus.

There clearly has been a strong undercurrent that has been moving the visible Church away from the center of the Rock. Obviously, different congregations have been boxed in by man's religions, dulled down by worldly influences, and experienced a shift from Christ-centered leadership to man-centered rule. As a result, these local bodies are also witnessing what I refer to as the "powerless pulpit." A "powerless pulpit" is a pulpit that has no means by which to impact people's lives. Without the right impact flowing from the pulpits, an identity crisis can erupt in those who are part of these congregations. These individuals will actually feel disconnected and confused about their lives in Christ.

There are a couple of reasons why pulpits are proving to be powerless in churches. The first reason is that congregations are not prepared or opened to any spiritual revolution that could be created by a pulpit that is aflame with the power of God. Many of these individuals in such congregations still find their identification with the world and not in the Jesus of the Bible. Some have been conditioned by heretical presentations and have been indoctrinated by man in some way. As a result, these individuals have not really accepted the call of Jesus to become His disciples. Because of this unreceptive attitude of those who sometimes represent the majority in certain congregations, pastors who could bring life back to the pulpit are passed over, disregarded, or shunned.

The second reason has to do with those who hold the title or position of a pastor. Many have given way to or fallen prey to the compromising, worldly, and heretical environment and philosophies that are invading much of the visible Church. Such pastors are nothing more than the "walking dead." They have no flame of inspiration (fire from the throne), light (resurrection life), or heavenly perspective to pass on the torch that has been entrusted to the true Church of Jesus. Therefore, dulled down, lifeless congregations and "dead" pastors are being drawn together, creating a dangerous scenario for those who innocently find themselves in such an environment.

As you consider this environment, you will realize that it enables people to *play* Church rather than become *part* of the living Church, Body, or extension of Jesus Christ. The other aspect of this worldly, religious environment is that it makes people feel good about their spiritual conditions. In other words, they actually believe that Jesus came to save them *in* their sin and not *from* it. This type of condition is actually making people feel good in their wretched, condemned state about their compromise with the world, as they merrily continue on their way to hell.

In order to understand the impact that every Christian pulpit should be making, we have to understand what constitutes a "pulpit." This is an important way to address attitudes towards the idea or concept of "pulpit" as a means to come to terms with their purpose.

To understand the purpose of pulpits, we have to consider their meaning. Since pulpits are not mentioned in the Bible, we must look to the secular dictionary to understand the premise of the attitudes that have been developed towards these objects. My dictionary gave a couple of definitions for the word "pulpit."[1]

The first definition is that a pulpit is an elevated platform or high reading desk that is used for preaching or to conduct worship service. Another meaning that the word "pulpit" is associated with is the preaching profession, and, in some cases, it is used to identify a person with a religious position.

As we consider these meanings, we can begin to see the attitude that has been developed towards the concept of the pulpit. First, it is a place of veneration, but whom or what is being exalted? It is a place where something is actually being staged. However, anything that is stage in relationship to God's kingdom often points to schedules that are controlled by man. These elevated places also can point to possible pretense or hypocrisy that has been promoted, encouraged, or condoned through the means of entertainment that has been clearly inspired by the world.

The word "pulpit" is also associated with a profession, but does the presence of the pulpit distinguish the person or does the person define the significance of such a place based on what is being proclaimed from this elevated place? It also points to position. Does a pulpit give a person authority or does the person's authority empower the place of the pulpit?

There was an incident in which a man was asked to inform the congregation of upcoming activities. He was a teacher by profession and

---

[1] Webster's Dictionary

Challenging the Christian Life

admitted that he had secretly longed to stand behind the church's pulpit. However, when he was standing behind the pulpit, informing the congregation of the upcoming activities, he felt intimidated by it. He realized that it was not just a matter of standing behind it, but of being equipped to actually fulfill the actual purpose for which it was designated.

In dealing with the issues of the pulpit, I have noticed a pulpit has no real meaning other than what people associate with it. Pulpits vary in sizes, looks, and presentations. Mere man may stand behind these objects, but, otherwise, it stands silent most of the time.

It is clear that the pulpit has no purpose outside of simply serving as a stand on which information can be placed. This stand, in many cases, has been elevated so the crowds or masses can see the speakers. Take away the pulpit and the stage, and the person who was elevated will once again be placed on equal footing with everyone else. This shows us that the real importance of the pulpit does not necessarily rest with the one who is speaking.

This brings us to the information or messages, which can include songs, that are being delivered from the pulpit. The purpose of the pulpit is to share, proclaim, or bring forth some kind of message. Clearly, people are not there to watch an individual simply stand behind a pulpit, rather they are present to hear what a person has to say in regard to a subject or matter. In summation, they are there to hear the message.

Sadly, man has been improperly exalted above the message, drowning out the real purpose for a pulpit. Consider for a moment, if people are present to simply venerate a man behind the pulpit instead of hearing the message, they are basically wasting their time. Granted the validity of man will be tested and established by his message, but the impact of the message will hinge on whether man has the necessary authority to deliver it. Therefore, the real purpose of a pulpit is to deliver an important message that will prove to be viable to the lives of others.

As I have stood behind different pulpits to share a message in regard to my faith, I have regarded them as altars, tables, or a place of exaltation. For example, it is from the altar of the pulpit that preachers or speakers offer up some type of sacrifice to God. These sacrifices must be holy to be considered acceptable to God. Acceptable sacrifices will emit some type of fragrance that will prove to be well-pleasing to God, bringing Him glory.

To me, a pulpit is a table of showbread. At this table, the bread of the Word will be broken and presented as food to sustain the inner lives of those who are present. For some, the bread must be dissolved into the milk of pure doctrine for them to drink of it. For others, it must be presented with the meat of righteousness to ensure maturity. Such impartation can prove challenging to any messenger, but the main goal of the messenger is to ensure that such priceless food is not flung at the people, but that it is actually being imparted to them.

This brings us to whom or what needs to be exalted from the Christian pulpit. There is only One person who deserves to be exalted from the pulpits of the churches that has His name associated with them, and that is the Lord Jesus Christ. It is His Gospel that must be proclaimed. He is the bread from heaven that must be properly imparted into the lives of His people, and it is the flow of His life that serves as a sweet savor to God.[2] It is from such a pulpit that man ceases to be the center of attention, as the message is empowered, and the people impacted.

When we consider what the real purpose of the pulpit is, we must examine why it has become powerless. Perhaps it is obvious to some. Instead of offering sacrifices that are pleasing to God, there are those who use the pulpit to offer up profane offerings to God that are emitting a stench to Him. Rather, than imparting the Word to feed the souls of people, leaders are feeding the people's minds with a mixture of worldly philosophies, such as psychology, along with what I consider to be nothing more than Biblical notions.

Biblical notions are when man takes a subject out of the Bible and adjusts it to his own self-serving preference. One such preference is the notion that God's whole goal is to see man happy, enriched with the world's goods, and pursuing that which is pleasing to him. Such a notion is man-centered, which makes it humanistic to the core. To offer this type of combination to God would be the same as offering strange fire to Him. Such fire resulted in the death of Aaron's sons and, sadly, is resulting in a tidal wave of destruction that will take many unsuspecting people into judgment.

Obviously, to offer unacceptable mixtures from the pulpits would render such pulpits powerless. In such cases, the preacher simply becomes an entertainer, and the message becomes nothing more than fluff that contains the residues of poison and death for those who partake of it.

Are there any pulpits in your life? Take time to examine them to see what kind of offering is being made by the leaders. If the strange or profane is being offered to God, flee from such a place for the wrath of God will be abiding on such a pulpit.

---

[2] John 6:35; 12:32; 2 Corinthians 2:15-16; Hebrews 5:11-14

12

THE PLACE OF WITNESS

When people stray from the center after finding themselves in an identity crisis, they begin to struggle to bring back some order, meaning, and purpose in their lives. In their desperate attempts, they often jump on the pendulum that is now beginning to swing from side to side in regard to the issues that have caused a tidal wave of confusion.

Cleary, the pendulum is swinging in Christendom. Those who try to gauge which side of the pendulum they want to associate with find themselves being flung into extremes. Even truth that is taken into any extreme becomes a point of deception. After all, God does not deal in extremes, but operates from the center of what is true, pure, and just. Center points to balance, not chaos, sanity rather than ridiculousness, and clarity instead of confusion.

Obviously, the sane action to take is to avoid the pendulum that is swinging into the extreme areas of religion and come back to center in order to establish what is sound. The prophet Haggai actually instructed the people of Israel to consider their ways. According to the *Strong's Exhaustive Concordance,* "consider" in this text pointed to coming back to center in order to establish the acceptable and right order.

As the problem in the visible Church gains the momentum of a tsunami, the debate rages on among those who are trying to bring some type of semblance to the Church before the momentum causes many to become shipwrecked in their faith. But such attempts result in some of these well-meaning people desperately snatching at straws that have already been flung up in the air by the present winds of judgment.

It does appear as if a great dam of destruction has broken, and its waters are sweeping many away from the sanity and safety of truth. However, the key is not to stop the flow of waters, for they will come, but to properly identify and address the breach that has been made through apparent compromise and neglect. No doubt, there could be various issues sighted as to the reason for this great breach, but, once again, I would like to weigh in on this matter with my conclusion. Much of the breach has occurred because the pulpit has been rendered powerless.

God has a clear order. This order has been distinguished by clear Scriptural guidelines. In fact, you can actually see God work within these guiding principles. One of the rules that has been brought out through Scripture has to do with witnesses.

A matter can only be confirmed by two or three witnesses.[1] It is not proper to take the word of one witness as being valid. When we consider the concept of one, we realize there is one who is the beginning, fulfillment, and end to all that is trustworthy, and that is God. However, even God confirms a matter with at least three witnesses. Granted, He could rightfully stop with two witnesses, for the number "two" points to agreement, but God usually confirms a matter with three witnesses, which points to the completion or entirety of a matter.

We can see the grouping of these three witnesses in Scripture. In 1 John 5:7-8, we are told there are three that bear record in heaven and three that bear witness in earth. Those who verify the record in heaven are the Father, the Word (Jesus), and the Holy Spirit. Their agreement actually establishes the record that the witnesses in earth will, in turn, establish as being true. These three witnesses of earth are the Spirit, the water (Word), and the blood of Jesus (covenant). What is the record that is being established and confirmed? "And this is the record, that God hath given to us eternal life, and this life is in his Son. He that hath the Son hath life; and he that hath not the Son of God hath not life" (1 John 5:11-12).

There are also three witnesses that confirm the matters of God's existence and character, especially when it comes to His creation, beginning with what has been clearly established in man. There is the witness of the conscience of man that serves as the inner witness that God truly exists. This is why the Apostle Paul warns those who fail to pursue and agree with this witness will end up with a reprobate mind that no longer retains any real knowledge of God.

The second witness of God's existence and His character is creation itself. It allows man to see his Creator's majesty and incredible ways. Because of these two witnesses, man will not be able to hide behind ignorance concerning the existence and character of God. In fact, God will not wink at such ignorance that manifests itself in unbelief; rather, He is commanding men to repent of such darkness to avoid judgment.[2]

Finally, the third witness that confirms God's existence is man himself. Scripture describes man as being nothing more than a clay vessel. However, if the life of Jesus is present in this vessel, man is not only part of the covenant established by the blood of Jesus, but he becomes a living, walking epistle who is read by others.[3] It is through the vessel of man that God verifies the testimony concerning the record of heaven, which must always be in accordance to the witnesses in earth.

This brings us to the three witnesses involved in declaring salvation. As clay vessels, believers possess the life of Christ. It is Jesus' life that is being offered and poured out from these vessels into others. It is the resurrection power associated with this incredible life that serves as the

---

[1] Deuteronomy 17:6-7; Matthew 18:16
[2] Acts 17:30-31; Romans 1:18-32
[3] 2 Corinthians 3:2-3; 4:7

first witness to the work of salvation. The second witness is the seal of the Holy Spirit. It is the power and work of the Spirit that is developing the very life of Christ in believers. The final witness that God uses to proclaim and verify the matter of salvation is man's voice. A good example of this can be found at Jesus' baptism as recorded in John 1:15-34. There were three that verified the record that He was the Son of God. The Father introduced Him as the Son, the Holy Spirit came upon Him to identify Him as the Son of God to the third witness, John the Baptist. It was John who introduced Jesus to others as being the Son of God.

Man is commissioned to testify of, as well as establish, this record through the preaching of the Gospel and through discipling, which is impartation of the Word though such means as teaching.[4] As you consider these three witnesses involving man, it is important to understand that the life of Christ in believers serves as an earthly witness that can be observed by others, the seal of the Spirit as a heavenly witness which points to connection, identity, and power with heaven, and the voice of man as the verbal witness that can be heard by others.

This brings us to the matter of the pulpits that stand in the Christian churches. The reason that so many are powerless is because the necessary witness is missing. Without the witness, nothing will be firmly established in the hearts and minds of God's people. Many will walk away with a vague concept of something, but there will be no clear witness that will bring clarity and revelation to a matter.

Why is the necessary witness missing? The reasons vary, but one of the main reasons is that the actual record is missing from much of the preaching and teaching. The purpose of the pulpit is to declare the record that has been firmly established in heaven. The record has to do with the eternal life that can only be obtained through Jesus. This record points to the Gospel which is the power of God onto salvation.

If the record is missing, what does man preach or teach from the pulpits? Sadly, at best, it is a mixture of worldly philosophies and Scriptural doctrine, and, at worst, it is a blatant attack against Scripture. A good example of blatant attack against the Gospel is Social Justice. This gospel substitutes faith toward God with "good works" and replaces righteous judgment with perverted "justice" that penalizes that which is decent, right, and moral.

One of the unholy mixtures in the Church today is what watchmen in the Church refer to as psychobabble. This psychological jargon takes Scriptural principles and institutes them into the philosophy of psychology. When you take an unholy mixture in which self must be esteemed to give a person a good sense of self-worth, you simply make such people feel good about the wretched condition of their lives. As a result, the Gospel is changed from the need to be saved *from* sin to being saved *in* sin. Instead of God being the center of a matter, man is

---

[4] Matthew 28:18-20; Mark 16:15-16; Galatians 2:20; Ephesians 1:9-14

made the center as people take Scriptural truths and try to revolve them around the idol of self.

The record clearly exalts Jesus as God Incarnate. It reveals man needs to be saved from the dictates and consequences of sin. Granted, the cross is about man's need to be saved, but Jesus is being exalted and esteemed on the cross, not man. In fact, the cross shows man he must cease in or die to his old ways in order to take on the very life of Christ. Once a person becomes totally identified with the cross, it ceases to be about him or her and becomes a matter of the life of Christ being established and brought forth in the person.

If the record is present, but the pulpit remains powerless, it is because the connection with heaven is missing. Jesus never spoke outside of what His Father commanded. In other words, as man, He was connected to the throne of God. He often separated Himself from the crowds to seek the Father in prayer. No doubt, He was receiving inspiration and instruction from the throne.

There is only one means by which believers can truly be connected to heaven, and that is through the Spirit of God. It is the Spirit who guides each of us in all truth.[5] He is the One who inspires and empowers us. However, inspiration of the Spirit comes from the throne, and His power comes only through humility, submission, and obedience.

Some pastors have zeal for God, but lack inspiration. Other pastors have formulas, but lack power. Some of these leaders have a set procedure for how they conduct services, but there is no real humility or sincere dependency (faith) that identifies them to the throne of God. Therefore, pastors or leaders who do not understand how to give way to the Spirit will never have the connection that will identify them to heaven. They are, thereby, rendered ineffective to impact the spirits and souls of men from their pulpits.

This brings me to the subject of preaching and teaching. As the vessel, man's voice simply becomes the means by which God's heart is being proclaimed and presented. Much of the heavenly connection has been taken out of these two presentations because man is either promoting personal agendas or worldly philosophies. He has a mixture where the Word of God is adjusted to fit into the presentation.

These two types of presentations also differ. Preaching stirs up, for it calls for some type of response. For example, the initial call in John the Baptist and Jesus' preaching was for people to repent. Inspired teaching from the throne of God does not simply inform us of doctrinal or kingdom matters, but it will challenge us on a personal basis to assimilate the ways of righteousness into our lives through obedience. Both inspired preaching and teaching will bring us to the crossroads of decision as to whether or not we will abandon all to follow Jesus in a sold-out, consecrated life.

---

[5] John 16:7-13

Real preaching has almost ceased in some pulpits. Instead of people being stirred up towards God concerning matters of sin, redemption, and eternal life in order to properly respond, they are being pumped up to feel as if they have had some religious experience. Some want to feel as if they have been entertained in some sentimental, religious way. Others may see it as a time to catch up on their rest as they are put to sleep by a lifeless message or presentation. However, such exercises speak of the ways of the flesh, and the Holy Spirit will have no part in activities that are clearly being orchestrated by man.

The teaching that is taking place may give some information, but it is directed at the mind, which takes on the form of conceit. Such information has no means by which to transform the mind. It is only revelation brought forth by the Holy Spirit that has the ability to transform the mind. In fact, such revelations come by way of man's spirit with the intent to enlarge his mind to receive the revelation.

Due to the abuses taking place from behind the pulpit, there are some who want to do away with godly responsibilities, such as preaching, to deal with the abuses and problems that are plaguing the visible Church. This would not be dealing with abuses or problems; rather, it would prove to be disobedient. We, as Christians, have been commissioned to preach the Gospel and to disciple (teach) followers of Jesus to observe His Word. Jesus both preached to the crowds and taught them, but He was inspired, empowered, and effective. There was no unholy mixture in what He presented.

It is clear why some pulpits are powerless. Those who stand behind them are failing to maintain the record of heaven through the power of the Spirit, the assimilation of the Word, and the putting on of the godly life wrought by the blood of Jesus.

How about you? Are you exposed to the ineffective work of the "powerless pulpit" or are you becoming established in your own life in Christ? Remember, it is *your* life in Christ.

13

THE SWORD

We have been considering the "powerless pulpit." Obviously, it is the record or message that is being delivered that will determine if the pulpit possesses any real substance behind it. However, there are also other reasons for a "powerless pulpit."

I have witnessed people who delivered the proper record or message, but there was no flame, life, or power to it. You can have the message, but, if you do not have the attitude to reinforce such a record, it will mean nothing to those who hear it.

What kind of attitude must those in the Christian pulpits have towards their place or position behind the pulpit? The Apostle Paul gives us insight into the type of attitude that must be evident when sharing heaven's record. Those who are proclaiming the message must realize they are in a battle for souls that is raging between light and darkness. These individuals must not only recognize this battle, but they must know how to bring the distinction between that which is of darkness and that which belongs to the light.

In Ephesians 6, we as Christians are given an armor that enables us to stand in faith, withstand with assurance, and stand in confidence in the battle. However, we have also been given a sword. This sword is powerful. Once it is properly being executed against the real enemy, it will put him on the run. In fact, the sword is also a surgical knife that will expose the inner disposition or spirit of man. It will cut with truth, break down with conviction, and divide with purifying fire as a means to cleanse and bring healing, spiritual wholeness, and maturity to believers.

The Apostle Paul identifies this sword as being the Word of God. Jesus said of His words that they have Spirit and life. In other words, the witness of the Spirit is confirmed by the Word of God as it becomes milk and meat to the soul, renewing the inner man of the believers.

When the Holy Spirit sets God's people apart, it is referred to as the work of sanctification. Sanctification points to cleansing for the purpose of preparing the vessel to be made fit for the Master's use. Preparation of this nature entails establishing a right environment as a means for us, as believers, to offer each of our bodies as consecrated, living sacrifices that will be brought into compliance to the good, acceptable, and perfect will of God.[1]

The Holy Spirit distinguishes the believer by the work of sanctification that takes place in the inner man, but believers are also cleansed or sanctified through the truth of the Word.[2] Such cleansing cannot occur unless there is obedience. Obedience leads to conduct that will clearly distinguish or set believers a part from the dictates of self and the influence of the world.

When you study the work of God's uncompromising truth, you will realize that it separates in order to bring spiritual liberty to the life of a person. His truth establishes the environment in which a person can find his or her life in Christ. Such a liberating environment also allows the person to properly receive and to move forward to discover his or her potential in the kingdom of God.

Jesus spoke of the separation that the sword of truth would bring in Matthew 10:32-35. As you study these Scriptures, you can begin to see how sharp the truth of God's Word is. In Matthew 10:32, Jesus was talking about men denying Him before others. Keep in mind Jesus is the essence of all truth. If a matter does not line up to who He is, express His likeness in attitude and conduct, and become an example of His righteousness, man will, in essence, be denying him in some way. Such denial means that a person is denying any real association or agreement with the record of heaven and disowning any point of identification of the revelation that has been clearly brought forth in the Word of God. Matthew 10:31 actually identifies one of the main reasons people disassociate themselves with Jesus—fear.

Man often fears being associated with truth that is considered narrow and unloving by the world. Jesus explained why man has such a negative, repulsive response to this sharp sword. He stated that the truth takes away the cloak that hides the sin of man. This cloak is in place because man's natural preference is to maintain the darkness of his evil deeds, rather than having his deeds brought to the light by truth and reproved.[3]

The truth of God's Word brings a contrast between light and dark. It will call man to decide between the darkness of death and the light of life. It will ultimately make man responsible for his ways. However, truth that has not been anointed and inspired by heaven will be void of its sharpness. In other words, it is incapable of making any inroads into the soul and spirit of man.

Powerless truth has only the capacity to impact the intellect of man in the ways of information, facts, and doctrine, but not to expose the state of man's spirit and soul. Even though such lifeless truth may be correct, if it lacks the power to become revelation. Such information will simply feed

---

[1] Romans 12:1-2; 1 Peter 1:2
[2] John 17:17
[3] John 3:19-21; 15:22

the conceit of man, making him indifferent to the reality of God and his responsibility towards Him.

God's truth can only become life or revelation when the Spirit of God is anointing it with the sharpness to penetrate the spirit of man with the reality of God and His ways. The Spirit will use the Word of truth to convict people of their sin (revealing their real spiritual state), reprove them of righteousness (bringing contrast between light and darkness), and warn them of judgment to come (contenting and exhorting man to repent before it is too late).[4]

This brings us to man's emphasis. If man is emphasizing the intellect according to man's take on theology and doctrine, the Holy Spirit will have no platform on which to make the truth sharp with conviction, righteousness, or judgment. Without the light of conviction that brings contrast, the Spirit will be prevented from bringing individuals to the place of conviction, understanding, and revelation. However, if man is emphasizing the record established in heaven according to the authority of the throne, the Holy Spirit will confirm, empower, and reveal the truth of it to open hearts.

The next aspect of truth is that it will divide where there is no real spiritual agreement. Although Jesus is the Prince of Peace, His sword of truth will bring contrast in order to establish a point of agreement. Most people prefer their personal reality to God's unchanging truth. These same people may use the same terminology, but the spirit or intent behind their words is different in meaning, causing them to be far from the truth. As long as you remain surface with these people, they are able to hold onto their reality in darkness. However, when the sharpness of truth begins to penetrate these people's perceptions, conflict will naturally arise. It is at this point that any unholy attachments between people are cut, ripped, and torn, bringing separation. As Jesus pointed out in Matthew 10:35-36, such separation often begins in the home.

It is on the home front that our level of love for our Lord is often tested. The main reason people give into fear is because their love for God is fickle, weak, fleshly, and immature in light of the devotion they may have towards earthly family members or friends. This is why the Apostle John made this statement in 1 John 4:18-19, "There is no fear in love, but perfect love casteth out fear, because fear hath torment, He that feareth is not made perfect in love. We love him, because he first love us."

Jesus also stated that if a person loves family members more than Him, he or she will not be worthy to be considered as one belonging to Him. It is at this point Jesus reminded His followers that they must deny self of such entanglements and pick up their cross to ensure total separation from the world. This separation allows people to follow Him, and, as they follow Him, they will gain their life in Him. He also later

---

[4] John 16:7-11; Ephesians 5:11-15

Challenging the Christian Life

identified those who are His family members as those who do the will of the Father.[5]

The sword of truth is meant to cut away that which has not been sanctified, rip away that which defiles, and tear away that which belongs to the old ways to ensure separation from that which entails unholy agreements. Truth is meant to put us on the same page as God in the matter of attitudes toward sin and the world. A right attitude is needed to establish righteousness according to the life of Jesus and to produce godly conduct that brings a clear distinction from that which belongs to darkness.

Sadly, people mishandle the truth by adjusting it to their particular reality. Adjusting truth renders it ineffective. The Holy Spirit will have no acceptable premise to bring revelation, causing the Word to fall by the wayside to be trampled by unbelief. Hence enters the warning that those who mishandle truth according to unrighteous motives and emphases will find themselves subject to the wrath of God.[6]

Without the powerful challenge of the sword of truth, man will be left in his dull state of compromise, darkness, and defeat. Since the truth is the only means by which to set the captive free, such a person will never know the victory of truth that will bring him or her to the blessed liberty of knowing God. Therefore, Christian pulpits that do not know how to use God's Word as the sword of truth will fail to do battle for the souls of men.

This brings us back to the fact that the pulpit is a place to do battle. The truth must cut the necessary swath through congregations in order to bring the contrast that will serve as a mirror to those who call themselves Christians. The real spiritual state of people must be exposed so that the enemies of their souls can be properly discerned, addressed, and defeated. People must be given a choice of what head they will individually come into subjection to (Adam or Christ), what master they will serve (sin or God), and what husband they will submit to (the Law or the risen Christ).[7]

This brings us to the territory that is the focus of this unseen battle. The battleground comes down to faith. Although we have already dealt with the matter of faith in this book, we must once again examine it in light of the powerless pulpit. Repetition of spiritual truths causes us to approach such subjects from different angles. However, that which is of the truth will be confirmed in greater ways.

Jude wanted to talk about salvation, but instead, he found himself contenting or wrestling for the faith that was first delivered to the saints. As already stated, there are many counterfeit faiths being presented to Christendom. However, there is only one true faith according to the

---

[5] Matthew 10:37-39; 12:46-50
[6] Romans 1:18
[7] Romans 5-7

Bible, and Jesus wondered if He would find it when He came back as the King of kings and Lord of lords.[8]

We must constantly remind ourselves that faith is a choice. We must choose to believe and appropriate the Word as being true and not debate, adjust, or reject it. The true faith described in the Word comes by hearing the Word of God. As believers, we are to walk in obedience to the Word of God by faith. Acceptable faith will direct its sole confidence, hope, and expectation towards the one true God. Such faith is the only means to please God.

In the armor of God, faith is the shield that gives us the confidence to stand on the truth of God when encountering the enemy, to withstand with His truth when attacked, and, when all is said and done in the battle, to continue to stand steadfast because of the truth of God's Word. We also know that faith is eternal and that at the end of it is our salvation. The Apostle Paul made the statement at the end of his life that he had kept the faith. Due to the importance of possessing the true faith, we are once again reminded of the apostle's exhortation to examine ourselves to see whether we are established in this faith. This faith can only be identified by the very life of Christ being present in us. It is His life that serves as our only true identification with Him and our hope of eternal glory.[9]

When God's shepherds stand behind pulpits, they must understand that they are contending for the faith that was first delivered to the saints. The battle can only be fought and won when the truth of God's sword is being presented under the anointing, inspiration, and power of the Spirit. It is the sharpness and power of truth that will liberate souls to pursue, possess, and maintain this faith through the course of their lives. However, the battle can prove to be extreme, intense, and overwhelming to the shepherds. Satan attempts to rob God's people of unfeigned faith, the world strives to replace faith with worldly methods, and man's religion adjusts faith according to humanistic philosophies, while the darkness of unbelief slowly dulls the mind of man towards the Spirit's overtures and hardens his heart towards the truth.

Since faith has been replaced by methods and philosophies, the record of heaven is no longer emphasized in many of the pulpits and teachings. Fleshly entertainment that excites the soul of man has taken the place of the move and work of the Holy Spirit. Meanwhile, the darkness of unbelief is invading the souls of men in the name of religion. This darkness is perceived as light, but, in reality, it is simply blinding these poor souls to the destruction that is awaiting them.

When the Apostle Paul exhorted people to examine to see if they were in the faith, he was establishing what each Christian must do to see if they are even in the same ballpark as God. When it comes to the

---

[8] Luke 18:8; Ephesians 4:5; Jude 3
[9] Romans 10:17; 1 Corinthians 13:13; 2 Corinthians 13:5; Ephesians 6:16; Colossians 1:27; 2 Timothy 4:6-7; Hebrews 6:1; 11:1, 6; 1 Peter 1:9; 5:9

matter of their salvation, people can believe they are saved and say they are saved, but, if they do not possess the true faith of the Bible, they remain lost.

What about you? When was the last time you actually examine yourself to see if you are on the same page as God when it comes to your faith?

14

PLACE OF AUTHORITY

We have been considering the reasons for the "powerless pulpit." We have looked at the record of heaven not being proclaimed or established through teaching. We know that, without the anointing of the Spirit, any such presentation will be lifeless, and, if the Word of truth is not sharpened by the Spirit, it will not impact anyone. When we combine these three elements together, we will be able to pinpoint one major reason for the pulpit being powerless. There is no authority present. Without authority, a preacher or teacher will not have the power to reinforce what is true.

How does one obtain authority? Authority can only be given by those who possess it. When you study Scripture, you realize there is only one who holds all authority, and that is God. God clearly stipulates where authority has been given in the home, church, and His kingdom. Therefore, we can only reason that a pulpit that proves to be powerless does not have God's confirmation or approval. Without God's confirmation, a preacher or shepherd's word will not possess any real credibility. Granted, these religious leaders' words may sound entertaining and great and have the means to inspire the sentiment of the soul of man to respond, but they will never penetrate the spirit of man. It is in the spirit that man will know a matter is from God.

Authority has to do with rights that warrant a person's positions and claims with the intent to influence people concerning a matter. God must ordain a matter before it can be given credence. Once he ordains a matter, then He must ordain the person who will be entrusted to testify, proclaim, or present it to others. Such ordination signifies that God's authority is behind it, thereby giving the person who is ordained the right to influence people to weigh a matter out to ensure it has been properly sanctioned. The Bereans are a good example of those who weighed out the preaching of Paul as to whether his message was truly sanctioned by God.[1] Once the authority of Paul's words was confirmed as being ordained by God, these people could readily receive his preaching, teachings, and instructions as truth.

This brings us back to what will warrant or sanction preaching or teaching from God's servants? As someone who has wrestled with this matter in the past, I have discovered some simple truths. Although,

---

[1] Acts 17:10-12

sometimes authority is interchanged with the word "power," there is a difference between these two words. Authority gives us the right to carry out a matter, while power enables us to carry it out. Without proper authority, power can prove to be abusive. After all, authority defines the purpose and direction of power that has been bestowed, while power will confirm the authority of the message that is presented.

When you listen to people, they mostly desire power as a means to exalt themselves and validate their claims. But, without proper authority, power has no real eternal purpose to it. If authority is clearly established in my life, power will naturally follow.

Sadly, I have watched people who held places of authority fail to be established in their positions. These people tried to exert power in their positions as a means to bring people into line with their agendas, but such self-serving methods do not possess the credibility to properly influence people. These particular individuals did not realize that sanctioned authority must be present to bring order to the situation.

There are four reasons why people mishandle authority. The first one is inexperience. Inexperienced people tend to become prideful when they are entrusted with authority they have not been prepared to walk in, rather than seeing it as a grave responsibility. This is why the Bible tells us not to place novices in leadership positions.

Another way authority is mishandled is through abusing one's position. People who abuse authority have never learned how to recognize or respect it in other people's lives. They see authority as their personal platform to exert their agendas, selfishness, and demands on others.

The third way people mishandle authority is through neglect. They do not recognize the responsibility established by their position. As a result, they become indifferent to their responsibility and drop the ball in terms of ensuring respect, discipline, and order.

Without discipline in the environment, chaos will prevail, preventing people from being prepared to properly receive. A chaotic environment will create disrespect towards all authority. We can see this in the case of many homes. Children call the shots, rather than the parents who were given the authority by God to influence their children by training them in the ways of righteousness.

Righteousness expresses itself by recognizing and honoring that which possesses authority. Since the ways of righteousness are missing in these homes, there is chaos. The children struggle with their place in the family as they lack any sense of real security. Insecurity turns into anger as these children begin to express their frustration by becoming disobedient and disrespectful towards their parent's authority. Eventually, this disrespect will take root and create lawlessness in the children. Lawlessness refuses to respect any authority or boundaries.

The fourth way people mishandle authority is by overstepping it. These are the people who add their own twists or standards to what they have been entrusted with. When people overstep their boundaries, it often causes confusion and division in a matter.

When it comes to our authority as Christians, we must understand where it comes from and how it is to be properly established in our lives. We know our power comes from the Holy Spirit. However, this power is to be clearly tested, disciplined, and executed according to the authority we possess. Keep in mind that authority comes from those who have the right to sanction or ordain a matter. As Christians, our authority comes from Jesus. The reason I say this is because of what Jesus said in John 17:18, "As thou hast sent me into the world, even so have I also sent them into the world." Since Jesus sent us forth, our authority comes from Him.

Clearly, Jesus has a reason to send us forth into the world. But, what has He entrusted to us? We already know that we have been entrusted with the record of heaven. However, we must consider how this record will establish us in our authority.

There are a couple of ways we, as Christians, become established in this authority. The first aspect of authority that must be present to verify our credibility is agreement. There is no way a person of authority can entrust you or me with a matter unless there is agreement. Jesus brought this out in John 17:21, "That they all may be one, as thou, Father art in me, and I in thee, that they also may be one in us; that the world may believe that thou hast sent me."

At the very core of the record of heaven is the Person and work of Jesus. Who is the person of Jesus? We have already addressed this issue, but we must recognize that it is hard for people to realize that the great debate at the heart of heaven's record is Jesus' identity. As pointed out, some say that Jesus is just a "good" man, a "great" prophet, a high-ranking angel, or one of the way-showers of this present age. Some claim His conscience is what prevails in the world and that possessing it causes them to become deified. However, such beliefs are contrary to the record of heaven.

Obviously, Jesus can be anyone or anybody. He can be given certain entitlements, but, if He is not revealed to the spirit or heart of man by heaven, man will erect a lifeless or conceptual Jesus. This Jesus may run parallel with the Bible, or he may even line up to the Bible's revelation, but such a Jesus will lack authority.

There is only one real Jesus. He can only be known when He is unveiled by heaven to our spirits. The Jesus of the Bible is not a theory, image, or fantasy. He is a living Person. In fact, the record of heaven declares that Jesus is fully God and fully man. He is God who came in the flesh to walk in the midst of man, ultimately dying on the cross for the sins of man.

Once again, we are reminded that the Apostle Paul described Jesus' coming in the flesh as being the mystery of godliness that was clearly revealed to man.[2] The mystery of godliness identifies the reality of God (manifested in the flesh), His witness (justified and upheld in the Spirit), His confirmation (seen of the angels), proclaimed as Lord and Savior (preached unto the Gentiles), received as truth (believed on in the world), and ensured His Person and work (received up into glory).

In light of this record, can people believe another Jesus and be saved, or are they actually neglecting such a great salvation? Keep in mind, Jesus is the essence of truth. If a person does not believe the record concerning Jesus, he or she will not possess the light of God. In fact, such individuals are calling God a liar because he or she will not receive the truth, regardless of the clear record that has been presented in His Word, confirmed by His Spirit, and established by the covenant wrought by Jesus' blood.[3]

One of the reasons pulpits remain powerless is because the people who stand behind them have not believed the record concerning Jesus. The Father draws people to the Son, Jesus invites people to come to Him, and the Holy Spirit leads a person into all truth concerning Him.[4] Since these people do not believe that Jesus is who the Bible ascribes Him to be, they have no agreement with heaven; therefore, they have no authority. The Apostle Paul made this statement about those who are being tossed to and fro by every wind of doctrine: "Till we all come in the unity of the faith, and of the knowledge of the Son of God, unto a perfect man, unto the measure of the stature of the fullness of Christ" (Ephesians 4:13).

Without agreement with heaven, a person can be assured that Jesus will never send him or her forth to carry out a mission. Such a person would not have the credibility to back up his or her claims.

This brings us to the second point about authority. Without authority, one does not have the power to make an eternal impact. In Matthew 28:18b-20, Jesus gave this commission to His disciples,

> All power is given unto me in heaven and in earth. Go ye, therefore, and teach all nations, baptizing them in the name of the Father, and of the Son, and of the Holy Ghost, Teaching them to observe all things whatsoever I have commanded you; and, lo, I am with you always, even unto the end of the world. Amen.

Keep in mind that authority defines our responsibility, while power enables us to carry out our commission.

Jesus clearly stipulated why He was sending us out in the world. Our commission is two-fold in these Scriptures. We are to teach all nations to observe all things concerning the matters of heaven. Teaching points to instructing people how to effectively live the Christian life. Observing all things involves obeying what He has established as our responsibility.

---

[2] 1 Timothy 3:16
[3] Romans 3:1-4; Hebrews 2:3
[4] John 6:44; 7:37-38; 14:26; 16:13-14

Observation of His commandments will ensure us that He will be with us, even to the end of the age.

The second part of this commission is to baptize people in the name or according to the character of the Father, of the Son, and of the Holy Ghost. Once again, we have the three witnesses of heaven that remind us of the record that was set forth. Water baptism points to total identification with Jesus in His life and work. Such identification will have no meaning if a person fails to live the life that is associated with it.

Likewise, our heavenly authority has no meaning or purpose if we do not fulfill our commission. Authority will be present in obedience, but missing in disobedience. Sadly, there are those who stand behind Christian pulpits, preaching another Jesus, operating according to a different spirit, and adhering to another gospel. These people's words will not possess any power, their works will be considered reprobate, and they will stand condemned by the Judge of heaven.

Do you sense authority coming from the pulpit of your fellowship? If not, it could be because your pastor has never really been ordained by heaven to be in his position, or, perhaps, the words he speaks do not have power behind them because he is not really fulfilling his commission. Only you can discern if the particular pulpit at your church building possesses the authority to impact the eternal destination of the souls of people.

15

VISION

When we consider the possible reasons that some of our pulpits in America and throughout the world are "powerless," we must examine the concept of vision. Vision has to do with the vantage point from which we consider a matter. The wisest man in the Old Testament stated that people who did not possess vision would perish.[1]

It must be noted that people examine all things from what they consider to be their particular vantage point. Some believe their intellectual abilities are a vantage point. Others perceive their sentimental insights, particularly those that involve religion and its practices, as vantage points. Some consider their vantage point in light of the ability to logic out a matter, while there are those who see their superior position because of the facts they possess.

When we consider these vantage points, we must recognize that our frame of reference or our worldview is usually what serves as our vantage point. However, such a perspective has been greatly influenced by the world's philosophies. Whenever the things of the flesh or the world are involved when it comes to our point of consideration, we must acknowledge that we are earthbound. In fact, our perceptions taint what we do perceive because we cannot see beyond self or above the influences or activities of the world.

The Apostle Paul spoke of blindness that plagues man who relies on the vantage point of the world. He explained that the god of this present age or world has actually blinded such people towards the light of the true Gospel, ensuring their spiritual destruction. Jesus also explained the delusion that is established by this false light or vantage point when He declared that, even though such understanding is darkness, it will seem as if it is light to the spiritually blind. Such a darkness of delusion can prove great since it is blinding these people to the destructive path they are on.

"Powerless pulpits" lack spiritual vision. Granted, some pastors have a vision for church growth, bringing in more money, and establishing greater outreaches, but such vision reveals that the pastor is earthbound. When we consider what the Word of God states, we must recognize that God did not send His disciples out to build greater church buildings,

---

[1] Proverbs 29:18

establish greater ministries, develop better methods to gain financial support, or devise noteworthy plans to reach many people. Jesus' instructions to the disciples were clear: preach the Gospel and teach people to observe or obey His commandments.

Since our Lord's instructions are clear, why is it that some Church leaders are emphasizing the pursuits of the world? Granted, such pursuits may sound noble and acceptable, but such emphasizes or pursuits will not bring salvation to any one. Such promotion is nothing more than advocating a social gospel that may help, impress, and attract people, but salvation will still be missing from the agenda.

A man stated his concern for the particular church he was affiliated with. He shared how he remembered when they preached the Gospel and the members were alive with inspiration. However, he recently noticed that nothing was really happening. As a church body, they appeared to be in a time warp in which they could not move backward to clearly discern their condition or forward in spiritual growth.

Since I had no first-hand knowledge of the church, my guess was that the leadership may have started off right, but it got off track. I then explained that all a church body has to do to get off track is change its emphasis from what Christ has ordained and commissioned His Church to do to something that is earthbound and will ultimately prove lifeless and uninspired.

There was a pastor of a big church who admitted to me that he had created a monster that he barely could keep ahead of. In fact, I wondered how much of his time he had to put in trying to finance the monstrosity that he had developed in his attempts to look like a successful pastor of a growing church. I observed him preaching about causes, while tacking a weak gospel on the end of his message to justify his preaching. What I did not see was people truly coming to salvation.

As we consider the pursuit and emphasis of some Christian Churches, it is becoming more apparent that the pastors, along with some who are in their congregations, have lost their way. The main reason people do not know where they are going is because they have lost sight of where they started from. In summation, they have lost their focus. They have become entangled in the terrain of the world and loaded down by the endless demands of a self-serving, religious lifestyle that leaves them empty and full of despair.

The Apostle Paul explained what the Christian's vantage point should be in Ephesians 2:6, "And hath raised us up together, and made us sit together in heavenly places in Christ Jesus." Positionally, we have been placed in high places in Jesus. For Christians, this position means that their vantage point is a heavenly one and not earthbound by worldly aspirations that have no sense of the spiritual or eternal perspective. When we compare the heavenly vantage point to the earthbound one, the contrast is quite clear. Those who have an earthbound vantage point have no vision past this present world. Without a heavenly vision, there is no direction, inspiration, or real purpose. Without spiritual vision, man is not only blind to the paths and traps of destruction and death, but he is assured of losing his way and possibly his very soul.

In his book *God's Goal: Christ as All in All,* Manfred Haller stated that the main problem with the Church at Ephesus, mentioned in Revelation 2:1-7, is that the people had lost their vantage point of being seated in heavenly places with Christ. Even though they were technically on, they had lost their sense of true identification, direction, and purpose. Clearly, it was not just a matter of doing "good" works and standing for truth, it was a matter of viewing all things from the heavenly perspective. It is the heavenly perspective that keeps the influences and demands of this present age in the right order.

Obviously, there are pastors who have fallen into the traps of the world. They are viewing matters from the premise of the world. As a result, their pulpits have been rendered powerless by worldly compromises, emphases, and agreements.

Obviously, our pulpits must be taken back. For this to happen, pastors, teachers, and leaders need to align their vision to that which is ordained by God, exalted in the heavenlies, and possesses the eternal. It is from this vantage point that pastors and congregations can experience the fire and power of heaven.

In order to possess a heavenly perspective, God's people must come to terms with what it means to possess such a vantage point. We were given this prophesy concerning the last days in Acts 2:17-18,

> And it shall come to pass in the last days, saith God, I will pour out of my Spirit upon all flesh; and your sons and your daughters shall prophesy, and your young men shall see visions, and your old men shall dream dreams; And on my servants and on my handmaidens I will pour out in those days of my Spirit, and they shall prophesy.

It is important to note that, in the last days, God will pour out His Spirit upon all flesh. On Pentecost, the beginning of the end days started for this present age. Granted, for the Church, it has been a long stretch of two thousand years as far as the last days. But, the most important aspect about the age of the Church will be the presence and power of the Spirit. He will not only reside in believers, but He will be poured out on believers to empower them to walk out their Christian lives, boldly carry out their commission, and inspire the direction of their vision. Obviously, the vision that every believer must possess will be marked by the presence of eternity. It will not be based on what we know or understand as Christians; rather, it will be inspired by the Holy Ghost.

The Holy Spirit is the one who gives revelations to believers. A revelation is the unveiling of a spiritual truth or matter about our Lord to bring inspiration, instruction, wisdom, and spiritual growth to Christians. Such unveiling is God's way of speaking His reality into the hearts of His people. However, this spiritual reality will not only leave people with a greater understanding of Scripture, but also a greater sense and knowledge of the character and ways of God.

In the youthful days of the prophet Samuel, it says that the word of the Lord was rare, and that there was no open or frequent vision in those days. The people of Israel had the Law, but an ongoing revelation or unveiling of God's heart and truths were missing due to the sin of the priesthood. However, this environment changed when Samuel was a man. It is said that Samuel grew and the Lord was with him. But, one of the reasons the Lord was with Samuel is that he did not let the words he proclaimed as both man and prophet fall to the ground.[2] He held them tight and maintained their integrity.

Remember, when we consider matters through the glasses of the flesh and the world, all we see will be darkened, tainted, or perverted. However, when we possess the heavenly vantage point, we are considering everything through the Person of Jesus Christ. We have been seated in high places *in* Christ who will serve as the frame or glasses through which we examine all matters.

This brings us to the work of the Spirit. He is the one who leads us into all truth about Jesus. He leads us to an understanding of Christ in order to unveil Him to us in a greater measure. Each unveiling brings us to a greater knowledge of Jesus that will even more so transform how we look at life through our now enlarged perspective that has lifted us to greater heights in His glory.

The Bible clearly brings out and confirms the truth about revelation. Such heavenly vision is what the Lord's people must pursue, possess, and live in accordance to. Each vision simply enlarges the person's understanding of God. There are four examples we are going to consider.

The first example is Moses. Moses ascended into the presence of God on Mount Sinai. He was there for forty days and nights and received the Law. However, his request after Mount Sinai revealed the type of focus that was inspired and defined by his experience in the presence of God. Heed what he asked of God in Exodus 33:18, "And he said, I beseech thee, show me thy glory." Moses was not seeking personal greatness, nor would he settle for simply experiencing God's presence. His heart was panting after an even greater revelation of Him that could only be unveiled in the light of His unending glory.

The prophet Isaiah's vision revolutionized his life.[3] He saw the Lord sitting upon a throne, high and lifted up, as his train filled the temple. We cannot begin to comprehend the indelible impact that this vision had on Isaiah. He sensed his unworthiness in light of the Lord's holiness. He cried out to be purged, and, once he stood purged, he was ready to offer his services, even in light of the fact that people would not hear him in their state of spiritual dullness.

Clearly, revelation has the ability to revolutionize God's people. However, the vision is of God's greatness or majesty. Such visions will

---

[2] 1 Samuel 3:1, 17-18

[3] Isaiah 6

humble and cause His true servants to avail themselves to His mission. A vision that beholds the majesty of the Son of God will transform and enlarge one's spiritual ability to see into the depths of God's character. It will also allow His saints to witness incredible aspects of the heights and brightness of His glory, even in spite of the present darkness of the age that may surround them.

The Apostle Paul actually loss his physical eyesight when he encountered the true light of the world.[4] The reality of our vision is that the physical eyes cannot behold the glory of God without being blinded by it. Such glory will reveal the darkness of one's soul, as it envelops him or her with the sense of total depravity and hopelessness. The example that Paul leaves us with is that the only way we will not be blinded by the heavenly light is to allow God to open the spiritual eyes of our hearts so we can truly behold the Son of God.

The Apostle Paul explained that there is a veil or covering over our spiritual eyes that prevent us from seeing the Lord in the spirit. He stated that only the Lord can take away the veil so we can see Him in His glory. As we come into the place of witnessing His glory and partaking of His very life, we will actually begin to take on His glory and reflect it to the world.[5]

The Apostle John also received an unveiling of Christ in Revelation 1. In fact, the whole theme of the book is Christ being unveiled as God, and coming back as victorious King and righteous Judge. Granted, many perceive Jesus as Savior and Lord, but, when Jesus comes back to claim the throne of David, He will come as the great Alpha and the never-ending Omega to execute judgment on the rebellious world. His entrance is going to cause those who have opposed Him to beg the rocks to fall on them as a means to hide them from His face that will reveal the extent of His great wrath that is ready to be poured out.[6]

Amazingly, John's reaction to the new revelation of the Christ was unexpected, but it sends a clear message to each of us. This apostle had been part of the inner group who witnessed miracles and the parting of Christ's humanity to reveal His glory as deity on the Mount of Transfiguration. He had laid his head on Jesus' chest the night He was betrayed. Jesus had entrusted the care of His mother, Mary, to him. He had been tempered by persecution, refined by the fires of adversity, and firmly established on the immovable Rock of Jesus. However, when Jesus was unveiled to him in Revelation, he fell at Jesus' feet as if dead. Jesus lifted him up and introduced Himself as the "I am" that lived, was put to death, but now is alive evermore. He is the one who now holds the keys of hell and death.[7] As reminded by Hebrews 2:14 in regard to the keys, "Forasmuch, then, as the children are partakers of flesh and blood,

---

[4] Acts 9
[5] 2 Corinthians 3:6-18
[6] Revelation 6:16-17
[7] Revelation 1:17-18

he also himself likewise took part of the same, that through death he might destroy him that had the power of death, that is the devil."

As we meditate on each of these examples, we, as believers, must realize that our vision must be the Son of God. As each of us considers these men, we can see that they were not seeking greater ministry, acknowledgment, methods, or miracles; rather, they were seeking to behold their Lord in greater measure.

If God people's vision was heavenward, their vantage point would be from and through Jesus. From this vantage point, they would and will be able to view the finished work of redemption, the ongoing ministry of Jesus as the High Priest, and the reality of God's heart toward the loss world. Such a perception will allow them to experience the leading of the Spirit according to God's eternal plan.

Pulpits that are aflame with the presence and power of the Spirit are pulpits where the pastor, leader, or teacher has beheld the Son of God on a continual basis. They have established and disciplined this heavenly focus by daily aligning their vision heavenward towards the One who sits on the right hand of God. As they align their vision upward, they set their affections on Jesus, knowing that they are dead, in Him, to their self-lives and the influences of the world. As these people set their hearts towards Jesus, their faith in Him becomes steadfast as they truly connect to the throne, heart, and purpose of God. In light of their heavenly connection, they also know that, because of their new lives in Jesus, they are actually hid in Him, and, when He appears, they are confident that they will also appear with Him in glory.[8]

How many leaders have you met that possess a heavenly focus? If you have met such a person, you might have taken note of their eyes. There is something about their eyes that can draw you to them, while causing you to feel unnerved and exposed. It is as though the penetrating ability of these individuals' eyes is capable of undoing a person. The transparency of their eyes reveals a light that is not of the present world; therefore, they are capable of penetrating its thick darkness. The intensity of their eyes is like a fire that burns through the coverings, masks, and cloaks to reveal the heart of a matter. Ultimately, the eyes of these people will reveal that they have seen into heaven itself.

In summation, these people have seen the essence of beauty, heard unspeakable words that cannot be comprehended by fleshly ears, and witnessed the miraculous, for they have beheld the mystery of godliness as described by Isaiah 9:6. They have seen the one who is too wonderful to comprehend. They have heard His wisdom as the ultimate Counselor. They have experienced His power as The Mighty God. They have been touched by His love as The Everlasting Father. They have smelled and partaken of the sweetness of His peace as the Prince of Peace. They have indeed beheld the Son of God in His glory.

---

[8] Colossians 3:1-4

What about you? Have you recently beheld the Son of God? Is He your focus, or is your vision limited by that which has no connection to the depths or heights of the eternal and the heavenly?

Part IV

COMING BACK TO CENTER

16

ARISE SLEEPING CHURCH

What does it mean for the Church of Jesus to come back to the center of what is truly inspired by the Spirit and established by the truth? We know that the real Church is local, national, and universal. The first thing we must recognize is not everyone who calls themselves Christian is part of Jesus' Body. Not every denomination or belief that wears the handle of being Christian represents or advocates the interests of the kingdom of heaven. The images that are being presented by some of the visible Church may have another spirit behind their religious cloaks or robes. The gospel that is being presented in some camps may be watered-down with compromise, perverted with worldliness, or tainted with poisonous heresy.

When it comes to the universal Church, it is hard to say how much of it, if any, has strayed from the center. Due to some of the influences and inroads worldly Christianity has made into certain mission fields, I realize that there are those who belong to the universal Church who have adopted worldly, greedy, unscriptural attitudes of the western Church. Much of the Church is being persecuted in different places throughout the world. The stories of Christians being persecuted for the sake of Christ are incredible, yet these people know they only have one life to offer, and they are willing to offer their bodies as living sacrifices to their precious Lord and on behalf of the living testimony He has established in the hearts of many.

The environment of the local churches around the world, along with their challenges, will vary. This is why studying the epistles and the seven churches in Revelation 2-3 shows how each church had a different struggle keeping to the center of Spirit and truth. Some local churches seemed more successful than other bodies. The main factors that caused the difference were probably being determined by the quality of leadership and environment. For example, in Romans, Paul dealt with the realities of the simple Gospel, which included sin, faith, justification, reconciliation, identification, and the work of the Spirit. The first letter to the Corinthians dealt with carnality, discipline, and the Oral Law of the

Jews, while the second letter addressed such subjects as consolation, repentance, ministry, and benevolence. Galatians confronted the place the Law was to have in the Christian's life. Ephesians addressed our inheritance as believers, Philippians dealt with what constituted godly attitude, Colossians contended with the matter of Christ's deity and pre-eminence, and Thessalonians spoke of the Christian's assurance and blessed hope.

The question is what kind of exhortation needs to be given to the Church in America? Granted, there are many different bodies, but the issue comes down to the prevailing environment that can be clearly discerned on a national level. Is there such an environment present? I believe there is. Due to the compromise with the world, some of the Church is basically asleep. Like the idolatrous people of Israel, this unholy agreement with the world has caused the hearts of some in the Church to become gross, their ears dull of hearing, and their eyes closed to the reality around them. The problem is that they have no intention of being converted to that which would oppose their particular reality in order to truly be healed by God's truth.

This brings us to the challenge that is confronting the American Church. The Apostle Paul made this statement, "That he might present it to himself a glorious church, not having spot, or wrinkle, and any such thing; but that it should be holy and without blemish" (Ephesians 5:27). Jesus is coming for a Church that is chaste, not one that reveals inconsistencies due to moral deviations, unholy alliances, and unscriptural variations in its foundation and conduct.

Sadly, much of the Church in America has become another subculture in the midst of many multi-cultures. The problem is that it is simply going with the waves of tolerance that have been rolling through America. However, Christianity was never meant to become a subculture with its own lingo and ethnic practices. Christianity is about living the life of Jesus in the midst of the world. It is the distinction of His life that will identify and distinguish the Christian in the world. After all, as believers, our commission is not to get others to agree or share in the subculture of Christianity; it is to offer the life-giving message of Jesus so that people can become the children of God. As children of God, these people will not only be identified with an eternal inheritance that is not of this present world, but they also will become citizens of a heavenly kingdom that will distinguish them as priests and kings.

With this in mind, the Church in America must come to terms with what it will take to ensure that it possesses such a chaste environment. After all, how much of the Church is finding itself riding the high wave of living a worldly lifestyle that enjoys and partakes of temporary benefits, while trying to maintain an active testimony of separation and distinction from such influences?

The truth is that we are living in precarious times. The wave that America has been enjoying is beginning to slam against the shore of reality. It is about to reap the whirlwind of judgment due to its idolatry and its overindulgence in selfishness, rebellion, immorality, and hatred towards God. Although many live in denial about this nation's condition, as well as deny the Scriptures that address the last days, if Americans remain unrepentant, this great nation will inevitably become shipwrecked as it hits the rocks of destruction. Its demise will expose the attitude many have developed towards it for the last four decades. Like Jerusalem during God's judgment on it, America will become a byword that once was marked by greatness, but, because the values that were written into her very fiber have been compromised, mocked, and discarded by the unchecked agendas of the wicked, it could very well end up lying in utter ruin. In summation, some of the people of America are literally pulling this nation down around their ears.

What will happen to the visible Church since aspects of it are part of this wave of destruction? It is important to point out that many people in America are asleep to the impending destruction. They are caught up with fantasies and notions that are blinding them to the collision course this nation is on. Sadly, much of the Church that has been riding this wave is asleep as well.

Therefore, the first course of action is that the sleeping members of the Church must awake from their spiritual dullness to properly face the course this nation is on. Once they face it, they must take responsibility for not only their spiritual condition, but the condition of this nation. By compromising with the world, much of the visible Church has failed to bring a viable contrast between light and dark. Without distinction from the world, it does not possess the authority it needs to warn and exhort others.

It must be noted that Christians are not only called to be preachers and teachers, but watchmen. They are not only to guard their inward condition, their homes, and their churches against invading enemies, but they are to watch the condition of the times that they are living in. After all, watchmen are to warn others of what is coming on the horizon. However, when Christians are sleeping instead of watching, they will not be ready to hear the warnings or prepared to properly respond.

It is important at this time to point out that the destruction that has been prophesized concerning the end of the last days will not be expected by most people. Many will be asleep, snuggled under the covering of a false peace. The destruction that is coming will come as a thief, ready to rob, kill, and destroy.[1] It will not sneak through the door, it will suddenly knock it down. This is why the Apostle Paul reminded Christians in 1 Thessalonians 5:5-9 that they are children of the light. As a result, they must not sleep as others who refuse to face the reality of the times; rather, they must be watching and sober-minded. He goes on to say that those who are asleep are as if they are drunk in the night. Therefore, as alert Christians, we must put on the breastplate of faith and love, as well as the helmet that serves as the hope of salvation to

---

[1] John 10:10; 1 Thessalonians 5:2-4

maintain our spiritual edge as watchmen. As reliable watchmen, we will be guarding with the sword of truth against the invasion of darkness, knowing we will ultimately be spared from God's wrath to come.

Clearly, those of the Church must awake before it is too late to not only sound the warning, but to be prepared to act. The Apostle Paul's instructions were clear about Christians who are drunk with sleep. He commanded them to awake and arise from the state of death, enabling Christ to give them the light to see what is going on. [2]

The apostle went on to command these sleepy individuals to awake to righteousness and cease from sinning. Keep in mind that the drunken state of slumber is the result of many of these individuals partaking of the world to the point they are intoxicated by it. In their state, the darkness of unbelief has overtaken them because they not only have become unfruitful and barren in their knowledge of Jesus, but they are also suffering from a famine of the Word of God. They have failed to fill their lives up with the things of God by following after righteousness that establishes a person on the Rock, faith that is directed towards God, charity that is expressed in benevolent actions, and the peace that comes only from Christ.[3]

In Romans 13:11-14 the Apostle Paul exhorted believers to awake, knowing the time. Clearly, for us in this age, time is short, and the reality of the fullness of salvation is nearer than when each of us first believed. The night that has engulfed many in this present age has been far spent; therefore, it is time to cast off the works of darkness that have been at work in our lives and put on the armor of light. To put on the armor of light simply means to put on the Lord Jesus with the intent of walking in integrity according to all that is upright before Him. If we put on the life of Jesus, we will not make provision for the flesh, thereby, putting off its lust with its rebellion, drunken ways, immoral practices, covetous pursuits, contrary attitudes, and jealous demands.

The challenge is clear. As the Church, we must awake from beneath the dark cover of deception, repent of our hardened hearts of idolatry, and ask the Lord to take the veil of compromise from our eyes and the plugs of indifference from our ears. We must allow the heavy hand of the Potter to soften our hearts with humility to ensure that we are able to respond to His conviction. We must desire Him to heal our eyes with the salve of truth so they can clearly see the destruction that is coming on the horizon and cleanse our ears in order to hear what the Spirit is saying so that we can respond to the call of God.

At this time in history, God is shaking America as never before. The markets are in chaos, as the great idol of wealth is beginning to be broken up in various pieces, and its remaining residues taken out into the ocean of foolishness by the great wave of judgment. The banks are beginning to hoard money, creating an environment of financial

---

[2] Ephesians 5:14
[3] Amos 8:11; 1 Corinthians 15:34; 2 Timothy 2:22; 2 Peter 1:8-9

depression, smaller businesses are now becoming casualties to greed, and the American lifestyle is dissipating as despair is taking hold of many families.

Due to the recent elections of 2008, the government is now purporting socialistic practices that are anti-God, anti-Israel, and contrary to the Constitution of this nation. In these wicked people's quick attempt to socialize all institutions to bring them under the government as a means to usher people into communistic control and oppression, America will cease to exist, along with its government. What is sad is these leaders are foolishly fouling their own nest, as the powers of the world are considering how to divide this country which is clearly split in its philosophies.

The question is where is the Church of America? How much of the Church is being shipwrecked by the shaking that is taking place because it has been asleep? Sadly, being shipwrecked at the point of faith is not the same as being cleansed. It simply shows that faith has not been towards God, and such revelation will leave those who feel the sharpness of the rocks, reeling in utter despair. Once again, faith is not refined by the rocks of judgment, but by the fiery ovens of adversities.[4]

Remember, the Church will be presented to Jesus in a chaste state. No doubt, God is beginning the process. As stated, judgment does not refine, it simply reveals the quality of something in order to separate it for the purpose to purify it or to deliver it to wrath. Judgment is a dividing point, a crossroad where a decision will be required by the person who is facing the devastation. Will the person choose to trust God, humble self to seek His face, or will he or she allow the waves of judgment to take what is left of his or her shambled lives in Christ out into the ocean of wrath and destruction?

Those who belong to the true Church of Jesus must choose to trust Him, regardless of what is going on. Those who experience any type of shipwreck of their lives in Christ must realize it is the result of them failing to truly hide in the ark of Christ. They have allowed the currents of the world to move them towards this point, rather than giving way to the powerful air currents of the Holy Spirit.

The Church must be purified by the washing of the Word or the fire of the Holy Spirit. If it is not purified by God's tools, He will use adversities such as persecution, losses, and failure to rid His people of the various contaminates of self, the world, and works of darkness.

However, as His people, we must be part of the cleansing that must take place in our lives to ensure a chaste environment in our homes and for the Church. James 4:6-10 talks about what it means to be cleansed. Those who need to be purified must first come to a state of humility. From this premise, they can actually submit themselves before God. Such submission will allow them to actually resist the devil, causing him to flee.

---

[4] 1 Timothy 1:19; 1 Peter 1:5-9

Since the interference of darkness is no longer present, God's people are able to repent. Repentance is a turning away from in order to draw near to God, enabling Him to draw near to humble individuals with the intent to lift them up out of the mire of their pits. It is within His presence that people's hands can be cleansed from touching that which is unclean, and hearts can be purified from divided loyalties. As His people become afflicted in their spirits because of what their treacherous actions have cost God. Their souls will become mournful as their sins are revealed. From this premise, they will begin to be broken at the point of their pride, as they feel the depth of heaviness tighten its vice-grip on their feeble frames of humanity.

Brokenness of spirit towards sin is a much-needed sacrifice before God that would produce the environment of healing, reconciliation, and restoration. It is able to ensure the revival of the spirit, the transformation of the soul, and the reformation of one's outer conduct.

How many of those who claim to be part of Jesus' Church would be willing to go through such a process to gain His life and ensure a right inward environment? The problem is that many of these individuals do not see how far from the center they are. They perceive themselves good enough in regard to their Christian life. They do not realize that their perceptions about religious matters are serving as their personal center; rather than God, whose thoughts and ways are far above man's.

This brings us to the need of contrast. Without the mirror of truth, man will never see how far from the center he is. To sense his spiritual plight, he must have a revelation of how the Christian life will express itself. After all, it must be an expression of Jesus and not of man's best attempts or the world's best presentation. There is no substitution to this life.

In the next chapter, I am going to rise up the mirror of the real purpose and working of the Church. I am then going to follow it up in the next chapter with how the Body of Christ has been divided as a means to conquer it. Ultimately, in the final chapter, I will be ending with the promise that has been given to those who are truly members of the Body of Christ.

Meanwhile, consider if you are riding the wave of the world. Perhaps you have already hit the rocks of the shoreline of reality, and your faith has been left shipwrecked as you are struggling with what to do next. Maybe you are aware that something is not quite right about your spiritual life and understanding. The answer can be found in humility before God, submission to His Spirit, and obedience to His Word.

17

UNVEILING THE MYSTERY

We have considered the different aspects of the challenge confronting the Church. The members of this body need a spiritual vision or revelation that will awake them from any spiritual slumber as a means to encourage them to finish the course set before them. Vision or focus is vital because it allows the person to keep his or her eyes on the goal. As we consider the different paths that some of the professing Church have taken, we must consider if many in this visible Church lack such vision when it comes to the function, purpose, and goal God established in regard to the Body of Jesus.

Obviously, before we can actually confront the problems ailing the professing Church, we must first establish God's perspective of it. Even though this book has brought glimpses of the purpose of the Body of Christ, it needs to be clearly established. In Ephesians 5:22-33, the Apostle Paul explained how marriage pointed to the type of relationship that Jesus wanted with His Church.

The mystery that was unveiled by Christ in regard to the Church is that He wanted to be one with this Body as He is one with the Father. Godly marriage was to unveil such a relationship of oneness to the world. We are given insight into this very fact in John 17:23, "I in them, and thou in me, that they may be made perfect in one; and that the world may know that thou hast sent me, and has loved them, as thou has loved me."

We know that the Church's commission is to preach the Gospel and disciple believers to be followers of Christ. However, its authority to do so comes from the Head, Jesus Christ. Its power is realized when that oneness or agreement with Jesus is present. Jesus confirmed this very fact when He stated that, where there are two or three in agreement, matters can be accomplished and brought forth through prayer.[1]

As we consider the oneness that should be present in marriage, we even become more aware of how such agreement is brought forth. Marriage points to a vow, a covenant, and walking as one in a way that will serve as a living testimony. A vow is where a person agrees to fulfill certain requirements in regard to his or her relationship with the other party. A vow in marriage points to the act of consecration in which the couple separates from all others in order to separate themselves to each

---

[1] Matthew 18:19-20

other. Therefore, the couple's vow is one of faithfulness towards one another.

A covenant is perpetual or ongoing. It points to the responsibilities that those who enter this agreement must maintain in order to ensure the integrity of their relationship. In marriage, the woman must submit to that which is worthy, her Lord Jesus, to ensure the *intent* of the marriage, and man must love his wife as Christ loved the Church to ensure the *integrity* of this relationship.

In the past, covenants usually entailed the offering of sacrifices to show commitment to this agreement. These sacrifices sealed the agreement as being true. In the covenant of marriage, sacrifices are also required. Submission points to the voluntary sacrifice of consecration that had to be made with every offering made by the priest. Without the consecration or separation unto God, sacrifices do not possess any real distinctions that are clearly marked by true devotion. These types of sacrifices emitted smoke or a fragrance that was pleasing to God. Although such sacrifices represented reasonable service, they also spoke of man's desire to please God and show due service and honor to Him.

As the voluntary sacrifice, the wife is able to submit to her husband in light of her devotion to the Lord. Such godly submission will ensure a sacrifice that will emit the fragrance that is pleasing to God. It will not only be an upright offering that comes out of real servitude towards the family, but will also ensure the flavor or environment of the family.

The husband must present the mandatory or required sacrifice in regard to his marriage. Jesus was the sin or the required sin offering on behalf of His Church. It was His blood that established the New Testament covenant. In the Old Testament, the sin offering also pointed to the life of an animal being sacrificed as a means to cover the sins. For the husband to honor or prefer his wife's best interests above himself, he must become the mandatory sacrifice to ensure the well-being of the marriage relationship. Although the husband's sacrifice ensures the integrity of the covenant established with his wife, it is a necessary or required sacrifice that will also secure the sanctity of this relationship.

The purpose for covenant in the marriage is to ensure the environment of agreement. This is where the husband and wife walk together, yoked by the same common purpose, goal, and focus in their lives. Amos 3:3 brings this out. How can two walk together unless there is agreement? Such agreement points to oneness in spirit, intention, and life.

When we consider the oneness or agreement that a married couple should have, we must realize that it points to the fact that marriage is to serve as a living testimony or witness of the reality of Christ and His Church. This is why godly marriages have the potential to be ongoing. They will actually leave an ongoing witness for generations to come. Depending on the length of their lives together, this witness can be made evident and carried forth through the couple's children, grandchildren, and great grandchildren.

This brings us to another important aspect of the Church in regard to being one with Jesus. When Jesus spoke of being one with the Father, He also stated that He was in the Father and the Father was in Him. There is no debate that the Father and Jesus share the same nature, status, and abilities. But, what does it mean for the members of the Church to be in Christ, and Christ in His Body.

Our place in Christ points to our position, but Christ in us points to His life being in us. Positionally, we know that we have been placed in heavenly places with Christ, and that we are actually hid in Him. Since we have been placed in Him, we have all matters that pertain to our spiritual well-being and godliness available to us. The four main virtues of heaven that have been made available in Christ are wisdom, righteousness, sanctification, and redemption.[2]

"Heavenly places" points to our vantage point. We are to consider all matters according to Jesus' wisdom (His Word), in light of His righteousness (His godly examples), through His sanctification (His Spirit), and from His redemption (His work). Such a vantage point will lift us above the envies and jealousies of worldly wisdom, the depravity of personal righteousness, the defilement of the world, and the wretched philosophies of our present age.

Being in Christ reminds us of the environment that we have been placed in to ensure our vantage point. We must never consider matters from a worldly perspective or make conclusions based on introspection according to the self-life. We must be lifted above such limited perceptions in order to see it from the heavenly perspective. Any other perspective will cause great delusion or great bondage.

This brings us to the second aspect of our Christian life, and that is Christ in us. We know that Christ must become our heavenly perception of wisdom, our robe of righteousness, our place of sanctification, and our point of redemption. However, Christ in us speaks of His life.

The members of the true Church of Jesus are identified as living stones that make up a spiritual house, a holy priesthood. The reason that believers are identified in this way is because they possess the very life of Christ. It is His life that makes every believer a living stone, and His Church a living organism, a corporate Body that functions according to its Head.

Although we have already dealt with the subject of how Christians comprise the Church, we have not fully dealt with what it means for the life of Christ to be present in the Church. We know that we are in Christ who must serve as our all in all when it pertains to godliness. However, we also must realize that Christ must be in all aspects of our lives as a means to possess all that pertains to life.

---

[2] 1 Corinthians 1:30; Ephesians 2:6; Colossians 3:3; 2 Peter 1:3-4

Consider what the Apostle Paul stated in Colossians 3:11, "Where there is neither Greek nor Jew, circumcision nor uncircumcision, barbarian, Scythian, bond nor free, but Christ is all, and in all." The real Body of Christ cannot be divided. There may be members of the Church divided, which will cause inconsistencies within local bodies, but the Church of Jesus is not fragmented. His Spirit and life identify each member with His Body. However, as members of this Body, we can see from this Scripture that, regardless of our earthly heritage, our religious status before others, our earthy identity, or our state, it is all about Christ becoming all to, in, and through His Body.

If Jesus is all that the Church is about, our status in the world does not matter. As believers in Christ, we have no real past. We stand equal in importance when it comes to the function of His whole Body. We have no identification other than the Spirit. Our heritage can be traced back to the cross and our spiritual state is that of a bondservant, consecrated unto God for His service.

Christ is not only what the Church should be about, He also must be what the Church becomes. The Church must resonate with His life. He must be the center of every function and activity of His Body. His life must be found in every corner, closet, entryway, room, and court of each member of this living building. He must be found in every decision, practice, and activity. In essence, the Body must take on the agenda, purpose, and focus of its Head. It must be established in the fullness of Christ's life as each member takes on His likeness. The Apostle Paul brought this out in Ephesians 4:13, "Till we all come in the unity of the faith, and of the knowledge of the Son of God, unto a perfect man, unto the measure of the stature of the fullness of Christ."

God's goal was to reveal His Son to the world. In order to do this, He wanted to positionally establish man in the fullness of Christ, so that the life of Christ could fill up every aspect of man with His likeness. The Apostle Paul confirmed this in Ephesians 1:22-23, "And hath put all things under his feet, and gave him to be the head over all things the church, which is his body, the fullness of him that filleth all in all."

It is important to point out that the Christian life is complete. We do not possess a partial life of Christ. This complete work and life of Christ was necessary to defeat the complete work of sin and death. Jesus did not just go to the cross; He gave up His life on it. Because of who Jesus is and what He has done, the members of His Church are associated with the word "all".

A good example of this association can be found in Colossians 1:16-20. In these Scriptures, we know *all* things are associated with Jesus because He is Creator of *all* things, visible and invisible, along with *all* powers that exist in this world and in the unseen world. He existed before *all* things, and, because of Him, *all* things exist. He is the Head of the Church, the beginning of the first-born of creation that He might have pre-eminence in *all* things. It pleased the Father that in him should *all* fullness of the Godhead dwell. As a result of His redemption, He has reconciled *all* things unto Himself.

As we consider the word "all," it points to the sum of everything. In Christ, as His saints we have *all* comfort, grace, joy, peace, knowledge, wisdom, revelation, and riches bounding towards us. If we are abiding in love, faith, and obedience, we can be assured that *all* things will work for our good, and that *all* our needs will be supplied to us. We also can trust that *all* of His promises will be brought forth, and that we are heirs with Him in *all* things. Because of our lives in Christ, we know that we can do *all* things through Him.[3]

Obviously, it is God's goal to completely fill Jesus' Church with the fullness of His life. The Apostle Paul confirmed this in Ephesians 4:10, "He that descended is the same also that ascended up far above all heavens, that he might fill all things." God is the One who is working in all to bring about this glorious fullness of His Son within His Body.

The Apostle Paul also made this statement in Ephesians 3:17-19,
> That Christ may dwell in your hearts by faith; that ye, being rooted and grounded in love, May be able to comprehend, with all saints, what is the breadth, and length, and depth, and height, And to know the love of Christ, which passeth knowledge, that ye might be filled with all the fullness of God.

Clearly, the vision the Church must have is that its main goal must be to possess the fullness of Christ. The fullness of Christ points to the abundant life that He made reference to in John 10:10. It is this fullness of His life within the Body that not only establishes complete oneness with the Head and in the Body, but serves as a living testimony of the reality of Christ in the world. It is in this oneness that His life will flow, authority will stand, and power is able to come forth.

Sadly, the visible Church does not display such oneness. In fact, it appears religiously active, but it is lifeless in so many ways. Not only are much of the practices of the visible Church not about Jesus, but they clearly do not display the fullness of His life. As a result, many of the sheep are scattering in search of the fullness that is eluding them. These sheep may not exactly know what they are seeking, but they have a sense of a destiny that is far greater and more encompassing than what they have witnessed.

It is easy to talk about what is wrong with the professing Church, but the challenge is to bring the contrast and heavenly vision to wake it up enough to see its plight. Even though those who are spiritually dulled down may hear words, they will not comprehend, and, although they may see the truth, they will not understand. Sadly, this state will keep these individuals from being converted so that they can be spiritually healed.[4]

---

[3] Romans 8:28; 15:13-14, 2 Corinthians 1:3, 20; 9:8; Philippians 4:12, 19; Colossians 1:9, 2:2-3; Hebrews 1:2

[4] Matthew 13:13-16

Challenging the Christian Life

What kind of vision do you have in regard to the true Church of Jesus? If you do not have the vision set forth in Scripture, ask the Holy Spirit to revive your heart with this vision. Such revival will take away any spiritual dullness of compromise from your ears, and to allow the Spirit to put healing salve on any area where there is blindness in your eyes so that you can behold what is in the heart and mind of God. As you allow God to do this incredible surgery on you, consider the real challenge set before you as one of the many living stones that have been designated to make up God's spiritual building.

18

DIVIDE AND CONQUER

Jesus taught that a house divided against itself will fall.[1] We know from Scripture that the Church of Jesus is considered both a body and a house. This brings us to an important challenge. We know what happens to a house that is divided, but what happens to a body that finds itself opposing its very function? It may be hard to understand, but a physical body can turn against itself. In fact, a good indication that a body is turning against itself is allergies. There are known cases where people have become allergic to everything because their bodies were overwhelmed by their inability to function properly.

Regardless of all the activities of the professing Church, it is not functioning according to the Bible. One of the obvious fruits of this malfunction is schisms or divisions. Instead of local churches serving as one Body, most of them have been broken up into separate groups. For example, within a local body, there are the adults who are often being placated with a form of knowledge, but such knowledge rarely brings them to the real knowledge of Jesus.[2]

There are the teenagers who are being presented with a worldly Christianity that is void of truth and holiness. Granted, they are allowed to rock out with ungodly music that stirs up rebellion in the name of Christ, but there is no real semblance of holiness in any of it. These poor young people are not necessarily being prepared to separate themselves from the things of the world that entangle their youthful lusts into the endless web of vanity, defilement, and hopelessness. It appears that, in many cases, they are not being challenged to come to terms with a holy God that cannot be seen unless they come to a state of holiness. To come to such a state, they must cease exposing themselves to the silly, foolish, and sensual ways of the world and begin to expose themselves to the power of the uncompromised Word of God.

What about our children? Instead of challenging the foolishness bound up in their hearts, they are being entertained with the foolish things of the world.[3] Our children are becoming so separated from reality that they are not able to distinguish what is real. Thanks to *Veggie Tales*,

---

[1] Matthew 12:25
[2] 2 Timothy 3:7
[3] Proverbs 22:15

Challenging the Christian Life

King David is some silly vegetable who takes on Goliath who is nothing more than a big pickle.

My question is where is the sobriety towards the serious matters of God? As I read the Bible, I wonder how can the older women teach the younger women to be godly if the Body is separated according to personal preference? How can godly men teach the younger men to be godly if they are separated into groups according to age? How can our children understand that they are part of a Body if they are simply being entertained with the rest of the children during Sunday services? How can the different members of the Body find their place in the Body if the Body is not functioning as a Body?[4]

The Bible clearly shows us how the members of Jesus' Body are to function. There are no such worldly practices of separations based on age groups found in the Bible. It is up to the elders to teach the young people how to be godly. Although I have no problem with the concept of Sunday school, I believe that Sunday school is not a place of entertainment, but one of teaching our children the seriousness of loving God. However, the concept of children's church is unscriptural. Children need to learn how to be part of the Body. This is vital if they are to understand order and to learn that they belong to the Body. This will help them to find their place in the Body as they understand that they are a vital part of ensuring not only a healthy Church, but one that also functions correctly according to Scriptural teachings.

In the former fellowship we were overseeing, the children learned what it meant to be part of our Body. The adults of the Body were actively involved in the children's lives. These children were memorizing the books of the Bible, as well as Scriptures that included the Romans' Road in Sunday school. They were encouraged to share what they had learned with the adults and to pray about matters that were affecting the Body. They were constantly being nurtured in the ways of God according to the effectual working of the whole Body.

The youth who were part of the fellowship did not attend a separate Sunday school class. They were part of the adult class where they were expected to learn. They were given Bible Studies to complete during the week, as well as the responsibility of memorizing Scripture weekly. They were also responsible to share these Scriptures with the adults during the Sunday morning class. They were being brought up in the environment of the Body where they were being equipped to stand strong in order to overcome the wicked one with the Word of God.[5] These young people were involved with decision making in spiritual and administrative matters, as well as evangelism and ministry. As a result, some in the fellowship discovered that God's design for the Body clearly works, if it is properly applied.

---

[4] 1 Corinthians 12:12, 18-25; 1 Timothy 5:1-2; 1 Peter 5:5
[5] 1 John 2:13-14

The division that is prevalent in the Church proves the world has been influencing the Church. The more the world influences the philosophies and practices of the professing Church, the more division will occur, not only in the Church, but in families as well. As people identify themselves according to group or denomination, rather than Jesus, or stand on a mixture of theology, rather than truth, and promote religious or worldly practices instead of honorable conduct towards God and others, there will be no real agreement in spirit or truth.

The professing Church is becoming more fragmented. Sadly, what those in this religious system are becoming allergic to as this time draws closer to the end of this present age is the truth. God's truth is actually insulting much of the professing Church. Such truth serves as a sharp sword that will divide asunder the attitude of the soul and the disposition of the spirit. It will expose the workings of the joints and marrow as to the quality of life that is in operation in the Body, and it will reveal the source of wisdom that is inspiring the thoughts, as well as the motivations of the heart.[6]

As the sword exposes the real workings of the professing Church, clear distinction will be made between those who love the truth and those who insist on their own reality concerning the matters of religion.[7] It will divide those who are simply playing church from those who are the Church. It will expose the limitations of denominations and the pettiness of man's doctrine. Ultimately, it will expose who people are truly serving: the Lord of the Church or the god of this present age.

The sword of the Word is constantly coming down in the professing Church. Granted, it is not being brought down by some religious denomination or system; rather, it is being brought down by those who will not compromise the truth of God to fit into the different religious systems or movements. These firebrands will not budge from the Rock of ages and from the spirit or intent of the Word of God. Granted, they have their own opinions about different issues, but their faith towards God has established them upon the one true foundation of Christ, lined them up to Him as the cornerstone, and has brought them into maturity or perfection according to His leadership as the Head and Lord of the true Body. They will also not be moved away from the intent or spirit of truth, nor will they agree with another gospel. Like the Apostle Paul, these individuals will insist on integrity in all matters concerning the function of the Body.

It is important to point out that there is a difference between the servants of God who are being led by the Spirit and those who are walking according to their own religious agendas. Those who have their own agendas walk according to their own drumbeat. Such people take pride in the fact that they do not fit into the system, but they also have not really allowed God to place them in the Body. They are doing their own thing. Such people may possess the truth, but they lack Christian

---

[6] Hebrews 4:12
[7] 2 Thessalonians 2:10-12

character. Their way of thinking still reveals they are leaning on their own worldly understanding and ways. Therefore, these people may have an understanding of truth, but they do not possess the truth because the attitude and life of Jesus are not prevalent in their approach and conduct when it comes to the matters of life and others. Real servants of God stand out because they are distinct from the world, not because they are proving to be contrary to the religious system.

As the sword of truth comes down, the separation between the light of truth and the delusion of darkness becomes more distinct. Instead of people walking between two opinions, they are being brought to a place of decision and identification. The place of decision comes down to what light they choose to walk according to.[8]

The Apostle Paul tells us that Satan also comes as an angel of light. He has his own army of false apostles and ministers who are capable of transforming themselves into a form of righteousness, but their works are bent on destruction. Satan's light is disguised or counterfeited in many ways. There is the light of self-righteousness for those who want to be the judge, expert, and authority of religious matters, rather than humble, discerning servants in the matters of God. There is the light of knowledge. This arrogant knowledge sees itself as being superior, but it lacks true wisdom and love, revealing the foolishness of this type of light. There is the light of the New Age, where the mind of man is exalted and mystical experiences of the occult are embraced. There is the light of success that considers quantity rather than quality. There is the light of false happiness that encourages every type of pagan, fleshly pursuit to secure a temporary façade of satisfaction.[9]

There is also the light of false religion. Since the Holy Spirit has lifted from the unholy mixture of the world in the professing Church, He has left an empty vacuum that is being filled with every type of Jesus imaginable, as well as worldly practices, methods, and pursuits that have some stamp of religion upon them, but are void of the identifying mark of the Spirit of God and His truth. Obviously, so much of what people perceive to be "Christian" has no life in it.

Since people must have some religious experience to give them a sense of security, there are always those who see the opportunity to capitalize upon such a vacuum. They simply counterfeit what is missing with such things as legalism. Legalism is so oppressive, cruel, bitter, and unrealistic to the spirit that it becomes repulsive.

People can also take their religious pursuits to the other extreme of legalism. The other extreme opens the door to doctrines of demons and lying signs and wonders. These counterfeits will fill the insatiable hole with fleshly worship that is totally pagan and experiences that are demonically inspired. These two extremes show scorn towards the real

---

[8] 1 Kings 18:21; Joel 3:14; Ephesians 5:8-17; 1 John 1:3-7
[9] Matthew 7:1-5; 1 Corinthians 8:1-3; 2 Corinthians 11:13-15; 1 Timothy 6:5-12; Hebrews 5:12-14; James 2:5; 3:13-18

work of the Spirit and prove to despise the real intent of the Bible. Granted, these different approaches use certain parts of the Bible, but, ultimately, they confuse or neglect the real issue of salvation.[10]

Satan does not care what extreme people operate within, just as long as they do not come back to the center of whom God is and His truth. He does not care if such individuals have a whole lot of truth in one area, as long as they do not come into balance where the Spirit or personal conduct is concerned. He does not care if people swing on a high due to a religious spirit, while holding onto some small semblance of truth, as long as they never really discover what it means to experience the Lord in His glory, enabling them to discern their true spiritual condition. He does not care because it is all a form of his worldly darkness that is blinding minds to the true light of Jesus' Gospel.

As you begin to study the condition of the visible or professing Church, you can see three types of environments in operation because of these extremes. Keep in mind that the professing Church is in the boiling pot of the world. Many well-meaning people are being conditioned to regard the matters of God according to a lifeless, twisted, or demonic environment. However, you can find the true Church functioning, even in spite of the boiling pot.

Since we are discussing the Church, let us now consider how it operates according to these environments. First, you have those of the Church who operate as the actual _Body_ of Jesus. This group of people realizes that they must come into one accord to grow up together into the Head. This will ensure that they will properly function as a body according to the vision, plan, and purpose of God. The challenge for the real Body of Jesus is that the members will taste various forms of oppression and persecution since they will not bow down to what is considered normal by the rest of the religious world.

The second group is made up of people who are part of the different _congregations_. People who are part of congregations come together to receive instruction and to worship according to a set schedule or pattern. The problem with many of the people in this particular group is that they maintain their personal identity or selfishness, while settling for some religious environment. In other words, they are not coming together as a means of submitting to one another to ensure the complete function of the Body. They may have agreement with those in the congregation, but they also reserve their right to determine the type of investment, if any, they may make in the kingdom of God.

The final group is made up of people who see themselves as part of the _audience_. These people come to some type of church building to be entertained. They are seeking a "Disneyland" environment to maintain their identity to the world, while being associated with some type of religious experience. Since this form of worldly religion entertains them, they can enjoy what they consider the best of both worlds.

---

[10] Matthew 23:3-4, 28; 2 Thessalonians 2:8-9; 1 Timothy 4:1-2; Hebrews 2:3

Challenging the Christian Life

This brings us to the next group of people that must be considered in light of the three groups found in churches—the leaders. The type of leadership that is in place will depend upon the flavor of the group they are overseeing. Deep calls to deep. You will not find a true servant overseeing an audience any more than you will see the true Body of Jesus accepting a charlatan, performer, or entertainer as its leader. There are three types of leaders. These leaders set up the religious environment that will be prevalent in the local bodies.

Before we address the subject of leaders, let us consider the environments that will be in operation. There are four types of environments. They are classified as fundamental, charismatic, the social club, and that of Spirit and truth. Each environment has its own emphasis. In the fundamental environment, the emphasis is to get back to the basic truths of Christianity. Such an emphasis is sound, but there is one problem, and that is much of it lacks the Spirit. It often proves to be lifeless.

The boundaries for each Christian are Spirit and truth. The Spirit is the one who maintains the integrity of truth. With the Spirit, truth is properly discerned.[11] Without this integrity, such truths will lack life. Truths that lack life will become indifferent, judgmental, and cruel.

A. W. Tozer explained how Fundamentalism fell victim to its own virtues, as the voice of the prophet was silenced by the cult of textualism.[12] Textualism operates according to the same premise as the scribes did in Jesus' day. It is where man decides how Scripture must be interpreted and understood by those who are being perceived as laity. Instead of touting phylacteries and enlarged borders on their garments as they did in Jesus' day, the scribes of today take pride in their various college degrees.[13] No doubt, Fundamentalism initially appeared to be an answer to the insanity that was taking place in the religious world, but all it did was establish its own cult mentality as people were made subject to the interpretation of man. Such interpretation of what is truth becomes the superior standard, rather than the simple truths of the Bible. It is from this premise that all spiritual matters are judged.

Once again, we are reminded that the ways of man and the world never really change. The religious system that put man in bondage during Jesus' day still exists; only it is being sold under the guise of Fundamentalism to the laity. The deeds and doctrines of the Nicolaitans of Revelation are now being sold to Christians through Replacement Theology. As Solomon tells us, there is nothing new under the sun.[14] In Christendom, we can find repackaged heresy that is always being sold under new names and titles.

---

[11] John 4:23-24; 16:13; 1 Corinthians 2:10-16
[12] Keys to the Deeper Life; A. W. Tozer, © 1957, 1984 by Creation House; Clarion Classics, Published by the Zondervan Publishing House, pg. 19
[13] Matthew 23:5
[14] Ecclesiastes 1:9

This brings us to the Charismatic movement. This movement swung in the opposite direction from Fundamentalism. This is where the finger pointing comes into play. You have the Fundamentalists calling the Charismatic people insane and ridiculous. You have the Charismatic people calling the Fundamentalists dead and judgmental. Who is correct? Sadly, both can prove to be correct. The Charismatic movement sought after spirit in order to have evidence of some spiritual life and experiences. However, in some cases there was no discernment of the spirit that was coming through the door. It did not seem to matter whether the spirit in operation was lining up to the Word of God. As a result, the antichrist spirit came in with various New Age and occult experiences. Since these experiences seemed so real, many embraced them as being reality. Out of this unholy mixture came methods and practices that the professing Church has embraced. Such methods and practices include Positive Confession and visualization. However, the latest practice in this long line of ungodly exercises that have been paraded and exalted through each antichrist movement in the Christian realm is contemplative prayer.

The next environment is the social club. Clearly, those of the Fundamental and the Charismatic camps would never come into agreement. They are poles apart in their emphasis. Hence, welcome the emergent church. The emergent church is nothing more than a big social club with a "Disneyland" atmosphere. The emergent church plays both sides of the two religious poles by not insulting anyone. For example, the truth and Gospel are presented in an extremely watered-down state, but it will satisfy the mentality of those who are seeking some form of religious truth. To satisfy the other group, the true Spirit has been counterfeited in the worship service. Therefore, on one side is the Fundamentalist who hears a semblance or appearance of the truth along with the Gospel being alluded to, and, on the other side, there are ample opportunities for those in the Charismatic camp to have a satisfying emotional experience. As a result, both groups can happily sit in the boiling pot of the world with some semblance of agreement at the expense of both Spirit and truth. Needless to say, the environment that is being established by the emergent church is ushering in the one-world religious system under the guise of Social Justice that will fall under the complete control of the antichrist spirit.

This brings us to the final environment: that of Spirit and truth. The integrity of truth is upheld in this environment to ensure that the Holy Spirit has freedom to move upon hearts and lives as He imparts, prepares, teaches, and guides the Body of Christ. Souls are saved, lives are changed, and people are healed and restored. This is where true worship occurs and service is defined and often becomes sacrificial for the glory of God.

It is within these environments that you can also find different types of leadership. There are the true shepherds of Jesus, the hireling shepherds, and the wolves. Within the first three environments, you will find that the true leaders (shepherds) are either frustrated, stifled, or in despair as they must constantly contend for the faith that was first delivered to the saints. Some of these leaders are actually being abused and driven out of some of the local churches.

There are also the hireling shepherds and wolves who will see the first three environments as platforms on which to fulfill their personal agendas, as they strive to undermine the Spirit and integrity of truth in the fourth environment. Sometimes, these false shepherds manage to split a local body in their attempt to gain control over the sheep. Needless to say, the real flock of God will find itself in the middle of a chess game, where the members perceive themselves as being pawns. Let us now consider how these three types of leaders operate.

The real shepherd has a distinct heart, calling, and emphasis. This shepherd's heart is towards the Lord and His sheep. The Chief Shepherd, Jesus Christ, has called this individual into this position. Out of loving devotion for the true Shepherd and with deep humility, meekness, and trepidation, this shepherd will always lead the sheep towards the reality of Jesus. This shepherd is not in competition with the Chief Shepherd, for this committed leader has one goal, and that is God must be glorified in His fold. The true shepherd knows that, unless the sheep learn to hear the voice of their Chief Shepherd, they will never know a satisfying life. This humble shepherd is not in this vocation because of money, importance, or prestige, but because of the faithfulness that comes out of loving and knowing the Chief Shepherd. The main responsibility of this shepherd will serve as this individual's constant emphasis and pursuit, and that responsibility is to feed the sheep of God to ensure spiritual maturity.[15]

The hireling shepherd comes in many forms. The many different seminaries have formed many of these imposters. Sadly, these seminaries, with their mixtures of theology and worldly philosophies, such as Psychology, produce what we call cookie-cutter ministers that often promote atheistic, amoral, New Age, and liberal views. In other words, they have been cut out of the same worldly or religious cloth. These individuals may start out with a call, but, because of the non-inspired, worldly influence that has invaded much of the professing Church's way of thinking, such callings can be drowned out by skepticism and unbelief. Such individuals are like those of Ephraim. They become a half-baked cake that has never been turned and baked on the other side. On one side, they look like they may have the spiritual goods to lead the people of God, but, on the other side, there is carnality, pride, and immaturity.[16]

Being a pastor to the Body of Christ is both a calling and a vocation. However, the calling can be defiled and confused by the ways of the world, and the vocation replaced by the wrong emphasis. Wrong

---

[15] John 10:4; 1 Peter 5:1-4
[16] Hosea 7:8-15; Colossians 2:8

emphasis will lack the right heart. Ultimately, such misdirected emphasis often embraces the attitude of the subculture that we refer to as Christianity to hide immature, fleshly devotion. As such a person loses heart, he or she will become blinded by the philosophies and practices of the world that have been packaged as acceptable Christian practices.

Hireling pastors often end up feeding the flock what I call placebo truths that are surrounded by a worldly emphasis. Worldly emphasis will change the intent of truth as it feeds the sheep sugar-coated poisons of heresy. Wrong spiritual diets always strip the truth of its power and authority to impact others and will ultimately rob the professing Church of life as it causes it to become sluggish. Such shepherds become void of godly concern for the flock and its spiritual growth. Eventually, the real sheep will become disillusioned because they do not hear the voice of the true Shepherd coming forth out of the mouth of these false shepherds. They will eventually scatter as they seek pastures that are satisfying and clean water that is able to revive them once again.[17]

Wolves are different from hireling shepherds because their main goal is to seek a following. The hireling shepherd often sees God's flock as an opportunity to do good or make a difference. Since their motive is self-serving, such shepherds end up fleecing the sheep or abandoning them altogether to become prey to the wolves. However, a wolf sees the flock as a means to survive. These individuals seek out the sheep not only to fleece them, but to also feed their overrated ego. If the poor sheep fail to serve the purpose of the wolf, they will taste the hatred and cruelty of these leaders.

In their delusion, such wolves perceive that it is the sheep's responsibility to sacrifice all to meet their personal desires and agendas, rather than the other way around. Granted, they will throw bones at the miserable little creatures to keep them unaware of what is really happening around them, but these wolves have no intention of serving the sheep. Ultimately, they will sacrifice the sheep who refuse to follow them, as well as condition those who do follow into obeying only their voice, making them two-fold the children of hell that they are themselves.[18]

Those who are strong sheep will confront these heretics with the Word of God.[19] However, if the wolf fails to repent, then all sheep must flee from the leadership of such a self-serving, cruel, unreasonable individual.

This brings us to the Word of God. The unbelief of the *world* will always attack or undermine the authority of the Word. The skepticism of man will always downplay the ways of faith towards the validity of the Word by perverting or applying the Word in an unrealistic way. In such an environment, the Word never becomes personal so that those hearing

---

[17] Ezekiel 34; John 10:1-5
[18] Matthew 7:15; 10:16; John 10:8-10
[19] Titus 3:10-11

or receiving it can clearly discern their own spiritual condition. Rather, it becomes judgmental towards others.

Worldly knowledge will make the Word appear obsolete or metaphoric, rather than absolute. Spiritualizing the things of God will make the truth of the Word appear inferior when considered in its unadulterated form. Obviously, the Word of God has been misused, abused, and neglected. It is often being presented lightly, as "fluff" if you will, rather than in the salty form that brings contrast to heal wounds, as well as necessary judgment or separation. It has been sugar-coated with misinterpretation, rather than allowed to serve as the sharp two-edged sword that reveals the vanity and frivolous ways of such interpretations. It has been paraphrased according to the popular winds of the time and translated according to the environment of the age (generally from Gnostic sources that our spiritual forefathers rejected as fables). In each worldly, uninspired paraphrase and translation of God's Word, the spirit or intent has been changed to cover up the insidious handling of it.[20] These attempts have a goal, and that is to condition God's people to embrace the unholy mixture of the world with the things of God. These unholy mixtures cleverly render the powerful Christian life into a worldly subculture that fits nicely into the various activities of the world. [21]

As for the *wolves,* they will use the Word as a blindfold or a club. In other words, they will cleverly use the Word as a means of blinding the sheep to their real intentions, all the while changing the intent of Scripture to subtly line their poor followers up to their way of thinking. If the sheep fail to line up to their leaders' insane reality, the leaders will use the Word as a club to beat them into total subjection to their abominable leadership, often leaving the poor sheep wounded and in total despair.

The *hireling* shepherds will twist the Word to give the impression that they are feeding the sheep, but, in reality, there is no real substance behind any of it. In the end, the sheep will fall victim to malnutrition. Such sheep often become prey to the winds of false doctrines and the various wolves that present themselves as apostles, prophets, and ministers of righteousness.

As you study these different environments in operation, you can see how they result in division. In the _Body_, the division comes when the Father prunes away the members that are void of any real life or fruit.[22]

For those in the _congregations_, the division comes when the wind blows through their ranks. The wind can be that of the Holy Spirit who serves as the fire that will test and purify the believers to reveal their real level of devotion. Or, it could be the wind of persecution that will purge to

---

[20] 2 Timothy 2:15

[21] If you would like to understand how to properly divide the Word of truth, see the author's book, *My Words Are Spirit and Life* in Volume One of the foundation series.

[22] John 15:1-8

bring distinction between those who are standing on the Rock and those who are standing on the shifting sands of self-righteousness. Finally, there are also the winds of false doctrines that will sweep away those who are unstable into the tidal wave of delusion.[23]

God simply turns the *audiences* of the professing Church over to their lusts. There is no place of real conviction because the glory of God's holiness has been changed into the latest form of entertainment. It is hard to say how much of the knowledge of the true God is retained in such an environment, but, if there are any sheep in such a place, eventually they will have to repent and come out and be separate from the charade.[24]

As you can see, the professing Church is being divided in various ways, but what about the true Church of Jesus? Is it being divided, refined, and/or defined by the separation that is taking place in the professing Church? More importantly, what division do you belong to? Are you part of the Body, being established according to the leadership of the Head? Perhaps, you are part of a congregation that has gone through some challenges and separation. Maybe, you have fallen into the lie and façade of being part of the popular audiences. It is time to make sure you are truly part of the universal Church that is neither limited by walls, nor defined by denomination or established by man's doctrine. Rather, your identification is truly in Christ in light of His wisdom, with Him in His righteousness, through His sanctification, and according to His work of redemption.

---

[23] Matthew 7:24-27; John 16:8; Acts 2:1-21; Ephesians 4:14; 2 Thessalonians 2:3, 10-12; 2 Timothy 3:12

[24] Romans 1:23-25; 2 Corinthians 6:14-18; Hebrews 12:14

19

THE GATES OF HELL WILL NOT PREVAIL

Whatever happened to the Church? We know that the face of the professing Church has changed according to the different winds that have blown through the ages. For me, in my initial Christian years, it was all about denomination. The most asked question was, "What denomination, or I should say "particular religious box", do you belong to?" This was so that you could be classified as being Fundamental, Charismatic (Pentecostal), or Liberal. In today's age of mega-churches and the endless stream of false apostles and prophets hitting the scene with their own brand of heresy, the popular question for today is, "Who is your covering?"

Regardless of the question, the real concern, in most instances, is not about one's soul; rather, it is about whether you fit into the newest presentation of the latest wind of worldly, lifeless, and uninspired nonsense that is taking the professing Church by storm. Much of the visible Church appears as if it does not care if you are on your way to eternal damnation. All it seems to care about is that you do not go against the grain of its worldly systems, controlled arenas, and delusions that are presently in operation. Clearly, as the professing Church is conditioned by the different winds of the doctrines of man and demons that blow through Christendom, it is becoming more allergic to the unadulterated truth of the Bible. In fact, some of those professing to be Christians would not recognize the Biblical presentation of what true Christianity constitutes any more than they would recognize the true Jesus of the Bible.

The question we must now pose is whatever happened to the true Church of Jesus? Obviously, the true Church constitutes the saints that truly have received the life of Jesus and have maintained that life by faith. As you study the lives of these saints, the answer to what has happened to the true Church is quite simple and obvious. From the time the world started coming into the midst of the professing Church and gaining a foothold into its way of thinking, the real Church has been continually coming out from the influence of the world and becoming separate from the religious system.

The true Church continues to discover the same truth: *it can never change the environment of the world, but the world can change it.*

Therefore, the members of the true Church are constantly separating from the influence of the age they are living in to ensure their status as God's children, kings, and priests.[1] As a result, they have consistently proved to be worthless to the world, insulting and irritating to the religious system, and immovable when assaulted by the changing winds of doctrine of both men and devils.

Members of this true Church of Jesus are being constantly challenged to discover true Christianity in the midst of the counterfeits. Most blood-bought saints start out being part of the professing Church. In their initial Christian lives, they are told what to think, how to conduct themselves, and what is true. But eventually, as they grow in Christ, they find themselves hitting the ceiling of their denomination and knocking their heads against doctrine that is an ungodly mixture void of life and revelation. Even in the midst of this conditioning, the saints do sense a stirring of the Spirit within them. There is a realization that there is so much more to this incredible life. At first, they fumble in their search, but, eventually, they begin to realize what that more is. It is more of God.

Once they recognize that their true desire is to see, know, and experience the fullness of their Lord and the life He has for them, they begin to recognize the signs of leanness in their spirit that are being unveiled to them. They will begin to see that the leanness is caused by the limitations of man and the defilement of the world. Such leanness of spirit will eventually become unbearable to these individuals. Therefore, some of these believers find themselves stepping outside of the "box." Granted, they usually find themselves in another "box," but at least the next "box" allows them a bit more room to explore the unlimited depths of their infinite God from a different perspective.

Once these seeking saints encounter the limitation of the next "box", their restlessness will fan into a flame, causing them to come out and be even more separated. They eventually discover that their sincere desire to know God leads them on an incredible journey. This journey leads them into secret places where they begin to experience Him. It also takes them through the barren wilderness of the present age.

In this barren wilderness, these saints discover that the religious attempts and experiences of man can only bring them so far in their spiritual search. As they begin to see that the light of denominations and traditions will eventually restrict their present growth, they quickly find themselves in another barren place, where they must choose to cling to the Rock. These stout, hearty individuals refuse to be cut out of the same religious cloth as others have been. They want to find their own place, identity, and life in Jesus. This identity will not be based on some denominational box that is inadequate or some movement that is clearly moving outside of the Scriptural boundaries of the Word of God.

The restlessness in the spirit of these individuals is the Holy Spirit, always calling them outside of limitations in order to come higher in their

---

[1] John 1:12; 2 Corinthians 6:14-18; Revelation 1:6

Challenging the Christian Life

lives in Christ. However, such a journey will take them into valleys of despair. God must go deeper in a person's character before he or she can come higher in his or her life with Him. These individuals may be sitting in congregations, but they have developed a secret life in God that makes them distinct in ways that cannot be explained. They may be in a group of religious people, but these individuals will never really belong to the group, for they continue to travel the course that God has prepared for them. Their walk of faith will lead them outside of the camp of religion with its traditions and activities into the wilderness of preparation.[2] In essence, these individuals are always being prepared to meet God in their incredible journey, in spite of the darkness of the present age.

This brings us to the statement that Jesus made in Matthew 16:18, "And I say also unto thee, That thou art Peter, and upon this rock (Jesus) I will build my church, and the gates of hell shall not prevail against it." (Parenthesis added.)[3] The professing Church may have changed throughout the ages, but the real Church of Jesus remains the same. Although hell may do all it can to replace the work of the Holy Spirit, redefine the foundation of Jesus, adjust the cornerstone of who He is, and make true faith worthless with unholy agreements, misdirected loyalties, and alliances, the true Church never moves from the Rock that it has clearly been established upon. Granted, it may become confused, oppressed, and occasionally lost in the midst of the onslaught of counterfeit presentations, but it will always come back to the Rock.

The reason the true Church will come back to the Rock of ages, is because its heart will not be satisfied unless it is lined up to the cornerstone. The spirit of the true Church will not settle for a different faith because nothing else makes sense outside of Jesus as its Head (His leadership), serving as its Vine (the source of life), partaking of Him as its Bread (the place of nourishment and communion), and being firmly established on Him as its Foundation (knowing and experiencing spiritual stability).

The true Church of Jesus has a clear understanding that the Lord has redeemed it.[4] It does not belong to itself. It does not represent self-interests. It is not here to be popular or to fit into this world. It stands upon truth, regardless of how unpopular, it withstands with truth, regardless of the possible rejection and persecution it may experience, and it is always determined to stand because of truth, regardless of the extent of darkness that is invading the souls of others. It is here to function according to the leadership, life, and purpose of Jesus Christ. In Him, this unique Body that is known as the Church stands complete. But, without Him, the Church knows it is void of life and purpose.

---

[2] 2 Timothy 4:7; Hebrews 13:10-14
[3] 1 Corinthians 10:4
[4] 1 Corinthians 6:17-20; 7:22-24

The Apostle Paul gave us insight into what the true Church of Jesus has been experiencing for the past 20 centuries. He made this statement in 2 Corinthians 4:7-11,

> But we have this treasure in earthen vessels, that the excellency of the power may be of God, and not of us. We are troubled on every side, yet not distressed; we are perplexed, but not in despair; Persecuted, but not forsaken; cast down, but not destroyed; Always bearing about in the body the dying of the Lord Jesus, that the life also of Jesus might be made manifest in our body. For we who live are always delivered unto death for Jesus' sake, that the life also of Jesus might be made manifest in our mortal flesh.

Members of the Body who truly gain a sense of who they are in Christ realize they are simply clay vessels. As vessels formed by the influences of the world, the members of Christ' Body are aware that they were found by God to be marred vessels. Marred by sin, they had to be purged. The only way they could be purged was to be broken so that the Potter could once again take them through a process that would make them sanctified vessels that could possess the priceless gift of the life of Jesus.[5]

For the saint who understands the necessity for such a process, he or she is humbled. In humility, the members of the Body of Christ realize that the Christian walk is contrary to what is nominal and acceptable, even to the religious world. A. W. Tozer best described the type of creature that saints become in his book *The Radical Cross*. Tozer pointed out that the saints will put themselves in jeopardy in order to be safe in Christ. To save their lives, they will lose them. They humble themselves so that they can be lifted up. They are strongest when they are the weakest. They are spiritually poor so they can make others rich. They possess the most after they have given most everything away. They experience the heights of God when they are the lowest. They are more aware of sin when they are sinless in their walk. They know the most when they realize they know nothing outside of Jesus. For the saints, the most is accomplished when they are standing still before the Lord, waiting for His instruction. In heaviness they manage to rejoice as they keep their hearts in the state of gladness during times of grave sorrow.[6]

Tozer explained that the real character of Christians is being revealed constantly in their attitude towards salvation. They believe they are saved presently, but they expect to be saved later and look forward to a future salvation. These individuals fear God, but do not live in fear of Him. In God's presence they feel overwhelmed and totally exposed, but there is no place they would rather abide. They know that they have

---

[5] Leviticus 11:32-33; Jeremiah 18:1-4; 2 Timothy 2:19-21

[6] The Radical Cross: Living the Passion of Christ; A. W. Tozer, © 2005 by Zur Ltd; pg. 102

been cleansed from sin, but they are keenly aware that they have nothing to offer Him according to their flesh. Although they are lowly, they know what it means to talk to the King of kings. Even though they are aware of being insignificant, they also know how important they are to God.[7]

It is such an attitude that makes the members of Jesus' Body vessels that are trustworthy to carry the prize possession of His life everywhere they go. They are like the woman who anointed Jesus for His burial. They are always ready to be sacrificially broken at the feet of Jesus so others can experience the fragrance of His sweet life.[8]

For this reason, the true Body of Jesus stands distinct. This distinction can cause its members to experience trouble from all sides. Satan stirs up such trouble to wipe out the reflection of Jesus' life. If need be, he stirs up the religious people with jealousy, inspires the world to placate sin by offering up the truth with flattery, bullying, or persecution, and blinds the masses to the fact that they are being led as sheep to the slaughter, while rejecting and crucifying the truth.[9] However, in such trouble, the true Body of Christ will not give way to the distress that may encamp about them.

Granted, the Body will surely become perplexed by the mocking attitudes and actions of those who claim to be religious or godly. The members of His Body will also struggle with the unpredictable opposition that accompanies these individuals as they resist the truths and ways of God in the name of Jesus or righteousness. Even though reasoning may elude these saints as to the insanity that often operates in the name of religious righteousness, they will not allow themselves to wallow in despair.

In many parts of the world, the true Church tastes the bitter sweetness of persecution. On one hand, the members of this eternal Body marvel that all false religions of the world fear Christianity. If these deluded persecutors' perception is true, why fear a simple message of the Gospel? However, these enemies of Christianity do fear it because it represents truth. Such truth will set the captive free from the clutches of religion and various delusions. Therefore, these false religions must snuff out the light of true Christianity. However, the more they try, the greater the light burns in the hearts of those who love and know their Lord. These saints know that the Lord will never forsake them in their time of persecution.

Some members of the Church are being cast down into the miry pits of rejection and oppression. Like the prophet Jeremiah, they will faithfully and obediently labor in these dark pits because of their faith towards God and His Word. Ultimately, their bodies may be destroyed, but their souls will be preserved by the faithfulness of God. These individuals are

---

[7] Ibid, pg. 103
[8] Matthew 26:6-13; 2 Corinthians 2:14-16
[9] Isaiah 53:6

assured of a better resurrection. They will know that it is through such sanctifying fires that the Church of Jesus will be refined and presented as a Body without spot and wrinkle.[10]

The Apostle Paul also reminded us in Romans 8:36-37, "As it is written, For thy sake we are killed all the day long; we are accounted as sheep for the slaughter. Nay, in all these things we are more than conquerors through him that loved us." Once again, we are reminded that, as believers, we must become identified with Jesus in His death, burial, and resurrection. The apostle explained in 2 Corinthians 4:11-12 that death is always working in each of us as the servants of God. We are bearing in our life of worship and service the reality of Jesus' death on our behalf. Therefore, we are constantly being led to the slaughter so that His life can manifest itself in and through our bodies. It is all about His glory being reflected in our very countenance.[11]

The Bible is clear that God always has a remnant that will remain true to Him, regardless of the darkness of the present age that is invading the hearts and minds of people. These saints will not bow to Baal in any way. They will not give honor or preference to any idolatrous altar. They may be weary behind the closed doors of their hidden life in Christ, but they will remain true. They will stand distinct from the world as strangers and pilgrims in spite of the rejection and persecution. Like Peter, these saints realize that there is no other to whom they can turn who has eternal life.[12] As a result, they cling faithfully to Jesus as they rest in His glorious hands.

In this place of abiding, they will stand firmly upon Him as their foundation; they will continue to line up to Him as the precious cornerstone, find abiding joy in His Word, and know that He is the source of their unwavering faith. Ultimately, they will be able to claim and verify the promise that Jesus gave His disciples, which is, the very gates of hell will not prevail against His Church.

Is this your claim? Are you a member of the true Church of Jesus? Perhaps you are limited by some type of "box," but are restless in your soul. Seek God as to what you must do in your particular barren wilderness. God may call you aside, apart, or into a secret place with Him.

Maybe you see that the particular doctrine that you have been established in lacks real power and revelation; therefore, you are ready to rethink what you have been conditioned to believe. If so, put aside what you think you know and understand, approach the Bible to believe it, and ask the Spirit to give you God's perspective. You might even be someone who is in a religious environment that makes no sense, but you do not know where to go. Flee to God and asked Him for more of

---

[10] Jeremiah 18:19-23; Matthew 10:28; Ephesians 5:27; Hebrews 11:35
[11] Romans 12:1; 2 Corinthians 3:18
[12] John 6:68-69

Himself. Come under His Spirit and be led to those pastures and waters that will satisfy your hungry soul.

Remember, the great cloud of witnesses proves that, since we are God's people, we do not have to settle for a substandard existence or accept lifeless religious presentations or an inconsistent life. We do not have to become part of the subculture of the professing Church to simply belong. We do not have to allow the winds of the present age to influence us. As believers, we can find our lives in Christ as we are established on the foundation, defined according to the cornerstone, and free to discover the unfeigned faith that was first delivered to the saints. Perhaps, in the darkness of the present age we live in, we will develop a life that God considers a sweet sacrifice that even the world is not worthy of witnessing and tasting.

The bottom line is that, as a believer, it is your life, your choice, and your sacrifice. When all is said and done, you alone will answer for what you did with the life of Christ that was so wonderfully entrusted to you as one of the many members of His living, eternal Body, the Church.

WOMEN'S PLACE IN THE KINGDOM OF GOD
(An Exposition)

Book Five

Copyright © 2006 by Rayola Kelley
Originally copyrighted © 1993 by Rayola Kelley

INTRODUCTION

This book has gone through various stages of development and growth to ensure a balanced perspective about women in the kingdom of God. Women who desire to serve God outside of the acceptable roles of conventional Christianity often enter a war zone. The invisible battle they encounter has nothing to do with their call, "per se," or with their abilities, but rather, with their gender.

No doubt, there are differences between men and women. The distinction is clearly defined by physical appearance and function. Women's scriptural responsibility in the family is irrevocably outlined, but their place in the kingdom of God has been a matter of controversy through the ages.

Battling prejudice born out of cultural and religious influences has left many women frustrated and often angry. Bound by man's tradition and unrealistic standards (and, in some incidents, a few misconstrued scriptures), many women find themselves victims of their own sex.

A casual observation of most of the world's cultures verifies the fact that women are indeed victims. Treated as substandard, they have often been deprived of the basics of human rights and dignity.

When considering these societies, it is interesting to note their pitiful condition. Plagued with insurmountable problems, they are crumbling from within. On the other hand, cultures that recognize the human dignity of women have flourished. Can we, therefore, conclude from this observation that the success of a society rests, at least in part, on how women are regarded?

The subject of women's place in the kingdom of heaven has haunted me. Desirous to serve God, I found myself corralled in unsatisfactory roles. These controlled roles stifled and robbed me of my need to please my Lord.

In my frustration, I began to seek God's perspective on women. If His perspective was in compliance with man's conventional beliefs, I was willing to deny the raging fire in my own soul and submit to such boundaries. If they did not agree, I had no choice but to consider them to be mere man's concepts or limited, prejudicial interpretations and could, therefore, reject them.

I reasoned that the kingdom of God belonged to God alone. Isaiah 55:8-9 declares God's ways are higher than man's ways. I knew in my heart the call and fire in my spirit could not be left in the hands of human reasoning.

Faithful to His Word, God answered my prayers. He revealed priceless information to me over the years. My findings not only upheld the fire in my spirit, but also set me free to pursue a life of service beyond normally acceptable boundaries.

My prayer is that these findings will set others free. God's perspective must replace the ideology man has conveniently hid behind as a cover for insecurity and pride. The liberty of the Spirit must reign where prejudice formerly dictated. Truth must overcome ignorance and Satan's lies. God must truly become Lord in those areas where man has unscripturally exalted his own authority.

No one will deny God has established sound rules for the home. However, the Bible is also clear regarding orderly and godly conduct as a requirement for both sexes. In the kingdom of God, Jesus is LORD! He determines the position each servant is to have in His work. His decision will not be based on sex. Galatians 3:26-28 states,

> For ye are all the children of God by faith in Christ Jesus. For as many of you as have been baptized into Christ have put on Christ. There is neither Jew nor Greek, there is neither bond nor free, there is neither male nor female; for ye are all one in Christ Jesus. (Emphasis added.)

1

INSPIRATION OR TRADITION?

Based on 2 Timothy 3:16, few Christians will question the validity of the Bible. This scripture states, All scripture is given by inspiration of God, and is profitable for doctrine, for reproof, for correction, for instruction in righteousness." Clearly, the Word is meant to bring forth correction in how we think, act, and conduct the affairs of our lives. It is to bring us to a place of right standing before God and upright or honorable conduct towards others. The purpose for this instruction in righteousness is to bring perfection or maturity in our lives that will express itself in good works.[1]

The author of the Word of God is the Holy Spirit. Since the Holy Spirit is behind the inspiration, integrity, and validity of the Word, we must conclude that it is not just a book with various statements that is meant to only reach the intellect. Rather, it is a book that can only be discerned and understood from the basis of spirit. Jesus stated that His words are spirit and life. [2] Therefore, only the Holy Spirit can bring the proper perspective to spiritual matters, producing the life that will speak of righteousness. The Apostle Paul verified this fact in 1 Corinthians 2:13-14,

> Which things also we speak, not in the words which man's wisdom teacheth, but which the Holy Ghost teacheth; comparing spiritual things with spiritual. But the natural man receiveth not the things of the Spirit of God; for they are foolishness unto him: neither can he know them, because they are spiritually discerned.

During my years of ministry, I discovered that Christians have one of three perceptions by which they evaluate scriptural principles. These perceptions are based on Spirit and truth, a literal perception, or religion and tradition.

These perceptions vary in approach, attitude, and action towards the Word of God. For example, the perception that is based on Spirit and truth is a perspective that desires to line up with God's heart (intent) and thoughts toward a matter. The Holy Spirit becomes the teacher who will be allowed to convict of sin and to reprove believers as to what is

---

[1] John 6:63; 2 Timothy 3:17
[2] 2 Peter 1:20-21

righteousness and what will serve as judgment. His ultimate goal is to lead each of us to the truth of Jesus Christ and His teachings.[3]

The Holy Spirit will establish us on the foundation of Jesus Christ. This means He will compare spiritual things with spiritual things as precept is carefully placed upon precept (doctrine), and lines of truth upon lines of truth.[4] As the foundation is established, it will unveil Jesus Christ to us, in us, and through us.

As we allow the Holy Spirit to use the Word in the right manner, the Word becomes a sharp sword that will penetrate the soul and spirit, exposing our motives, dispositions, and attitudes. Such a dividing is able to produce humility, meekness, and submission. It will bring liberty to the soul, allowing us the freedom to discover God and to move forward in service and worship before Him.[5]

Clearly, if the Holy Spirit is missing, the Word of God will never make an impact on our lives. It will be lifeless and maintained on an intellectual level that will keep us indifferent to the heart of God and the reality around us.

This brings us to the other two approaches. The literalist approach to the Bible is to accept the letter of the Scripture. This may seem appropriate, but there is one problem with this approach—it will lack spirit. It will fail to consider matters in light of the spiritual aspect. Therefore, discerning the intent of Scripture in light of the complete Word of God will be absent.

The Word of God speaks of the mystery that is hidden in Scripture. This mystery was unveiled, but there is great depth to the mystery that the carnal finite mind will fail to see unless the Holy Spirit reveals it. To lack the right spirit in approaching the Bible will cause understanding to become dead-letter, or, in other words, it will lack the life to impact the soul and spirit of man.[6]

Any perception based on religion or tradition also has the opposite effect in a person's life. Jesus declared that such an approach actually nullifies the Word of God. A person who operates from this perspective will try to adjust the Word to his or beliefs or practices, rather than allow the Word to line him or her up to the nature of his or her Holy God. Thus, the Word is rendered powerless to change the lives of these types of individuals. This is a dangerous practice. Jesus advocated that religious practices may give the appearance of righteousness, but the inward man lacks life. He described such individuals as white sepulchers that appear beautiful on the outside, but, from within, are full of dead men's bones and uncleanness.[7]

---

[3] John 16:7-15; 1 John 2:27
[4] Isaiah 28:10, 13; 1 Corinthians 3:11
[5] John 4:24; 8:32; 2 Corinthians 3:17; Hebrews 4:12
[6] Romans 7:6; 2 Corinthians 3:2-3, 6; Ephesians 3:3-5; Colossians 2:2-3
[7] Matthew 15:6; 23:27

To adjust the Word of God to personal beliefs is the same as adjusting the narrow path that leads to life, making it more acceptable as one merrily goes on his or her way to hell.[8] Sadly, it is a natural tendency of man's religion to adjust the narrow path established by Jesus, while submitting to a religious lifestyle that displays an outward righteousness, but is devoid of a right heart attitude. Jesus made mention of this heart condition. He said that even though some religious people honored Him with their lips, their hearts were far from Him. Matthew 15:8 identifies the source behind traditions as belonging to man and not inspired by the Holy Spirit. The result of tradition is bondage and death. We read this declaration from Jesus in Matthew 23:13 and15,

> But woe unto you, scribes and Pharisees, hypocrites! for ye shut up the kingdom of heaven against men: for ye neither go in yourselves, neither suffer ye them that are entering to go in...Woe unto you, scribes and Pharisees, hypocrites! for ye compass sea and land to make one proselyte, and when he is made, ye make him twofold more the child of hell than yourself.

These religious people used the Word of God for their own purposes. They made it ineffective with their own interpretations, resulting in death. This is why the Apostle Paul made this reference in 2 Corinthians 3:6, "Who also hath made us able ministers of the new testament; not of the letter, but of the spirit: for the letter killeth, but the spirit giveth life."

Jesus came to set us free, not to enslave us with more rules. His light burden is to love Him, and His easy yoke is to learn of Him.[9] Obviously, it is important that we consider our perception. As Christians, it is our responsibility to handle the Word correctly in all spiritual matters. This would include the subject of women's place in the kingdom of God. We must approach a matter in the right spirit in order to end with truth that ensures the integrity of God's character and the pure intent of His Word. It is such an approach that will allow the Word of God to have its way in our lives.

I have learned that I must hold my opinions lightly and be quick to discard every belief that does not maintain spirit and truth. I am obligated to test all of my beliefs to determine whether they bring me liberty in the spirit, or bondage as a result of man-made rules.

This study about women may challenge your perception. Remember, challenges are positive as long as you do as the Bereans did in Acts 17:11. They were eager to receive the message of truth, but they also examined it to see if it was true or consistent with what they already knew to be true. After all, there are no inconsistencies in God's truth.

Obviously, the real issue is not whether something agrees with a particular way of thinking, but whether it agrees with God. As I have confronted this issue of women's place in God's kingdom, I have

---

[8] Matthew 7:13-14
[9] Matthew 11:28-20

Challenging the Christian Life

discovered that people who stumble over this issue err in one of three ways: 1) they are either erring in how they handle the Word of God due to their approach; 2) they are erring due to ignorance about the cultural, religious, and political influences of that day; and/or 3) they are erring in their knowledge and attitude about the character of God.

My hope is that reader will examine this information in light of the complete Word of God to ensure its spirit and integrity. I pray he or she will allow the Holy Spirit to form his or her conclusions, rather than traditional religious beliefs that are often literal in their interpretation. I hope each person will see my goal in writing this book is to help anyone who might be in bondage concerning this particular issue.

As you read this material, open your heart and mind to the Holy Spirit. Give Him permission to help you explore this controversial subject in a way that will be both pleasing to Him and liberating for you!

2

A WOMAN CALLED "ADAM"

A very important question to ask about women is why did God create Eve? The old standby answer comes from Genesis 2:18, "And the LORD God said, It is not good that the man should be alone; I will make him an help mate for him."

We know that God brought every creature to Adam to name. However, according to Genesis 2:20, there was no real suitable helper to be found in all of creation.

The general consensus is that woman was formed from the side of man to serve as his helper. This belief has given way to attitudes marking women with a stigma of inferiority and servitude. But, is this a correct attitude?

In his viewpoint about the term "helper", Skip Moen pointed out that God did not refer to Eve as woman, wife, or female. It was Adam who first called her "woman" because she was taken out of his side.[1] According to Moen, the word "helper" comes from the Hebrew word "ezer," which points to masculine gender. He also pointed out it is the same word or noun that is used to describe God's relationship to Israel. In other words, God is the helper (protector and provider) of His chosen people.

Moen points out other uses of the word "helper" in the Bible that give the sense of "save from danger," "deliver from death," and "succor". Clearly, this word carries the concept of someone who has superior strength in the matter of being a helper, provider, and protector, rather than one who is inferior.

By using this term, God is clearly establishing the fact that woman was not created from the standpoint of being inferior, but equal. Why should this surprise us? After all, if woman was taken out of man, one could only reason that she is of the same quality and caliber as Adam and is, therefore, equal to him.

What or who reduced women to a substandard or inferior state? Obviously, God did not put woman in such a light. In fact, He initially foreshadowed, in the garden, the reality that it was through woman the Messiah would come to save and deliver those who believe. There can only be one explanation of why women have been displaced into an

---

[1] Genesis 2:22

inferior position and existence. It must be due to the effect of sin working within the human heart and mind.

We must gain God's perspective to see if woman is capable of being the "helper," equal in every way that God intended her to be. To understand it in a proper perspective, it is important that we consider all of scripture concerning the creation of man.

Genesis 5:1b-2 states, "In the day that God created man, in the likeness of God made he him; Male and female created he them; and blessed them, and called their name Adam, in the day when they were created." Keep in mind that woman was in Adam when he was formed from the dust of the earth. God already acknowledged that He had created both of them. When God created man, He made <u>them</u> in His likeness. He called them both "Adam" or "man," which means red, signifying the earth. This shows God made no distinction between man and woman, displaying equality in importance and purpose.

We know woman was fashioned from the side of Adam.[2] One cannot help but note Christ's words on this subject in relationship to the sanctity of marriage in Matthew 19:4-5, "And he answered and said unto them, Have ye not read, that he which made them at the beginning made them male and female. And said, For this cause shall a man leave father and mother, and shall cleave to his wife: and they twain shall be one flesh?" In light of this consideration, we can possibly see how marriage would be symbolic of restoring man back to his original state. But, all of this speculation still brings us back to a woman called "Adam."

Can we assume the conventional belief surrounding the forming of woman was simply based on Adam's need for a helper? Is there more to the story? Keep in mind that "helper" pointed to one who was equal and had the strength to provide what was necessary, as well as protect. But, in what way would woman serve as such a helper? To examine this issue further, we need to consider the fall of man.

The popular approach of the Church has been to focus on the woman. After all, she was the one deceived by the master of deception. She confessed to this truth in Genesis 3:13. Although many have falsely accused Eve of lying about being deceived, the Apostle Paul concurred with her in the New Testament in 2 Corinthians 11:3 and 2 Timothy 2:14.

In 2 Corinthians 11:3, the Apostle Paul stated that the serpent beguiled Eve. "Beguiled" in this text means to seduce wholly.[3] In 1 Timothy 2:14, Paul told us that woman was in transgression because of this deception. Clearly, Eve had no intention of being deceived and giving in to Satan's temptation in the garden.

The normal procedure is to point the finger of mockery at the woman's vulnerability to Satan's lies. This mockery could be justified if Satan's ability to deceive was limited to women alone. But, as we see in

---

[2] Genesis 2:21-22
[3] Strong's Exhaustive Concordance of the Bible, #1818

2 Corinthians 11:3, Paul was concerned about men falling for Satan's lies as well.

Those who point their fingers at the obvious manage to ignore the true cause behind man's fall. Paul told us in 1 Timothy 2:14 that Adam <u>was not deceived</u>, therefore Adam deliberately sinned. Job 31:33 gives us this special insight about Adam's condition, "If I covered my transgressions as Adam, by hiding mine iniquity in my bosom."

Adam had transgression hidden in his heart. In other words, he was already considering transgressing the covenant that God had made with him. Such an attitude is considered treachery. What was the covenant? It was not to eat of the tree of knowledge of good and evil.[4] Clearly, something was amiss in Adam's character. His spiritual condition was revealed even more when he blamed not only woman for his disobedient decision, but God as well! It was, after all, God who gave him a woman. We read Adam's accusation in Genesis 3:12, "And the man said, The woman whom <u>thou</u> gavest to be with me, she gave me of the tree, and I did eat." (Emphasis added.)

For Adam to blame a holy, perfect God for his <u>own</u> sinful action should serve as a powerful clue to Adam's inward spiritual condition. This brings us to the real truth about fallen man ascribed in Romans 5:12, "Wherefore, as by one man sin entered into the world, and death by sin; and so death passed upon all men, for that all have sinned."

Sin and its consequence came through Adam and <u>not</u> Eve! Sin existed in Adam's heart before he even fell in the garden. The proof of this is evidenced in his attitude towards God's provision and command.

We know that, after God had finished creating man on the sixth day, he looked upon his creation and considered that "it was very good" (Genesis 1:31b).

In Genesis 2:18, we see a change from God's first declaration of "it was very good" to "it is not good." What happened between the sixth day of creation and God's declaration in Genesis 2:18? Adam had it all. He was complete as part of God's creation and had fellowship with God. He lived in Paradise.

The first clue there was a problem is seen in Adam's disregard for God's provision. In Genesis 2:16-17, we are given this insight. God commanded Adam to freely eat from any tree in the garden, except the tree of the knowledge of good and evil

We know from Genesis 2:9 that one of the trees Adam could have eaten from was the tree of life. But, according to Genesis 3:22, Adam did not eat of the tree of life. This verse reads, "And the LORD God said, Behold, the man is become as one of us, to know good and evil: and now, lest he put forth his hand, and take also of the tree of life, and eat, and live for ever"

Adam could have chosen life, but instead he chose death. Adam also showed disregard for his responsibility in the garden. In Genesis

---

[4] Genesis 2:16-17; Hosea 6:7

1:26, we see how God gave man rule over His creation. In Genesis 2:15, we read that his responsibility in the garden was to dress and keep it.

The word "dress" implies work that is done from the basis of servitude, while "keep" means to put a hedge about, protect, guard, attend to, preserve, regard, serve, and watch.[5] Since there were no thistles, sweat, or struggle with the ground until after the fall, what did Adam have to oversee? Perhaps his work had to do with protecting his domain from Satan, guarding his relationship with his Creator, attending to the matters of the heart, preserving the perfect environment, regarding the covenant with his God, serving in humility, and watching over the complete welfare of the garden.

Keep in mind that Adam had rule over the garden. He had an obligation to keep it. If he was dedicated to God, devoted to his wife, and responsible towards what had been entrusted to him, why did he allow the presence of Satan to intrude into this perfect paradise?

Some Bible scholars feel the real meaning behind Adam "being alone" in Genesis 2:18 actually implies there was a separation occurring between Adam and his God. Adam was created in the image of God. He lived in a perfect environment. How could this perfect picture change unless Adam began to change?

Based upon these conclusions, some Bible scholars believe God formed woman for the sole purpose of pointing Adam back to Himself. In Professor Katharine C. Bushnell's studies on this subject, she noted that the late Dr. Alexander Whyte, in his book *Bible Characters*, maintained this concept. He wrote, "There must have been something of the nature of a stumble, if not an actual fall, in Adam while yet alone in Eden . . . Eve was created to 'help' Adam to recover himself, and to establish himself in Paradise, and in the favor, fellowship and service of his Maker."

Bushnell also pointed out that other respected Bible scholars of her time (1923) were in agreement with these conclusions, but they were being ignored by the generality of Bible expositors.[6]

The idea that a woman called "Adam" was formed to point man back to God as a means to confront or protect him from giving way to moral deviation that was present in his character is indeed a challenge to traditional views. The general approach to this subject has left woman scorned, and that without mercy or forgiveness. She has been left "holding the bag" for not only man's initial fall, but also his succession of sins. However, the question we must seriously ask ourselves is who has failed who?

Scripture clearly reveals Adam's failure, not only to his Creator and the Creation, but also to woman. One must ask, why was woman deceived in the first place? Deception comes out of ignorance of God. This ignorance could have only existed because the man who walked

---

[5] Strong's Exhaustive Concordance of the Bible; # 5647 & 8104
[6] God's Word To Women; study note 32

with God did not take the responsibility to lead his wife into an intimate understanding or fellowship with her Creator.

On this note I will leave the reader to ponder these inspiring and challenging thoughts by W.L. Heslop,

> Adam was first formed, and then Eve. She was taken out of man and builded for the man as a helper, guide, philosopher, and friend. As the last created, the woman was the best and most honored of all. She was not made directly from the dust of the ground, but builded from a living, warm portion of man's body. Man was created from the cold, soulless dust. The woman was one step farther removed from the earth than the man, and was intended to pull man upward and heavenward. *(Seed Thoughts)*

3

CURSED OR BLESSED?

During the ERA movement in the 1970s, a well-known TV preacher blamed woman's dissension on their husbands. At the time, I felt it quite noble for him to elude that men might have played an invisible role in this movement.

Attitudes from both the secular and Church world have helped fuel the fire of this movement. Although the ERA movement is motivated by a sinister plan to destroy the family and this nation and usher in Communistic, humanistic ideology, it would serve each of us well if we would consider the prevalent attitudes surrounding women. Obviously, the problem does not solely rest on the shoulders of one particular gender, but with the blatant reality that attitudes towards gender are often conditioned according to cultural and religious influences.

Unhappy women, who are unaware of the underlying goal of ERA, have joined their ranks to vent suppressed anger and frustration. Striving to maintain some measure of dignity, respect, consideration, and control over their lives, these ladies have become mere puppets to a movement that will sacrifice them in the end.

The question is how can we change this movement? I have already alluded to the problem. The answer is simple; it begins with changing attitudes. Because of one wrong action in the Garden, women have been plagued for centuries by stories making them accursed. Pagan tales such as Pandora's Box have sent subliminal messages promoting attitudes which make women scapegoats for every ailment of society.

What about the Church? Are attitudes towards women inspired by pagan and unfounded beliefs? Those in the Church who harbor wrong attitudes would answer with a resounding "No!" They would then back their answer with a few scriptures, taken out of context, to justify both their unscriptural attitudes and actions.

Let us now begin to examine our attitudes in light of the Word of God. Many misconceptions have been established by the types of emphasis church leaders have put on the fall of man. When we think of the fall, we automatically focus on Eve being deceived. According to popular belief, because she was deceived, she received a curse from God, which she and those of her gender must forever endure. To guarantee she pays for leading Adam down the wrong path, she, along with all other females, must gracefully bear this curse of being regarded and treated as substandard, foolish, and insignificant. After all, isn't it their deserved lot in life?

Consider that sin and death came through <u>one</u> man. The Apostle Paul mentioned this fact eight times. He identified the culprit to be Adam in two of these scriptures.[1]

We know Eve was truly deceived, but Adam was not. According to Job 31:33, Adam had sin hidden in his heart. We know from the Genesis account that, instead of owing up to his actions, he blamed both Eve and God. Was it Adam or Eve who rebelled against God?

Let's just assume for a moment that women <u>are</u> cursed. Does this idea that all women must pay in some way really line up to the complete counsel of God? Ezekiel 18:19-20 gives us this insight,

> Yet say ye, Why? Doth not the son bear the iniquity of the father? When the son hath done that which is lawful and right, and hath kept all my statutes, and hath done them, he shall surely live. The soul that sinneth, it shall die. The son shall not bear the iniquity of the father, neither shall the father bear the iniquity of the son; the righteousness of the righteous shall be upon him, and the wickedness of the wicked shall be upon him.

Has God changed? Are women to be held accountable for Eve's response in the garden or for their own actions? Galatians 3:13 gives this decisive blow to the concept that women are under a curse, "Christ hath redeemed us from the curse of the law, being made a curse for us; for it is written, Cursed is everyone that hangeth on a tree."

Christ brings liberty from the curse, not bondage. Those who believe upon Him are no longer under a curse. We must ask why are there those in the Church who insist on putting women under some curse in the name of Christ? What are they really hiding?

It is amazing to me that Christian men and women would stand behind this idea. Basically, what this perception says is that woman's lot as a wife is a matter of a curse and not a privilege. If this is true, why marry? One must also ask, where does the dignity of the husband rest when their wife's submission is solely motivated and maintained by a curse, and not because of love and commitment? Where is the sweet victory?

According to Katharine C. Bushnell, the Babylonian Talmud inspired some of the church's belief and attitude.[2] These writings are not a translation of scripture, but a collection of Jewish traditions. They came from what was known as the Oral Law of the Jews. This law was not written down until 100 AD.[3] However, it stood as law for how women were to conduct themselves. The Talmud actually pronounced ten curses on women. These ten curses have demoted women from the

---

[1] See Romans 5:14-19; 1 Corinthians 15:22; 1 Timothy 2:14
[2] God's Word To Women, study notes 102-106 & 132
[3] Difficult Sayings (article)

status of a human being to a depraved object that has no rights because of Eve's action.

I realize some Christians are armed with their "pat" scriptures to justify their beliefs. One such scripture is found in Genesis 3:16. Some uphold that God pronounced a curse on Eve, but did He? Let us examine this incident.

Eve was deceived. She did not evade this truth. She simply confessed it to God.[4] In Genesis 3:14, we see God putting the blame on the serpent for deceiving her and pronouncing a curse on the creature, "And the LORD God said unto the serpent, Because thou hast done this, thou art cursed above all cattle, and above every beast of the field; upon thy belly shalt thou go, and dust shalt thou eat all the days of my life."

In Genesis 3:17-19, we see God declaring the consequences Adam must face because of his rebellion. However, in close proximity of these two declarations (verses 17 and 19), we see Him saying this to the serpent about Eve in Genesis 3:15, "And I will put enmity between thee and the woman, and between thy seed and her seed; he shall bruise thy head, and thou shalt bruise his heel."

In Romans 16:20, we see Paul identifying Satan as the one who will be crushed, "And the God of peace shall bruise Satan under your feet shortly. The grace of our Lord Jesus Christ be with you. Amen."

We see God bringing a separation between Eve and Satan. Remember, it was Satan who used the serpent to deceive. We must note that we do not see this enmity being put between Adam and Satan.

Hebrews 2:14 tells us that Jesus Christ was the promise mentioned in Genesis 3:15 that would bring victory, "Forasmuch, then, as the children are partakers of flesh and blood, he also himself likewise took part of the same, that through death he might destroy him that had the power of death, that is, the devil."

We know that the offspring mentioned in Genesis 3:15 are those who are born of the spirit. In John 1:12-13, we read this promise, "But as many as received him, to them gave he power to become the sons of God, even to them that believe on his name; Who were born, not of blood, nor of the will of the flesh, nor of the will of man, but of God."

Consider how this spiritual birth has nothing to do with the plan or decision of man, nor will it be the result of a husband's attempt. This birth will come out of the will of God and it will be executed through a woman.

In fact, the promise of the coming Messiah was very real among the young maidens of the Orthodox Jewish Belief. It was the longing of all believing Jewish handmaidens to be the mother of the Messiah.

In Genesis 3:15, we see God bestowing the greatest promise on Eve. The question we must consider is why would God pronounce a blessing on Eve and then turn around and curse her? In Bushnell's book *God's Word to Women*, she explained how the curse was a product of Satan and not a consequence determined by God. Satan hated the

---

[4] Genesis 3:13

woman. Remember that God had put enmity between her and him. God gave a promise of redemption that would come through woman. By revealing the original meaning of the Hebrew translation of this scripture, Bushnell uncovered a mistranslation that has served to carry out the very hatred Satan has towards the vessel God would one day use to bring about His plan of redemption.

This hatred would put woman under bondage. It would encourage hatred in the one closest to her who would have the responsibility to love her as his own body.

Let us look at this deviation in translation that Bushnell exposed with her expertise of the Hebrew language. For history's sake, she posed that the original translation was lost with an earlier Greek version that came into being around 175 A.D. Instead of the following translation, "Unto the woman he said, I will greatly multiply thy sorrow and thy conception; in sorrow thou shalt bring forth children", Bushnell cited this to be the correct translation taken from the Septuagint, "Unto the woman He said, "A snare has increased your sorrow and your sighing . . ."[5]

The snare is Satan who waits to bring sorrow upon women of all ages. This sorrow becomes evident as women in every generation watch their children suffer, not only due to the travail of birth, but to the hardness of those who travel the way of transgression, as well as Satan's destruction of their spiritual well-being. We can even see a prophetical culmination of this truth in the life of Mary, the mother of Jesus.

Mary had considered herself blessed to be entrusted with the Messiah, but then came the sorrow as she stood at the foot of His cross.[6] The prophet Simeon described her future sorrow with these words in Luke 2:35, "Yea, a sword shall pierce through thy soul also, that the thoughts of many hearts may be revealed."

Think about how broken Mary's heart must have been. She witnessed the incredible price of Adam's disobedience, as well as the reality of Satan's hatred and goal to destroy souls for eternity.

There has been confusion over the second part of Genesis 3:16 concerning a woman's rights and place in the Church. It has served as a frame of reference for the interpretation of other scriptures pertaining to women. For this reason, Bushnell referred back to various versions in her book, including the Septuagint, to establish the correct translation. Instead of this translation, "...and thy desire shall be to thy husband, and he shall rule over thee," the correct translation should be rendered: "You are turning away (from Me) to your husband, and he will rule over you."[7]

An Italian Dominican monk by the name of Pagnino replaced the word "turning" with the word "desire." In this context, the word "desire"

---

[5] God's Word To Women; study notes 117-120
[6] John 19:25
[7] God's Word To Women; study notes 124-126, 130-137

means lust.⁸ According to Pagnino's take on this text, the woman's lust would totally hinge on her husband. Lust is totally associated with the works of the flesh.⁹ According to James 1:14-15, such lust ends in death.

When we consider this concept, we see it is not realistic. A woman would have to be a robot to adhere to this perception, for she would have to lose her personality and individuality and cease to feel or think. She would end up serving the whims of her husband's appetites and demands, regardless of the spiritual implications of a matter. This would make her a slave to something that could easily prove to be sinister and ungodly. In fact, her husband would serve as her god or lord, which is scripturally unacceptable. As the Bible has pointed out, people can only serve one master at a time, and there is only one God and one Lord. Obviously, man in his fallen state of sin is unable to fill such a billing, even in the capacity of a husband.¹⁰

The Apostle Peter settled the issue of who women must obey in Acts 5:29b, "We ought to obey God rather than men."

In 1 Corinthians 6:20, the Apostle Paul stated we were bought with a price; therefore, we should glorify God in our bodies and spirits. He goes on to say in 1 Corinthians 7:23 that, since we are bought with a price, we must not be servants of men. Clearly, as believers we are not here to serve mere man, but the living God who redeemed us with the blood of His Son.

By honestly studying the Word of God, we can safely conclude that the translation that stands consistent in light of other scriptures is the word "turning." In Genesis 3:16, God was actually telling Eve that, since she was turning away from Him to be with Adam, she would come under the rule of her husband. Sadly, the rule of men is often according to their selfish, arrogant dispositions. Rather than serving as the example of Christ's meek leadership, they come across as tyrannical dictators that simply see their wives as substandard and a possession.

Many have made Adam look noble by stating that it was Adam's love for Eve that inspired his treachery against God's covenant. It is time to set the record straight as to who gave up what. If Adam loved Eve, why didn't he lead her away from the serpent and his temptation? After all, Genesis 3:6 states he was <u>with</u> her during the temptation. If he loved Eve, why didn't he lead her <u>away</u> from the tree of knowledge <u>to</u> the tree of life? True love desires to protect.

God expelled <u>the man</u> Adam from the garden, lest he would eat of the tree of life.¹¹ Granted, the term "man" could apply to both Adam and Eve. However, it is interesting to note that the LORD God sent him forth from the garden. If Bushnell is correct about the translation of Genesis

---

⁸ Ibid, study notes 141-144
⁹ Galatians 5:16-21
¹⁰ Isaiah 43:10-11; Matthew 6:24; Ephesians 4:4-6; 1 Corinthians 8:5-6
¹¹ Genesis 3:22-24

3:16b, the woman had a choice to remain under God's rule or follow Adam. Inevitably, God already knew she would choose to follow Adam. If this is true, there is nowhere in scripture where we can find that God actually expelled Eve. She simply followed Adam. She left the garden and the protective rule of her Creator. If this is so, because of Eve's choice to follow Adam, many women have tasted the cruelty of man's rule through the ages.

Is woman cursed or blessed? Let me answer the question according to my perception of the information that we have been considering. Because Eve was blessed by God, she became cursed by Satan. This curse has made her a target and a victim by those who have never allowed themselves to be separated from the darkness of their own hearts and from the god of this world.

Women, the only way you can cease to be a victim is to reverse Eve's decision. Come back and submit yourself under the protective hand of your loving Creator. He has a garden prepared for each of you. This garden overflows with love, joy, peace, mercy, grace, purity, and liberty. Above all else, know that your eternal bridegroom, Jesus Christ, is waiting for you with open arms.

4

THE STRUGGLE INTENSIFIES

One of my struggles with the issue of women in God's kingdom has been how it has been presented in the Word of God. For all of my Christian life, I have believed that all Scriptures have been inspired just as the Word declares.[1] Clearly, any literalist would conclude from the few Scriptures that make reference to women that they are to be strictly seen and not heard.

To conclude that a few Scriptures might be improperly handled would appear to put serious doubt on the rest of the Word of God. As a woman, I struggled with this very issue. If a person took liberty with Genesis 3:16, then how many other men have taken liberty with the rest of the Word of God?

My struggle to uphold the integrity of the Word of God was intense enough that I was almost willing to let the issue of women slide. On the other hand, was I willing to sacrifice my life in God to keep a façade of calmness? Is the Word of God so weak that it cannot be challenged?

As I studied the character of God, I realize that the truth will stand any challenge. However, truth had to be defined. Such definition would come down to the God of the Bible. All truth would line up to His character. It would be consistent to His Spirit and ways. As I studied deliverance, I realized God's truth does not put people in bondage; rather, it brings liberty to them.[2]

Since truth will stand in the midst of all challenges, all discrepancies or places of confusion in God's Word must be honestly challenged. As I considered the complete Word of God, I had no doubt all Scriptures have been inspired, but that does not mean man has not occasionally taken liberty with them. Bu, such inconsistencies will be discovered when compared with the complete Word of God.

Another matter that I am sure of is that the intent of the Word has always been maintained. If you consider the sure Word of God, it comes down to prophecy.[3] In other words, we can be sure of the validity of the Word of God because of prophecy, not because of technicality. Even in the Gospels, there are what some consider discrepancies when, in fact, they represent different eye-witness presentations of something. For

---

[1] 2 Timothy 3:16
[2] John 8:32-36; 14:6; 2 Corinthians 13:8
[3] 2 Peter 1:20-21

example, not every witness sees or hears the same thing. However, when you study the different incidents in the Gospels, you will clearly see the consistency of the spirit or intent behind each incident.

This brings me to the matter of spirit. In spite of the few discrepancies, I have encountered in my studies of God's Word, if a person approaches a matter in the right spirit, the so-called "discrepancies" will not change a person's perception, attitude, or conduct. In other words, if a man is righteous, the few Scriptures that appear to disparage women will not change the righteous ways of how he already looks, regards, or treats women. Questionable Scriptures will only advance those who are hiding behind indoctrination, prejudices, personal agendas, and ignorance.

Hence, enter the discrepancies. It is important to consider in what ways the various translators throughout the years might possibly take liberty with Scripture. Could they honestly take liberty with God's character, Law, history, or dealings with man? The answer is not really. God's character is clearly seen throughout His Word, His Law is indelibly established, His dealings with man are a matter of record, and history has its own checks and balances. For example, you could not change King David's sins of adultery and murder without throwing out Psalm 51. The history of the kings was also a matter of record.

However, the places in which man could take liberty with the Word would be at points of semantics, instructions, cultural influences, and customs. For example, the word "man" in Scripture does not necessary mean just men, but can be an indefinite pronoun that can embrace the concept of someone, anyone, or a certain one. For example, in Matthew 16:24 where Jesus stated if any man will come after me, "man" in this text means anyone.[4]

Obviously, the call to preach the Gospel and make disciples is not just extended to men, but to women as well. This means women must preach and teach. Therefore, the term "men" in such Scripture as 2 Timothy 2:2 where it talks about faithful men who are competent to teach others can be a generic term for mankind or a human being.[5]

Another term that can include women is the "position of a bishop." This term is actually the feminine word "episcope". The position of bishop was the same as the elder. In Titus 2:3-4, elder women were instructed to teach and admonish the younger women. Obviously, this required the elder women to take authority over others, but, apparently, it was not just restricted to instructing women about their conduct in the matters of life. The qualities established for both elder women and men in 1 Timothy 3:2-3 and Titus 1:8-9 sound like the same qualities that were established for those in the office of elders.[6]

---

[4] Difficult Sayings (article)
[5] Ibid
[6] Ibid

Phoebe was a deacon. Although the word "deacon" was translated as minister and servant when referring to her, she was a powerful influence in the early Church.[7] According to historical information, she was widely traveled and had a legal mind. She argued cases for the churches in the courts of her land. She was an evangelist and superintendent of at least two churches.[8] Clearly, the Apostle Paul recognized her leadership because he told those at the Roman Church in Romans 16:1 to give her any help she may need from them.

Obviously, by changing the meaning or representation of a word, one can change the impact it might have in a matter. I remember watching a movie about the history of Texas. There was one woman who proved to be instrumental in some of the major events surrounding the state's fight for independence from Mexico. When the history book came out, the woman's part was conspicuously missing. Upon commenting on the obvious absence of her name and deeds, it was pointed out that men wrote the history. Remember, it was men who translated the Word of God. How much these men might have let personal bias affect them is a matter of speculation, but the results can be somewhat clearly seen in the confusion, misunderstandings, and divisions that a few Scriptures have created in this area.

We are about to consider the few Scriptures that have been used to put women in their so-called "place" in the kingdom of God. As we consider these Scriptures in light of the whole Word of God, we must consider if any liberty was possibly taken in regard to these Scriptures. As you are about to see, these Scriptures will be considered from various points. As these different points are brought out, we each must conclude that these Scriptures must not be taken at face value. Rather, they must be discerned in light of Spirit and truth.

Obviously, these few Scriptures could put women in bondage, but the rest of the Written Word does not condone such bondage. These Scriptures could justify prejudice towards women, but the whole counsel of the Word of God never makes such sins of the heart or attitudes justifiable. Such Scriptures could encourage ignorance towards the ways of God, but the knowledge of the character and attitude of Jesus would reveal such ignorance as darkness.

We must allow the truth of God's character and ways test these few Scriptures. It is from this basis that we can be assured of properly being impacted by His character and attitude towards a matter, and not by our own conclusions. Remember that we will not only be judged for what we believe, but for what is truly in our hearts.

We can also put religious cloaks over the prejudice and hardness of our hearts, but they will not hide our real attitude about a matter. This was brought out in an encounter I had with a man over this very subject.

---

[7] Romans 16:1
[8] Women in Today's Church, page 16

I had thought this man to be godly. He appeared to stand for truth. Although I had a couple of "red flags" go up when I met him, I just accredited his indifferent attitude to his frustration. He seemed hard, skeptical, and unreceptive towards the moving of the Spirit. Later, I realized my "red flags" were clearly warning me that his man had some unresolved issues in his life.

These unresolved issues made him hard about matters that challenged his personal perception. Ultimately, in his mind, he became the final authority on Scriptural issues, proving that he was unteachable and cruel when challenged to reconsider his attitude and presentation.

This man's real attitude was brought out over the issue of women in ministry. If a woman's writing and teachings were referenced by heretics, he basically blamed these men's heretical views on the woman's influence. In other words, if a woman was spiritually involved in any man's spiritual development, she was to blame for any of his spiritual deviation from the truth. It was as if man cannot be really held responsible for his moral or scriptural deviation as long as a woman could be found to blame.

If you questioned this man about my perception of him, he might deny my conclusion, but his attitude and handling of our disagreement spoke volumes about his inward disposition and spirit. Later, he even wrote his opinions about this matter. In his writing, he clearly was taking liberty in using Scripture to justify his ungodly attitude. His lovely wife even backed him up in another article. Needless to say, regardless of her sincerity about this matter, would she dare to even disagree with him?

Perhaps this man is loving and respectable to his wife. However, such respect may hinge on her totally agreeing with him. Obviously, the man's reaction reveals that he has unresolved issues of the heart. Whether his attitude towards women is a matter of prejudice, cultural conditioning, traumatic experiences, or wrong teaching, the man has taken liberty with Scripture to justify his miserable attitude in his own eyes.

For us, it was not just a matter of agreeing to disagree; it was a matter of having no basis of agreement at the point of spirit. We know a person by his or her fruit. Obviously, if the right spirit is in place, the fruit and agreement will be there, in spite of the disagreement. Ultimately, the attitude of Jesus and not man's opinions will be exalted, bringing agreement and peace.

The question is, are we willing to truthfully consider these few Scriptures from different angles in light of the complete counsel of God's Word? The purpose for such examination is to reveal wrong thinking, attitudes, and conduct. Will truth be opposed by hiding behind wrong spirits and wickedness? It is our choice whether we choose to love truth or give way to our own selfish preferences and conclusions.

5

THE TRUTH ABOUT MARRIAGE

Since we have discussed attitudes and whether woman was cursed or blessed in the garden, we can begin to consider the implications of women in marriage. As Christians we must ensure that we have the mind of Christ concerning this subject.

Through many years of attending different churches, I have often found the emphasis concerning marriage centers around the woman's responsibility to submit. The motivation of this focus can often be traced back to Genesis 3:16.

This lopsided presentation has given the husband an unfair and, at times, abusive leverage. To know whether teachings and attitudes about marriage need to be re-examined, simply observe the condition of marriages within the Church.

Sadly, statistics reveal the world is reflected within the Church where divorce and remarriage are concerned. Domestic violence and abuse are not unheard of among churchgoers. The marriage bed has become defiled by sexual practices encouraged by perversion.[1] This perversion has invaded the minds of those who refuse to separate themselves from the world's entanglements. The result is the destruction of this sacred institution.

God established the first principle governing marriage before the fall of man in the garden. Jesus reiterated this principle in Matthew 19:4-5, "...Have ye not read that he who made them at the beginning, made them male and female; And said, For this cause shall a man leave father and mother, and shall cleave to his wife, and they twain shall be one flesh?"

Let us examine what this verse actually says. First of all, it is the man who is to leave his family and be united to his wife. It amazes me that many can quote this scripture in reference to marriage and still believe it is the woman who must initially give up all to please her husband. Granted, Psalm 45:10, tells the woman to forget her people. Obviously, to be made one with her husband, the woman must cleave to him as well. But, clearly it is up to parents to ensure that the husband will regard their daughter in a proper way before they release her to his care.

---

[1] Hebrews 13:4

Rayola Kelley

Archaeologists have actually found evidence that reveals early civilizations practiced the principle of marriage God laid down in the garden. The matriarchs, as well as the patriarchs, influenced these early people. It was the woman who held the household property; therefore, kinship came through her.[2]

Professor Flinders Petrie, an archaeologist, made this statement, "The early ideal in the East was separate worlds of men and women while women retained their own rights and property."

These findings would indeed throw doubt on accepted attitudes and beliefs governing women in marriage today. All too often, it has been assumed that women must give up everything for the man's pleasures. But we must keep in mind that it was Eve who moved herself out from under the protection of her Creator to come under the rule of her husband. The result of her action has allowed Satan to use husbands who lack love as a tool to demean the dignity and importance of women, not only in marriage, but also in the kingdom of God.

We can see why God set down this principle. It keeps the woman under the protection of her parents, protected from abusive and harsh husbands. This rule governed the customs of great people of the Bible such as Jacob and Samson. In Genesis 31, for example, we see Jacob going to his wives and explaining his need to separate himself from their father. In Genesis 31:14-16, we find the women making the final decision about taking their children and following him,

> And Rachel and Leah answered and said unto him, Is there yet any <u>portion</u> or <u>inheritance</u> <u>for</u> <u>us</u> <u>in</u> <u>our</u> <u>father's</u> <u>house</u>? Are we not counted of him as strangers? For he hath sold us, and hath quite devoured also <u>our</u> <u>money</u>. For all the riches which God hath taken from our father, <u>that is</u> <u>ours</u>, and <u>our</u> <u>children's</u>; now then, whatsoever God hath said unto thee, do. (Emphasis added.)

In Samson's situation, we discover that he left his wife in her father's care in Judges 14:19-15:1. We observe in the account of Rebekah that her family had to give permission for her to be taken to Isaac. In Genesis 24:58, we see her family giving her a choice of whether or not she wanted to go.

In the case of the Shunammite woman in 2 Kings 4:8-36 and 8:1-6, we are able to make some interesting observations. In 2 Kings 8:1, we read how the prophet Elisha went to the woman (and not her husband) with the following instruction, "Then spoke Elisha unto the woman, whose son he had restored to life, saying, Arise, and go thou and thine household, and sojourn wheresoever thou canst sojourn; for the LORD hath called for a famine, and it shall also come upon the land seven years."

Nowhere in Scripture is it stated this woman was a widow at this time. In fact, the verse states <u>family,</u> which implies the contrary. 2 Kings

---

[2] God's Word to Women; study notes 53, 58-62

8:2 tells us the woman obeyed and ended up in the land of the Philistines for seven years.

Although the command came from a prophet, a woman executed it. Upon her arrival back in her country, we find her going to the king to request the return of <u>her house and land</u> in 2 Kings 8:5. Due to her identification to the prophet, Elisha, in 2 Kings 8:6, we read the king's response to her, "And when the king asked the woman, she told him. So the king appointed unto her a certain officer, saying, Restore all that was hers, and all the fruits of the field since the day that she left the land, even until now."

This brings us to the subject of marriage in the New Testament. To gain a correct perspective of marriage, one must understand what this sacred institution represents. Marriage is to serve as a representation of the relationship of Christ with His Church. The Apostle Paul confirmed this in Ephesians 5:32, "This is a great mystery, but I speak concerning Christ and the church."

Godly husbands and wives are to become one in spirit, identity, and purpose, just as believers must become one with Christ. To become one means agreement. This implies restoration. Man, once again, becomes complete when united with his particular Eve. Not only is he made whole because he is one with woman who was taken from his side, but, since he is born again, he also now has fellowship with his Creator.

Christians must come to terms with the relationship the Church is to have with Christ. We must examine marriage in light of the example Jesus left for us. Our Christian life and this relationship must function within two godly boundaries—submission and love.

In Ephesians 5:22, a wife is instructed to submit to her husband. According to Roy B. Blizzard, Jr.'s article, submission in this text should be translated as "adapt." "Adapt" has different meanings, but one meaning is to reconcile or bring into one unit.[3] What is the real intent behind godly submission? Submission implies giving way to something that is worthy for the benefit of the whole. No matter how you look at it, submission does not mean coming into subordination under man. After all, there is a difference between submission and subordination.

Pastor W.L. Myers, in his excellent little book entitled *Does God Call Women to Preach?*, made this statement, "God did not give man a slave but a help-mate." Women, therefore, must not allow themselves to become subordinate to their husbands.

Women are to submit or adapt to their husbands, <u>as unto the Lord</u>. They must take the example of true submission from Jesus Christ. Jesus was a submissive servant who served as a perpetual sacrifice before God. He had one goal—to be obedient to the Father. Philippians 2:7-8 confirms this, "But made himself of no reputation, and took upon him the form of a servant, and was made in the likeness of men; And, being

---

[3] Webster's New Collegiate Dictionary

found in fashion as a man, he humbled himself and became obedient unto death, even the death of the cross."

Jesus clearly adapted Himself to carry out the will of the Father. To bring forth a ministry of reconciliation, He had to take on the disposition of a servant and allow Himself to be fashioned as a man.[4] In light of Jesus' example, wives are being called to a place of servitude, and, like their Lord, they must do all things for the glory of God. They are to live a life of obedience and commitment, not to their husbands, but to their Creator. In a sense, they must become perpetual living sacrifices for the benefit of their families.

A woman must first please God. Godly submission to her husband will be a natural extension of her service to her Lord and Savior. However, if a husband's request proves to be contrary to her Lord, she must submit to the righteousness of her Lord and not the wicked demands of her husband. Scriptural examples concur with this truth. For example, Abigail's disobedience to her husband prevented King David from committing sin and resulted in saving her entire household. On the other hand, because of her compliance with her husband deceitful ways, Sapphira lost her life.[5]

The Apostle Paul reminded each believer that he or she must be led by the Spirit of God.[6] This applies to women. The Spirit must instruct us, as godly women, in our ways, ensure an upright attitude, and guide us in our examples. As a result, the Apostle Paul made this statement regarding all Christians in Ephesians 5:21, "Submitting yourselves one to another in the fear of God."

Christian living and responses are applicable to all Christians. Submission to his wife must be implemented in the husband's response, just as a wife must love her husband.[7] Love should be the motivation for all responses, and submission is not only a form of honoring someone, but serves as the outward response of godly love. Therefore, love and submission walk hand in hand.

The responsibility of the husband is awesome. He must have the same commitment of love towards his wife as Christ does towards the Church. Christ was first in showing His commitment and devotion to the Church. He gave up His identity to become identified with His Church. Paul brought His commitment to the forefront with this instruction to the husbands in Ephesians 5:25, "Husbands, love your wives, even as Christ also loved the church, and gave himself for it."

A wife's position of servitude stipulates a life that serves as a perpetual living sacrifice on behalf of her family for the glory of God. As for the husband's responsibility, we see an example that goes a step farther. The husband must become the actual sacrifice for the benefit of

---

[4] 2 Corinthians 5:18-19
[5] 1 Samuel 25; Acts 5:1-11
[6] Romans 8:14
[7] Titus 2:4

the family. To be a sacrifice means one gives up his or her rights and life. Sadly, the focus is usually on the husband's position as the "head" of the family, rather than the sacrificial life he is called to live before his family.

According to *Vine's Expository Dictionary of Biblical Words*, "headship" is not just a position of authority. The other meaning that upholds the intent of this position is leadership that is defined and maintained by example. 1 John 4:19 concurs with leadership by example, "We love him, because he first loved us."

Christ's example to His followers persuaded them to follow Him. He was/is not a harsh, demanding dictator. Although He deserves our undivided attention and adoration, He desires us to follow Him because we love Him.

He has left this same example for the husband to follow. A husband's headship is not defined by position, but by the example of love. Adam failed to lead Eve away from temptation and deception. He, in a sense, sacrificed her when it came time to own up to his own actions.

By examining the husband's scriptural responsibility, husbands have been given a second chance to do right by their wives. They must become a sacrifice in order to lead their wives by example in the ways of righteousness.

The Apostle Paul gave this instruction in Ephesians 5:28, "So ought men to love their wives as their own bodies. He that loveth his wife loveth himself."

Men, it is easy to advocate your position in the family, but there is a price. The price is your pride, ego, and worldly leadership. The truest form of spiritual leadership is servitude.[8] Servitude or submission is a product of the love of God working in our hearts. Submission implies sensitivity to the needs of others. Real submission will fulfill Paul's instruction found in Ephesians 5:21.

Marriage is also representative of both Christ's first and second comings. Bushnell pointed out this truth as follows,

> And then they (Adam and Eve) were separated during a "deep sleep," which came upon Adam. So Christ was with us, and then separated from us by the "deep sleep" of death, while we came, as it were, from His riven side, by faith in His shed blood. Adam was separated, that he might be reunited to Eve, in greater joy than ever, --And one day Christ will come again "to our joy,"—for it was "expedient" for Him to go, and return again, He told us.[9]

The Jewish marriage ceremony also points to the second coming of Christ. The procedure begins with a Shadchan or marriage broker who is hired by parents to find a mate for their son or daughter. Ruth Specter

---

[8] Matthew 20:25-28
[9] God's Word to Women; study notes 50-51

Lascelle relates this procedure to the Father sending the Holy Spirit to draw the spiritual bride to His Son, Jesus Christ.[10]

Bible teacher and author, Zola Levitt, added more insight about the wedding preparation. In his presentation, he shared how the groom had to prepare the honeymoon cottage before the wedding feast could actually take place. Jesus assured his disciples of a similar preparation for the Church in John 14:2-3.

This building project took the better part of a year. Upon completion of the building, the groom's father would make the final determination as to when it was finished. We see this similarity in Christ coming for His Church in Matthew 24:36, "But of that day and hour knoweth no man, no, not the angels of heaven, but my Father only." All the Church can do is wait and be ready for the unexpected arrival of her bridegroom. Jesus confirmed this in Matthew 25:10-13. Only those with the oil of the Holy Spirit will be prepared for the coming of the bridegroom.

Do our attitudes and responses uphold the sanctity of marriage? Are they motivated by the love of God or by prejudice and hatred that hide behind self-righteousness and a few misconstrued scriptures? Christians must examine their position concerning marriage. After all, it is symbolic of the type of relationship the Creator desires with man now, and will have in the future.

---

[10] John 16:13-15

6

UNVEILING THE TRUTH

The Apostle Paul made this statement in 2 Corinthians 13:8, "For we can do nothing against the truth, but for the truth."

Jesus is the summary of all truth.[1] In the end, truth will either justify or judge man. Therefore, each of us must ask ourselves whether rejection of truth at any level of our Christian life ultimately means we will miss our Savior. Rev. Payne-Smith made this statement, "Give men what proof you will, but seldom do they find more than what it suits them to find. If what is said agrees with their preconceived notions, well; if not, they reject it."

I have had no illusions while writing this book about those who have already made convenient and selfish determinations concerning the subject of women in the Church. I realize the saying, "A man persuaded against his will, is of the same opinion still," remains true today. My goal is to simply educate those who are struggling with this issue and who desire God's perspective. Admittedly, women are not the only ones desiring illumination on this matter, any more than men are the only culprits in stifling women from being what God wants them to be in His kingdom.

Three most quoted scriptures that put women in their so-called "proper place" in the Church promote bondage, while denying human dignity. These verses have been used to hammer women into a box which some refuse to be reconciled to. The result is these women are accused of being rebellious or of having a "Jezebel Spirit" if they fail to come into compliance with the box that has been established for them. In the next three chapters, we will be examining these scriptures, but first we must examine the attitude of the one who wrote the instructions.

The writer of the verses in question was the Apostle Paul. In Galatians 3:26-29, we have already made reference to the Apostle Paul's attitude towards the issue of women in the kingdom of God, "For ye are all the children of God by faith in Christ Jesus. For as many of you as have been baptized into Christ have put on Christ. There is neither Jew nor Greek, there is neither bond nor free, there is neither male nor female; for ye are all one in Christ Jesus."

If we belong to Christ, we are heirs of God's promise, thereby establishing equality among all believers. In Galatians 5:1, we see that

---

[1] John 14:6

the culmination of Paul's desire for all believers is that they maintain their freedom in Christ. The harsh reality is that there are so many people who want to bring us into bondage one way or the other.

Obviously, the Apostle Paul was fighting for the liberty of all believers. He made no distinction in the case of women. In fact, we see him commending women for laboring in the Gospel.[2] In 1 Corinthians 9:5, we see him defending himself for having a woman as part of his traveling ministry team. But, in 1 Corinthians 11:1-16, 14:34-35, and 1 Timothy 2:9-15, we see instructions which appear contrary to the liberty Paul had so adamantly stood for in his letter to the Galatians. Did Paul have a change of heart, or are there explanations that will not only maintain his attitudes, but will ensure continuity with the rest of the Word of God?

There are explanations. They involve understanding cultural and historical events surrounding the people these letters were addressed to. Now, keep in mind that Paul was addressing real people and real problems. For instance, if he were to write a letter to the church in America today, what issues would he address, and would they be applicable to people who might live a hundred years from now? If such a letter was written and Christ tarried, would it bring understanding or confusion to future generations if they did not first consider the problems and times to which it was addressed to ensure the intent and principle of a spiritual matter?

This is why confusion exists over the instructions in question. In order for people to have the correct perspective, they must first understand the issues and problems confronting these different bodies of believers.

In the case of the Corinthian Church, their greatest influence and distraction came from those trying to bring in Judaism. If the Judaizers were successful, it would mean bondage for the believers. The Apostle Paul was, therefore, contending with Jewish traditions, something he was quite familiar with because of having been a Pharisee. In fact, we see him clearly referring to two distinct laws in his first letter to the Corinthians. In 1 Corinthians 9:9 he referred to the Law of Moses (the Torah), while in 1 Corinthians 14:34 he was clearly referring to another law.

The other law he referred to was known as the Oral Law of the Jews. The Oral Law was a re-interpretation of the Mosaic Law. These re-interpretations became traditions that were adhered to, even though they were simply re-interpretations of a Law that clearly stood on its own merits. This particular law was directed at issues that affected the Jewish people's daily life. As previously stated, the Oral Law of the Jews was passed down orally until it was written down in 100 A.D. The writing

---

[2] Romans 16:1-3, 12-13

Challenging the Christian Life

became known as the Mishnah, the Palestinian, or the Babylonian Talmuds.[3]

Jesus referred to the affect that Jewish tradition had on those who followed them in Matthew 23:4, 5a and 13,

> For they bind heavy burdens and grievous to be borne, and lay them on men's shoulders, but they themselves will not move them with one of their fingers. But all their works they do to be seen of men...But woe unto you, scribes and Pharisees, hypocrites! For ye shut up the kingdom of heaven against men; for ye neither go in yourselves, neither suffer them that are entering to go in.

If improperly interpreted or applied, these Jewish traditions had the means to show extreme prejudice against women and treat them as cursed. Lascelle confirmed this prejudice when sharing about her orthodox Jewish upbringing. Her grandfather would say a prayer that all orthodox Jewish men repeat. It goes like this:

> Blessed art Thou, O Lord our God, King of the Universe Who hath not created me a <u>slave</u>.
> Blessed are Thou, O Lord our God, King of the Universe Who hath not created me a <u>Gentile</u>.
> Blessed are Thou, O Lord our God, King of the Universe Who hath not created me a <u>woman</u>.[4]

This attitude was never upheld or condoned by the Written Law. In fact, we see Jesus condemning Jewish traditions, but He both quoted and fulfilled the Written Law. We must not forget about the Apostle Paul. He was a Pharisee, and, in Galatians 3:28, he reversed this whole concept. He stated that, in Christ, there is neither *bond* nor free, Jew nor *Gentile*, male nor *female*. [5]

In 1 Corinthians 11:1-16, Paul was dealing with the Jewish custom of veiling. The men wore what they called a tallith or prayer shawl. This shawl was both a sign of reverence before God and of condemnation of sin. In 1 Corinthians 11:4, Paul condemned this practice. He stated, "Every man praying or prophesying, having his head covered, dishonoreth his head." Who is the head of man? The Apostle Paul answered that question in the previous Scripture, Jesus Christ.

You must compare Scripture with Scripture to understand the real implication behind Paul's instruction. We know there is no condemnation for those who are in Christ Jesus and are walking after the Spirit; therefore, there is no shame.[6] In his internet article, Blizzard tells us that "head" in 1 Corinthians 11:3 means image or reflection. We know that Moses covered the heavenly reflection displayed by his countenance

---

[3] Difficult Sayings (article)
[4] Also see Jewish Faith and the New Covenant, page 53
[5] Matthew 5:17-20; 22:34-40
[6] Romans 8:1

when he came down from the mountain, but we are told in 2 Corinthians 3:18 that we are to reflect the Lord's glory.[7]

In the case of women, it was a different issue. Women did not practice veiling. The Old Testament only records two events where women veiled themselves. Rebekah put on a veil when she first saw Isaac, possibly to show reverence for the sorrow he felt over his mother's death. Tamar used a veil to keep Judah from recognizing her. It is interesting to note that Judah mistook Tamar for a prostitute because her face was veiled. Remember, being veiled implied sin and guilt, and Christ took away sin and guilt on the cross.[8]

It tells us man is head of the woman. But we must note the term "man" is used, and not husband. Who is the head of the woman in marriage and in ministry? It is the Man, not a man. In other words, it is the man, Christ Jesus. Granted, godly women have a responsibility to give way to their husbands in a godly way, but they will still reflect the glory of their Lord.

According to 1 Corinthians 11:6, Paul gave the woman liberty to choose whether she wanted to wear a veil or not. He implied that if she wore a veil, she must understand it represented neither reverence nor guilt. Once again, we are reminded that the veil was taken away so all of Jesus' followers could reflect Him. It is the life of Christ in every believer that serves as the light to those who are lost.

Here we have the truth behind veiling. All Christians must reflect Christ, and not their personal best. If they hide behind a veil, the light of Christ cannot shine forth to serve as a living testimony.[9] With this in mind, what about the credibility of the other instructions concerning women in 1 Corinthians 11:1-16? We once again see reference to "headship" in the New Testament. One of its meanings is leadership through example. However, according to Bushnell, "head" in the Old Testament means first in order.[10]

The usage of "head" in 1 Corinthians 11:3 illuminates its simplicity in Scripture, for man was created first, then woman. Ethel Ruff, an ordained Baptist minister, made this interesting observation about the order of creation in her book, *When the Saints Go Marching,*

> So it was that the human pair, 'them,' originally had dominion. That man was placed here first is no proof of his superiority, for creation was in the ascending order, lowest to the highest, and Eve came last. It has been argued that man was superior in intellect, for he named the beasts, birds, etc. But Eve named her children. (Genesis 4:25, emphasis added)

Let us just say for a moment that the term "head" points to superiority and subordination. Here is another interesting observation about the

---

[7] Consider 2 Corinthians 3:13-18
[8] Genesis 24:65; 38:14-15; 2 Corinthians 5:21
[9] Matthew 5:14
[10] God's Word to Women, study note 276

concept of "head" in 1 Corinthians 11:3. We are told God is the head of Christ, yet Philippians 2:9 tells us, "Wherefore, God also hath highly exalted him, and given him a name which is above every name." Jesus in His humanity reflected the glory of the Father. He not only was equal with the Father, He existed before all creation, and was willing to come into a place of submission to His Father.

God exalted Christ. Christ, the head of man, became a servant to man. We see this in His example in John 13:3-15. How can man, therefore, exalt himself above his wife and claim to be her superior, especially when he is commanded, in 1 Peter 3:7, to give her honor as unto a weaker vessel to ensure that his prayers will not be hindered. To properly give his wife honor, he would have to humble himself and prefer her betterment over his personal desires and needs.

We can debate "headship" where woman is concerned, but there is only one true "head" over all believers in relationship to authority, Jesus Christ.[11] It was Christ who purchased the Church with His blood. Therefore, every Christian owes Him complete adoration and commitment. Every Christian should bring glory to Him.

But some may argue, a woman must be in subjection to her husband. According to Bushnell, subjection does not mean obedience, but rather a yielding up of one's will or rights in preference to another.[12] This definition is consistent with the instructions found in Romans 12:10-11 in relationship to honoring one another in brotherly love, and in Ephesians 5:21 where each believer must submit to one another out of the fear of the Lord.

Another subject of debate has been the length of a woman's hair. 1 Corinthians 11:15 states, "But if a woman have long hair, it is a glory to her; for her hair is given her for a covering." Paul was asking a question and not making a statement. Hair cannot possibly serve as a woman's spiritual covering or determine her level of commitment to God or her husband. Granted, it can be a source that reflects or enhances her beauty, but it should never hold any place of authority. According to scripture, it is God who covers the head in the day of battle, and the Holy Spirit is the One who serves as the real covering over God's saints. If anything is to cover the Christian's head, it must be the spiritual helmet of salvation.[13]

Clearly, the Apostle Paul was contending with Jewish customs in 1 Corinthians 11. We actually see him referring to these as customs in 1 Corinthians 11:16. He made this comment, "But if any man seem to be contentious, we have no such custom, neither the churches of God." Can you clearly grasp his message? He stated there is no such custom, especially in the churches. It is easy to see Paul was refuting Jewish

---

[11] Ephesians 4:15
[12] God's Word to Women, study note 293
[13] Psalm 140:7; Isaiah 30:1; Ephesians 6:17; 1 Thessalonians 5:8

customs that did not represent the real spirit, heart, or mind of the new Church.

The Law given to Moses was to lead people to Christ. Many of the Jewish customs and practices served as shadows that pointed to Jesus Christ. To argue over these issues and to insist that people adhere to them would not only be unprofitable, but it would be putting grievous burdens that had no ability to neither impact a person's spirit nor change his or her life.[14]

There is confusion regarding 1 Corinthians 11:1-16. We could debate the meanings behind each scripture, but the conclusion would be the same: it was a matter of Jewish customs and not the inspiration of the Holy Spirit. These passages are in stark contrast to the rest of Scripture. As Christians, we have no agreement with beliefs that take away from the message of Christ and put people in bondage. It is time we focused on the truth governing all Christians.

Ruth Specter Lascelle found liberty from Jewish traditions when she met her Messiah. She spent many years serving her Savior and Lord as a missionary, evangelist, Bible teacher, and author. In response to the Jewish Orthodox prayer she heard from her grandfather throughout her early years, she penned this testimony,

> After I became a believer in the Lord Jesus as my Messiah, I could recreate that prayer that my grandfather prayed and which Paul prayed (before his conversion) and which orthodox Jewish men today pray—
> Blessed art Thou, O Lord our God, King of the Universe Who hath recreated me and I am no longer a slave (to sin).
> Blessed art Thou, O Lord our God, King of the Universe Who hath recreated me and I am no longer a heathen.
> Blessed art Thou, O Lord our God, King of the Universe Who hath recreated me and I am now a SON OF GOD!

Men and women have the same inheritance in the kingdom of God. The truth that must govern us, as believers, is the reality that men and women are all "sons or children," bought with the precious blood of Jesus. How can Christians quibble about superiority and importance when being a "child of God" should be considered the greatest position an individual holds? This position not only determines our relationship here on earth with our Creator, but also guarantees us a heavenly inheritance for eternity.

---

[14] Acts 15:19-20; Galatians 3:21-24; 4:9-10; Colossians 2:16-17; Titus 3:9

7

RESTRAINT OR PERSECUTION?

In 1 Timothy 2:9-15, we see Paul's instructions concerning women's dress and conduct. We could accept these scriptures at face value and settle for their implication without question. However, would our interpretation of these verses be consistent with the entire Word of God?

A few questions need to be asked before we examine these verses. Paul never advocated a dress code anywhere else in scripture, so why here? Both knowledge and attitude will not only always inspire conduct for women, but men as well. This is evident throughout Scripture. But, why make such an emphasis of it with this body of believers? Is there an explanation that will put this focus in perspective?

The answer is yes. There were cultural issues and possibly circumstances that called for wise restraint on the part of the women who belonged to this particular body. With this in mind, let us examine these scriptures in light of the rest of the Word of God and the times in which these people lived. 1 Timothy 2:9 states, "In like manner, also, that women adorn themselves in modest, apparel, with shamefacedness and sobriety, not with broided hair, or gold, or pearls, or costly array."

When we consider other Scriptures, we know that God does not look at the outward appearance of man. The Apostle Peter talked about the need for women to possess inward beauty, rather than outward vanity. Solomon declared that charm is deceptive and beauty fleeing, but a woman who fears God should be praised.[1]

Since dress is no more an indication of Christianity than are religious acts, we must take time to consider if there were events that deemed these instructions necessary. According to my studies there are a couple of possibilities.

This letter was written to Timothy who was overseeing the Church at Ephesus. Ephesus was famed for its heresies and female supremacy in various cults. For example, there were temple prostitutes at the shrine of Diana that wore outlandish apparel. Naturally, the apostle would want Christian women to remain distinct from such associations.[2]

Another explanation has to do with historical events. There were dangerous circumstances that were developing that required extremely

---

[1] 1 Samuel 16:7; Proverbs 31:30; 1 Peter 3:3-4
[2] Difficult Sayings (article)

wise decisions on the part of the Church. These wise responses could mean life or death for the believers.

Nero was in power in Rome at the time the Apostle Paul wrote this letter. Nero's second wife was a Jewess and supported the Oral Law of the Jews. Because of her belief, she hated Christians. Needless to say, her hatred influenced policy and attitudes that resulted in the severe persecution of Christians. This hatred and persecution were clearly reinforced when Nero blamed Christians for his own actions resulting in the burning of Rome. After this false accusation, the persecution of Christians escalated into unspeakable atrocities.

This persecution penetrated the outer areas of the Roman Empire. One of the cities within reach of Rome was Ephesus. We must understand that women did find liberty in Christ. This liberty brought a change in dress and conduct that was decisively different from their Jewish counterparts. According to Pastor George Watkins, Roman soldiers watched for women who displayed a change in dress and conduct. If they spotted a woman with such freedom, they would follow her in hopes of discovering the church. This could spell persecution and death for members of God's family.[3]

It was also pointed out that "professing" in 1 Timothy 2:10 is "epaggellomai" and was also in regard to those who were offering promises through public speaking, such as political candidates and false teachers.[4] If Christian women were publicly speaking in regards to salvation, Paul could be instructing them to be discrete and distinct, confirming their testimony by godly works, and not outward vanity.

Clearly, Paul was telling Christian women to dress in a moderate way to maintain a distinction, as well as for their possible protection. Obviously, Paul's instructions show godly wisdom that all Christian women should adhere to. God is interested in inward beauty and not outward vanity. As a result, there must be a distinction from the world's idea of beauty and the right attitude that will outshine all vanity and become an attraction to those who are lost.

This brings us to the next instruction found in 1 Timothy 2:11, "Let the woman learn in silence with all subjection." Under Jewish tradition, women were not allowed to learn about Scriptural matters. As new converts in Christ, these women were given the necessary liberty to learn about their God. What does it mean to learn in silence? "Silence" in this Scripture could be better translated as "a calm quietness."[5] To effectively learn, there must be quietness of the mind to listen, hear, and retain. There are so many activities that can rob, kill, and destroy the impact of the Word. It was also pointed out that learning requires asking

---

[3] Women in Today's Church, pages 26-27
[4] Difficult Sayings (article), Consider Strong's Concordance, #1861 and 2 Peter 2:19
[5] Ibid, consider #2271

questions, but all conduct must be done in an orderly manner.[6] Once again, Christian women are called to show discretion and restraint in their conduct.

According to other scriptures, these women were not to remain passive students. Teaching in God's kingdom has two goals that produce action and results. These goals are found in Ephesians 4:11-13. They are to prepare God's people for service and to bring them to spiritual maturity. These goals can be summarized in the concept of edification. Christians, regardless of gender, must be brought to maturity in order to discern good and evil. The writer of Hebrews actually rebuked believers who refused to come to such maturity.[7]

There must never be a professional student in the kingdom of heaven. Instruction should bring a Christian to a life of service, which brings glory to his or her Lord and edifies the Body. By obeying these instructions, believers will begin to exemplify Christ and His righteousness in their lives. According to Romans 8:29, Christians have been predestined to be conformed to the very image of Christ.

1 Timothy 2:12-14 states, "But I suffer not a woman to teach, nor to usurp authority over the man, but to be in silence. For Adam was first formed, then Eve. And Adam was not deceived, but the woman being deceived, was in the transgression."

There has been much controversy and abuse surrounding these verses. The first abuse can be found with the first sentence of 1 Timothy 2:12, which states that a woman must not teach. Many have interpreted this to mean women are not to teach even in Sunday school. This is unrealistic and unscriptural. We are reminded of Titus 2:3-4, which instructs older women to teach the younger women proper conduct towards their husbands and children. This clearly involves taking authority over others.

The Apostle Paul commended Timothy's grandmother and mother in 2 Timothy 1:5 for their influence on Timothy's life. Acts 18:26 tells us that Priscilla, along with her husband, taught Apollos the way of God in a more adequate manner. In these scriptures, we see women instructing and influencing women, children, and men.

These scriptural truths hint at another meaning behind this instruction. What is it? Let us continue to examine these verses. The next instruction is: "...nor to usurp authority over the man..." In the King James Version, the word "usurp" is added to this scripture. Pastor W. L. Myers stated in his book that this instruction can only be applied to husbands and wives. He reproved those who refuse to see both the singular tense of both genders in this verse. He declared the real meaning of this instruction is, "No woman (wife) can usurp authority over the man, her husband."

---

[6] 1 Corinthians 14:33
[7] Hebrews 5:11-14

Myers also insisted that the word "usurp" does not mean what many perceive it to mean. He declared the word "usurp" means to take possession by force. The woman must not lord a matter over her husband or demand total subjection.

This could be correct, but does it run consistent with the rest of the text in this chapter? In his article, "Difficult Sayings," Jonathan Went, discussed the word "authority" in this Scripture. The Greek word for it is "authentein," which means, "one acting by his own authority, or being dominating." Although "authentein" is never used in the other places where Paul speaks of authority, this Scripture is basically denouncing a woman from acting out of control or intentionally, without being in proper submission to her husband or father.

However, we must remember that, according to the complete text, the Apostle Paul was not making reference to husbands and wives in these Scriptures, but Church conduct. In her explanation of this series of verses, Bushnell stated the purpose of these scriptures was simply for the protection of women.[8] The Jews were angered at the prospect of women being educated. The apostle was stating that, if a woman was sincere about learning, she had a right to do so, but she must do it in meekness to ensure order and not draw attention to herself. At the same time, he also put a restraint on women teaching men due to the perilous times in which they lived as a means to protect them from the long reach of Rome, as well as the local church.

In her response to the word "usurp," Bushnell stated it cannot be found in the original text, therefore one must conclude it has been added.[9]

Although Bushnell, Myers, and Went had different approaches to explain the meaning of these scriptures, they had the same conclusion. The popular interpretation of these scriptures by the Church today is contrary to the spirit and truth of the Word and must be challenged.

1 Timothy 2:14 states, "And Adam was not deceived, but the woman, being deceived was in the transgression." My conclusion is that this scripture focuses on the real purpose behind this series of instructions in 1 Timothy. The issue inspiring these verses was the woman's right to learn. 1 Timothy 2:14 reinforces this by reminding us that Eve was deceived. We must take this one step further by asking ourselves, "Why was she deceived?" Hosea 4:6 tells us that people perish from lack of knowledge. Ephesians 4:14 instructs people to cease being children and become mature in their knowledge of the Lord so they will no longer be tossed to and fro by every changing wind of doctrine.

Eve was deceived because she lacked instruction. The only way to prevent this from occurring again was to guarantee women the right to receive instruction. Therefore, the rules of conduct put forth in Timothy were not to put women in total subjection to men, but to secure their right

---

[8] God's Word to Women, study notes 336-337
[9] Ibid, study note 337

to learn in the midst of cultures that were critical of such learning, while ensuring their safety.

The last scripture attached to these instructions is 1 Timothy 2:15. It states, "Notwithstanding, she shall be saved in childbearing, if they continue in faith and charity and holiness with sobriety." Many have interpreted this scripture to mean that salvation will come to women if they have children. Many cults have practiced this, resulting in abuse. However, Christians should know that the scripture is in reference to the seed of the woman, Jesus Christ.[10]

It amazes me that Paul would once again make reference to woman's part in salvation. It is as though he wanted to reiterate the importance of woman in the plan of salvation. Christ came to earth via woman (Mary), and it is only through Christ that redemption can be obtained. How could man consider woman to be less important than he? After all, God used a woman, not a man, to bring forth His plan of salvation in the form of His Son. If it was not for the woman, man would still be miserably lost.

To add an interesting note, it is believed by some that 1 Timothy 2:11-12 was added 115 AD, fifty years after Paul's martyrdom.[11] If this is true, clearly liberty has been taken with God's Word. But, even if the liberty was not taken, what would the Apostle Paul say to the Church today concerning their handling of this passage of Scripture? Would he be appalled at the knowledge that words he penned to protect and ensure women the right to learn are now being used by some of the Church to persecute and enslave them? What a sad irony this would be to a man who fought long and hard for spiritual liberty for all the children of God.

---

[10] Genesis 3:15
[11] Difficult Sayings (article)

8

BETWEEN A ROCK AND A HARD PLACE

In response to the treatment of women in the church, Pastor George Watkins of Mt. Vernon, Washington began the introduction of his small book *Women in Today's Church* by stating that 50 percent of God's Church is being held in bondage by generations of misunderstanding and misinterpretation. He was referring to women's place and role in the kingdom of God. Watkins maintained that if liberty was afforded to the women of God, it would result in 100 percent destruction of the kingdom of Satan.

The title of this particular chapter is not only a cliché, but also a description of what women must confront in order to serve God. Often condemned by man if she does, and disobedient to God if she does not, women find themselves struggling to overcome obstacles their male counterparts do not encounter in a life of service. It is as though women have been destined to only be seen and not heard in the Church. The final product has weakened the Church and strengthened Satan's work.

We have already examined two sets of controversial scriptures in regard to women. Now, let us consider the last of these controversial Scriptures. 1 Corinthians 14:34-35 states, "Let your women keep silence in the churches; for it is not permitted unto them to speak, but they are commanded to be under obedience, as also saith the law. And if they will learn anything, let them ask their husbands at home; for it is a shame for women to speak in the church."

Once again, we are confronted with what could be considered an unshakable rule governing women in the Church. However, we must observe these verses in light of the rest of God's Word.

In 1 Corinthians 14:26, we begin to see the accepted and popular presentation of these two scriptures losing credibility as part of the inspired text, "How is it, then, brethren? When ye come together, every one of you hath a psalm, hath a doctrine, hath a tongue, hath a revelation, hath an interpretation. Let all things be done unto edifying." (Emphasis added)

We know terms such as the "sons of God" and "brothers or brethren" apply to both men and women. If it is difficult for a person to accept that the instruction of verse 26 applies to women, all we need to do is refer them to the words "every one." Note that this scripture verse had to have been written a few minutes before verses 34-35. Did the Apostle Paul suddenly change his mind?

Some maintain that verses 34 and 35 are only applicable for husbands and wives. This may be a quick way to bring the discussion to an end, but what about single women? Where do they fit in Church procedure?

The Apostle Paul clearly dealt with the subject of single women in 1 Corinthians 7:25 and 34,

> Now concerning virgins, I have no commandment of the Lord; yet I give my judgment, as one that hath obtained mercy of the Lord to be faithful...There is difference also between a wife and a virgin. The unmarried woman careth for the things of the Lord, that she may be holy both in body and in spirit; but she that is married careth for the things of the world, how she may please her husband.

There is no instruction for the single woman to remain silent or come under the control of man. In fact, Paul commended unmarried women for their devotion solely to the Lord. If 1 Corinthians 7:34-35 were only applicable to married women, does it mean God excludes married women alone from speaking in the church?

Acts 2:17-18 declares,

> And it shall come to pass in the last days, saith God, I will pour out of my Spirit upon all flesh; and your sons and your <u>daughters</u> shall prophesy, and your young men shall see visions, and your old men shall dream dreams; And on my servants and on my <u>handmaidens</u> I will pour out in those days of my Spirit, and they shall prophesy. (Emphasis added)

There is no indication that God was making a distinction based on sex or marital status in this declaration. Both men and women would be moved by the Holy Spirit in prophecy.

Prophecy is when one speaks forth truths to the Church. This was not uncommon in the new Church. This gift was for the edification of the Body and it was not limited to men. Acts 21:9 tells us that Philip had four daughters who had the gift of prophecy. 1 Thessalonians 5:19-20 commands us not to quench the Spirit and despise not prophesyings.

How can a godly woman, married or single, remain silent when prompted by the Holy Spirit? Who would be willing to quench the Spirit? On the other hand, how can all women be strictly accountable to two scriptures that are inconsistent with the rest of the Word?

In Corinthians, we see a pattern. Remember, the apostle Paul was dealing with the infiltration of Judaism into the Corinthian Church. It is believed that Paul referred to another source, such as a letter written to him, which he quotes before writing his stand on these issues. For instance, in 1 Corinthians 8:1 we read, "Now as touching things offered unto idols..."

In 1 Corinthians 10:23, we read a statement that was being quoted and answered, "All things are lawful for me, but all things are not expedient; all things are lawful for me, but all things edify not."

In 1 Corinthians 14:34-35, we can identify this pattern. For instance, let us focus on this statement, "...for it is not permitted unto them to speak..." Paul is not making a command here, but referring to something alien to church conduct. While we may be uncertain of the source Paul was referring to throughout the letter, we are sure of the inspiration behind these two scriptures. Note the last part of verse 14:34, "...as also saith the law."

The Apostle Paul was not stating "our law" or "my law," but "the law." Clearly, the apostle was not laying personal claim to this law in regard to the Church. Therefore, what law was Paul making reference to? The attitudes toward women in these two verses are clearly in accordance with the Oral Law of the Jews. (Note: Remember the Oral Law of the Jews is not contained within the Old Testament.) Paul was quoting the Oral Law of the Jews and not the written Law of Moses.

The tradition of the Oral Law was to separate men and women into different sections during religious teaching and worship. Apparently, if an issue confused some women during service, they would disrupt the services by yelling the question to their husbands from their section. To keep order, it was commanded for women to refrain from asking the question until they were in the confines of their homes.

It appears as if Paul was referring to the Oral Law of the Jews to give the Corinthians a comparison in regard to order. After all, the theme of 1 Corinthians 14 is about order in the Body when it came to the inspirational gifts of speaking in tongues and prophesies. Apparently, the Corinthians did not display order in the use of these gifts, and, since they were leaning towards the Oral Law of the Jews, Paul was possibly using it to drive home a point in relationship to order. Clearly, it was not to establish a law for women in the middle of establishing the proper order for Church conduct in regards to the use of the gifts of the Holy Ghost.

We ultimately see a blatant rebuke in Paul's next statement which many seem to ignore when using these scriptures to "put women in their place" in God's kingdom. "What? Came the word of God out from you? Or came it unto you only" (1 Corinthians 14:36)? The Apostle Paul was exhorting his hearers to agree with his evaluation about the proper conduct and order, as far as the instruction he put forth concerning the gifts.

Who would display such conceit towards godly instruction? In Jesus' condemnation of the teachers of the law and the Pharisees, He referred to them as hypocritical experts of the Law that put people in bondage.[1] Such people missed the whole point because they always missed God in a matter. Paul concluded with this challenge in 1 Corinthians 14:37-38, "If any man think himself to be a prophet, or spiritual, let him

---

[1] Matthew 1:20;23

acknowledge that the things that I write unto you are the commandments of the Lord. But if any man be ignorant, let him be ignorant."

Needless to say, most people use these couple of Scriptures in 1 Corinthians 14 to determine women's place in the Church, but, if you note, Paul did not end with the subject of women, but with prophesy and tongues. Then, he made this statement, "Let all things be done decently and in order."

The burden of proof in regard to the debate that was evident concerning proper attitudes and practice for the local body at Corinth fell on those who were promoting Jewish traditions. If they were followers of Jesus, they had to prove it by submitting to the instructions Paul set down. If they did not, Paul instructed those around them to leave them in their ignorance.

In the information contained in his article, Went pointed out the similarities between 1 Timothy 2:11-12 and 1 Corinthians 14:35. If the Scriptures in Timothy were added 50 years after Paul's martyrdom, then most likely the same liberty was taken with the couple of inconsistent Scriptures found in 1 Corinthians 14. After all, altering a few Scriptures here or there will not do any real harm, or will it?

However, as we approach 1 Corinthians 14, Paul was not establishing a separate law for women. He had already stipulated the one law that all Christians were to adhere to in Romans 8:2, and that is the law of the Spirit of the life in Christ Jesus. Whether these Scriptures were added, or Paul was making reference to the Oral Law of the Jews to bring contrast, they were not meant to put women in bondage. Clearly, the Apostle Paul discredited the attitudes and instructions the Oral Law maintained towards women. Surely, Paul was aware that, even in the Old Testament, women also enjoyed great religious freedom. In one quick swoop of the pen, he put all into scriptural perspective in Galatians 3:28. Why is it today that some have a tendency to focus on a few verses, while ignoring the rest? Paul's test remains the same. If someone claims to be spiritual, let him or her line up with his instructions. If they do not follow them, then leave them to their preferred ignorance.

Let Romans 12:16 summarize the proper attitude among Christians, regardless of gender, "Be of the same mind one toward another. Mind not high things, but condescend to men of low estate. Be not wise in your own conceits."

9

THE LAST SHALL BE FIRST

What does it mean to be the greatest in the kingdom of heaven? Matthew 20:26b-27 gives us the answer, "...but whosoever will be great among you, let him be your minister, And whosoever will be chief among you, let him be your servant."

Greatness in the kingdom of heaven is not determined by title, position, or rank, but by genuine servitude. As servants of God, Christians become vessels in the hand of the Great Potter, or instruments in the hand of the Great Conductor. After all, it is Christ's life that believers are manifesting, it is the Father's business they must carry out, and it is the power of the Spirit that ensures all spiritual matters are brought to completion. Obviously, it is not a matter of position, rank, or gender, rather it comes down to what we will allow God to do in us, through us, and with us as His vessels and instruments.[1]

God is clearly not impressed or persuaded by positions. He is no respecter of persons.[2] In fact, God considers Christian attitudes and responses foremost. We see Him guarding against any favoritism in the Church as well. 1 Corinthians 12:22-25 states,

> Nay, much more those members of the body which seem to be more feeble, are necessary: And those members of the body, which we think to be less honorable, upon these we bestow more abundant honor; and our uncomely parts have more abundant comeliness. For our comely parts have no need; but God hath tempered the body together, having given more abundant honor to that part which lacked. That there should be no schism in the body, but that the members should have the same care one for another.

To avoid schisms or divisions in the Body, the Lord exalts those parts that seem less honorable to the same place as the rest of the members of the Body. Obviously, there is no preference, exaltation, or honor given to certain members of the Body, regardless of the preference that may be shown by those who are part of the Church.

We have to keep in mind that God is the potter. He chooses what vessels He will use and how He will use them. Vessels do not hold ranks, nor are they considered on the basis of gender. Such vessels do

---

[1] Luke 2:49; 24:49; Romans 6:13-16; 9:20-21; Galatians 2:20
[2] Romans 2:11; Ephesians 6:9

not make decisions concerning their use, whether in regard to self or to others. Some of the vessels we perceive to be least might be the very vessels God will bestow honor upon. For other vessels that we would choose to exalt, He may pass by. We judge by the outward appearance, but God's considers the heart.[3]

God is not limited by the vessel He uses. He can use a donkey, as He did in the case of Balaam. He will use young people. For example, it was upon the suggestion of a young Jewish girl that Naaman sought out Elisha for healing. The prophet Jeremiah referred to himself as a child.[4] Luke 2:8-17 tells us the angels pronounced Christ's birth to shepherds who were the first to proclaim that the Messiah was born. Shepherds were considered to be the dregs of society.

Matthew 3:4 gives us this description of John the Baptist, "And the same John had his raiment of camel's hair, and a leathern girdle about his loins; and his meat was locusts and wild honey." How many of our churches today would accept John the Baptist into their midst, let alone acknowledge him as a prophet?

Jesus initially called fishermen, not merchants or the educated, to follow Him in order to become fishers of men.[5] As for the Apostle Paul, we gain this insight about him in 2 Corinthians 10:10: "For his letters, say they, are weighty and powerful, but his bodily presence is weak, and his speech contemptible."

In Luke 19:35-40 we read how the Pharisees criticized the people paying homage to Christ. Jesus made this response in Luke 19:40b, "I tell you that, if these should hold their peace, the stones would immediately cry out."

Once again, God will not be limited by the vessels He chooses to use. Some vessels are used for dishonorable purposes like Pharaoh and Judas Iscariot. Other vessels are used for noble purposes like Peter and Paul. The vessels of dishonor are destined for destruction, while the vessels of honor will bring glory to God. The determination of which vessel a person becomes originates with his or her heart response towards God. Noble vessels have an available heart to God and will allow themselves to be set apart for His use and glory.

2 Timothy 2:19-22 talks about the different vessels in the house of God. Some of these vessels are made of gold and silver, but some of wood and clay. The use of these vessels may be honorable or dishonorable, but those who desire to be used in an honorable way must cleanse themselves and submit to the Holy Spirit. It is the Spirit of God that will make a vessel holy and useful for the Master's use, ready to do any good work.

The Apostle Paul gave us insight in these Scriptures in 2 Timothy as to how to cleanse ourselves, "Flee also youthful lusts, but follow

---

[3] Romans 9:21-23
[4] Numbers 22:28-32; 2 Kings 5:1-15; Jeremiah 1:6
[5] Matthew 4:18-22

righteousness, faith, charity, peace with them that call on the Lord out of a pure heart" (2 Timothy 2:22).

Our God is sovereign. He decides who he will use and how He will use each vessel. 1 Corinthians 12:11 and 18 confirms this same type of sovereign work within the Church, "But all these worketh that one and the selfsame Spirit, dividing to every man severally as he will…But now hath God set the members, every one of them in the body, as it hath pleased him." (Emphasis added)

The real issue in the kingdom of God is not what type of vessel God chooses to use, but whether a vessel is being used by God. The real test of the vessel does not rest with status, rank, or gender, but with the message. If God wants to use a vessel that might be unacceptable to man, He will do so in spite of man's unwillingness to accept it. After all, it is not up to God to lower His ways to compliment man's prideful, vain perception, but, rather, it is up to man to first humble himself in preparation in order to adjust his base ways to the higher purpose of God.

God uses the most unlikely vessels as a test to the wise and strong. By using the foolish, weak, base, and despised, He illuminates the true works of darkness in the hearts of men. Decisions that are made as hidden works of darkness are exposed. Either the individual will repent of darkness, or he or she will continue to give way to his or her sin.[6]

This brings us to the subject of God using women in His kingdom. If any one vessel has been classified as being foolish, weak, base, and despised, it has been the woman. Although not necessarily earned, this description has been readily placed upon females.

1 Peter 3:7 gives this command, "In like manner, ye husbands, dwell with them according to knowledge, giving honor unto the wife, as unto the weaker vessel, and as being heirs together of the grace of life; that your prayers be not hindered." In this Scripture, we see a reference made concerning woman being the weaker partner. In what way is a woman weaker? We know that, in the area of physical strength, she is not equal, but what about spiritually? The only way a woman is weaker, spiritually speaking, is in marriage. Because of her position of servitude and the wrong attitudes that can be firmly in place in people's way of thinking, she is at the mercy of her husband. The Apostle Peter established both the attitude and response a husband must have toward his wife to ensure her dignity and safety within this relationship. The husband must honor her. In other words, he must exalt her to the proper place in their relationship to ensure his prayers remain effective.

All too often, a woman finds herself becoming, not only under subjection to her husband at home, but also to every man in the church. There are no scriptural grounds for this practice in the Body of Christ.

---

[6] John 3:19-21; 1 Corinthians 1:25-29

The Church is the bride of Christ. Each believer makes up this bride. Christ is the head and Lord of His Body. He will not take second position to the rule of man in any believer's life.

Jeremiah 17:5 and 7 warns us not to lean on the arm of the flesh in any type of dependency or reliance. To do so would put us under a curse. Blessing only comes out of trusting the Lord and putting confidence in Him.

We know from Scripture woman was made last, but we also read in the Word that women were the first ones to be used by God in many situations. Some Bible scholars maintain the first one to believe the message of redemption was Eve. The word "Eve" means the "mother of all living." Adam did not give her this name until after the fall in the Garden of Eden.[7]

Adam knew the consequence for his act of disobedience was death or separation from God. What type of life was Adam referring to in giving Eve her name—the mere physical life of mankind or the eternal life that would come through Christ?

Eve believed God when He promised redemption. This was made evident when Cain was born. According to Bushnell, the original translation of Genesis 4:1 should read, "I have gotten a man, --even 'The Coming One!'"[8]

"The Coming One" means "Jehovah." "Jehovah" in Greek means "Lord," Although Cain was not the "Promised One," Eve's belief in the "Coming One" qualified her to be a believer. John 1:12 declares, "But as many as receive him, to them gave he power to become the sons of God, even to them that believer on his name."

It is interesting to note women were the first to name the Lord Jesus Christ. Eve was the first one to refer to Him as "Jehovah" or "Lord". Hannah was the first to call Him "The Anointed One" or "The Christ."[9] Mary, the mother of Christ, was the first one told to call Him "Jesus" in Luke 1:31.

Philippians 2:9-11 states this about the name of the Lord Jesus Christ, "Wherefore, God also hath highly exalted him, and given him a name which is above every name, That at the name of Jesus every knee should bow, of things in heaven, and things in earth, and things under the earth, And that every tongue should confess that Jesus Christ is Lord, to the glory of God the Father."

We can conclude that God not only chose woman to bring forth His Son, but, from all appearances, He also ordained that they would be the first ones to declare His Son's name. Acts 4:12 summarizes the significance of this name, "Neither is there salvation in any other; for there is no other name under heaven given among men, whereby we must be saved."

---

[7] Genesis 3:20
[8] God's Word to Women, study note 77
[9] 1 Samuel 2:10

Rayola Kelley

This brings us to women's responses towards the Christ. Women may have been formed last, but many times they were first to perform God's work in the kingdom. Anna was a prophetess who spent forty-four years of her life in the temple. When Mary brought Jesus to the temple to be dedicated, Anna recognized Him to be "The Messiah" or "The Christ." Luke 2:38 tells us that she went forth and spoke to all of them there who were looking for redemption in Jerusalem. Because of her response, Anna is considered to be the <u>first</u> evangelist to the Jews.

Mary, the sister of Martha, was the <u>first</u> to anoint Jesus for His burial.[10] Jesus made this statement about her action in Matthew 26:13, "Verily I say unto you, Wherever this gospel shall be preached in the whole world, there shall also this, that this woman hath done, be told for a memorial of her."

Mary Magdalene was the <u>first</u> one to witness the empty tomb. She would also be the <u>first</u> one to proclaim Jesus' resurrection to the disciples who were in hiding. Lydia was the <u>first</u> convert in Europe. We know the <u>first</u> church in Europe met in her home in Philippi. Later, this church would be commended by Paul in his epistle to the believers of this new body.[11]

In Luke 18:14b we read this principle, "...for everyone that exalteth himself shall be abased; and he that humbleth himself shall be exalted."

As I studied how women were the first in many situations, I remembered the words of Luke 18:14. It is obvious that women have been made the tail in so many areas relating to the kingdom of God. In spite of man's rush to subject and subdue womankind, God has raised many godly women into places of greatness. These places not only reveal women quietly running the spiritual race, but they show them pressing past man-made obstacles to be all that their Lord ordained them to be. Because of their availability, they have been chosen first in many instances, therefore, exalting them in the kingdom of God.

Jesus made this statement in Matthew 19:30, "But many that are first shall be last, and the last shall be first." The meaning of this scripture has other applications than my use of it regarding women, but, nevertheless, the implications remain true.

Considering my struggle over the subject of women in God's kingdom, I had to face my own fears. Initially, I could not understand how God could put women into bondage. My overwhelming fear was that God would turn out to be the "male chauvinist" the few misconstrued, out-of-context scriptures purported Him to be. I was uneasy that, just because of something beyond my control, meaning my gender, I would be condemned to a life I could never accept in my heart.

Pushing past anxieties and risking my faith, I set out in search of truth. Truth never fails those who desire to find it. It did vindicate my scriptural perception of God. He does not "change like shifting

---

[10] John 12:3-7
[11] Matthew 28:1-10; John 20:1-18; Acts 16:11-15, 40; Philippians 4:10-19

Challenging the Christian Life

shadows."[12] He looks at the heart and not the gender. He sits on the throne and uses what vessel He will. He exalts those who are abased.

The result of my search for truth confirmed what I had suspected all along. God does not have favorites. I am now stronger in my belief. My discouragement has turned into joy, my oppression into liberty, and my adversity into victory. Through it all, I gained insight into my true identity in the kingdom of God. I do not stand before God as a "woman," but as "His child." I do not have to accept the crumbs of man when my Lord has offered me a full meal—for He is the Bread of Life and the Giver of Living Water.

I have learned it is okay to be last, for it is in one's weakness that God's greatness is learned. It is because of need that many accept God's invitation to sup with Him. It is in the darkest of times of such need that some will come out with a greater revelation of Jesus. It is in lack that others learn contentment in Christ

In my struggle, I have learned it is not ministry that verifies spiritual success. Spiritual success is grasped when one learns to lose in order to gain. As believers, we must all forsake our self-importance in order to gain Christ. After all, Christ is our reward and inheritance. If we have Christ, we have it all.

Now I can truly say, "Thank you God, for making me last."

---

[12] James 1:17

10

CAN WOMEN BE ENTRUSTED?

We have already discussed how God chooses the most unlikely vessels to use for His glory. His decision is not based on sex, as many have tried to prove by using certain passages of scripture. The major issue in the kingdom is quite simple; what vessel can God entrust with his work?

Throughout scripture, we see God commending women. We already know God used a virgin by the name of Mary to bring forth His Son. In Judges 4-5, God entrusted the prophetess, Deborah, to lead the armies of Israel into a victorious battle. In the book of Esther, we read of God's miraculous intervention to save the nation of Israel when He moved Mordecai's niece, Esther, into a position of intercession with the king on behalf of His people.

Although a source of much controversy in the Church, Rebekah took action on what God revealed to her about her two sons. Bear in mind that Isaac dealt in the realm of both the material world and the tradition in determining which son would inherit the promise. Rebekah saw beyond to God's plan. Her intervention may be classified as deceptive, but, nevertheless, it was a fulfillment of God's will.[1]

In Judges 13:3, we read of the angel first appearing to Samson's mother to declare his conception. In 1 Samuel 1:26-28, we see how it was Hannah who dedicated Samuel to the Lord. It was the harlot, Rahab, who hid the two spies from Israel's enemies in Jericho. A Moabite woman named Ruth left home and family to follow her mother-in-law to her homeland, Israel. Both of these pagan ladies are named in the lineage of Jesus.[2]

Scripturally, we see women being used in every facet in the kingdom of God. Like Deborah, some were leaders of God's people. In the New Testament, Phoebe would be Deborah's counterpart. Once again, we are reminded that this godly woman served in the position of a deacon. There was also Junia. According to the spelling of the name, it points to a woman who was noted among the apostles.[3]

Women were also used in temple work. Exodus 38:8 and 1 Samuel 2:22 imply women served in the tabernacle at stated intervals, as did the priests. Numbers 6:2 tells us that women could be Nazarites. Exodus

---

[1] Genesis 25:22-23
[2] Joshua 2, Ruth 1; Matthew 1:5
[3] Difficult Sayings (article)

Challenging the Christian Life

38:8 states, "And he made the laver of brass, and the foot of it of brass, of the looking glasses of the women assembling, which assembled at the door of the tabernacle of the congregation."

Ruth Specter Lascelle made this comment about Exodus 38:8, "In typology the Laver represents the WORD OF GOD. The looking-glasses were made of highly polished brass (copper) into which the women would look to see a reflection of themselves. The Word of God is like a mirror which reflects what we look like and it tells of a remedy whereby we can be cleansed. These looking-glasses were donated by the Jewish women for the building of the Laver."

In the New Testament, the believer serves as the temple of the Holy Spirit. The Apostle Paul encouraged the single women to remain so and consecrate themselves totally to God.[4] 1 Peter 2:5 says, "Ye also, as lively stones, are built up a spiritual house, and holy priesthood, to offer up spiritual sacrifices, acceptable to God by Jesus Christ."

We can clearly see that women's roles have not varied in either of the testaments. Women have been placed in spiritual leadership positions. For instance, Moses' sister, Miriam, was a prophetess. She was accredited with leading the children of Israel, along with Moses and Aaron.[5]

The priests went to the prophetess, Huldah, to find out the mind of the Lord in 2 Kings 22:14-20. The word "prophecy" is described by Paul in 1 Corinthians 14:3 in this manner: "But he that prophesieth speaketh unto men to edification, and exhortation and comfort."

Pastor W. L. Myers explained in his book, *Does God Call Women to Preach?*, that the meaning of prophecy in 1 Corinthians 14:3 can be ascribed to the definition of preaching as well. Preaching is more than proclaiming; it edifies, exhorts, and comforts.

Acts 21:8-9 tells us, "And the next day we that were of Paul's company departed, and came unto Caesarea; and we entered into the house of Philip, the evangelist, who was one of the seven, and abode with him. And the same man had four daughters, virgins, who did prophesy." According to historical information, these four women evangelized throughout the then known world. They preached in parks, in public buildings, and in halls.[6] This should not surprise us since a Christian's commission is to preach the good news to all creation.[7]

Obviously, preaching is not limited to men. Every time a woman proclaims Christ, she is fulfilling her commission. We know Anna and Mary Magdalene were evangelists, but so was the woman at the well. While Jesus was talking to His disciples about the harvest field, the Samaritan woman was sharing Christ with the men of the city.[8]

---

[4] 1 Corinthians 6:19-20; 7:25-26, 34-35
[5] Exodus 15:20-21; Micah 6:4
[6] Women In Today's Church, page 20
[7] Mark 16:15
[8] John 4:28-29

According to archaeological findings, etchings and paintings have been found on the walls of catacombs depicting women preaching and serving communion.[9] Acts 1:14 tells us that women were part of the group waiting to be endued with power from above.[10] Therefore, these women had to be declaring the Gospel along with the men.

Some would contend that the commission of proclaiming the Gospel is different from the position of being a preacher. I realize there is a position of shepherd or pastor in the church, but there is no scriptural reference to stipulate this position is limited to a man. Recent history even proves differently when you consider the staggering work done by women on the mission field.

Again, we must refer back to the definition of prophecy. Prophecy involves forth-telling, expounding scripture for the purpose of instruction. The Apostle Paul made this statement in 1 Corinthians 14:1, "Follow after charity, and desire spiritual gifts, but rather that ye may prophesy." According to Paul, prophecy was beneficial for the building up of the Church. He desired that all would have this gift.

Preaching by women can be found in the Old Testament. Psalm 68:11 says, "The Lord gave the word; great was the company of those who published it." Lascelle gives this insight into this Scripture,

> The word "company" is in the feminine gender. The words of action (i.e. "proclaimed" or "published") telling what this feminine "company" is doing, is also in the feminine gender, since this is the proper Hebrew grammar. The word "company" implies that it is an army that assembles by troops. These words, "assembling" and "assembled" (KJV) in Exodus 38:8 along with the word "company" in Psalm 68:11 tells that the Lord gave the WORD (the Laver) and there was a feminine army who published or PREACHED it! The R.V. gives it as "The Lord giveth the Word. The WOMEN that publish the tidings are a great host.

Godly women comprise a powerful army in God. They have led God's people in various ways. They have been pillars in the Church. They faithfully served alongside the Apostle Paul in the harvest field. We see Paul commending some of these women for their commitment to the Gospel in Romans 16:3, 6 & 12.

Paul referred to Priscilla as a fellow worker. According to *Vine's Expository Dictionary of Biblical Words*, "fellow workers" implies equality in importance and position. He acknowledged Mary, Tryphena, Tryphosa, and Persis' hard work in the Lord. In Romans 16:13, the Apostle Paul sent a greeting to Rufus and his mother whom Paul also claimed to be his mother. Was Rufus' mother Paul's biological mother or did he consider her to be his spiritual mother?

---

[9] Women In Today's Church, page 29
[10] Luke 24:49

Bible scholars note that Priscilla's name was used before her husband's name in a couple Scriptures such as Acts 18:18 and Romans 16:3. According to the culture of that time, putting Priscilla's name first indicated leadership or importance in that particular reference. Based on my various studies, she appears to be the dominant minister and teacher in this husband-and-wife team. We know Priscilla played a major role in instructing Apollo.[11] Many believe she was the believing wife Paul made reference to in 1 Corinthians 9:5 (Refer to 1 Corinthians 16:19). According to Romans 16:3, she had risked her life for Paul and other believers.

This brings me to the unrealistic mindset some church leaders have adopted towards women holding leadership positions in the Church. Quick to accept women as missionaries in foreign countries, some of these same leaders hypocritically deny these same women the position and recognition in the Church in America. These women have served as apostles, prophets, evangelists, pastors, and teachers on the mission field. They have laid down their lives for the Gospel; yet, they still cannot be entrusted with leadership positions in the Church. It appears as if some men are trying to maintain their comfortable positions behind the pulpit in the name of scriptural instruction, while ignoring the price their female counterparts have had to pay to serve on the mission field.

In fact, the latest ratio of women to men in the mission field is sixteen women to one man. Certain men can go around advocating why women must come into bondage to their way of thinking because of a few Scriptures, but statistics reveal that it is the women that continue to work in the harvest field. Where would the souls that have been affected by their devotion be today if women would have come into submission to a few misused Scriptures, rather than faithfully adhered to their high calling?

One must wonder what happened from the time women of the new Church were used in a powerful way to the present time. Obviously, women have been demoted to the position of silent, mindless zombies in the scheme of things, who have no other option but to become subservient to all of man's conclusions and whims. Some believe it had to do with the pressures of what would be more accepted by the culture and the societal values within the last part of the first century of the new Church. These pressures resulted in women's roles being minimized.[12] Apparently, in the attempt to justify this unfounded demotion, Scriptures were either adjusted in their presentation or added.

Regardless of this mindset, the Word establishes the truth about women. God has entrusted women with much. They were in the upper room at Pentecost and named among those of "whom the world was not worthy" in Hebrews 11. Their actions were upheld by the Lord to serve as a memorial and example to others. They preached, held leadership

---

[11] Acts 18:18-19, 24-26
[12] Difficult Sayings (article)

positions, and worked hard for the kingdom of God. They even suffered and died for the sake of their Lord and the furtherance of the kingdom of God.

Here is a simple question, If God entrusted women with leadership in the kingdom of God, then who is mere man within his religious organization, to declare certain areas off limits to them? Whose kingdom is being "protected" from the influence of women—God's kingdom or man's?

11

LET MY HANDMAIDENS GO!

I have learned true service to God hinges on having the liberty to be what God desires us to be. In Exodus, God made this request of Pharaoh, "Let my people go." The reason that Pharaoh had to let the people go was so that they could serve and worship God.[1]

Humankind has been formed by God to worship and be in fellowship with Him. It is only in a growing relationship with God that we, as believers, will glorify Him. However, it takes the liberty of the Spirit to worship God in spirit and truth. It is truth that makes us free to discover the reality of our Lord and Savior, and to be all that He desires us to be in His kingdom.[2]

People who are in bondage cannot be available to God. They are too busy striving to serve two masters. Divided loyalties bring nothing but frustration and double-mindedness that lead to spiritual, mental, and emotional instability.[3] God was clearly asking Pharaoh to let His people go to worship Him. This worship involved offering sacrifices. Romans 12:1 instructs us to offer our bodies as a living sacrifice, which is our reasonable service.

Christians must have liberty in the Spirit in order to present their bodies as a living sacrifice. This sacrifice is necessary to ensure a life that will do that which is good, acceptable, and according to God's perfect will.[4].

Jesus made this statement in Matthew 12:48b-50 about who was part of the family of God, "...Who is my mother? And who are my brethren? And he stretched forth his hand toward his disciples, and said, Behold my mother and my brethren! For whosoever shall do the will of my Father, who is in heaven, the same is my brother, and sister, and mother."

Jesus made no distinction of gender when He made reference to the family of God. He revealed the simple ingredient to be a part of His family—doing the will of the Father.

---

[1] Exodus 7:16; 8:20; 9:1, 13
[2] John 4:24; 8:32-36; 2 Corinthians 3:17
[3] James 1:8
[4] Romans 12:2

Who determines the will of the Father? Romans 11:33-34 informs us that the riches of the wisdom and knowledge of God are unsearchable. There is no way mere man can know the mind of the Lord for himself or others. It is only by the Holy Spirit that we can discover, know, and experience the depth of God and come to terms with what is His personal will for our lives.

Many times, man has put God in a box. He has tried to confine God's ways to fit his understanding and pride. But God's ways and thoughts are higher than ours. They are righteous and perfect; therefore, there is no inconsistency in His dealings with man.[5]

How can man ensure he is lining up with the ways of God? Proverbs 4:7 instructs us to get wisdom, no matter how much it might cost us. Psalm 111:10 tells us the fear of the Lord is the beginning of wisdom. Ecclesiastes 12:13 summarizes the whole duty of man as fearing God and keeping His commandments. Philippians 2:12 commands us to work out our salvation in fear and trembling. Although Proverbs 31 is often quoted to show woman how she is to act, the secret behind all godly women is revealed in Proverbs 31:30, "Favor is deceitful, and beauty is vain, but a woman who feareth the LORD, she shall be praised." The fear of the Lord is an awesome reverence towards God. This reverence will hate evil, serve as one's confidence towards God, and become a fountain of life.[6]

Fear of God is also vital if one is to see the importance of doing it God's way. Man is quick to lose sight of the holiness of his God. It is easy for man to take lightly the things of God. However, when one has the fear of the Lord, he or she keeps the reality of God's righteousness before his or her eyes.

Another aspect of the Christian life is love or charity. Love is the heartbeat of Christianity. It is a commitment to be right before God and to do right by those around us. This love is patient and kind. It is not envious, proud, or rude. It is not selfish; therefore, it does not demand its own way. It is meek (teachable) in nature, pursues peace, desires truth, and remains faithful. It is benevolent, which means it will possess good will and kindness.[7]

This love must be evident in everyone who claims to be a Christian. It must exist between believers and between husbands and wives. It results in submission, and it ultimately serves as the test of true Christianity.[8]

God's love is sacrificial. It will deny self and exalt the needs of others. It will not value the ways of man, but seeks to please God. It does not desire to control. Rather it desires to see one discover his or her real potential in God. It does not rejoice in the iniquity of bondage,

---

[5] Psalm 18:30; Isaiah 55:8-9
[6] Proverbs 8:13; 14:26-27
[7] 1 Corinthians 7:3; 13; 1 John 3:10
[8] 1 John 3:14-15

but in truth reigning in a situation. It is real and persevering. Above all else, it will bring glory to God.[9]

Satan hates God and His people. One of his greatest devices is bondage. He does not care how he secures the captivity of people, whether he uses the different fears that plague us or the sin that can so easily beset us. He does not care if he uses lies, adjusts the Word, man's religion, or the wickedness of others, he wants people to be in bondage to his ways of death and destruction. Such bondage implies control and inferiority. Inferiority among humanity is a product of an outward judgment based on man's standards. Such judgment proves to be unmerciful. It is contrary to the very nature of God's love, mercy, compassion, and grace.[10]

Bondage destroys not only its victims, but also those who are part of the enslaving process. Individuals who enslave others will ultimately find themselves in bondage themselves. Galatians 6:7-8 confirms this principle, "Be not deceived, God is not mocked, for whatsoever a man soweth, that shall he also reap. For he that soweth to his flesh shall of the flesh reap corruption; but he that soweth to the Spirit shall of the Spirit reap life everlasting."

Liberty is associated with the Spirit of God, and bondage with the flesh of man. It is clear that the Holy Spirit must be evident in our attitudes, ways, and practices if we are going to reap eternal value. In Exodus 10:7-11 we read that Pharaoh agreed to allow the men to go worship God, but not the women or the children. Moses refused to accept his stipulation. God's demand remained the same, "Let <u>my people</u> go . . ."

If Christian women are in bondage in any way, God's command is the same for today as it was during Moses' day. He wants those who are Pharaohs in heart to let His handmaidens go to worship Him! Although they came out of the side of man, they came from the heart of God. They do not belong to man. They are not here to serve man's whims. They are here to bring glory to their Creator.

As long as women are in bondage to man's religious standards, the Church remains in captivity, for when one member suffers, the whole body suffers.[11] There is nothing more heart wrenching than to watch an individual who desires liberty in God be put down in the name of Christ because of physical traits (gender) the person had no power in determining.

This captivity will benefit no one but the kingdom of darkness. It will keep women who have the call of God and the desire, devotion, and ability to serve Him from making a vital difference in the Church, as well as in the lives of those who live in darkness.

---

[9] John 3:16; 13:34-35; 1 Corinthians 13:6-7; 1 John 3:16

[10] John 8:44; Romans 6:6-7; 2 Timothy 1:7; 2:26; Hebrews 12:1
    James 2:13

[11] 1 Corinthians 12:26

Like Barak, who submitted to the leadership of Deborah, it is a show of faith to let God use the vessel He chooses. Although Deborah helped lead the army, Barak was still accredited with conquering kingdoms. His name is listed with the great heroes of the faith in Hebrews 11. After all, true faith is letting God be God. If God chooses woman to lead, so be it. Great men of faith will always submit, for there is only one correct goal in the kingdom of God—to glorify God and to build up His people.

Although the entire Church today does not promote the bondage that enslaves women, those who do are adhering to Satan's rules. As long as they insist on maintaining this bondage, the Church is being held in a cage. Like Israel, true worship cannot occur until all of God's people are set free to present themselves as living sacrifices for His glory. Without humility and worship, there is no revival. If there is no revival, the demons dance with joy because they are gaining ground.

The kingdom of God is not a matter of competition. If there is a job to do, who cares what type of vessel is used as long as the job gets done for the glory of God and the benefit of His kingdom? Myers made this statement in his book *Does God Call Women to Preach?*

> Some preachers remind me of Joshua, when he came running in, eyes blared, nostrils dilated crying, 'My Lord, Eldad and Medad do prophesy in the camp.' But Moses said, 'Son, I wish all God's people were prophets.' (Numbers 11:28, 29). Moses was not envious. He was not afraid the ladies would root him out of his pulpit. Neither am I.

Church, what will it be? Liberty for all or bondage? There is no middle ground. Liberty must happen on an individual level before it can occur collectively. It begins with the heart, invades the attitude, and results in submission, not only to God, but also to each other.

If you are a woman who feels the oppression of religious bondage, take heart! Like Israel, God will intercede on your behalf and force the issue of liberty for you. He provided the means by which Pharaoh would let His people go. The means was the Passover Lamb.

Women, you have a Passover Lamb. His name is Jesus Christ. All you have to do is present yourself to Him as a living sacrifice. Once you come under His reign, He will fight for you. In the end, you will be able to sing a song of victory like the people of Israel in Exodus 15:1-3, 11, 13, 17-18,

> I will sing unto the LORD, for he hath triumphed gloriously...The Lord is my strength and song, and he is become my salvation; he is my God, and I will prepare him an habitation; my father's God, and I will exalt him. The LORD is a man of war; the LORD is his name...Who is like unto thee, O LORD, among the gods? Who is like thee, glorious in holiness, fearful in praises, doing wonders?...Thou in thy mercy hast led forth the people whom thou hast redeemed; thou has guided them in thy strength unto thy holy habitation...Thou shalt bring them in, and plant them in the mountain of thine inheritance, in

the place, O LORD, which thou has made for thee to dwell in, in the sanctuary, O Lord, which thy hands have established. The LORD shall reign forever and ever.

BIBLOGRAPHY

Strong's Exhaustive Concordance of the Bible; James Strong, © 1986 assigned to World Bible Publishers, Inc

Webster's New Collegiate Dictionary; © 1976 by G. & C. Merriam Co.

Encyclopedia of Sermon Illustrations; ©1988 Concordia Publishing House

Deeper Experience Of Famous Christians; by James Gilchrist Lawson; © 2000 by Barbour Publishing Inc.

The Way; (Devotional) by Stanley Jones © 1946 by Stone & Pierce

Vine's Expository Dictionary of Biblical Words; © 1985 by Thomas Nelson, Inc., Publishers

A Dwelling Place For God; by Ruth Specter Lascelle; © 1990 by Hyman Israel Specter, Van Nuys CA.

Principles of Holiness, Charles G. Finney, © 1984 by Louis G. Parkhurst Jr.

The Power of the Spirit, William Law, © 1971, CLC Ministries International

Tozer on Christian Leadership, © 2001 by Christian Publications, Inc.

Out of the Labyrinth, L. H. Lehmann, Published by Chick Publications, 1982

Occult Invasion, Dave Hunt, © 1998, Harvest House Publishers

Matthew Henry's Commentary on the whole Bible, © 1991 by Hendrickson Publishers, Inc.

Royal Way of the Cross; Fenelon; © 1982 by the Community of Jesus, Inc.

Encyclopedia of Sermon Illustrations; ©1988 Concordia Publishing House

Will the Real Heretics Please Stand Up; © 1989, 3RD edition, © 1999 by David W. Bercot

The Gifts of the Spirit; by Harold Horton, © 1934

The Four Hundred Silent Years; H. A. Ironside; 16th printing 1980; Loizeaux Brothers

A Glimpse at Early Christian Church Life; Tertullian, © 1991 by David W. Bercot

Nicolaitanism (The Rise and Growth of the Clergy), F. W. Grant, Believers Bookshelf Inc.

Smiths Bible Dictionary; William Smith, Thomas Nelson Publishers

A Woman Rides the Beast; © 1994 by Dave Hunt, Published by Harvest House Publishers

Keys to the Deeper Life; A. W. Tozer, © 1957, 1984 by Creation House; Clarion Classics, Published by the Zondervan Publishing House

The Radical Cross: Living the Passion of Christ; A. W. Tozer, © 2005 by Zur Ltd.
Lectures on Colossians; H. A. Ironside; 15TH printing, May 1978; Published by Loizeaux Brothers, Inc.
The Pilgrim Church; Edmund Broadbent; © 1999, Gospel Folio Press
Women In Today's Church; George Watkins; ©1984
The Laver (Article); Ruth Specter Lascelle
Jewish Faith and the New Covenant; Ruth Specter Lascelle © 1980
When Saints Go Marching; Ethel Ruff; 1957
Does God Call Women To Preach?; Rev. W. L. Myers; 1948
God's Word to Women (1923) 100 Bible Studies by Katharine C. Bushnell
Finding the Reality of God, Paris W. Reidhead, © 1989
You Will Receive Power, William Law; © 1997 by Whitaker House

Internet Articles:

Today's Word; Skip Moen, At Gods Table. com. ©2003
Roy B. Blizzard. Jr.; Article posted February 09, 2006
"Difficult Sayings" Jonathan Went; © 2002-2005;
   http://www.studylight.org/col/ds/

About the Author

Rayola Kelley, an ordained minister of the Gospel, was born again and saved out of a cult in 1976 while serving in the U.S. Navy. Her spiritual journey continued through extensive discipleship, before following the Lord's call upon her life into full-time ministry over 30 years ago, when, with Jeannette Haley, founded Gentle Shepherd Ministries.

Through the years, Rayola's gift of teaching the Word has opened many doors for her to teach adult Sunday school, oversee a fellowship for over 30 years, hold evangelistic meetings in churches, conduct seminars, and speak at retreats. She has served in jail ministry, and is well known for her gift of spiritual insight and counseling. Upon being called to be a missionary in America, Rayola, along with Jeannette Haley established different fellowships where intense Bible Studies and discipleship training were conducted to equip believers for the ministry. These different mission fields in America entailed working in various churches as well as working with other cultures such as Korean and Hispanic nationalities.

Rayola, along with co-laborer Jeannette Haley, (professional artist, author of Christian novels, Bible Studies and stories for children) began sending out a monthly newsletter containing articles for the Body of Christ in 1997 which continues to grow. Ms. Kelley has authored over 55 books, and numerous Bible Studies including an advanced Discipleship Course (available in both English and Spanish) that is being used in countries such as Africa, Bulgaria, Israel, Ireland, India, Cuba, and Pakistan. Among her many books is *"Hidden Manna"* which deals with destructive cycles in people and relationships, and *"Battle for the Soul"* which presents a clear picture of the battle that rages in the soul. She has written seven in-depth devotional books, including both the Old Testament and New Testament devotional study which takes the reader through the entire Bible in one year. All of her books are hard-hitting, bottom-line spiritual food for the hungry and thirsty soul to "chew" upon in order to *"grow strong in the Lord, and in the power of His might."*

Rayola currently resides in Oldtown, ID and she continues to fulfill Christ's commission to make disciples through teaching, spiritual counseling, and writing.

Please visit Gentle Shepherd Ministries Web Site at: www.gentleshepherd.com for further information, and to access her challenging and informative audio sermons.

Other books by Rayola Kelley:

Hidden Manna
Battle for the Soul
Stories of the Heart
Transforming Love & Beyond
The Great Debate
Post to Post: (1) Establishing the Way
Post to Post: (2) Walking in the Way
Post to Post: (3) Meditations Along the Way

Volume One: Establishing Our Life in Christ
Includes the following books:
My Words are Spirit and Life
The Anatomy of Sin
The Principles of the Abundant Life
The Place of Covenant
Unmasking the Cult Mentality

Volume Two: Putting on the Life of Christ
Includes the following books:
He Actually Thought It Not Robbery
Revelation of the Cross
In Search of Real Faith
Think on These Things
Follow the Pattern

Volume Three: Developing a Godly Environment
Includes the following books:
Godly Discipline
Prayer and Worship
Don't Touch That Dial
Face of Thankfulness
ABC's of Christianity

Volume Four: Issues of the Heart
Includes the following books:
Hidden Manna (Revised)
Bring Down the Sacred Cows
The Manual for the Single Christian Life
Parents are People Too

Volume Six: Developing Our Christian Life
Includes the following books:
The Many Faces of Christianity
Possessing Our Souls
Experiencing the Christian Life
The Power of Our Testimonies
The Victorious Journey

Volume Seven: Discovering True Ministry
Includes the following books:
From Prisons and Dots to Christianity
So You Want To Be In Ministry?

Devotions
Devotions of the Heart: Books One and Two
Daily Food for the Soul: Books One and Two

Gentle Shepherd Ministries Devotion Series
Being a Child of God
Disciplining the Strength of our Youth
Coming to Full Age

Nugget Books
Nuggets From Heaven
More Nuggets From Heaven
Heavenly Gems
More Heavenly Gems
Heavenly Treasures

Gentle Shepherd Ministries Series:
The Christian Life Series
What Matter Is This?
The Challenge of It
The Reality of It
The Leadership Series
Overcoming
A Matter of Authority and Power
The Dynamics of True Leadership

Books By Jeannette Haley
Books co-authored with Rayola Kelley:
Hidden Manna (original)
The Many Faces of Christianity (Volume 6)
Post to Post 3: Meditations Along the Way

Other Books:
Rose of Light, Thorn of Darkness (Volume 7)
Interview in Hell (Volume 7)
Interview on Earth (Volume 7)
The Pig and I
Reflections of Wonder (Devotional)

Children's Books:
Little Stories for Little People
Traveler's Tales
The Adventures of Zack and Mira
The Adventures of Paul and Dana
(A House on the Beach)
The Monster of Mystery Valley

www.ingramcontent.com/pod-product-compliance
Lightning Source LLC
Chambersburg PA
CBHW021953160426
43197CB00007B/120